Lecture Notes in Computer Science 2910

Edited by G. Goos, J. Hartmanis, and J. van Leeuwen

Springer
Berlin
Heidelberg
New York
Hong Kong
London
Milan
Paris
Tokyo

Maria E. Orlowska Sanjiva Weerawarana
Michael P. Papazoglou Jian Yang (Eds.)

Service-Oriented Computing – ICSOC 2003

First International Conference
Trento, Italy, December 15-18, 2003
Proceedings

Springer

Volume Editors

Maria E. Orlowska
University of Queensland, School of ITEE
Brisbane Qld 4072, Australia
E-mail: maria@itee.uq.edu.au

Sanjiva Weerawarana
University of Moratuwa, Sri Lanka and IBM TJ Watson Research Center
19 Skyline Drive, Hawthorne, NY 10532, USA
E-mail: sanjiva@us.ibm.com

Michael P. Papazoglou
Tilburg University, Computer Science Department, INFOLAB
Room 711, P.O. Box 90153, 5000 LE Tilburg, The Netherlands
E-mail: mikep@uvt.nl

Jian Yang
Tilburg University, INFOLAB
P.O. Box 90153, 5000 LE, Tilburg, The Netherlands
E-mail: Jian.Yang@uvt.nl

Cataloging-in-Publication Data applied for

A catalog record for this book is available from the Library of Congress.

Bibliographic information published by Die Deutsche Bibliothek
Die Deutsche Bibliothek lists this publication in the Deutsche Nationalbibliografie; detailed bibliographic data is available in the Internet at <http://dnb.ddb.de>.

CR Subject Classification (1998): C.2, D.2, D.4, H.4, H.3, K.4.4

ISSN 0302-9743
ISBN 3-540-20681-7 Springer-Verlag Berlin Heidelberg New York

Springer-Verlag is a part of Springer Science+Business Media

springeronline.com

Printed in Germany

Typesetting: Camera-ready by author, data conversion by PTP-Berlin, Protago-TeX-Production GmbH
Printed on acid-free paper SPIN: 10972267 06/3142 5 4 3 2 1 0

Preface

Welcome to the proceedings of the inaugural International Conference on Service-Oriented Computing (ICSOC 2003). This was the first of a series of events that will evolve over the coming years, and we were happy to hold the event in Trento, where the idea for this conference was born. Trento is a lovely city with many Renaissance buildings, testimony to its great medieval past, and has a bustling modern university ready to master the future.

The participants visited Trento at the beginning of the winter season, with excellent opportunities for skiing and hiking. The city offers many other tourist attractions, some of which, we hope, the participants took the opportunity to enjoy.

Service Oriented Computing (SOC) is the new emerging paradigm for distributed computing and e-business processing which has evolved from object-oriented and component computing to one that enables us to build agile networks of collaborating business applications distributed within and across organizational boundaries.

ICSOC aims to become the flagship conference in the area of service-oriented computing, which is attracting more and more researchers and practitioners from both academia and industry. The beginnings are extremely promising, beyond our most optimistic expectations. We were deluged by requests for further information from all parts of the world and by a very high number of submissions. In fact, the success of a conference depends on the quality of the papers and on the organizational efforts of the conference officers and secretariat.

On the research side, exciting new areas in service computing, including service modeling, composition, business transactions and collaborations, service development and management, P2P and Grid computing, mobile computing, and security, were reported in the conference, in conjunction with keynote addresses and informative tutorials offered by leaders in the field.

We received an impressive collection of 181 papers in response to the call for papers. This shows a growing community of researchers addressing this challenging field. The program committee members considered all the papers very carefully. Each paper was reviewed by at least three (and in many cases four) reviewers. The reviews concentrated primarily on originality, high quality and relevance to the theme of the conference. In the end, 38 outstanding papers (about 20 % of the submissions) were accepted for presentation. The reasons for choosing so few were not only to make sure that the papers presented were of the highest quality, but, just as important, we wanted to avoid parallel sessions and thus facilitate interaction and exchange of ideas among participants.

Our special thanks go to the authors for submitting their papers to the conference, to the program committee members, and to the numerous reviewers who did an excellent job in guaranteeing that the articles in this volume are of very high quality. We also would like to acknowledge the keynote speakers, panelists and tutorial speakers for their excellent contributions to the program of this vibrant conference.

On the organization side, we are indebted to all the conference officers and to the conference secretariat of the University of Trento for their generous, invaluable help and support in all aspects of the organization of this conference. In particular, the local arrangements team, led by Vincenzo D'Andrea and Marco Aiello, did an outstanding job under great time pressure. Fabrizio Sannicoló also did an excellent job programming and maintaining the automated conference system.

If you attended the conference we are sure that you will remember it and the excellent social program that was arranged. Special thanks are also due to all of our kind sponsors: IBM, Springer-Verlag, and the University of Trento.

September 2003

Fabio Casati
Bernd Krämer
Maria Orlowska
Mike Papazoglou
Sanjiva Weerawarana

ICSOC 2003 Conference Organization

ICSOC 2003 was organized by the Department of Computer Science, University of Trento.

Conference Chairs

Conference Chairs	Fabio Casati, HP Labs, Palo Alto, USA Bernd Krämer, FernUniversität, Hagen, Germany
Program Chairs	Maria E. Orlowska, DSTC/Univ. of Queensland, Australia Mike P. Papazoglou, Tilburg Univ., Netherlands Sanjiva Weerawarana, IBM, TJ Watson Research Center, USA
Tutorial Chair	Barbara Pernici, Politecnico di Milano, Italy
Panel Chairs	Paul Grefen, Eindhoven University of Technology, Netherlands Colette Rolland, Univ. of Paris, France
Awards Chair	Stefan Tai, IBM TJ Watson Research Center, USA
Industrial Papers Chair	Christoph Bussler, Digital Enterprise Research Institute, Ireland
Publicity Chairs	Athman Bouguettaya, Virginia Tech., USA Willem-Jan van den Heuvel, Tilburg Univ, Netherlands
Proceedings Chair	Jian Yang, Tilburg Univ, Netherlands
International Liaison Chairs	Charles Petrie, Stanford Univ., USA Thomas Risse, Fraunhofer, IPSI, Germany Makoto Takizawa, Tokyo Denki Univ., Japan
Organizing Chairs	Marco Aiello, Univ. of Trento, Italy Vincenzo D'Andrea, Univ. of Trento, Italy

Program Committee

Nabil Adam	Rutgers Univ., USA
Marco Aiello	Univ. of Trento, Italy
Mikio Aoyama	Nanzan Univ., Japan
Grigoris Antoniou	Univ. of Crete, Greece
Carlo Batini	AIPA, Italy
Boualem Benatallah	UNSW, Australia
M. Brian Blake	Georgetown Univ., USA
Sjaak Brinkkemper	Triffit, and Vrije Univ., Netherlands
Tiziana Catarci	Univ. of Rome, Italy
Vincenzo D'Andrea	Univ. of Trento, Italy
Valeria de Antonellis	Univ. of Brescia, Italy
Alex Delis	Univ. of Athens, Greece
Schahram Dustdar	Vienna Univ. of Technology, Austria
David Edmond	QUT, Australia
Ian Foster	Univ. of Chicago, USA
Brent Hailpern	IBM TJ Watson Research Center, USA
Jos van Hillegersberg	Erasmus Univ., Rotterdam, Netherlands
Paul Johannesson	Stockholm Univ., Sweden
Rania Khalaf	IBM TJ Watson Research Center, USA
Craig Knoblock	Univ. of Southern California, USA
Manolis Koubarakis	Technical Univ. of Crete, Greece
Winfried Lamersdorf	Hamburg Univ., Germany
Paul Layzell	UMIST, UK
Doug Lea	SUNY Oswego, USA
Frank Leymann	IBM Software Group, Germany
Oscar Pastor López	Universidad Politècnica de València, Spain
Maurizio Marchese	Univ. of Trento, Italy
Fabio Massacci	Univ. of Trento, Italy
Massimo Mecella	Univ. of Rome, Italy
Giacomo Piccinelli	Univ. College London, UK
Dimitris Plexousakis	Univ. of Crete, Greece
Michael Rosemann	QUT, Australia
Matti Rossi	Helsinki School of Economics, Finland
Wasim Sadiq	SAP Corporate Research, Australia
Karsten Schultz	SAP Corporate Research, Australia
Santosh Shrivastava	Univ. of Newcastle, UK
Maarten Steen	Telematica Instituut, Netherlands
Patrick Strating	Telematica Instituut, Netherlands
Eleni Stroulia	Univ. of Alberta, Canada
Zahir Tari	RMIT, Australia
Paolo Traverso	IRST, Italy
Aad van Moorsel	Hewlett-Packard, USA
Carlos Varela	Rensselaer Poly. Inst. USA
Benkt Wangler	Univ. of Skövde, Sweden
Roel Wieringa	Twente Univ., Netherlands
Andreas Wombacher	Fraunhofer Inst., Germany
Steve Vinoski	Iona, USA
Yanchun Zhang	Univ. of Southern Queensland, Australia

Table of Contents

Service Description

Service Composition

Quality of Service Models

Service Personalization

Service Semantics

Business Processes and Transactions

Business Collaborations

Service Request and Coordination

Service Security and Reliability

Infrastructure for Service Delivery

Service P2P and Grid Computing

Service and Mobile Computing

Service Computing and Applications

Capabilities: Describing What Services Can Do*

Phillipa Oaks, Arthur H.M. ter Hofstede, and David Edmond

Centre for Information Technology Innovation - Faculty of Information Technology
Queensland University of Technology
GPO Box 2434, Brisbane, QLD 4001, Australia
{p.oaks,a.terhofstede,d.edmond}@qut.edu.au

Abstract. The ability of agents and services to automatically locate and interact with unknown partners is a goal for both the semantic web and web services. This, "serendipitous interoperability", is hindered by the lack of an explicit means of describing what services (or agents) are able to do, that is, their capabilities. At present, informal descriptions of what services can do are found in "documentation" elements; or they are somehow encoded in operation names and signatures. We show, by reference to existing service examples, how ambiguous and imprecise capability descriptions hamper the attainment of automated interoperability goals in the open, global web environment. In this paper we propose a structured, machine readable description of capabilities, which may help to increase the recall and precision of service discovery mechanisms. Our capability description draws on previous work in capability and process modeling and allows the incorporation of external classification schemes. The capability description is presented as a conceptual meta model. The model supports conceptual queries and can be used as an extension to the DAML-S Service Profile.

1 Introduction

In recent times the Semantic Web, and Web Services have converged into the notion of self-describing semantic web services. These are web services that provide and use semantic descriptions of the concepts in their domain over and above the information provided by WSDL[1] and UDDI[2]. Two W3C groups (Semantic Web and Web Services) have described a need for service descriptions that are sufficiently expressive to allow services to be located dynamically without human intervention. The requirements for the W3C's Web Services Architecture and Web Services Description working groups describe the need for "semantic descriptions that allow the discovery of services that implement the required functionality" [1]. The Web Ontology Language (OWL) requirements describe "serendipitous interoperability" as the ability of devices to "discover each others'

* This work is supported by the Australian Research Council SPIRT Grant "Self-describing transactions operating in a large, open, heterogeneous and distributed environment" involving QUT, UNSW and GBST Holdings Pty Ltd.

[1] http://www.w3.org/TR/wsdl12/

[2] http://www.uddi.org

M.E. Orlowska et al. (Eds.): ICSOC 2003, LNCS 2910, pp. 1–16, 2003.

functionality and be able to take advantage of it" [2]. This sentiment can also be applied to web services.

At present web services are described using the Web Services Description Language (WSDL). WSDL only provides for the description of web service interfaces. There are two alternative ways of dealing with this as far as determining the capability of the service is concerned. The first way is for users to manually search for services and read the documentation to see what the service can do, then hard wire the service invocation and interaction. The second way is to locate services based on matching keywords representing the required capability with words used in the interface description. This is particularly prone to problems, as most software developers use names and words idiosyncratically according to their local culture, rules and naming conventions. These conventions often require words to be mashed together, and the words may or may not bear any relevance to what the service actually does. In the world of web services it is no longer possible to assume that all users will share the local conventions of the service provider.

Service descriptions must explicitly state what they can do, and the context the service operates on and within. The advantage of this higher level capability description, is that users can select and use specific functionality. This is in contrast to the current situation, where service users must make their own determination of the functionality and requirements of each operation.

To enable the dynamic discovery of services, a mechanism is required to describe behavioural aspects of services, i.e. what services do. A semantic description of services should include the following: the capabilities a service can provide, under what circumstances the capabilities can be provided, what the service requires to provide the capability, and what results can be delivered. The description should also provide references to definitions of all the words and terms it uses. The capability description has to provide enough information for users to identify and locate alternative services without human intervention. Non-functional aspects of services, such as cost and quality of service [3] are necessary for the evaluation, selection, and configuration of services following their discovery. A description of these aspects is outside of the scope of this work.

In this paper we are concerned with advertising web services in such a way that the discovery of their capabilities can be automated. Although the other phases of service interaction, such as evaluation, selection, negotiation, execution and monitoring are important, the discovery phase is the crucial first step.

2 Existing Work in Capability Description

A set of criteria for evaluating capability description languages were described by Sycara et.al. [4] in reference to agent capabilities. These requirements include expressiveness, abstraction, support for inferences, ease of use, application on the web, and avoiding reliance on keyword extraction and comparison. We believe these high level criteria are also relevant in the context of semantic web services but they do not address the specific requirements of dynamic web service discovery. To address these requirements, a capability language should provide:

1. The ability to declare what action a service performs.
2. The ability to allow a capability to have different sets of inputs.
3. The ability to declare preconditions and effects in some named rule definition language.
4. The ability to describe objects that are not input but are used or affected by the capability.
5. The ability to refer to ontological descriptions of the terms used in the description and thus place the use of the terms in context.
6. The ability to make explicit the domain or context in which the service operates.
7. The ability to classify capabilities based on aspects of the description enabling exact or partial matches between required and provided capability descriptions.

The genesis of the requirements is illustrated below, and we refer to them using this notation (req. 1) with the number corresponding to the requirement listed above.

There are several areas where we draw from existing work in capability description. We were influenced by the conclusions drawn in [5] and [6], where it was concluded after reviewing various description mechanisms and languages, that frame based representations were the most expressive and flexible means to represent the capabilities of intelligent agents. We start with an overview of case frames and look at several capability representations based on them, in the context of software agents and software reuse. Then we look at one of the current mechanisms for describing web services to see how well it provides a description of service capabilities.

Case Frames. [7] Much of the work in agent capability description has been based on the work of Charles Fillmore. We briefly review this work to understand why case frames are used to describe what agents and services do, and how they have been adapted over time.

Fillmore proposed a structure, called a case frame, to describe information about a verb. Each case describes some aspect of the verb and a completed case frame describes an action, its context and its consequences. The case frame provides a mechanism to state the who, what, where, when, how questions for actions. Fillmore elaborated several cases and postulated that other cases may exist. The base cases he described for verbs or actions are:

- Agentive - who does the action.
- Dative - who it happens to.
- Instrumental - what thing is involved.
- Factive - the object or being resulting from the action.
- Locative - where the action happens.
- Objective - things affected by the action.

In the context of semantic web service descriptions the case frame provides a convenient way of structuring the description of what behaviours, actions or capabilities a service provides.

For the purpose of representing service capabilities within a case frame structure, we can assume the agentive case implicitly represents the service itself and the dative case implicitly represents the service user, so these do not have to be elaborated explicitly. This does however imply that the capability description of a service is always from the perspective of what the service (as the agentive case) does or provides. For example, a service that provides goods that customers can buy, is a selling service. A service that finds and buys the lowest priced goods is a purchasing service.

The instrumental case represents things involved in the action. In the following paragraphs we will see how this has been used to represent the inputs for an action.

The objective case represents those objects that are involved in the performance of a service but not explicitly provided as inputs by the user. For example, a third party web service may offer to search for books by looking in the Amazon book catalog[3]. A user then may decide to use the third party service because they are unable to access Amazon directly and have heard that Amazon provides a competitively priced delivery service.

The factive case represents the results of the action and, in subsequent work discussed below, has been translated to represent the outputs or effects of an action.

In recent times Fillmore has been involved with the Berkeley FrameNet project[4], which is in the process of describing the frames (conceptual structures) of many verbs in common use [8]. The FrameNet system will be useful for the automated generation of descriptions, by providing base frames for many different kinds of service capabilities. For example the FrameNet frame for the verb sell contains the cases; *Buyer, Seller, Money, Goods, Rate, Unit, Means and Manner.* These are the possible cases for sell, therefore a description of a selling capability will need to incorporate some if not all of these cases to be effective.

2.1 Capability Descriptions for Software Agents

EXPECT [9,10] provides a structured representation of goals, based on verb clauses, it allows the representation of both general and specialized goals for agent planning systems. The structured representation allows reasoning about how goals relate to one another and allows inexact matching for loose coupling between representations of goals and capabilities descriptions. The representation is tied to a domain ontology to ensure the terms have consistent semantics amongst all users.

The verb clause consists of a verb and one or more roles or slots (cases). The role can represent objects involved in the task, parameters, or a description of the task. Roles can be populated by different types of objects including; concepts or instances from some ontology, literals, data types, sets, or descriptions.

---

[3] `http://www.amazon.com`

[4] `http://www.icsi.berkeley.edu/~framenet/`

An example (from [10]) of an Expect capability description for calculating the weight of objects is shown below:

```
((name calculate-total-cargo-weight-objects)
 (capability (calculate (obj (?w is (spec-of weight)))
   (of (?fms is (set-of (inst-of object))))))
 (result-type (inst-of weight))
 (method (sum (obj (r-weight ?fms)))))
```

When we apply the criteria from [4] noted above, this description would succeed on the expressiveness and inferences criteria but fail on ease of use and web applicability. Apart from keywords in the name "calculate-total-cargo-weight-objects", there is little in this capability description that could be used for discovery .

A consistent semantics is necessary for the representation of the structure of the capability description. However, in an open environment there will be many diverse contexts in which the capability description is used. This means a single ontology for the representation of the *content* of the description is not feasible.

The advantage of this description is the ability to use a rule notation to express conditions and effects. The use of rules to describe aspects of capabilities was also advocated in [6] where the ability to explicitly declare which rule language was being used is also provided (req. 3). The disadvantage of this capability description is that it would require training in order to write the descriptions.

Language for Advertisement and Request for Knowledge Sharing (LARKS) [11, 4] is a refined-frame based language for the specification of agent capabilities. It comprises a text description of the capability, with a structured description of the context, types, input, output, and constraints of an agent. An ontological description of terms used in the description can also be provided. The primary purpose of a LARKS specification is to allow inferencing and efficient accurate matchmaking.

In the current environment, where ontologies are proliferating, it is more likely that terms will be described by reference to external ontologies, rather than incorporated as an ontological description within the capability description itself (req. 5).

LARKS does not provide sufficient information in the form of a structured description of its purpose to enable discovery. The example below (from [4]) shows a capability description for a portfolio agent.

```
Context:            Stock, StockMarket;
Types:              StockSymbols = {IBM, Apple, HP},
                    Money = Real;
Input:              symbol:StockSymbols;
                    yourMoney:Money;
                    shares:Money;
Output:             yourStock:StockSymbols;
                    yourShares:Money;
                    yourChange:Money;
```

```
InConstraints:        yourMoney >= shares*currentPrice(symb);
OutConstraints:       yourChange =
                          yourMoney-shares*currentPrice(symb);
                      yourShares = shares;
                      yourStock = symbol;
ConcDescriptions:
TextDescription:      buying stocks from IBM,Apple,HP
                      at the stock market.
```

The information available for discovery is the unstructured text description "buying stocks from IBM, Apple, HP at the stock market", thus leaving keyword extraction as the only way of deciding what the service actually does. The capability of the agent being described is unclear, is it buying stocks on the stock market or directly from the company at the stock market?

In terms of the criteria, the language is expressive, and it allows inferences. It appears to be easy to use, although the example has an error[5] and other inconsistencies. This representation does not do well on the web applicability criteria but it has been used as the basis of the web accessible DAML-S Profile, which we look at in section 2.3.

The lack of an explicit action description means the capability has to be derived from keywords and unstructured text descriptions, but the advantages of this description mechanism are the ability to refer to ontological description of terms, comprehensive coverage of constraints and effects (rules) (req. 3), input/output (data), and the context the service operates in (req. 6). The ability to "matchmake" (req. 7) based on IOPE's was reported in [11].

2.2 Capability Description for Reuse

Web services are software, so we draw on work that has been done in the context of describing the capabilities of reusable software.

Reuse of Software Artifacts (ROSA). [12] The ROSA system is used for the automated indexing and retrieval of software components. In contrast to faceted classification, ROSA uses a conventional case frame structure, along with constraints and heuristics, to automatically extract lexical, syntactic and semantic information from free text software descriptions.

The automated interpretation of descriptive phrases into case frames makes this a potential tool for the generation and indexing of web service capability descriptions. However, apart from a few papers preceding [13] we have not been able to access this promising resource. Similar work has been reported in [14], where a web interface allows the entry of natural language descriptions of required components.

In terms of the criteria ROSA is expressive and capable of supporting inferencing. Comparisons are easily made between the "normalized" internal representations. ROSA is easy to use as the descriptions can be made in free text

[5] Input *shares* has to be a quantity to have meaning in the OutConstraint *yourChange*

and automatically translated into a structured description. The use of WordNet implies the use of other ontologies could also be supported (req. 5).

ROSA, being intended for the manual discovery of reusable software assets, rather than global automated web service invocation, does not deal with the possibility that some capabilities may be context dependent, if that is the case then the context should be made explicit (req. 6).

2.3 Web Service Description

DAML-S Pro le [6] [15,16,17] builds on work on LARKS and ATLAS[7]. The DAML-S profile is a "yellow pages" description of a service, it is intended to specify what the service requires and what it provides. The service capability is described in terms of input and output parameters, preconditions and effects (IOPEs). The description also includes the service profile name, a text description, a reference to a Process specification (how it works), a service category (NAICS etc), and a quality rating. The profile allows the definition of service parameters to describe (non-functional) aspects of the service such as "MaxResponseTime", and information about the service provider or requester, such as their name, title, address, web URL etc.

The DAML-S Profile has further refined the basic case frame down to the description of capabilities only in terms of IOPEs. In the process it has lost the ability to explicitly declare what the service actually does. It has also lost the ability to describe the objects that are used but are not inputs in the description of the service [18].

To illustrate several points the extract below has been taken from the DAML-S V0.7 Congo Book example service profile description. The example represents the information in the profile that is machine processable and the types of the IOPE's.

```
serviceName                 Congo_BookBuying_Agent
textDescription             This agentified service provides
                            the opportunity to browse a book
                            selling site and buy books there
NAME                        TYPE
(Inputs)
bookTitle                   xsd:string
signInInfo                  CongoProcess:SignInData
createAcctInfo              CongoProcess:CreateAcct
creditCardNumber            xsd:decimal
creditCardType              CongoProcess:CreditCardType
creditCardExpirationDate    time:TemporalEntity
deliveryAddress             xsd:string
packagingSelection          CongoProcess:PackagingType
DeliveryType                CongoProcess:DeliveryType
```

[6] http://www.daml.org/services/daml-s/0.7/

[7] http://www-2.cs.cmu.edu/~softagents/larks.html, http://www.daml.ri.cmu.edu/index.html

```
(Outputs)
EReceipt               CongoProcess:EReceipt
ShippingOrder          CongoProcess:ShippingOrder
AccountType            CongoProcess:CreateAcctOutputType
(Preconditions)
AcctExists             CongoProcess:AcctExists
CreditExists           CongoProcess:CreditExists
(Effects)
BuyEffectType          CongoProcess:BuyEffectType
```

The lack of an explicit means of declaring what the service actually does means that keyword extraction from the service name and description is necessary to discover the service's capabilities (req. 1). In this example, this is made more difficult by the description which states it is a BookBuying_Agent when it is a service that sells books.

In the text accompanying the example it is implied that the service provides two capabilities, "catalog browsing" and "selling books", neither of these are clear from the information provided in the form of IOPEs. In fact, there are also the implied capabilities to "accept credit card payments from the customer", to "check the customers credit availability" and to "deliver books to the customer". On one hand, it could be argued that these are capabilities that do not need to be exposed for discovery, on the other hand they are implicitly exposed by being declared as input parameters in the service profile.

The problem seems to be that the service profile does not have a mechanism to explicitly declare that a service may comprise several capabilities; and that each capability may have a different set of IOPEs. In addition, it needs to be able to hide the IOPEs that are not directly related to discovery.

Recent work by Sabou [19] in using DAML-S to describe a web service has revealed problems with describing services that may have alternative (sets of) inputs. The problem arises mainly in terms of the binding to WSDL, but it highlights the case where each capability provided by a service may have its own sets of alternative inputs (req. 2).

It is possible that the explicit declaration of capability has been replaced by the explicit declaration of the effects of the service. This is a valid modeling choice if it is used correctly. For example, instead of saying "we have the capability to sell books", the service could say "the effect of this service is that a book is purchased". The example does not support this interpretation.

In terms of the criteria, DAML-S has the potential to be sufficiently expressive to model both atomic and complex services and allows description at an abstract level. Being based on DAML+OIL/OWL it is implicitly capable of supporting inferencing and machine processing. The language appears easy to use well (and poorly). It is the best example of a web enabled language for the automated exchange and processing of capability information that we have looked at.

The shortcomings of the DAML-S Profile are the inability to describe the actual action performed (req. 1), and to describe the objects it may use or affect that are not provided as inputs (req. 4). It should also be possible to associate (sets of) inputs with specific capabilities (req. 2).

3 A Conceptual Model of Capability

In this section we present a conceptual model (figure 1) for capability descriptions. We believe that the model fully delivers all the requirements listed in section 2 and also satisfies the criteria proposed in [4]. In addition to the requirements and criteria, this model of capability descriptions is sufficiently detailed to facilitate the location of functionally equivalent or similar services. It is expressive enough to model simple atomic services as well as the functionality of complex, possibly composed, services. The model will allow the creation of capability descriptions that work human to human as well as machine to machine [20], because ultimately it is people who design and create software applications.

The capability description is presented as an Object Role Modeling (ORM) [21] model. ORM is a well known visual conceptual data modeling technique. The advantages of using ORM are that it has an associated modelling methodology and conceptual query language. It is implementation independent and has a formal semantics. It also has the advantage of being able to include a sample population, shown below the fact types, which helps to validate the model and demonstrate how it is used.

We briefly describe some of the main concepts of ORM is to assist the reader to interpret the schema presented below. The ellipses represent entity types (e.g. *Capability*), while the boxes represent the roles played by the entities in a fact type and a fact type can consist of one or more roles. Double arrows represent uniqueness constraints over roles (e.g. a *Capability* has at most one output Signature set), while solid dots represent mandatory role constraints (e.g. every *Capability* has an action *Verb*). A string, in parenthesis below the name of an entity type (e.g. *(id)*), indicates the presence of a value type with a name which is the concatenation of that entity type name and that string. In this case instances of the value type uniquely identify instances of that entity type (e.g. *Signatureid* is a value type providing identification for entity type *Signature*).

The sample population demonstrates the description of three capabilities. The first capability is the ability to book tickets for a performance of the opera "Carmen", at the Queensland Performing Arts Center (QTAC). The second capability provides valuations for pre-war Belgian stamps, and the third capability retrieves ontologies that contain a given string.

A *Capability* is described, in the first instance, by an action *Verb* that expresses what the capability does (req. 1). To allow for the fact that different verbs may be used to express the same action, synonyms are provided directly, and a definition is available in an *Ontological source* (e.g. dictionary, thesaurus, ontology, specification or standard) (req. 5). The ability to provide alternatives to the primary verb assists similarity matching of capabilities (req. 7).

From the case frame point of view, we have modelled cases as roles. We have grouped the roles according to the type of objects that play those roles. We distinguish between cases that play an informational role, such as *location, topic, manner* etc., from roles that are played by a *Signature*, and roles that are played by *Rules*.

A *Signature* represents a set of *Parameters*. A capability can have zero or more *input*, *uses* and *a ects* signature sets, including the empty set (req. 2, 4).

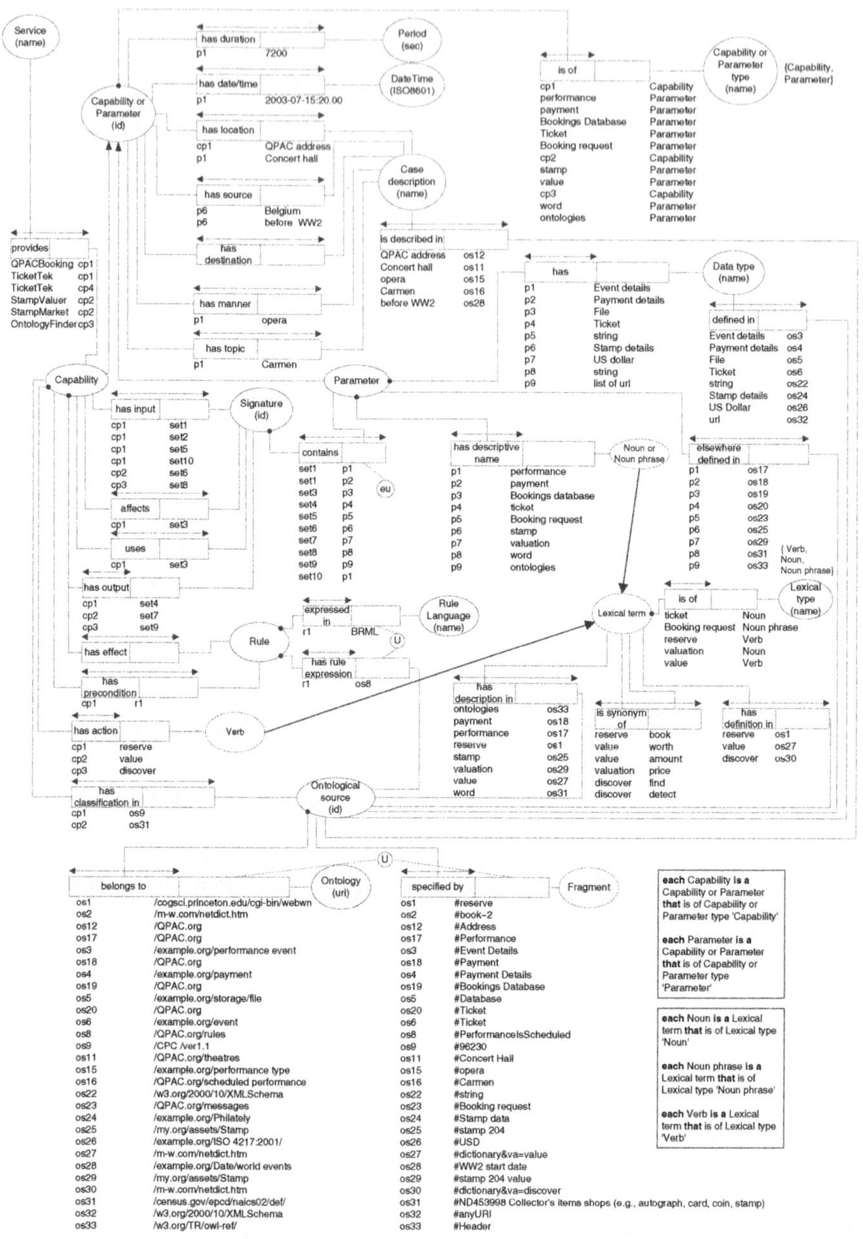

Fig. 1. A conceptual meta model of capability

For example, a service may take as input a name (string) and an age (integer), or an email address (URI) and an age (integer), or nothing at all. Each signature set must contain a different combination of elements, this is shown by the "eu" constraint [22] on the role that connects to Parameter. Each Parameter and its associated *Data type* are defined in an Ontological source (req. 5).

The *output* role is constrained to have only one signature set, as we take the view that different output set would represent a different capability.

We created a supertype *Capability or Parameter* so we could share the definition of the informational roles, location etc. between the two types Capability and Parameter. These roles are played by a *Case description* described in an Ontological Source (req. 5).

We have distinguished the cases for preconditions and effects (PEs) and modelled these as roles played by Rules; as opposed to the input and output (IO) roles played by Signatures. This is because rules and signatures are fundamentally different and require a different treatment in the conceptual model. Each rule is associated with a named *Rule Language* and a rule expression (req. 3) in an Ontological source.

The use of an explicit domain or context identifier (req. 6) is provided by the role *has classi cation*. The classification itself is contained in an Ontological source.

An issue that may cause confusion, is that in this model we show verbs, nouns and noun phrases as subtypes of *Lexical term*. There is potentially a problem if the same word is used as a noun and as a verb. For example, the verb 'reserve' has 'book' as a synonym, however the noun 'book' would have a completely unrelated set of synonyms. We think this problem may be resolved by using a namespace identifier in conjunction with the word, rather than the abbreviated version shown in the model.

In terms of Fillmore's cases (section 2) the Agentive case is the service providing the capability, and the Dative case is the user, these are implicit. The Instrumental case is modeled as the *has input* and *uses* roles. The Factive case is modeled as the *has output* and *has e ect* roles. The Objective case is shown as the role *a ects*, and the Locative case can made explicit using *has location*, *has source* and *has destination* for both capabilities and parameters.

3.1 Evaluation of the Model

In this section we show how our capability description model satisfies the requirements listed in section 2.

1. The action declaration is explicitly provided by the role has action. The verb representing the action is defined in an ontological source. Alternative action words such as synonyms that are equivalent to the primary verb in this context can also be defined using the role has synonym. The explicit provision of alternative terms assists in service matching.
2. The model provides for different sets of inputs by allowing a capability to have different signatures for the roles has input, uses and effects. The signature is a possibly empty set of parameters. Each parameter is declared with a name (by convention the name should indicate its purpose) and its data type. However, the model does not only rely on descriptive parameter names it also allows both the parameter and its data type to refer to external definitions for more information.

3. Preconditions and effects can be defined by reference to an expression, using a named rule language, in an ontological source. The use of an explicit name for the rule language caters for the fact that web enabled rule languages are still being developed and until a clear favourite emerges, it is safer to explicitly state which one applies.
4. Objects that may be used or affected by the capability, but are not part of the input provided by the user, can be explicitly described using the uses and affects roles.
5. Most of the elements in the model can make reference to an ontological source for further information and clarification on how terms are intended to be used in the context of the capability.
6. The domain or context the capability operates within is made explicit by the has classification in role. Categorization schemes such as UNSPSC[8] and NAICS[9] can be used to describe the context in which a capability is performed.
7. The capability description provides many aspects that can be used for classifying capabilities. The has classification in role is similar to the level of classification available in UDDI. However, this capability description allows classification along much broader lines including the type of action performed, the location of the service, its manner of operation, and its topic of concern amongst others.

3.2 Querying the Model

A collection of capability descriptions can be easily queried using a conceptual query langauge like ConQuer [23,24]. An implementation of ConQuer is available in the Active Query tool, but we have been unable to access it yet, so the syntax shown below is based on the references above, rather than the output of the software tool. For users unfamiliar with ConQuer, the tick symbol is similar to the SQL select clause and these elements are returned or displayed. The +-symbol should be interpreted as "and", and alternatives are shown explicitly as "or".

The ability to query a collection of capability descriptions, based on the conceptual model, is of benefit to those users who have specific requirements beyond the types of input and output parameters provided by WSDL. Conceptual queries can access any of the objects and the relationships between objects shown in the model. The ability to make queries at the conceptual level will also be of benefit to service composers, allowing them to determine in advance what kinds of capabilities are available, and what kinds of objects a particular capability uses and has an effect upon in the performance of its function. This kind of information about the side-effects of a service or capability are important, and as far as we know are not available in any other structured service description mechanism. All of the major elements in the model provide the ability to access

[8] Universal Standard Products and Services Classification (UNSPSC), `http://eccma.org/unspsc/`

[9] North American Industry Classification System (NAICS), `http://www.ntis.gov/product/naics.htm`

further information in the form of ontologies, to assist with disambiguation and clarification.

Two examples of the types of queries the model can support are shown below.

1. Find a service that will allow me to book tickets for the opera "Carmen" and tell me when and where it will be held.

```
√ Service
  +- provides Capability
            +- has output Signature
                       +-contains Parameter has Datatype "Ticket"
            +- has input Signature
                      +- contains Parameter
                               +- has descriptive name Noun or Noun
                                  phrase "performance"
                                  or is synonym of Noun or Noun phrase
                                     "performance"
                               +- has manner Case description "opera"
                               +- has topic Case description "Carmen"
                               √ has date time DateTime
                               √ has location Case description
```

2. Find me a service that provides stamp valuations and show the type of input the service requires. Use the NAICs code 452998 that covers many types of specialist retailers including "Collector's items shops (e.g., autograph, card, coin, stamp)", to narrow the search.

```
√ Service
  +- provides Capability
            +- has classification in Ontological source
                                +- belongs to Ontology
                                   "www.census.gov/epcd/naics02/def/"
                                +- specified by Fragment
                                   "ND453998 Collector's items shops
                                   (e.g., autograph, card, coin, stamp)"
            +- has output Signature
                       +- contains Parameter
                                 +- has descriptive name Noun or Noun
                                    phrase "valuation"
                                    or is synonym of Noun or Noun
                                       phrase "valuation"
            +-has input Signature
                      contains Parameter
                            √ has Data type
```

4 Realisation

Various existing services and tools can be used to automate the generation of capability descriptions. The FrameNet frame [8] for the selected operation can be used as the basis of the capability description. Natural language descriptions [13,14] can be used along with WordNet verb synsets (groups of related terms) to generate alternative verbs, nouns and noun phrases to populate the capability description.

Alternatively, the MIT Process Handbook[10] could be used to describe a capability as is, or with case refinements as described by Lee and Pentland in [25]. A capability could be declared to be equivalent to some process in the handbook, or it could be a specialization or generalization of a process description in the handbook. Klein and Bernstein [26] also suggest using the Process Handbook as a means to describe and locate semantic web services, and they provide the basis of a query language to use as an alternative to manual navigation of the handbook.

The more publicly accessible external classification schemes, standards, specifications, ontologies and other sources of information that are used in the capability description, the more likely it is that interaction partners will be able to find a common ground for understanding the terms the service uses.

5 Conclusion

The capability description we introduced in this paper can be used to advertise the capabilities of web services. The structure can also be used by service composers and planners to describe what they expect services to provide. Service composition planners can use the conceptual query language to interrogate a collection of capability descriptions. In addition, this capability description can be readily translated into a machine processable ontology. An explicit structured description of service capabilities allows the dynamic location of services based on their advertised capabilities rather than keyword searches and this will improve the efficiency and effectiveness of the discovery process.

One issue that still needs to be addressed is the specialization (by extension or restriction) of capability descriptions for specific contexts. The semantics of this are complex, as a capability description could potentially be both extended with additional cases, and existing cases could have their range of values restricted or removed.

The capability description we propose is not trivial, it will require much greater effort on the part of those describing services. We believe this level of complexity is unavoidable if we want to be able to achieve the goal of automated ad-hoc interaction between web services.

References

1. Haas, H., Orchard, D.: Web Services Architecture Usage Scenarios, W3C Working Draft 30 July 2002 (2002) Available from: `http://www.w3.org/TR/ws-arch-scenarios/`, (11 March 2003).
2. Heflin, J.: Web Ontology Language (OWL) Use Cases and Requirements, W3C Working Draft 31 March 2003 (2003) Available from: `http://www.w3.org/TR/webont-req/`, (15 April 2003).

10 `http://ccs.mit.edu/ph/`

3. O'Sullivan, J., Edmond, D., ter Hofstede, A.: What's in a service? Towards accurate description of non-functional service properties. Distributed and Parallel Databases Journal - Special Issue on E-Services **12** (2002) 117–133
4. Sycara, K., Widoff, S., Klusch, M., Lu, J.: LARKS: Dynamic Matchmaking Among Heterogeneous Software Agents in Cyberspace. Autonomous Agents and Multi-Agent Systems (2002) 173–203
5. Wickler, G., Tate, A.: Capability representations for brokering: A survey (1998) Submitted to Knowledge Engineering Review, December 1999. Available from: `http://www.aiai.ed.ac.uk/~oplan/cdl/cdl-ker.ps`, (4 October 2002).
6. Wickler, G.J.: Using Expressive and Flexible Action Representations to Reason about Capabilities for Intelligent Agent Cooperation. PhD thesis, University of Edinburgh, Edinburgh, UK (1999)
7. Fillmore, C.: The Case for Case. Universals in Liguistic Theory. Holt, Rinehart and Winston, New York (1968)
8. Fillmore, C.J., Wooters, C., Baker, C.F.: Building a Large Lexical Databank Which Provides Deep Semantics. In: Proceedings of the Pacific Asian Conference on Language, Information and Computation, Hong Kong, Language Information Sciences Research Centre, City University of Hong Kong, PACLIC 15 (2001)
9. Swartout, W., Gil, Y., Valente, A.: Representing Capabilities of Problem-Solving Methods. In: In Proceedings of 1999 IJCAI Workshop on Ontologies and Problem-Solving Methods, Stockholm, Sweden, CEUR Publications (`http://sunsite.informatik.rwth-aachen.de/Publications/CEUR-WS/Vol-18/`) (1999)
10. Gil, Y., Blythe, J.: How Can a Structured Representation of Capabilities Help in Planning? (2000) In AAAI 2000 workshop on Representational Issues for Real-world Planning Systems.
11. Sycara, K.P., Klusch, M., Widoff, S., Lu, J.: Dynamic service matchmaking among agents in open information environments. SIGMOD Record **28** (1999) 47–53 `citeseer.nj.nec.com/article/sycara99dynamic.html`, (1 February 2002).
12. Girardi, M.R., Ibrahim, B.: Using English to Retrieve Software. The Journal of Systems and Software, Special Issue on Software Reusability **30** (1995) 249–270
13. Girardi, M.R.: Classification and Retrieval of Software through their Descriptions in Natural Language. PhD thesis, University of Geneva (1995) Ph.D. dissertation, No. 2782.
14. Sugumaran, V., Storey, V.C.: A Semantic-Based Approach to Component Retrieval. The DATA BASE for Advances in Information Systems **34** (2003) 8–24 Quarterly publication of the Special Interest Group on Management Information Systems of the Association for Computing Machinery (ACM-SIGMIS).
15. Denker, G., Hobbs, J., Martin, D., Narayana, S., Waldinger, W.: Accessing Information and Services on the DAML-Enabled Web. In: Second International Workshop on the Semantic Web - SemWeb'2001, Workshop at WWW10, Hongkong (2001)
16. Ankolekar, A., Burstein, M., Hobbs, J.R., Lassila, O., Martin, D.L., McIlraith, S.A., Narayanan, S., Paolucci, M., Payne, T., Sycara, K., Zeng, H.: DAML-S: Semantic Markup For Web Services. In: Proceedings of SWWS' 01 The First Semantic Web Working Symposium, Stanford University, CA, USA (2001) 411–430
17. Paolucci, M., Sycara, K., Kawamura, T.: Delivering Semantic Web Services. In: Proceedings of the twelfth international conference on World Wide Web, WWW2003, Budapest, Hungary, ACM, ACM Press (2003)

18. Wroe, C., Stevens, R., Goble, C., Roberts, A., Greenwood, M.: A Suite of DAML+OIL Ontologies to Describe Bioinformatics Web Services and Data. International Journal of Cooperative Information Systems **12** (2003) 197–224
19. Sabou, M., Richards, D., van Splunter, S.: An experience report on using DAML-S. In: Proceedings of the Twelfth International World Wide Web Conference Workshop on E-Services and the Semantic Web (ESSW '03), Budapest (2003)
20. Kovitz, B.: Ambiguity and What to Do about it. In: Proceedings IEEE Joint International Conference on Requirements Engineering, Essen, IEEE (2002) 213
21. Halpin, T.: Information Modeling and Relational Databases: from conceptual analysis to logical design. Morgan Kaufmann Publishers, San Diego, CA, USA (2001)
22. ter Hofstede, A.H.M., van der Weide, T.P.: Deriving Identity from Extensionality. International Journal of Software Engineering and Knowledge Engineering **8** (1998) 189–221
23. Bloesch, A.C., Halpin, T.A.: ConQuer: A Conceptual Query Language. In Thalheim, B., ed.: Proceedings of ER'96: 15th International Conference on Conceptual Modeling. Lecture Notes in Computer Science v. 1157, Cottbus, Germany, Springer Verlag (1996) 121–133
24. Bloesch, A.C., Halpin, T.A.: Conceptual Queries using ConQuer-II. In: Proceedings of ER'97: 16th International Conference on Conceptual Modeling. Lecture Notes in Computer Science v. 1331, Los Angeles, California, Springer Verlag (1997) 113–126
25. Lee, J., Pentland, B.T.: Grammatical Approach to Organizational Design (2000) Available from: `http://ccs.mit.edu/papers/pdf/wp215.pdf`, (24 April 2003).
26. Klein, M., Bernstein, A.: Searching for services on the semantic web using process ontologies. In: Proceedings of SWWS' 01 The First Semantic Web Working Symposium, Stanford University, California, USA (2001) 431–446 Available from: `http://www.daml.org/services/daml-s/2001/05/`, (20 September 2001).

Representing Web Services with UML: A Case Study

Esperanza Marcos, Valeria de Castro, and Belén Vela

Kybele Research Group
Rey Juan Carlos University
Madrid (Spain)
{e.marcos, vcastro, b.vela}@escet.urjc.es

Abstract. Nowadays services are one of the most important issues in the scope of the Web Information Systems (WIS). Although, there is a great amount of Web services, still it do not exist methods or modelling techniques that can guarantee quality in services and service-oriented applications development. MIDAS is a model-driven methodology for the development of WISs and is based on UML, XML and object-relational technology. Web services represent a new dimension in WIS development, in which the systems are constructed by means of transparent integration of services available in the Web. WSDL is the language proposed by the W3C for Web service description. In this paper, an UML extension for Web services modelling defined in WSDL is described through a case study.

1 Introduction

In the last decade the Web has become one of the main channels to share and to spread information. Services are one of the most important issues in the scope of Web Information Systems (WIS). One of the central ideas of this approach is that future applications will be conceived like a collection of services available through the Web. So, for example, companies and organizations could encapsulate their business processes and publish them like services in the Web, or request other available services and integrate them to their applications, to provide new solutions.

Several technologies, such as JAVA or .NET allow implementing this kind of applications. However, there is not any solid methodological basis for service-oriented system and Web services development. For this reason, new methods or modelling techniques are needed to guarantee the quality in service-oriented WIS and Web services development. In the last years a large amount of modelling techniques and methodologies for the development of WIS [5,8,11] and service-oriented WIS [15] have appeared. MIDAS [13,4] is a model-driven methodology for the development of WIS, that proposes to use standards in the development process It is based on UML [2], XML [3] and object-relational technology [7]. MIDAS selects, adapts and integrates, if possible, the best techniques and notations of existing methodologies and also defines some new ones if necessary. Thus, for example, the UML extension for object-relational database design [12,14] and the UML extension to represent XML Schemas [16] have been defined.

Fig. 1 shows the MIDAS architecture, which has a system core that represents the domain and business models. Over this central core we define a ring which includes

M.E. Orlowska et al. (Eds.): IC-SOC 2003, LNCS 2910, pp. 17–27, 2003.

both the structural and the behavior dimension of the system. The core and this ring represent the technology and platform independent modeling. The external ring focuses on the different platforms and supported technologies. We will focus on the behavioral dimension of MIDAS, which is the marked part in figure and we propose to model the systems behavior with Web Services.

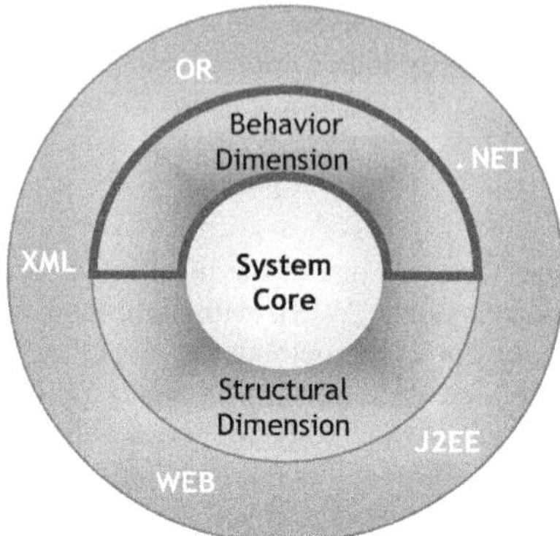

Fig. 1. MIDAS Architecture

The Web Services technologies provide a neutral language that accelerates integration of applications inside and outside the enterprise [10]. A Web service is a software system designed to support interoperable machine-to-machine interaction over a network. It has an interface that describes a collection of operations that will be accessible through the Web by means of standardized XML messaging. Web Services Description Language (WSDL) is the language to describe Web Services proposed by the W3C [17]. In this paper an UML extension for Web Services modelling based on WSDL is proposed. This extension has two purposes: to make easy both, the Web Services documentation at a high level of abstraction and the automatic generation of Web services description in WSDL from UML diagram.

Some other works related with Web services modelling and automatic WSDL code generation have appeared during the last years [1,20]. However these proposals have some limitations with respect to our goals. The extension proposal in [1] is not complete, since it does not allow operations and parameters modelling, neither relations between these components and others like input or output messages. Since one of our goals is to make easy the automatic generation of Web services description in WSDL from UML diagram, it will be necessary to define modelling guidelines that allow representing all the needed issues for Web services description maintaining the main benefit of modelling that is the reality abstraction. XMLSPY5 [20] case tool allows automatic generating of WSDL documents, but starting from its own graphical notation instead of from an UML diagram.

The rest of the paper is organised as follows: section 2 WSDL metamodel is described. In section 3 the UML extension for Web services modelling through a case study is proposed; finally, section 4 sums up the main conclusions and further research topics.

2 The WSDL Metamodel

WSDL [17,18] is a markup language proposed by the W3C for describing Web services. A WSDL document is an XML document which specifies the operations that a service can perform. One of the advantages of WSDL is that it enables separating the abstract functionality description offered by a service from description of concrete details, such as "how" and "where" that functionality is offered [6,9].

WSDL describes Web services through the *messages* that are exchanged between the service provider and requestor. An exchange of messages between the service provider and requestor are described as an *operation*. A collection of operations is called a *port type*, which define the service interface in abstract way. The *binding* between a *port type* and concrete network protocol and message format define the service interface in concrete way.

Fig. 2 shows the WSDL metamodel represented by an UML class diagram. The shadowed components represent the concrete issues of service description and the rest represent abstract issues of service description.

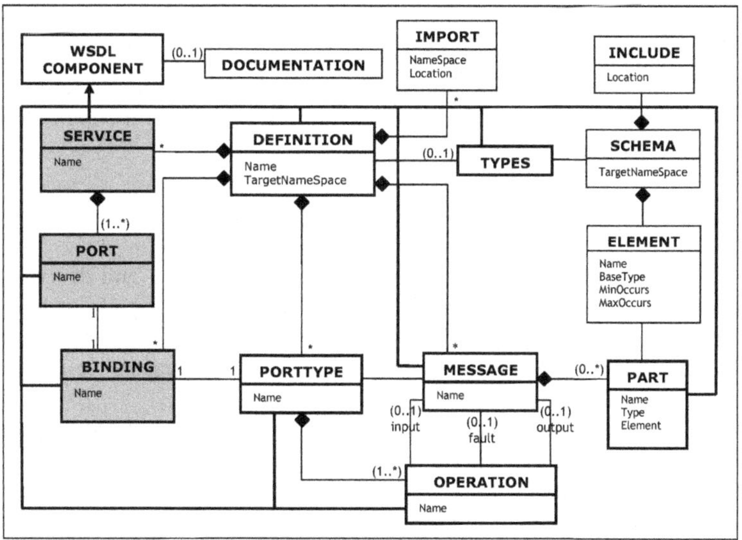

Fig. 2. WSDL metamodel represented in UML

A WSDL document contains a version number and a root DEFINITION component. It has a *Name* and *TargetNameSpace* attribute and zero or more namespaces. The namespaces are used to avoid naming conflicts when several services or applications are integrated. A DEFINITION component contains: a TYPES component and zero or more MESSAGE, PORTTYPE, BINDING and SERVICE components. All WSDL components can be associates with a DOCUMENTATION component.

A TYPES component is used for data type definitions which will be used in messages. For this purpose, WSDL is based on XML Schema [19] and contains a SCHEMA component in which, namespaces and data types are defined. WSDL allows to include XML Schemas documents defined previously, for that uses a INCLUDE component which indicates the document location. In the same way the

IMPORT component is used to reuse WSDL documents, the document name and location are needed.
The PORTTYPE component is the most important component in WSDL, since it describes the operations that the service realizes, that is, the interface. The OPERATION component groups the set of messages that will be interchanged between service provider and requester. Each operation can be associated with one, two or three messages, that is, one *input message*, one *output message* or both, and optionally *fault message*. A MESSAGE contains a *Name* attribute and zero or more PART components. The PART component describes one portion of particular message that Web service sends or receives. The type associated to a PART can be a base type XSD (int, float, string, etc.) or a type defined in the TYPES section. In this last case, the data type can be associated through a *type* or *element* attribute.
A BINDING component describes the binding of a PORTTYPE component and associated operations to concrete message format and communication protocol, such as SOAP, HTTP or MIME [18]. WSDL defines different components to describe each one of these protocols. However a detailed discussion on message format and communication protocol is beyond the scope of the present paper and will be boarded in future works.
A SERVICE component contains a *Name* attribute and describes the set of PORTs that a service provides. A PORT component contains a *Name* attribute. It is related with the BINDING component that describes how and where (by *location* attribute) to interact with the service interface.

3 Extended UML for Web Services Modelling

In order to represent each one of proposed elements by WSDL and described in the previous section, it will be necessary to extend the UML using its own extension mechanisms [2]. As we have already said, WSDL uses XML Schema for data type definitions that will be used for message sending. For this reason we use the UML extensions to represent XML Schemas proposed in [16].
The proposed extension for Web services modelling will be described through a case study. Firstly, we explain the criteria that have been used for the definition of UML extension. Next, in section 3.2 we describe in detail the service and next we formalize the extension explaining the use of proposed stereotypes.

3.1 Design Guidelines for the Definition of UML Extension

To choose the stereotypes necessary to represent in UML all the components of WSDL and their relations the following criteria are used:

- DEFINITION components have been considered as stereotyped classes because they are explicitly defined in WSDL and constitute the root component that groups all the used elements.
- TYPES and SCHEMA components have been considered stereotyped compositions with <<*TypeSchema*>> and represent the relation between a DEFINITION component and the data type definitions.
- MESSAGE, PART, PORT TYPE, OPERATION, BINDING, PORT and SERVICE components have been considered stereotyped classes because they represent important components and explicitly defined in WSDL.

- MESSAGE components will be related to the DEFINITION component, by means of a composition and must be associated, at least, one PART component.
- PART components will be related to the MESSAGE component that it used, by means of a composition. In addition the will have associate the data types that will be used in the message. Each PART component must be associate to only one MESSAGE component.
- PORTTYPE component will be related to the DEFINITION component, by means of a composition and will have associated, at least, one OPERATION component.
- OPERATION components will be related by means of an aggregation to the PORTTYPE component that defines its. In addition the MESSAGE component that its use, will have associated.
- BINDING components will be related to the DEFINITION component, by means of a composition and must be associated to one PORT TYPE component.
- PORT components will be related to only one SERVICE component and must be associated to only one BINDING component.
- SERVICE components will be related to the DEFINITION component, by means of a composition and must be associate, at least, one PORT component.

3.2 Web Services Modelling: A Case Study

We present the UML extension for web services modelling. For this, we have taken as a case study a flight information service of an airport called *"FlightService"*. Fig. 3 shows the *"FlightService"* Web service description in WSDL.

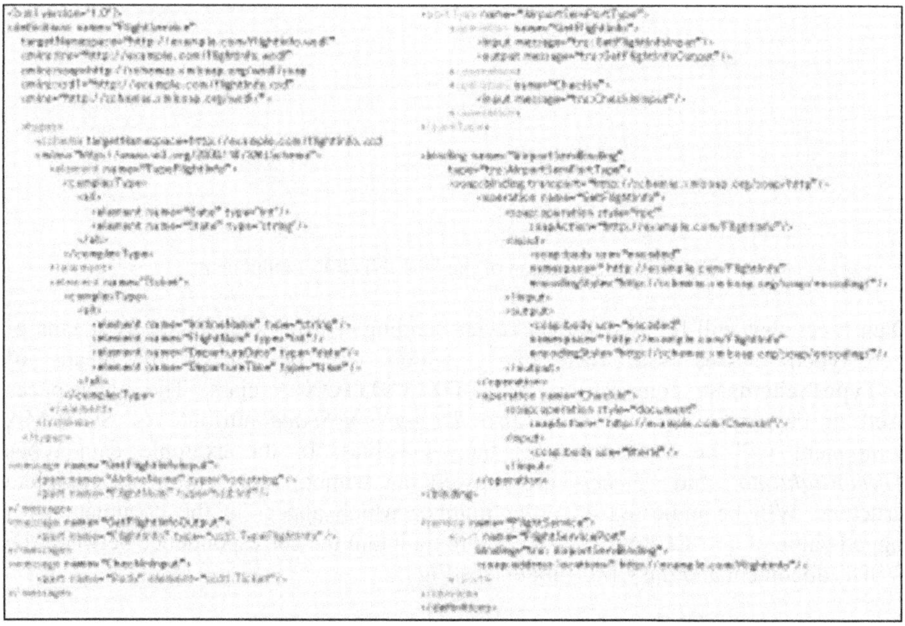

Fig. 3. WSDL description of a "FlightService" Web service

The Web service defines two operations *"GetFlightInfo"* and *"CheckIn"*. The operation *"GetFlightInfo"* has two messages, an input and an output message. The input message *"GetFlightInfoInput"* contains two parts: *"AirlineName"* and *"FlightNum"*, which use a base type XSD, string and int, respectively. The output message "*GetFlightInfoOutput*" has only one part *"FlightInfo"*, this part uses the element *"TypeFlightInfo"* as a data type, which is associated through a *type* attribute. The operation *"CheckIn"* contains only one input message *"CheckInInput"*. This message has only one part *"Body"*, which use the element "Ticket" as a data type and is associated through an element attribute.

The port type *"AirportServPortType"* groups the operations that will be performed by the service. The link between this port type and the SOAP protocol is described by the *"AirportServBinding"* element.

The service has only one port *"FlightServicePort"*, which defines through an URL the Web service location.

The UML extension to represent a Web service will be described considering the design guidelines previously established in section 3.1. Next, we will explain the used stereotypes for each component, its constraints and its tagged values.

DEFINITION component will be represented by means of stereotyped class **<<DEFINITION>>**. The *Name* attribute will be the name of the class and *TargetNameSpace* attribute will be represented as a class attribute. The used namespaces will be included as tagged values. Tagged values will be associated to element that defines its as a note, see Fig. 4.

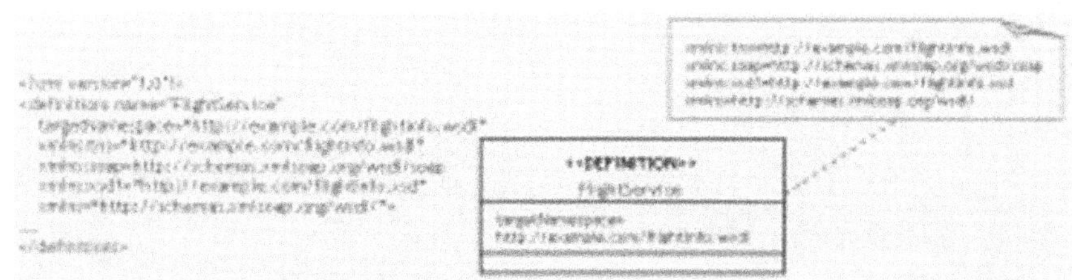

Fig. 4. Representation of the DEFINITION component

Data types that will be used for messages sending will be represented by means of stereotyped classes **<<ELEMENT>>**, which will be related by means of **<<TypesSchema>>** composition, to **<<DEFINITION>>** class. The namespaces used in data type definitions as also *TargetNameSpace* attribute of SCHEMA component will be represented as tagged values. In the example data types *"TypeFlightInfo"* and *"Ticket"* are showed but without representing its complete structure. Will be indicated an order number which appear in the document as a tagged value of a **<<ELEMENT>>** class to maintain the correspondence between the WSDL document and the UML model, see Fig. 5.

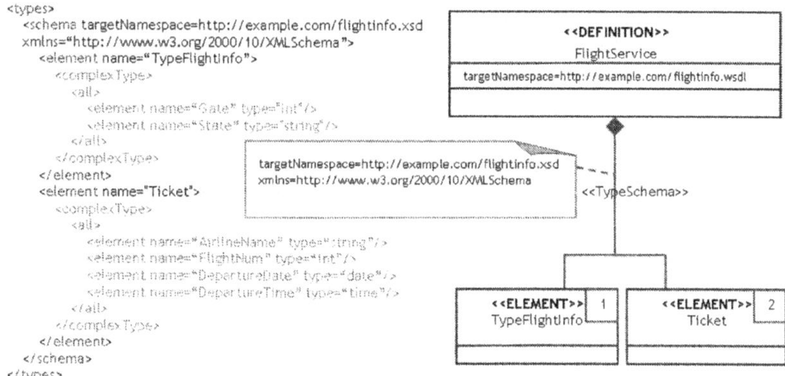

Fig. 5. Representation of the ELEMENT, TYPES and SCHEMA components

MESSAGE component will be represented by means of a **<<MESSAGE>>** stereotyped class. The *Name* attribute will be the name of the class and will have an order number as a tagged value. All **<<MESSAGE>>** classes will be related to a **<<DEFINITION>>** class by means of a composition. The PART component of each message will be represented by means of a **<<PART>>** stereotyped class that will have an order number as a tagged value with the message order number as prefix. In the example, the "*GetFlightInfoInput*" message has two parts which use a base type that are represented as a class attribute. The "*GetFlightInfoOutput*" message contains one part which has associated the "*TypeFlightInfo*" data type through a *type* attribute that has been previously defined. Therefore, the existing association between "*FlightInfo*" part and "*TypeFlightInfo*" element is stereotyped with **<<part_type>>**. The "*CheckInInput*" message contains one part which has associated the "*Ticket*" data type through a *element* attribute that has been previously defined. Therefore, the existing association between "*Body*" part and "*Ticket*" element is stereotyped with **<<part_element>>**. The **<<MESSAGE>>** class will have associated, at least, one **<<PART>>** class and each **<<PART>>** class will be associate to only one **<<MESSAGE>>** class, see Fig. 6.

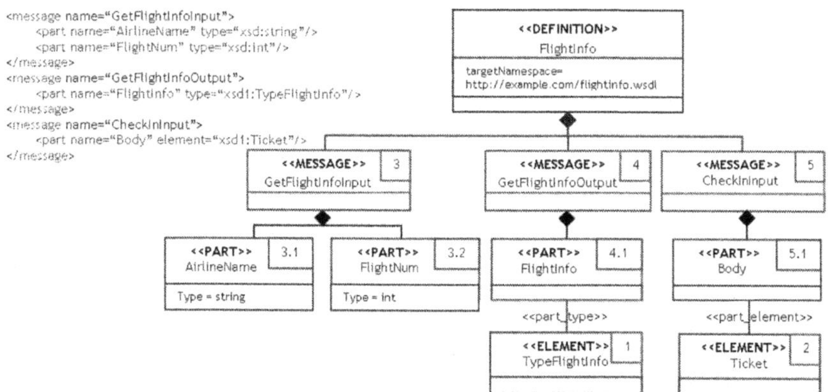

Fig. 6. Representation of the MESSAGE and PART components

PORTTYPE component will be represented by means of a **<<PORTTYPE>>** stereotyped class. The *Name* attribute will be the name of the class and will have an order number as a tagged value. The **<<PORTTYPE>>** classes will be related to a **<<DEFINITION>>** class by means of a composition. To represent OPERATION component, a **<<OPERATION>>** stereotyped classes will be used, that will have an order number as a tagged value with the PORTTYPE order number as prefix. A **<<PORTTYPE>>** class will have to be associated, at least, one **<<OPERATION>>** class by means of a composition. Each operation will be associated with the messages that it use and association stereotypes will be **<<input>>**, **<<output>>** or **<<fault>>** depending on the way which messages are used, see Fig. 7.

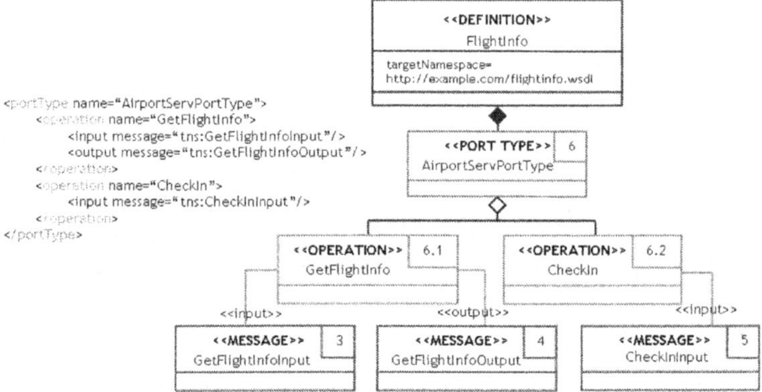

Fig. 7. Representation of the PORTTYPE and OPERATION components

BINDING component will be represented by means of a **<<BINDING>>** stereotyped class. The *Name* attribute will be the name of the class and will have order number as tagged value. The **<<BINDING>>** classes by means of a composition to a **<<DEFINITION>>** class and it will be related by means of an association to a **<<PORTTYPE>>** class that it describes. In the example BINDING component is showed without representing connection with SOAP protocol, see Fig. 8.

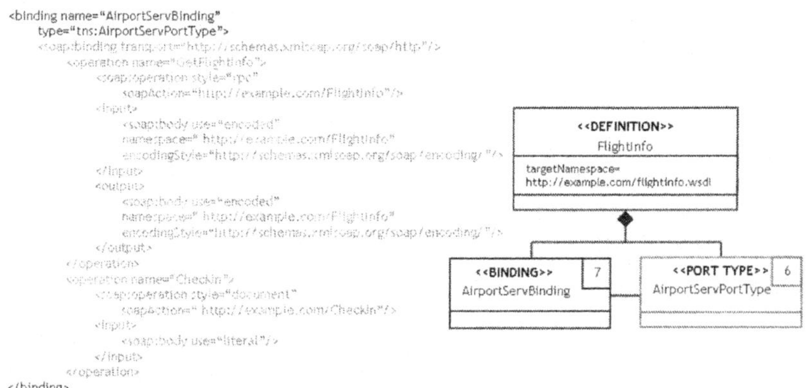

Fig. 8. Representation of the BINDING component

In order to represent SERVICE component a **<<SERVICE>>** stereotyped class will be used. The *Name* attribute will be the name of the class and will have an order number as a tagged value. The **<<SERVICE>>** classes will be related to a **<<DEFINITION>>** class by means of a composition and must be composite, at least of one **<<PORT>>** class which represent PORT component. This class will be related by means of an association to a **<<BINDING>>** class. The **<<PORT>>** class will have an order number as a tagged value with the SERVICE order number as prefix. The *Location* attribute indicates the service URL and will be represented like a class attribute. The **<<PORT>>** class will be related with only one **<<BINDING>>** class, see Fig. 9.

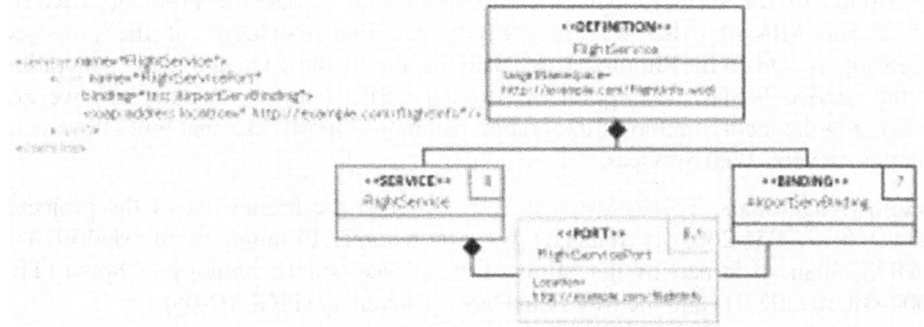

Fig. 9. Representation of the SERVICE and PORT components

Fig. 10 shows the UML representation of "FlightService" Web service taken as case study, using the defined extensions.

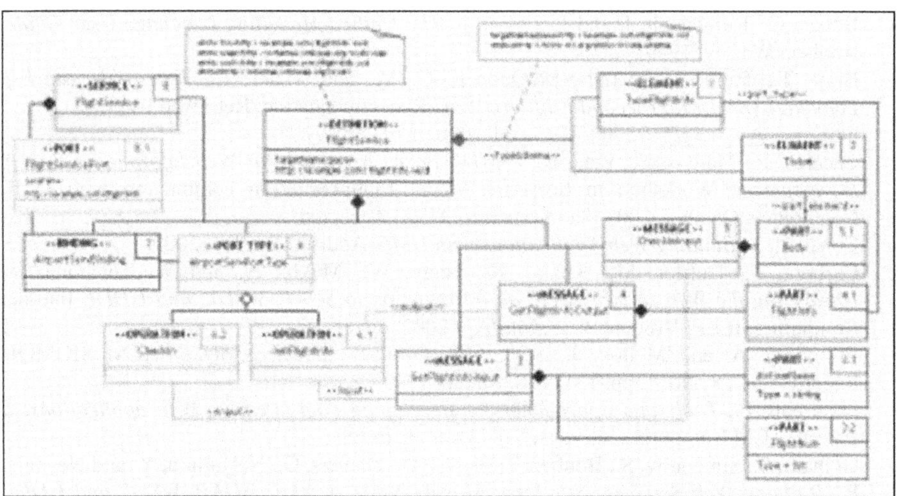

Fig. 10. UML representation of "FlightService" Web service

4 Conclusions and Further Research Topics

In this paper we have presented, by mean of a case study, an UML extension to model Web services defined in WSDL. This proposal is integrated in MIDAS, a methodological framework for WIS development, which proposes UML for the whole system modelling.
Firstly we have described the WSDL metamodel using UML. Next, a Web service which offers airport flight information and its UML graphical representation has proposed using the defined extension.
Actually we are working in the definition of the necessary extensions for the complete description of the service, including the connection to specific protocols (SOAP, HTTP and MIME). Also we are studying the implementation of the proposed extension as Add-In for Rational Rose, with the aim to allow the automatic generation of the service WSDL description of, from a UML diagram. In addition we are working in the incorporation of integration techniques in MIDAS that will allow us to compose several Web Services.

Acknowledgements. This research is carried out in the framework of the projects: *EDAD* (07T/0056/2003 1) financed by Autonomous Community of Madrid and *DAWIS*, financed in part by the Ministry of Science and Technology of Spain (TIC 2002-04050-C02-01) and the Rey Juan Carlos University (PIGE 02-05).

References

1. Armstrong, C., *Modeling Web Services with UML.* OMG Web Services Workshop 2002. Retrieved from: http://www.omg.org/news/meetings/workshops/webservices_2002.htm, 2003.
2. Booch, G., Rumbaugh, J. and Jacobson, I., *The Unified Modelling Language User Guide.* Addison Wesley, 1999.
3. Bray, T., Paoli, J, Sperberg-McQu4een, C. M. and Maler, E., *Extensible Markup Language (XML) 1.0 (Second Edition),* W3C Recommendation. Retrieved from: http://www.w3.org/TR/2000/REC-xml-20001006/, 2000.
4. Cáceres, P., Marcos, E., Vela, B., *A MDA-Based Approach for Web Information System Development.* Workshop in Software Model Engineering in conjunction with UML Conference. October, 2003. San Francisco, USA. Accepted.
5. Conallen, J., *Building Web Applications with UML.* Addison Wesley, 2000.
6. Curbera, F., Duftler, M., Khalaf, R., Nagy, W., Mukhi, N. and Weerawarana, S., *Unraveling the Web services web: an introduction to SOAP, WSDL, and UDDI.* Internet Computing, IEEE, Volume: 6, 2 , Mar/Apr 2002, pp. 86–93.
7. Eisenberg, A. and Melton, J., *SQL:1999, formerly known as SQL3.* ACM SIGMOD Record, Vol. 28, No. 1, pp. 131–138, March, 1999.
8. Fraternali, P., *Tools and approaches for developing data-intensive Web applications: a survey.* ACM Computing Surveys, Vol. 31, nº 3, 1999.
9. Graham, S., Simeonov, S., Boubez, T., Davis, D., Daniels, G., Nakamura, Y. and Neyama, R., *Building Web Services with Java: Making Sense of XML, SOAP, WSDL and UDDI.* SAMS, 2002.
10. Gottschalk, K., Graham, S., Kreger, H. and Snell, J., *Introduction to Web services architecture.* Retrieved from: http://researchweb.watson.ibm.com/journal/sj/412/gottschalk.html, 2003.

11. Koch, N., Baumeister, H. and Mandel, L., *Extending UML to Model Navigation and Presentation in Web Applications*. In Modeling Web Applications, Workshop of the UML 2000. Ed. Geri Winters and Jason Winters, York, England, October, 2000.
12. Marcos, E., Vela, B., and Cavero, J. M., *Extending UML for Object-Relational Database Design*. Fourth Int. Conference on the Unified Modelling Language, UML 2001, Toronto (Canadá), LNCS 2185, Springer Verlag, pp. 225–239, 2001.
13. Marcos, E., Vela, B., Cáceres, P. and Cavero, J.M., *MIDAS/DB: a Methodological Framework for Web Database Design*. DASWIS 2001. Yokohama (Japan), November, 2001. LNCS-2465. Springer Verlag. ISBN 3-540-44122-0. September, 2002.
14. Marcos, E., Vela, B. and Cavero, J.M., *Methodological Approach for Object-Relational Database Design using UML*. Journal on Software and System Modeling (SoSyM). Springer-Verlag. Ed.: R. France and B. Rumpe. Accepted to be published.
15. Rodríguez, J.J., Díaz, O. and Ibánez, F., *Moving Web Services Dependencies at the Front-end*. Engineering Information Systems in the Internet Context 2002, pp.221–237, 2002.
16. Vela, B. and Marcos, E., *Extending UML to represent XML Schemas*. The 15th Conference On Advanced Information Systems Engineering (CAISE'03). CAISE'03 FORUM. Klagenfurt/Velden (Austria). 16–20 June 2003. Ed: J. Eder, T. Welzer. Short Paper Proceedings. ISBN 86-435-0549-8. 2003
17. W3C *Web Services Description Language (WSDL) Version 1.2*. W3C Working Draft 3 March 2003. Retrieved from: http://www.w3.org/TR/wsdl12/, 2003.
18. W3C *Web Services Description Language (WSDL) Version 1.2: Bindings*. W3C Working Draft 3 March 2003. Retrieved from: http://www.w3.org/TR/2003/WD-wsdl12-bindings-20030124/, 2003.
19. W3C XML Schema Working Group. *XML Schema Parts 0-2:[Primer, Structures, Datatypes]*. W3C Recommendation. Retrieved from: http://www.w3.org/TR/xmlschema-0/, http://www.w3.org/TR/xmlschema-1/ and http://www.w3.org/TR/xmlschema-2/, 2001.
20. XMLSPY 5. Retrieved from: http://www.xmlspy.com/features_wsdl.html, 2003.

A Peer-to-Peer Advertising Game*

Paolo Avesani and Alessandro Agostini

ITC-IRST,
Via Sommarive 18 - Loc. Pantè, 38050 Povo, Trento, Italy
{avesani,agostini}@itc.it

Abstract. Advertising plays a key role in service oriented recommendation over a peer-to-peer network. The advertising problem can be considered as the problem of finding a common language to denote the peers' capabilities and needs. Up to now the current approaches to the problem of advertising revealed that the proposed solutions either affect the autonomy assumption or do not scale up the size of the network. We explain how an approach based on language games can be effective in dealing with the typical issue of advertising: do not require ex-ante agreement and to be responsive to the evolution of the network as an open system. In the paper we introduce the notion of advertising game, a specific language game designed to deal with the issue of supporting the emergence of a common denotation language over a network of peers. We provide the related computational model and an experimental evaluation. A positive empirical evidence is achieved by sketching a peer-to-peer recommendation service for bookmark exchanging using real data.

1 Introduction

A recent evolution of architectures for distributed systems attempts to overcome the narrow view of client-server approach to promote a fully distributed view, where every host can play both the role of service provider and service consumer at the same time. Napster [18] and Gnutella [10] are only the most well known examples of peer-to-peer architectures, mainly designed to support file sharing. However, this kind of architectures are going to be used in the field of e-learning [8], database [9] and knowledge management [13].

The peer-to-peer view [17] sustains a service oriented approach with the design and deployment of software components. In such a case a service may perform a task on demand but at the same time it may become a consumer of another service to accomplish the original commitment. In this twofold perspective of provider and consumer, a common language is crucial to support the peers interoperability independently from the specific role. Let us consider a very simple scenario of information retrieval: we need a language to support the service advertising, for example to express capability like *I m able to deliver*

* This work was funded by Fondo Progetti PAT, EDAMOK (*"Enabling Distributed and Autonomous Management of Knowledge"*), art. 9, Legge Provinciale 3/2000, DGP n. 1060 dd. 04/05/01.

M.E. Orlowska et al. (Eds.): ICSOC 2003, LNCS 2910, pp. 28–42, 2003.

contents on topic x , and we need a language to express the query, for example to formulate needs like *I m looking for contents on topic y* .

More generally the issue of a common language has to deal with the problem of semantic interoperability, that received an increasing attention after the success of the XML-based protocols. Nevertheless, XML-based protocols succeeded to provide an effective standard for the interoperability at the syntactic level, but the related semantics problem remains an open issue. Usually, the semantics of a new XML-protocol has to be agreed in advance. Such a process of negotiation is performed off-line and it doesn't allow to capture the evolutionary dinamics of an open network of peers. The consortia arranged to manage these agreements on semantics of a given protocol, moreover, are very slow in including new extensions.

A solution to the problem of a common language agreement has been proposed by DAML [11] and OIL [5]. The idea is to design a well defined ontology and refer to it to decode the semantics of a given interaction protocol [12,19,20]. We can refer to these approaches as solutions based on an *ex-ante* agreement: first let agree on semantics, then let use it. A drawback of ex-ante approaches is the underlying assumption of a centralized management of knowledge representation. As mentioned before, this solution is not responsive with respect to the ontology evolution and it contradicts the working assumption that aims to see the peers as autonomous (and not only distributed) sources of knowledge.

More recently there is a new kind of approach that aims to preserve the autonomy assumption while supporting an *ex-post* agreement view: first let use a semantics, then let map it to others. The basic idea is to allow the single peers to define its own semantics and then finding a pairwise mapping with other peer's semantics [1,4,7,14,15]. While this way to proceed represents a meaningful enhancement with respect to the ex-ante approaches, a couple of factors are neglected that are very crucial in a peer-to-peer architecture. The first is that, in an open world, peers join and leave the network; a mapping-based solution doesn't provide the opportunity to exploit past mapping efforts when a new peer join the network and a new custom mapping must be defined from scratch. The second critical factor is related to the scalability issue. Since a peer has to mantain a pairwise mapping for each other peer of the network, this solution requires a quadratic effort with respect to the size of the peer network.

We argue that instead of pursuing a pairwise custom language, the interoperability effort should be devoted to achieve a common language shared by all the peers. Language games [21,23], introduced by Steels in robotics [22], can be considered a powerful tool to support the emergence of a common language among a community of peers preserving their autonomy. Naming games, a specific type of language game, allow to achieve a shared denotation language through an iterative process of pairwise interactions. We claim that naming games can be an effective approach to the challenge of delivering service advertisement in an open network of peers.

In the following we introduce an extension of the naming game model, namely *advertising game*, to deal with the issue of achieving an ex-post agreement on an advertising language. A shared advertising language, differently from the mapping approach, requires only one mapping for each peer, therefore this solution is linear with respect to the size of the peer network. Advertising games differ from naming games because they have to deal with *indirect* feedbacks that introduce a component of uncertainty in the interaction process.

In Section 2 we illustrate a reference example that refers to a recommendation service over a peer-to-peer network. Nevertheless we believe that advertising game can have a great impact even in the field of semantic web and mutiagent systems, where the issue of capabilities language plays a similar role to advertising.

After a brief presentation of the general definition of naming game in Section 3, we introduce the advertising game model in Section 4 and the related computational schema. A more formal definition of the advertising game model is illustrated in [2]. Section 5 is devoted to present the results of the experimental evaluation performed using real world data.

2 A P2P Recommendation Service

To better understand how a language game approach can be effective in supporting the service advertising over a network of peers, let us introduce a reference scenario concerned with the delivery of bookmark recommendation services.

We conceive a community of users where each of them organizes his own bookmarks in the usual fashion of folders and subfolders. A folder can be considered representative of a topic of interest and the folder's contents, i.e. the URI, are the goods that can be shared among the users. Users autonomously collect bookmarks and organize them according to their topics of interest using directory path to uniquely refer to a folder and using a mnemonic label, i.e. the directory name, to denote the semantics of folder contents, i.e. a concept or a category. Of course, we assume to have a peer per user.

Once a user joins the network for the first time he has to deal with the following problems: how to share own topics of interest, i.e. bookmark's folders, and how to look for bookmarks according to his topics of interest. The first issue is concerned with service advertising (advertising language), the second issue is concerned with information retrieval (inquiring language). These issues are associated to the two roles that a peer can play over the network: as service provider and as service consumer respectively. The goal is to define a denotation language that may support both the purposes, advertising and inquiry, exploiting the mutual dependency that holds between an advertising language and an inquiring language.

Let us suppose that our user has a folder devoted to advertising topic. To correctly publish over the network the capability to support recommendation, i.e. new bookmarks, on this topic it is needed to assess what is the right denotation. A correct denotation allows to prevent misunderstanding in taking advantage of the recommendation service: if the user publishes an advertising service recommendation (i.e. capability to deliver advertising related bookmarks), how will be

```
<TopicAdvertisement>
  <Name>...</Name>
  <Topic>...</Topic>
</TopicAdvertisement>
```

```
<TopicQuery>
  <Name>...</Name>
  <Topic>...</Topic>
</TopicQuery>
```

Fig. 1. XML Communication Protocol. On the left hand side a sketch of the protocol to support the advertising of a new topic of interest, i.e. a folder to collect and to share bookmarks according to a predefined category. On the right hand side a sketch of the protocol to support an inquiry over the network to receive recommendations on related bookmarks.

interpreted by other peers? Will the label advertising be interpreted like a capability to deliver bookmarks related to companies that offer TV broadcasting advertisements, or like bookmarks on web services and the related techniques to support the advertising step? The answer of course is user dependent because the right interpretation is given by the expectation of the user that performs a query to other peers using the same denotation. If the user asks for *advertising* bookmarks recommendations, a satisfactory suggestion will include bookmarks that can be stored in the local folder with the same mnemonic label, i.e. interpretations of seeker and provider overlap.

Therefore the mutual dependency between the advertising language and the inquiring language can be exploited to assess the better way to publish over the network the own recommendation service. Before to advertising a new topic the user will try to refer to the other peer's recommendation services checking whether the denotation is consistent with the local working hypothesis. Of course the user can take into account the choice performed by other users or he can ignore them. A denotation not compliant with other users choices will affect the reliability of the services delivered over the network.

The open challenge is to arrange an interaction strategy that brings the peers to adopt a denotation language that reduces the misunderstanding between advertisements of recommendation services and queries for recommendation services. The ultimate goal is to promote the emergence of a shared language where all the users adopt the same denotation for the topic that has to be referred to.

In Figure 1 it is sketched a pairwise protocol to support the communications among peers: a topic advertising protocol and a topic inquiring protocol. Both protocols are defined by a pair: a label to denote the topic of interest, and the reference to the original encoding of a topic (see Figure 2 and Figure 5 for an example). In our example a topic is defined by the name of the directory that hosts the bookmark's folder, by the name of the folder and by the bookmarks stored in the folder.

From the point of view of the single peer a denotation language can be conceived as a mapping between a collection of words and a collection of topics. The name of the folder can be considered the topic's denotation choosen locally by a single peer.

```
<topic>
   <directory>/top/home/cooking/soups_and_stews/fish_and_seafood<\directory>
   <name>fish and seafood</name>
   <bookmark>...</bookmark>
   <bookmark>...</bookmark>
   ...
   <bookmark>...</bookmark>
</topic>
...
<topic>
   <directory>/top/home/cooking/soups_and_stews/beef<\directory>
   <name>beef</name>
   <bookmark>...</bookmark>
   <bookmark>...</bookmark>
   ...
   <bookmark>...</bookmark>
</topic>
```

Fig. 2. Topic XML Schema. A couple of examples of directories extracted from Google's web directories; each directory is defined by an identifier (in this case the full path), a name that should provide a mnemonic support to detect the related category associated to the directory (the local denotation), and finally a collection of bookmarks as defined in a following figure.

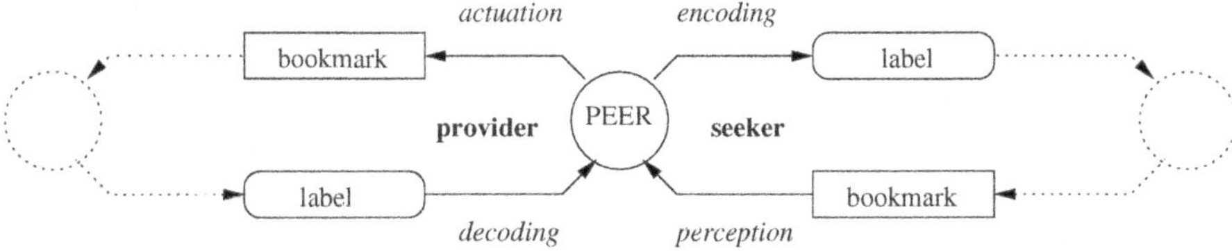

Fig. 3. Twofold Peer's Roles. The schema shows the four basic interactions according to the two roles a peer plays interacting with other peers: provider and seeker.

Figure 3 summarizes what happens in our scenario based on a peer-to-peer bookmark recommendation service. The interaction of a peer with an other peer differs with respect to the role it assumes in the interaction: provider or seeker. When the peer plays the role of provider he receives in input a label that refers to a topic of interest formulated by the sender. In this case the peer performs a *deconding* step to find what kind of topic is denoted by the given label. The next step is an *actuation* step that selects from the related folder the most novel bookmarks and sends them to the inquiring peer. From the other side when a peer plays the role of seeker the first step is an *encoding* step. Given a topic of interest, e.g. a bookmark's folder, the denotation is obtained looking at the lexical relation that binds a word to this topic. The word is sent to the other peers to look for novel bookmarks on related topic. The following step is a *perception* step that is in charge to assess whether the recommended bookmarks, received from the other peers, are compliant with the inquired topic and then can be stored in the associated folder.

It is worthwhile to note that the *encoding* and *decoding* steps are supported by the same common language, i.e. the mapping between words and topics, while the two steps of *actuation* and *perception* allows to be effective in delivering recommendation and to assess the compliance of the language (as by-product of recommendation service invocation).

Let us proceed to show how such a common denotation language can be achieved by an ex-post agreement approach using naming game.

3 A Naming Game Approach

Language games have been introduced to study language formation and evolution interacting with visually grounded robots [22]. A typical kind of language game is "naming," that is, how vocabulary and meanings are learned individually and a shared lexicon eventually emerges in a group of agents. The problem of naming may be expressed in game-theoretical terms, and was extensively studied as naming games in [24]. In short, each "player" (or even agent, peer, ...) has a set of words and a set of objects, and randomly associates a word to an object, called "the topic," to form his local lexicon. It is assumed that all the agents gain a positive payoff in cooperating "but only if they use the same language". A naming game is a coordination game and it is repeatedly played among randomly chosen pairs of players. Thus, a naming game involves a different couple of agents at each repetition of playing. By definition a naming game is adaptive, in the sense that the players in the game change their internal state. A reason for changing is to be more successful in playing future games.

More formally a naming game is defined by a set of peers $\mathcal{P}$, of size $\mathcal{N}_\mathcal{P}$ where each peer $p \in \mathcal{P}$ has a set of objects $\mathcal{O}_p = \{o_1, \ldots, o_n\}$ of size $\mathcal{N}_\mathcal{O}$. The objects are shared among the peers. A lexicon $\mathcal{L}$ is a relation between objects and words, where it is assumed that they are composed using a shared and finite alphabet. Lexicon is extended with a couple of additional information: the number of times the relation has been used and the number of times the relation was in successful use. Each peer $p \in \mathcal{P}$ has his own lexicon drawn from the cartesian product $\mathcal{L}_p = \mathcal{O}_p \times \mathcal{W} \times \mathcal{N} \times \mathcal{N}$, where $\mathcal{W}$ is a set of words and $\mathcal{N}$ the natural numbers to represent the peers' preferences. The lexicon may include synonymous words, two words associated to the same object, and homonymous words, the same word can be associated to two different objects. A peer $p \in \mathcal{P}$ is then defined as a pair $p =< \mathcal{L}_p, \mathcal{O}_p >$.

A naming game is an iterative process where at each step two peers are selected to interact together. Two different roles are given to them: a speaker p_s and a hearer p_h. The interaction proceed as follows. First the speaker p_s randomly selects a topic from his set of objects, then he encodes the topic o_i through a word w_j. The word is choosen accordingly to the current version of the local lexicon $\mathcal{L}_s$ (local to speaker p_s). The denotation of object o_i is obtained looking at the most successful word (a word w_j is more successful than a word w_k iff $< o_i, w_j, u_j, s_j > \in \mathcal{L}_s$, $< o_i, w_k, u_k, s_k > \in \mathcal{L}_s$, $u_j \geq u_k$ and either $s_j/u_j > s_k/u_k$ or $s_j/u_j = s_k/u_k$ and $u_j > u_k$). If the are more successful words a random choice is performed. The hearer p_h decodes the word w_j retrieving the associated object. Whether the object referred by the hearer is the same selected by the speaker both of them give a positive reinforcement to their lexica updating the following relations: $< o_i, w_j, u_j + 1, s_j + 1 >\in \mathcal{L}_s$ and $< o_i, w_j, u_j+1, s_j+1 >\in \mathcal{L}_h$. If the hearer replies with an object $o_l \neq o_i$, it means that the communication failed, the peers' lexicon is updated with a negative reinforcement increasing only the counters of lexical relation (while the counters of successful use of the lexical relation remain the same): $< o_i, w_j, u_j + 1, s_j >\in \mathcal{L}_s$ and $< o_i, w_j, u_j + 1, s_j >\in \mathcal{L}_h$.

Of course a next stage of the game may involve the same pair of peers with inverted roles. After a certain number of iterations, and under given conditions, the game brings the peers to converge to the same lexicon. It means that even though the lexical relation of different peers are not the same, given a topic all peers select the same word as the most successful denotation. In this case the communication between two peers becomes effective because it can't occur a misleading denotation or ambiguous words.

As mentioned before the final result of the game is a common denotation language. It is not stored on a specific server devoted to this purpose but it is encoded in a distributed way. Each peer has his own mapping table, the lexicon, that provides the support for the advertising and inquiring tasks. The distributed representation of the language, although introduces some redundancy, it allows the whole system to be fault tolerant, no one single point of failure, but mostly important it allows the peers to be responsive to the evolution of the language. Language can be evolve because new peers join the network, new words are introduced in the lexicon or new topics have to be delivered over the network. The issues related to the language evolution are deeply analyzed in the spatially distributed game [24] but they are not the goal of this paper.

We prefer to focus our attention to a crucial assumption that underlies the naming games. The key step of the peers interaction is represented by the assessment phase. The assessment step is in charge to check whether, given a word, the two peers refer to the same topic. This test is the precondition of the reinforcement policy because provides a reliable feedback on the lexical relations of the peers. But there is a further inherent condition that has to be satisfied when two peers interact together: the communication channel has to transfer contents that belong to a shared space. It is the case of words but not of the topics. Since topics represent abstract concepts or categories the encoding in terms of bookmarks's folders is local to a single peer. We have already seen in Figure 2 that a peer implicitly defines a topic through a folder pathname and a folder name. It straightforward to notice that in our case it doesn't exist the opportunity for the peers to assess the agreement on lexicon because the topic representations, even according to a common syntax, doesn't refer to a common semantics. Two peers can refer the same topic arranging the bookmark folders in different directories and giving to the folder a mnemonic label that respects their preferences[1].

[1] May be the double denotation of a topic may be misleading. It is important don't confuse the label of the folder, that plays the role of the local denotation of the topic, with the word defined in the lexicon, that globally defines the denotation for the same topic.

A trivial solution to this issue can be arranged looking at the approaches adopted in the semantic web and web services: they suppose the availability of a centralized representation of the topics where their meanings are well defined. It will be in charge of the peers to qualify their topics with respect to such a kind of catalog. The naming game will be accomplished comparing the $c(o_i) = c(o_j)$, where $c : T \rightarrow I$ is a function that takes in input a topic $t \in \mathcal{T}$ and gives in output the index $i \in \mathcal{I}$ of a common referenced representation (where $\mathcal{I}$ is the set of all the meanings indexed by a unique identifier i) . Of course this solution drastically reduces the advantages of a naming game approach.

The challenge is to preserve the language game framework while supporting the assessment step without any further condition of ex-ante agreements.

4 Advertising Game

We have seen in the previous section that if we allow the peers to encode locally their topics of interest, some communication issues may arise. If denotation is matter of negotiation and the representation is autonomously managed the only way to support the assessment of topic meaning is through the exchange of examples.

In our scenario the examples take the form of bookmarks. Bookmarks belong to a common space of the peers and can be shared among them. The link between topics and bookmarks can be defined providing a more detailed view of the two tasks of a peer: actuation and perception.

Actuation can be modeled as a function $f_a : \mathcal{T} \longrightarrow 2^{\mathcal{O}}$ that takes in input a topic and gives in output a subsample of objects. In our scenario bookmarks play the roles of objects and each of them can be considered as an example of a given topic. Actuation function has a stochastic component therefore two subsequent invocations of $f_a(t_k)$ not necessarily produce the same outcome. For example when a peer has to provide a recommendation on a given topic he can sample the related folder selecting the most novel bookmarks; of course the novelty of a bookmark is a time dependent notion therefore the sample may include time by time different bookmarks. From this example it is straightforward to notice that the definition of the actuation function is local to the peer because each of them can have a specific bias in sampling bookmarks for a given topic. Nevertheless, we make the assumption that given a topic $t_k \in \mathcal{T}$ and two peers p_i and p_j, the peers' actuation functions satisfy the following condition:

$$\cup_{n=1}^{\infty} f_{a_{p_i}}^{n}(t_k) = \cup_{n=1}^{\infty} f_{a_{p_j}}^{n}(t_k).$$

It means that, independently from the local encoding of the topic, if the meaning selected by two peers is the same, then an infinite iteration of samples produces the same set of bookmarks.

From the other side we model the perception task as a function $f_p : 2^{\mathcal{O}} \longrightarrow \mathcal{T}$ that takes in input a sample of objects, i.e. bookmarks, and gives in output an hypothesis of topic that may subsume such a sample. Of course the hypothesis formulated by the perception function is sensitive of the size of the sample. Given the assumption above on the actuation function, we may conclude that given a sample large enough, virtually infinite, it is possible to assess correctly the topic that underlies the sample generation.

Given the two definitions above, actuation and perception respectively, it s possible now to resume the naming game illustrated in advance and to show how it can be extended in an advertising game. Two are the main variations on the naming game scheme: the first is concerned with the hearer p_h ,the second with the speaker p_s. In the advertising game the hearer once received a word w_k from the speaker, he first decodes as usual w_k in the related topic t_k accordingly with his lexicon, then instead of sending t_k to the speaker, he applies an actuation step communicating $f_{a_h}(t_k)$, i.e. a set of bookmarks representative of the topic t_k. From the other side the speaker, differently from the naming game, doesn't receive a topic t_k but a sample of bookmarks; then he has to perform a perception step, i.e. $f_{p_s}(f_{a_h}(t_k))$, to obtain an hypothesis on the topic selected by the hearer. The assement process can now be carried on easily checking the condition $t_k = f_{p_s}(f_{a_h}(t_k))$.

The schema above introduces the notion of *undirect* feedback because the assessment is inherently uncertain. The uncertainty is related to the reinforcement policy: are we correctly rewarding a positive reinforcement (both denotation and perception hypotheses are correct) or are we erroneously penalizing with a negative reinforcement (drawing wrong conclusions from the error prone perception results)? Of course increasing the amount of examples, i.e. bookmarks, provided each other by the peers, it is possible to reduce the uncertainty virtually to achieve a *direct* feedback.

It is worthwhile to remark that, in the new advertsing game model, peers exchange only words and bookmarks, neither of them affect the assumption of autonomy. Moreover no additional ex-ante agreement is required excepted the communication protocol.

5 Experimental Evaluation

The next step is to put the advertising game model to work to provide some empirical evidence of its effectiveness. Let us resume our scenario concerned with a peer-to-peer bookmark recommendation service. To define a referenced set of topics we looked at the Google web directory [6]. We considered a snapshot of the whole directory, more specifically the Google:Top>Home>Cooking subdirectory. A collection of topics has been encoded accordingly to the XML protocol shown in Figure 2. The single topic has been derived from a node of the Google's structure using the path and the node label as unique identifier. Then accordingly to the bookmark's XML protocol shown in Figure 5 we encode the web pages classified under the given node recording the URI, a web page excerpt and the related preprocessed text that allows to obtain a collection of lemmata as abstract representation of the web page content.

```
procedure Advertising-Game(P, L, F_a, F_p):
    Initialize-Lexica(L_p)
    while not Exit-Condition
        p_s ← Random-Sample(P)
        p_h ← Random-Sample(P)
        t_s ← Random-Sample(T_s)
        w_s ← Lexical-Encoding(L_s)
        t_h ← Lexical-Decoding(w_s)
        B_h ← Topic-Actuation(t_h)
        t_h^s ← Topic-Perception(B_h)
        if t_s = t_h^s
            then L_s ← Lexical-Reward(t_s, w_s)
            else L_s ← Lexical-Penalize(t_s, w_s)
        endif
    endwhile
    end Advertising-Game
```

Fig. 4. Advertising Game Loop. A snapshot of the basic loop of an advertising game. Detailed parameters like the size of the bookmarks samples in the actuation step are omitted.

Figure 4 shows a snapshot of the basic loop designed for advertising game. Actuation functions have been uniformly modelled with a random choice without assigning specific biases to different peers. Perception functions have been modelled by a nearest neighbour classifier based on prototypes [16]. Given a sample of bookmarks, and their related encoding in terms of boolean vector of terms, a prototype is built averaging the different vector representations summarizing a new boolean vector representative of the original sample of bookmarks [3]. The new representation, i.e. the prototype, is compared with the prototypical encoding of the topics through a nearest neighbour rule. In this way it is possible to make an hypothesis on topic given a sample of bookmarks. After the perception step the game follows the same schema illustrated in the naming game model.

The performance of the advertising game is evaluated computing the level of agreement on a common denotation language achieved by the whole set of peers. The denotation agreement is computed looking at a triple $< p_i, p_j, t_k >$ checking whether both p_i and p_j have selected the same word w_h to denote the topic t_k, where $p_i, p_j \in \mathcal{P}$ and $p_i \neq p_j$. The whole agreement is defined as the ratio between the denotation agreements and all the possible communications, i.e. all the triple of the cartesian product $\{\mathcal{P} \times \mathcal{P} \times \mathcal{T}\}$.

The first set of experiments aimed to assess how much the advertising game is effective in supporting the emergence of a common denotation language, even though not all peers play against every other peer. Therefore we arranged an advertising game with 20 peers, 20 topics and 20 words. At each stage a peer playing the role of speaker selected an hearer from a subset of peers, namely his neighbours. We then repeated such a kind of games using a different scope of the peer neighbourhood. Figure 6 shows the results of experiment plotting

```
<bookmark>
  <uri>
    http://www.fish2go.com/rec_0120.htm
  </uri>
  <excerpt>
    Finnan Haddie and Watercress Soup: made with smoked haddock,
    potatoes, watercress, and milk.
  </excerpt>
  <lemmata>
     smoke,watercress,make,haddock,milk,potato,soup
  </lemmata>
</bookmark>
...
<bookmark>
  <uri>
    http://www.bettycrocker.com/default.asp
  </uri>
  <excerpt>
    Crunchy Snacks from Betty Crocker: collection of sweet
    and savory snack recipes which pack a crunch, from healthy
    vegetables to s'mores.
  </excerpt>
  <lemmata>
     snack,collection,recipe,healthy,savoury,vegetable,sweet
  </lemmata>
</bookmark>
```

Fig. 5. Bookmark XML Schema. A couple of bookmark examples extracted from the web directory of Google; each bookmark is defined by its URI, a short description that summarizes the page content, and the result of text processing step that after discarding the stop-words reduces the words to their lemmata.

on the x axis the iterations of a pairwise peer interaction, and in the y axis the percentage of agreement on a common denotation language. Although the restriction of a peer to play only with its neighbours the agreement evaluation was performed considering the hypothesis of full connectivity. The plots shown how the advertising game is effective in supporting the agreement on a common denotation language, although the scope is quite narrow. Even with a set of neighbours based on 30% of the peers the game converges. We didn't explore further smaller subsets of neighbours because in this case it is required to do more precise hypothesis on the network topology.

Thanks to these results we can claim that an advertising game doesn't require a synchronization among the peers to be effective. It means that it is not needed for all the peers to be connected with every other peers. This property is really crucial for the peer-to-peer architectures where the peers join and leave the network asynchronously. But these results are meaningful even from the practical point of view because they enable the opportunity to have an ef-

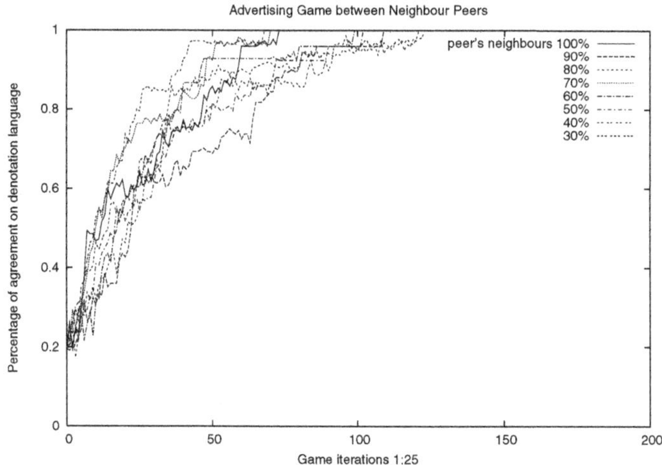

Fig. 6. Advertising Game Evaluation (1). The plot shows the performance of an advertising game where the peers play only with their neighbours. The different curves refer to the scope of the neighbourhood with respect to the size of the network.

fective communication between two peers, i.e. a non ambiguous denotation of a topic, although they have never "meet" before. Looking at our example on bookmark recommendation service it means that if a new user join the network, as a peer, s/he can look for novel bookmark recommendation listening the other peers advertisements without engaging with them a time consuming and bandwidth expensive assessment (of course assuming to have played in advance an advertising game with my neighbours).

The second experiment was concerned with the evaluation of the impact of an indirect feedback on the advertising game. Actuation and perception steps introduced an uncertainty factor because replaced the denoted topics with a sample of their examples. Therefore when the sample of examples is enough large to identify without ambiguity the related topic we fall into the case of naming game because we are facing with a kind of *direct* feedback. We can have different degree of uncertainty depending on the amount of ambiguous examples, i.e. bookmars, may be delivered by the actuation step.

Figure 7 shows the results of such kind of experiment. The different curves in the plot refer to the increasing ambiguity in pairwise peers interaction. It is worthwhile to underline that even though the uncertainty of an *indirect* feedback the advertising games succeed to find an agreement. Still with a 50% of ambiguous examples the network of peers achieves a common denotation language. Differently from the previous case it takes much more interactions to find an agreement, in average four times with respect to a *direct* feedback (pay attention to the different scale of the two plots in Figure 6b). It has to be observed that the performance at the beginning is not meaningful because we didn't ini-

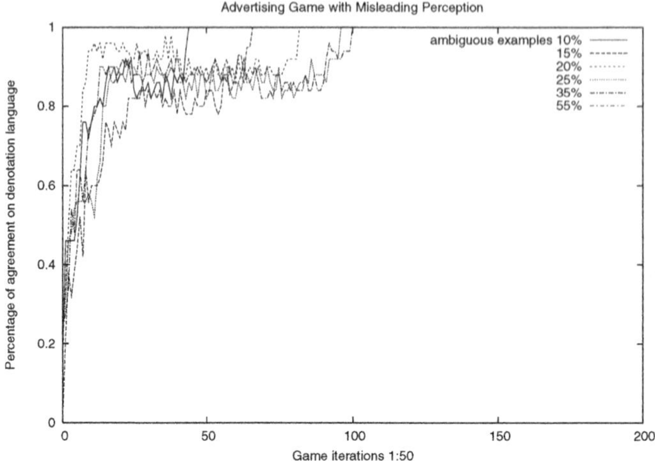

Fig. 7. Advertising Game Evaluation (2). The plot shows the performance of an advertising game when the perception can be misleading. The different curves refer to the percentage of ambiguous objects.

tialize the lexicon of the different peers with a predefined bias, but we simply started with the empty hypotheses.

These results are promising because they provide an evidence that advertising games can be an effective solution to the advertisement issue of distributed systems. Nevertheless, the optimal solution is in finding a trade-off between the bandwidth saving, i.e. small samples of examples, and the ambiguity reduction, i.e. large samples of examples. It would be trivial to enhance the performance of the advertising game without to take into account the scalability issue of bandwidth consumption.

6 Conclusion and Future Work

Advertising plays a key role in delivering service oriented recommendation over a peer-to-peer network. A review of the current approaches to the problem of advertising revealed that the proposed solutions affect the autonomy assumption or don't scale with respect to the size of the network. We explained how an approach based on language games can be effective in dealing with the typical issue of advertising: do not require ex-ante agreement and to be responsive with respect to the evolution of the network scenario both at the level of peers and topics. Nevertheless, naming games are not a satisfactory model for advertising because it doesn't allow to manage a local encoding of topics. We then introduced the notion of advertising game and the related computational model. An empirical evaluation on a real setting data allowed to provide a positive evidence of the proposed model.

As we have already argued, the advertising game is sensitive to the size of the bookmarks samples because if it is increased we overload the network, while if it is decreased we affect the base of induction of the perception. A new challenge arises for the advertising games: how to extend the base of induction without affecting the network overload. The exploitation of the interaction history or strategies based on multicast may help to enhance the current model.

A further critical assumption of the current setting is the homogeneous definition of the perception functions. It is really crucial to investigate what happens when different peers adopt different perception functions or different loss functions.

References

1. Y. Tzitzikas and C. Meghini. *Ostensive Automatic Schema Mapping for Taxonomy-based Peer-to-Peer Systems.* Springer-Verlag LNAI, vol. 2782, 2003.
2. A. Agostini and P. Avesani. Advertising games for web services. In R. Meersman, Z. Tari, and D. Schmit, editors, *Eleventh International Conference on Cooperative Information Systems (CoopIS-03)*, Berlin Heidelberg, 2003. Springer-Verlag LNCS.
3. R. Baeza-Yates and B. Ribeiro-Neto. *Modern Information Retrieval.* Addison Wesley, 1999.
4. Sonia Bergamaschi, Silvana Castano, and Maurizio Vincini. Semantic integration of semistructured and structured data sources. *SIGMOD Record*, 28(1):54–59, 1999.
5. Jeen Broekstra, Michel C. A. Klein, Stefan Decker, Dieter Fensel, Frank van Harmelen, and Ian Horrocks. Enabling knowledge representation on the web by extending RDF schema. In *World Wide Web*, pages 467–478, 2001.
6. Google Web Directory. `http://www.google.com/dirhp`.
7. AnHai Doan, Pedro Domingos, and Alon Y. Halevy. Reconciling schemas of disparate data sources: A machine-learning approach. In *SIGMOD Conference*, 2001.
8. Edutella. `http://edutella.jxta.org`.
9. I. Zaihrayeu F. Giunchiglia. Making peer databases interact, a vision for an architecture supporting data coordination. In *International Workshop on Cooperative Information Agents (CIA-2002)*, volume 2446 of *Lecture Notes in AI.* Springer Verlag, 2002.
10. Gnutella. `http://gnutella.wego.com`.
11. J. Hendler and D.L. McGuinness. Darpa agent markup language. *IEEE Intelligent Systems*, 15(6), 2000.
12. Michel Klein, Dieter Fensel, Atanas Kiryakov, and Damyan Ognyanov. Ontology versioning and change detection on the web. In *International Semantic Web Working Symposium*, 2001.
13. G. Mameli M. Nori M. Bonifacio, P. Bouquet. Kex: a peer-to-peer solution for distributed knowledge management. In *Proceedings of the Fourth International Conference on Practical Aspects of Knowledge Management (PAKM-02)*, volume 2569 of *Lecture Notes in AI*, pages 490–500. Springer Verlag, 2002.
14. Jayant Madhavan, Philip A. Bernstein, and Erhard Rahm. Generic schema matching with cupid. In *The VLDB Journal*, pages 49–58, 2001.
15. Bernardo Magnini, Luciano Serafini, and Manuela Speranza. Linguistic based matching of local ontologies. In *Workshop on Meaning Negotiation (MeaN-02)*, Edmonton, Alberta, Canada, July 2002.

16. Tom M. Mitchell. *Machine Learning.* McGraw-Hill, 1997.
17. G. Moro and M. Koubarakis, editors. *Agents and Peer-to-Peer Computing*, Berlin Heidelberg, 2002. Springer-Verlag LNCS 2530.
18. Napster. `http://www.napster.com`.
19. Wolfgang Nejdl, Boris Wolf, Changtao Qu, Stefan Decker, Michael Sintek Ambjrn Naeve, Mikael Nilsson, Matthias Palmer, and Tore Risch. Edutella: A p2p networking infrastructure based on rdf. *Computer Networks Journal, Special Issue on Semantic Web (to appear)*, 2003.
20. M. Paolucci, T. Kawmura, T. Payne, and K. Sycara. Semantic matching of web services capabilities. In *First International Semantic Web Conference*, 2002.
21. L. Steels. Grounding symbols through evolutionary language games. In A. Cangelosi and D. Parisi, editors, *Simulating the evolution of language*, pages 211–226. Springer Verlag, London, 2001.
22. L. Steels. Language games for autonomous robots. *IEEE Intelligent systems*, pages 17–22, October 2001.
23. L. Steels and F. Kaplan. Bootstrapping grounded word semantics. In T. Briscoe, editor, *Linguistic evolution through language acquisition: formal and computational models*, chapter 3, pages 53–73. Cambridge University Press, Cambridge, 2002.
24. L. Steels and A. McIntyre. Spatially distributed naming games. *Advances in complex systems*, 1(4), January 1999.

Automatic Composition of *E*-services That Export Their Behavior*

Daniela Berardi, Diego Calvanese, Giuseppe De Giacomo, Maurizio Lenzerini, and Massimo Mecella

Dipartimento di Informatica e Sistemistica
Università di Roma "La Sapienza"
Via Salaria 113, 00198 Roma, Italy
lastname@dis.uniroma1.it

Abstract. The main focus of this paper is on automatic *e*-Service composition. We start by developing a framework in which the exported behavior of an *e*-Service is described in terms of its possible executions (execution trees). Then we specialize the framework to the case in which such exported behavior (i.e., the execution tree of the *e*-Service) is represented by a finite state machine. In this specific setting, we analyze the complexity of synthesizing a composition, and develop sound and complete algorithms to check the existence of a composition and to return one such a composition if one exists. To the best of our knowledge, our work is the first attempt to provide an algorithm for the automatic synthesis of *e*-Service composition, that is both proved to be correct, and has an associated computational complexity characterization.

1 Introduction

Service Oriented Computing (SOC [16]) aims at building agile networks of collaborating business applications, distributed within and across organizational boundaries.[1] *e*-Services, which are the basic building blocks of SOC, represent a new model in the utilization of the network, in which self-contained, modular applications can be described, published, located and dynamically invoked, in a programming language independent way.

The commonly accepted and *minimal* framework for *e*-Services, referred to as Service Oriented Architecture (SOA [17]), consists of the following basic roles: *(i)* the *service provider*, which is the subject (e.g., an organization) providing services; *(ii)* the *service directory*, which is the subject providing a repository/registry of service descriptions, where providers publish their services and requestors find services; and, *(iii)* the *service requestor*, also referred to as client, which is the subject looking for and invoking the service in order to fulfill

* This work has been partially supported by MIUR through the "Fondo Strategico 2000" Project *VISPO* and the "FIRB 2001" Project *MAIS*. The work of Massimo Mecella has been also partially supported by the European Commission under Contract No. IST-2001-35217, Project *EU-PUBLI.com.*

[1] cf., Service Oriented Computing Net: http://www.eusoc.net/

M.E. Orlowska et al. (Eds.): ICSOC 2003, LNCS 2910, pp. 43–58, 2003.

some goals. A requestor discovers a suitable service in the directory, and then it connects to the specific service provider and uses the service.

Research on *e*-Services spans over many interesting issues regarding, in particular, composability, synchronization, coordination, and verification [21]. In this paper, we are particularly interested in automatic *e*-Service composition. *e*-Service *composition* addresses the situation when a client request cannot be satisfied by an available *e*-Service, but a *composite* *e*-Service, obtained by combining "parts of" available *component* *e*-Services, might be used. Each composite *e*-Service can be regarded as a kind of client wrt its components, since it (indirectly) looks for and invokes them. *e*-Service composition leads to enhancements of the SOA, by adding new elements and roles, such as brokers and integration systems, which are able to satisfy client needs by combining available *e*-Services.

Composition involves two different issues. The first, sometimes called *composition synthesis*, or simply *composition*, is concerned with synthesizing a new composite *e*-Service, thus producing a specification of how to coordinate the component *e*-Services to obtain the composite *e*-Service. Such a specification can be obtained either *automatically*, i.e., using a tool that implements a composition algorithm , or *manually* by a human. The second issue, often referred to as *orchestration*, is concerned with coordinating the various component *e*-Services according to some given specification, and also monitoring control and data flow among the involved *e*-Services, in order to guarantee the correct execution of the composite *e*-Service, synthesized in the previous phase.

Our main focus in this paper is on automatic composition synthesis. In order to address this issue in an effective and well-founded way, our first contribution is a general formal framework for representing *e*-Services. Note that several works published in the literature address service oriented computing from different points of views (see [11] for a survey), but an agreed comprehension of what an *e*-Service is, in an abstract and general fashion, is still lacking. Our framework, although simplified in several aspects, provides not only a clear definition of *e*-Services, but also a formal setting for a precise characterization of automatic composition of *e*-Services.

The second contribution of the paper is an effective technique for automatic *e*-Service composition. In particular, we specialize the general framework to the case where *e*-Services are specified by means of finite state machines, and we present an algorithm that, given a specification of a target *e*-Service, i.e., specified by a client, and a set of available *e*-Services, synthesizes a composite *e*-Service that uses only the available *e*-Services and fully captures the target one. We also study the computational complexity of our algorithm, and we show that it runs in exponential time with respect to the size of the input state machines.

Although several papers have been already published that discuss either a formal model of *e*-Services (even more expressive than ours, see e.g., [7]), or propose algorithms for computing composition (e.g., [15]), to the best of our knowledge, the work presented in this paper is the first one tackling simultaneously the following issues: *(i)* presenting a formal model where the problem of *e*-Service composition is precisely characterized, *(ii)* providing techniques for computing *e*-Service composition in the case of *e*-Services represented by finite state machines, and *(iii)* providing a computational complexity characterization of the algorithm for automatic composition.

The rest of this paper is organized as follows. In Section 2 and 3 we define our general formal framework, and in Section 4 we define the problem of composition synthesis in such a framework. In Section 5 we specialize the general framework to the case where *e*-Services are specified by means of finite state machines, and in Section 6 we present an EXPTIME algorithm for automatic *e*-Service composition in the specialized framework. Finally, in Section 7 we consider related research work and in Section 8 we draw conclusions by discussing future work.

2 General Framework

Generally speaking, an *e*-Service is a software artifact (delivered over the Internet) that interacts with its clients in order to perform a specified task. A client can be either a human user, or another *e*-Service. When executed, an *e*-Service performs its task by directly executing certain actions, and interacting with other *e*-Services to delegate to them the execution of other actions. In order to address SOC from an abstract and conceptual point of view, several facets may be identified [5], each one reflecting a particular aspect of an *e*-Service during its life time. Here, we focus on two of them, namely, *(i)* the *e*-Service *schema*, specifying functional requirements[2], i.e., what an *e*-Service does; *(ii)* an *e*-Service instance, that is an occurrence of an *e*-Service effectively running and interacting with a client. In general, several running instances corresponding to the same *e*-Service schema may exist, each one executing independently from the others.

In order to execute an *e*-Service, the client needs to *activate* an instance from a deployed *e*-Service. In our abstract model, the client can then interact with the *e*-Service instance by repeatedly *choosing* an action and waiting for either the fulfillment of the specific task, or the return of some information. On the basis of the information returned, the client chooses the next action to invoke. In turn, the activated *e*-Service instance executes (the computation associated to) the invoked action; after that, it is ready to execute new actions. Under certain circumstances, i.e., when the client has reached his goal, he may explicitly *end* (i.e., terminate) the *e*-Service instance. However, in principle, a given *e*-Service instance may need to interact with a client for an unbounded, or even infinite, number of steps, thus providing the client with a continuous service. In this case, no operation for ending the *e*-Service instance is ever executed.

When a client invokes an *e*-Service instance e, it may happen that e does not execute all of its actions on its own, but instead it *delegates* some or all of them to other *e*-Service instances. All this is transparent to the client. To precisely capture the situations when the execution of certain actions can be delegated to other *e*-Service instances, we introduce the notion of *community* of *e*-Services, which is formally characterized by:

[2] An *e*-Service schema may also specify non-functional requirements, such as those concerning quality or performance. However, non-functional requirements go beyond the scope of this paper.

- a finite common set of actions Σ, called the *action alphabet*, or simply the *alphabet* of the community,
- a set of e-Services specified in terms of the common set of actions.

Hence, to join a community, an e-Service needs to export its service(s) in terms of the alphabet of the community. The added value of a community is the fact that an e-Service of the community may delegate the execution of some or all of its actions to other instances of e-Services in the community. We call such an e-Service *composite*. If this is not the case, an e-Service is called *simple*. Simple e-Services realize offered actions directly in the software artifacts implementing them, whereas composite e-Services, when receiving requests from clients, can invoke other e-Service instances in order to fulfill the client's needs.

Notably, the community can be used to generate (virtual) e-Services whose execution completely delegates actions to other members of the community. In other words, the community can be used to realize a target e-Service requested by the client, not simply by selecting a member of the community to which delegate the target e-Service actions, but more generally by suitably "composing" parts of e-Service instances in the community in order to obtain a virtual e-Service which "is coherent" with the target one. This function of composing existing e-Services on the basis of a target e-Service is known as e-Service composition, and is the main subject of the research reported in this paper.

3 *E*-service Schema

From the external point of view, i.e., that of a client, an e-Service E, belonging to a community C, is seen as a black box that exhibits a certain *exported behavior* represented as sequences of atomic *actions* of C with constraints on their invocation order. From the internal point of view, i.e., that of an application deploying E and activating and running an instance of it, it is also of interest how the actions that are part of the behavior of E are effectively executed. Specifically, it is relevant to specify whether each action is executed by E itself or whether its execution is delegated to another e-Service belonging to the community C with which E interacts, transparently to the client of E. To capture these two points of view we introduce the notion of e-Service schema, as constituted by two different parts, called *external schema* and *internal schema*, respectively.

Also e-Service instances can be characterized by an external and an internal view: further details can be found in [5].

3.1 External Schema

The aim of the external schema is to specify the exported behavior of the e-Service. For now we are not concerned with any particular specification formalism, rather we only assume that, whatever formalism is used, the external schema specifies the behavior in terms of a tree of actions, called *external execution tree*. The external execution tree abstractly represents all possible executions of all possible instances of an e-Service. Therefore, any instance of an e-Service executes a path of such a tree. In this sense, each node x of an external execution tree represents the history of the sequence of actions of all *e*-Service instances[3], that have executed the path to x. For every action a belonging to the alphabet Σ of the community, and that can be executed at the point represented by x, there is a (single) successor node $x{\cdot}a$. The node $x{\cdot}a$ represents the fact that, after performing the sequence of actions leading to x, the client chooses to execute action a, among those possible, thus getting to $x{\cdot}a$. Therefore, each node represents a choice point at which the client makes a decision on the next action the *e*-Service should perform. We call the pair $(x, x{\cdot}a)$ *edge* of the tree and we say that such an edge is *labeled* with action a. The root ε of the tree represents the fact that the *e*-Service has not yet executed any action. Some nodes of the execution tree are *nal*: when a node is final, and only then, the client can stop the execution of the *e*-Service. In other words, the execution of an *e*-Service can correctly terminate only at these points[4].

Notably, an execution tree does not represent the information returned to the client by the *e*-Service instance execution, since the purpose of such information is to let the client choose the next action, and the rationale behind this choice depends entirely on the client.

Given the external schema E^{ext} of an *e*-Service E, we denote with $T(E^{ext})$ the external execution tree *speci ed* by E^{ext}.

3.2 Internal Schema

The internal schema specifies, besides the external behavior of the *e*-Service, the information on which *e*-Service instances in the community execute each given action. As before, for now, we abstract from the specific formalism chosen for giving such a specification, instead we concentrate on the notion of *internal execution tree*. An internal execution tree is analogous to an external execution tree, except that each edge is labeled by (a, I), where a is the executed action and I is a nonempty set denoting the *e*-Service instances executing a. Every element of I is a pair (E', e'), where E' is an *e*-Service and e' is the identifier of an instance of E'. The identifier e' uniquely identifies the instance of E' within the internal execution tree. In general, in the internal execution tree of an *e*-Service E, some actions may be executed also by the running instance of E itself. In this case we use the special instance identifier `this`. Note that, since I is in general not a singleton, the execution of each action can be delegated to more than one other *e*-Service instance.

An internal execution tree *induces* an external execution tree: given an internal execution tree T_{int} we call *o ered external execution tree* the external execution tree T_{ext} obtained from T_{int} by dropping the part of the labeling denoting the *e*-Service instances, and therefore keeping only the information on the actions. An internal execution tree T_{int} *conforms to* an external execution tree T_{ext} if T_{ext} is equal to the offered external execution tree of T_{int}.

[3] In what follows, we omit the terms "schema" and "instance" when clear from the context.

[4] Typically, in an *e*-Service, the root is final, to model that the computation of the *e*-Service may not be started at all by the client.

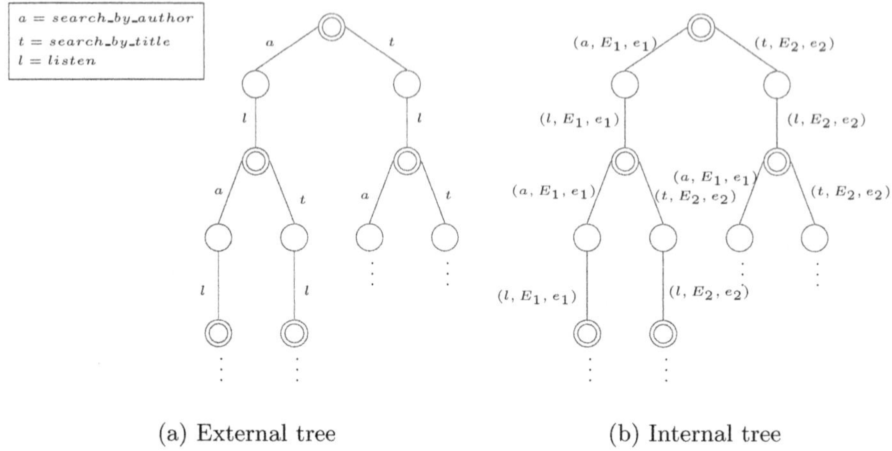

(a) External tree (b) Internal tree

Fig. 1. *E*-service execution trees

Given an e-Service E, the internal schema E^{int} of E is a *speci cation* that uniquely represents an internal execution tree. We denote such an internal execution tree by $T(E^{int})$.

We now formally define when an e-Service of a community correctly delegates actions to other e-Services of the community. We need a preliminary definition: given the internal execution tree T_{int} of an e-Service E, and a path p in T_{int} starting from the root, we call the *projection* of p on an instance e' of an e-Service E' the path obtained from p by removing each edge whose label (a, I) is such that I does not contain e', and collapsing start and end node of each removed edge.

We say that the internal execution tree T_{int} of an e-Service E is *coherent* with a community C if:

- for each edge labeled with (a, I), the action a is in the alphabet of C, and for each pair (E', e') in I, E' is a member of the community C;
- for each path p in T_{int} from the root of T_{int} to a node x, and for each pair (E', e') appearing in p, with e' different from `this`, the projection of p on e' is a path in the external execution tree T'_{ext} of E' from the root of T'_{ext} to a node y, and moreover, if x is final in T_{int}, then y is final in T'_{ext}.

Observe that, if an e-Service of a community C is simple, i.e., it does not delegate actions to other e-Service instances, then it is trivially coherent with C. Otherwise, it is composite and hence delegates actions to other e-Service instances. In the latter case, the behavior of each one of such e-Service instances must be correct according to its external schema.

Example 1. Figure 1(a) shows (a portion of) an (infinite) external execution tree representing an e-Service that allows for searching and listening to mp3 files[5].

[5] Final nodes are represented by two concentric circles.

In particular, the client may choose to search for a song by specifying either its author(s) or its title (action `search_by_author` and `search_by_title`, respectively). Then the client selects and listens to a song (action `listen`). Finally, the client chooses whether to perform those actions again.

Figure 1(b)[6] shows (a portion of) an (infinite) internal execution tree, conforming to the previous external execution tree, where all the actions are delegated to e-Services of the community. In particular, the execution of `search_by_title` action and its subsequent `listen` action are delegated to instance e_2 of e-Service E_2, and `search_by_author` action and its subsequent `listen` action to instance e_1 of e-Service E_1. □

4 Composition Synthesis

When a user requests a certain service from an e-Service community, there may be no e-Service in the community that can deliver it directly. However, it may still be possible to synthesize a new composite e-Service, which suitably delegates action execution to the e-Services of the community, and when suitably orchestrated, provides the user with the service he requested. Formally, given an e-Service community C and the external schema E^{ext} of a target e-Service E expressed in terms of the alphabet Σ of C, a *composition* of E wrt C is an internal schema E^{int} such that *(i)* $T(E^{int})$ conforms to $T(E^{ext})$, *(ii)* $T(E^{int})$ delegates all actions to the e-Services of C (i.e., `this` does not appear in $T(E^{int})$), and *(iii)* $T(E^{int})$ is coherent with C.

The problem of *composition existence* is the problem of checking whether there exists some internal schema E^{int} that is a composition of E wrt C. Observe that, since for now we are not placing any restriction of the form of E^{int}, this corresponds to checking if there exists an internal execution tree T_{int} such that *(i)* T_{int} conforms to $T(E^{ext})$, *(ii)* T_{int} delegates all actions to the e-Services of C, and *(iii)* T_{int} is coherent with C.

The problem of *composition synthesis* is the problem of synthesizing an internal schema E^{int} for E that is a composition of E wrt C.

An *e-Service Integration System* delivers possibly composite e-Services on the basis of user requests, exploiting the available e-Services of a community C. When a client requests a new e-Service E, he presents his request in the form of an external e-Service schema E^{ext} for E, and expects the e-Service Integration System to execute an instance of E. To do so, first a *composer* module makes the composite e-Service E available for execution, by synthesizing an internal schema E^{int} of E that is a composition of E wrt the community C. Then, following the internal execution tree $T(E^{int})$ specified by E^{int}, an *orchestration engine* activates an (internal) instance of E, and orchestrates the different available e-Services, by activating and interacting with their external view, so as to fulfill the client's needs.

[6] In the figure, each action is delegated to exactly one instance of an e-Service schema. Hence, for simplicity, we have denoted a label $(a, \{(E_i, e_i)\})$ simply by (a, E_i, e_i), for $i = 1, 2$.

The orchestration engine is also in charge of terminating the execution of component *e*-Service instances, offering the correct set of actions to the client, as defined by the external execution tree, and invoking the action chosen by the client on the *e*-Service that offers it.

All this happens in a transparent manner for the client, who interacts only with the *e*-Service Integration System and is not aware that a composite *e*-Service is being executed instead of a simple one.

5 *E*-services as Finite State Machines

Till now, we have not referred to any specific form of *e*-Service schemas. In what follows, we consider *e*-Services whose schema (both internal and external) can be represented using only a *nite number of states*, i.e., using (deterministic) Finite State Machines (FSMs).

The class of *e*-Services that can be captured by FSMs are of particular interest. This class allows us to address an interesting set of *e*-Services, that are able to carry on rather complex interactions with their clients, performing useful tasks. Indeed, several papers in the *e*-Service literature adopt FSMs as the basic model of exported behavior of *e*-Services [7,6]. Also, FSMs constitute the core of statecharts, which are one of the main components of UML and are becoming a widely used formalism for specifying the dynamic behavior of entities.

In the study we report here, we make the simplifying assumption that the number of instances of an *e*-Service in the community that can be involved in the internal execution tree of another *e*-Service is bounded and fixed a priori. In fact, wlog we assume that it is equal to one. If more instances correspond to the same external schema, we simply duplicate the external schema for each instance. Since the number of *e*-Services in a community is finite, the overall number of instances orchestrated by the orchestrator in executing an *e*-Service is finite and bounded by the number of *e*-Services belonging to the community. Within this setting, in the next section, we show how to solve the composition problem, and how to synthesize a composition that is a FSM. Instead, how to deal with an unbounded number of instances remains open for future work.

We consider here *e*-Services whose external schemas can be represented with a finite number of states. Intuitively, this means that we can factorize the sequence of actions executed at a certain point into a finite number of states, which are sufficient to determine the future behavior of the *e*-Service. Formally, for an *e*-Service E, the external schema of E is a FSM $A_E^{ext} = (\Sigma, S_E, s_E^0, \delta_E, F_E)$, where:

- Σ is the alphabet of the FSM, which is the alphabet of the community;
- S_E is the set of states of the FSM, representing the finite set of states of the *e*-Service E;
- s_E^0 is the initial state of the FSM, representing the initial state of the *e*-Service;
- $\delta_E : S_E \times \Sigma \to S_E$ is the (partial) transition function of the FSM, which is a partial function that given a state s and an action a returns the state resulting from executing a in s;

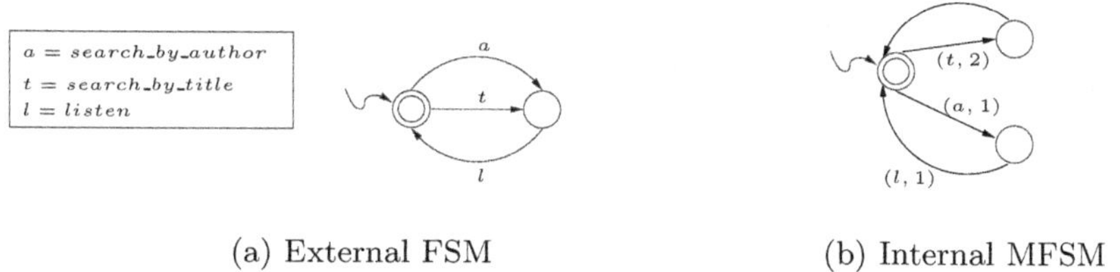

(a) External FSM

(b) Internal MFSM

Fig. 2. E--service specification as FSM

- $F_E \subseteq S_E$ is the set of final states of the FSM, representing the set of states that are final for the e-Service E, i.e., the states where the interactions with E can be terminated.

The FSM A_E^{ext} is an external schema in the sense that it specifies an external execution tree $T(A_E^{ext})$. Specifically, given A_E^{ext} we define $T(A_E^{ext})$ inductively on the level of nodes in the tree, by making use of an auxiliary function $\sigma(\cdot)$ that associates to each node of the tree a state in the FSM. We proceed as follows:

- ε, as usual, is the root of $T(A_E^{ext})$ and $\sigma(\varepsilon) = s_E^0$;
- if x is a node of $T(A_E^{ext})$, and $\sigma(x) = s$, for some $s \in S_E$, then for each a such that $s' = \delta_E(s, a)$ is defined, $x \cdot a$ is a node of $T(A_E^{ext})$ and $\sigma(x \cdot a) = s'$;
- x is final iff $\sigma(x) \in F_E$.

Figure 2(a) shows a FSM that is a specification for the external execution tree of Figure 1(a). Note that in general there may be several FSMs that may serve as such a specification.

Since we have assumed that each e-Service in the community can contribute to the internal execution tree of another e-Service with at most one instance, in specifying internal execution trees we do not need to distinguish between e-Services and e-Service instances. Hence, when the community C is formed by n e-Services $E_1, \ldots, E_n$, it suffices to label the internal execution tree of an e-Service E by the action that caused the transition and a subset of $[n] = \{1, \ldots, n\}$ that identifies which e-Services in the community have contributed in executing the action. The empty set $\emptyset$ is used to (implicitly) denote `this`.

We are interested in internal schemas, for an e-Service E, that have a finite number of states, i.e., that can be represented as a Mealy FSM (MFSM) $A_E^{int} = (\Sigma, 2^{[n]}, S_E^{int}, s_E^{0\ int}, \delta_E^{int}, \omega_E^{int}, F_E^{int})$, where:

- $\Sigma, S_E^{int}, s_E^{0\ int}, \delta_E^{int}, F_E^{int}$, have the same meaning as for A_E^{ext};
- $2^{[n]}$ is the output alphabet of the MFSM, which is used to denote which e-Service instances execute each action;
- $\omega_E^{int} : S_E^{int} \times \Sigma \to 2^{[n]}$ is the output function of the MFSM, that, given a state s and an action a, returns the subset of e-Services that executes action a when the e-Service E is in the state s; if such a set is empty then `this` is implied; we assume that the output function ω_E^{int} is defined exactly when δ_E^{int} is so.

The MFSM A_E^{int} is an internal schema in the sense that it specifies an internal execution tree $T(A_E^{int})$. Given A_E^{int} we, again, define the internal execution tree $T(A_E^{int})$ by induction on the level of the nodes, by making use of an auxiliary function $\sigma^{int}(\cdot)$ that associates each node of the tree with a state in the MFSM, as follows:

- ε is, as usual, the root of $T(A_E^{int})$ and $\sigma^{int}(\varepsilon) = s_E^{0\ int}$;
- if x is a node of $T(A_E^{int})$, and $\sigma^{int}(x) = s$, for some $s \in S_E^{int}$, then for each a such that $s' = \delta_E^{int}(s,a)$ is defined, $x \cdot a$ is a node of $T(A_E^{int})$ and $\sigma^{int}(x \cdot a) = s'$;
- if x is a node of $T(A_E^{int})$, and $\sigma^{int}(x) = s$, for some $s \in S_E^{int}$, then for each a such that $\omega_E^{int}(s,a)$ is defined (i.e., $\delta_E^{int}(s,a)$ is defined), the edge $(x, x \cdot a)$ of the tree is labeled by $\omega_E^{int}(s,a)$;
- x is final iff $\sigma^{int}(x) \in F_E^{int}$.

As an example, Figure 2(b) shows a MFSM that is a specification of an internal execution tree that conforms to the external execution tree specified by the FSM of Figure 2(a). Indeed the MFSM in the figure compactly represents the e-Service whose internal execution tree is shown in Figure 1(b). In general, an external schema specified as FSM and its corresponding internal schema specified as MFSM may have different structures, as the example shows.

Given an e-Service E whose external schema is an FSM and whose internal schema is an MFSM, checking whether E is well formed, i.e., whether the internal execution tree conforms to the external execution tree, can be done using standard finite state machine techniques. Similarly for coherency of E with a community of e-Services whose external schemas are FSMs. In this paper, we do not go into the details of these problems, and instead we concentrate on composition.

6 Automatic *E*-service Composition

We address the problem of actually checking the existence of a composite e-Service in the FSM-based framework introduced above. We show that if a composition exists then there is one where the internal schema is constituted by a MFSM, and we show how to actually synthesize such a MFSM. The basic tool we use to show such results is reducing the problem of composition existence into satisfiability of a suitable formula of Deterministic Propositional Dynamic Logic (DPDL), a well-known logic of programs developed to verify properties of program schemas [12].

We start from a set $\mathcal{P}$ of atomic propositions and a set $\mathcal{A}$ of *deterministic* atomic actions and we define DPDL formulas as follows:

$$\phi \longrightarrow P \mid \neg\phi \mid \phi_1 \wedge \phi_2 \mid \langle r\rangle\phi \mid [r]\phi$$

where P is an atomic proposition in $\mathcal{P}$ and r is a regular expression over the set of actions in $\mathcal{A}$. That is, DPDL formulas are composed from atomic propositions by applying arbitrary propositional connectives, and modal operators $\langle r\rangle\phi$ and $[r]\phi$.

The meaning of the latter two is, respectively, that there exists an execution of r reaching a state where ϕ holds, and that all terminating executions of r reach a state where ϕ holds. Let u be an abbreviation for $(\cup_{a\in\mathcal{A}}a)^*$. Then $[u]$ represents the *master modality*, which can be used to state universal assertions.

A DPDL interpretation is a (deterministic) Kripke structure of the form $\mathcal{I} = (\Delta^\mathcal{I}, \{a^\mathcal{I}\}_{a\in\mathcal{A}}, \{P^\mathcal{I}\}_{P\in\mathcal{P}})$, where $a^\mathcal{I} \subseteq \Delta^\mathcal{I} \times \Delta^\mathcal{I}$ is a partial function from elements of $\Delta^\mathcal{I}$ to elements of $\Delta^\mathcal{I}$, and $P^\mathcal{I} \subseteq \Delta^\mathcal{I}$ are all the elements of $\Delta^\mathcal{I}$ where P is true. Such interpretation is then extended to formulas and complex actions in a standard way, see [12] for details.

DPDL enjoys two properties that are of particular interest for our aims. The first is the *tree model property*, which says that every model of a formula can be unwound to a (possibly infinite) tree-shaped model (considering domain elements as nodes and partial functions interpreting actions as edges). The second is the *small model property*, which says that every satisfiable formula admits a finite model whose size (in particular the number of domain elements) is at most exponential in the size of the formula itself.

Given the target e-Service E_0 whose external schema is a FSM A_0 and a community of e-Services formed by n component e-Services $E_1, \ldots, E_n$ whose external schemas are FSMs $A_1, \ldots, A_n$ respectively, we build a DPDL formula Φ as follows. As set of atomic propositions $\mathcal{P}$ in Φ we have *(i)* one proposition s_j for each state s_j of A_j, $j = 0, \ldots, n$, that is true if A_j is in state s_j; *(ii)* propositions F_j, $j = 0, \ldots, n$, denoting whether A_j is in a final state; and *(iii)* propositions $moved_j$, $j = 1, \ldots, n$, denoting whether (component) automaton A_j performed a transition. As set of atomic actions $\mathcal{A}$ in Φ we have the actions in Σ (i.e, $\mathcal{A} = \Sigma$). The formula Φ is built as a conjunction of the following formulas.

- The formulas representing $A_0 = (\Sigma, S_0, s_0^0, \delta_0, F_0)$:
  - $[u](s \to \neg s')$ for all pairs of states $s \in S_0$ and $s' \in S_0$, with $s \neq s'$; these say that propositions representing different states are disjoint (cannot be true simultaneously).
  - $[u](s \to \langle a\rangle\mathtt{true} \wedge [a]s')$ for each a such that $s' = \delta_0(s, a)$; these encode the transitions of A_0.
  - $[u](s \to [a]\mathtt{false})$ for each a such that $\delta(s, a)$ is not defined; these say when a transition is not defined.
  - $[u](F_0 \leftrightarrow \bigvee_{s\in F_0} s)$; this highlights final states of A_0.
- For each component FSM $A_i = (\Sigma, S_i, s_i^0, \delta_i, F_i)$, the following formulas:
  - $[u](s \to \neg s')$ for all pairs of states $s \in S_i$ and $s' \in S_i$, with $s \neq s'$; these again say that propositions representing different states are disjoint.
  - $[u](s \to [a](moved_i \wedge s' \vee \neg moved_i \wedge s))$ for each a such that $s' = \delta_i(s, a)$; these encode the transitions of A_i, conditioned to the fact that the component A_i is actually required to make a transition a in the composition.
  - $[u](s \to [a]\neg moved_i)$ for each a such that $\delta_i(s, a)$ is not defined; these say that when a transition is not defined, A_i cannot be asked to execute in the composition.
  - $[u](F_i \leftrightarrow \bigvee_{s\in F_i} s)$; this highlights final states of A_i.

- Finally, the following formulas:
  - $s_0^0 \wedge \bigwedge_{i=1,\dots,n} s_i^0$; this says that initially all e-Services are in their initial state; note that this formula is not prefixed by $[u]\cdot$.
  - $[u](\langle a\rangle\mathtt{true} \rightarrow [a]\bigvee_{i=1,\dots,n} moved_i)$, for each $a \in \Sigma$; these say that at each step at least one of the component FSM has moved.
  - $[u](F_0 \rightarrow \bigwedge_{i=1,\dots,n} F_i)$; this says that when the target e-Service is in a final state also all component e-Services must be in a final state.

Theorem 1. *The DPDL formula Φ, constructed as above, is satis able if and only if there exists a composition of E_0 wrt $E_1,\dots,E_n$.*

Proof (sketch). "$\Leftarrow$" Suppose that there exists some internal schema (without restriction on its form) ${E_0}^{int}$ which is a composition of E_0 wrt $E_1,\dots,E_n$. Let $T_{int} = T({E_0}^{int})$ be the internal execution tree defined by ${E_0}^{int}$.

Then for the target e-Service E_0 and each component e-Service E_i, $i = 1,\dots n$, we can define mappings σ and σ_i from nodes in T_{int} to states of A_0 and A_i, respectively, by induction on the level of the nodes in T_{int} as follows.

- base case: $\sigma(\varepsilon) = s_0^0$ and $\sigma_i(\varepsilon) = s_i^0$.
- inductive case: let $\sigma(x) = s$ and $\sigma_i(x) = s_i$, and let the node $x \cdot a$ be in T_{int} with the edge $(x, x \cdot a)$ labeled by (a, I), where $I \subseteq [n]$ and $I \neq \emptyset$ (notice that `this` may not occur since T_{int} is specified by a composition). Then we define

$$\sigma(x \cdot a) = s' = \delta_0(s, a)$$

and

$$\sigma_i(x \cdot a) = \begin{cases} {s_i}' = \delta_i(s_i, a) & \text{if } i \in I \\ s_i & \text{if } i \notin I \end{cases}$$

Once we have σ and σ_i in place we can define a model $\mathcal{I} = (\Delta^{\mathcal{I}}, \{a^{\mathcal{I}}\}_{a\in\Sigma}, \{P^{\mathcal{I}}\}_{P\in\mathcal{P}})$ of Φ as follows:

- $\Delta^{\mathcal{I}} = \{x \mid x \in T_{int}\}$;
- $a^{\mathcal{I}} = \{(x, x \cdot a) \mid x, x \cdot a \in T_{int}\}$, for each $a \in \Sigma$;
- $s^{\mathcal{I}} = \{x \in T_{int} \mid \sigma(x) = s\}$, for all propositions s corresponding to states of A_0;
- $s_i^{\mathcal{I}} = \{x \in T_{int} \mid \sigma_i(x) = s_i\}$, for all propositions s_i corresponding to states of A_i;
- $moved_i^{\mathcal{I}} = \{x \cdot a \mid (x, x \cdot a)$ is labeled by I with $i \in I\}$, for $i = 1,\dots,n$;
- $F_0^{\mathcal{I}} = \{x \in T_{int} \mid \sigma(x) = s$ with $s \in F_0\}$;
- $F_i^{\mathcal{I}} = \{x \in T_{int} \mid \sigma_i(x) = s_i$ with $s_i \in F_i\}$, for $i = 1,\dots,n$.

It is easy to check that, being T_{int} specified by a composition E_{int}, the above model indeed satisfies Φ.

"$\Rightarrow$" Let Φ be satisfiable and $\mathcal{I} = (\Delta^{\mathcal{I}}, \{a^{\mathcal{I}}\}_{a\in\Sigma}, \{P^{\mathcal{I}}\}_{P\in\mathcal{P}})$ be a tree-like model. From $\mathcal{I}$ we can build an internal execution tree T_{int} for E_0 as follows.

- the nodes of the tree are the elements of $\Delta^{\mathcal{I}}$; actually, since $\mathcal{I}$ is tree-like we can denote the elements in $\Delta^{\mathcal{I}}$ as nodes of a tree, using the same notation that we used for internal/external execution tree;
- nodes x such that $x \in F_0^{\mathcal{I}}$ are the final nodes;
- if $(x, x \cdot a) \in a^{\mathcal{I}}$ and for all $i \in I$, $x \cdot a \in moved_i^{\mathcal{I}}$ and for all $j \notin I$, $x \cdot a \notin moved_j^{\mathcal{I}}$, then $(x, x \cdot a)$ is labeled by (a, I).

It is possible to show that: *(i)* T_{int} conforms to $T(A_0)$, *(ii)* T_{int} delegates all actions to the e-Services of $E_1, \ldots, E_n$, and *(iii)* T_{int} is coherent with $E_1, \ldots, E_n$. Since we are not placing any restriction on the kind of specification allowed for internal schemas, it follows that there exists an internal schema E_{int} that is a composition of E_0 wrt $E_1, \ldots, E_n$. □

Observe that the size of Φ is polynomially related to the size of A_0, $A_1, \ldots, A_n$. Hence, from the EXPTIME-completeness of satisfiability in DPDL and from Theorem 1 we get the following complexity result.

Theorem 2. *Checking the existence of an* e-*Service composition can be done in EXPTIME.*

Observe that, because of the small model property, from Φ one can always obtain a model which is at most exponential in the size of Φ. From such a model one can extract an internal schema for E_0 that is a composition of E_0 wrt $E_1, \ldots, E_n$, and has the form of a MFSM. Specifically, given a finite model $\mathcal{I} = (\Delta^{\mathcal{I}}, \{a^{\mathcal{I}}\}_{a \in \Sigma}, \{P^{\mathcal{I}}\}_{P \in \mathcal{P}})$, we define such an MFSM $A_c = (\Sigma, 2^{[n]}, S_c, s_c^0, \delta_c, \omega_c, F_c,)$ as follows:

- $S_c = \Delta^{\mathcal{I}}$;
- $s_c^0 = d_0$ where $d_0 \in (s_0^0 \wedge \bigwedge_{i=1,\ldots,n} s_i^0)^{\mathcal{I}}$;
- $s' = \delta_c(s, a)$ iff $(s, s') \in a^{\mathcal{I}}$;
- $I = \omega_c(s, a)$ iff $(s, s') \in a^{\mathcal{I}}$ and for all $i \in I$, $s' \in moved_i^{\mathcal{I}}$ and for all $j \notin I$, $s' \notin moved_j^{\mathcal{I}}$;
- $F_c = F_0^{\mathcal{I}}$.

As a consequence of this, we get the following result.

Theorem 3. *If there exists a composition of E_0 wrt $E_1, \ldots, E_0$, then there exists one which is a MFSM of at most exponential size in the size of the external schemas A_0, $A_1, \ldots, A_n$ of E_0, $E_1, \ldots, E_n$ respectively.*

Proof (sketch). By Theorem 1, if A_0 can be obtained by composing $A_1, \ldots, A_n$, then the DPDL formula Φ constructed as above is satisfiable. In turn, if Φ is satisfiable, for the small-model property of DPDL there exists a model $\mathcal{I}$ of size at most exponential in Φ, and hence in A_0 and $A_1, \ldots, A_n$. From $\mathcal{I}$ we can construct a MFSM A_c as above. It is possible to show that the internal execution tree $T(A_c)$ defined by A_c satisfies all the conditions required for A_c to be a composition, namely: *(i)* $T(A_c)$ conforms to $T(A_0)$, *(ii)* $T(A_c)$ delegates all actions to the e-Services of $E_1, \ldots, E_n$, and *(iii)* $T(A_c)$ is coherent with $E_1, \ldots, E_n$. □

In [4] a detailed example is provided, that explains the composition synthesis algorithm step by step.

From a practical point of view, because of the correspondence between Propositional Dynamic Logics (which DPDL belongs to) and Description Logics (DLs [8]), one can use current highly optimized DL-based systems [3][7] to check the existence of e-Service compositions. Indeed, these systems are based on tableaux techniques that construct a model when checking for satisfiability, and from such a model one can construct a MFSM that is the composition.

7 Related Work

Up to now, research on e-Services has mainly concentrated on the issues of *(i)* service description and modeling, and *(ii)* service composition, including synthesis and orchestration.

Current research in description and modeling of e-Services is mainly founded on the work on workflows, which model business processes as sequences of (possibly partially) automated activities, in terms of data and control flow among them (e.g., [18,19]). In [14] e-Services are represented as statecharts, and in [7], an e-Service is modeled as a Mealy machine, with input and output messages, and a queue is used to buffer messages that were received but not yet processed.

In our paper, we model e-Services as finite state machines, even if we do not consider communication delays and therefore any concept of message queuing is not taken into account. Indeed, from the survey of [11], it stems that the most practical approaches for modeling and describing e-Services are the ones based on specific forms of state machines. Additionally, our model of e-Service is oriented towards representing the interactions between a client and an e-Service. Therefore, our focus is on action sequences, rather than on message sequences as in [7], or on actions with input/output parameters as in [15].

Orchestration requires that the composite e-Service is specified in a precise way, considering both the specification of how various component e-Services are linked and the internal process flow of the component one. In [11], different technologies, standards and approaches for specification of composite e-Services are considered, including BPEL4WS, BPML, AZTEC, etc. In [11] three different kinds of composition are identified: *(i)* peer-to-peer, in which the individual e-Services are equals, *(ii)* the mediated approach, based on a hub-and-spoke topology, in which one service is given the role of process mediator, and *(iii)* the brokered approach, where process control is centralized but data can pass between component e-Services. With respect to such a classification, the approach proposed in this paper belongs to the mediated one. Analogously, research works reported in [9,19,13] can be classified into the mediated approach to composition. Conversely in [10] the enactment of a composite e-Service is carried out in a decentralized way, through peer-to-peer interactions. In [7], a peer-to-peer

[7] In fact, current DL-based systems cannot handle Kleene star. However, since in Φ, $*$ is only used to mimic universal assertions, and such systems have the ability of handling universal assertions, they can indeed check satisfiability of Φ.

approach is considered, and the interplay between a composite *e*-Service and component ones is analyzed, also in presence of unexpected behavior.

The *DAML-S Coalition* [2] is defining a specific ontology and a related language for *e*-Services, with the aim of composing them in automatic way. In [20] the issue of service composition is addressed, in order to create composite services by re-using, specializing and extending existing ones; in [15] composition of *e*-Services is addressed by using GOLOG and providing a semantics of the composition based on Petri Nets. In [1] a way of composing *e*-Services is presented, based on planning under uncertainty and constraint satisfaction techniques, and a request language, to be used for specifying client goals, is proposed. *e*-Service composition is indeed a form of program synthesis as is planning. The main conceptual difference is that, while in planning we are typically interested in synthesizing a *new* sequence of actions (or more generally a program, i.e., an execution tree) that achieves the client goal, in *e*-Service composition, we try to obtain (the execution tree of) the target *e*-Service by *reusing* in a suitable way fragments of the executions of the component *e*-Services.

8 Conclusions

The main contribution of this paper wrt research on service oriented computing is in tackling *simultaneously* the following issues: *(i)* presenting a formal model where the problem of *e*-Service composition is precisely characterized, *(ii)* providing techniques for computing *e*-Service composition in the case of *e*-Services represented by finite state machines, and *(iii)* providing a computational complexity characterization of the algorithm for automatic composition.

In the future we plan to extend our work both in practical and theoretical directions. On one side, we are developing a DL-based prototype system that implements the composition technique presented in the paper. Such system will enable us to test how the complexity of composition in our framework impacts real world applications. On the theoretical side, we will address open issues such as the characterization of a lower bound for the complexity of the composition problem. Additionally, we plan to extend our setting, by taking into account the possibility that the target *e*-Service is underspecified, as well as the presence of communication delays and of an unbounded number of active instances.

References

1. M. Aiello, M.P. Papazoglou, J. Yang, M. Carman, M. Pistore, L. Serafini, and P. Traverso. A Request Language for Web-Services Based on Planning and Constraint Satisfaction. In *Proc. of VLDB-TES 2002*.
2. A. Ankolekar, M. Burstein, J. Hobbs, O. Lassila, D. Martin, D. McDermott, S. McIlraith, S. Narayanan, M. Paolucci, T. Payne, and K. Sycara. DAML-S: Web Service Description for the Semantic Web. In *Proc. of ISWC 2002*.
3. F. Baader, D. Calvanese, D. McGuinness, D. Nardi, and P. Patel-Schneider. *The Description Logic Handbook: Theory, Implementation and Applications.* CUP, 2003.

4. D. Berardi, D. Calvanese, G. De Giacomo, M. Lenzerini, and M. Mecella. Automatic Composition of *e*-Services. Technical Report DIS 22–03 (`http://www.dis.uniroma1.it/~berardi/publications/techRep/TR-22-03.pdf`).
5. D. Berardi, D. Calvanese, G. De Giacomo, M. Lenzerini, and M. Mecella. A Foundational Vision of *e*-Services. In *Proc. of WES 2003.*
6. D. Berardi, F. De Rosa, L. De Santis, and M. Mecella. Finite State Automata as Conceptual Model for *e*-Services. In *Proc. of IDPT 2003*, to appear.
7. T. Bultan, X. Fu, R. Hull, and J. Su. Conversation Specification: A New Approach to Design and Analysis of E-Service Composition. In *Proc. of WWW 2003.*
8. D. Calvanese, G. De Giacomo, M. Lenzerini, and D. Nardi. Reasoning in Expressive Description Logics. *Handbook of Automated Reasoning*, ESP, 2001.
9. F. Casati and M.C. Shan. Dynamic and Adaptive Composition of *e*-Services. *Information Systems*, 6(3), 2001.
10. M.C. Fauvet, M. Dumas, B. Benatallah, and H.Y. Paik. Peer-to-Peer Traced Execution of Composite Services. In *Proc. of VLDB-TES 2001.*
11. R. Hull, M. Benedikt, V. Christophides, and J. Su. E-Services: A Look Behind the Curtain. In *Proc. of PODS 2003.*
12. D. Kozen and J. Tiuryn. Logics of programs. *Handbook of Theoretical Computer Science — Formal Models and Semantics*, ESP, 1990.
13. M. Mecella and B. Pernici. Building Flexible and Cooperative Applications Based on *e*-Services. Technical Report DIS 21–2002 (`http://www.dis.uniroma1.it/~mecella/publications/mp_techreport_212002.pdf`).
14. M. Mecella, B. Pernici, and P. Craca. Compatibility of *e*-Services in a Cooperative Multi-Platform Environment. In *Proc. of VLDB-TES 2001.*
15. S. Narayanan and S. McIlraith. Simulation, Verification and Automated Composition of Web Services. In *Proc. of WWW 2002.*
16. M. Papazoglou. Agent-Oriented Technology in Support of e-Business. *Communications of the ACM*, 44(4):71–77, 2001.
17. T. Pilioura and A. Tsalgatidou. *e*-Services: Current Technologies and Open Issues. In *Proc. of VLDB-TES 2001.*
18. H. Schuster, D. Georgakopoulos, A. Cichocki, and D. Baker. Modeling and Composing Service-based and Reference Process-based Multi-enterprise Processes. In *Proc. of CAiSE 2000.*
19. G. Shegalov, M. Gillmann, and G. Weikum. XML-enabled Workflow Management for *e*-Services across Heterogeneous Platforms. *VLDB Journal*, 10(1), 2001.
20. J. Yang and M.P. Papazoglou. Web Components: A Substrate for Web Service Reuse and Composition. In *Proc. of CAiSE 2002.*
21. J. Yang, W.J. van den Heuvel, and M.P. Papazoglou. Tackling the Challenges of Service Composition in *e*-Marketplaces. In *Proc. of RIDE-2EC 2002.*

Service Discovery and Orchestration for Distributed Service Repositories

Ioannis Fikouras and Eugen Freiter

Bremen Institute of Industrial Technology and Applied Work Science (BIBA),
Hochschulring 20, 28359 Bremen, Germany
{fks,fre}@biba.uni-bremen.de
http://www.biba.uni-bremen.de

Abstract. Driven by the need for transparent discovery and orchestration of composite services out of elementary services, this paper introduces an innovative approach to Distributed Composite Services Orchestration and Discovery. The proposed concept is based on Variant Configuration theory and Distributed Service Repositories. The authors proceed to describe parts of the specification of a middleware platform based on the proposed concept capable of addressing the need for seamless discovery and composition of distributed services. This study was conducted as part of project NOMAD (IST-2001-33292) and presents the concepts behind the NOMAD Composite Service Configurator and its integration in the Distributed Service Repository.

1 Introduction

Significant technological advances in recent years in the areas of mobile devices and wireless communications were accompanied by infiltration of all aspects of our lives by all sorts of new Internet based services. Mobile communications and the Internet have been the two major drivers of consumer demand for new services in the last decade of the twentieth century [1].

Mobile phones are already pervasive in all major developed economies as well as in an increasing number of developing ones. The average mobile penetration in Europe in 2002 reached 72.4 per cent [2] and internet penetration in EU homes reached 38 per cent in December 2001 [3]. In November 2001, almost 50 per cent of the population over 15 years used the Internet either stationary or mobile. The rate of Internet take up by businesses is far higher at almost 90 per cent of enterprises with more than ten employees. Furthermore, it is forecasted that by 2005 an increasing portion of Internet users will be using wireless devices such as web-enabled cell phones and PDAs to go online and the number of worldwide Internet users will nearly triple to 1.17 billion [4]. By that time, a variety of different wireless network platforms with different properties, capable of transporting Internet traffic will be available [5]. In addition, the turn of operators towards license-free frequencies [6] and their eventual congestion will lead to the realisation of alternative dynamic network structures, namely Internet compatible, multi-hop, ad-hoc networks.

M.E. Orlowska et al. (Eds.): ICSOC 2003, LNCS 2910, pp. 59–74, 2003.

1.1 Problem Statement and Motivation

In spite of repeated past forecasts of the contrary, mobile Internet access today accounts for less than 10 per cent of those online globally even though the number of mobile users greatly exceeds the number of Internet-users [8]. However, it is expected that as early as 2005 over one half of the Internet population will consist of mobile access devices [4]. In countries with low Internet penetration wireless Internet devices will be the primary or only Internet access means.

The advent of the mobile Internet depends on the corresponding evolution of a new type of services vital for providing concrete added-value to users [9] resulting in motivation to adopt the new technology. In an environment with the potential for true global user mobility, a paradigm shift from stationary to mobility aware services and from a provider or operator-centric service model to a user-centric view [10] will be witnessed. Main characteristics of the new paradigm are:

- **User centricity**: Use of all available means to free the user from established restricting structures in order to offer the best possible service.
- **Mobility awareness**: Use of all data concerning the user's position, movement and direct environment or context for the provision of services.

A Composite Service Discovery technology addressing these issues was researched and developed by Project NOMAD (IST-2001-33292). This paper will present the concepts behind the NOMAD Composite Service Configurator and its integration in a Distributed Service Repository.

Sections 2 and 3 of this paper give an overview of existing approaches to Service Orchestration and Distributed Service Repositories. Section 4 proceeds to explain the NOMAD Composite Services data model while Section 5 describes how a configuration engine for Composite Services can be integrated in an LDAP repository. Section 6 provides the overall conclusions.

2 Approaches to Service Orchestration

Orchestration of Services is usually based on the concepts of Knowledge-based Variant Configuration. Case-based, rules-based and the Object Oriented approach including the concept of "Lean Configuration" are briefly illustrated in the following sections.

2.1 Knowledge-Based Variant Configuration

Knowledge-based Variant Configuration [18] is a process were complex products are composed out of elementary components. A Configurator is an expert system that supports this process and thereby uses predefined goals as well as expert knowledge. Design goals can be constraints, functional requirements, predetermined components or various quality criteria [19]. Such systems do not follow a single predefined method, but rather a strategy based on a series of small steps, each step representing a certain aspect or assumption leading to the configuration of the composite service.

Configuration is therefore considered as the solution to a single exercise and not the solution to a whole problem or problem class that has first to be methodically analysed. This implies the following:

- The set of all possible solutions is finite.
- The solution sought is not innovative, but rather is a subset of the available parts.
- The configuration problem is known and well defined.

2.2 Rules-Based Configuration

Existing configuration systems like JSR 94 [33] are based on knowledge bases consisting of a description of all the available components (objects) and an accompanying set of rules that define how specific objects should behave under defined conditions and thereby control the flow of configuration [24].

Consequently configuration rules are structured according to the "if-then" principle familiar from various programming languages. The "if" part of a rule contains the conditions under which the actions defined in the "then" part rule should be applied [30]. A configuration problem described using rules based concepts is composed of the following three elements [20]:

- Facts describe conditions that are necessary for configurations.
- Rules describe the relationships between facts and describe actions to be takes.
- Enquiries describe the problem to be solved.

The aim is to acquire answers to the questions posed with the help of the rules defined based on the known facts [20].

Rule-based systems are easy to implement due to the simplicity of the individual rules, but are hard to maintain after reaching a certain complexity. Production rules based systems are maintained by highly qualified knowledge engineers that must have considerable knowledge on the products in question and on the configurations system and most importantly the defined rules. Furthermore rule-based systems are usually restricted to a single knowledge domain in order to prevent the exponential complexity necessary for multiple rules-sets for multiple domains.

2.3 Case-Based Configuration

Case-based orchestration makes use of libraries containing similar problems and predefined solutions in order to formulate new composite services [34] thereby reducing the configuration problem to the following steps:

- The search for a similar case.
- The transformation of the original case to fit the current requirements.

The second step is where case-based configuration differs from other case-based methods, i.e. case-based reasoning or diagnosis where no such transformation is needed [32]. Collected knowledge can be used for further configuration under the following conditions:

- Creation and maintenance of appropriately organised libraries containing problems, solutions as well as the used process.

- Existence of algorithms and heuristics for the selection of appropriate cases from the library.
- The integration of case-knowledge in the configuration process. This includes procedures for checking case consistency and case transformation [31].

Configurations created on the basis of such a library can often be less efficient than others created with more conventional means. This is mainly due two the following characteristics of case-based methods:

- Resulting configurations are not fully compliant to the current requirements, but rather adapted products that were originally designed for different requirements.
- Changes in the knowledge domain can not be integrated in the case library without changing all relevant cases resulting in configurations that are sometimes not up-to-date [31].

2.4 Object-Oriented Variant Configuration

Object-oriented Variant Configuration is based on the concept of iterative composition of the final product out of a set of elementary components that have been previously organised according to a product data model into a structure, known as the object hierarchy that contains all knowledge related to the product in question. The relationships between components and how they fit together are described with the help of constraints.

Constraints are constructs connecting two unknown or variable components and their respective attributes, which have predefined values (taken from a specific knowledge domain). The constraint defines the values the variables are allowed to have, but also connects variables, and more importantly, defines the relationship between the two values [21]. In other words, constraints contain general rules that can be applied to make sure that specific components are put together in a correct fashion without having to specify any component-related rules or calculations [21]. The *constraint* satisfaction problem is defined as follows [22]:

- There is a finite set of variables $X = \{x_1, \ldots, x_n\}$.
- For each variable x_i, there exists a finite set D_i of possible values (its domain).
- There is also a set of constraints, which restrict the possible values that these variables are allowed to take at the same time.

The object hierarchy contains all relevant objects and the relationships between them in an "is-a" relationship that defines types of objects, object classes and subclasses, and their properties. The configuration process creates objects on the basis of this information according to the products being configured. In one specific hierarchy (as depicted in the following figure for the configuration of automobiles, classes for specific car types (i.e. coupé, minivan, etc.) are connected by "is-a" relationships to the main "car" class. This hierarchy also allows the breakdown of a product into components with the help of further "has-parts" relationships. These "has-parts" relationships are the basis for the decision-making process employed to create new configurations. An example of such a relationship would be the relationship between a chassis and a wheel. A chassis can be connected to up to four wheels in a passenger car, but the wheels are represented only once, with an appropriate cardinality (see Fig.1).

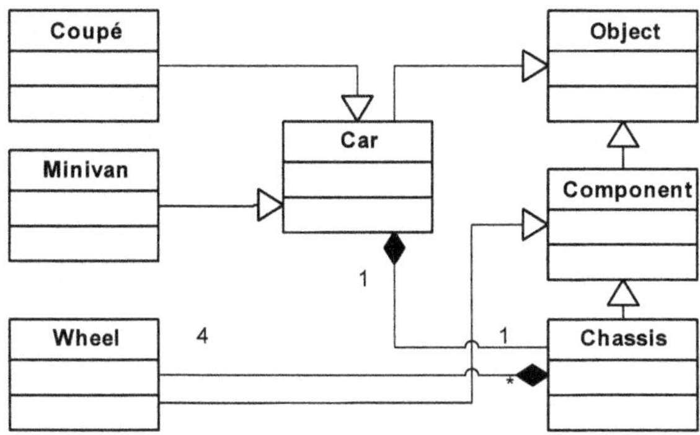

Fig. 1. Example object hierarchy of a specific product domain

The greatest hurdle to be resolved when creating new configurations is the fact that the software is required to make decisions that are not based on available information. Such an action can possibly lead to a dysfunctional composition or simply to a combination that does not conform to user requirements. In this case all related configuration steps have to be undone (backtracking) in order to return to a valid state. The longer it takes for the configuration to detect that a mistake has been made, the more difficult it is to correct the error in question [19]. The configuration process itself is composed of three phases [24]:

- Analysis of the product in order to define possible actions.
- Specification of further configuration actions.
- Execution of specified actions.

These actions are:

- *Disassembly of the product into its components.* This is meant to reduce the complexity of the problem and create a large number of smaller objectives in the manner of conventional top-down specification.
- *Assembly of components, integration and aggregation.* This step creates a product out of its components in a bottom-up manner.
- *Creation of specialised objects.* Object classes are specialised through the definition of subclasses.
- *Parameterise objects.* Define attributes and parameters for the specified objects that can be used for the application of constraints or other configuration mechanisms.

Object-oriented configuration is a modern approach to variant configuration suitable for complex structures in arbitrary product domains. Furthermore this approach allows for simplified maintenance of established service repositories through clear hierarchical structures.

2.5 Lean Configuration

The "Lean Configuration" [25] approach (developed in the course of the INTELLECT IST-1999-10375 Project) to variant configuration is object oriented, but reduces the configuration process to a search problem by eliminating the complex, computationally intensive and error-prone first two steps of object oriented configuration thereby eliminating the need for back-tracking.

The reduction in complexity is realised by the usage of correctly configured, complete compositions as the basis for interactive configuration. As long as the user uses a pre-configured composition as a template for the new variant the configuration process can be transformed into a search problem and, specifically, a search for the next component to be exchanged. The Configurator supplies the user with lists of components that (a) are comparable to the service being exchanged and can be safely used in place of the component to be removed or (b) are compatible to existing services and can be safely added to the configuration. This mechanism ensures that the configuration is constantly in a correct state.

3 Distributed Service Repository Approaches

Discovery of a requested service can typically be accomplished in two separate manners:

- by directly contacting a known address that can supply the client with information on the available services as is currently implemented by UDDI[12].
- per broadcast. Broadcasts can be either focused on the local network or use mechanisms like multicast to reach a much larger group of service agents without the need for predefined addresses; an example for such protocols is Service Location Protocol (SLP) [13].

A major disadvantage of broadcast solutions is that they can produce enormous amounts of unnecessary traffic that grows exponentially with the number of hops (Time To Live, TTL) the broadcast is allowed to traverse (i.e. the number of networks it is allowed to flood). Furthermore such broadcasts are necessary every time the mobile node changes its environment (i.e. after a handover) or in some cases even every time a certain service is desired. Small TTLs on the other hand reduce the amount of signalling traffic generated, but coupled with the discrepancy between the networked and the physical world [14]; can lead to ineffective service discovery queries. Even clients and service providers in close physical proximity are not guaranteed to find each other due to possibly large "virtual" distances separating them in the Internet [14].

Centralised Service Repositories suffer from scalability issues that are usually addressed with the help of replication. Replicated repositories are however neither truly scalable, nor transparent due to the fact that updates occur only periodically. Existing technologies like UDDI v1 are considered to scale only moderately. The UDDI Replication and Scalability team is as of the writing of this document considering a distributed architecture for future revisions of its specification.

A distributed service repository based on a distributed directory like LDAP (Lightweight Director Access Protocol) can provide both a more scalable and more efficient solution. In addition to the performance benefits offered by LDAP, work within the NOMAD project is also progressing on an LDAP based distributed UDDI repository for providing compatibility with WebService technologies [15]. Within Project NOMAD an existing Free software UDDI repository (SOAPUDDI) is extended to support LDAP as a universal distributed backend to service repositories.

3.1 Lightweight Directory Access Protocol

In LDAP, directory entries are arranged in a hierarchical tree-like structure called the Directory Information Tree (DIT). Traditionally [16], this structure reflected the geographic and/or organisational boundaries. Entries representing countries appeared at the top of the tree. Below them are entries representing states and national organisations. Below them might be entries representing organisational units, people, printers, documents, or anything else. In addition, the tree may also be arranged based upon Internet domain names. This naming approach is becoming increasing popular as it allows for directory services to be locating using the Domain Name System (DNS).

An entry is referenced by its distinguished name, which is constructed by taking the name of the entry itself (called the Relative Distinguished Name or RDN) and concatenating the names of its ancestor entries. For example, the entry for Ioannis Fikouras in the Internet naming example above has an RDN of uid=fks and a DN of uid=fks,ou=PPC,o=BIBA,c=DE".

Data on services stored in an LDAP distributed database can be spread across multiple LDAP servers. These servers are typically responsible for specific regions of the LDAP directory tree.

4 NOMAD Composite Services Data Model

This section introduces the NOMAD Composite Services Data Model starting with the NOMAD Mobility Aware Services Taxonomy and continuing with the various component and workflow types.

4.1 Mobility Aware Services Taxonomy

The following simple taxonomy is used as the basis for defining different types of Elementary Services and the relationships between them in the context of mobility aware Composite Services Configuration. This categorization is achieved mainly based on the type of functionality the Elementary Services offer. Services can thus belong to the following groups (see Fig.2):

- Stationary or Mobile
- Of limited availability or unlimited availability
- Information services

The defining attribute of stationary services is their fixed position. Such services are usable only by users in their immediate vicinity, as opposed to mobile Services that can change their location. An example for a stationary service would be a service provided in a physical store i.e. a haircut, a meal, etc., whereas mobile services could be taxis, couriers, etc that can change their location to meet the user. Mobile services can be of a logistical nature, but are not restricted to transportation services. In order to combine multiple stationary services into a composite service, logistics (mobile) services are required if both stationary services are in different physical locations. Combinations of multiple mobile services are also possible.

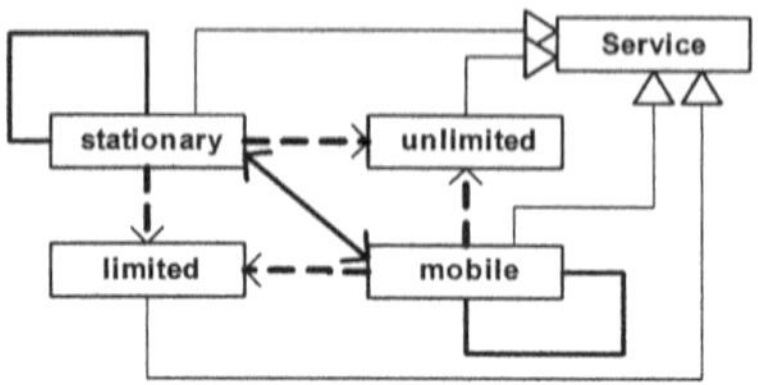

Fig. 2. NOMAD elementary services

Information Services are considered to be a special type of stationary services as they lack a number of characteristics thereby posing a smaller amount of requirements to the configuration process. An example for such a service could be an Internet based weather report system. This type of facility does not have a physical location, is nevertheless stationary, but does not require a mobile service to get connected to other services. Ubiquitous connectivity is assumed to be provided by networks. Networking facilities provided by the NOMAD integrated network platform [27] are assumed to be always available.

Services with limited availability are services that are provided based on the availability of finite resources. Such services usually require additional actions in order to handle reservations, prevent overbooking, etc. An example for such a service would be any facility that can accommodate a limited amount of customers (i.e. hotel, restaurant, etc.) Services that service customers on a FIFO basis and simply serve all incoming requests are considered to be services with an unlimited capacity. Both services with limited and unlimited capacities can be either stationary or mobile.

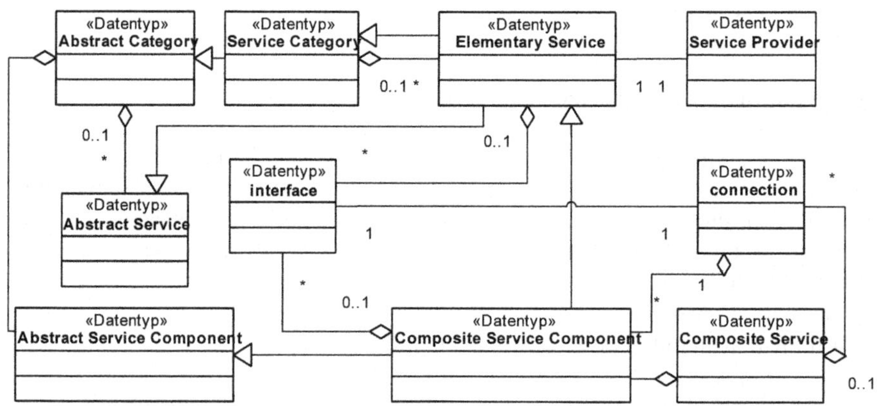

Fig. 3. Composite Services Data Model

4.2 NOMAD Composite Services Component Types

The NOMAD Composite Services Data Model divides services conceptually into two categories, *Elementary Services* and *Composite Services*. Elementary Services represent a specific instantiation of a service and contain all data needed to describe it. They inherit a set of general attributes available to all services from the *Abstract Service* data-type. *Composite Services* consist of groups of *Composite Service Com-*

ponents derived individually from Elementary Services. Composite Service Components inherit their attributes from Elementary Services, as well as attributes related to workflow management from the *Abstract Service Component* datatype. The purpose of these components is to describe the exact composition of the service, including data on which components are connected, by what *Interfaces* and in what order. Connections between such components are described additionally with the help of *Connection* components (see Fig.6).

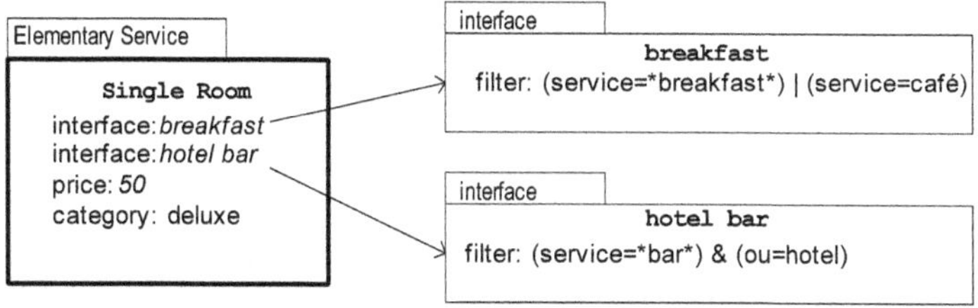

Fig. 4. Elementary Services with two Interfaces

Service Categories descend from the *Abstract Category* datatype and implement a means of grouping elementary services into sets according to functional criteria. These sets are meant to simplify and optimise the composite service configuration process, by providing predefined groups of components that can be used to reduce the amount of services the Configurator has to process in his/her search for suitable components.

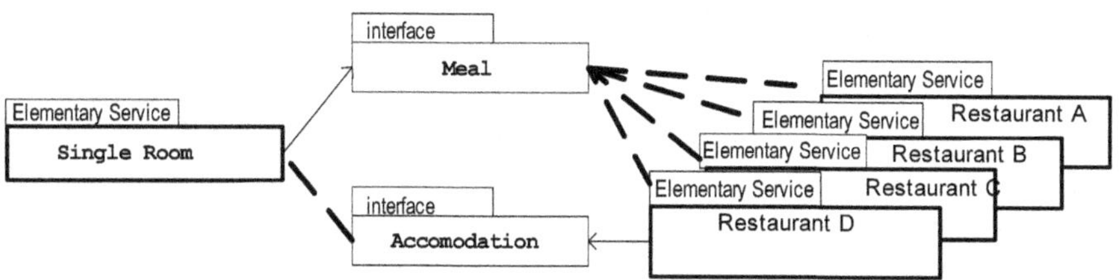

Fig. 5. Elementary Service "socket" (left) with multiple "plugs"(right)´

4.2.1 Composite Services, Interfaces, Connections, and Workflows

Interfaces between components implement constraints and as such offer mechanisms for determining whether Elementary Services are suitable for integration into a composite service (see Fig.6). The requirements that need to be fulfilled for a successful composition are derived both from Components connected to the Interface, as well as from user preferences or *Connection* components. Interfaces can be defined between Elementary Services, Composite Services, Service Categories and Service Providers and are a part of Elementary Services. Interfaces are mainly used to determine whether two Elementary Services fit, whereas Connection components describe a specific bond between two Composite Service Components.

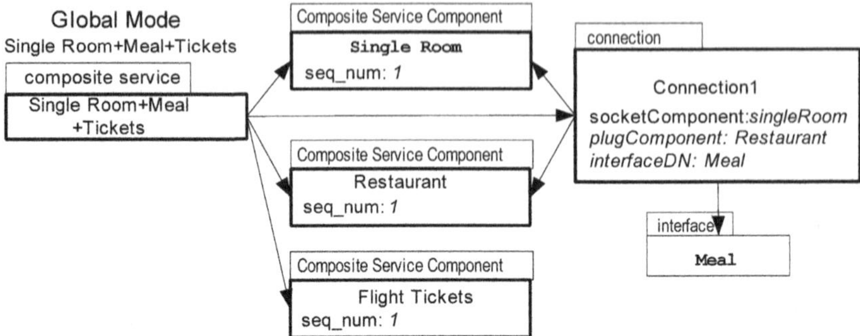

Fig. 6. Composite Service with Global Workflow Model

The relationship between interfaces and elementary services matched by the filters contained in an interface resembles the one between plugs and sockets, whereby interfaces as sockets match multiple plugs. Henceforth, connections to Elementary Components that have a direct reference to an interface via its unique identifier will be referred as "sockets" and components that are matched by a socket will be referred to as "plugs". An interface object is not restricted in its scope to use by only one pair of Service Components, but rather implements a generic rule (constraint) that can be used by multiple components for describing their interfaces.

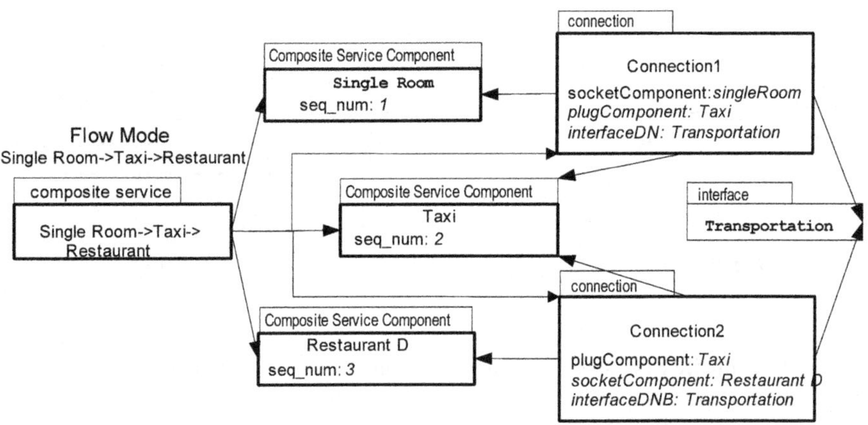

Fig. 7. Composite Service with Flow Model Workflow

An elementary component can be connected to multiple interfaces and can act as a plug and or a socket (see Fig.5) depending on whether it is executing a search for a compatible component (through one of its interfaces) or being the target of such a search. Provided that multiple interfaces are available, all plugs corresponding to the filters in the interface objects are possible composition candidates. A positive match between two components however requires matching interfaces in both directions. In turn, this causes the Configurator to backtrack the connection between the plug and the socket in order to make sure that the plug also fits the socket.

When modifying existing Composite Services (i.e. when exchanging one Service Component for another) the Configurator needs to know precisely how components are connected to each other, to avoid altering the structure of the composition by using a different interface for connecting the new component with the rest of the composition. Connection components are therefore used for storing information on the connections between composite service and the corresponding interfaces (see Fig.7).

NOMAD Composite Services are assembled as a set of Composite Service Components arranged according to a specific type of workflow. Workflow functionality is introduced based on mechanisms specified by WSFL [26] (WebServices Flow Language) in order to ensure WebService compatibility. Composite Services can thus have one of the following types of workflow: *Flow Model, Global Model* and *Recursive Composition.*

- A Flow Model is a linear workflow where each service has to be executed in a specific sequence. The correct sequence of execution is stored within the Composite Service Components.
- Global Models provide a description of how the composed services interact with each other. This type of workflow requires no additional considerations.
- Recursive composition of services provides scalability to the composition language and support for top-down progressive refinement design as well as for bottom-up aggregation. Recursive composition of services is made possible by the loosely couple nature of NOMAD Composite Services. New Composite Services can be composed out of existing compositions by merging the existing groups of components into new bigger compositions.

5 Composite Services Schema and Engine Integration

Current implementations of LDAP offer flexible database integration mechanisms that make the coupling of a large variety of systems possible through a simple and well documented interface. Servers like the OpenSource product OpenLDAP [17] are based on a modular front-end-backend architecture that allows that usage of the LDAP front-end with arbitrary back-ends. Such back-ends would traditionally be relational or other databases (SQL, BDB, LDBM, etc.), programmable back-ends (i.e. perl, tcl, etc.) or even other LDAP servers, LDAP proxies and other constructs. OpenLDAP can be configured to serve multiple back-ends at the same time. This means that a single OpenLDAP server can respond to requests for many logically different portions of the LDAP tree, using the same or different back-ends for each part of the DIT.

Middleware for the management and configuration of composite services can be thus integrated as an additional backend. This backend would be responsible for resolving queries regarding Composite Services based on defined constraints. The Configurator itself could also use the LDAP distributed database as a source for data on elementary services. Such queries would then be referred to the appropriate LDAP-Node within the DIT. The Configurator itself can also be implemented locally as supporting module for the local Service Discovery node or be installed centrally.

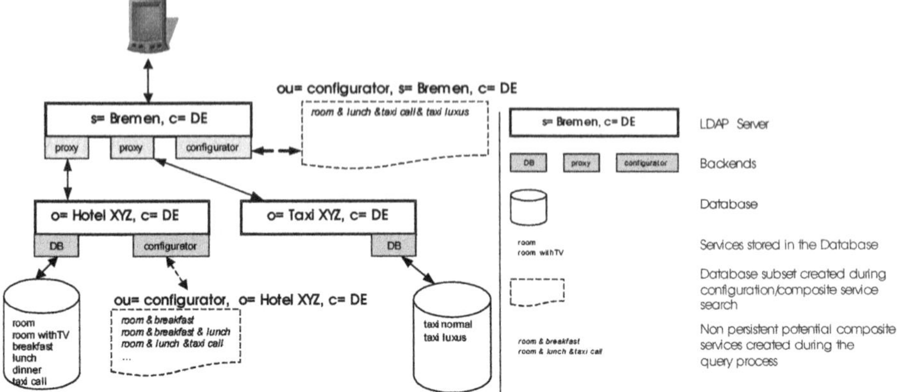

Fig. 8. Distributed Directory hierarchy with multiple Configurator Engines

A Composite Service Configurator can be configured to receive service discovery queries directed to the LDAP DIT node they are attached to. This is achieved by designating the Configurator back-end as responsible for a predetermined branch of the DIT. The Configurator being one of many possible back-ends of a single LDAP server can be restricted to a portion of the branch covered by the directory server itself. This allows for standards conform access the Configurator via LDAP queries. At the same time the Configurator has full access to all the LDAP DIT and can itself use LDAP queries to gather information on additional services, as well as access other Configurators located in different parts of the distributed directory. Such an arrangement allows for recursive creation of composite services, were a Configurator can consult any number of other Engines providing some subset of the overall composite service.

The Configurator handling Composite Services for a Service Repository in the area of Bremen (see Fig.8) could for instance be set-up as one of the back-ends for a Directory Server with the distinguished name (DN) "s=Bremen, c=DE". Queries related to elementary services under the aforementioned DN are automatically handled by the root directory server or forwarded to other associated directory servers handling smaller branches of the local DIT (i.e. Hotel XYZ, Taxi XYZ, etc.). Queries related to composite services on the other hand are addressed to a specific branch of the DIT (ou=configurator, s=Bremen, c=DE) and are forwarded to the Configurator back-end.

5.1 LDAP Composite Services Schema

The domain specific knowledge required for Service Composition is hard-coded into an LDAP schema [28]. Elementary Service types that are to be part of the composition process are described in this schema. LDAP schemata are Object Oriented and consist of definitions of Object Classes defined as a collection of attributes with clearly defined datatypes. Object Classes may inherit attributes from multiple other such classes. The Composite Services schema thus defines the attributes describing the services, as well as the interfaces required for service composition. Component attributes are statically defined in the LDAP schema of the directory server and have either a MUST (compulsory) or MAY (optional) status. Individual instantiations of the services may only vary in their choice of attributes, and possibly additional optional attributes not used for composition purposes.

The following code is a simplified representation of an LDAP v3 schema with respective object definition in LDIF [29] format for Composite Service Components, Composite Services, Interface and Connection components.

```
objectclass (1.1.4.2.1 NAME 'serviceComponent'

DESC 'Composite Service Component'

SUP elementaryService, abstractServiceComponent

MUST (seqNumber $ elementaryServiceDN )

MAY interfaceDN )

dn: cn=flight,cn=Fly&Drive, …

objectclass: abstractServiceComponent

objectclass: elementaryService

objectclass: serviceComponent

elementaryServiceDN: cn=flight,ou=KLM,o=Transport, …

seqNumber: 1

dn: cn=RentAcar, cn=Fly&Drive, …

objectclass: abstractServiceComponent

objectclass: elementaryService

objectclass: serviceComponent

elementaryServiceDN: cn=rentAcar,ou=AVIS,o=Transport, …

interfaceDN: cn=AVIS_interface,cn=Fly&Drive, …

seqNumber: 2
```

Service Components inherit attributes from the Abstract Service Component and the Elementary Service, such attributes include the sequence number used for implementing the workflow. Furthermore a Service Component contains a direct connection to the Elementary Service it represents and its related interfaces.

```
objectclass (1.1.1.2.1 NAME 'Interface'

DESC 'Interface object'

MUST (cn $ filter)

MAY availability )

dn: cn=AVIS_interface,cn=Fly&Drive, ...

objectclass: interface

filter: &((objectclass=flight)(destination=Bremen)
(class=first))
```

The actual task of defining the relationship between two elementary services is accomplished by Interface objects. Interfaces are separate objects that contain LDAP filters or DNs describing the compatible components, as well as additional attributes specifically related to the interface and are linked to a specific component via their Distinguished Name (DN), a unique identifier positioning the object within the LDAP Directory Information Tree (DIT).

LDAP filters defined in an Interface object effectively represent preconditions that have to be met in order to achieve a working composition. Valid operators used for constraint resolution are all the operators supported by the LDAP filter specification [23] and include basic operations like “equal”, “not equal”, “greater than” and “less than”. The filters contained in an interface object make use of standardised attributes defined in the schema for the required type of service. The use of non-standardised attributes is possible, but may lead to ineffective queries.

```
objectclass (1.1.5.2.1 NAME 'connection'

DESC 'Connection in Composite Service'

MUST (cn $ plugComponent $ socketComponent $ interface)
)

dn: cn=Fly&Drive_Connection,cn=Fly&Drive, ...

objectclass: connection

plugComponent: cn=FlyTicket,cn=Fly&Drive, ...

socketComponent: cn=CarRental,cn=Fly&Drive, ...

interface:cn=AVIS_interface,cn=Fly&Drive, ...
```

Connection objects describe a specific connection between two Service Components. As such these objects contain the unique identifier of the plug and the socket components involved as well as the interface describing compatible Elementary Services.

6 Conclusions

This paper has shown the need for transparent discovery and orchestration of composite services out of elementary services. Furthermore an approach was illustrated for Distributed Composite Services Orchestration and Discovery based on Variant Configuration theory and a Distributed Service Repository. The authors propose the implementation of a middleware platform capable of addressing the issues identified and proceed to describe parts of its specification.

Acknowledgements. Project NOMAD (IST-2001-33292) is funded by the European Commission within the IST Programme of the FP5. The authors wish to express their gratitude and appreciation to the European Commission and all NOMAD partners for their strong support and valuable contribution during the various activities presented in this paper.

References

1. ITU Internet Reports 2002: Internet for a Mobile Generation, International Telecommunication Union, September 2002, http://www.itu.int/osg/spu/publications/sales/mobileinternet/
2. Mobile and internet penetration rates increase 08/08/2002, http://www.europemedia.net/
3. eEurope Benchmarking Report, European Commission, http://europa.eu.int/information_society/eeurope/benchmarking/index_en.htm
4. eTForecasts, Internet Users Will Surpass 1 Billion in 2005, http://www.etforecasts.com/pr/pr201.htm
5. Niebert, N, "Convergence of Cellular and Broadband Networks towards Future Wireless Generations", In Wireless Strategic Initiative (WSI) Book of Visions 2000 – Visions of the Wireless World Workshop, Brussels 2000
6. Mohr, W., "Alternative Vorschläge zur Spektrumsnutzung für IMT-2000/UMTS", Spektrumsworkshop ITU-R, October 2000, Geneva, Switzerland
7. Katz, HR, Brewer, AE, "The Case for Wireless Overlay 'Networks", In: SPIE Multimedia and Networking Conference (MMNC'96), January 1996, San Jose, CA, USA
8. Keryer, P. (2000), Presentation at the workshop: Visions of the Wireless World, 12th December 2000, Brussels
9. Pöyry, P., Repokari, L., Fournogerakis, P., Fikouras, I., "User Requirements for Seamless and Transparent Service Discovery", In: Proceedings of eChallenges 2003, 22–24 October 2003, Bologna, Italy, to be published
10. Fikouras, I., Wunram, M., Weber, F., "Seamless Integration of Mobile Products and Services – User-centricity and Mobility Awareness for mCommerce", In: Proceedings of the Wireless World Research Forum (WWRF) Kick-off meeting, Munich 2001
11. Gilder, G., "Telecosm : How Infinite Bandwidth Will Revolutionize Our World", Free Press, September 11, 2000
12. Universal Description, Discovery and Integration of WebServices (UDDI), http://www.uddi.org/
13. Guttman, E., Perkins C., Veizades J. and Day M., "Service Location Protocol, Version 2", RFC 2608, June 1999

14. Ioannis Fikouras, "Peer-to-peer Service Engineering for Integrated Networks", In: Wireless Technology 2002 Business Briefing, World Markets Research Centre, London, UK, Pages 88–91
15. B. Bergeson, K. Boogert, "LDAP Schema for UDDI" draft-bergeson-uddi-ldap-schema-01.txt, May 2002
16. RFC2253 "Lightweight Directory Access Protocol (v3): UTF-8 String Representation of Distinguished Names.
17. http://www.OpenLDAP.net
18. Tank, W., Wissensbasiertes Konfigurieren: Ein Überblick. Künstliche Intelligenz (KI) 1 1993
19. Neumann B. (1988) Configuration expert systems: a case study and tutorial. Proc. Conf. on AI in manufacturing, Assembly, and Robotics, Oldenbourg
20. Lunze, J. Künstliche Intelligenz für Ingenieure. München, Wien: Oldenburg Verl. 1994
21. Tsang, E.P.K., Foundations of Constraint Satisfaction, Academic Press, London and San Diego, 1993
22. Barták, R., in Proceedings of Week of Doctoral Students (WDS99), Part IV, MatFyzPress, Prague, June 1999, pp. 555–564
23. Howes, T., "The String Representation of LDAP Search Filters" RFC 2254, December 1997
24. Cunis R., Günter A., Strecker H. (1991) Begriffshierarchie-orientierte Kontrolle. In Das PLACON-Buch. Informatik Fachberichte Nr. 266. Springer, Berlin, Heidelberg
25. Fikouras, I., Detken, K., Lean Configuration: Interactive 3D Configuration for E-Commerce Environments, In: J. Gasos, K-D. Thoben (Eds.), "E-Business Applications: Technologies for Tomorrow's Solutions", Springer, Berlin, 2002
26. Prof. Dr. Frank Leymann, WebServices Flow Language (WSFL 1.0), May 2001, www.ibm.com/software/solutions/ webservices
27. Koojana Kuladinithi, Andreas Könsgen, Stefan Aust, Nikolaus Fikouras, Carmelita Görg Ioannis Fikouras, "Mobility Management for an Integrated Network Platform", 4th IEEE Conference on Mobile and Wireless Communications Networks, Stockholm September 2002
28. M. Wahl, T. Howes, S. Kille, "Lightweight Directory Access Protocol (v3)" RFC2251-2256, 2829–2831, December 1997
29. G. Good, "The LDAP Data Interchange Format (LDIF) - Technical Specification" RFC2849, June 2000
30. Bense, H; Bodrow, W. Wissensbasierte Dialogführung für ein Beratungssystem zum Softwarequalitätsmanagement. In Objektorientierte und regelbasierte Wissensverarbeitung. Heidelberg, Berlin, Oxford: Spektrum, Akad. Verl., 1995
31. Cunis, R; Günter, A; Strecker, H. Fallbasiertes Konstruieren mit Bibliothekslösungen. In Das PLACON-Buch. Springer, Informatik Fachberichte Nr. 266 1991
32. Günter, A; Dörner, H; Gläser, H; Neumann, B; Posthoff, C; Sebastian, H-J. Das Projekt PROCON: Problemspezifische Werkzeuge für die wissensbasierte Konfigurierung. Technische Uni Chemnitz, Martin-Luther Uni Halle-Wittenberg, Uni Hamburg, Technische Hochschule Leipzig, Technische Hochschule Zwickau. PROCON-Bericht Nr.1, 1991
33. Alex Toussaint, BEA Systems, Java Specification Requests, Java Rule Engine API , http://www.jcp.org/en/jsr/detail?id=94
34. Limthanmaphon, B. and Zhang, Y. (2003). Web Service Composition with Case-Based Reasoning. In Proc. Fourteenth Australasian Database Conference (ADC2003), Adelaide, Australia. Conferences in Research and Practice in Information Technology, 17. Schewe, K.-D. and Zhou, X., Eds., ACS. 201–208.

Model Driven Service Composition

Bart Orriëns, Jian Yang, and Mike. P. Papazoglou

Tilburg University, Infolab
PO Box 90153, 5000 LE, Tilburg, Netherlands
{b.orriens,jian,mikep}@kub.nl

Abstract. The current standards for web service composition, e.g. BPEL. neither cater for dynamic service composition nor for dynamic business configuration. Our firm belief is that business processes can be built dynamically by composing web services in a model driven fashion where the design process is controlled and governed by a series of business rules.
In this paper we examine the functional requirements of service composition and introduce a phased approach to the development of service compositions that spans abstract definition, scheduling, construction and execution. Subsequently, we analyze the information requirements for developing service compositions by identifying the basic elements in a web service composition and the business rules that are used to govern the development of service compositions.

1 Introduction

The platform neutral nature of web services creates the opportunity for enterprisers to develop business processes by using and combining existing web services, possibly offered by different providers. By selecting and combining the most suitable and economical web services, business processes can be generated dynamically by observing the changing business conditions.

Current composite web service development and management solutions are very much a manual activity, which require specialized knowledge and take up much time and effort. This applies even to applications that are being developed on the basis of available standards, such as BPEL4WS [4] or BPML [2]. Due to a vast service space to search, a variety of services to compare and match, and different ways to construct composed services service composition is simply too complex and too dynamic to handle manually. To automate the development of service compositions, we require a systematic way of analyzing their requirements and modelling the activities involved in them just as we do with software development. The benefits of adapting a service development methodology for service composition is that we gain much more insight in the process of constructing service compositions so that we can better manage their implementations.

In this paper we use a model driven approach to facilitate the development and management of dynamic service compositions. The central notion in this

M.E. Orlowska et al. (Eds.): ICSOC 2003, LNCS 2910, pp. 75–90, 2003.

approach entails separation of the fundamental composition logic from particular composition specifications (e.g., BPEL and BPML) in order to raise the level of abstraction. This allows rapid development and delivery of service compositions based on proven and tested models, as such supporting the service composition life-cycle. The proposed approach uses UML as the method for modelling service compositions. This will enable us to develop technology independent composition definitions, which can subsequently be mapped to a specific standard (e.g. BPEL) automatically. Furthermore, in addition to UML we use the Object Constraint Language (OCL) [9] to express business rules that govern and steer the process of service composition.

Business rules are precise statements that describe, constrain and control the structure, operations and strategies of a business. They can express e.g. pricing and billing policies, quality of service, process flow - where they describe routing decisions, actor assignment policies, etc - regulations, and so on. In current web service technology solutions, such rules are deeply embedded in the implementation of processes, leaving the user with little empowerment to manage and control them and eventually the processes themselves. When business rules are relative to business processes, these statements should be extracted from the application code in order to be more easily managed (defined and versified) and consistently executed. Our thesis is that we can use business rules to determine how a service composition should be structured and scheduled, how the services and their providers should be selected, and how service binding should be conducted. This paves the way towards developing dynamic service compositions.

The paper is structured as follows: In Section 2 we explain the functional requirements for service composition development. Then we examine the information model and business rules required for the development of compositions. In Section 4 we describe the process of service composition development. Section 5 highlights related work and our contribution. We present our conclusions and future research in section 6.

2 Functional Requirements of Service Composition

When considering service compositions it is useful to identify two main use cases: service composition development and service composition management. During the process of service composition development, the application developer interacts with the service composition system to generate a business process by composing services. The use case starts when the developer sends a request. The system at the end produces an executable service composition.

In the second use case the application developer interacts with the service composition system to execute and manage compositions. This use case begins when the developer indicates that he wants to execute a service composition. In response the system gathers the required information and subsequently executes the composition. During run-time the developer may interact with the service composition system to make modifications, e.g. change service providers.

In this paper we only concentrate on the first use case, i.e., the development of compositions.

This paper advocates a phased approach to service composition development. The activities in this approach are collectively referred to as the *service composition life-cycle* [13]. Four broad phases are distinguished spanning composition *de nition*, *scheduling*, *construction* and *execution*, as shown in Fig. 1.

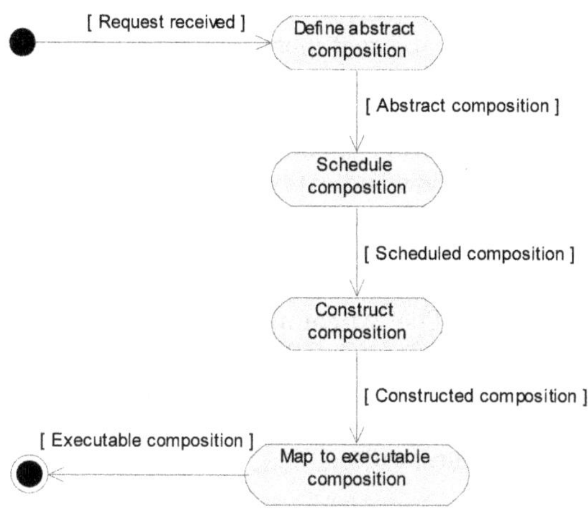

Fig. 1. Service composition life cycle

The idea behind the phased approach to service composition development is to start with an abstract definition and gradually make it concrete so that we can generate executable service processes from these abstract specifications.

The system starts in the *De nition phase* with an *abstract composite service*, which specifies the constituent activities of a composite service, the constraints under which they operate, their informational requirements, and the exceptional behavior that may occur during their execution

In the *Scheduling* phase of the approach, the service composition system determines how and when services should run and prepares them for execution. Its main purpose is to make the definition developed in the definition phase concrete by correlating messages to express data dependencies, and synchronizing and prioritizing the execution of the constituent activities. During this phase the system may generate alternative composition schedules and present them to the application developer for selection.

Next, the service composition system proceeds with the *Construction phase* to construct an unambiguous composition of concrete services out of a set of desirable or potentially available/matching constituent services. Similar to the scheduling phase the system may produce alternative construction schemes (e.g. varying in quality or price) from which the application developer can select.

Lastly, during the *Execution phase* the service composition system prepares the constructed composed services for execution. This phase maps the resulting specification to an executable web service orchestration language (e.g. BPEL).

3 The Information Model for Service Composition Development

The information model (IM) is an abstract meta-model that represents the building blocks of all possible service compositions. The IM models the components required for a given composition as well as their inter-relationships. Relationships in the IM indicate how a composition is constructed. For example, a relationship between an activity and a flow indicates that this activity is used in the flow. We model all the required information as classes containing special purpose attributes so that this information can be captured and described. A service composition derived on the basis of the IM generates a specific instance of this model by populating its classes. The IM comprises classes referred to as *service composition classes*, while the instances of these classes are referred to *composition elements*. Relationships between composition classes, i.e., how to relate a certain activity to a flow, how to relate a service to an activity, and so on, are determined on the basis of business rules.

3.1 Service Composition Classes and Elements

The IM is based on generic service composition constructs derived after a thorough study of the current standards (e.g. BPEL, BPML). Based on this study we have identified the following service composition classes: **activity, condition, event, flow, message, provider** and **role**. These classes and their inter-relationships are illustrated in Fig. 2, and presented in what follows.

- **Activity:** This abstract class represents a well-defined business function (similar to e.g. basic activities in BPML). It contains four attributes: `name, function, input, output`. An instance of this class can be defined as follows:

  ```
  Activity: (
  name="flightActivity"
  function="flightTicketBooking"
  inputs="departureDate,returnDate,from,to"
  outputs="airline,flightNr,seatNr"
  )
  ```

  This example shows an activity named "flightActivity" that is meant for booking a flight ticket. It requires several input parameters to carry out this task, such as, for instance, departure and return date. The output parameters of this class include the airline name, and the flight and seat number.

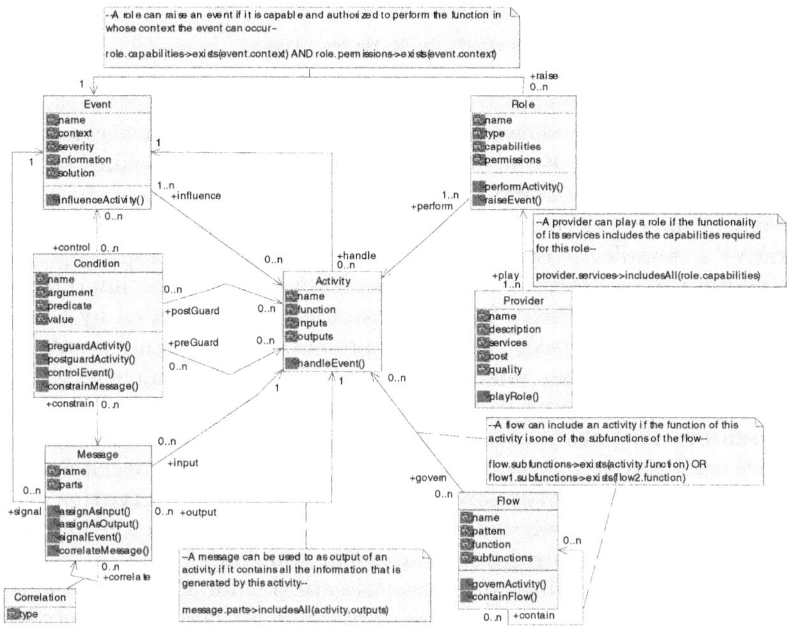

Fig. 2. Service composition model

- **Condition:** This class constrains the behavior of the composition by controlling event occurrences, guarding activities and enforcing pre-conditions, post-conditions and integrity constraints. To achieve this a condition class has four attributes, `name, argument, predicate, value`. A typical post-condition for "flightActivity" could be that "a seat has been reserved".
- **Event:** This abstract class describes occurrences during the process of service composition and its impact on an activity. These can be both of a normal and exceptional nature (e.g. encompassing WSDL faults). An instance of this class can be defined as follows:

```
Event: ( name="seatAvailabilityError"
context="flightTicketBooking"
severity="unrecoverable"
information="seatStatus"
solution="abandonCompositionExecution" )
```

  This example illustrates an event class called "seatAvailabilityError". If the attribute "Severity" in this event class is set to "unrecoverable", then the execution needs to be abandoned. To signal the occurrence of "seatAvailabilityError" a "seatStatus" message must be sent.
- **Flow:** This abstract class defines a block of activities and how they are connected. An example of an instantiation of the flow class can be:

```
Flow: (
name="TravelPlanFlow"
function="travelPlanning"
subfunctions="(flightTicketBooking,hotelRoomReservation)"
pattern="sequential"
)
```

The above example shows a flow named "TravelPlanFlow whose function is "travelPlanning". Its subfunctions are "flightTicketBooking" and "hotelRoomReservation". These subfunctions are carried out in a "sequential" manner (indicated by the pattern attribute). Other patterns include "iterative", "parallel", "conditional", etc, as described in [13].

- **Message:** This abstract class represents a container of information (like e.g. properties in BPEL). Messages are used and generated by activities as input and output, respectively. They are also used to signal events, and can be correlated to other messages to express data dependencies. They have attributes such as name and parts.
- **Provider:** This abstract class describes a party offering concrete services, which can play a role(s) at runtime. A provider class declares attributes such as name, description, services, cost and quality. (Observe that no WSDL constructs are used here to describe providers to maximize the independency of the IM model with regard to particular standards)
- **Role:** This class provides an abstract description for a party participating in the service composition. Roles are responsible for performing activities and raising events. An instance of this class can be:

```
Role: (
name="flightRole"
type="airline"
capabilities="(flightTicketBooking,cancelTicketBooking)"
permissions="(flightTicketBooking)"
)
```

The above example describes "flightRole" as being of the type "airline", both capable and authorized to book flight tickets.

Please observe that the above model closely resembles standard workflow meta-models, which have been developed (e.g. by the WfMC [12]). This is not surprising, since service composition is in many ways similar to workflow, e.g. concerning task structuring, transition conditions, roles, and etceteras. However, in the IM these are perceived and subsequently represented from a service oriented point of view. Also, some concepts like events are often not defined workflow meta models (e.g. in [12]), but they are an important part of the IM.

Now, at this stage it is easy to understand that the difference between an abstract, scheduled, and constructed service composition lies in the absence of specific composition elements or associations between these elements. More specifically, the service composition system starts by only specifying activities, messages and constraints elements in the abstract based on the user requirements and leave the **flow, role, providers** elements unspecified. Then it can progress from an abstract service composition specification to an executable composition by gradually generating these elements on the basis of applying business rules and seeking user input. This is discussed in what follows.

3.2 Service Composition Rules

A concrete service composition needs to link elements such as "service provider" to "service", "service" to "activity", "activity" to "flow", and so on, as indicated in Fig. 2. These associations in a service composition IM are constrained by means of business rules. Fig. 2 shows some examples of these rules, referred to as *composition rules*, as notes attached to associations between service composition classes.

Composition rules are expressed in the Object Constraint Language (OCL) [9]). We apply such rules to constrain composition element attributes values and associations. An example of an attribute constraint is `activity.function="FlightTicketBooking"`, specifying that the function of an activity must be "FlightTicketBooking". The expression `activity.input -> notEmpty` is an example of an association constraint, depicting that the "input" of the activity must not be empty, i.e., an activity must always be associated with an input message.

Service composition comprises a number of composition rules that in our approach are classified into five broad categories of rules, namely structural, behavioral, data, resource and exception rules. These categories of business rules are discussed in what follows. To illustrate the concepts that we introduced we will use the composition elements illustrated in Table 1 to 7. In reality composition will likely be much harder as they may involve complex matching algorithms and conformance rules, which are not elaborated in this paper to provide more intuition.

Table 1. Activity elements

Label	Name	Function	Inputs	Outputs
Activity1	flight	flightTicketBooking	departureDate,from,to	flightNr,seatNr
Activity2	hotel	hotelRoomReservation	checkinDate,duration,	hotelName
Activity3	car	carRental	period	pickupDate,carType
Activity4	stop	stopExecution	none	none

Table 2. Condition elements

Label	Name	Argument	Predicate	Value
Condition1	destinationCheckCondition	from	!=	to
Condition2	seatReservedCondition	seatNr	!=	-1
Condition3	seatUnavailableCondition	seatStatus	=	unsuccessful
Condition4	departureDateCondition	departureDate	>	currentDate

Structural rules: rules in this category are used to guide the process of structuring, scheduling and prioritizing activities within a service composition. An example of a structural rule in this category can be defined as:

```
structuralActivity: flow.subfunctions->exists(activity.function)
OR flow1.subfunctions->exists(flow2.function)                (1)
```

Table 3. Event elements

Label	Name	Context	Severity	Information	Solution
Event1	seatUnavailableException	flightTicketBooking	unrecoverable	seatStatus	stopExecution

Table 4. Flow elements

Label	Name	Function	Subfunctions	Pattern
Flow1	hotelCarFlow	hotelCar	hotelRoomReservation,carRental	ParallelWithSynchronization
Flow2	travelFlow	flightHotelCar	flightTicketBooking,hotelCar	Sequential

Table 5. Message elements

Label	Name	Parts	Correlations
Message1	flightReservationData	departureDate,returnDate,from,to	
Message2	hotelRoomBookingData	checkinTime,duration,roomType	checkinTime=arriv-time
Message3	carRentalData	period,carType,insurance	
Message4	flightTicket	airline,dept-time,arriv-time,flightNr,seatNr	
Message5	hotelRoomConfirmation	hotelName,period,roomNr	
Message6	carRentalApproval	carType,pickupLoc,pickupDate,period,dropOffLoc	
Message7	seatUnavailableSignal	seatStatus	

Table 6. Provider elements

Label	Name	Description	Services	Cost	Quality
Provider1	KLM	Royal Dutch Airline	flightSearching,flightTicketBooking	expensive	high
Provider2	MartinAir	Dutch Airline	flightSearching,flightTicketBooking	cheap	average
Provider3	Hertz	Car Rental Company	carRental	expensive	high
Provider4	Dollar	Car Rental Company2	carRental	average	average
Provider5	HotelDirect	Hotels Worldwide	hotelRoomReservation	cheap	average

Table 7. Role elements

Label	Name	Type	Capabilities	Permissions
Role1	flightRole	airline	flightTicketBooking,bookingCancellation	flightTicketBooking
Role2	hotelRole	hotelBroker	hotelRoomReservation	hotelRoomReservation
Role3	carRole	carRentalCompany	carRental,carSale	carRental

Suppose we have a travel plan composition consisting of flight ticket booking, hotel reservation and car rental activity, i.e., `Activity1-3` in Table1. One of the first concerns that a designer would face is to schedule these activities. We can observe from the structural rule (1) that we may only include an activity in a flow if its function attribute coincides with one of the subfunction attributes in a flow element. Consequently, `Activity1` in Table 1 can be included in `Flow2` in Table4. In a similar manner `Activity2` and `Activity3` can also be both included in `Flow1` (since the functions of `Activity2` and `Activity3` are subfunctions of `Flow1`). This yields the two flows: `Flow1` and `Flow2`. In order to merge these flows, we need to re-apply the structural rule (1). This time the rule indicates that we may include `Flow1` in `Flow2`. As a result we have a composition in which the activities are scheduled in accordance with the specified dependencies and priorities, and the association instances are created by linking `Activity1` with `Flow2`, `Activity2-3` with `Flow1`, and `Flow1` with `Flow2`.

Data rules are used to control the use of data in a composition, i.e., how messages are related to each other, what is the necessary input/output message for an activity. There are four data rules: *assignAsInput, assignAsOutput, signalEvent* and *correlateMessage*. These are defined as follows:

```
assignAsInput:     message.parts->includesAll(activity.inputs)
assignAsOutput:    message.parts->includesAll(activity.outputs)
signalEvent:       message.parts->includesAll(event.information)
correlateMessage: message1.part != message2.part AND
                   message1.correlations->includes(message2.part)    (2)
```

To illustrate how the data rules *assignAsInput* and *assignAsOutput* are applied, we try to determine the input and output message for `Activity1` (Table 1). The rule *assignAsInput* indicates that a message is only suitable if it includes all the information required by the activity. `Activity1` requires an input message containing a departure date, a starting point and a destination. This is satisfied by `Message1` (Table 5) as it provides the required data. In a similar fashion we can derive the output message for `Activity1`. It must be noted that `Message1-3` are not suitable, since the outputs of `Activity1` are not all contained in one of these messages. However, `Message4` turns out to be suitable (even though it contains additional information).

We use the rule *signalEvent* to determine which message signals the occurrence of an event. To illustrate this, we consider as example `Event1` (Table 3), which describes a seat unavailability exception. The rule `Event1` also indicates that an appropriate seat status needs to be included in its signal. Thus the only message satisfying this requirement is `Message7`.

Lastly, messages may be correlated to express dependencies between data in a composition. The creation of such correlations is governed by a special rule called *correlateMessage*. This rule specifies that a correlation exists if a part attribute in a message is correlated to a part attribute in another message. For example, in `Message2` "checkinDate" must be equal to "arriv-time". Therefore `Message2` can be correlated with `Message4` by applying the rule *correlateMessage*.

Behavioral rules are used to derive conditions for guarding activities, controlling event occurrences and enforcing integrity constraints. We may define the following behavioral rules:

```
preguardActivity:   activity.inputs->exists(condition.argument)
postguardActivity:  activity.outputs->exists(condition.argument)
controlEvent:       event.information->exists(condition.argument)
preserveIntegrity: message.parts->exists(condition.argument)    (3)
```

The first two rules derive the pre- and post-conditions of an activity, respectively. In particular, the rule *preguardActivity* specifies that a condition can guard the execution of an activity only if its argument constrains an input of the activity. In other words, pre-execution guards can be based solely on information that is used as activity input. Take `Condition1` (in Table 2) for example, it constrains the inputs "from" and "to" of `Activity1` by stating that the starting place must not be equal to the destination. Therefore, `Condition1` can guard the execution of `Activity1` according to rule *preguardActivity*.

Another important use of conditions is to control how events can be raised by indicating in which situations they may occur. For this purpose the rule *controlEvent* is used to specify that if a condition constrains part of the information required to signal the event, then it can control the occurrence of that event. To understand this, we consider `Event1` (in Table 3) and `Condition3` (in Table 2). Rule `Event1` represents a seat unavailability exception, therefore it should only occur if no seats can be reserved. The rule `Condition3` can be used to constrain its occurrence, since this condition checks the value of "seatStatus" which is "information" required by `Event1` according to rule *controlEvent*.

Finally, conditions can be used to influence integrity constraints. For example, the rule *preserveIntegrity* guides the creation of constraints by establishing associations between **condition** and **message**. More specifically, rule *preserveIntegrity* specifies that only if the argument of the condition refers to a part in a given message, then the condition can be used to enforce data integrity. For instance `Condition4` (in Table2), which specifies a constraint that the departure date for the flight must always be greater than the current date, has an argument "departureDate". This argument is part of `Message1` (in Table5). Consequently, rule *preserveIntegrity* helps establish a valid association between `Condition4` and `Message1`.

Resource rules are provided to guide the use of resources in the composition in terms of selecting services, providers, and event raisers.

```
performActivity: role.capabilities->exists(activity.function)
                 AND role.permissions->exists(activity.function)
raiseEvent:      role.capabilities->exists(event.context)
                 AND role.permissions->exists(event.context)
playRole:        provider.services->includesAll(role.capabilities)(4)
```

The rule *performActivity* regulates which role is responsible for carrying out an activity in the composition. It indicates that this can only be the case whenever a role is capable and authorized to perform the function in the activity. For instance, in the case of `Activity1`, rule *performActivity* indicates that a role both capable of and authorized to book flight tickets needs to be found. As a result of this `Role1` (in Table 7) is selected to handle the functions of `Activity1`.

Roles are also responsible for raising events. The requirements for doing so are expressed by the rule *raiseEvent*. This rule specifies that a role must be capable of and authorized to perform the function in those contexts where the event can occur. For instance, only role `Role1` can raise event `Event1` according to rule *raiseEvent*. This is due to the matching of the attribute "context" in `Event1` with the "capabilities" and "permissions" attributes in `Role1`.

At runtime roles are carried out by concrete service providers. To guide the selection process for each role we use the rule *playRole*. This rule controls selection by demanding that a provider's services must provide the functions for which the role is capable of and authorized to perform. This means that, for example, `Role1` requires that a service provider must offer a service with flight ticket booking. According to this rule, *playRole* `Provider1` (Table 6) is the first suitable provider.

Exception rules are finally used to guide the exceptional behavior regarding service compositions. In this case the *in uenceActivity* is used to determine which events can affect an activity at run-time, while the rule *handleEvent* governs how these events are to be handled. These rules are defined as follows:

```
influenceActivity: event.context->includes(activity.function)
handleEvent:       activity.function=event.solution        (5)
```

Rule *in uenceActivity* specifies that for an event to impact an activity at run-time, the context in which the event occurs must be equal to the function of the activity. According to this rule an event such as `Event1` can only influence an activity whose function is the attribute "flight-ticket-booking". As a result, the only element with which an association can be established is `Activity1`.

Knowing which activity is affected by which event is relatively useless if it is not clear how this event is handled. Each event specifies in its "solution" attribute the preferable way to react to its occurrence. The rule *handleEvent* is used for this purpose by specifying that an activity can only handle an event if its "function" is equal to specified "solution" in the respective event. For `Event1` this means finding an activity whose function is to "stop execution" of the composition. Accordingly, `Activity4` is assigned to handle `Event1`.

4 Service Composition Development Process

In this section we use the constructs we introduced in the previous to show how to construct service compositions. We assume that already defined composition elements, such as the ones described in Table-1, as well as all composition elements in Tables 2 to 7, are stored in the repository of the service composition tool (see Fig 3). We also assume that the user is interested in booking a flight from New York to Vancouver with departure date July 15th, and return date August 22th. Furthermore, the user needs to reserve a hotel room and rent a car.

The process of designing a composite service for this travel example becomes a matter of applying the composition rules to incrementally construct composition elements and associations. Again we use the composition elements in Table 1 to 7 for this example. The user triggers a request by either writing an application program that retrieves existing activity elements and tries to combine them in a composite service or by issuing a request expressed in a formal XML based request language such as the one described in [1], [10]. The process of constructing composite services out of elementary activities can proceed in accordance with the steps of the algorithm found in Fig. 4, and is described in the following. To describe this process we will use the travel example we introduced in the previous.

The service composition development system receives the user request and enters the *De nition* phase of the algorithm depicted in Fig. 4. In the first

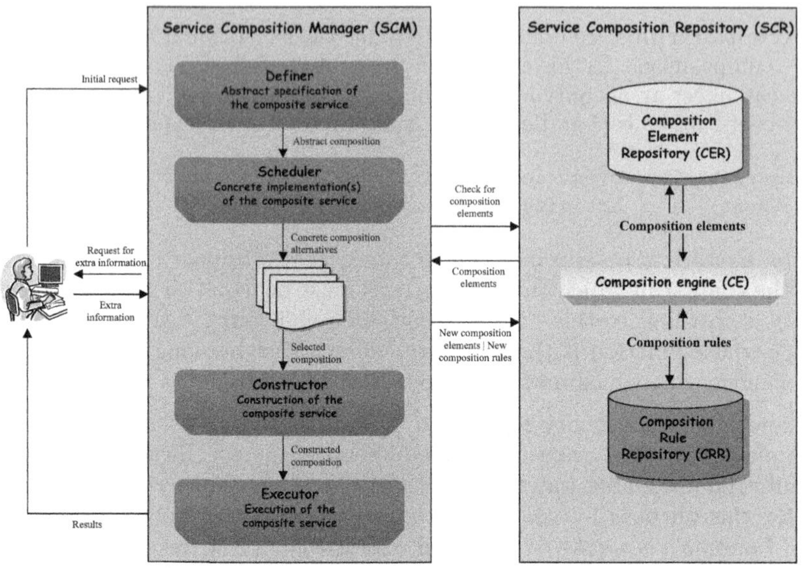

Fig. 3. Architecture for the Service Composition Development System

instance the system attempts to *determine/select activities* that satisfy a user request. As a result of the request expressed above, `Activity1, Activity2` and `Activity3` (in Table 2) are added to the composition. Subsequently, for each activity the service composition development system tries to *add message exchanging behavior*. To achieve this the system must determine for each activity what type of messages it should use as input and generate as its output messages. For example, for `Activity1` message `Message1` is found as input and `Message4` as output. As a result these elements are added to the composition.

The next steps in the algorithm *de nes exceptional behavior* for the service composition by applying the rule `influenceActivity` for events and activities possible to determine possible event occurrences. For example, for `Activity1` `Event1` (Table 4) is found as an influencing event. If an event influences an activity, subsequently the event raiser, signal and handler need to be determined. For `Event1` this is done as follows:

1. Apply `raiseEvent` to **role** to determine the role raising the event. For `Event1` `Role1` (Table 8), is found.
2. Apply `signalEvent` to **message** to derive the message signalling the event occurrence. As a result `Message7` is found for `Event1`.

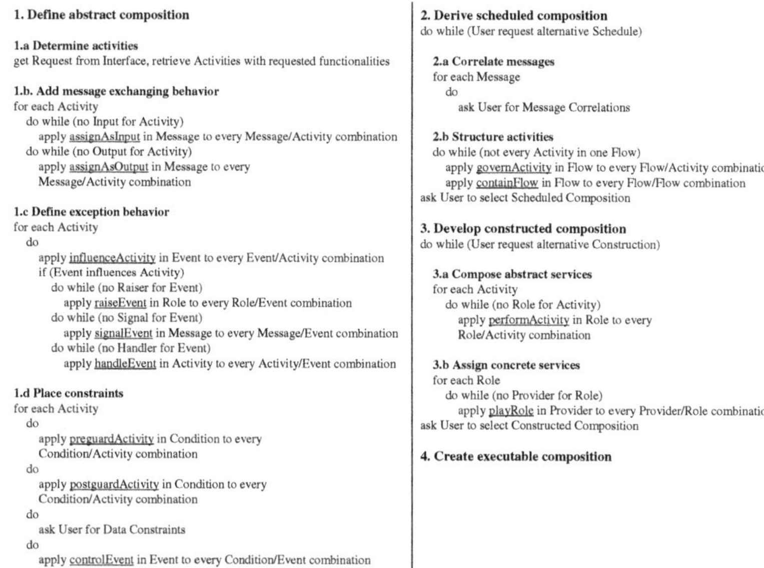

```
1. Define abstract composition

1.a Determine activities
get Request from Interface, retrieve Activities with requested functionalities

1.b. Add message exchanging behavior
for each Activity
  do while (no Input for Activity)
    apply assignAsInput in Message to every Message/Activity combination
  do while (no Output for Activity)
    apply assignAsOutput in Message to every
    Message/Activity combination

1.c Define exception behavior
for each Activity
  do
    apply influenceActivity in Event to every Event/Activity combination
    if (Event influences Activity)
      do while (no Raiser for Event)
        apply raiseEvent in Role to every Role/Event combination
      do while (no Signal for Event)
        apply signalEvent in Message to every Message/Event combination
      do while (no Handler for Event)
        apply handleEvent in Activity to every Activity/Event combination

1.d Place constraints
for each Activity
  do
    apply preguardActivity in Condition to every
    Condition/Activity combination
  do
    apply postguardActivity in Condition to every
    Condition/Activity combination
  do
    ask User for Data Constraints
  do
    apply controlEvent in Event to every Condition/Event combination

2. Derive scheduled composition
do while (User request alternative Schedule)

  2.a Correlate messages
  for each Message
    do
      ask User for Message Correlations

  2.b Structure activities
  do while (not every Activity in one Flow)
    apply governActivity in Flow to every Flow/Activity combination
    apply containFlow in Flow to every Flow/Flow combination
ask User to select Scheduled Composition

3. Develop constructed composition
do while (User request alternative Construction)

  3.a Compose abstract services
  for each Activity
    do while (no Role for Activity)
      apply performActivity in Role to every
      Role/Activity combination

  3.b Assign concrete services
  for each Role
    do while (no Provider for Role)
      apply playRole in Provider to every Provider/Role combination
ask User to select Constructed Composition

4. Create executable composition
```

Fig. 4. Algorithm for the Service Composition Development Process

3. Apply `handleEvent` to **activity** to determine the activity that will handle the event. For example `Activity4` is found for `Event1`.

Following the definition of exceptions, necessary constraints (if any) are placed on the service composition. The constraints under which the composition is to be executed are depicted in condition elements. These can be predefined, e.g., pre-condition, post-condition, or user specified, e.g., data constraints. As an example we can derive pre-conditions for the activities in the composition by applying `preguardActivity` for each activity. This means that for `Activity1` condition `Condition1` applies.

Next, the abstract composition is made more concrete by entering the *Scheduling* phase in the algorithm. During this phase we need to *correlate messages* and *structure activities*. Correlations are usually context-dependent and thus cannot be derived by a general business rule. Instead they can be defined for each message by the user. This may, for instance, mean that for the travel request we consider, the user may wish to define a correlation between "arrivtime" in `Message4` and "checkinDate" in `Message2` to ensure that he will have a hotel room the day he arrives. Following this, activities must be structured. This is accomplished by applying the `governActivity` and `containFlow` structuring operations which group related activities into a single flow. The construct `governActivity` can be applied to both `Activity2` and `Activity 3` (Table 1) to indicate that they can be included in `Flow1` (Table 5). It can also be applied to `Activity1` to include it in `Flow2`. Finally, the constructs `Flow1` `Flow2` can be combined into a single flow using `containFlow` to create a complete activity schedule. The correlation and structuring sub-steps may be repeated to generate additional schedules that may be relevant to a user request.

During the next step the algorithm enters *Construction* phase during which the scheduled composition will turn into an unambiguous composition of concrete services. First the algorithm *composes abstract services* by associating each activity with a role, specifying the requirements for a party interested in carrying out the activity. This is accomplished by applying the operation `performActivity` for each activity until a role has been found. For example, for `Role2` can be found for `Activity2`. As a last sub-step in the construction phase *concrete services are selected* for the roles in the composition. For this purpose the operation `playRole` is applied to each role, resulting in, for example, `Provider2` (Table 6) as the first suitable provider for `Role2`. The construction sub-steps can be repeated to create multiple concrete compositions for the user to choose from.

The final step in the algorithm is the *Execution* phase during which the constructed composition is mapped to an executable format in a service composition language, e.g., BPEL. Such a translation can be likely done without too much difficulty, however, we do not elaborate on it here due to space limitations.

It is not necessary that every composition needs to go through each individual step discussed in the previous. If, for example, part of a composition is already partially constructed with some of the composition elements defined, the model only needs to be completed and mapped to an executable format.

5 Related Work

Most of the work in service composition has focused on using work flows either as a engine for distributed activity coordination or as a tool to model and define service composition. Representative work is described in [3] where the authors discuss the development of a platform specifying and enacting composite services in the context of a workflow engine.

The workflow community has recently paid attention to configurable or extensible workflow systems which present some overlaps with the ideas reported in the above. For example, work on flexible workflows has focused on dynamic process modification [8]. In this publication workflow changes are specified by transformation rules composed of a source schema, a destination schema and of conditions. The workflow system checks for parts of the process that are isomorphic with the source schema and replaces them with the destination schema for all instances for which the conditions are satisfied.

The approach described in [6] allows for automatic process adaptation. The authors present a workflow model that contains a placeholder activity, which is an abstract activity replaced at run-time with a concrete activity type. This concrete activity must have the same input and output parameter types as those defined as part of the placeholder. In addition, the model allows to specify a selection policy to indicate which activity should be executed.

In [14] authors developed an agent-based cross-enterprize Workflow Management System (WFMS) which can integrate business processes on user's demand. Based on users' requirements, the integration agent contacts the discovery agent to locate appropriate service agents, then negotiates with the service agents about task executions. Authors in [15] proposed a dynamic workflow system that is capable of dynamic composition and modification of running workflows by using a business rule inference engine. However these two approaches are more of the focus of dynamic process execution and management.

Our approach differs from the above work as regards supporting the dynamic composition of web services in the following manner:

- We propose a model driven approach towards service composition, which covers the entire service composition life cycle ranging from abstract service definition, scheduling, construction, execution and evolution. By raising the level of abstraction compositions developed in our approach are flexible and agile in the face of change.
- Service compositions are defined in terms of basic abstract elements, i.e. *composition elements*, which are used to construct a concrete service composition specification. This design process is governed by *composition rules*, supporting highly flexible composition development.
- Business rules are classified based on the requirements of service composition, something which to the best of our knowledge has not been addressed in work related to business rule classification, such as [5],[7] and [11].

6 Conclusions and Future Research

Current standards in service composition, such as BPEL, are not suitable for dealing with the complex and dynamic nature of developing and managing composite web services to realize business processes. With a vast service space to search, a variety of services to compare and match, and different ways to construct composed services, manual specification of compositions is an almost impossible task requiring specialistic knowledge, taking up much time and effort. The challenge is thus to provide a solution in which dynamic service composition development and management is facilitated in an automated fashion.

In this paper we have presented a phased approach to service composition development conducted on the basis of abstract constructs provided by a model driven architecture. Service compositions are constructed in a piecemeal fashion by progressing from abstract service descriptions to more concrete ones on the basis of a set of business rules that synthesize the activities in a composition. This approach makes service composition more flexible and dynamic compared to current standards and recent research activities.

The work presented herein is at an initial stage. Several issues including the mappings and conformance between compositions need to be further investigated and verified in a formal manner. In addition, a change management sub-system to control the evolution of business rules and service composition specifications needs to be developed.

References

1. Aiello et al. A request language for web-services based on planning and constraint satisfaction. VLDB Workshop on Technologies for E-Services (TES02), 2002.
2. Business Process Modelling Initiative. Business Process Modeling Language, *June 24, 2002, http://www.bpmi.org*
3. F. Casati, S. Ilnicki, L. Jin, V. Krishnamoorthy, M.C. Shan. Adaptive and Dynamic Service Composition in eFlow, *HP Lab. Techn. Report, HPL-2000-39.*
4. F. Curbera, Y. Goland, J. Klein, F. Leymann, D. Roller, S. Thatte, S. Weerawarana. Business Process Execution Language for Web Services, *July 31, 2002, http://www-106.ibm.com/developerworks/webservices/library/ws-bpel/*
5. Business Rules Group. Defining business rules, what are they really?, *July 2000, http://www.brcommunity.com*
6. D. Georgakopoulos, H. Schuster, D. Baker, and A. Cichocki. Managing Escalation of Collaboration Processes in Crisis Mitigation Situations. *Proceedings of ICDE 2000, San Diego, CA, USA, 2000.*
7. B. von Halle. Business rules applied: Building Better Systems Using the Business Rule Approach, *Wiley & Sons, 2002*
8. G. Joeris and O. Herzog. Managing Evolving Workflow Specifications with Schema Versioning and Migration Rules. *TZI Technical Report 15, University of Bremen, 1999.*
9. Object Management Group. Object Constraint Language, *http://www.omg.org/docs/formal/03-03-13.pdf*
10. M.P. Papazoglou, M. Aiello, M. Pistore, J. Yang Planning for Requests against web-Services *IEEE Data Engineering Bulletin*, vol. 25, no.4, 2002.
11. R. Veryard. Rule Based Development, *CBDi Journal, July/August 2002*
12. Workflow Management Coalition. The Workflow Reference Model, *http://www.wfmc.org/standards/docs/tc003v11.pdf*
13. J. Yang, M.P. Papazoglou. Service Component for Managing Service Composition Life-Cycle, *Information Systems, Elsevier, June, 2003*
14. Liangzhao Zeng, Boualem Benatallah, and Anne H. H. Ngu. "On Demand Business-to-Business Integration", *CooPIS01, Trento, 2001*
15. Liangzhao Zeng, David Flaxer, Henry Chang, Jun-Jang Jeng. PLM_{flow}-Dynamic Business Process Composition and Execution by Rule Inference, *TES2002, Hong Kong, 2002*

Automating the Procurement of Web Services*

Octavio Martín-Díaz, Antonio Ruiz-Cortés,
Amador Durán, David Benavides, and Miguel Toro

Dpto. de Lenguajes y Sistemas Informáticos
E.T.S. de Ingeniería Informática, Universidad de Sevilla
41012 Sevilla, España - Spain
Phone: +34 95 455 3871 Fax: +34 95 455 7139
{octavio,aruiz,amador,mtoro}@lsi.us.es
benavides@us.es

Abstract. As government agencies and business become more dependent on web services, software solutions to automate their procurement gain importance. Current approaches for automating the procurement of web services suffer from an important drawback: neither uncertainty measures nor non-linear, and complex relations among parameters can be used by providers to specify quality-of-service in offers. In this paper, we look deeply into the roots of this drawback and present a proposal which overcomes it. The key point to achieve this improvement has been using the constraint programming as a formal basis, since it endows the model with a very powerful expressiveness. A XML-based implementation is presented along with some experimental results and comparisons with other approaches.

Keywords: software procurement, web services, quality-of-service, traders.

1 Introduction

As government agencies and business become more dependent on web services, software solutions to automate their procurement gain importance. It is generally assumed that decision criteria for choosing software packages stems from the user requirements they should fulfill. There are different types of requirements such as managerial, political, and, of course, quality requirements. There are a number of approaches which automate some activities of the procurement, most of them focus in quality requirements. However, these approaches suffer from several drawbacks that hamper their use when requirements that providers guarantee include uncertainty measures, non-linear and complex relations among parameters. In fact, if we want to achieve a competitive technology based on web services, their quality-of-service is an important issue to be taken into account, becoming one of challenges to be solved in the near future [31].

In this context, software procurement [4,5] becomes web services procurement (WSP), an activity focussed on the acquisition of web services required by a web-

* Supported by the Spanish Interministerial Commission on Science and the Spanish Ministry of Science and Technology under grants TIC2000-1106-C02-01, TIC2003-02737-C02-01 and FIT-150100-2001-78.

M.E. Orlowska et al. (Eds.): ICSOC 2003, LNCS 2910, pp. 91–103, 2003.

service-based system, thus it is a critical activity for current web system developers. Some typical tasks involved in WSP are:

- Specification of demands and offers, which should be checked for consistency in order to verify they do not contain any inner contradiction.
- Search of offers, which should be checked for conformance in order to verify they fulfill the demand, so that the selection is limited to such offers.
- Selection of the best choice according to the assessment criteria which is included in the demand.

In this paper, we present a proposal to automate the procurement of web services. Our proposal improves on others in that it supports a symmetric specification model. Thus, providers can include in their offers requirements as complex as customers include in their demands. The key point to achieve this improvement has been using the constraint programming as a formal basis, since it endows the model with a very powerful expressiveness. A XML–based implementation is presented along with some experimental results and comparisons with other approaches.

The rest of the paper is structured as follows. In Section 2, we introduce the notions of asymmetric and symmetric specification models, as well as an overview of related works. In Section 3, we propose the use of constraint programming as a means of achieving a symmetric specification model. In Section 4, we present briefly the main implementation aspects of our run-time framework, together with some experimental results. Finally, in Section 5 we summarise the presented work and the immediate future work.

2 Symmetric versus Asymmetric Models

2.1 Asymmetric Models

Let S be a multidimensional space whose dimensions are given by domains of quality-of-service parameters. Traditionally, a demand (δ) has been viewed as a subspace in S, whereas an offer (ω) has been viewed as a point in S. Thus, checking the conformance amounts to checking whether the point (the offer) belongs to the subspace (the demand) or not. See Figures 1.a and 1.b, respectively. This checking can be computed easily by evaluating ω in δ. As an example, if a web service owns the offer $\omega = \{MTTF = 120\}$, then it is conformant to the demand $\delta_1 = \{MTTF \geq 100\}$ because $120 \geq 100$, but not to the demand $\delta_2 = \{MTTF > 120\}$ because $120 \not> 100$.

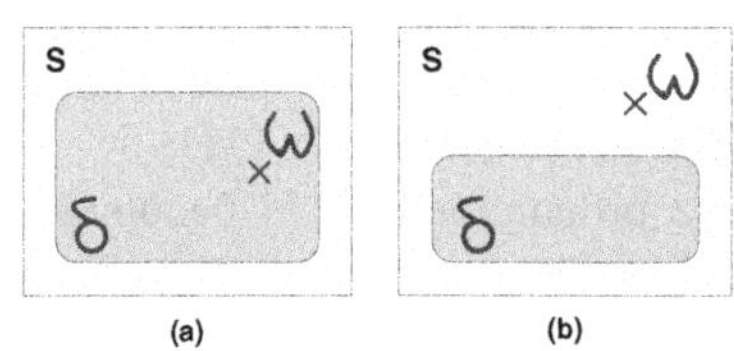

Fig. 1. Conformance in asymmetric models.

This interpretation of conformance results in a model which is asymmetric with regard to the expressiveness of quality-of-service specifications. This semantics makes very difficult to specify offers when it is needed something else than a point, as an example to specify some uncertainty or a space. As most of programming languages are able to check if a point is inside a space, whereas checking if a space includes another space is a hard question, most of platforms have adopted an asymmetric specification model. As well, these approaches with an asymmetric model usually own a limited expressiveness because conditions are restricted to simple expressions involving single parameters, so complex expressions are not allowed.

2.2 Symmetric Models

Alternatively, an offer can be also considered as a sub-space, just as demands, so that it represents the ranges of quality-of-service values that the corresponding web service guarantees to supply. In this way, an offer (ω) is conformant to a demand (δ) whenever the offer's sub-space is inside the demand's sub-space (see Figure 2.a), otherwise the offer is not conformant (see Figure 2.b). As an example, if a web service owns the offer $\omega = \{MTTF >= 120\}$, then it is conformant to the following demand $\delta_1 = \{MTTF >= 100\}$, but not to the demand $\delta_2 = \{MTTF > 120\}$ because the offer's instance value $\{MTTF = 120\}$ is out of the demand's space.

This interpretation of conformance results in a symmetric model because quality-of-service in demands and offers can be specified in the same way. This semantics makes the offer guarantee the complete range, not only a concrete value, i.e., we can not make any assumption on a concrete value, because it is equally possible any value in the sub-space, and there is no control to get a concrete value. As well, symmetric approaches usually achieve a greater deal of expressiveness to specify quality-of-service, since there is usually no restriction on the number of involved parameters or type of operators, so that non-linear or more complex expressions are allowed.

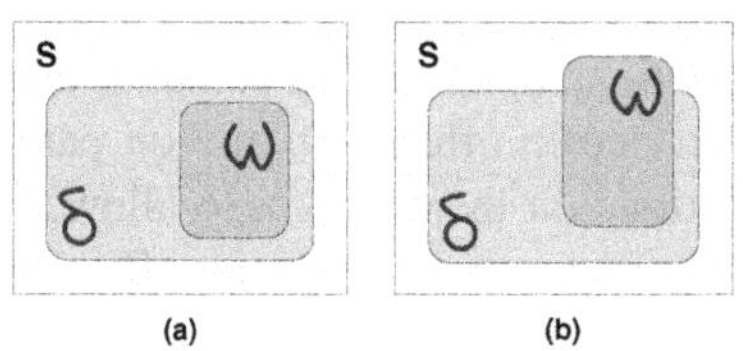

Fig. 2. Conformance in symmetric models.

2.3 Related Work

Figure 3 shows a comparative study among the most prominent (as far as we know) quality-aware approaches to WSP. Briefly:

The Reference Model	Static View: The Lexicon					Dynamic View: The Process Model
	Stakeholders	Quality-of-Service Documents	Catalogues, Parameters & Measures			
			Data Structuring	Customer's	Provider's	
IBM's WSME MME	Providers Costumers	Advertisements Queries Agreements	Data Dictionary: pre-def. basic types sequences records	Name-Value Pair Properties Static/Dynamic Binding Scripts for Rule-based Reqs.		Advertisement/Submission Query/Submission Matchmaking Selecting Providers' Offers
HP's MME Service	Advertisers Requestors	Service Offers & Requests	DAML+OIL Ontology: datatypes and types subsumption	Composition Single-Parameter Constraints on Parameters of Service (expandable)		Advertising Querying Browsing
UDDIe	Providers Consumers	Publishing Inquiry	*Blue Pages*	Single-Par. Conditions on Properties (Qualifiers)	Name-Value Pair Properties	Publishing Search and Discovery
Our Proposal	Providers Costumers	Demands Offers Agreements	Catalogues: pre-def. basic types catalogue extension basic and derived p.	Composition Multiple-Parameter Constraints on Parameters of Service		Creating Catalogues Offers Submission Demands Submission Matchmaking

Fig. 3. A comparison of quality-aware approaches to WSP.

- The *UDDI Extension* (UDDIe) [28] is based on the UDDI (Universal Description Discovery and Integration) services. UDDIe owns an asymmetric model when specifying demands and offers.
- The HP's *Matchmaking Engine* (MME) [10] is based on the DAML (DARPA Agent Markup Language) semantic web language [2]. It is the closest proposal to ours, because it owns a symmetric model to specify quality-of-service, and it uses constraints to do it, so it owns a great expressiveness. As well, it uses a Description Logic DL's solver as a mean of carrying out the WSP-related tasks. Nevertheless, there is not currently any DL's solver version able to process some of the most complex expressions which can be specified in MME.
- The IBM's *Web Services Matchmaking Engine* (WSME) [12], which is related to *Web Service Level Agreement* (WSLA) [15,17], is based on the CORBA/ODP trader service. It owns an asymmetric model and there is no optimation of the selection because search results are only the lists of conformant offers. Nonetheless, there is a difference: relationships between demands and offers are bilateral. In the same way quality-of-service in offers is based on parameter/value pairs whereas demands impose conditions on them, it is also allowed that demands define their own quality-of-service parameters whereas the offers impose conditions on them. As an example, let an offer be given by the following quality-of-service specification $\omega = \{me.MTTF = 120 \ \& \ your.nationality \in \{BE, \ldots, UK\}\}$ and a demand $\delta = \{me.nationality = \{IS\} \ \& \ your.MTTF > 100\}$, then the offer ω is not conformant to the demand δ, because the condition it imposes on the demand (the Europe Union membership) is not fulfilled, despite of the offer fulfills conditions imposed by the demand.
- Other languages for specifying quality-of-service and trader services the *Quality-of-service Modeling Language* (QML) [8], the NoFun language [6], and the CORBA trader service [22]. These proposals are not directly related to WSP.

3 Supporting WSP with Constraint Programming

We have chosen mathematical constraints as the way of specifying quality-of-service in demands and offers. In this way, checking conformance can be carried out just as a constraint satisfaction problem (CSP) or a constraint satisfaction optimisation problem (CSOP) [7,11,18,29]. In general, CSP-based modelling is quite simple and intuitive (in most cases) in the context of problems which we are dealing with. Constraint programming is an excellent support for symmetric specifications models, because it makes possible to check whether a space is included in another one, being these spaces treated as constraints. Our proposal owns a symmetric specification model with a great deal of expressiveness because of using constraints.

3.1 Constraint Programming in a Nutshell

Constraint Programming (CP) has recently attracted high attention among experts from many areas because of its potential for solving hard real-life problems. Not only it is based on a strong theoretical foundation, but it is an attracting widespread commercial interest, as well. Constraints formalise those dependencies in physical worlds and their mathematical abstractions naturally and transparently. A constraint is simply a logical relation among several variables, each taking a value in a given domain. The constraint thus restricts the possible values that variables can take, and it represents a partial information about the variables of interest. An important feature of constraints is their declarative manner, i.e., they specify what relationships must hold without specifying a computational procedure to enforce them. CP is the study of computational systems based on constraints. The idea of CP is to solve problems by stating constraints (requirements) about the problem area and, consequently, finding solution satisfying all the constraints.

The earliest ideas leading to CP may be found in the Artificial Intelligence dating back to sixties and seventies. The scene labelling problem [30] is probably the first constraint satisfaction problem that was formalised. The main step towards CP was achieved when Gallaire [9] and Jaffar & Lassez [14] noted that logic programming was just a particular kind of constraint programming. The basic idea behind Logic Programming (LP), and declarative programming in general, is that the user states what has to be solved instead of how to solve it, which is very close to the idea of constraints. Therefore the combination of constraints and logic programming is very natural, and Constraint Logic Programming (CLP) makes a nice declarative environment for solving problems by means of constraints. However, it does not mean that CP is restricted to CLP. Constraints were integrated to typical imperative languages like C++ and Java, as well.

The nowadays real-life applications of CP in the area of planning, scheduling and optimisation rise the question if the traditional field of Operations Research (OR) is a competitor or an associate of CP. There is a significant overlap of CP and OR in the field of NP-Hard combinatorial problems. While the OR has a long research tradition and (very successful) method of solving problems using linear programming, the CP emphasis is on higher level modelling and solutions methods that are easier to understand by the final customer. Most recent advances promise that both methodologies can exploit each other, in particular, the CP can serve as a roof platform for integrating various constraint solving algorithms including those developed and checked to be successful in OR. As the above paragraphs show, the CP has an inner interdisciplinary nature. It combines and exploits ideas from a number of fields including Artificial Intelligence, Combinatorial Algorithms, Computational Logic, Discrete Mathematics, Neural Networks, Operations Research, Programming Languages, and Symbolic Computation.

Currently, we see two branches of CP, namely constraint satisfaction and constraint solving. Both share the same terminology but the origins and solving technologies are different. The former deals with problems defined over finite domains and, currently, probably more than 95% of all industrial constraint applications use finite domains. Therefore, we deal with constraint satisfaction problems mostly in this paper. The latter shares the basis of CP, i.e., describing the problem as a set of constraints and solving these constraints. But now, the constraints are defined (mostly) over infinite or more complex domains. Instead of combinatorial methods for constraint satisfaction, the constraint solving algorithms are based on mathematical techniques such as automatic differentiation, Taylor series or Newton method.

Constraint Satisfaction Problems [29] have been a subject of research in Artificial Intelligence for many years. A Constraint Satisfaction Problem (CSP) is defined as a set of variables each ranging on a finite domain, and a set of constraints restricting all the values that variables can simultaneously take. A solution to a CSP is an assignment of a value from its domain to every variable, in such a way that all constraints are satisfied at once. We may want to find: i) just one solution, with no preference as to which one, ii) all solutions, iii) an optimal, or at least a good solution, given some objective function defined in terms of some or all of variables. Solutions to a CSP can be found by searching (systematically) through all possible value assignments to variables.

In many real-life applications, we do not want to find any solution but a good solution. The quality of solution is usually measured by an application dependent function called objective function. The goal is to find such solution that satisfies all the constraints and minimise or maximise the objective function, respectively. Such problems are referred to as Constraint Satisfaction Optimisation Problems (CSOP), which consists of a standard CSP and an optimisation function that maps every solution (complete labelling of variables) to a numerical value [29].

3.2 Consistency and Conformance

Whenever a new demand or offer is submitted, its consistency needs to be checked, i.e., whether or not it contains any inner contradiction. This is interpreted as a CSP, so that if the corresponding CSP is satisfiable, then the demand or offer can be considered as consistent. The corresponding CSP for a demand or offer is composed of all the constraints it contains. On the other hand, the best choice selection regarding with a demand implies the previous checking for conformance, because the search is reduced to conformant offers. As we are using constraint programming, checking of conformance lies in determining whether each and every solution to the offer's CSP is also a solution to the demand's CSP.

In this way, the corresponding CSP for checking the conformance is constructed according to the definition given in [18]:

$$conformance(\omega, \delta) \Leftrightarrow sat(c_\omega \wedge \neg c_\delta) = false$$

where ω is the offer and c_ω its corresponding CSP, δ is the demand and c_δ its corresponding CSP, and sat is a function that we identify with the CSP solver which is being used. It can be applied on a CSP c so that it returns one of the following results: $true$ if c is satisfiable, $false$ if not, and $\perp$ if the solver cannot determine whether c is satisfiable or not.

3.3 Optimality

More often than not, it is possible to have several offers which are conformant to the same demand for a web service, then we should select that offer which is the best choice. This selection is carried out according to the assessment criteria the customer includes in his or her demand. These criteria may be given by utility functions [3,16,21] which, in general, have the signature $\mathcal{U} : \pi \rightarrow [0, 1]$ where π is the measuring domain of a quality-of-service parameter. Utility functions assign an utility assessment (ranging from 0 to 1) to every quality-of-service value it can take, so the greater the assessment, the better the consideration of the customer. Therefore, utility functions allow the establishment of an objective criteria, given by customers, in order to select those offers which better fulfill the demands. Figure 4 shows several utility functions corresponding to examples in this section.

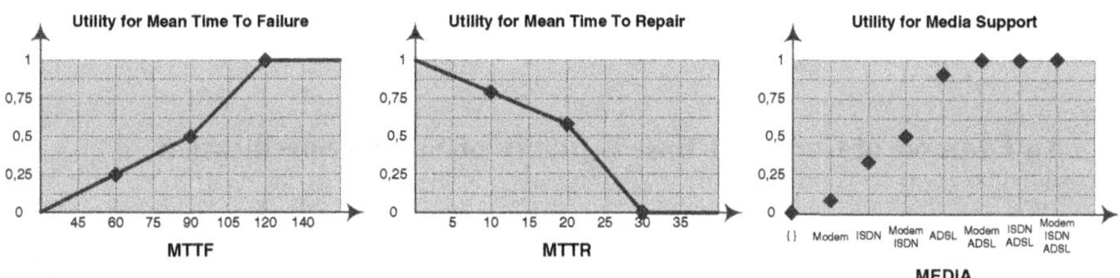

Fig. 4. Utility functions for $MTTF$, $MTTR$, and $MEDIA$.

Although we can make use of any kind of function to specify utility functions, linear piecewise functions are often the preferred. As an example, the utility function for a numeric quality-of-service parameter can be defined by means of polylines determined by a sequence of coordinate points such as $(x_1, u_1), (x_2, u_2), \ldots, (x_n, u_n)$, where every x represents a value in the measuring domain of the quality-of-service, and u its assessment in the range [0,1]. The corresponding utility function is then given by:

$$\mathcal{U}(x) = \begin{cases} u_1 + \frac{u_2 - u_1}{x_2 - x_1}(x - x_1) & \text{if} \quad x_1 \leq x < x_2 \\ \ldots & \\ u_{n-1} + \frac{u_n - u_{n-1}}{x_n - x_{n-1}}(x - x_{n-1}) & \text{if } x_{n-1} \leq x \leq x_n \\ \perp & \text{if } x < x_1 \text{ o } x > x_n \end{cases}$$

We are not usually interested in computing the utility assessment of an unique quality-of-service parameter, but on maximising the global assessment of offers in order to select the best one, being these offers conformant to the demand. Nevertheless, we can not compute the maximum offers' utility assessments when comparing them. As an example, let the following offers $\omega_1 = \{60 \leq MTTF \leq 120\}$ and $\omega_2 = \{90 \leq MTTF \leq 110\}$. Intuitively, the first is better, because if $MTTF = 120$ then $\mathcal{U}(\omega_1) = 1$. However, the offer is guaranteeing the complete range, not only a concrete value, so we can not make such assumption because it is equally possible that $MTTF = 60$, and there is no control to get a concrete value. Therefore, we compare the minimum utility assessments of offers. In this way, the latter offer is the better, because if $MTTF = 90$ then $\mathcal{U}(\omega_2) = 0.5$, whereas the worst assessment of the first offer is 0.25, at most. Formally, the best offer (ω_S) can be defined as:

$$\omega_S = \omega \in \Omega_\delta \cdot \ \forall \omega_i \in \Omega_\delta - \{\omega\} \ \ \mathcal{U}^\delta(\omega) \geq \mathcal{U}^\delta(\omega_i)$$

where ω and ω_i stand for offers in the set Ω_δ of conformant offers to the demand δ, and the $\mathcal{U}^\delta(\omega)$ utility function of an offer ω according to assessment criteria in demand δ is defined as:

$$\mathcal{U}^\delta(\omega) = \underset{st \ c_\omega}{min} \ \textstyle\sum_{\pi \in c_\omega} w_\pi^\delta U^\delta(\pi)$$

where π represents a quality-of-service parameter which is involved in the offer's CSP c_ω, and $U^\delta(\pi)$ its utility function, and w_π^δ its assigned weight, according to assessment criteria in demand δ. On the other hand, weights are needed to express that a quality-of-service parameter is preferred to another.

3.4 An Example of Contraint-Based Quality-of-Service Specification

Figure 5 shows several catalogues, demands, and offers written in QRL [23,26], the language which we have defined for specifying quality requirements. Figure 4 shows the graphical representation of utility functions appearing in Figure 5. These demands and offers will be used in the examples along these paragraphs.

In this case, the involved quality-of-service parameters are the `Mean Time To Failure` (MTTF), the `Mean Time To Repair` (MTTR), and the `Media Support` (MEDIA). Note the included demand and offers are all consistent, because their corresponding CSP are satisfiable, as well as offers are conformant to the demand, because the corresponding CSP for checking the conformance are not satisfiable, according to definitions in Section 3.2.

Since both offers are conformant to the demand, we will have to compute the utility functions to compare them. According to definitions in Section 3.3, both offers own $U(MTTF = 110) = 0.83$ and $U(MTTR = 10) = 0.8$, `velazquez` owns $U(MEDIA) = 1$, and `zipi` owns $U(MEDIA) = 0.5$. Therefore, utility assessment of `velazquez` is $0.9 * 0.83 + 0.05 * 0.04 + 0.05 * 1 = 0.84$, and utility assessment of `zipi` is $0.9 * 0.83 + 0.05 * 0.04 + 0.05 * 0.5 = 0.815$, so the best offer is `velazquez`.

```
// A catalogue of Reliability-related QoS parameters
catalogue Reliability {
  MTTF {
    description: "Mean Time to Failure";
    domain: real [0,+inf) minute;
  };
  MTTR {
    description: "Mean Time To Repair";
    domain: real [0,+inf) minute;
  };
}

// A catalogue of Multimedia-related QoS parameters
catalogue Multimedia {
  MEDIA {
   description: "Media Support";
   domain: set { modem, ISDN, ADSL };
  }
}
```

a) Catalogues of quality-of-service parameters.

```
// Web service demand for IVideoServer
using Reliability, Multimedia;
demands for IVideoServer {
  D1: MTTF / (MTTF + MTTR) >= 0.9;
  D2: MEDIA includes {modem,ISDN};
}
assessment {
  MTTF {90, { (0,0), (90,0.5), (120,1) } };
  MTTR {05, { (0,1), (20,0.6), (30,0) } };
  MODEM {05,
    case MEDIA = { } : 0.01;
    case MEDIA = {modem} : 0.1;
    case MEDIA = {ISDN} : 0.3;
    case MEDIA = {ISDN,modem} : 0.5;
    case MEDIA = {ADSL} : 0.9;
    case MEDIA = {modem, ADSL} : 1;
    case MEDIA = {ISDN, ADSL} : 1;
    case MEDIA = {modem, ISDN, ADSL} : 1;
  }
}
```

b) A demand.

```
// Web service offer supplied by Velazquez
using Reliability, Multimedia;
offer for IVideoServer {
  O1: MTTF >= 110 and MTTF <= 120;
  O2: MTTR > 5 and MTTR <= 10;
  O3: MEDIA = {ADSL,ISDN,modem};
}
```

```
// Web service offer supplied by Zipi
using Reliability, Multimedia;
offer for IVideoServer {
  O1: MTTF >= 110 and MTTF <= 120;
  O2: MTTR > 5 and MTTR <= 10;
  O3: MEDIA = {ISDN,modem};
}
```

c) Several offers.

Fig. 5. Demands and offers written in QRL.

4 Implementation and Experimental Results

4.1 Overview of the Prototype's Architecture

We are developing a prototype of a run-time framework for WSP [19,20,24,27], whose preliminary version is available at `http://www.lsi.us.es/~octavio`. In this paper, we give a brief review, together with some experimental results we have recently obtained. A components view of the run-time framework is shown in Figure 6.

Selecting a multi-level architecture along with the deployment of the components as web applications or web services have been critical design decisions. Components are split up among the upper user-interface level, the intermediate service and utility levels, and the bottom repository level. These components can be reusable and interchangeable. Service level includes those components which implement the `IImportService` interface (functions related to submission of demands and searching for best conformant offer), and the `IExportService` interface (functions related to submission of offers).

These components have need of invoking checkings for consistency, conformance, and optimum search. These functions are implemented by the Quality Trader Web Service [19] at the utility level. Each function has a similar operation:

1. It takes the involved demands and offers written in XML as parameters.
2. It invokes the appropriate XSLT transformations in order to generate automatically the corresponding CSP.

3. It invokes a CSP solver which processes the CSP in order to get the result, which is finally returned.

The CSP solver which is invoked is ILOG's OPL Studio [13], which is an integrated development environment for mathematical programming and combinatorial optimisation applications. The OPL language (OPtimisation Language) is used to define CSP and CSOP models.

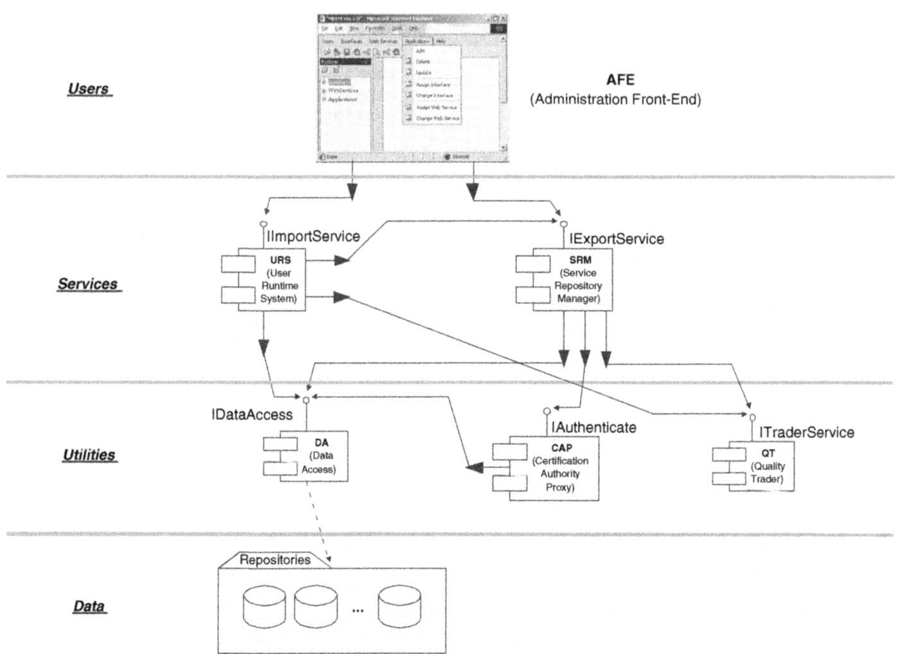

Fig. 6. Architecture of the run-time framework.

4.2 Experimental Results

Recently, we have carried out several tests, in order to get measures about performance of quality trader. We have implemented the first prototype in a Microsoft .NET environment, using the Visual Studio C#-based utilities and compilers. The main characteristics of the server computer are an AMD Athlom XP 1.8Gb processor with 560 Mb RAM. These tests have been focussed on latency of consistency, which is possibly the simplest of operations which are involved in WSP. In this paper, latency means the time from invokation of operation to return of a result. Figure 7 summarises the time our implementation took to check the consistency of a demand (of course, it could have been an offer).

Experimental data have been specified in this way: the Nth execution involves a QoS specification containing N constraints. Each QoS specification is constructed according

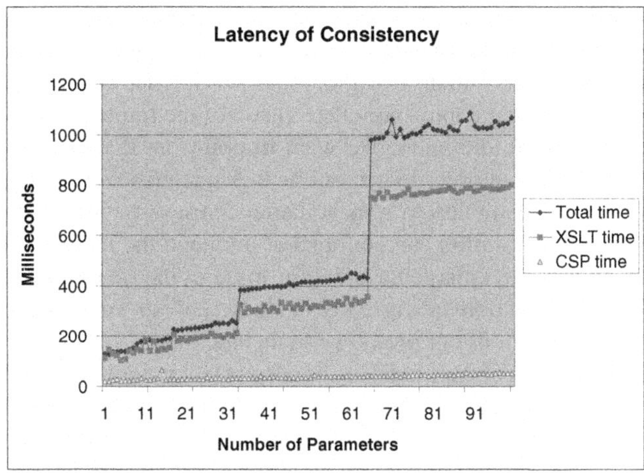

Fig. 7. Average time to check the consistency.

to this criteria: the first constraint involves a single integer-typed parameter, the second constraint involves a real-typed parameter, the third a set-typed parameter, the fourth an enumerated-type parameter, the fifth a boolean parameter, and so on, up to N constraints. Consistency of every QoS specification has been checked up to 50 times, so that 7 shows the average latency of invokations.

Figure 7 shows that XSLT processing is roughly implying up to 80 per cent. In this way, a first conclusion is that another alternative should be studied in case of a final version of the platform, such as the use of compilers or similar. XML and XSLT are good solutions for a prototype version, but it is not an efficient solution at all. On the other hand, XML and XSLT are (nearly) the universal standard of communications on the Internet, and it owns a very high versatility because it makes easier any adaptation, as well as the treatment of corresponding XML schemas as truly ontologies on QoS specification. We have used the Microsoft DOM library, so that another alternative is the use of components with improved XSLT-related functions, such as SAX, or similar.

5 Conclusions and Future Work

In this paper, we have presented our run-time framework for automating WSP. The solution is based on usage of mathematical constraints in order to specify quality-of-service in demands and offers, so we have achieved a lot of interesting properties. First, it owns a great deal of expressiveness, allowing non-linear or more complex expressions involving multiple parameters to be specified. As the same expressiveness is allowed to specify quality-of-service in demands and offers, our approach is symmetric. As well, our approach includes the possibility to express the assessment criteria, which is very important to select the best choice according to a demand.

Currently, we have developed a prototype of the run-time framework. It includes a quality trader web service as the core component, which offers services such as the checking for consistency and conformance, and the search/selection of the best choice. Preliminar experimental results have been presented, standing out the marked influence of XSLT processing in perfomance of the trader service. However, new experiments have to be carried out to get a more complete vision of the framework perfomance.

Regarding with the future work, we want to point out that our approach can be extended in several ways in order to achieve new characteristics: the inclusion of temporality in constraints, the inclusion of negotiation clauses to improve the flexibility of the model whenever no solution can be found at first, and the inclusion of importance and soft clauses in order to enlarge the solution space of the search. In fact, definitions of temporality and negotiation are currently in study [25], so we are beginning the first phases of the improvement of our prototype to include them.

Finally, the integration of our model on the current technology is also a pending work. We are aware of the uselessness of our approach if we do not have a working prototype integrated with any of them, such as UDDI or similar. In this way, our quality trader is a component leveled at the top of a pyramid, wherein the lowerer levels are devoted to functional-aspects of WSP [1]. This stage of development is currently starting, but we hope to have a completely functional prototype in the very near future.

References

1. A. Beugnard, J-M. Jézéquiel, N. Plouzeau, and D. Watkins. Making components contract aware. *IEEE Computer*, pages 38–45, July 1999.
2. Joint US/EU Agent Markup Language Committee. DARPA Agent Markup Language. Technical report, US's DARPA Defense Advance Research Projects Agency and EU's IST Information Society Technologies, 2000. `http://www.daml.org`.
3. J.J. Dujmovic. A Method for Evaluation and Selection of Complex Hardware and Software Systems. In *Proceedings of the 22nd International Conference for the Resource Management and Performance Evaluation of Enterprise Computing Systems*, volume 1, pages 368–378, 1996.
4. B. Farbey and A. Finkelstein. Software acquisition: a business strategy analysis. In *Proc. of the Requirements Engineering (RE'01)*. IEEE Computer Society Press, 2001.
5. A. Finkelstein and G. Spanoudakis. Software package requirements and procurement. In *Proc. of the 8th Int'l IEEE Workshop on Software Specification and Design (IWSSD'96)*. IEEE Press, 1996.
6. X. Franch and P. Botella. Putting non-functional requirements into software architecture. In *Proc. of the IXth Intl. Workshop on Software Specification and Design*, Ise-Shima (Isobe), Japan, April 1998.
7. E.C. Freuder and M. Wallace. Science and substance: A challenge to software engineers. *Constraints IEEE Intelligent Systems*, 2000.
8. S. Frolund and J. Koistinen. QML: A language for quality of service specification. Technical Report HPL-98-10, Hewlett–Packard, 1998.
9. H. Gallaire. Logic programming: Further developments. In *Proc. of the IEEE Symposium on Logic Programming*, pages 88–96, Boston, 1985. IEEE-CS Press.
10. J. González-Castillo, D. Trastour, and C. Bartolini. Description logics for matchmaking of services. Technical Report HPL-2001-265, Hewlett-Packard, 2001.
11. P. Hentenryck and V. Saraswat. Strategic directions in constraint programming. *ACM Computing Surveys*, 28(4), December 1996.
12. Y. Hoffner, S. Field, P. Grefen, and H. Ludwig. Contract-driven creation and operation of virtual enterprises. *Computer Networks*, (37):111–136, 2001.

13. ILOG. OPL Studio. `http://www.ilog.fr`.
14. J. Jaffar and J.L. Lassez. Constraint logic programming. In *Proc. of the ACM Symposium on Principles of Programming Languages*, pages 111–119, Boston, 1987.
15. A. Keller and H. Ludwig. The WSLA framework: Specifying and monitoring service level agreements for web services. Technical Report RC22456 (W0205-171), IBM International Business Machines Corporation, 2002.
16. J. Koistinen and A. Seetharaman. Worth–based multi-category quality–of–service negotiation in distributed object infrastructures. In *Proceedings of the Second International Enterprise Distributed Object Computing Workshop (EDOC'98)*, La Jolla, USA, 1998.
17. H. Ludwig, A. Keller, A. Dan, and R.P. King. A service level agreement language for dynamic electronic services. Technical Report RC22316 (W0201-112), IBM International Business Machines Corporation, 2002.
18. K. Marriot and P.J. Stuckey. *Programming with Constraints: An Introduction*. The MIT Press, 1998.
19. O. Martín-Díaz, A. Ruiz-Cortés, D. Benavides, A. Durán, and M. Toro. A quality-aware approach to web services procurement. In *Fourth International VLDB Workshop Technologies for E-Services, Springer LNCS 2819*, pages 42–53, Berlin, Germany, 2003.
20. O. Martín-Díaz, A. Ruiz-Cortés, R. Corchuelo, and A. Durán. A Management and Execution Environment for Multi-Organisational Web-based Systems. In *ZOCO: Métodos y Herramientas para el Comercio Electrónico*, pages 79–88, San Lorenzo del Escorial, Spain, 2002.
21. L. Olsina, D. Godoy, G. Lafuente, and G. Rossi. Specifying Quality Characteristics and Attributes for Websites. In *Proceedings of the Web Engineering Workshop, in conjunction with 21st International Conference on Software Engineering (ICSE)*, pages 84–93, May 1999.
22. OMG. Trading Object Service Specification. Technical report, Object Management Group, 2000. Version 1.0.
23. A. Ruiz-Cortés. *A Semi-qualitative Approach to Automated Treatment of Quality Requirements (in Spanish)*. PhD thesis, E.T.S. de Ingeniería Informática. Dpto. de Lenguajes y Sistemas Informáticos. Universidad de Sevilla, 2002.
24. A. Ruiz-Cortés, R. Corchuelo, and A. Durán. An automated approach to quality-aware web applications. In *Enterprise Information Systems IV*, pages 237–242. Kluwer Academic Publishers, 2003.
25. A. Ruiz-Cortés, R. Corchuelo, A. Durán, and M. Toro. Enhancing Win–Win requirements negotiation model. In *Applied Requirements Engineering*. Catedral, 2002.
26. A. Ruiz-Cortés, A. Durán, R. Corchuelo, B. Bernárdez, and M. Toro. Automated Checking of Quality Requirements in Multi-Organisational Systems (in Spanish). In *4th Workshop on Requirements Engineering (WER'01)*, pages 195–201, Buenos Aires, Argentina, 2001.
27. A. Ruiz-Cortés, R. Corchuelo, A. Duran, and M. Toro. Automated support for quality requirements in web-services-based systems. In *Proc. of the 8th IEEE Workshop on Future Trends of Distributed Computing Systems (FTDCS'2001)*, Bologna, Italy, 2001. IEEE Press.
28. A. ShaikhAli, R. Al-Ali O. Rana, and D. Walker. UDDIe: An extended registry for web services. In *Proc. of the IEEE Int'l Workshop on Service Oriented Computing: Models, Architectures and Applications at SAINT Conference*. IEEE Press, January 2003.
29. E. Tsang. *Foundations of Constraint Satisfaction*. Academic Press, London, 1995.
30. D.L. Waltz. *Understanding line drawings of scenes withshadows*. Psychology of Computer Vision, New York, 1975.
31. Gerhard Weikum. The Web in 2010: Challenges and opportunities for database research. *Lecture Notes in Computer Science n° 2000*, 2001.

A Quality of Service Management Framework Based on User Expectations

Vikas Deora, J. Shao, W. Alex Gray, and Nick J. Fiddian

School of Computer Science
Cardiff University
Cardiff, UK
{v.deora,j.shao,w.a.gray,n.j.fiddian}@cs.cf.ac.uk

Abstract. The ability to gauge the quality of a service is critical if we are to achieve the service oriented computing paradigm. Many techniques have been proposed and most of them attempt to calculate the quality of a service by collecting quality ratings from the users of the service, then combining them in one way or another. We argue that collecting quality ratings alone from the users is not sufficient for deriving a reliable or accurate quality measure for a service. This is because different users often have different expectations on the quality of a service and their ratings tend to be closely related to their expectations, i.e. how their expectations are met. In this paper, we propose a quality of service management framework based on user expectations. That is, we collect expectations as well as ratings from the users of a service, then calculate the quality of the service only at the time a request for the service is made and only using the ratings that have similar expectations. We give examples to show that our approach can result in a more accurate and meaningful measure for quality of service.

1 Introduction

There is a growing interest in service oriented computing (SOC) in recent years [1,2,3,4]. Central to SOC is the notion of *service* which can broadly be considered as a software component that represents some computational or business capability. By allowing services to be advertised declaratively, discovered dynamically and invoked remotely, SOC makes it possible for users to locate, select and execute services without having to know how and where they are implemented. This new computing paradigm offers great potential for agent-based e-commerce applications [5,6,7]. For example, vendors may wish to identify suitable partners from time to time to form a virtual organisation [8] so that they together can compete better in the market, and consumers would always want to select the services that best serve their interests. All such "match-making" tasks can potentially be performed by the agents automatically in an SOC environment.

In this paper, we consider the problem of quality of service (QoS) management in SOC. This is an important problem to consider because, just like in any other business environment, it is possible to have several service providers (SP)

M.E. Orlowska et al. (Eds.): ICSOC 2003, LNCS 2910, pp. 104–114, 2003.

offering the same service but with different qualities in an SOC environment. It is essential, therefore, that an agent should select a service that meets not only the required capability with the lowest possible price, but also the quality requirement. Various methods for modelling, calculating and monitoring QoS have been proposed in the literature [9,10,11,12], especially for web services and multi-agent systems [13,14,15]. A common approach is to collect quality ratings from the users of a service and then aggregate them in one way or another to derive the quality of the service. The following example explains this.

Suppose that we have three SPs who offer a multimedia news service to PDA or mobile phone users. Suppose also that there are six users (or their agents) who have used the services, and each of them has been asked to rate the quality of the service he or she has used in terms of news update frequency. Table 1 below shows the quality ratings collected from the users, where ratings are expressed as real numbers in $[0, 1]$ with 0 representing the most unsatisfactory quality and 1 the most satisfactory.

Table 1. Collected Quality Ratings

Users	SP1 update frequency	SP2 update frequency	SP3 update frequency
A1	0.3		0.3
A2	0.8	0.9	
A3	0.3		1.0
A4		0.8	
A5	0.5		0.1
A6	0.6	0.3	
Aggregate rating	0.50	0.67	0.47

For simplicity of presentation, we assume that the aggregate quality rating for each SP is derived by combining the individual ratings using a simple arithmetic average. So according to Table 1, SP2 offers the best service with respect to news update frequency.

While various methods may be employed to aggregate the collected ratings more rationally, for example, using a weighted average so that the reputation or trust of the user may be taken into account [16,14], this approach to quality rating calculation suffers from two fundamental weaknesses:

- First, users are invited to rate a service in "absolute" terms, e.g. 0.3 or 0.8 out of 1.0 in our example. Such quality ratings may not be very meaningful or can even be misleading in some cases, because the context within which the ratings are derived is not known. For example, A1 rated SP1 low perhaps because SP1's news update was not frequent enough for him or her, but this does not necessarily mean that the same frequency is not good enough quality for someone else, e.g. for A2.

– Second, the aggregate quality rating for a service is derived "statically" using all the ratings collected from the users. This does not take into account the fact that some of the ratings may not be relevant to a particular quality assessment request. For example, if the request was to assess the quality of SP1, SP2 and SP3 in terms of their ability to update news at least 4 times a day, then A6's rating should not be included in the quality calculation if A6 had expected a minimum of 8 updates per day from SP2.

In this paper, we address the above two problems by introducing a new model for collecting and monitoring QoS "relatively". That is, we attempt to collect from service users QoS ratings as well as their expectations on QoS, so that we can measure QoS in relative terms, i.e., how well a delivered service meets users' expectations. Based on user expectations, we also propose to calculate the quality of a service dynamically at the time a request for QoS assessment is made, and use only the ratings that have similar expectations. We show that our approach can result in a more accurate and meaningful measure for quality of service.

The rest of the paper is organised as follows. Section 2 introduces our framework for managing QoS information. Section 3 discusses how we calculate QoS based on user expectations and gives examples to show how our approach works. Related work is considered in Section 4, and finally Section 5 presents conclusions and discusses future work.

2 The QoS Model

To develop a QoS management model, it is essential to understand what the term *quality* actually entails. Unfortunately, what defines quality is vague, and different views exist in different studies and from different perspectives [10,11, 17,12]. The following three views are, however, most common.

– Quality as Functionality. This view considers quality in terms of the amount of functionality that a service can offer to its users. For example, if SP1 allows you to select different positions of cameras from which you may watch a football game, and if this functionality is not provided by SP2 or SP3, then SP1 can be considered as offering a better quality than SP2 and SP3 do.
– Quality as Conformance. This view sees quality as being synonymous with meeting specifications. For example, if SP1 specified in its service agreement that it would provide 1 Mb/s bandwidth for its news service and SP1 did provide users with 1 Mb/s bandwidth (or more) at all times in its operation, then SP1 is usually considered as offering good quality of service.
– Quality as Reputation. This view links quality to users' perception of a service in general. It is worth noting that this perception is typically built over the time of the service's existence. For example, the BBC news service is generally considered to be offering good quality to its users, due to its reputation built over many years as a news service provider.

These different views of quality require QoS to be monitored and measured differently. Quality as functionality characterizes the design of a service and can only be measured by comparing the service against other services offering similar functionalities. Quality as conformance, on the other hand, can be monitored for each service individually, and usually requires the user's experience of the service in order to measure the "promise" against the "delivery". Finally, reputation can be regarded as a reference to a service's consistency over time in offering both functionality and conformance qualities, and can therefore be measured through the other two types of quality over time.

While it is possible to establish all three types of quality for a service in an SOC environment, it is perhaps most interesting and relevant to understand how quality as conformance may be monitored. In this paper, therefore, we adopt the conformance view and define QoS to be a degree of satisfaction that the user has experienced after using a service. More specifically,

Definition 1. *let S be a service and $A_1, A_2, \ldots, A_n$ be a set of attributes that describe S and upon which we wish to monitor the quality for S. Assume that for each A_i, A_i^a is the advertised quality (or the quality that the service provider promised to o er), and A_i^d is the delivered quality (or the actual quality that the service provider delivered). Then the QoS for A_i is given by*

$$Q_{A_i} = f(A_i^a, A_i^d)$$

where f is a function that calculates the conformance between A_i^a and A_i^d.

The above definition captures the notion of conformance generically, but does not specify how A_i^a and A_i^d may be obtained and Q_{A_i} may be calculated. In practice, it may not be realistic to expect every A_i to have an A_i^a value specified by the service provider, and its A_i^d value monitored and Q_{A_i} calculated by the system automatically. Often, we need user feedback to help assess the quality of a service.

While the need for involving users in QoS assessment is well recognised, existing methods tend to collect quality ratings only from the users. This is inadequate if we wish to measure quality as conformance according to Definition 1. In this paper, we propose to collect "fuller" ratings from the users and then to use such ratings to assess QoS.

Definition 2. *Let U be a user and A be an attribute of a service S. A quality rating on A by U is a triple*

$$\langle E_u(A), P_u(A), R_u(A) \rangle$$

where $E_u(A)$ represents the quality that U expects from A, $P_u(A)$ the actual quality of A perceived or experienced by U after using S, and $R_u(A)$ the quality rating that U gives to A.

Collecting $\langle E_u(A), P_u(A), R_u(A) \rangle$ from users can perhaps be considered as a way of "materialising" the conformance calculation function introduced in

Definition 1. Instead of relying on the system for monitoring A_i^d and calculating Q_{A_i}, we obtain $P_u(A_i)$ and $R_u(A_i)$ from the user. The use of $E_u(A_i)$ represents a shift from using SP advertised values to user expectations on quality in QoS calculation. This is significant. While some correlation between A_i^a and $E_u(A_i)$ can be expected - users are likely to be influenced by advertisement in forming their expectations, expectations are not solely based on advertisement. Other factors, such as the user's past experience with the service, the price the user is paying for the service, or the recommendation by a friend for the service can all influence the user in forming his or her expectation on the quality of the service. Thus, by including user expectations as part of user rating on a service, we can hope to interpret such ratings more accurately and meaningfully.

To explain how the proposed QoS model works, consider the example we gave in the Introduction again. Suppose that we still ask the six users to rate the new services in terms of update frequency, *fr*, but this time use the expectation model we introduced here. Assuming that we represent $E_u(\text{fr})$, $P_u(\text{fr})$ and $R_u(\text{fr})$ all as real numbers in $[0, 1]$, Table 2 below shows the ratings collected from the users.

Table 2. Expectation based Quality Ratings

Users	SP1 $\langle E(\text{fr}), P(\text{fr}), R(\text{fr})\rangle$	SP2 $\langle E(\text{fr}), P(\text{fr}), R(\text{fr})\rangle$	SP3 $\langle E(\text{fr}), P(\text{fr}), R(\text{fr})\rangle$
A1	$< 0.9, 0.7, 0.3 >$		$< 0.7, 0.5, 0.3 >$
A2	$< 0.4, 0.4, 0.8 >$	$< 0.5, 0.5, 0.9 >$	
A3	$< 0.8, 0.6, 0.3 >$		$< 0.4, 0.5, 1.0 >$
A4		$< 0.6, 0.6, 0.8 >$	
A5	$< 0.9, 0.7, 0.5 >$		$< 0.9, 0.5, 0.1 >$
A6	$< 0.9, 0.7, 0.6 >$	$< 0.7, 0.5, 0.3 >$	

How a user arrived at a particular rating may never be known to us, but it is interesting to speculate what the ratings shown in Table 2 might suggest. The majority of the users of SP1 and SP3 seem to have high expectations (probably as the result of some effective recommendations or advertising effort), but do not seem to get what they expect (perhaps due to the unexpected level of business that SP1 and SP3 have got themselves into). SP2, on the other hand, is the opposite: users do not have high expectations but are generally satisfied with the service. In the following section, we show how this difference in expectation is taken into account when assessing QoS for services.

3 Collection and Calculation of QoS Ratings

In this section, we consider how the QoS ratings may be collected from the users and be used in the calculation of QoS by the Quality Assessment (QA) agent that we are currently constructing as part of the CONOISE project (`www.conoise.org`). The basic system architecture is outlined in Figure 1 below.

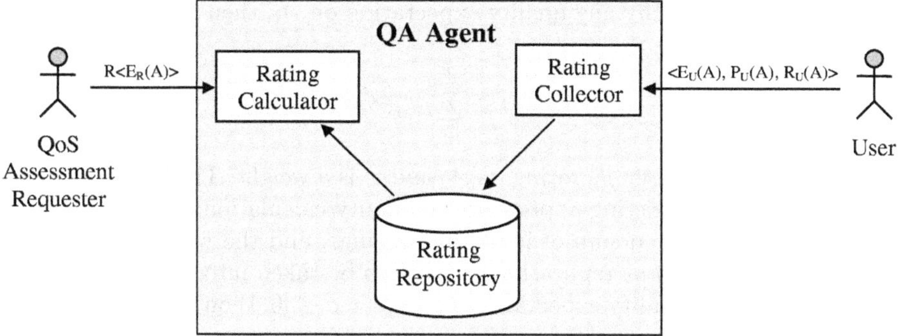

Fig. 1. The system architecture of the QA agent

The QA agent consists of two main components. The Rating Collector is responsible for soliciting quality ratings from the users. In this paper, we have assumed that the users are willing, when asked, to return quality ratings on the services they have used and their ratings can be trusted. We have also assumed that all three elements of a user rating, $E_u(A)$, $P_u(A)$ and $R_u(A)$, are expressed as real numbers in $[0, 1]$. These simplification assumptions have resulted in a fairly straightforward process for collecting ratings from the users, but they may not be particularly realistic for many practical applications. To relax these assumptions, it is possible to incorporate some more advanced techniques into our QA agent, so that issues such as how to collect quality ratings from users or agents whom we can not fully trust may be addressed [18,16,19,14].

The Rating Calculator is responsible for calculating QoS from the collected ratings. To aggregate individual ratings into an overall assessment of quality for a given service S, two calculations are necessary:

1. combining individual ratings for each A_i of S into an aggregate rating for A_i, and
2. combining the ratings for individual A_i's into an overall rating for S.

Currently, we treat all quality attributes of a service to be of equal importance and the overall rating for S is derived by a simple average of the individual ratings for its attributes. But it is possible to consider a weighted average so that the fact that some attributes are more significant than others may be taken into account [20].

How to combine individual ratings for each A_i into an aggregate one, however, needs some explanation. In contrast to many existing methods which simply aggregate *all* the collected ratings on A_i, our approach is to selectively aggregate only the ratings that have similar expectations. That is, we allow a quality assessment request R to specify a quality expectation, $E_R(A_i)$, on A_i, and derive an aggregate quality rating for A_i by using only the ratings in the Rating Repository that have similar expectations to $E_R(A_i)$. More specifically,

- If R does not specify any quality expectation on A_i, then $Q(A_i)$, the quality rating for A_i, is

$$Q(A_i) = \sum_{j=1}^{k} w_j \times R_j(A_i)$$

  where $R_j(A_i)$ is user j's rating on A_i and w is a weight. This is equivalent to the majority of existing approaches to quality calculation: the overall rating for A_i is a weighted sum of individual ratings, and the weights are used to allow factors such as reputation or trust to be taken into account [16,14].
- If R specifies a quality expectation $E_R(A_i) = \alpha \in [0, 1]$ on A_i, i.e. the quality expectation on A_i is α, then

$$Q(A_i) = \sum_{j=1}^{m} w_j \times R'_j(A_i)$$

  where $R'_j(A_i)$ is the element of the rating $\langle E'_j(A), P'_j(A), R'_j(A)\rangle$ in the Rating Repository whose corresponding expectation element $E'_j(A_i)$ is *similar* to $E_R(A_i) = \alpha$. In this paper, we use a simple criteria for determining whether the two are similar: $E'_j(A_i)$ and $E_R(A_i) = \alpha$ are compatible if $|E'_j(A_i) - \alpha| \leq \delta$, where δ is a constant. However, more complex forms of similarity test are possible, for example, by specifying quality expectations as "ranges" over $[0, 1]$ (instead of *points*) and by allowing fuzzy matching between $E'_j(A_i)$ and $E_R(A_i) = \alpha$.

By aggregating individual quality ratings dynamically at the time when a QoS assessment request is made and by comparing the raters' and the requester's expectations on qualities, our approach is able to calculate QoS in "context", that is, to use the ratings which are actually relevant to the context within which the QoS assessment request is made.

Now consider our example and Table 2 again. Suppose that the QA agent has been asked to assess QoS for all three SPs in terms of news update frequency, given $E_R(\text{fr}) = \text{unspecified}$, $E_R(\text{fr}) = 0.5$ and $E_R(\text{fr}) = 0.8$, respectively. Assuming that we have $\delta = 0.1$, the result of calculation by the QA agent is given in Table 3.

As can be seen from Table 3, the quality ratings for SPs can vary with respect to expectations. For example, when the expectation is $E_R(\text{fr}) = 0.5$, SP3 emerges to be the best service provider, whereas when the expectation is changed to $E_R(\text{fr}) = 0.8$, we have SP1 as the winner. This is in contrast to conventional approaches to quality calculation that do not consider user expectations (equivalent to setting $E_R(\text{fr}) = \text{unspecified}$, resulting in SP2 being the best provider for all cases), our method gives a more meaningful rating for a service on a case-by-case basis.

Table 3. Calculated quality ratings for SPs

Expectation	SP1 aggregate rating	SP2 aggregate rating	SP3 aggregate rating
$E_R(\text{fr})$ = unspecified	0.50	0.67	0.47
$E_R(\text{fr}) = 0.5$	0.80	0.85	1.00
$E_R(\text{fr}) = 0.8$	0.43	0.30	0.20

Finally, it is worth mentioning that although $P_u(A_i)$, the quality perceived by the user, is not used in quality calculation in this paper, it can play an important role in deriving more accurate quality assessment. For example, by monitoring the relationship between $R_u(A_i)$ (the verdict) and $|E_u(A_i) - P_u(A_i)|$ (the basis for the verdict) over a period of time with sufficient rating data, we can determine whether a particular user has been harsh or lenient in rating the services. By factoring such knowledge into quality calculations, we can deliver more accurate QoS assessment of services.

4 Related Work

There exist a large number of proposals in the literature for managing QoS as reputation or trust for service providers. These approaches, e.g. [21,16,19,14], typically seek to establish the quality of a service by gathering ratings from the users who have used the service, but do not consider the context within which the ratings are derived. The need for having some contextual information alongside the ratings themselves has been identified only recently. For example, Maximilien and Singh [20] suggest that some attributes be used to describe the ratings and users be allowed to define their preferences on the importance of individual ratings. While this work is similar to the method proposed here in principle, it does not include user expectations as part of the context, and thus does not help to identify the reasons behind the ratings given by users.

Our approach to include expectations as part of QoS management was inspired by work done in the area of marketing, where user expectations are commonly collected as a way of understanding quality. For example, the SERVQUAL system [12] uses the difference between what consumers expect and what they perceive to determine product/service quality, so that quality may be improved to meet users' expectations better. Our approach however differs from marketing-based ones in that we do not directly use expectations to calculate the actual quality of a product or service, but as a basis for determining which ratings are relevant to a given QoS assessment request.

The idea of using similar expectations in assessing QoS is also akin to the concept of *collaborative ltering* [22]. In collaborative filtering, users are categorised into several groups and the users in the same group are considered to have the same "likes" and "dislikes", or expectations. This common expectation is then used to determine or predict if a given item (e.g. a book) would be of any interest to a particular user. We also use similar expectations to determine the quality of a service for a given quality assessment request in our QoS management framework, but there is a fundamental difference between our work and that in collaborative filtering: we do not attempt to classify users (raters and requesters). The groups of users who have similar expectations are formed dynamically in our model, based on the given QoS assessment request and the criteria for similarity measures.

It is worth noting that quality management has also been considered in other research areas [9,10,17,23,24]. For example, Mecella et al. [17] have designed a broker which can select the best available data from a number of different service providers based on a specified set of data quality dimensions such as accuracy, completeness, currency and consistency. In [9,10], QoS management for network resources has been considered. These studies aim to identify and establish suitable quality matrices for specific services in specific application areas, so that the quality of these services can be meaningfully gauged. In contrast, the quality management model proposed in this paper assumes the availability of appropriate quality attributes (or matrices), and is designed to address the problem of how qualities of similar services may be compared based on user ratings and expectations.

5 Conclusion

In this paper, we have introduced a user expectation based framework for modelling and calculating QoS in an SOC environment. This framework is founded on the following basic observation: if A rates the quality of S as x, then this rating is only meaningful to B if A and B have similar expectations on S. So instead of aggregating all the quality ratings collected from the users of services, we propose to calculate QoS dynamically at the time a QoS assessment request is made, and use only the ratings that have similar expectations to that of the request. This, as we have shown in the paper, can lead to more accurate and meaningful rating in QoS assessment.

The work reported in this paper is still at an early stage, and a number of issues still need to be investigated. First, there is a need to consider how user expectation may be best represented. The current real-number based representation is rather limited, and does not allow the user to specify, for example, the minimum and maximum expectations. Second, better techniques for matching expectations need to be developed, particularly for expectations that are not expressed as simple real numbers. We envisage that some reasoning mechanisms will be required. Finally, there is a need to consider what happens when there are no matching expectations when assessing QoS, or the so-called "cold start" problem [25]. This is particularly interesting to consider in our quality model, as tightening or relaxing similarity measures in the model can have a direct impact on matchable expectations.

Acknowledgments. This work is supported by British Telecommunications plc, and we wish to thank the members of the CONOISE project team for their constructive comments on this work.

References

1. Casati, F., Shan, M.C.: Definition, execution, analysis, and optimization of composite e-services. Data Engineering Bulletin **4** (2001) 29–34
2. Leymann, F.: Web services: distributed applications without limits. In: Proceedings of 10th Conference on Database Systems for Business. (2003) 2–23
3. Piccinelli, G., Stammers, E.: From e-processes to e-networks: an e-service-oriented approach. In: Proceedings of 3rd International Conference on Internet Computing. (2002) 549–553
4. Rust, R.T., Kannan, P.K.: E-service: a new paradigm for business in the electronic environment. Communications of the ACM **46** (2003) 36–42
5. He, M., Jennings, N.R., Leung, H.: On agent-mediated electronic commerce. IEEE Trans on Knowledge and Data Engineering **15** (2003) 985–1003
6. Jennings, N.R., Faratin, P., Norman, T.J., O'Brien, P., Odgers, B.: Autonomous agents for business process management. International Journal of Applied Artificial Intelligence **14** (2000) 145–189
7. Papazoglou, M.P.: Agent-oriented technology in support of e-business. Communications of the ACM **44** (2001) 71–77
8. Petersen, S.A., Gruninger, M.: An agent-based model to support the formation of virtual enterprises. In: International ICSC Symposium on Mobile Agents and Multi-agents in Virtual Organisations and E-Commerce. (2000)
9. Aurrecoechea, C., Campbell, A.T., Hauw, L.: A survey of qos architectures. Multimedia Systems Journal **6** (1998) 138–151
10. Chalmers, D., Sloman, M.: A survey of quality of service in mobile computing environments. IEEE Communications Surveys and Tutorials **2** (1999) 2–10
11. Lee, Y.W., Strong, D.M., Khan, B.K., Wang, R.Y.: Aimq: a methodology for information quality assessment. Information and Management **40** (2002) 133–146
12. Parasuraman, A., Zeithaml, V.A., Berry, L.L.: Reassessment of expectations as a comparison standard in measuring service quality: implications for future research. Journal of Marketing **58** (1994) 201–230
13. Trzec, K., Huljenic, D.: Intelligent agents for qos management. In: Proceedings of First International Conference on Autonomous Agents and Multi Agent Systems. (2002) 1405–1412
14. Yu, B., Singh, M.: An evidential model of distributed reputation management. In: Proceedings of First International Conference on Autonomous Agents and Multi Agent Systems. (2002) 294–301
15. Zeng, L., Benatallah, B., Dumas, M., Kalagnanam, J.: Quality driven web service composition. In: Proceedings of Twelfth International Conference on World Wide Web. (2003) 411–421
16. Mui, L., Mohtashemi, M., Halberstadt, A.: A computational model of trust and reputation. In: Proceedings of 35th Hawaii International Conference on System Sciences. (2002) 2423–2431
17. Mecella, M., Scannapieco, M., Virgillito, A., Baldoni, R., Catarci, T., Batini, C.: Managing data quality in cooperative information systems. In: Proceedings of 10th International Conference on Cooperative Information Systems. (2002) 486–502

18. Braynov, S., Sandholm, T.: Incentive compatible mechanism for trust revelation. In: Proceedings of First International Conference on Autonomous Agents and Multi Agent Systems. (2002) 310–311
19. Schillo, M., Funk, P., Rovatsos, M.: Using trust for detecting deceitful agents in artificial societies. Applied Artificial Intelligence, Special Issue on Trust, Deception and Fraud in Agent Societies (2000) 825–848
20. Maximilien, E.M., Singh, M.: Conceptual model of web service reputation. SIGMOD Record, ACM Special Interest Group on Management of Data (2002) 36–41
21. Maes, P., Guttman, R.H., Moukas, A.G.: Agents that buy and sell. Communications of the ACM **42** (1999) 81–91
22. Herlocker, J., Konstan, J., Riedl, J.: Explaining collaborative filtering recommendations. In: Proceedings of ACM 2000 Conference on Computer Supported Cooperative Work. (2000) 241–250
23. Burgess, M., Gray, W.A., Fiddian, N.: Establishing a taxonomy of quality for use in information filtering. In: Proceedings of 19th British National Conference on Databases. (2002) 103–113
24. Wang, R.Y., Strong, D.M.: Beyond accuracy: what data quality means to data consumers. Journal of Management Information Systems **12** (1996) 5–34
25. Schein, A., Popescul, A., Ungar, L., Pennock, D.: Methods and metrics for cold-start recommendations. In: Proceedings of 25th Annual International ACM SIGIR Conference on Research and Development in Information Retrieval. (2002) 253–260

Reflective Architectures for Adaptive Information Systems

Andrea Maurino, Stefano Modafferi, and Barbara Pernici

Politecnico di Milano,
Dipartimento di Elettronica e Informazione,
Piazza Leonardo da Vinci, 20133 Milano, Italy
{maurino, modafferi, pernici}@elet.polimi.it

Abstract. Nowadays the anytime/anywhere/anyone paradigm is becoming very important and new applications are being developed in many contexts. The possibility of using applications along a wide range of devices, networks, and protocols raises new problems related to delivery of services. Current academic and industrial solutions try to adapt services to the specific distribution channel, mainly by changing the presentation of the service. In this paper, we reverse this perspective by using adaptive strategies to try to adapt the delivery channel to services as well. We present a possible architecture and focus our attention on the use of reflective components in the adaptive process. Using the reflection principle, we are able to evaluate the channel constraints and the conditions in which the distribution channel is working at a specific time. This information, built with service, user, and context constraints, is used as input to adaptive strategies to change the current channel characteristics, to new ones satisfying all the requirements. If this kind of adaptation is not possible, we consider the different QoS levels offered by the service and the user's readiness to accept a downgraded service provisioning.

Keywords: Adaptive information system, reflective architecture

1 Introduction

In the last years, the design and development of information systems have significantly changed due to new network architectures and devices, which increase the number of distribution channels available for delivering of information or services. In the anytime/anywhere/anyone paradigm [18], a novel generation of applications [9] modify themselves according to the change of context, or to specific application constraints; for example, adaptive hypermedia applications [5,1, 20] modify data presentation according to the specific client browser capability. The goal of this paper is to present an architecture of a reflective adaptive system and adaptation strategies at different levels. First, we consider the possibility of modifying the distribution channel by means of adaptive information systems based on reflective architectures. The principle of reflection [10] is mainly studied in the programming language community and it consists in the possibility of

M.E. Orlowska et al. (Eds.): ICSOC 2003, LNCS 2910, pp. 115–131, 2003.

system inspecting and adapting itself by using appropriate metadata. In [6,12], the use of reflective architectures has been proposed as a new design principle of middleware, but the adaptivity is in charge of applications only; other papers [16,7] have considered the use of non-reflective adaptive channels, but they consider only the network as channel. Clearly adaptive distribution channels may be also used with adaptive applications to create a novel generation of multichannel adaptive information systems. The middleware architecture we present allows overcoming existing limitations of information systems by means of modification of controllable components of distribution channels, identified through their description, and according to the specific context and level of Quality of Service (QoS) requested by users. The distribution channel delivers *e*-Services in order to satisfy a given QoS. If the user-specified quality level cannot be satisfied then our strategies try to adapt the distribution channel to a reduced QoS level still acceptable for the user. If the downgrading of QoS levels is still not sufficient, then other alternatives to provide the service are considered according to the users and service constraints.

The paper is organized as follows: in Section 2, we present the requirements of a reference example used to show, throughout the paper, how our architecture is able to adapt the distribution channel to deliver *e*-Services; Section 3 shows the distribution channel model representing metadata used by the reflective architecture. In Section 4, we present the general architecture and then we describe adaptive strategies in Section 5. Section 6 explains the adaptations functions used in our strategies. Finally, Section 7 discusses the state of art of adaptive information systems.

2 Reference Example

The reference example taken from the banking information system domain is based on a service that "*allow users, through Internet, to see in real time interviews with nancial analysts*". This activity requires the delivery of real time videos along Internet, with some mandatory minimum requirements: the user device must be audio enabled and due to the real time nature of the service the channel bandwidth is also relevant. The information system has to negotiate with the user a reasonable minimum channel bandwidth that s/he accepts to see the video in an acceptable mode from her/his point of view.

3 Distribution Channel Model

The distribution channel model adopted in this paper defines the metadata needed for adaptation functionalities. Developing our first proposal in [13], we specify this information at three different levels of abstraction. The conceptual level specifies the general characteristics of service distribution; at logical level, we characterize such general characteristics; at technological level, technical tuning parameters are specified.

At each level, characteristics may be either observable or controllable, or both, yielding different levels of possible adaptation. In the following, we illustrate the three levels in detail.

3.1 Conceptual Model

We consider a conceptual distribution channel as an access point to a specific set of information or execution services. This level corresponds to channel definitions as they are viewed from the commercial point of view. For instance, a service can be provided via web, via a call center, or using short messages. In the description of distribution channels at conceptual level, a service can be viewed as a functionality with a set of constraints. If requirements for invoking the service on each channel on which it is provided, and for providing the results of the service itself, are given, the service is well described for the distribution channel.

At this level a distribution channel is defined as:

- **Set of services**: each distribution channel supplies a specific set of services
- **Technological features**: each distribution channel has specific technological features characterizing the definition of channel.

Reference example. Within a banking information system, we consider the Internet banking channel as the one requiring that customers interact with the Bank information system by means of an Internet connection. Customers access the Bank application (typically a web site) through a login/password mechanism. After the authentication phase, they may carry out services according to their personal profile. The technological constraints in this case require that the provider provides the service through a web server, a http connection, and a video-player plugged in the browser on the client side.

3.2 Logical Model

From the logical point of view, we characterize a distribution channel as composed of (see Fig.1):

- The *user device* of application users,
- The *network interface* through which the device is connected to the *network*,
- The *network* used to transfer information,
- The *application protocols* used by *e*-Services.

Each element composing the distribution channel is characterized by a number of *attributes* (e.g., device screen resolution or network topology). Each attribute is associated with a value, which can be numeric, as for example in the case of the device weight, or a set of numbers, or a mathematical function, e.g., the graph function describing the network topology. The service delivery is affected by user requirements. To specify them, we introduce the concept of *rating*

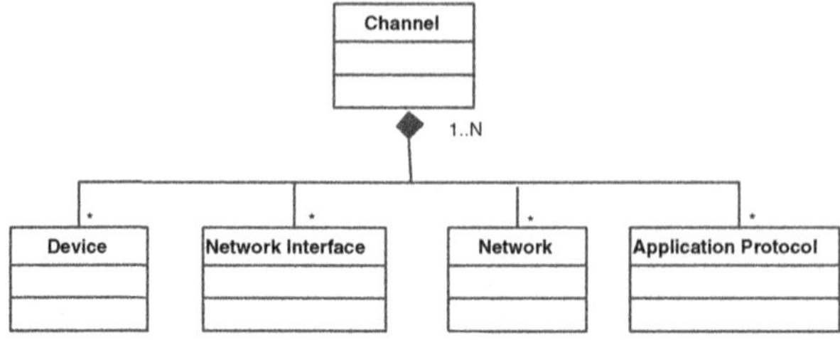

Fig. 1. UML specification of logical distribution channel components

class, which associates qualitative values (e.g., "fast" or "slow") to attributes in a given application domain. Rating classes are defined thanks to a measurement scale applied on measurable attributes. The scale has to be at least ordinal, but it can be also interval, ratio or absolute [15]. The rating classes are used to describe QoS levels offered by a given *e*-Service. An example of QoS levels is shown in Fig.2, where the quality dimension "speed" is associated with three different quality level: "very high", "high", and "medium". For each quality level a minimum value is defined.

```
<QualityLevels ServiceID="S1">
  <Dimension name="speed">
    <Level name="very high">
      <LogicalAttribute name="Bandwidth">
        <Condition type="greaterThan" unit="Kbps">512</Condition>
      </LogicalAttribute>
    </Level>
  </Dimension>
  <Dimension name="speed">
    <Level name="high">
      <LogicalAttribute name="Bandwidth">
        <Condition type="greaterThan" unit="Kbps">150</Condition>
      </LogicalAttribute>
    </Level>
  </Dimension>
  <Dimension name="speed">
    <Level name="medium">
      <LogicalAttribute name="Bandwidth">
        <Condition type="greaterThan" unit="Kbps">128</Condition>
      </LogicalAttribute>
    </Level>
  </Dimension>
  ...
</QualityLevels>
```

Fig. 2. Example of QoS levels

Reference example. According to the business requirements of the banking information system, we define the domain specific relevant attributes for all the four components previously defined.

Table 1. The 5 tuples of Internet banking channel used in the examples

Internet Banking	Device					Interface		Network			Protocol		
	Type	Screen resolution	Number of colors	Audio	Input Device	Type	Transfer rate	Type	Transfer rate	Security	Type	Standar-disation	Security
n1	PC	C	C	O	O	Network Card	C	Wired	O	O	HTTP/SSL	O	O
n2	PC	C	C	O	O	Modem	C	Wired	O	O	HTTP/SSL	O	O
n3	TV	O	O	O	O	Modem	C	Wired	C	O	HTTP/SSL	O	O
n4	Mobile Phone	O	O	O	O	GPRS	C	GPRS	O	O	HTTP	O	O
n5	PDA	C	C	O	O	GPRS	C	GPRS	O	O	HTTP	O	O

C=Controllable attributes O=Observable attributes

The first element describing a distribution channel is the device on which the end-user interacts. Within the financial application domain, we consider as relevant attributes for this component: the *screen resolution* and the *number of colors*, which are relevant when the information system wants to send users graphical information. Other key attributes are the *audio support* describing the presence or absence of audio cards inside the device and the *input device* used by customers; this attribute is relevant in the definition of the best interaction methods. The second component is the network interface representing the connection between devices and transmission media. It is worth noting that a device can access different networks by means of different interfaces; for example, a PC can access the Internet via LAN through a network card or via PSTN by means of an analogical modem. In the financial context, we consider that the only relevant attribute is the *Transfer rate* achievable by the specific interface.

The next component describing a distribution channel is the network. It includes all physical structures, hardware components and protocols defining a network infrastructure. In this component, we include all protocols covering the first four levels of the ISO/OSI protocol stack. Within the bank information system, we identify as relevant attributes for the network the *transfer rate* and the *security* level that it offers.

We also consider as a distribution channel component the set of application protocols allowing users to interact with the information system. We identify two interesting attributes: the *security* support and the *standardization* of the application protocol, which is an important feature for reusing existing application parts.

3.3 Technological Model

From a technological point of view a distribution channel is defined by a tuple of specific instances of device, network interface, networks and application protocols. If a value does not exist we assume that it is *null*. At technological level, it is possible to define attributes as *observable* (e.g. device position), if a software layer allows only showing their values to the information system; or *controllable* (e.g. bandwidth or screen resolution), if it is also possible to modify them. It is worth noting that a logical model can be instantiated with several tuples having at least one common attribute value. For example the logical distribution channel Internet (described in Section 3.2) is composed of a set of tuples each one characterized by the use of the HTTP as application protocol.

Reference example. An example of the technological model applied to Internet banking channel is shown in Table.1, where for each attribute and for each tuple, we indicate if it is observable (O) or controllable (C).

4 General Architecture

Fig.3 shows the general architecture and its relationships with clients and services. Three are the layers composing our architecture; they are:

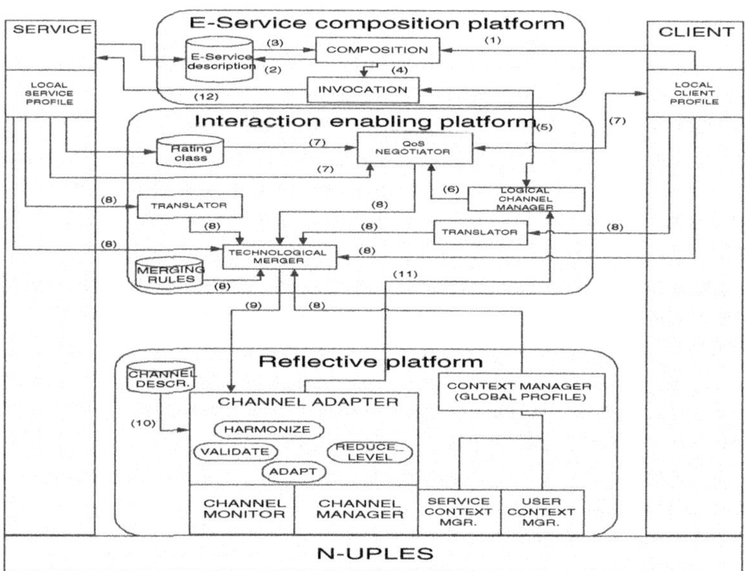

Fig. 3. General architecture

- *e-Service composition platform*, which is in charge of receiving the client request, selecting *e*-Service(s) satisfying it, and invoking the selected *e*-Service(s).
- *Interaction enabling platform*, which is the core of our architecture, because it is in charge of collecting constraints from *e*-Services, clients and context,

determining the QoS for each *e*-Service according to the client profile and selecting the best channel where the *e*-Service can be delivered.
- *Re ective platform*, which is in charge of adapting the selected distribution channel according to the constraints obtained from the Interaction enabling platform and monitoring if the distribution channel along which an *e*-Service is delivering respects the QoS level chosen by user.

Our architecture interacts with the client, which can be a user or a software agent, and with the *e*-Service. It is worth noting that the general architecture is decentralized so it is possible that all components of each layer are distributed over a number of hosts.

4.1 Constraints

In this paragraph we introduce the concept of technological constraints. They are given by service and user, through local and global profiles, and by context, and they are collected by *Technological merger* (see Fig.3), which sends them, opportunely integrated, to the Reflective platform.

Let T_c be the set of *Technological Constraints* associated with a tuple.

Because there exist different QoS levels that user might accept, there will exist a set of T_c for each tuple. We indicate with Δ_T this set of T_c.

Each element $T_{c_i}^j$ is defined as

$$T_{c_i}^j = \langle v_{min_i}, v_{max_i}, attribute, component \rangle$$

where:

- the index i represents the tuple and the index j the instance of Δ_T we are considering;
- v_{min} and v_{max} are the minimum and the maximum of a mathematic function (i.e. the media or the peak or simply the identity function) calculated for each distribution channel attribute value;
- *attribute* and *component* are respectively the attribute and the component where the constraint is defined.

4.2 E-service Composition Platform

The first layer of our architecture is in charge of receiving the client requests, defining the appropriate (set of) *e*-Service(s) satisfying them. The goal is obtained by analyzing the static description of the requested *e*-Services and the functional and non-functional requirements of the client as described in [3]. The *e*-Service composition platform selects the best *e*-Service, and requests the Interaction enabling platform to find the best distribution channel. When the distribution channel is selected, the *e*-Service composition platform invokes the execution of the *e*-Service.

Reference example. Let us assume that a user requests the video streaming service about an interview of financial analysts. He sends his request (through arc (1) of Fig.3) to the *Composition* module, which queries the *e*-Service description repository and gets the description of *e*-Service S1 only (arcs (2) and (3) of Fig.3). The *Composition* module calls the *Invocation* module which passes to the *Logical channel manager*, in the Interaction Enabling Platform, the request of enabling the delivery of *e*-Service S1 (arc (5)).

4.3 Interaction Enabling Platform

The Interaction enabling platform collects all requirements from the client, the *e*-Service and the distribution channel in order to manage service delivery on a given distribution channel. The *Logical channel manager* module, according to the description of the *e*-Service received from the *Invocation* module, selects a technological distribution channel (that is, a given tuple). The *QoS negotiator*, invoked by the *Logical channel manager* (arc (6)), requests the sub-set of the local client profile involved in the definition of QoS levels related to the given *e*-Service. This information can be stored directly in the user device or in other hosts if the device has a very small amount of memory. The QoS levels acceptable for the end users are chosen among the ones available for the *e*-Service stored in the Rating class repository of Fig.3 (arc (7)). These different levels allow a flexible QoS managing policy, by modeling different satisfaction degrees for the client. The *Technological merger* module receives inputs (arc (8) of Fig.3) from the *QoS negotiator*, and non negotiable constraints from both client and service profiles. We identify two kinds of constraints: logical and technological. The former are related to logical features which do not refer to measurable attributes and they have to be translated into constraints on technological attributes. An example of logical attribute is the device graphical capability, which is the result of both screen resolution and number of colors of a given device at technological level. Technological constraints are related to technological attributes as described in Section 4.1. Logical constraints, coming from both user and service profile, are first translated into technological ones (by using appropriate *Translator* modules, which are different for both client and service). The *Technological merger* integrates all constraints by using the Merging rules repository and passes down to the Reflective platform the result of its elaboration and QoS levels expressed as sets of technological constraints, requesting to satisfy them.

Reference example. Continuing the example, the *Logical channel manager* invokes the *QoS negotiator* by passing the description of *e*-Service S1. This component finds in the Rating class repository the QoS levels shown in Fig.2.

In the example of Fig.2 the *e*-Service S1 is offered at several different QoS levels about the channel speed ("Very high", "high", "medium", etc.). The client (through his local profile) selects his best and worst acceptable level by defining a sorted sub set of QoS. They are then translated into technological constraints before passing them to the *Technological merger*. The translation considers that channel bandwidth depends on both the transfer rate of the Network interface and the Network. The *Technological merger* receives also another technological constraint specified by the *e*-Service S1 requiring that the client device must have the audio card turned on to allow user to listen to the interview. This requirement is mandatory in order to deliver the *e*-Service; consequently it has not been included in the definition of the QoS level.

Let $n3$, described in Table 1, be the tuple chosen by the *Logical channel manager*. Let be

$$\begin{cases} \langle 0, 128kb/s \rangle \text{ for Transfer rate of Interface} \\ \langle 0, 10Mb/s \rangle \text{ for Transfer rate of Network} \\ \langle Off, On \rangle \text{ for Audio of Device} \end{cases}$$

the range of values in which the distribution channel we are considering can work.

The *Technological merger* module generates the following constraints:

$$\begin{cases} \text{level } 0 \begin{cases} \langle 150kb/s, *, Transfer\ rate, Interface \rangle \\ \langle 150kb/s, *, Transfer\ rate, Network \rangle \\ \langle On, On, Audio, Device \rangle \end{cases} \\ \\ \text{level } 1 \begin{cases} \langle 128kb/s, *, Transfer\ rate, Interface \rangle \\ \langle 128kb/s, *, Transfer\ rate, Network \rangle \\ \langle On, On, Audio, Device \rangle \end{cases} \end{cases}$$

where $*$ means that a maximum value is not given.

This output represents the two acceptable technological QoS levels for the user. The chosen tuple and the set of technological QoS levels, that is the set of technological constraints, are sent to the Reflective platform.

4.4 Reflective Platform

The central element of the Reflective platform is constituted by metadata, that is, the description of distribution channels built by using the model shown in Section 3 and stored in the Channel description repository. The availability of this characterization allows the platform to evaluate if constraints can be satisfied.

The *Channel monitor* module is in charge of measuring the current values of the attributes describing the selected distribution channel. Its information is used by the *Channel adapter* module, which first evaluates if all constraints can be satisfied for the tuple chosen by the upper layer from a hypothetical point of view; that happens if the current working point of tuple satisfies constraints or if it is possible to modify the distribution channel attributes values according to constraints. If there is the theoretical possibility of adaptation, then the *Channel manager* module realizes the modification of the distribution channel by invoking the appropriate software components. If one or more attributes cannot be modified, for example because the network manager does not accept the request of additional bandwidth, the Reflective platform reduces QoS levels and tries to modify the current tuple according to the new values. The reduction of QoS levels is executed also if there are no acceptable hypothetical solutions. If the Reflective platform does not satisfy the client request at least at the lower level of the QoS assigned, then it advises the *Logical channel manager* module (arc 11 in Fig.3), which will select another tuple according to the *e*-Service description. The Reflective platform has also the goal of monitoring and, if necessary, adapting tuples along which *e*-Services are delivering services. Finally the *Service context manager* and the *User context manager* modules measure the behavior of *e*-Services and users to build their global profiles (realized by the *Context manager* module).

5 Adaptive Strategies

We consider that the adaptation of distribution channels to services means to find and, in case, modify, if it exits, a tuple satisfying all constraints.

Let a working point (Wp) be the set of all attribute values carried out by Channel Monitor in a given instant for the given tuple.

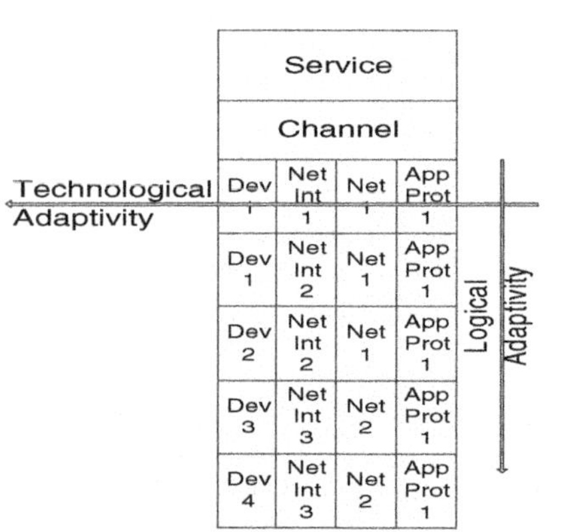

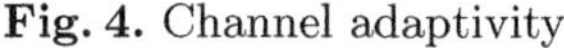
Fig. 4. Channel adaptivity

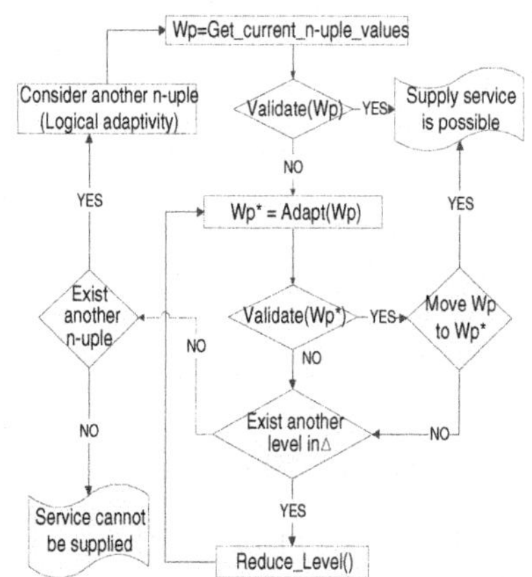

Fig. 5. Adaptive flow-chart

Fig.4 shows the two strategies of adaptivity we consider; logical and technological, which are developed in sequence, in particular:

- The "*Technological Adaptivity*" represents the tuning phase on the single tuple, i.e. the attempt to change some attributes of the given tuple to satisfy constraints, and it is realized by the Reflective platform
- The "*Logical Adaptivity*" represents the possibility of using a different tuple of the same logical distribution channel, it is realized by the Interactive enabling platform.

Fig.5 shows the flow-chart of adaptive strategies mainly realized by the *Channel adapter* module, while the concrete movement of working point is realized by the

Channel manager and the selection of alternative tuples is in charge of the Interaction enabling platform. Hereafter we consider the "Technological Adaptivity" only.

The $Validate()$ function evaluates if the current tuple working point satisfies the conditions required by constraints. In this case the service is supplied along the current tuple, otherwise the *Adapt*() function (see Section 6.2) proposes an acceptable working point available for such tuple (Wp^*). The new point is, then, evaluated again by the $Validate()$ function. If it satisfies constraints then the *Channel manager* module tries to change the current working point of the selected tuple. If it is impossible to move the current tuple working point, due to technical limitations or because Wp^* does not satisfy the constraints, then the *Channel adapter*, by means of the *Reduce_level*() function, tries to progressively reduce QoS levels, according to the service and user requests, looking for an existing QoS level satisfying them. After each invocation of the *Reduce_level*() function, the *Adapt*() function is invoked.

If technological adaptation fails, the information system, within the Interaction enabling platform, selects another tuple, QoS levels and constraints, and the technological adaptive strategy starts again.

This iterative process ends when a tuple satisfying all constraints is found or when no tuple can deliver the service. In this case the *Logical channel manager* tries to use multichannel delivery strategies selecting an alternative delivery channel, if possible, for the given *e*-Service.

6 Adaptive Functions

As shown before, adaptive strategies are executed in two phases: theoretical and practical. For the theoretical study the *Channel adapter* module has to know the channel structure. It obtains this information from the Channel description repository. It is worth noting that the designer has to write some functions defining the relationship between two or more technological constraints of a specific tuple to express them in a compatible way. These functions are named *Harmonize Functions* as shown in Fig.3.

Following the direction of most recent literature [2], to adapt means looking for an admissible solution minimizing the distance between service directive and channel availability to maximizing the QoS. It is clear that this concept of QoS is dynamic [17,14,19], because channel conditions vary both in time and space.

The *Adapt*() function realizes such algorithm, while the $Validate()$ function detects if the working point, current or proposed by the *Adapt*() function, satisfies the constraints. In the next sections we explain more in depth these functions.

6.1 Validate Function

The $Validate()$ function evaluates if current attribute values, that is, the current working point, (Wp), satisfy all constraints. Formally

$$Validate() : \{A\} \rightarrow \{[0,1] \in N\}$$

where $A = \langle A_o \cup A_c \rangle$ is the set of attributes composed by the union of observable (A_o) and controllable attributes (A_c) of a given tuple. The result of $Validate$ function is 1 if Wp satisfies all constraints, it is 0 otherwise.

Let C_A the hypercube formed by the union of theoretical available working points included between all v_{min} and all v_{max} carried out from Interaction enabling platform and let C_C the hypercube formed by all theoretical working points of a given tuple; it results that acceptable solutions are those included in the intersection of C_A and C_C.

Each edge hypercube C_{C_i} (resp. C_{A_i}) of C_C (resp. C_A) associated with the generic attribute (i) is defined as follows:

$$\begin{cases} [v_{i_{min}}; \infty[& \text{if constraints are like } \langle v_{i_{min}}, *, i, component\rangle \\ [v_{i_{min}}; v_{i_{max}}] & \text{if constraints are like } \langle v_{i_{min}}, v_{i_{max}}, i, component\rangle \\ [0; v_{i_{max}}] & \text{if constraints are like } \langle *, v_{i_{max}}, i, component\rangle \\ [0; \infty] & \text{if there are no associated constraints} \end{cases}$$

It is worth noting that an attribute domain can be discrete rather than continuous and all Wp are included in C_C.

The $Validate()$ function is defined as follows:

$$Validate(Wp) \mid_{C_A, C_C} = \begin{cases} 1 & \text{if } Wp \in (C_C \cap C_A) \\ 0 & \text{otherwise} \end{cases}$$

A hypercube can have an infinite extension along variables associated with constraints where $v_{i_{max}}$ is not defined. Moreover if an attribute allows only a value, the hypercube loses one dimension.

According to the flow-chart of Fig.5 the $Validate()$ function is also invoked each time a new Wp is proposed by the *Adapt*() function as shown in next Section.

6.2 Adapt Function

The *Adapt*() function is used to move the current channel working point to C_A hypercube, that is, to a new one respecting the constraints requested from e-Service and user. Thus it receives as input a working point (Wp) and return as output another working point (Wp^*).

Notice that *Adapt*() function does not change the working point, it only detects if there exists a hypothetical point in the solution space where all constraints are satisfied. The result of function is:

$$Wp^* = Adapt(Wp) \mid_{(C_A, C_C)} = argmin(\| Wp; C_A \|)$$

The *Adapt*() function looks for a point in C_C having the minimum distance from C_A.

Fig.6 shows a graphical representation of the *Adapt*() function by considering only two continuous attributes. There exists an overlapping area between the two

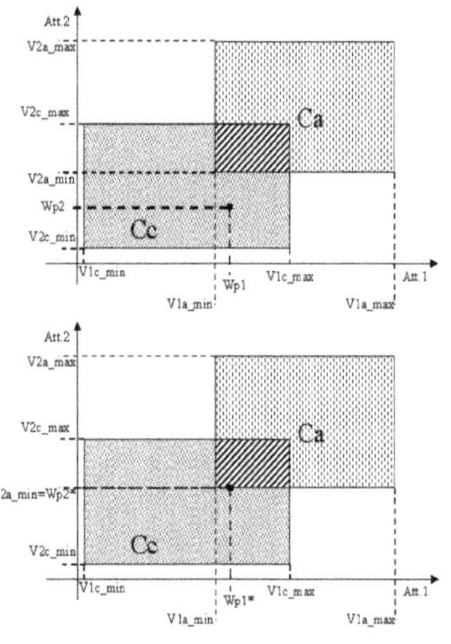

Fig. 6. Adapt() function behavior when there exists a no-empty intersection

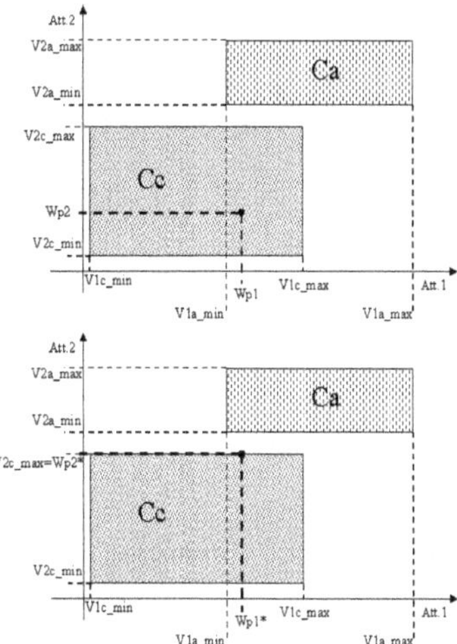

Fig. 7. Adapt() function behavior when there exists an empty intersection

areas C_A and C_C; consequently the *Adapt*() function will define a Wp^* as shown. Conversely, Fig.7 shows the case in which there exists an empty intersection between the two constraint sets. In this case the *Adapt*() function returns a new Wp^* point, that is the best working point available for the current tuple, however, using $Validate()$ functions the *Channel adapter* module will notice that Wp^* does not satisfy constraints and thus it will try to relax one or more constraints (that is to widen C_A) by using the *Reduce_Level*() function described in Section 6.3.

Reference example. Considering that the current tuples is $n3$, let C_A be:

$$C_A = \begin{cases} \langle 150kb/s, \infty \rangle & \text{for Network} \\ \langle 150kb/s, \infty \rangle & \text{for Interface Network} \\ \langle On, On \rangle & \text{for Audio} \end{cases}$$

where values are related to the best QoS level chosen by user.

Let C_C be the following:

$$C_{C_{n3}} = \begin{cases} \langle 0kb/s, 128kb/s \rangle & \text{for Network} \\ \langle 0kb/s, 128kb/s \rangle & \text{for Interface Network} \\ \langle Off, On \rangle & \text{for Audio} \end{cases}$$

Let we suppose that the current working point is:

$$Wp = \begin{cases} 64\ kb/s & \text{for Network} \\ 64\ kb/s & \text{for Interface Network} \\ On & \text{for Audio} \end{cases}$$

Calculating the $Validate()$ function on these values we obtain

$$Validate(Wp)\ |_{C_A,C_C} = 0$$

Then the *Channel adapter* module tries to adapt distribution channel by calculating the *Adapt*() function:

$$Wp^* = Adapt(Wp) = \begin{cases} 128\ kb/s & \text{for Network} \\ 128\ kb/s & \text{for Interface Network} \\ On & \text{for Audio} \end{cases}$$

but the output of $Validate()$ is still the same

$$Validate(Wp^*)\ |_{C_A,C_C} = 0$$

6.3 Reduce_level Function

Let Δ_T be the ordered set of QoS levels acceptable for a given tuple by service and user, generated by the Interaction enabling platform. Each QoS level is composed by a set of constraints T_c (Section 4.1), that is different levels may have different T_c. The *Reduce_level*() function tries to downgrade the C_A of one level. This operation is strongly related to the tuple the *Channel adapter* module is considering; so the function tries to relax attribute constraints that are still not respected looking for closest downgrading level allowed for the tuple. Formally:

$$Reduce\_level() : \{C_A\} \rightarrow \{C_A\}$$

In particular

$$C_A^{new} = Reduce\_level(C_A)\ |_{\Delta_T}$$

It is hopefully that this new C_A is formed by satisfable constraints for the channel characteristic. The reduction process is progressive and it ends if no other level is available or if an acceptable one exists.

Reference example. By continuing the reference example the *Channel adapter* module controls if it is possible to provide a downgraded service. For this goal it uses the *Reduce_level*() function.

$$C_A^{new} = Reduce\_level(C_A)\ |_{\Delta_T} = \begin{cases} \langle 128Kb/s, \infty \rangle \\ \langle 128Kb/s, \infty \rangle \\ \langle On, On \rangle \end{cases}$$

Consequently, by remembering that

$$Wp^* = \begin{cases} 128\ kb/s & \text{for Network} \\ 128\ kb/s & \text{for Interface Network} \\ On & \text{for Audio} \end{cases}$$

we obtain
$$Validate(Wp^*)\ |_{C_A,C_C} = 1$$

because
$$(C_C \cap C_A \neq \emptyset)\ \wedge\ (Wp^* \in C_C \cap C_A)$$

That is, the current working point is now acceptable and it is the same of the lower bound asked after relaxation. We suppose that all the modification of attribute values are executed without failures; the *e*-Service provisioning can now start (arc (12) in Fig.3) and it will be monitored by *Channel monitor* module in order to respect the requested constraints during all the provisioning period.

7 Related Work

The field of adaptive information systems is new and relatively unexplored. The use of reflective architecture for mobile middleware is discussed in [12,4]; other work [6] use the reflection principle to support the dynamic adaptation of applications. However, none of these papers mention the possibility to assign the task of adaptation to the distribution channel instead of application; in our opinion, our approach simplifies the design and implementation of *e*-Services because they do not have to realize adaptive behaviors.
The concept of dynamic service provisioning and dynamic QoS [19,14] involves both channel and application issues; moreover the new wireless networks and devices increase the complexity of solutions. Different approaches are being developed; in [7,16] the possibility of adapting the network by maximizing the network efficiency looking at its intrinsic parameters is investigated. In the same direction other systems [2] try to consider features regarding users, but their channel idea is simply the network and their adaptation process consider a simple user-profile containing information about user preferences and past behavior. Other approaches [1,20] try to adapt applications to the distribution channel; they consider the channel as an only-observable system and try to adapt the application to it; some systems put their attention above all on the presentation of the information delivering on a channel; important examples of this approach are defined in the field of adaptive hypermedia [8,5].

The enriched definition of distribution channel [13] distinguishes our approach from others, because we consider a distribution channel as a tuple of four different components and the network is only one of them, thus our approach is at a higher level of abstraction. Moreover our strategies try to adapt the distribution channel before trying adaptive application strategy to supply at least a downgraded service.

8 Conclusion

In this paper we presented adaptive information systems to deliver *e*-Services by means of reflective architectures. The use of reflection principle, obtained by using a high level description of distribution channels, allow us to define adaptive strategies to modify the distribution channel itself (viewed as a tuple of four different components) to *e*-Services. Two levels of adaptability are considered: logical and technological. The former, realized in the Interaction enabling platform, selects the tuple where the *e*-Service has to be delivered. The latter strategy tries to modify the controllable attributes of current tuple to satisfy constraints. If it is impossible to adapt the selected tuple, then the Interaction enabling platform selects an alternative tuple. This is the first proposal to design a new generation of multichannel adaptive information systems. We are now studying more efficient logical adaptive strategies in the selection of the tuple where to deliver the service, and how to assign each architectural components in a distributed information system; we are also evaluating how a service can select another logical distribution channel. Another problem we are studying is channel monitoring in mobile systems and adaptive networks.

Acknowledgments. This work has been developed within the Italian MURST-FIRB Project MAIS (Multi-channel Adaptive Information Systems) [11].

References

1. G. Ammendola, A. Andreadis, and G. Giambene, *A software architecture for the provision of mobile information services*, Softcom, International Conference on Software, Telecommunications and Computer Networks (Dubrovnik (Croatia) and Ancona, Venice (Italy)), October 2002.
2. G. Araniti, P. De Meo, A. Iera, and D. Ursino, *Adaptively control the QoS of multimedia wireless applications through "user profiling" techniques*, IEEE Journal On Selected Areas in Communications (JSAC) (2003), Forthcoming.
3. L. Baresi, D. Bianchini, V. De Antonellis, M.G. Fugini, B. Pernici, and P. Plebani, *Context-aware composition of e-services*, In Proc. of VLDB Workshop on Technologies for E-Services (TES'03) (Berlin, Germany), 2003.
4. G. Blair, A. Andersen, L. Blair, G. Coulson, and D. Gancedo, *Supporting dynamic QoS management functions in a reflective middleware platform*, IEEE Proceedings – Software, 2000.
5. P. Brusilovky, *Adaptive hypermedia*, User Modeling and User Adapted Interaction **11** (2001), no. 1–2, 87–100.
6. L. Capra, W. Emmerich, and C. Mascolo, *Reflective middleware solutions for context-aware applications*, Lecture Notes in Computer Science **2192** (2001).
7. A. Hac and A. Armstrong, *Resource allocation scheme for QoS provisioning in microcellular networks carrying multimedia traffic*, International Journal of Network Management **11** (2001), no. 5, 277–307.
8. A. Kobsa, J. Koenemann, and W. Pohl, *Personalized hypermedia presentation techniques for improving online customer relationships*, The Knowledge Engineering Review **16** (2001), no. 2, 111–155.

9. J. Krogstie, *Requirement engineering for mobile information systems*, Proc. of International Workshop on Requirements Engineering: Foundation for Software Quality (Interlaken, Switzerland), 2001.
10. P. Maes, *Concepts and experiments in computational reflection*, In Proc. of Object-Oriented Programming Systems, Languages, and Applications (OOPSLA) (Orlando, Florida, USA), vol. 7, ACM Press, 1987, pp. 147–155.
11. MAIS_Consortium, *MAIS: Multichannel Adaptive Information Systems*, http://black.elet.polimi.it/mais/.
12. V. Marangozova and F. Boyer, *Using reflective features to support mobile users*, In Walter Cazzola, Shigeru Chiba, and Thomas Ledoux, editors, On-Line Proceedings of ECOOP'2000 Workshop on Reflection and Metalevel Architectures, June, 2000.
13. A. Maurino, B. Pernici, and F.A. Schreiber, *Adaptive behaviour in financial information system*, Workshop on Ubiquitous Mobile Information and Collaboration Systems (Klagenfurt/Velden, Austria), June, 2003.
14. K. Nahrstedt, D. Xu, D. Wichadakul, and B. Li, *QoS-aware middleware for ubiquitous and heterogeneous environments*, IEEE Communications Magazine **39** (2001), no. (11), 140–148.
15. N.Fenton, *Software metrics, a rigorous approach*, Chapmann & Hall, 1991.
16. R. Raymond, F. Liao, and A. T. Campbell, *A utility-based approach for quantitative adaptation in wireless packet networks*, Wireless Networks **7** (2001), no. 5, 541–557.
17. D. Reiniger, R. Izmalov, B. Rajagopalan, M. Ott, and D. Raychaudhuri, *Soft Qos control in the watmnet broadband wireless system*, IEEE Personal Communications Magazine **Feb** (1999), 34–43.
18. K. Siau, E.P. Lim, and Z. Shen, *Mobile commerce: Promises, challenges, and research agenda*, Journal of Database Management **12** (2001).
19. R. Steinmetz and L. Wolf, *Quality of service: Where are we?*, Proc. of IFIP International Workshop on Quality of Service (IWQOS'97) (New York City, New York, USA), IEEE Press, 1997, pp. 211–222.
20. V. Zariskas, G. Papatzanis, and C. Stephanidis, *An architecture for a self-adapting information system for tourists*, Proc. of the Workshop on Multiple User Interfaces over the Internet: Engineering and Applications Trends (in conjunction with HCI-IHM'2001) (Lille, France), 2001.

E-healthcare via Customized Information Services: Addressing the Need for Factually Consistent Information

Syed Sibte Raza Abidi[1] and Yong Han Chong[2]

[1]Faculty of Computer Science, Dalhousie University, Halifax B3H 1W5, Canada
sraza@cs.dal.ca
[2]School of Computer Sciences, Universiti Sains Malaysia, Penang 11800, Malaysia
thestep@cs.usm.my

Abstract. Web portals provide an efficient gateway to a broad range of E-services, resources and information. Web portals need to evolve towards being *adaptive* in nature, so that the ensuing E-services provided by them are dynamically tailored to meet the diverse needs of its users. This paper explores the use of intelligent techniques, in particular *constraint satisfaction* methods, to develop adaptive E-services that provide customized and factually consistent information to users. We model the generation of customized information content as a constraint satisfaction problem—a solution is derived by (a) satisfying user-model constraints with information document selection constraints; and (b) establishing inter-document consistency when dynamically combining heterogeneous information documents. The work is applied in an *E-Healthcare* setting leading to the generation of personalized healthcare information.

1 Introduction

Web portals provide an efficient gateway to a broad range of open, remote and ubiquitous electronic services, resources and information—the so-called E-Services portfolio [1, 2]. The emergence of vertical portals—i.e. portals offering services and content aimed for a specific community—such as *Enterprise information portals*, *Knowledge portals* and *Internet portals* allow access to enterprise-specific information/services for an audience that have may have different goals, interests, preferences, intellectual levels and consumption capacity [3, 4].

A web portal interacts with a broad-base of heterogeneous users. Hence, a *one size fits all* model for web content and service design does not necessarily satisfy the entire spectrum of user needs/goals. Given that it is impossible to develop an exclusive web portal for each user class, one solution is to develop *adaptive web portals*—i.e. develop a base-set of both generic E-services and information content that can be dynamically tailored to meet the diverse goals/needs of the users [5]. This brings to relief an interesting constraint satisfaction problem, whereby the problem space on the one hand encompasses a wide diversity of E-service/information needs of the

M.E. Orlowska et al. (Eds.): ICSOC 2003, LNCS 2910, pp. 132–148, 2003.

users, and on the other hand a profusion of generic E-services/information content. Our novel constraint satisfaction based solution therefore involves matching the specific user needs/goals with the most effective and appropriate E-service/information content. Our IC approach goes even further; we argue that the customization of both E-services and information content should not only be limited to satisfying the user profile, rather it is important that any dynamically customized (a) E-service should satisfy all business rules; and (b) information content should be factually and contextually consistent—i.e. no aspect of the customized information content should appear to be in contradiction with any other information simultaneously presented to the user. Hence constraint satisfaction methods need to be applied at two levels: (1) satisfying the user-profile constraints when selecting from generic E-services/information content; and (2) satisfying the factual consistency between the selected information content in order to ensure that the cumulative information content is factually consistent.

This paper explores the use of intelligent techniques, in particular *constraint satisfaction* methods, to develop adaptive E-services that provide customized information services via a web portal. Adaptive E-services and information presentation have been pursued using adaptive hypermedia systems in conjunction with model-based and rule-based methods [6]. In our work, we present a novel approach whereby we model the generation of adaptive and customized information content as a constraint satisfaction problem—a solution is derived by (a) satisfying user-model constraints vs. information/service selection constraints; and (b) establishing information content consistency when combining heterogeneous information objects by satisfying information consistency constraints associated with each selected information object. We argue that, establishing the factual consistency of the information provided to users is an important, yet often neglected, issue. Functionally, it is possible that the combination of two information objects, both relevant to the user model, can inadvertently lead to a contradictory situation—i.e. one recommending whilst the other restricting from an action/decision at the same time. Hence, information customization methods need to check whether two information objects can be amicably synthesized—i.e. they jointly do not lead to any contradictions—to generate personalized information content. We believe that the incorporation of constraint satisfaction based information customization methods within E-services setting can reduce the cognitive overload experienced by E-service users and also improve the usability, acceptance and effectiveness of an interactive vertical portal.

We present an *Information Customization* (IC) framework that (a) generates personalized information via the dynamic selection and synthesis of multiple topic-specific documents that are deemed relevant to a user profile [7]; (b) satisfies the factual, contextual and functional consistency of the compiled personalized information via inter-document constraint satisfaction; and (c) delivers the personalized information via a vertical portal. A unique hybrid of adaptive hypermedia and *Constraint Satisfaction* (CS) methods is suggested to realize an IC framework that maximizes collaboration and minimizes conflicts between a set of hypermedia documents whilst generating personalized information. IC is achieved by satisfying user-model constraints and inter-document (factual consistency) constraints using a variety of CS methods. This work is applied to an experimental *E-Healthcare* setting that provides personalized healthcare information in the realm of a patient empowerment programme [8].

The paper is organized as follows: In section 2 we provide an overview of IC in general. In section 3 we briefly introduce constraint satisfaction methods and then lead to our constraint satisfaction based IC methodology. In section 4, we discuss the IC methods that we have developed. In section 5 we present a working example of IC, vis-à-vis personalizing healthcare information, using our IC methodology and methods. Finally, in section 6 we present our conclusions and future outlook.

2 A Brief Overview of Information Customization

At the forefront of adaptive services initiatives are adaptive hypermedia systems [9, 10, 11, 12] that provide an umbrella framework incorporating hypermedia, artificial intelligence and web technology to develop and deploy web-based dynamically adaptive E-service systems [5].

IC research offers interesting insights into ways for (a) profiling users based on information about the user's demographic data, knowledge, skills, capabilities, interests, preferences, needs, goals, plans and/or usage behaviour; and (b) pro-actively adapting the content, structure and/or presentation of hypermedia objects, based on the user's profile, to make an ostensive impact on the user. Each of the above-mentioned IC modalities involves different methods and strategies, for instance:

- *Content adaptation* is achieved via page variants [13], fragment variants [14, 7], Adaptive stretchtext [15] and adaptive natural language generation methods [16]. Our work is based on the notion of fragment variants, whereby fragments of texts are authored to cover the entire diversity of the topic, where each text fragment corresponds to a particular user characteristic. At runtime, a set of fragments is amalgamated to realize the final personalized document.
- *Structure adaptation* involves the dynamic changing of the link structure of hypermedia documents. Collateral structure adaptation [15], link sorting [17], link annotation [18], and link removal/addition [19] are some of the methods used. Our work does not involve any structure adaptation, as this kind of adaptation is relevant to an existing hypermedia document/website.
- *Presentation adaptation* leads to changes in the layout of the hypermedia document. Typically, the changes involve text positioning (or focusing), graphics and multimedia inclusion/exclusion, background variations and GUI interface. In our work, the use of a presentation template allows for presentation adaptation based on the user's preferences and information browsing behaviour.

3 Our Information Customization Operational Framework

Constraints arise in most areas of human endeavor and we are used to solving them. In a computational sense, constraints mathematically formalize the dependencies in a physical world in terms of a logical relation among several unknowns (or variables), each taking a value from a defined domain. In principle, a constraint restricts the possible values that the variables can take whilst solving a problem. *Constraint programming* solves problems by stating constraints about the problem area and, consequently, finding solutions that may 'satisfy' all the constraints. A *Constraint Satisfaction Problem* is defined by a tuple $P = (X, D, C)$ where $X=\{X_1, \ldots, X_n\}$ is a finite set of *variables*, each associated with a domain of discrete values $D = \{D_1, \ldots, D_n\}$, and a set of constraints $C = \{C_1, \ldots, C_l\}$. Each constraint C_i is expressed by a relation R_i on some subset of variables. This subset of variables is called the *connection* of the constraint and denoted by $con(C_i)$. The relation R_i over the connection of a constraint C_i is defined by $R_i \subseteq D_{i1} \times \ldots \times D_{ik}$ and denotes the tuples that satisfy C_i. A solution to a constraint satisfaction problem is an assignment of a value from its domain to every variable, in such a way that every constraint is satisfied [20, 21, 22].

3.1 Information Customization Approach

Our CS-mediated IC approach specifically caters for the following operational conditions:

- A *user profile*, comprising a number of user-defining attributes, describes the characteristics of each user.
- IC is achieved using constraint satisfaction methods that involve the satisfaction of two constraints: (i) *user-model constraints* and (ii) *co-existence constraints.*
- The information content is organized as a corpus of *topic-specific hypermedia documents*, where each topic may be described by a number of documents.
- Each document is composed of two sections: (a) *Condition section* that specifies the conditions for the selection of the document; and (b) *Content section* that comprises the information content.
- The condition section comprises two types of conditions: (a) *document-selection conditions* that are compared with the user's profile in order to determine whether the said document is relevant to the user. A document is selected if *all* document-selection conditions are satisfied; and (b) *document-compatibility conditions* determine whether the said document can mutually co-exist with other selected documents—i.e. the selected documents do not suggest contradictory information.
- The content section is sub-divided into two segments: (i) *unrestricted content* segment which is available when the document is selected; and (ii) *restricted content* segment which has the same structure as the document itself, but is available for limited use, subject to the satisfaction of its associated conditions.

- The final *personalized information package* is a systematic collection of user-specific and mutually consistent hypermedia documents that is delivered to end-users using web-based mechanisms.

In line with our IC approach we have developed a Java-based IC system (see Fig. 1) to generate personalized healthcare information. The CS methods and the user-interface for the IC website have been developed in Java. The information content is written as XML documents, and is transformed to HTML to be *pushed* to the users via email. Also we have developed a dedicated XML-based document editor for medical professionals to author both the information content and associated constraints.

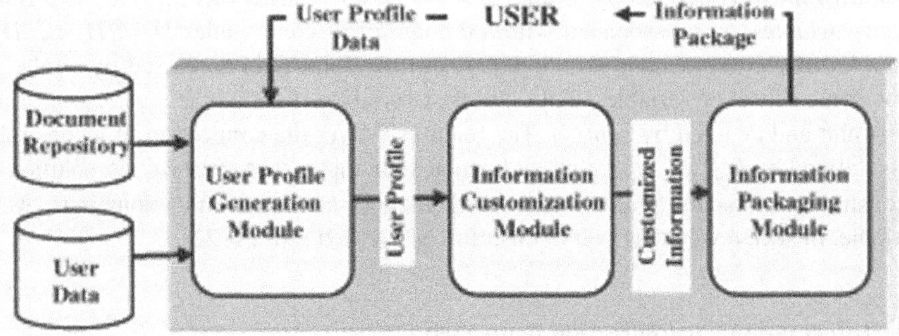

Fig. 1. The architecture of our IC system comprising 3 main modules

3.2 Operational Pre-requisites for Information Customization

We would like to point out that at present our IC approach presupposes the existence of the following pre-requisites (which are not addressed by us in this research).

- The content and constraints for each document is *a priori* specified by domain experts. We do not have a specific knowledge engineering methodology whereby domain experts can specify the content and the constraints for a variety of new topics and enhance existing ones. Hence, at present we work with a much smaller set of documents than required in a real-life setting.
- A complete user-profile is given. Our IC methodology addresses user profiling by acquiring current user data from an online data repository and subsequently verifying it with the user. However, at present the methods to generate the user-profile are not operational.
- The classification of the various topic-specific documents is predicated by a simple yet static domain-specific ontology. We foresee the need to develop means to enable the evolution of the ontology together with the automatic re-classification of the documents. At present, we do not focus on sophisticated methods for document classification, but intend to look into this issue in future research as it impacts IC.

4 Information Customization Methodology

The proposed IC methodology takes into account the above operational considerations and prerequisites, and provides a technical solution towards (a) the satisfaction of user-model constraints to select user-specific information; and (b) the satisfaction of co-existence constraints to ensure that the selected information is factually, functionally and contextually consistent. In principle, the above demands a conflict evaluation framework, hence we leverage variants of CS consistency-checking techniques and CS search algorithms to generate customize information. Below we list the distinct steps of our IC methodology (shown in Fig. 2).

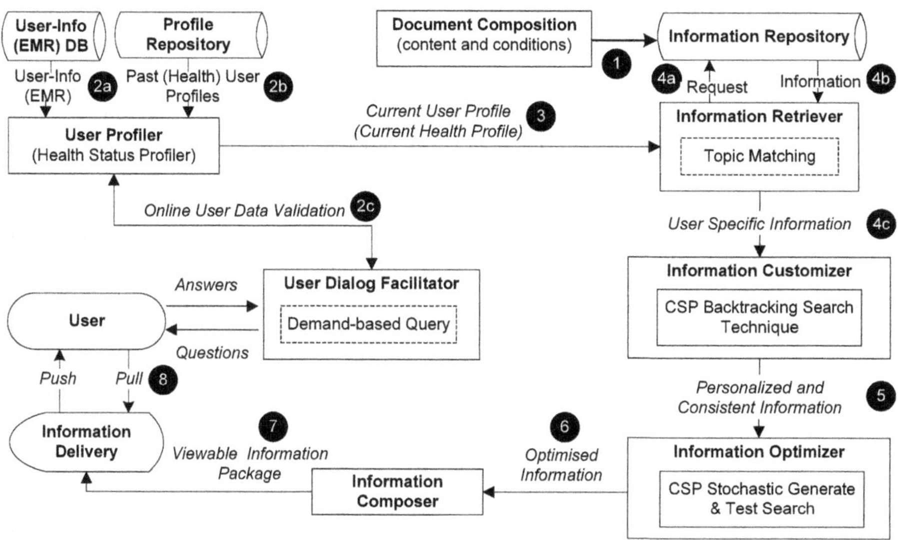

Fig. 2. Process flow for generating personalized and factually consistent information

Our IC methodology is used to generate personalized healthcare information, however we emphasize that the proposed IC methodology is applicable to other information dissemination problems.

1. ***Document composition***: For each topic-specific document, its information content and associated conditions need to be specified by the document authors. We use conditional frame-based representation for representing each document, as it supports our overall information customization strategy.
2. ***Acquisition of user- profile specific information:*** User-defining information can be acquired from stored personal records (in our case from user's electronic medical record with the permission of the user), past user-profiles, and if needed directly from the user via a web-based dialogue.
3. ***Generation of the user profile (i.e. user model):*** For optimal impact of the disseminated information, the user's profile needs to be current and accurate. Based on the collected user information, we prepare a representative user profile that serves as the basis for information customization.

4. ***Selection of user-specific information content:*** Based on the user-profile, relevant documents are selected from the document corpus. Document selection involves the use of CS techniques to satisfy the document-selection conditions of each document with the user's critical attributes noted in the user-profile. Here, we collect a set of *candidate documents* that individually are relevant to the user-profile.
5. ***Selection of factually compatible information content:*** Given a set of candidate documents, it is important to ensure that they can potentially co-exist without causing any factual inconsistency. We begin by establishing the minimum information coverage that is factually consistent—i.e. establishing the *core document set* which includes one document for each topic that need to be discussed in the final information package. We use a CS based backtracking search method to globally satisfy the document-compatibility conditions for all the selected documents—any document that is deemed factually inconsistent with the rest of the documents is discarded. The ensuing *core document set* covers each topic of interest; yet depict the minimum consistent information coverage that can be provided to the user.
6. ***Maximizing the information coverage:*** Given the core document set, we next attempt to maximize the information coverage by checking whether it is possible to include any previously non-selected candidate document to the core document set, whilst maintaining overall factual consistency. A CS based stochastic generate-and-test algorithm is used for this purpose. The outcome is the potential maximization of the information coverage (from the baseline determined by the core documents) manifested in terms of an optimized *presentation document set,* which constitutes the final personalized information content.
7. ***Preparation of information package:*** The information content (of the documents) within the *presentation document set* is in XML format. Depending on the user's viewing medium, the information content (in XML) is transformed to HTML, WML or PDF format to realize the personalized information package.
8. ***Delivery of information package:*** Finally, the personalized information package is delivered to the user over the Internet. Two delivery mechanisms are supported: (a) *push-based*—the information package is pro-actively e-mailed to the user, and (b) *pull-based*—the user retrieves it from the website.

5 Information Customization Methods

5.1 Information Representation

Our information representation scheme involves the binding of information content segments with a set of conditions [10, 11, 15, 23, 24], in the form of a *conditional frame* (shown in Fig. 3).

The notion of associating information content with its selection criteria is quite relevant in a healthcare setting where there is a necessity to ensure that any information provided to users is not only consistent with the individual's needs but it also should not inadvertently prove to be harmful, confusing and contradictory in any way. Note that, each condition is representation by the tuple *(type, value, weight)*. The weight defines the degree of restriction ranging from 0 to 1, where 0→ strictly not recommended and 1→ highly recommended.

	Document ID	Topic: abc Sub-Topic: abc-5
Conditions	Document Selection Conditions (DSC)	DSC(observation, high BP, 0) DSC(drug, motrin, 0)
	Document Compatibility Conditions (DSC)	DCC(diet, low calorie, 0) DCC(condition, hypertension, 0)
Content	Information Content	Unrestricted Content Segment
		Restricted Content Segment: DSC / DCC / Content

Fig. 3. Architecture of a conditional frame-based hypermedia document for IC

5.2 Constraint Satisfaction Methods for Information Customization

After having retrieved topic-specific documents relevant to a given user profile, here we illustrate the modelling of our information customization problem as a CS problem. The specification of a CS problem requires a set of variables, its domain values and constraints.

We define IC via CS problem-solving as (a) a set of information topics, represented in terms of *topic-variables* $X=\{x_1,...,x_n\}$, where for each topic-variable x_i, there is a finite set of (topic-specific) documents. The set of documents associated with each topic-variable is deemed as its domain, D_i; (b) a user profile represented as a single-valued *user-variable*; and (c) and two types of constraints—*user-model constraint* (UMC) and *co-existence constraint* (CoC). A solution to our CS problem is the systematic selection of the largest subset of documents for each topic-variable, in such a way that the ensuing user-model and co-existence constraints (amongst all selected documents) are fully satisfied. Such a CS solution can be obtained by searching, via CS search methods, the domain for each topic-variable.

5.2.1 User-Model Constraint Satisfaction: Generating the Candidate Document Set

A user-model constraint between a topic-variable and a user-variable is satisfied when all the documents in the domain of the topic-variable are consistent with user profile. The general idea is to compare the document-selection conditions (DSC) for each document with the user critical attributes (UCA) listed in the user profile. This is achieved by calculating the *conflict value* (CV), as shown below, between the DSC and UCA. A low CV value implies that the user-model constraint is not breached and that the document is seemingly relevant to the user, whereas a high CV value denotes the irrelevance of the document to the user. Typically, a user-defined threshold is used to determine the acceptable level of CV.

$$cv_{DSC}^{UCA} = \left|(weight)_{DSC}^{Doc} - (weight)_{UCA}^{UP}\right|,\ (type,value)_{DSC}^{Doc} = (type,value)_{UCA}^{UP}$$

$$0 \le cv_{DSC}^{UCA} \le 1,\ 0 \to \text{not breached},\ 1 \to \text{breached}$$

The conflict value for a DSC is the modulus of the difference between the weights of the DSC and the matching UCA. Note that a matching UCA has the same type and value as the DSC in question.

To satisfy the user-model constraint we employ a variation of CSP node-consistency technique—the *recursive-level node-consistency algorithm* [25]. The working of our modified recursive-level node-consistency algorithm is as follows: for each topic-variable, if the domain contains a document that is inconsistent to user profile, then that particular document is removed from the domain. Eventually, only documents that are consistent to user profile—i.e. relevant to user—are retained in each topic-variable's domain and the resulting set of user-specific documents are regarded as the candidate document set.

```
Algorithm Recursive-level NC
  for topic-var1 to topic-varm{m = no. of topics}
    for Doc1 to Docn {n = no. of documents in the domain
    of topic-vari}
      test UMC
      if UMC not satisfied {inconsistent with user
      profile}
        discard Doci
```

5.2.2 Co-existence Constraint Satisfaction: Generating the Core Document Set

Co-existence constraints between two topic-variables need to be satisfied to ensure that their respective selected documents are factually, procedurally and contextually consistent with each other. In practice, co-existence constraints between two topic-variables$_{A\&B}$ are satisfied if the selected documents from the domain of topic-variable$_A$ are consistent with selected documents from the domain of topic-variable$_B$. This implies that the document-compatibility conditions (DCC) of a document are not breached by the DCC of another document. A DCC is deemed to be 'breached' when the conflict value (cv), calculated as below, exceeds a predefined threshold.

$$cv_{DCC}^{DCC'} = \left|(weight)_{DCC}^{Doc} - (weight)_{DCC'}^{Doc'}\right|,\ (type,value)_{DCC}^{Doc} = (type,value)_{DCC'}^{Doc}$$

$$0 \le cv_{DCC}^{DCC'} \le 1,\ 0 \to \text{not breached},\ 1 \to \text{breached}$$

To satisfy co-existence constraints, we leverage two CSP search methods: (i) Backtracking (BT) Search; and (ii) Stochastic Generate Test (S-GT) Search. BT search method is used to search the candidate document space to generate the so-called *core document set*–the minimum set of mutually consistent documents such that there exists a single document to cover each topic of interest. BT search incrementally attempts to generate the core document set by (i) choosing an un-instantiated topic-variable, i.e. no document has yet been assigned to the topic-variable; (ii) choosing a candidate document from the domain of the un-instantiated topic-variable; (iii) checking whether the candidate document is consistent with documents that have already been selected to instantiate the other topic-variables; (iv) if the candidate document is consistent—implying that the co-existence constraint is satisfied—the candidate document is selected by instantiating the topic-variable, else the next candidate document within the domain of the same topic-variable is examined. Given that the co-existence constraint cannot be satisfied because all the candidate documents for a topic-variable have been checked, backtracking is performed to select the most recently instantiated topic-variable that may still have some alternative candidate documents. Search proceeds forward again based on the new instantiation of the said topic-variable. Successful BT search ensures that each topic-variable is instantiated with a document, thus resulting in the *core document set.*

5.2.3 Co-existence Constraint Satisfaction: Generating the Presentation Set

Extension of the core document set to the potentially larger presentation document set is performed via two methods: (a) *Stochastic Generate and Test* (S-GT) and (b) Document Swapping. The motivation for generating the presentation document set is to maximize the information coverage by selecting those candidate documents that do not violate the a priori established factual consistency of the core document set.

The working of the S-GT method is as follows: the non-selected candidate documents are randomly sequenced in N different sets. Each set is then systematically searched based on the order of the constituent documents in an attempt to include more documents into the core information set without violating the co-existence constraint (i.e. the factual consistency). Consequently, N presentation document sets are generated, whereby the presentation set with the most documents is selected. We argue that the S-GT method is suitable for this purpose because of its stochastic nature in selecting topic variables and evaluating the documents within their domain in a manner that avoids the 'unfair' effects resulting from a sequenced evaluation of documents as practised by most of the systematic search algorithms.

The application of the earlier CS solving techniques realize factually consistent information set, but the solution is not necessarily optimum—i.e. there may exist a possibility whereby a particular selected document may have caused multiple candidate documents to be discarded during the CSP search. To rectify this limitation, we have developed an information optimization mechanism, termed as *document swapping*, that 'swaps' a single selected document with multiple discarded candidate documents provided (a) the co-existence constraint is maintained and (b) the presentation document set still contains at least one document for each topic of interest. The outcome of this document-swapping technique is optimized presentation document set, which is the final CSP solution. The document swapping algorithm is given below:

Algorithm Document Swapping

```
for each document, Doc in the presentation set
  identify non-selected candidate documents that
  are inconsistent to Doc
    if size of non-selected candidate documents,
    N > 1
      if Doc is not the only document for a topic-
      variable
        apply S-GT algorithm to the non-selected
        candidate documents to generate N sets
          if size of the biggest set of candidate
          documents C > 1
             discard Doc
             append C to the presentation set
end Document Swapping
```

6 Working Example of Information Customization

We present a working example of information customization based on the methodology and methods defined above. We are able to partially show the generation of personalized and factually consistent healthcare information.

Step 1 - Generate current user health profile by collecting information from the user's EMR, past profiles and directly from the user. Table 1 shows an exemplar health profile.

Table 1. An exemplar health profile

<table>
<tr><td colspan="2">Name: abcd</td><td>ID: 5565248</td></tr>
<tr><td colspan="2">Health Problem</td><td>Date</td></tr>
<tr><td colspan="2">Diabetes</td><td>10 July 2003</td></tr>
<tr><td colspan="2">COPD</td><td>15 August 2003</td></tr>
<tr><td colspan="3">User Attributes</td></tr>
<tr><td>Type</td><td>Value</td><td>Validity</td></tr>
<tr><td>Age</td><td>32</td><td>1</td></tr>
<tr><td>Gender</td><td>Female</td><td>1</td></tr>
<tr><td>Blood type</td><td>O+</td><td>1</td></tr>
<tr><td>Family History</td><td>Diabetes</td><td>1</td></tr>
<tr><td>Allergy</td><td>Pollen</td><td>0</td></tr>
<tr><td>Diet</td><td>Vegetarian</td><td>0</td></tr>
<tr><td>Lifestyle</td><td>Smoker</td><td>1</td></tr>
<tr><td>Allergy</td><td>Seafood</td><td>1</td></tr>
<tr><td>Allergy</td><td>Dust</td><td>1</td></tr>
<tr><td>Condition</td><td>Pregnant</td><td>0</td></tr>
</table>

Step 2- Retrieve topic-specific documents for each health problem, stated in the user's health profile, from the document repository. This gives us the document set shown in Table 2. For CSP purposes, we need to define the topic-variable (*topic_var*) representing each health problem concerning the user. The domain for each topic-variable comprises the documents that correspond to the topic, shown in Table 3.

Table 2. Topic-specific documents for Diabetes and COPD.

Health Problems	Topic-Specific Documents	
	Treatment (T)	**Medication (M)**
Diabetes (D)	DT1	DM1
	DT2	DM2
	DT3	DM3
	DT4	DM4
COPD – Chronic Obstructive Pulmonology (C)	CT1	CM1
	CT2	CM2
	CT3	CM3

Table 3. Definition of variables for topics under diabetes and COPD

Health problem
Topic
Variable ::{Domain}

Diabetes
Treatment
topic_var1::{DT1, DT2, DT3, DT4}

Medication
topic_var2::{DM1, DM2, DM3, DM4}

COPD
Treatment
topic_var3::{CT1, CT2, CT3, CT4}

Medication
topic_var4::{CM1, CM2, CM3, CM4}

Step 3- Satisfy the user-model constraints to establish the candidate document set. Table 4 shows the result of the node-consistency algorithm on topic_var1, whereby only the relevant documents are selected.

Table 4. The candidate document set for the health problem diabetes

Doc	Document Selection Condition	Matching User Attribute from health profile	CV	Status
DT1	<family history, diabetes, 1>	<family history, diabetes, 1>	0	Retained
DT2	<lifestyle, smoker, 1>	<lifestyle, smoker, 1>	0	Retained
DT3	<condition, pregnant, 1>	<condition, pregnant, 0>	1	Discarded
DT4	<allergy, seafood, 1>	<allergy, seafood, 1>	0	Retained

Step 4- Satisfy the co-existence constraints to generate the core document set and presentation document set. Given the document co-existence conditions for each document (which cannot be shown due to lack of space), Table 5 shows the core set. Next, we apply the S-GT algorithm to maximize the information coverage. Table 6 shows the three random sets of non-selected documents, whereby the second random set best maximizes the information coverage. This is because CT4, which is inconsistent with both DM4 and DT4, was positioned only after DM4 in the random set. Such ordering of documents enabled DM4 to be selected first instead of CT4 and thus blocked CT4 to be selected subsequently. Without CT4 in the presentation set, DT4 can be next selected. Note that this is not possible for the other two random sets.

Table 5. Core document set resulting from BT search

Topic-variables	Domain (Candidate set)	Selected (Core set)	Discarded	None-selected
Topic_var1	DT1, DT2, DT4	DT1	-	DT2, DT4
Topic_var2	DM1, DM3, DM4	DM1	-	DM3, DM4
Topic_var3	CT1, CT2, CT3, CT4	CT3	CT1, CT2	CT4
Topic_var4	CM1, CM2, CM3	CM1	-	CM2

Table 6. An extended presentation document set resulting from S-GT search

Non-selected (Randomised order)	Documents selected	Documents discarded	Size
CT4, DT4, DM3, DM4, DT2, CM2	CT4, DM3, DT2	DT4, DM4, CM2	3
DM4, CT4, DT4, DM3, CM2, DT2	**DM4, DT4, DM3, DT2**	**CT4, CM2**	**4**
CM2, CT4, DM4, DT2, DM3, DT4	CT4, DT2, DM3	CM2, DM4, DT4	3

Step 5- Apply document swapping to optimize the presentation document set. Table 7 shows the presentation document set (comprising 8 documents) together with their conflicts with the non-selected documents. DT1 has been detected to be block the inclusion of CT1 and CM2. Via document swapping, DT1 can be discarded to select CT1 and CM2, without disturbing the factual consistency, thereby increasing the size of the (optimized) presentation document (as shown in Table 8). The resultant optimized presentation document set is the personalized and factually consistent information that need to be presented to the user.

Table 7. Presentation document set *before* optimization

		Non-selected documents				
		CT1	CT2	CT4	CM2	Conflicts
Presentation Set (size =8)	DT1	X	-	-	X	2
	DT2	-	-	-	-	0
	DT4	-	-	X	-	1
	DM1	-	-	-	-	0
	DM3	-	-	-	-	0
	DM4	-	-	X	-	1
	CM1	-	X	-	-	1
	CT3	-	-	-	-	0
Conflicts		1	1	2	1	

Table 8. Presentation document set *after* optimization

		Non-selected docs			Conflicts
		CT2	CT4	DT1	
Presentation Set (Size = 9)	DT2	-	-	-	0
	DT4	-	X	-	1
	DM1	-	-	-	0
	DM3	-	-	-	0
	DM4	-	X	-	1
	CM1	X	-	-	1
	CT3	-	-	-	0
	CT1	-	-	X	1
	CM2	-	-	X	1
Conflicts		1	2	2	

Step 6- Prepare the final information package based on the optimized presentation document set. The XML based documents are transformed to a pre-defined HTML template to realize an HTML based, including text and images, information package.

Step 7- Deliver the information package to the user via Internet mediated mechanisms. A push based mechanism is implemented to send the customized information package to the user via email.

7 Concluding Remarks

In this paper we presented and demonstrated a services-oriented information customization framework that leverages on a unique hybrid of adaptive hypermedia and constraint satisfaction methods. The work has direct implication towards efforts to retain a stable client-base for E-services via a web portal. It is routinely suggested that enterprises need to understand their customers in terms of their current needs, preferences and future goals. One way of manifesting this understanding of customer needs is to pro-actively customize services/information content, leading to improved customer relationship management (CRM). In fact, according to Brohman et al "CRM solutions are deemed to be so critical that investments in them continue to be funded, even in these days of shriveling IT budgets" [26]. We believe that our work, contributes to this end by presenting an information customization framework that provides adaptive personalized information content through a static user-model. Most importantly, the incorporation of constraint satisfaction methods ensure that not only the information content is consistent with the user-model but it is also factually, procedurally, and contextually consistent. Indeed, for effective CRM it is imperative to both account for and satisfy these qualitative constraints.

We conclude that person-specific customization of information viz. a user-model is a complex task that necessitates a systematic, pragmatic and multifaceted methodology. Previously, knowledge-based reasoning, case-based reasoning, natural language processing and other artificial intelligence methods have been successfully applied for user modeling and information personalization. In this paper, we have demonstrated the novel application of constraint satisfaction methods for information customization, which offers an interesting synergy between adaptive hypermedia and constraint satisfaction methods. From our experiments, we have concluded that (a) by varying the constraints the degree of information personalization can be modulated with interesting outcomes; and (b) apart from text-based hypermedia documents, other hypermedia objects such as picture, movie or sound-based documents can be used within the final information package.

Information personalization in an E-Healthcare context for the purposes for patient education and empowerment is quite prevalent [8, 27, 28] and there is a growing demand for adaptive websites that deliver personalized wellness maintenance information on an individual and community basis. We have applied our IC framework towards the dissemination of personalized healthcare information, for a limited number of medical problems, via a restricted website managed by medical professionals.

In conclusion, we believe that this is the first step towards the incorporation of constraint satisfaction within an IC paradigm. Also, the realization to ensure factual consistency when amalgamating heterogeneous information will lead to interesting research in adaptive service-oriented systems. Finally, we believe that the featured IC approach can be used for a variety of E-services for education material customization, stock market reporting and advice, tourist information and so on; the only limitation is the specification of co-existence constraints.

References

[1] Rust RT, Lemon KN, E-service and the consumer. *International Journal of Electronic Commerce,* Vol. 5(3), 2001 pp. 85–102.

[2] Helal S, Su S, meng J, Krithivasan R, Jagatheesan A, The Internet enterprise. *Proceedings of Symposium on Application and the Internet*, 2002.

[3] Zirpins C, Weinreich H, Bartelt A, Lamersdorf W, Advanced concepts for next generation portals. *Proceedings of 12th International Workshop on Database and Expert Systems Applications*, 3-7 Sept. 2001, pp. 501–506.

[4] Piccinelli G, Salle M, Zirpins C, Service-oriented modelling for e-business applications components. *Proceedings of 10th IEEE International Workshops on Enabling Technologies: Infrastructure for Collaborative Enterprises (WET ICE)*, 20–22 June 2001, pp. 12–17.

[5] Bogonikolos N, Makris C, Tsakalidis A, Vassiliadis B, Adapting information presentation and retrieval through user modeling. *Proceedings of International Conference on Information Technology: Coding and Computing*, 2-4 April 2001, pp. 399–404.

[6] Zhang Y, Im I, Recommender systems: A framework and research issues. *Proceedings of American Conference on Information Systems*, 2002.

[7] Fink J, Kobsa A, Putting personalization into practice, *Communications of the ACM*, Vol. 45(5), 2002.

[8] Abidi SSR, Chong Y, Abidi SR, Patient empowerment via 'pushed' delivery of personalized healthcare Educational content over the internet. *Proceedings of 10th World Congress on Medical Informatics*, 2001, London.

[9] Brusilovsky P, Methods and techniques of adaptive hypermedia. In *P. Brusilovsky, A. Kobsa and J. Vassileva (eds.): Adaptive Hypertext and Hypermedia.* Kluwer Academic Publishers, Dordrecht, 1998a, pp. 1–43.

[10] Brusilovsky P, Kobsa A, Vassileva J (Eds.), *Adaptive Hypertext and Hypermedia.* Kluwer Academic Publishers, Dordrecht, 1998b.

[11] Kobsa A, Personalized hypermedia presentation techniques for improving online customer relationships. *The Knowledge Engineering Review,* Vol. 16(2), 1999, pp. 111–155.

[12] Perkowitz, M, Etzioni O, Adaptive web sites. *Communications of the ACM*, Vol. 43(8), 2000, pp. 152–158.

[13] Henze N, Nejdl W, Extendible adaptive hypermedia courseware: integrating different courses and web material. In *P. Brusilovsky, O Stock & C Strappavara (Eds.) Adaptive Hypermedia and Adaptive Web-based Systems*, Springer Verlag, Berlin, 2000, pp. 109–120.

[14] Kobsa A, Muller D, Nill A, KN-AHS: an adaptive hypermedia client of the user modeling system BGP-MS. *Proceeding of the Fourth International Conference on User Modeling*, 1994, pp. 99–105.

[15] Boyle C, Encarnacion AO, MetaDoc: An adaptive hypertext reading system. *User Models and User Adapted Interaction,* Vol. 4(1), 1994, pp. 1–19.

[16] Ardissono L, Goy A, Tailoring the interaction with users in web stores, *User Modelling and User Adapted Interaction*, Vol. 10(4), 2000, pp. 251–303.

[17] Hohl H, Bocker HD, Gunzenhauser R, HYPADAPTER: an adaptive hypertext system for exploratory learning and programming, *User Modelling and User Adapted Interaction,* Vol. 6(2), pp. 131–155.

[18] Kaplan C, Fenwick J, Chen J, Adaptive hypertext navigation based on user goals and context, *User Modelling and User Adapted Interaction,* Vol. 3(3), pp. 193–220.

[19] Oppermann R, Specht M, A context sensitive nomadic information system as an exhibition guide, *Proceedings of the Handheld and Ubiquitious Computing Second International Symposium (HUC 2000)*, 2000, pp. 127–142.

[20] Tsang E, *Foundations of constraint satisfaction*. Academic Press, London, UK. 1993.

[21] Sabin D, Freuder E, Configuration as composite constraint satisfaction. *Proceedings of the Artificial Intelligence and Manufacturing Research Planning Workshop*, 1996, pp.153–161.

[22] Torrens M, Faltings B, SmartClients: Constraint satisfaction as a paradigm for scaleable intelligent information systems. *Workshop on Artificial Intelligence on Electronic Commerce, AAAI-99*, 1999, Orlando, Florida, USA.

[23] De Rosis F, Pizzutilo S, Russo A, User tailored hypermedia explanations. *INTERCHI'93 Adjunct proceedings*, Amsterdam, 1993.

[24] Beaumont IH, User modeling in the interactive anatomy tutoring system ANATOMTUTOR. *User Models and User Adapted Interaction*, Vol. 4(1), 1994, pp. 21–45.

[25] Barták R, Constraint programming: In pursuit of the holy grail. *Proceedings of the Week of Doctoral Students (WDS99),* Part IV, MatFyzPress, Prague, 1999, pp. 555–564.

[26] Brohman MT, Watson RT, Piccoli G, Parasuraman A, Data completeness: A key to effective net-based customer service systems. Communications of the ACM, Vol. 46(6), 2003, pp. 47–51.

[27] Bental D, Adapting web-based information to the needs of patients with cancer. *Proceedings of International Conference On Adaptive Hypertext and Adaptive Web-based Systems*, Trento, Italy, 2000, pp. 27–37.

[28] Wilke W, Bergmann R, Techniques and Knowledge Used for Adaptation During Case Based Problem Solving. Lecture Notes in Artificial Intelligence, Vol. 1416. Springer-Verlag, Berlin, 1998.

“Everything Personal, Not Just Business:” Improving User Experience through Rule-Based Service Customization

Richard Hull, Bharat Kumar, Daniel Lieuwen, Peter F. Patel-Schneider, Arnaud Sahuguet, Sriram Varadarajan, and Avinash Vyas

Bell Labs, Lucent Technologies
600 Mountain Avenue
Murray Hill, NJ 07974
{hull,bharat,lieuwen,pfps,sahuguet,sv5,vyasa}@lucent.com
http://db.bell-labs.com/

Abstract. The web and converged services paradigm promises tremendous flexibility in the creation of rich composite services for enterprises and end-users. The flexibility and richness offers the possibility of highly customized, individualized services for the end user and hence revenue generating services for service providers (*e.g.,* ASPs, telecom network operators, ISPs). But how can end-users (and enterprises) specify their preferences when a myriad of possibilities and potential circumstances need to be addressed? In this paper we advocate a solution based on policy management where user preferences are specified through forms but translated into rules in a high-level policy language. This paper identifies the requirements for this kind of interpretation, and describes the Houdini system (under development at Bell Labs) which offers a rich rule-based language and a framework that supports intuitive, forms-based provisioning interfaces.

1 Introduction

One main reason for the tremendous success of the Web is that it managed – since its early days – to establish a personalized relationship with its user. Wasn’t the “personal homepage”, the first Web killer app? At this point almost all web portals and web-based services offer some form of customization, from letting the end-user select what content is displayed and how, to storing end-user values (such as credit card information) to simplify future interactions, to providing alerts based on end-user requests. The next revolution of the web will be based on service-oriented programming, embracing both the web services paradigm and also *converged* (web and telecom) services, *i.e.,* services based on the evolving integration of the telephony network and the Internet through standards such as SIP, Parlay/OSA and 3GPP/3GPP2. With the next revolution, will the infrastructure in place now be sufficient for customizing and personalizing the web and converged services of the future? This paper argues that the answer is a resounding NO! The paper then introduces the Houdini policy management infrastructure being developed at Bell Labs, a framework that will be sufficient for this purpose.

The customization infrastructure commonly used in today’s web is *value-based*: the core logic of an application or service is essentially static, but end-users can insert

M.E. Orlowska et al. (Eds.): ICSOC 2003, LNCS 2910, pp. 149–164, 2003.

personalized values to obtain customized behaviors. The prototypical example is a typical on-line newspaper, which lets the user indicate what types of and how many stories should be displayed on her "front page". Consider now a composite web/converged service of the future, which itself is formed from tens or perhaps hundreds of individual services, that gather information from a myriad of sources and potentially invoke numerous side effects to fulfill an end-user's request (or an enterprise's request). Because of the vast richness and variability in composite web/converged services of the future, if only value-based customization were supported, then an end-user would be overwhelmed when inputting all of her preferences. What we need is *rule-based* customization, whereby end-users can express their preferences at a higher, more generalized manner than possible with value-based customization. With rule-based customization, the preferences of the end-user can translate into rules which impact both the values used by the web/converged service and also portions of the *core logic* of the service.

Policy management is not new. A policy management reference architecture that cleanly separates application logic from policy decisions has converged from the data networking and telecom communities [17,11]. But we argue here that current policy management solutions are not yet appropriate for service oriented programming applications for two reasons. The first reason concerns expressive power and performance. In typical IETF-style[17] policy management, the rules have an **if** *conditions* **then** *actions* format, where the actions cause side-effects outside of the rules engine; rule chaining is not supported. We show in this paper that in the context of web/converged services, rule chaining is desirable, to permit substantial succinctness and modularity in rule specifications. In typical production-style rules systems (*e.g.,* ILOG [18], CLIPS [22]) chaining is supported, but also recursion. We argue that this is beyond the needs of customization for future web/converged services, and leads to unnecessary overhead in terms of rules creation, rules maintenance, and runtime space and time consumption. We advocate here the use of production-style rules with chaining but no cycles as the appropriate balance between expressive power and performance. The rules system used in the Houdini framework is based on this balance. This rules system has recently been incorporated into Lucent's MiLife ISG product, a Parlay/OSA gateway that allows internet- and web-based applications to access data and services hosted in telecom networks.

The second short-coming of current policy infrastructures for customizing future web/converged services is the lack of simple, intuitive support for end-users to specify rich preferences. A key part of the Houdini framework is an approach in which end-users provision preferences using a forms-based interface. These preferences are converted into a collection of tables and rules that captures the preferences. End-users are aware of the high-level "flow" of logic that the ruleset will use to interpret the user's preferences, but are insulated from the the explicit rules underneath. Importantly, the use of the Houdini rules engine permits relatively inexpensive modifications and extensions to the provisionable content, and permits radically different provisionable content for different user groups.

The primary focus of this paper is on *rule-based customization*. As such, we do not address the issue of managing end-user profile data, and we touch on the issue of storing user preferences data in a cursory manner. Management of (possibly distributed) profile data is the subject of [25], and is the topic of several industry standards groups (3GPP GUP[1], OMA[3], Liberty Alliance[20]).

Paper organization: Section 2 illustrates the need for rule-based customization using a motivating example from web/converged services and two broad themes (service selection and privacy) that arise in web/converged services. We then (in Section 3) derive from the examples key requirements for customization in service oriented programming. In Section 4 we present the Houdini framework and explain how it satisfies those requirements. We contrast our proposal with related work (Section 5) before offering final remarks and conclusion (Section 6). The emphasis of the current paper is to motivate the use of a policy enablement reference architecture for service oriented programming and to introduce the Houdini framework that supports it. Further information about some aspects of Houdini, including preliminary benchmarks and more details on self-provisioning, are presented in [15,14].

2 Motivating Examples

This section presents three representative areas where service oriented programming will need a high degree of customization. The first, focused on "presence" [9] and "selective-reach-me" [25], is based on a composite of web and converged network services. It involves specifying intricate preferences about when and how an individual can be reached for interactive communication. The last two are more fundamental. The second concerns the selection of atomic services to form a composite service that meets the individual needs of a given user in a given context. The third concerns how end-users can specify policies about who can access personal information, when, and under what circumstances.

2.1 Presence and Selective-Reach-Me

With the emergence of pagers, mobile telephony, and wireless handhelds it is increasingly possible to contact people anytime, anywhere. People sometimes prefer to be contacted on a wireline phone because of voice quality. Instant messaging is also popular as a near-realtime mechanism for communication, *e.g.*, if someone is already in voice communication with someone else. People sometimes prefer not to be contacted at all, instead having messages routed to voicemail, email, or completely blocked. Because of this explosion of contact devices, two crucial emerging services are *Presence* and *Selective-Reach-Me* (SRM). Current products [19,26] support limited forms of presence and SRM capabilities, but the degree of customization provided by these is limited.

Figure 1 illustrates a possible architecture for supporting presence and SRM built around various web services. In particular, the Presence and SRM Web Server acts as a kind of hub/coordinator. It can obtain information from a user's calendar(s), address book, corporate directory, etc. (on the right side of the figure), and it can access raw presence information from various communication networks, and also invoke or re-route calls (bottom of figure). In this example, telecom and network services such as mobile phone presence are "wrapped" to act as web services, *e.g.*, according to the Parlay X [11] standards.

A truly useful Presence [9] service will (a) provide requesters with information about a person's presence across all the devices associated with the person, or simply suggest the best device(s) for communicating with the person, and (b) share the appropriately personalized subset of this information only with authorized requesters at appropriate times in appropriate contexts – to protect privacy. Furthermore, it is sometimes useful to display the person's degree of availability/interruptibility, so that requesters can exercise discretion about whether to attempt live communication, and through what medium.

SRM is an important "dual" of Presence, which allows people to "call people, not devices." More specifically, SRM allows a user to specify preferences about when she is available by what communication medium (wireline phone, wireless phone, IM, etc). This might be based on time of day; day of week; appointments listed in calendars; current presence, location, and availability; whether the person is currently on the phone and with whom; etc.

A tremendously broad variety of data may be relevant for determining a user's Presence, for determining how to share that presence information, and for determining the correct routing for an SRM call. For a class of typical office workers, these decisions can best be described (informally) in terms of a flow of logic, that starts with information about the user's typical schedule (*e.g.*, commute from 8:00 to 8:30, in office from 8:30 to 5:30, etc.), the user's calendar (showing meetings, with whom, and where), and recent device usage; and interprets those based on availability preferences ("if meeting with my boss then route subordinates to voicemail", "if meeting anyone else, then use speech-to-text and route calls to instant messaging and use text-to-speech for my responses (if any)"), hints about location ("if I used my office phone in the last 30 minutes then I'm probably still in my office, unless I have a meeting elsewhere or I typically go home at that time"), and other information (*e.g.*, looming deadlines tend to decrease degree of availability). Different classes of users will have different stereotypical patterns that can be customized. This will minimize their data entry, maximizing ease of use.

2.2 Service Selection

Through the use of standards such as WSDL and SOAP, and repositories such as UDDI for web service descriptions and URLs, the web services paradigm affords tremendous flexibility in dynamically selecting and composing services. Further, it is expected that over time the languages for describing web services will become richer [12], to include, for example, behavioral and other descriptions (*e.g.*, about function call sequencing and pre- and post-conditions). This permits personalization not only of the individual services, but also in selecting what services will be used to support a service request.

To illustrate, we recall one pragmatic approach to service selection and composition, that involves the use of hierarchical composition [6]. For this, it is assumed that a library is available that holds both "base" web services (*e.g.*, to make a flight reservation, to make a hotel reservation) and "template" web services (*e.g.*, that can invoke a flight reservation service followed by a hotel reservation service). A composite web service can be created dynamically by selecting first a top-level web service template (*e.g.*, to create a business or vacation trip itinerary with flights, car rentals, hotels, etc.), and then choosing additional template or base web services to fill in the "gaps" of that template; this process continues iteratively until there are no more "gaps".

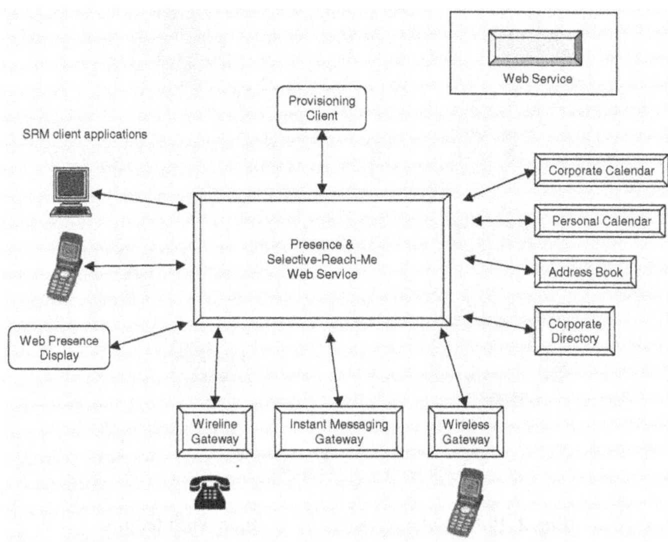

Fig. 1. Presence and SRM Service Architecture

The process of selecting template and base services will need substantial personalization. In the travel itinerary case just described, factors involved in making the selections will include the kinds of trip the person is planning, preferences about who is supplying services (*e.g.,* use Orbitz vs. Travelocity vs. a particular carrier's web service), transactional and quality-of-service guarantees provided by the services, their response times, the kinds of status reporting supported, the costs of the different services, the deals that they can access, etc.

More broadly, personalization in the selection of service will be relevant to any technology that is used for web service selection and composition, not just hierarchical composition. Also, this personalization will be relevant wherever dynamic service creation arises, including, *e.g.,* in the Presence and SRM services mentioned above.

2.3 Privacy Shield

One key aspect of customization is the sharing of personal information (see [25,7]). The end user is willing to share personal information in order to get a better user experience, but she wants to remain in control of what information is used, by whom and for what purpose. We designate this set of preferences as the user *privacy shield.*

As illustrated by the first motivating example, the end user may want to restrict access to information such as presence information (*e.g.,* buddy lists for instant messaging clients). For instance, a user is willing to share traveling information (*e.g.,* favorite airlines, preferred seating, diet, passport number) with authorized Web travel agents, shipping and billing information (*e.g.,* home address, preferred shipping method) with authorized e-retailers. A user is willing to share personal entries from her calendar with friends and family, corporate entries with co-workers, etc.

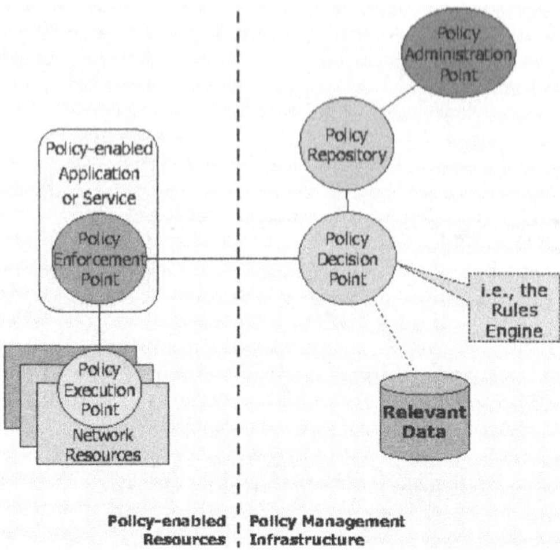

Fig. 2. Policy Management Reference Architecture

Reference [15] applies the Houdini framework to privacy shields stemming from mobility and ubiquitous computing. It also discusses related standards.

3 Requirements on Policy Infrastructure for Services

We now list six requirements on a service oriented programming infrastructure needed to support customization. The first requirement is at a meta-level – we argue that a policy-management infrastructure is needed. The remaining requirements focus on particular characteristics needed by that policy-management infrastructure.

Separation of Concerns: As illustrated in Section 2, there is a need for a high degree of customization in service oriented programming. Furthermore, different user groups will use different kinds of data and paths of reasoning to achieve their customization. Capturing all these variations within services is a daunting, if not impossible, task. Instead we advocate a substantial separation of the core service logic (which should reside in the service code) from the core customization decisions (which should reside in a policy infrastructure). Various standard bodies [17,11] have defined a reference architecture for policy management, identifying some key components and roles (see Figure 2):

- *Policy Enforcement Point*: in charge of asking for a decision and enforcing it (*i.e.,* invoking the required actions). In some cases, the enforcement point uses a *Policy Execution Point,* which is where the invoked actions are actually executed.
- *Policy Decision Point*: in charge of rendering a decision based on a ruleset and a context. The decision point only returns a decision and has absolutely no side-effect on the environment.
- *Policy Repository*: in charge of storing policies, *e.g.,* rulesets.
- *Policy Administration Point*: in charge of provisioning the rules (*i.e.,* letting the user access and modify directly or indirectly the rules that define her preferences) and other administrative tasks (*e.g.,* checking that the rules are valid).

Service-oriented programming should use the standard policy-management reference architecture in order to achieve a separation of concerns between core service logic and personalization.

We now turn to requirements on the policy management infrastructure itself, *i.e.*, the portion of Figure 2 to the right of the dashed line.

Can "scale" to a high degree of complexity: As illustrated by the examples of Section 2, the input data for customization decisions can be voluminous and highly varied in kind and richness (beyond string and numeric types). Customization decisions themselves can be very complex and may require a high-level expressive language to describe individual decisions and/or decision flows.

End-users may find it useful to conceptualize the data into different categories (*e.g.*, for SRM, data indicative of my current and future activity, data indicative of my location, data about the caller), and may conceptualize a flow of decisions based on that data. Users may want to incorporate heuristic and/or probabilistic reasoning, since the information available in the network is incomplete, and human behavior is non-deterministic.

A policy infrastructure must be rich enough to support this myriad of rich input data, and the ability to combine the data in complex ways.

Easy to provision for the end-user: In spite of the implicit variability and complexity of emerging composite services, preference provisioning must be conceptually straightforward for end users. If provisioning is too complex, then the vast majority of users will never bother to provision their preferences, and will lose many of the benefits of web- and converged-services. Although intricate rules might be used inside the policy infrastructure, the end-user must be able to specify his preferences by filling in tables, and making simple selections. One aspect of achieving this will be to support, for a single service such as SRM, different preferences-provisioning interfaces for different classes of users (*e.g.*, office worker, student, emergency worker).

A policy infrastructure must offer user-friendly provisioning interfaces that help the user specify and verify preferences and permit broad variations for different user groups.

Performance: The need for high performance is clear in the case of converged-network applications, such as SRM or mobile commerce, since users expect wireline and wireless telephony network responses at sub-second speeds. Users are more tolerant of services provided over the web, but adding more than a second or two for policy-enablement would be unacceptable. Since many composite web services will involve multiple decisions (either by a single atomic web services, or by multiple web services in a composition), the time for individual decisions must still be well under a second. Further, in order to be economically feasible this response time must be attainable even under heavy load (*e.g.*, 100K or more decisions per hour per processor).

A policy infrastructure must introduce very little overhead when added on top of an existing service.

Ease of Integration: Policy enabling an already existing service (or set of services) must respect the given architecture in terms of domain boundaries, security, etc. The policy component must adapt to the architecture.

*A policy infrastructure must be applicable to a variety of deployment architectures (*e.g., *client/server vs. embedded, centralized vs. distributed).*

Genericity and Extensibility: The proposed framework should not be specific to one application domain but capable of dealing with any kind of preferences. This implies that the framework is extensible in the sense that new data sources can be added and made accessible at the level of the evaluation context.

A policy infrastructure must be generic and extensible to enable it to easily adapt to changing application requirements.

The next two sections provide more detail about tools we are developing to support customization of web and converged services.

4 The Houdini Rules System

This section describes Houdini, which provides the core of our approach for customization in service oriented programming. In particular, we describe here the Houdini language and rules paradigm, and the Houdini engine. For completeness we also touch on the rules engine performance and provisioning infrastructure in Houdini, although these are considered in more detail elsewhere [14,15]. As will be seen below, the Houdini infrastructure has been developed to satisfy all of the requirements identified in Section 3. Houdini is intended primarily to serve as a Policy Decision Point in the sense of IETF/Parlay perspective on policy management. Houdini supports production-style rules and acyclic chaining. The language is side-effect free, i.e., the evaluation of a rule only affects variables inside the ruleset. This allows the solution to be high-performance and scalable with predictable run-times. Note that the rules language syntax is typically hidden from end-users, who are provided a forms-based interface for provisioning their preferences and changing them as desired.

The section begins with a description of the Houdini language, to provide an overview and insight into how it supports modular rule sets, and then moves to the system architecture, performance, and provisioning. A more detailed treatment of the language appears in our earlier work [13].

Rulesets and Variable Typing: Following the paradigm of policy enforcement points and decision points, Houdini provides an explicit notion of *ruleset*, *i.e.,* the set of rules that should be used for a given decision request. As described below, the Houdini rules language is strongly typed. In particular, all variables used by a ruleset have specified types. (We currently support scalars, record of scalar, list of scalar, and list of record). Furthermore, each ruleset has an explicit *input* and *output* signature, corresponding to the parameters passed in and out by decision requests made against the rule set.

All variables used in a ruleset, along with their types, must be specified explicitly during provisioning. The variable types are used for statically checking the rules at provisioning time, as well as validating decision requests at run-time. The types currently offered by the language support traditional types found in relational databases, *i.e.,*, *atomic types* (bool, char, int, float, string, time), *record types* (record of atomic types) and *collection types* (list of atomic or record types).

Houdini supports condition-action rules that take the form:

if (*condition*) **then** $action_1$**;** $action_2$**;** ... $action_n$**; end**

Conditions are arbitrary boolean expressions constructed out of Houdini types and the usual boolean operators. When a rule is invoked, the rule condition is evaluated, and if true, all rule actions are executed in the order in which they are specified. Actions operate only on the variables of the rulesets. There are no side-effects outside of the current evaluation context. In the current version of Houdini there are two kinds of action: variable assignment (=) and list-value assignment (+= to append).

Since Houdini follows the IETF/Parlay PEP/PDP model, the rules engine is not responsible for how the input data is obtained for a decision request. For example, if the rules engine is being utilized by a network service, and some input data values cannot be obtained due to some technical problems (*e.g.,* off-line, out of service, etc.), it is the responsibility of the PEP to generate meaningful data values for the given situation before passing them to the rules engine.

Also, various services may interpret the same raw data in different ways, *e.g.,*, a user's presence and availability may be different based on different applications / contexts. The Houdini rules language is expressive enough to allow different types of data interpretations to be specified in a flexible manner.

Single-valued vs. list-valued variables: Houdini supports operations with both single-valued and list-valued variables during rule evaluation. Houdini provides two mechanisms for working with list-valued variables. The first is through explicit built-in functions, that can manipulate a list as a whole (*e.g.,* aggregate operators such as `count`, `min`, `max`, `sort`, etc.) or combine lists in various ways. The second is to use the production system style of rule evaluation, in which an occurrence of a list-valued variable in a rule condition leads to consideration of the rule for each individual member of that variable. To differentiate between the use of a list-valued variable `listVar` for the first and second mechanism, Houdini uses '`listVar`' to refer to the collection as a whole, and uses '`?listVar`' to indicate that production system semantics should be used. We refer to occurrences of '`?listVar`' in a rule as an *element-wise occurrence*.

We now present a couple of rules to illustrate the Houdini syntax and semantics. The following rule (chosen from a representative SRM ruleset), specifies that if the boss calls while the callee is in a meeting with a subordinate (and possibly others), the callee is *Available* to the boss (in this case represented as 4 on a scale of 1 to 5). The variable `meeting_with` is list-valued, and has an element-wise occurrence here. (The `min` function is used because, for example, some other meeting participant might be providing a different value for `availability`.)

Rule for meetings

```
rule: check_availability_for_boss
if ((caller_relationship == "Boss") && (?meeting_with = "Subordinate"))
then
   availability = min(availability, 4);    /* 4 = Available */
end
```

Note that conditions can operate on both atomic (*e.g.,* `caller_relationship`) as well as record and collection (*e.g.,* `?meeting_with`) variables – they can handle both element-wise occurences and aggregate operators over whole lists.

The above rule explicitly refers to values such as "Boss" and 4. As an alternative, assume now that a list-valued variable `interrupt_table` is holding a family of records, each record corresponding to a category of caller, a category of meeting participant, and an availability level for that combination. In this case the following rule can be used in place of the above rule and other rules analogous to it.

Rule for availability

```
rule: check_availability_for_all
if ((?interrupt_table.caller == caller_relationship) &&
    (?interrupt_table.interacting_with == ?meeting_with))
then
   availability = min(availability, ?interrupt_table.in_meeting_availability);
end
```

Importantly, list-valued variables in Houdini can be used to support capabilities such as white-listing and black-listing. Note that Houdini provides a generic framework to which a particular application (like the one above) adds domain knowledge to specify what data is needed and what rules make sense. The rules interpret the data.

Rule Semantics: The semantics for rule execution follows the typical approach for forward-chaining production systems. We present here only the details of rule execution when element-wise list variables are present.

DEFINITION (SEMANTICS WITH ELEMENT-WISE VARIABLES). Given a production-style rule r, let $prod(r) = \{v_i \mid 1 \leq i \leq n,\ v_i$ is a variable with one (or more) element-wise occurrences in $r\}$. The execution semantics of r are defined as: $\forall(e_1, e_2, ..., e_n) \in (L_1 \times L_2 \times ... \times L_n)$, evaluate r by using e_i as the value associated with each occurrence of $?v_i$, for $1 \leq i \leq n$, where L_i is the list of current members associated with variable v_i for each i, and $\times$ is the cross-product operator. □

In other words, for each tuple of elements, one from each of the L_i's, the rule condition is evaluated, and if the condition is true, the rule actions are executed in the context of the list elements being operated on.

Ruleset Acyclicity: While Houdini does support forward chaining of rules, it restricts the chaining to be acyclic. The specific notion of acyclicity currently used is defined as follows.

DEFINITION (RULESET ACYCLICITY). Given a ruleset S, let $rules(S) = \{r \mid r$ is a rule in $S\}$. Also, given a rule r, let (where 'v' ranges over variables)

$$def(r) = \{v \mid v \text{ is defined in an action of } r\}$$
$$use(r) = \{v \mid v \text{ is used in condition or RHS of any assignment in an action of } r\}$$
$$use_c(r) = \{v \mid v \text{ is used in the condition of } r\}$$

Let $G(S) = (V, E)$ be a graph defined on a ruleset S where $V = \{r \mid r \in rules(S)\}$ and $E = \{(r_i, r_j) \mid (i \neq j,$ and $def(r_i) \cap use(r_j) \neq \phi)$ or $(i = j,$ and $def(r_i) \cap use_c(r_i) \neq \phi)\}$. Then S is *acyclic iff* $G(S)$ is acyclic. □

Essentially, for ruleset S, we define a graph $G(S)$ where each node in the graph corresponds to a rule in the ruleset S, and there is a directed edge from node r_i to a different node r_j *iff* there is a variable defined in r_i which is used in r_j. Also, there is a self-edge on a node r_i *iff* there is a variable defined in r_i which is also used in the condition in r_i. We say that S is acyclic if there are no cycles in $G(S)$ (including no self-edges).

The acyclicity condition restricts the Houdini rules' expressive power, in contrast with, *e.g.*, general-purpose production system engines like ILOG Rules, CLIPS, OPS5 (see related work in Section 5). However, the decision to restrict to acyclic chaining is based on the focus of Houdini, namely to support reasonably rich policy management for service oriented programming, especially in the time-constrained context of web and converged services. We have built several converged applications with Houdini (including presence, SRM, and location-based services), and lack of recursion was not a problem for any of them. We thus feel it provides a good compromise between performance and functionality. We note that our notion of acyclicity is more restrictive than, but in the same general spirit of, the notion of stratified logic (or datalog) programs.

Conflict Resolution, Priority, and Acyclicity: Conflict resolution is determined by two-levels of ordering of rules in a ruleset. The primary ordering is dictated by the acyclicity restriction on a ruleset S, i.e., rules are evaluated according to a topological sorted order of the graph $G(S)$. The secondary ordering criteria is based on explicit rule priorities, if given (note that in the examples presented above, the optional `priority` keyword has been committed). If explicit priorities are not specified, priorities are assigned based on the order of rules in the rules definition section (rules specified later in the section have higher priority). This secondary ordering is applied to the primary ordering, as long as it still results in the rules being evaluated in *some* topological-sort order of $G(S)$.

Note that because of the acyclicity restriction, each rule is considered for execution at most once. For rules affecting a given single-valued variable A, we can say that the "highest priority rule wins", or more precisely, that if multiple rules have the effect of assigning a value to A, then the rule with highest priority that executes with true condition determines the ultimate value of A. An analogous semantics is given in the case of rules that assign a value to list-valued variables.

Note also that domain experts produce the rulesets, so only they need to understand the conflict resolution—end users will simply fill out forms with their preferences.

Modularity: As mentioned earlier, each ruleset that can be evaluated in response to a decision request has an associated input/output signature. The variables that do not belong to this signature are termed as *intermediate* variables. The use of intermediate variables with forward-chaining allows one to construct modular rulesets, where each module corresponds to the set of rules used to define an intermediate or target variable.

We illustrate this with the SRM service. Based on a callee's network activity, a rule (or set of rules) can infer his location; based on his location, his calendar and his recent device usage, another rule set can infer his activity and the devices he can be reached at; based on his activity and caller identity, a rule set can decide to (not) try to allow the callee to be reached. Each of these sub-decisions can be thought of as a *module* within the overall ruleset. The combination of intermediate variables and the acyclicity of Houdini rulesets implies that the family of modules associated with a ruleset can be arranged in a directed acyclic graph that represents the flow of decisioning. This modular structure makes it easier to specify and reason about complex rulesets.

Validity Checking: Houdini provides the ability to perform validity checking on rulesets being provisioned. Various levels of validity checking are performed in the following order. First, *syntax checking* is performed to ensure that the ruleset conforms to the rules language grammar. Next, *type checking* is performed to verify that variables are used according to their types (*i.e.,* boolean variables should not be added together).

Acyclicity checking is then performed to make sure that the ruleset is acyclic (and also to generate an appropriate rule ordering for evaluation). Finally, *data dependency checking* is performed to ensure that (taking the optimistic view that all rule conditions will be true at run-time), if the rules are evaluated according to the order generated during acyclicity checking, no variables will be used before being defined (unless they are input variables); moreover after all rules are evaluated, all output variables must have been defined. Note that this obviously need not be true during run-time, but it does help catch some invalid rulesets. Thus, only limited run-time checking is needed.

Self Provisioning As noted above, Houdini provides a framework for self-provisioning of preferences, described in detail in [14,15]. Briefly, that framework includes three layers: (1) A front end that presents a series of forms through which end-users can fill in blanks and mark check-boxes in order to express their preferences; (2) A family of relational tables and rule *templates* are associated with the forms; and (3) The user preferences are mapped into tuples for the relational tables and/or *concrete* rules constructed from the rule templates. Users can also be provided with an image of the overall flow of decisioning, based on the DAG corresponding to (all or some) of the intermediate and target variables that are inferred.

Different families of users (*e.g.,* office working, road warriors, field service technicians, students, home-makers) can be provided with different sets of provisioning forms. Different sets of forms can also be provided for "naive" users vs. "power" users. Importantly, all of the provisioning interfaces can be supported by the same underlying policy management infrastructure, *i.e.,* there is no need to re-compile the policy engine or services when modifying or extending the family of data values that preferences are based on. Experts produce the forms and write the corresponding rules. End users simply fill out intuitive forms as described in [14,15].

Toolkit-based Architecture: The Houdini implementation has been structured around a *toolkit* approach, where the toolkit provides a collection of C++ classes containing the core functionality of loading/parsing/executing rulesets, with the application-specific portions (scheduling of events/processes/threads, communication with internal/external components) being layered on top of the toolkit to create the complete application. The Houdini framework is also extensible, allowing additional types and functions to manipulate them to be incorporated easily (the functions can be incorporated either at compile- or run-time).

Applications that wish to interact with a rules engine can incorporate the Houdini toolkit into the application itself, and call the Houdini API methods as necessary. Conversely, different protocols (*e.g.,* SOAP, CORBA, etc.) can be layered very easily on top of the Houdini API to create a stand-alone rules engine that can interact with various clients. Indeed, interfaces for SOAP and the CORBA-based Parlay/OSA standard have already been created for Houdini, in addition to a more direct TCP/IP interface. There are plans for a SIP interface as well.

Performance: Preliminary performance results on a Sun UltraSPARC-IIe with 1GB of main memory for the Houdini engine that we have developed at Bell Labs show that Houdini can execute on the order of 35K to 40K rules per second for the SRM service, and can render decisions in under 3 milliseconds [14,15]. This performance is clearly within the acceptable range for customization of web- and converged-services. We expect that this performance is substantially better than rules engines supporting full production system rules (with cycles), because of the substantial data structures needed in connection with the RETE algorithm [8] and its descendants. More performance details can be found in our related work [14,15].

Work is underway on performance improvements for Houdini. Some particular areas we are focusing on include decision caching, data caching, rule caching, taking advantage of common rule structures, etc. We also expect further optimizations will be possible for specific application contexts, *e.g.,* for a web services host or a telephony service provider.

5 Related Work

There are several other technologies that are potential solutions for the requirements described in Section 3, but all are missing something important that our solution offers.

Hard-coded solutions: The simplest solution is to just write code that implements the user preferences, but that can be customized by reading data provided by end users (usually in the form of tables). For example, end users could specify their whereabouts by entering information into a table of days and times. This solution has several advantages. First, it does not need a system to execute any rules. Second, it is relatively easy to write an interface for users to enter the table data. However, this solution is not sufficiently flexible for our purposes. It does not allow the computation of different information or differing control flow for different kinds of users. In certain cases though (*e.g.,* packet routing applications where extreme performance is needed), hard-coding is the only way.

Decision trees: Another solution is to use a form of decision tree [21], where the decision tree uses branching conditions to determine the action to take. Decision trees can be quite general, but decision trees of any reasonable size are difficult for end users to create, as it is difficult to keep track of the context of internal nodes and, moreover, it is hard to determine the correct structure of the tree.

"Simple" rule formalisms: Yet another solution is to use a simpler rule formalism, such as the no-chaining rule formalism in the IETF standards [17]. In this rule formalism, the effect of running a rule is to trigger some action external to the rule system, thus preventing one rule from affecting the behavior of another. This potential solution is again too limited as it prevents the computation of intermediate information and using this in later rules, such as computing whereabouts and using this to determine call acceptability in our SRM examples. This "simple rule formalism" approach has been embraced by some Web preference languages such as P3P/APPEL [27], PICSRules [28], and more recently XACML [23]. However, those languages are primarily designed to address privacy issues, and thus have either restricted vocabulary for rule conditions and actions (*e.g.,* APPEL), or no chaining (*e.g.,* PICSRules, XACML), and are not designed to be general purpose personalization languages.

More powerful formalisms: It would also be possible to use a more-powerful rule formalism. Many systems for such rule formalisms exist, such as OPS5 [5], CLIPS [22],

ILOG [18]. We compare Houdini directly with ILOG (however, some of the arguments can be applied to the other systems as well).

The core of the ILOG Rules engine [18] consists of a fast and robust implementation of the RETE[8] algorithm, which is recognized as the fastest and most efficient algorithm for production style rules with cycles. The ILOG rule language supports a rich set of data types, permitting the use of (C++ or Java) objects on both sides of the rules. Object properties and methods (possibly with some side effects) can be invoked. ILOG rules execution consists of rules, stored in an *agenda*, which execute against objects, stored in a working memory. Rule execution may modify working memory objects, therefore new rules may become eligible for execution and thereby added to the agenda.

The problem with this style of rules is that as soon as cycles are allowed it becomes dramatically harder to write correct rule bases or to estimate run-time – crucial in real-time, converged services. This would be a particularly difficult problem to overcome in our situation, as the actual creation of the rule bases is done by end users, with developers only providing rule templates.

In Houdini there is also a working memory to hold the "context", or set of variables being accessed and manipulated by the ruleset execution. However, because of the restriction to acyclic rulesets, a variable is not used or read until all writes (and overwrites) to it have completed. As a result, the "agenda" in Houdini is much less dynamic than in ILOG; in particular, the sequencing of rules is computed by the acyclicity condition and can be determined in advance. This reduces the possibility of unexpected interactions between rules, simplifies debugging, and simplifies the Houdini internal execution algorithms considerably.

We believe that there is little benefit to cycles in rules in service customization, so we do not feel that paying the performance penalty for going to a more-powerful rule formalism is justified.

6 Conclusions

This paper's core observation is that intelligent e-services arising from the web services paradigm and the converged network will need rule-based customization. Further, for these applications, the typical IETF-style rules language is not sufficient; rather, a production-style language that supports chaining but not recursion is appropriate. More broadly, the paper identifies requirements on the policy infrastructure needed in the realm, and describes a framework and the high-performance Houdini system under development at Bell Labs, that satisfies these requirements. It also discusses privacy and provisioning aspects.

This paper raises several areas for further investigation; we mention three here. An obvious topic is further optimization of rules systems based on Houdini-style rules. Some natural places to look are pre-"compilation" and caching of rulesets, and exploiting commonality across rulesets. The trade-off between storing preferences in rules, or in tables and using rules to interpret the tables, should be explored. It will also be useful to develop techniques to avoid "unnecessary" testing of conditions based on (design-time or run-time) analysis of the rulesets (as done for the Houdini rules language [16]; note that it was referred to as the Vortex rules language in that paper).

Research on personalization has focused mainly on automated discovery of user profile and preference data. Important recent work (*e.g.*, [2]) has focused on using data mining to discover user preferences in the form of association rules (i.e., no chaining). If a Houdini-based language is adopted for specification of user preferences in web and converged services, then it would be useful to extend the techniques of that work, to discover rulesets over the richer rules language.

The current paper has focused largely on providing a single rules engine that is used by a single web service, where that service typically plays the role of coordinator of other web services. In a composite web service, several of the individual services may be policy-enabled, perhaps using the same rules paradigm or perhaps using different ones. In spite of this distribution and possible heterogeneity, end-users should be able to specify a single set of "global" preferences, that are mapped appropriately to the participant e-services. Preliminary work in this direction is found in [24,4,13].

Acknowledgements. The authors would like to thank Prasan Roy for fruitful discussions on this paper.

References

1. 3GPP. Generic User Profile, 2001. http://www.3gpp.org.
2. G. Adomavicius and A. Tuzhilin. User profiling in personalization applications through rule discovery and validation. In *Proc. Fifth ACM SIGKDD Intl. Conf. on Knowledge Discovery and Data Mining*, 1999.
3. Open Mobile Alliance. http://www.openmobilealliance.org.
4. X. Ao, N. Minsky, and T. D. Nguyen. A hierarchical policy specification language, and enforcement mechanism, for governing digitual enterprises. In *Proc. of IEEE 3rd Intl. Workshop on Policies for Distributed Systems and Networks (Policy2002)*, 2002.
5. L. Brownston, R. Farrell, E. Kant, and N. Martin. *Programming Expert Systems in OPS5: An Introduction to Rule-Based Programming*. Addison-Wesley, Reading Massachusetts, 1985.
6. V. Christophides, R. Hull, and A. Kumar. Querying and splicing of XML workflows. In *Proc. of Intl. Conf. on Cooperating Information Systems (CoopIS)*, 2001.
7. C. Clifton, I. Fundulaki, R. Hull, B. Kumar, D. Lieuwen, and A. Sahuguet. Privacy-enhanced data management for next-generation e-commerce. In *Proc. VLDB*, 2003. To appear.
8. C. L. Forgy. Rete: A Fast Algorithm for the Many Pattern/Many Object Pattern Match Problem. *Artificial Intelligence*, 19:17–37, 1982.
9. PAM Forum. Presence and availability forum home page. http://www.panforum.org/.
10. Apache Foundation. Module mod_rewrite URL Rewriting Engine. http://httpd.apache.org/docs/mod/mod_rewrite.html.
11. Parlay Group. The Parlay Group – specifications. http://www.parlay.org/specs/index.asp.
12. R. Hull, M. Benedikt, V. Christophides, and J. Su. E-services: A look behind the curtain. In *Proc. ACM Symp. on Principles of Database Systems (PODS)*, pages 1–14, 2003.
13. R. Hull, B. Kumar, and D. Lieuwen. Towards federated policy management. In *Proc. IEEE Policy 2003*, 2003.
14. R. Hull, B. Kumar, D. Lieuwen, P. Patel-Schneider, A. Sahuguet, S. Varadarajan, and A. Vyas. A policy-based system for personalized and privacy-conscious user data sharing. Technical report, Bell Labs, 2003. http://db.bell-labs.com/project/e-services-customization/personal-data-sharing-2003-TM.pdf.

15. R. Hull, B. Kumar, D. Lieuwen, P. Patel-Schneider, A. Sahuguet, S. Varadarajan, and A. Vyas. Enabling context-aware and privacy-conscious user data sharing. In *Proc. IEEE Intl. Conf. on Mobile Data Management*, 2004. To appear.
16. R. Hull, F. Llirbat, B. Kumar, G. Zhou, G. Dong, and J. Su. Optimization techniques for data-intensive decision flows. In *Proc. IEEE Intl. Conf. on Data Engineering*, 2000.
17. IETF. Policy Framework, 2001. http://www.ietf.org/html.charters/policy-charter.html.
18. ILOG. ILOG Rules. http://www.ilog.com.
19. iMerge Enhanced Business Services (EBS). http://www.agcs.com/aboutv2/iMergeEBS/.
20. Liberty Alliance. http://www.projectliberty.org.
21. Tom Mitchell. Decision tree learning. In Tom Mitchell, editor, *Machine Learning*, pages 52–78. McGraw-Hill, 1997.
22. NASA. CLIPS. http://www.ghg.net/clips/CLIPS.html.
23. OASIS. XML Access Control Language. http://www.oasis-open.org/committees/xacml.
24. L. Pearlman, I. Foster, V. Welch, C. Kesselman, and S. Tuecke. A community authorization service for group collaboration. In *Proc. of IEEE 3rd Intl. Workshop on Policies for Distributed Systems and Networks (Policy2002)*, 2002.
25. A. Sahuguet, R. Hull, D. Lieuwen, and M. Xiong. Enter Once, Share Everywhere: User Profile Management in Converged Networks. In *Proc. Conf. on Innovative Database Research(CIDR)*, January 2003.
26. Appium Technologies. Fuzion-UC: Unified communications, October 1 2002. http://www.appium.com/pdf/fuzion_uc.pdf.
27. W3C. A P3P Preference Exchange Language (APPEL). http://www.w3.org/TR/P3P-preferences.
28. W3C. PICSRules. http://www.w3.org/TR/REC-PICSRules.
29. W3C. Platform for Internet Content Selection (PICS). http://www.w3.org/PICS.
30. W3C. Platform for Privacy Preferences Project (P3P). http://www.w3.org/TR/P3P.

VINCA – A Visual and Personalized Business-Level Composition Language for Chaining Web-Based Services

Yanbo Han[1], Hui Geng[1], Houfu Li[1], Jinhua Xiong[1], Gang Li[1], Bernhard Holtkamp[2], Rüdiger Gartmann[2], Roland Wagner[2], and Norbert Weissenberg[2]

[1]Institute of Computing Technology, Chinese Academy of Sciences, 100080, Beijing, China
[2]Fraunhofer Institute for Software and Systems Engineering, 44227, Dortmund, Germany
{yhan,genghui,lhfsday,xjh,gangli}@software.ict.ac.cn

Abstract. The paper presents a service composition language called VINCA, which differs from many existing ones in its emphasis on enabling business users to visually "program" from business view-point their personalized applications on the basis of Web-based services. VINCA embodies an integrated approach to mediating between diverse, rapidly changing user requirements and composites of individual services scattered over the Internet. The approach is targeted at application scenarios that require Web-based services be quickly assembled by non-computer professionals to fulfill certain spontaneous requirements. VINCA is developed within a real-world project for developing a service mediation platform for the Olympic Games Beijing 2008, on which an effective information system providing personalized and one-stop information services to the general public, should be based. In this paper, we introduce the main features and design rationales of VINCA with a scenario, and also discuss its implementation and application.

Keywords: Business-level service composition, Semantic Web services, On-demand and just-in-time application construction

1 Introduction

The Internet and the World-Wide Web opened up a new horizon for us to acquire information and also aroused our appetite for a more flexible and scalable computing infrastructure for building up cross-organizational information systems. In this connection, many efforts have in the past years been made on developing technologies and platforms for integrating autonomous, heterogeneous and Web-based services [Casa01][Sing01][Weis01]. The service-oriented technologies that are currently highlighted by the Web Service architecture are among the prominent outcomes. Web-based services for a wide range of purposes are beginning to

The research work is supported by the National Natural Science Foundation of China under Grant No. 60173018, the Key Scientific and Technological Program for the Tenth Five-Year Plan of China under Grant No. 2001BA904B07 and German Ministry of Research and Education under Grant No. 01AK055

M.E. Orlowska et al. (Eds.): ICSOC 2003, LNCS 2910, pp. 165–177, 2003.

proliferate. Service composition will play an essential role in making full use of these services as well as the Internet infrastructure, and a number of composition languages have been proposed [Andr03][Casa01][Kici01][Picc02]. Most of these languages were developed for software professionals and targeted at developing large-scale E-business applications and the like.

Meanwhile, we can also observe the trend towards user-centric and just-in-time application construction. Instead of constructing monolithic and wholly packed applications for business users, software professionals will be requested to concentrate more on establishing IT infrastructure and enabling environments, and to leave the job of configuring individual applications to business users in order to better cope with the diversity of user requirements and the uncertainty of Web-based resources. To date, there exists a wider spectrum of application scenarios that require Web-based services be quickly assembled and coordinated by non-computer professionals to fulfill certain spontaneous requirements. Examples of such application scenarios include dynamic supply chain management, handling of city emergency, and management of massive public events. In fact, we are undertaking a real-world project that bears exactly the same characteristics. The project is called FLAME2008, which is abbreviated from *A Flexible Semantic Web Service Management Environment for the Olympic Games Beijing 2008* [Holt03]. It is a Sino-German joint effort for developing a service mediation platform for the Olympic Games Beijing 2008, on which an effective information system providing personalised and one-stop information services to the general public, should be based. Adopting the service-oriented paradigm, we designed the service integration platform with a novel integrated approach called CAFISE [Han03] to mediating between diverse, rapidly changing user requirements and composites of individual services scattered over the Internet. A central element of CAFISE is the user-centric, business-level service composition language – VINCA, shortened from *A Visual and Personalized Business-level Composition Language for Chaining Web-based Services.*

The paper is organized as follows: Section 2 gives a brief overview of FLAME2008 and CAFISE to make clear the context of VINCA, and then discusses the business-end programming metaphor underlining the language. Section 3 describes the language and its enabling environment. A simplified application scenario is examined to evaluate the design of VINCA. Section 4 sums up with several concluding remarks.

2 Context and Positioning of VINCA

As mentioned earlier, the development of VINCA is driven by a set of practical requirements. To better explain the design rationales of the language, let us first get an overview of FLAME2008 project and the CAFISE approach. Thereafter, in line with the business-end programming metaphor, we discuss the positioning and design considerations of VINCA.

2.1 FLAME2008

As shown in Fig.2.1, FLAME2008 is to mediate between personalized requirements of different user groups (reporters, spectators, organizers, athletes, etc.) through different channels (stationary information kiosks, mobile devices, etc.), and a large pool of services provided by various parties (organizers, governmental organizations, profit-oriented service providers, etc.). Fig.2.2 goes further to illustrate the conceptual architecture of FLAME2008. Here, individual user requirements are resolved as FLAME2008-based applications, which are specific assemblies of Web-based services and are formed directly by business users in an easy and just-in-time manner. The major components shown in Fig.2.2 are to cover the following key aspects:

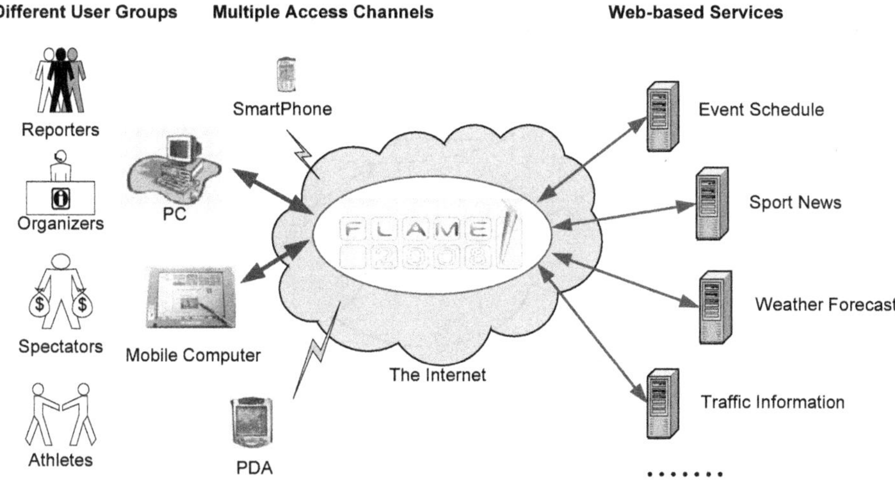

Fig. 2.1. Objectives of FLAME2008

Semantic Service Organization

In FLAME2008, Web-based services are at present based on Web Services. Although Web Service standards provide a basic means to encapsulate and register Web-based services, service registration alone is not enough to get all registered resources well organized for different purposes. FLAME2008 provides a mechanism to enable personalized organization of services on semantic level. The semantic descriptions are used for composing and matching services. As a basis for service semantics description we use ontologies. A more detailed discussion of the approach can be found in [Weis03]. Based on a set of given criteria including user context, services can be logically grouped into service communities with multiple layers. Business-oriented services can then be extracted from service communities.

Business-level Service Composition

For each eligible user, FLAME2008 manages a business-oriented logic view of all Web-based services made available to him or her according to his/her user context. The user can browse the resources and configure them according to their business needs. Through the business-end programming environment, they only need, based on predefined modeling elements and rules, to drag and configure the symbols representing services at different levels of granularity to express their business requirements. Since this issue is the main point of discussion in the paper, a separate section is devoted to it subsequently.

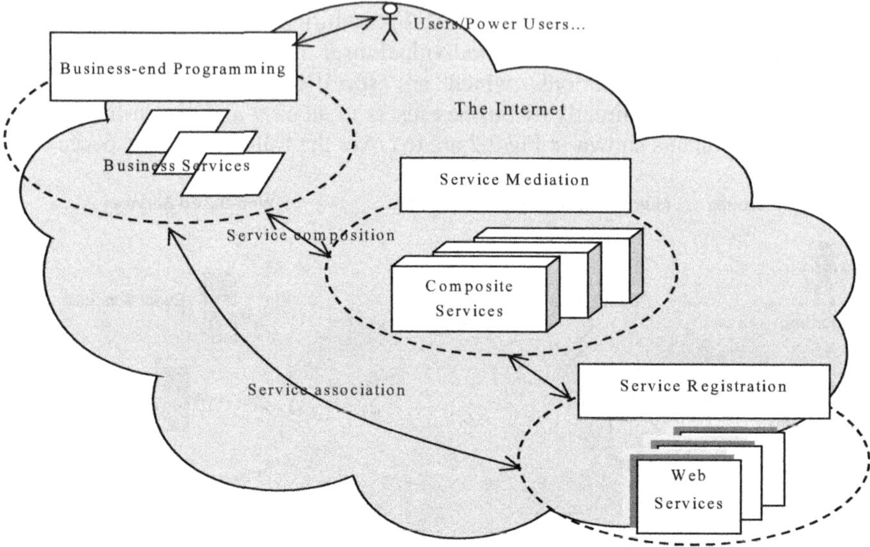

Fig. 2.2. Conceptual Architecture of FLAME2008

Service Mediation

With the help of ontology-based descriptions of service semantics, user demands that are captured with the business-level specifications are either matched directly with service offerings or related to a composition of a number of service offerings. VINCA is the language we developed for the business-level specifications. For the operational level composition of Web services, a subset of the standard Business Process Execution Language for Web Services - BPEL4WS [Andr03] is used. The mapping between our business-level models and BPEL4WS specifications is realized by the FLAME2008 platform. Derived from application scenarios that reflect a typical usage of a targeted user group, composition patterns can be predefined and used as a basis for individual cases. Composition of services can be performed either automatically based on a full-fledged composition pattern and related ontological descriptions or can be defined manually with the business-end programming environment.

2.2 The Business-End Programming Metaphor

The business-end programming metaphor advocates that business-level service composition should not be considered in computer programming logic as we usually do. We call the process, with which a business user configures his or her applications, business-end programming. To stress user involvement, we coined the term – power user. A power user is any business user who knows little about software programming but is capable of configuring his businesses with tool support. FLAME2008 aims at supporting power users in (re)configuring their service-based applications on their demand. Instead of directly introducing object-oriented concepts and technologies into a business domain as in [Sing01], our approach proposes to build an integrated model to cover business issues and software issues at the same time.

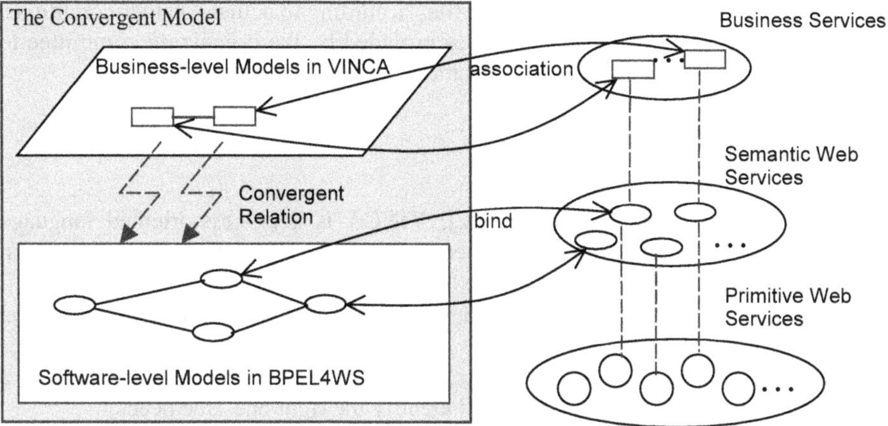

Fig. 2.3. The CAFISE Convergent Model

Highlight of the CAFISE approach is a convergent model - the CAFISE model, which is a grand model covering business issues and software issues simultaneously [Han03]. As shown in Fig.2.3, a CAFISE model has three related parts: a business-level model, a software-level model and a convergent relation as glue. Expressed by VINCA, business-level models are designed to reflect business requirements with a minimum set of business-end programming concepts and mechanisms, which are easy for a business user to understand and master. A business user can (re)configure his/her applications by building or editing business-level models. Software-level models deal with compositions of Web Services. CAFISE narrows the gap between the two levels with a convergent relation. The convergent relation helps to relate or map simple and intuitive business-level elements into more concrete and executable elements at software level.

3 Design, Implementation, and Application of VINCA

3.1 A Simplified Application Scenario

To better explain how VINCA works, the following imaginary example is used for subsequent discussions: In 2008, various parties will provide a large variety of information services for public uses, and VINCA is to help different groups of users to define their personalized "applications". Among the users is Mr. John Bull, a sport journalist. He is going to write a series of reports for his sport magazine during the Olympic Games. In his spare time, he also plans to visit some famous sights and meet some acquainted peers coming from other countries. Before he leaves for Beijing, he can use the FLAME2008-based information system to schedule his activities and enjoy the multitude of services. For a simplified example, in addition to making some online reservations, he orders his personalized weather information service and can arrange his meetings and sightseeing activities according to actual weather conditions. He can also subscribe information services provided by the organizing committee to periodically get the latest schedule information of press conferences.

3.2 Language Design

Like some other efforts [Krit01][Shen02], VINCA is a process-oriented language designed for visually capturing user's needs at a high abstraction level. Based on BPEL4WS, VINCA intends to take a step further towards:

- Adding semantic descriptions to Web services so that they can be composed at business level more easily.
- Organizing semantic Web services rationally into business services so that a business user can easily understand and identify the right ones she needs.
- Letting business users to visually configure business services with easy-to-use operations like drag-and-drop and letting the system to take over related tedious work of interconnecting Web services.
- Defining and making use of user context information so that users get more accurate and personalized information provided.
- Defining interaction channels and user interfaces flexibly.

In the context of the FLAME2008 project, the first working version of VINCA reported in the paper is proposed and implemented, answering partly the above-stated questions. VINCA deals with the following four aspects: service conglomeration, process specification, context specification and interaction specification. Surrounding VINCA process specifications, the other three components provide necessary support. In the subsequent parts, we informally describe these components.

3.2.1 Service Conglomeration

In FLAME2008, different users may "see" different sub-sets of all available resources in terms of her user context including preferences and privileges. As illustrated on the right side of Fig.2.3 shown above, FLAME2008 has three abstraction layers and provides a mechanism called service community [Cafi02] for organizing Web-based services. Each service community corresponds to an organized set of services with domain-specific semantics. Through this mechanism we get a uniform view of Web-based services and their semantics. Semantic services are attributed by a list of semantic descriptions, each of which refers to an ontology concept shared by all involved parties [Weis03]. In a business domain, services are often interrelated with each other in some common patterns. In a service community, a set of supplementary rules can be defined for member services to capture common patterns of interrelationship to improve efficiency or ensure correctness.

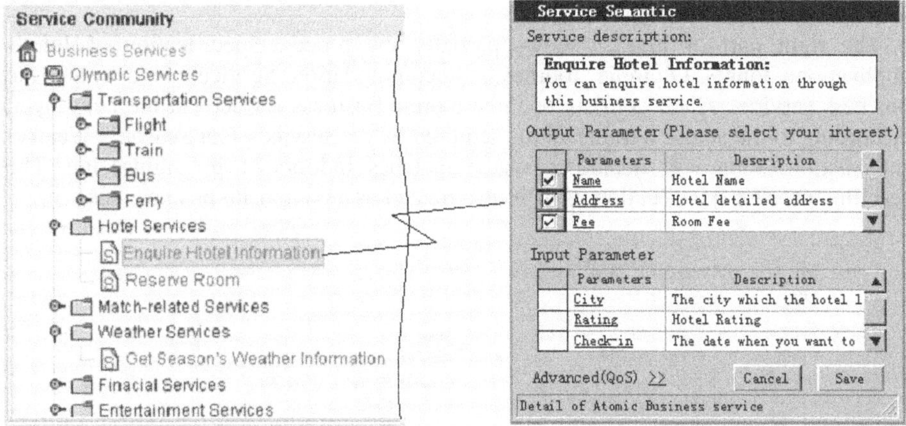

Fig. 3.1. Visualization of Business Services

As Fig.3.1 shows, business services are organized in terms of an application-specific classification for the purpose of navigation. In addition to its semantic description, a business service visually exposes to users a list of input and output parameters that are all in character form with separate type information. When composing services, users can either match the output and input parameters by drag-and-drop corresponding icons or specify certain parameter as "runtime decision". In the second case, the system will interact with users to acquire information at runtime. Each business service has a separate panel for specifying service qualities. This functionality is designed for more advanced users to specify her QoS requirements, such as cost, time of response and so on. Besides normal business services, there are composite business services that are pre-defined processes and can be used as if it were a normal business service. FLAME2008 cares about its updates in case its constituent member changes.

3.2.2 Process Specification

A VINCA process specification represents business logic from user's viewpoints. The left part of Fig.3.2 shows the graphical elements of VINCA process. For defining business-level processes, we adopt a Windows-Explorer-alike style. A node can be a service node or a control node, presenting a business service (either atomic or composite) or a control element expressing some control logic. Service nodes in the same column are ordered from top to bottom for activation. Composite service nodes can be unfolded into columns at the next layer, arranged from the left to the right. In order to specify the complete business logic, VINCA employs four kinds of control nodes linking business services: sequential link, concurrent link, decision point and repeat. Service nodes following a sequence link are ordered sequentially from top to bottom for activation. Sequential link is the default linkage mode between services. Service nodes following a concurrent link can be invoked in parallel. Decision point is associated with a condition expression and determines which one(s) of the following nodes can be activated. The control node - repeat – is also associated with a condition and the service nodes following it will be invoked repeatedly until the associated condition is satisfied.

The right part of Fig.3.2 shows partially the process specification of John's application: John's Olympic Journey. "Accommodation Service" is a composite business service, which consists of three atomic business services at the next layer. According to the actual weather status acquired by the service - Get Season's Weather Information, John will decide to watch matches indoors or go sightseeing. The resulting process specification itself is also treated as a composite business service.

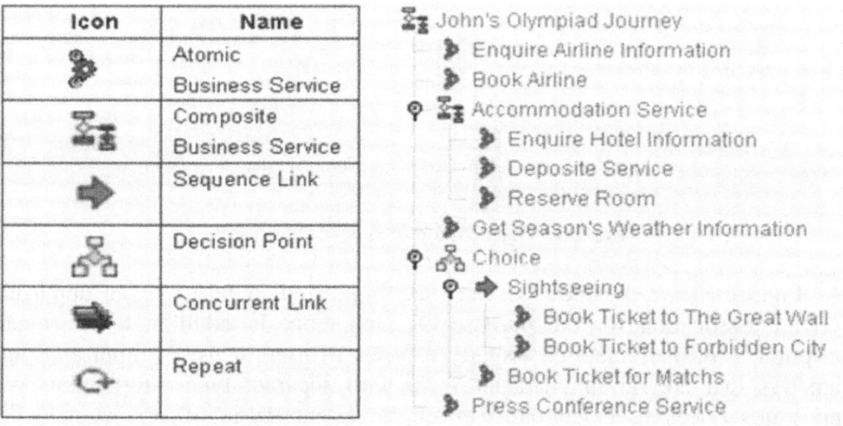

Icon	Name
	Atomic Business Service
	Composite Business Service
	Sequence Link
	Decision Point
	Concurrent Link
	Repeat

Fig. 3.2. A Snippet of VINCA Process Specification

3.2.3 Context Specification

One of the most important objectives of VINCA is to move as much as possible the complexity of a business-level specification to FLAME2008. Since a business user pays more attention to what a service does in their business terms, rather than how certain functionality is achieved or which service does the job, we need to hide all the details on the one side, and to supplement enough information for the step-wise refinement and interpretation on the other side. Thus, we have to define an effective context for the business-end programming environment. In fact, context-aware applications are gaining momentum due to the flexibility and extra functionality that context information brings [Brow97][Abow00]. User context is integrated into VINCA and serves as a reference in forming service communities and as a sort of implicit input in defining and executing a VINCA process specification. One VINCA process specification may associate with many context specifications, each of which is associated with a user.

In VINCA, user context is represented and organized in hierarchical, tree-like structure. In the upper-right corner of Fig.3.3, an exemplary user context of John is given: his information is organized in several layers. Internally, user context is expressed in XML. A user context consists of basic information, user preferences, and constraints such as time and location. Users may have multiple preference categories at the same time. Each preference category represents a category of interests. The categories share the same semantic infrastructure of VINCA service communities. The domain attribute can be linked to business service, and the keyword and value in item can be used to specify the non-functional requirements for the business service. Through these attributes (domain, keyword, value), the semantic of basic information or user preferences can be specified, similar to the semantic mechanism of service community. A user context may dynamically include new categories of preference when user interests change.

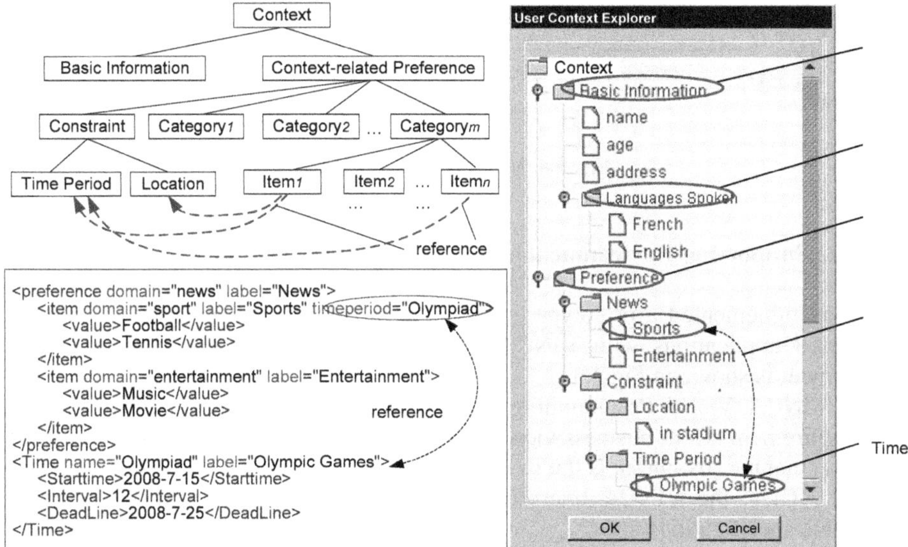

Fig. 3.3. Illustration of a User Context

3.2.4 Interaction Specification

Today, users have multiple choices to interact with an information system. In our scenario, John may interact with FLAME2008 using different devices such as ordinary desktop explorer, PDA, and smart phones in her preferred Also, interaction interfaces for individual services need to be defined. In VINCA, we introduce Interaction specification to deal with the above-mentioned problems. An Interaction specification describes the way of service delivery, and one may also define templates for user interactions.

In VINCA, Interaction specification consists three orthogonal parts: Channel, Template and Mode. Channel defines the terminal or client via which users interact with business application. A channel may be a kind of device, such as Personal Computer, Smart Phone or PDA, or a kind of client software, for instance Email client Outlook. Template specifies formats for capturing or delivering information. Mode describes how users will get or send information, it may be in a pull mode or a push mode. At present, FLAME2008 supports three kinds of interaction channels (PC Internet Browser, PDA Browser and Smart Phone Browser). Fig.3.4 gives an example of a VINCA interaction specification. The message exchanged between users and services is also illustrated here. The same message will be delivered to different channels in suitable formats, such as cHtml, HTML and WML, according to the interaction specification, resulting different effects.

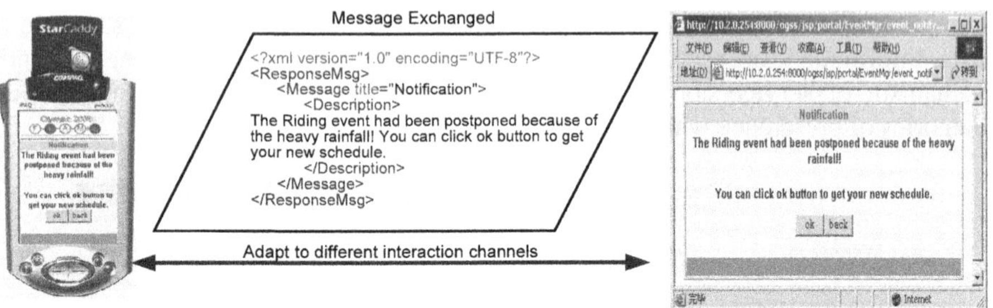

Fig. 3.4. Multiple Access Channels

3.3 The Supporting Environment of VINCA

We have implemented a prototype environment to support power users in building Web-based applications with VINCA. The system architecture of the supporting environment is shown in Fig.3.5.

The VINCA Visual Programming Environment enables power users to express their requirements from business viewpoint in a WYSIWYG (What You See Is What You Get) manner. Its output is the so-called VINCA program – a set of specifications in XML. Then, the VINCA Interpreter will transform them into BPEL4WS-alike executable specifications.

The BPEL4WS-based Running Environment is responsible for chaining Web-based services at operational level, and binding and invoking individual services. It consists of an event manager, an application scheduler, a location manager, a time manager and a process engine [Holt03].

3.4 Application

Fig.3.6 is a snapshot of a power user's working interface supported by the business-end programming environment. It is based on the simplified scenario discussed in Section 3.1. John or his secretary can take the role of a power user and sketch his schedule during the Olympic Games. When he arrives at Beijing, his application is triggered. Whenever he changes his mind or his predefined schedule is influenced by some unexpected factors, John can reconstruct his personal application in a just-in-time manner through directly composing business services made available to him through the service community.

A third-party agent, such as the Olympiad organizing committee, can define some common-used processes as value-added composite services (see the upper-right corner of Fig.3.6). Since these pre-defined composite services normally cannot 100-percent satisfy diverse requirements of different users; John as a power user can customize and extend his personalized service composite based on pre-defined composite services as well as basic business services available to him. The customized process is shown in the lower part of Fig.3.6.

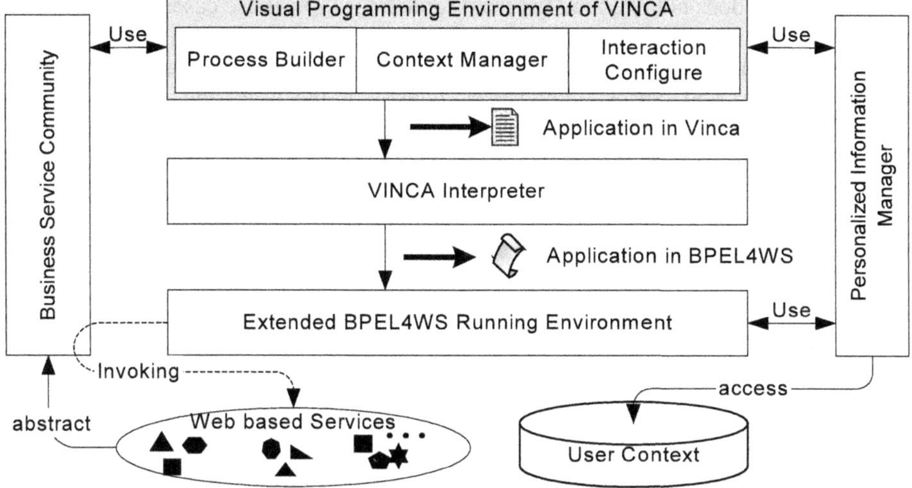

Fig. 3.5. The Supporting Environment of VINCA

Using the running example, we sum up how the VINCA-based approach works with the following major steps:

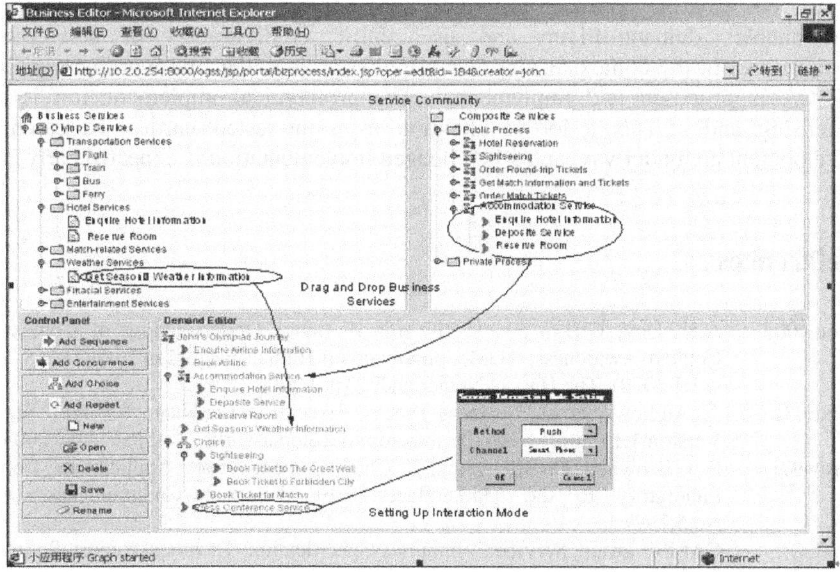

Fig. 3.6. Snap-shot of VINCA Programming Environment

Setting up a business program skeleton. The VINCA programming environment provides an intuitive way to use potential templates for setting up business program skeletons. Templates are actually also service composites maintained by the system and organized according to domain-specific classifications. With the help of templates, John does not need to start from scratch for typical use cases.
Checking and locating appropriate business services. For each power user, the VINCA programming environment filters out all available business services in terms of the privileges and corresponding user context of the user, and organizes them according to a domain-specific classification.
Completing the business program. After locating his desired services, John can drag and drop these services into the Business Program area, and use the control elements listed on the left side to glue them together. John can either explicitly specify the input-output relationships of interrelated services or leave them to be determined at runtime.
Defining the interaction modes. After getting the business program, John configures the interaction mode for his application. Then he can get the expected results in the way he defined in the interaction specification.

4 Conclusion

The central idea of the reported research is to let users "see" all the network-based resources available to them and "program" their personalized applications by configuring their resources in a straightforward manner using business-related concepts only. Based on the integrated model that relates some key elements of a business-level design issues and their counterparts in the software domain in a convergent way, our approach promotes the metaphor of business-end programming and enables demand-driven and user-centric configuration of service-based applications. In the context of the FLAME2008 project, the first working version of VINCA is proposed and implemented. The prototypical implementation is quite promising and attracts a lot of attention from interested parties. Research and development are underway, and a full-fledged implementation is expected early 2005.

References

[Abow00] A.K. Dey, G.D. Abowd, Towards A Better Understanding of Context and Context-Awareness, ACM Conference on Human Factors in Computer Systems (CHI 2000), The Hague, Netherlands, April 2000

[Andr03] T. Andrews, et al, Business Process Execution Language for Web Services Version 1.1, http://www-106.ibm.com/developerworks /ws-bpel/, May 2003

[Brow97] P. J. Brown, J. D. Bovey, and X. Chen, Context-Aware Applications: from the Laboratory to the Marketplace, IEEE Personal Communications,Vol.4, No.5,1997

[Cafi02] CAFISE group, Service Community Specification, Technical Report, Software Division, ICT of CAS, December 2002

[Casa01] F. Casati, M. Sayal, M. Shan, Developing E-Services for Composing E-Services, Advanced Information Systems Engineering: 13th International Conference, CAiSE 2001, Interlaken, Switzerland, June 4–8, 2001

[Han03] Y. Han, et al, CAFISE: An Approach Enabling On-Demand Configuration of Service Grid Applications, Journal of Computer Science and Technology, Vol.18, No.4, 2003

[Holt03] B. Holtkamp, R. Gartmann, Y. Han, FLAME2008-Personalized Web Services for the Olympic Games 2008 in Beijing, Proceedings of eChallenges 2003, Bologna, Italy, Oct. 2003 (to appear)

[Kici01] E. Kiciman, L.L. Melloul, A. Fox, Towards Zero-Code Service Composition, Proceedings of the Eighth Workshop in Hot Topics in Operating Systems (HotOS VIII), 2001

[Krit01] R. Krithivasan, A. Helal, BizBuilder- An e-Services Framework Targeted for Internet Workflow, Proceedings of the third Workshop on Technologies for E-Services (Tes'01), Springer lecture notes in Computer Science series, Vol.2193

[Picc02] G. Piccinelli, S. L. Williams, Workflow: A Language for Composing Web Services, Second International Workshop on Composition Languages In conjunction with 16th European Conference on Object-Oriented Programming (ECOOP), Málaga, Spain June 11, 2002

[Shen02] Q. Sheng, B.Benatallah, M.Dumas, E. Mak, SELF-SERV: A Platform for Rapid Composition of Web Services in a Peer-to-Peer Environment, VLDB 2002

[Sing01] M. P. Singh, Physics of Service Composition, IEEE Internet Computing, Vol.5, No.3, May/June 2001

[Weis01] J. B. Weissman, B. Lee. The Service Grid: Supporting Scalable Heterogeneous Services in Wide-Area Networks, Proceedings of Symposium on Applications and the Internet, January 2001

[Weis03] N.Weissenberg, R.Gartmann, An Ontology Architecture for Semantic Geo Services for Olympia 2008, in: IfGIprints 18, Proc. GI-Tage , Münster, June, 2003

Stepwise Refinable Service Descriptions: Adapting DAML-S to Staged Service Trading*

Michael Klein, Birgitta König-Ries, and Philipp Obreiter

Institute for Program Structures and Data Organization
Universität Karlsruhe
D-76128 Karlsruhe, Germany
{kleinm,koenig,obreiter}@ipd.uni-karlsruhe.de
http://www.ipd.uni-karlsruhe.de/DIANE/en

Abstract. In order for service-oriented architectures to become successful, powerful mechanisms are needed that allow service requestors to find service offerers that are able to provide the services they need. Typically, this service trading needs to be executed in several stages as the offer descriptions are not complete in most cases and different parameters have to be supplemented by the service requestor and offerer alternately. Unfortunately, existing service description languages (like DAML-S) treat service discovery as a one shot activity rather than as a process and accordingly do not support this stepwise refinement. Therefore, in this paper, we introduce the concept of partially instantiated service descriptions containing different types of variables which are instantiated successively, thereby mirroring the progress in a trading process. Moreover, we present possibilities how to integrate these concepts into DAML-S syntactically.

1 Introduction

In distributed environments, services offer an important possibility to enable cooperation among the participating devices. On the one hand, members can offer their resources as services and on the other hand, they can use the functionalities offered by other members in order to enable complex applications. When regarding typical distributed service-oriented systems like internet-based web services or services in peer-to-peer or ad hoc networks, we notice what they have in common is the fact that the participating devices are loosely coupled, only. In these environments, like on a public marketplace, services are traded, i.e. service offerers publish a description of their service, which are in turn searched by potential service users.

At first glance, this trading seems to be comparable to "normal" internet searches, e.g., for certain documents. However, when one takes a closer look, it becomes obvious that indeed this is *not* the case. Typically, service offers are

* This work is partially funded by the German Research Community (DFG) in context of the priority program (SPP) no. 1140.

M.E. Orlowska et al. (Eds.): ICSOC 2003, LNCS 2910, pp. 178–193, 2003.

not fixed descriptions of all execution details, but contain different categories of variables which have to be instantiated in subsequent steps of the service negotiation before the service can be executed properly. Consider, e.g., a printing service: The description has to be made in a generic way, i.e. leaving space for a user to specify the resolution and color type of the printout as well as the document he wants to have printed. Moreover, the service offerer cannot provide quality of service parameters like the time when printing will finish without knowing the size and format of the document[1].

Unfortunately, existing service description languages do not support incomplete service descriptions which can be successively completed in further steps. Therefore, in this paper, we present a novel approach to service trading which takes into consideration that service trading is an interactive process rather than a one-shot activity. The approach is mainly based on DAML-S [1] and additional service ontologies that have been developed in our research project DIANE (see [2,3]).

In Section 2, we will first analyze existing service description languages and shoe that most of them are not capable of accurately describing a configurable service. Therefore, we will examine typical stages of service trading in Section 3 using the printer example from above. Based on these deliberations, we will derive a generic state oriented service description language which describes the initial and resulting state of the service including fixed and variable parts. Each of these variable parts is expressed by a variable of a certain category exactly defining who has to instantiate it and when. It will turn out that the variables will not always be freely instantiatable and independent of one another. Therefore, we formalize instantiation restrictions for these variables in a next step in Section 4. Finally, in Section 5, we show how the approach could be integrated into DAML-S using a special valueless RDF construct. The papers ends with a conclusion and an outlook to future work in Section 6.

2 Related Work

In this section, we want to examine existing service description languages. Besides languages that are explicitly denoted to describe *services*, we also want to take a look at languages to describe methods and operation of *components* in a middleware environment (sometimes also called *component description languages*). Typically, these component services have a finer granularity than common web services, are often developed for a non-human use, and seldom implement a self-contained action (see [4]). In the following, we will refer to these component operations as *services*, too, and also denote their descriptions as *service descriptions*.

The most frequently used languages are **message oriented service description languages**. They try to describe a service by explaining the values that are entering and leaving the black box service (see Figure 1a). If the service is realized by methods of an object, this can be achieved by exporting the

[1] We will take a more detailed look at this printer example in Section 3.2.

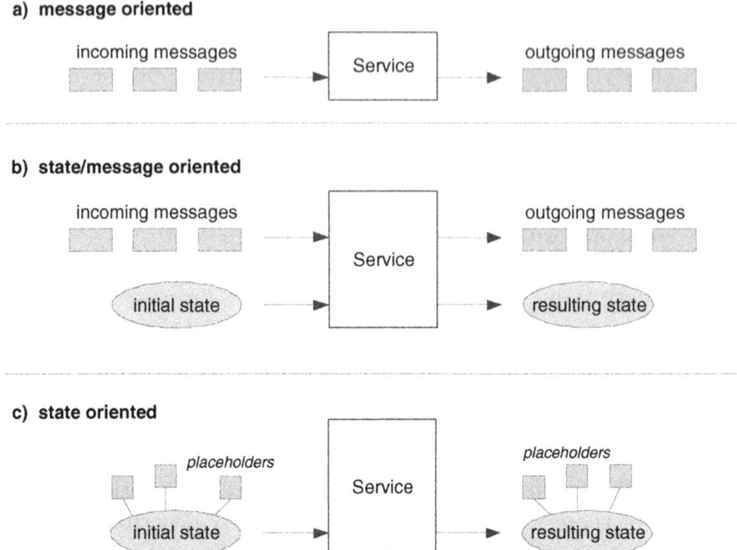

Fig. 1. Different types of service description languages: (a) Message oriented languages try to describe services by their incoming and outgoing data, (b) state/message oriented languages additionally express the functional semantics by describing the initial and resulting state, whereas (c) purely state oriented languages also omit the messages in favor of configurable placeholders in the state description.

interface of the class, which defines the ingoing method parameters as well as the outgoing method result. Well known *interface de nition languages* (IDL) are used in CORBA (as OMG IDL [5] or Java IDL [6]), Microsoft's RPC, COM and DCOM (as Microsoft IDL or MIDL [7]), in the area of web services (as Web IDL [8]) and also Java RMI [9], Jini [10] or Enterprise Java Beans [11] (as standard Java interfaces). On the other hand, languages like WSDL [12], e-Speak (used within Hewlett Packard's Web Services Platform [13]), the Collaboration Protocol Profile from ebXML [14] and IBM's Network Accessible Service Specification Language (NASSL) [15] more clearly point out the messages that enter and leave the service.

However, these message centered description languages suffer from one severe drawback: The semantics of the service is left open, i.e. the description leaves unspecified how inputs and outputs are connected and what side effects are performed. This functional semantics can only be guessed by a human user from the operation's name or a textual description. Because of their severe problems with respect to automatic service trading, we will not consider these languages any further.

This drawback is removed in **state/message oriented service description languages**. In addition to the flow of information, they try to capture the functional semantics by describing the state of the world before and after successful service execution (see Figure 1b). This can be achieved by the use of state ontologies like in DAML-S [1] (with extensions from [3]), OWL-S [16], and the Interagent Communication Language (ICL) from the Open Agent Architecture [17].

However, this mixed description consisting of message parts and state parts is problematic: First, the influence of the parameters stemming from the exchanged messages on the involved states is left open and therefore unclear[2]. Second, it is unclear when the messages between service requestor and executor have to be sent. Generally, the problem arises from the fact that in these descriptions the abstract service representation is intermixed with a concrete execution realization (i.e. by sending messages). On the other hand, the necessary description of the variable parts of the state is removed from their description and can only be guessed in the description of the exchanged messages. Other approaches try to capture the transition of states more accurately with the help of high level logical programming languages like Golog [18] or Abstract State Machines [19]. However, this leads to an non-declarative, but imperative description of the service action, which prevents a useful comparison with a service request.

As a consequence, the description of messages should be avoided in service description all together, which leads to purely **state oriented service description languages**. Here, the description of the states contains fixed parts, i.e. parts that are completely defined before service trading starts, as well as variable parts, i.e. placeholders which represent values that have to be negotiated before service execution can start (see Figure 1c). Similar ideas are included in LARKS [20], a language to describe agent capabilities. However, the process of correctly filling these values remains unclear. It turns out that each placeholder should be tagged with a label denoting by whom, when and how it should be filled in order to more clearly specify the process that is necessary to configure and execute this service. Nevertheless, the technical details of this configuration process (like the format of exchanged messages etc.) should be left open as they can be derived from the placeholders automatically. As the goal of this paper is to find a service description language for staged service trading, we will introduce a generic state oriented service description language by introducing the concept of states that are configurable with the help of variables and show how these ideas could be syntactically included into DAML-S.

3 The Process

As pointed out above, in contrast to simple internet or information retrieval searches, service trading is a complex, interactive process. In this section, we take a closer look at this process, its different stages, and their respective requirements.

[2] In DAML-S/OWL-S, these connections have to be explicitly listed in a separat part of the description, the so called *Service Model*, which normally is not taken into consideration when matching services within the phase of service trading.

3.1 General Trading Process and Variable Categories

In order to use a service in a loosely coupled, distributed environment, services have to be explicitly announced by their offerer (Stage 1). After that, from a client's point of view, the following three phases (consisting of six stages) can be noticed:

Phase I – Search
Sending a service request (Stage 2) and gathering service advertisements (Stage 3).

Phase II – Estimate
Requesting (Stage 4) and comparing estimates (Stage 5).

Phase III – Execution
Choosing a service (Stage 6) and receiving its results (Stage 7).

Typically, the service advertisements gathered in Phase I are not yet complete as different kinds of parameters are still missing. Therefore, in Phases II and III, the advertisements are successively specialized by instantiating these variables. We denote variables that are used within Phase II *estimate variables* and mark them with index e. Variables used in Phase III are called *execution variables* and are marked with an x. Furthermore, we distinguish variables based on the party that has to instantiate it. Variables that need to be instantiated by the client are called `IN` variables, the ones that are instantiated by the server are called `OUT` variables. To sum up, we differentiate between four *categories* of variables: $\texttt{IN}_e$, $\texttt{OUT}_e$, $\texttt{IN}_x$, and $\texttt{OUT}_x$. Consider as an example the printing service mentioned in the introduction. `IN` variables could be the document identifier and the desired resolution. While the latter needs to be specified during Phase II to allow for e.g. cost estimates, it is sufficient to provide the former in time for service execution, that is in Phase III. Examples for `OUT` variables are the printer location and the estimated completion time. Again, the latter needs to be instantiated for Phase II, the former is known at execution time, only.

3.2 Details of the Process

With the help of the variables introduced above, we can now take a more detailed look at the process of service usage. As identified above, we have seven stages:

(1) Service Announcement

Whenever a device wishes to make a service available to other members of the network, it needs to provide a service advertisement describing the service it is willing to offer. This service advertisement has then to be made known to potential service requestors. This is done by some kind of service discovery mechanism and is outside of the scope of this paper (see [21] for an overview). In [3], we have described a process and a tool to develop such service descriptions. In order for service descriptions to be of any use in a loosely coupled environment, an

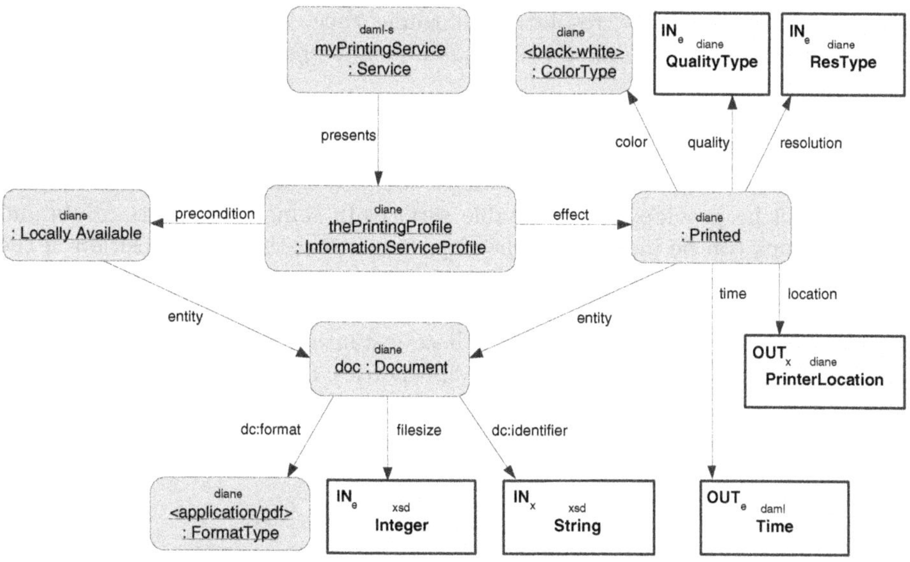

Fig. 2. Advertisement for a printing service.

ontology based approach is needed. In our approach, we distinguish three layers of service description. The top-layer contains the general structure of service descriptions. An example for such a top layer description is a modified DAML-S profile. Here, services are described by the initial states (preconditions) and the resulting states (effects). The middle layer specializes these general state descriptions for different service categories, e.g., information services, shopping services and so on. The specialization is achieved by restricting the types and cardinalities of the service's states. Finally, the third layer contains a collection of domain ontologies. A concrete service description is an instantiation of these three layers using one service category and one or more domain ontologies. However, there are certain aspects of a service (or more precisely the involved states) that cannot be completely instantiated at the time of service description. For these, the four categories of variables introduced above are used.

Consider as an example the advertisement for the printing service depicted in Figure 2. Generally, the service transforms the state of a document from LocallyAvailable (the precondition) to Printed (the effect). Notice that precondition and effect are connected via a common document instance. As mentioned above, some of the document's and state's attributes are already known and instantiated, others are undefined and therefore represented by variables. For example, as the service only allows to print PDF documents, the format of the document is already set. Also the color of the printout is defined: it will be black-white. Other values like the document's file size and its identifier as well as the printout's quality, resolution, finishing time, and output location[3] are unknown yet and will be filled in the subsequent steps.

(2) Service Search
If a client wants to use a certain service, it first has to find it. Therefore, it creates a *service request* containing at least the wished effects and wished outputs that should be provided by a suitable service. In some cases, also inputs and preconditions can be included in the request showing the initial position of the client before service execution. Like service advertisements, requests consist of instantiated and undefined parts. These undefined parts are also represented by variables (so called *placeholders*) whose instantiation can be restricted to a certain set of values by specially denoted properties. In Section 4, we will examine these restrictions in more detail. This request is dismissed to the discovery layer in order to find service advertisements that could be interesting for the client.

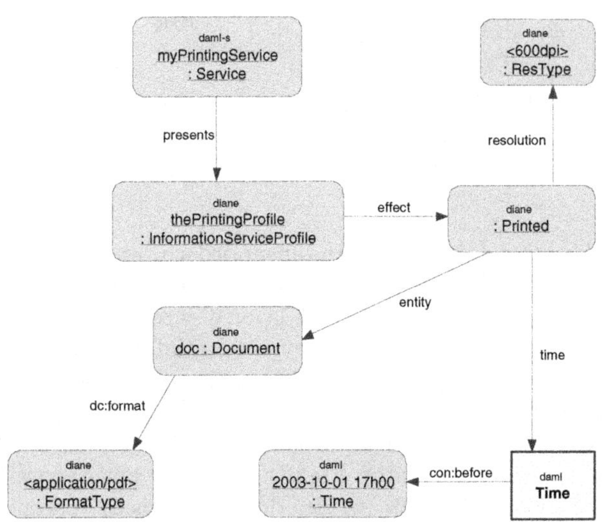

Fig. 3. Service request: Wants a PDF document to be printed in 600 dpi.

Figure 3 shows such a request. A user wants a PDF document to be printed in 600 dpi, which he specifies as effect of the requested service. The fixed values (600 dpi and PDF) are given as instantiated parts. On the other hand, the user does not want to restrict the finishing time of the output to an exact point in time, but wants to allow all times before a certain deadline. Therefore, he uses a placeholder of type Time that represents the finishing time and is restricted to values before 2003-10-01 17h00 by the special property con:before. Besides this

[3] This shows that this printing service automatically and dynamically chooses a device from a pool of physically distributed printers.

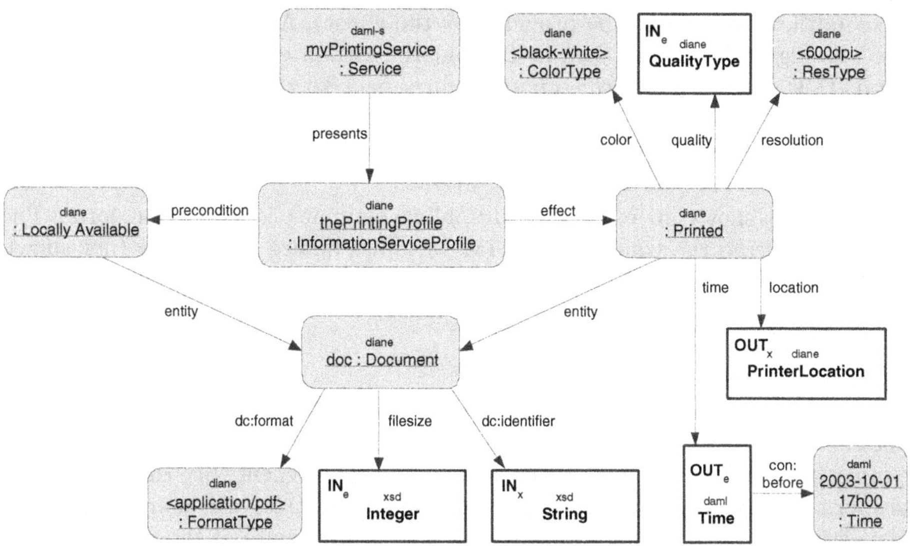

Fig. 4. Estimate Configuration Form.

condition, other instantiation restrictions are thinkable. In the following, we will denote them with the namespace con.

(3) Service Matching

When the discovery layer receives a request, it determines *possibly matching* advertisements for it. Generally, an advertisement possibly matches a request, if (a) all wished effect instances of the request can also be found in the advertisement and (b) there could be a variable binding so that the request and the advertisement are not contradictory. All possibly matching advertisements that can be found are further instantiated according to the restrictions from the requestor and sent back to it as an *estimate con guration form.*

In our example, the service request from Figure 3 possibly matches the advertisement from Figure 2 because the effect Printed matches and points to a PDF document in both cases. Moreover, the finishing time could match but cannot be determined exactly at this stage of service trading. It needs additional information like the concrete value for the $\mathtt{IN}_e$ variable standing for the document size to estimate the ending time. Therefore, this advertisement is a candidate which is further instantiated to the estimate configuration form from Figure 4. It differs from the service advertisements only in two places: the printout's resolution is now fixedly set to 600 dpi (as requested by the user) and the finishing time is restricted to values before a certain deadline with the condition con:before (also requested by the user).

(4) Estimate Configuration

In this stage, the service requestor collects the found service advertisements and filters out the ones that are not interesting for him (for instance because of a precondition that cannot be provided by the client). After that, he instantiates the missing $\texttt{IN}_e$ variables (i.e., he fills out the estimate configuration form) and sends this *lled estimate con guration form* back to the offerer to provide him with the information he needs for calculating an estimate. Notice that some of the $\texttt{OUT}_e$ variables could also be computed on the client side if the calculation formula was part of the service description.

Figure 5 shows an extract of this filled estimate configuration form. The user has entered the values for the $\texttt{IN}_e$ variables filesize and quality (not shown in the Figure). To calculate the estimated finishing time, this form is sent back to the offerer.

(5) Estimate Calculation

When the service offerer receives a filled estimate configuration form, it computes the complete estimate by filling out the missing $\texttt{OUT}_e$ values. Typically, this computation takes into account (a) the parameters of the client (like the document's size or the wished quality of the printout in our example) which are specified in the estimate configuration form and (b) the current state of the service offerer (like for example the current length of the printing queue). If these values fulfill possibly attached condition properties, this *service estimate* is sent back to the service requestor who also understands it as an *execution con guration form.*

Figure 6 shows the estimate for our example printing service computed from the values in the estimate configuration form. The only change is the value for the finishing time, which has been set to 2003-10-01 16h51 by the service offerer. As it is conform to the condition con:before, it is sent back to the requestor.

(6) Execution Configuration

In this stage, the service requestor collects the estimates and selects one of it. Typically, the main criteria for the selection are the values of the variables that had been placeholders in the service request. As these values have not been specified explicitly, the incoming estimates generally differ in these values and get comparable by them as a result. The chosen estimate serves as execution configuration form at the same time. The client specifies the $\texttt{IN}_x$ variables that are necessary for a proper execution of the service. Often, $\texttt{IN}_x$ variables are filled with values that should be known to the actual service executor only, in contrast

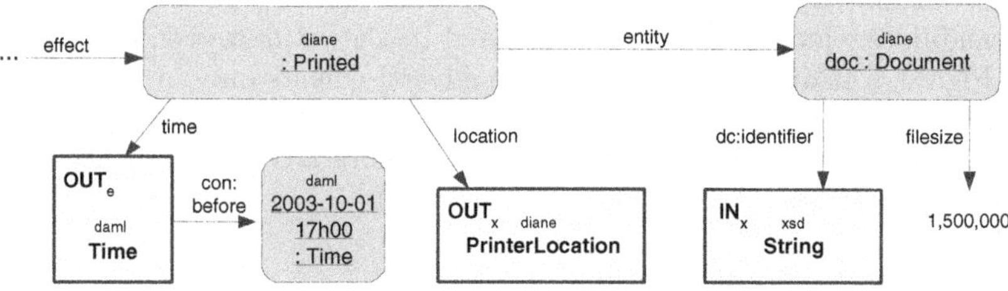

Fig. 5. Part of the Filled Estimate Configuration Form.

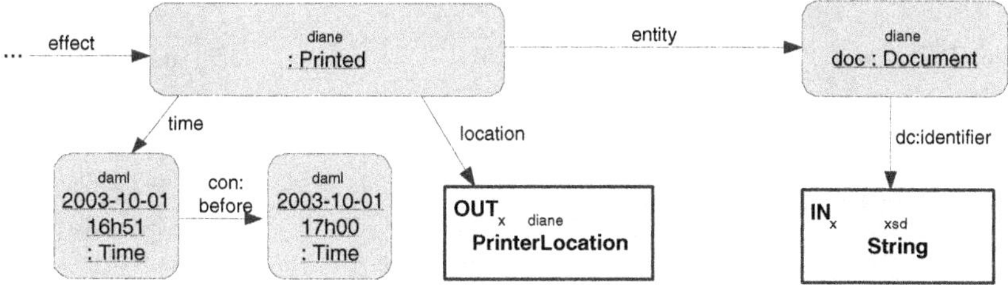

Fig. 6. Service estimate = Execution Configuration Form.

to $\mathtt{IN}_e$ variables, which can be freely disseminated to all possible service offerers. Then, the *lled execution con guration form* is sent back to the chosen service offerer.

In our printing example, the client has specified the $\mathtt{IN}_x$ variable dc:identifier, i.e. the location of the document to be printed (see Figure 7). Notice that for privacy reasons this URL should not be disseminated to every service offerer, especially as it is not necessary for service search and estimate calculation.

(7) Result Generation

The last step occurs after service execution. Then, the service executor instantiates the $\mathtt{OUT}_x$ variables. These contain values that can be determined not until the service execution starts. The resulting *service receipt* is sent back to the service requestor. In the case of our printing service, as soon as the executing printer is determined, the offerer fills in the location of this so that the user can fetch its printout there.

In Figure 8, the service executor has inserted the location of the printout as <room335>. The service description is now fully instantiated as it contains no variables anymore.

3.3 Conclusion

To sum up, service trading does not only consist of sending out a service request and picking the best from a list of received service offers, but the service offers

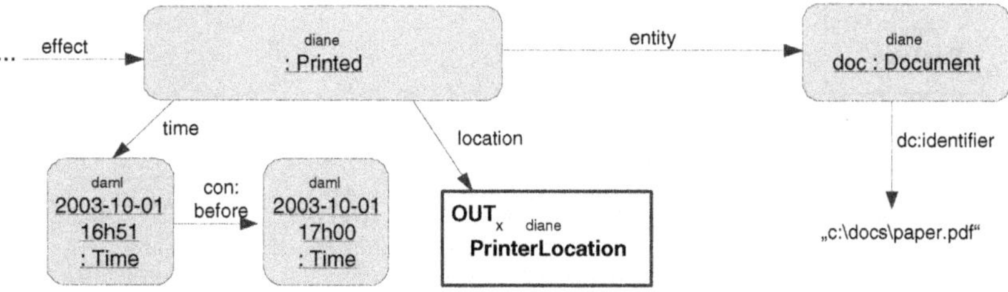

Fig. 7. Filled Execution Configuration Form.

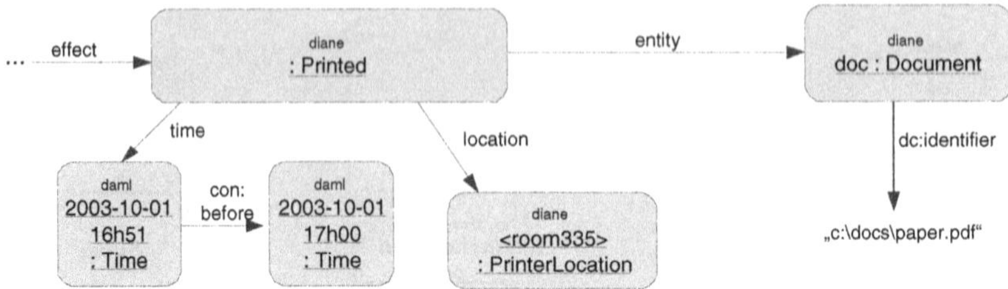

Fig. 8. Service Receipt.

(or more clearly the states involved in them) are developing in several steps. At the beginning, the descriptions contain different categories of variables, which are instantiated in each of the trading stages. Finally, the descriptions (and its states) are completely specified. Notice, that the realization of this instantiation process is explicitly left open. Typically, it is accomplished by sending messages containing the values of the instantiated variables.

4 Instantiation Restrictions on Variables

When a variable is instantiated, in principle, each value from its domain is legal and can be chosen. Often, this behavior is not desirable: (1) A service offerer might want to express that his service only allows, supports or provides certain values for the parameters. In the printer example, only resolutions from 150 to 300 dpi could be offered or the location of the printout could be restricted to rooms of the university. (2) A service requestor might want to express that placeholders in his request should only match certain values in advertisements. In the example in Figure 3, the ending time of the printout is restricted to time values before 2003-10-01 17h00.

Generally, two types of instantiation restrictions can be distinguished:

– **Restrictions concerning a single variable.** Restrictions of this type narrow the instantiation possibilities of one variable independently from other

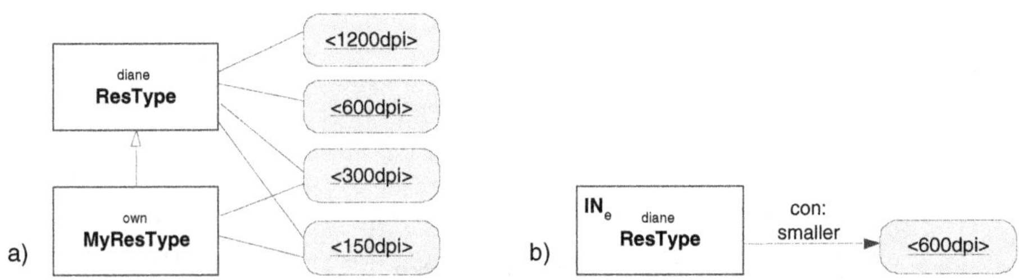

Fig. 9. Technical possibilities to restrict the instantiation of a single, independent variable.

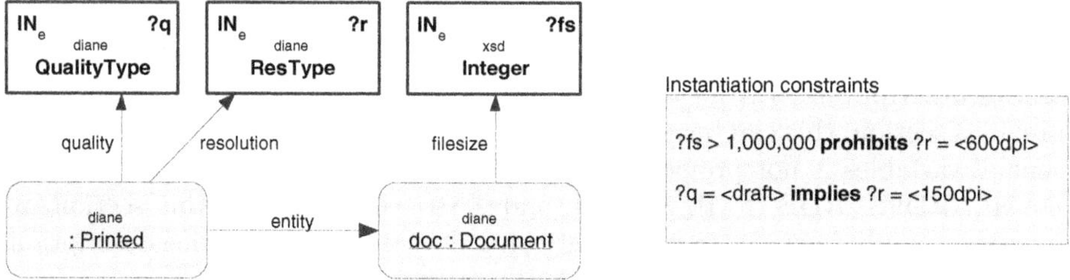

Fig. 10. Restricting several non-orthogonal variables by introducing variable names and an external dependencies list.

variables. Technically, this can be done with two different methods: (1) Introducing own user-defined classes and using them as type for the variable. This new class should be a subclass of the original class and narrow its domain. An example is depicted in Figure 9a. Here, the superclass ResType is an enumeration type describing general printer resolutions. It comprises the values <1200dpi>, <600dpi>, <300dpi>, and <150dpi>. The specialized subclass MyResType is also an enumeration type, but comprises only <300dpi> and <150dpi>. In a service description of a low resolution printer, MyResType could be used as class for the `IN` variable representing the resolution. (2) Inserting special properties that restrict the instantiation of the appropriate variable. In Figure 9b, the `IN` variable of type ResType is restricted with the property con:smaller to resolutions that are smaller than <600dpi>. Notice that these restricting properties can be recognized by their prefix con for constraint.

- **Restrictions concerning several variables.** Restrictions of this type limit the instantiation possibility of one variable with respect to the instantiation of another variable. This becomes necessary if the parameters of a service are not orthogonal, but partially exclude each other. In our printer example, the resolution variable could only be instantiable to <600dpi> if the file size is smaller than 1 MB. Moreover, the printing quality <draft> could always lead to a resolution of <150dpi>. As these restrictions can become very complex (by containing mathematical and logical formulae), they should be separated from the service description graph and collected in an additional constraint list[4]. As an additional requirement, variables with external instantiation dependencies need to have a unique name. Figure 10 shows a possibility to describe the above-mentioned dependencies of our printing service.

5 Syntactical Integration into DAML-S

The most important representative of ontology based service description languages is DAML-S (and its OWL-based pendant OWL-S) [1,16]. In the follow-

[4] Another possibility in RDF based service description would be reification.

ing, we will concentrate on DAML-S together with the state ontologies from [3]. We will examine how to enhance it with the possibility to express incomplete service descriptions, which can be completed successively. As pointed out in the previous section, this can be achieved by using variables. Unfortunately, the concept of variables is not provided in DAML-S and the standards it is based on: DAML, RDFS, RDF, XML Schema, and XML. Therefore, in this section, we propose a syntactical construct for enriching DAML-S based service descriptions (and also other DAML instance graphs) with variables.

Before presenting the construct, we want to explain some important requirements for it: First, as service descriptions are instance graphs, variables should also be regardable as instances of their domain without having been assigned a concrete value yet. This would avoid a mixture of classes and instances, which often leads to unclear semantics. Second, the construct needs to offer the possibility to express the name, the type, the category (i.e. $\texttt{IN}_e$, $\texttt{OUT}_e$ etc.), and possible instantiation constraints of the variable. When looking back to the variables used in the printing example, we observe that only variables of primitive XML schema datatypes (like `xsd:integer` or `xsd:string`, see [22]) as well as DAML enumeration types (like `diane:QualityType`) have been used. Therefore, we will concentrate on these two groups in the following, leaving out variables for general object types (which are not necessary in general as they can be composed of other types) and collection types (which we will have to examine more closely in future).

The construct we propose satisfies these requirements. It is based on the fact that the creation of a new DAML instance can be expressed indirectly with the RDF constructs `rdf:Description` and `rdf:ID`. Therefore, we can create a instance as follows:

```
<rdf:Description rdf:ID="filesizevalue"/>
```

Generally, the type of an instance can be denoted with `rdf:type`. As XML schema datatypes are accessible within DAML via the class `daml:Datatype`, we could specify an integer instance as follows:

```
<rdf:Description rdf:ID="filesizevalue">
  <rdf:type>
    <daml:Datatype rdf:about="xsd:integer"/>
  </rdf:type>
</rdf:Description>
```

Notice that this is an instance of an integer, but its value has not been specified yet. Therefore, this construct can be regarded as a variable and its value could be added in a later stage by inserting an `rdf:value` statement:

```
<rdf:Description rdf:ID="filesizevalue">
  <rdf:type>
    <daml:Datatype rdf:about="xsd:integer"/>
  </rdf:type>
```

```
  <rdf:value>1500000</rdf:value>
</rdf:Description>
```

To be able to express the category of such a variable, we introduce a new class and a new property:

```
<daml:Class rdf:ID="VariableCategory">
  <daml:oneOf rdf:parseType="daml:Collection">
    <Thing rdf:resource="#INe"/>
    <Thing rdf:resource="#OUTe"/>
    <Thing rdf:resource="#INx"/>
    <Thing rdf:resource="#OUTx"/>
  </daml:oneOf>
</daml:Class>

<daml:ObjectProperty rdf:ID="varCat">
  <daml:range rdf:resource="#VariableCategory"/>
</daml:ObjectProperty>
```

This allows us to express that `filesizevalue` is an $\mathtt{IN}_e$ variable:

```
<rdf:Description rdf:ID="filesizevalue">
  <rdf:type>
    <daml:Datatype rdf:about="xsd:integer"/>
  </rdf:type>
  <diane:varCat rdf:resource="#INe"/>
</rdf:Description>
```

Figure 11 shows a complete example by expressing the diagram from Figure 10 in DAML using the above-mentioned constructs. Besides XML schema datatype variables also variables with enumeration types are presented. Notice that the constraint restrictions concerning a single variable can be simply inserted into the description as DAML construct whereas restrictions concerning several variables are written down in a external file.

6 Conclusion and Future Work

In this paper, we have analyzed a typical process of service trading, which generally does not consist of a simple request/response step only, but more interactively extents to several stages. As the existing message and state/message oriented service description are not capable of accurately describing a configurable service, we have presented a generic state oriented service description, which describes the initial and resulting state of the service including fixed and variable parts. Each of these variable parts is labelled showing who should instantiate it, and in which stage and under what restrictions. However, the description explicitly lacks a concrete explanation of the exchanged messages as this can be derived

```
<diane:Printed>
  <diane:quality>
    <rdf:Description rdf:ID="?q"/>
      <rdf:type>
        <daml:Class rdf:about="diane:QualityType"/>
      <rdf:type>
      <diane:varCat>
        <diane:VariableCategory rdf:resource="#INe"/>
      </diane:varCat>
    </rdf:Description>
  </diane:quality>
  <diane:resolution>
    <rdf:Description rdf:ID="?r"/>
      <rdf:type>
        <daml:Class rdf:about="diane:ResType"/>
      <rdf:type>
      <diane:varCat>
        <diane:VariableCategory rdf:resource="#INe"/>
      </diane:varCat>
    </rdf:Description>
  </diane:resolution>
  <diane:entity>
    <diane:Document rdf:ID="doc">
      <diane:filesize>
        <rdf:Description rdf:ID="?fs">
          <rdf:type>
            <daml:Datatype rdf:about="xsd:integer"/>
          </rdf:type>
          <diane:varCat>
            <diane:VariableCategory rdf:resource="#INe"/>
          </diane:varCat>
        </rdf:Description>
      </diane:filesize>
    </diane:Document>
  </diane:entity>
</diane:Printed>
```

Fig. 11. DAML based description for the diagram from Figure 10.

automatically. Finally, we have presented a construct that allows a syntactical integration of the concepts into the service description language DAML-S.

In the future, we will examine possibilities how to automatically construct graphical user interfaces from such a configurable service description. Moreover, more complex dependencies between variables (e.g. those including time) and dependencies between several services (e.g. those between a storage and a retrieval service) will be analyzed.

References

1. Defense Advanced Research Projects Agency: DARPA agents markup language - services (DAML-S). (http://www.daml.org/services/)
2. Institute for Program Structures and Data Organization, Universität Karlsruhe: DIANE project. (http://www.ipd.uni-karlsruhe.de/DIANE/en)
3. Klein, M., König-Ries, B.: A process and a tool for creating service descriptions based on DAML-S. (http://www.ipd.uni-karlsruhe.de/DIANE/docs/KK03.pdf, submitted to 4th VLDB Workshop on Technologies for E-Services (TES'03))
4. Dumas, M., O'Sullivan, J., Heravizadeh, M., Edmond, D., Hofstede, A.: Towards a semantic framework for service description. In: 9th International Conference on Database Semantics, Hong-Kong, Kluwer Academic Publishers (2001)
5. Object Management Group: OMG IDL syntax and semantics. (http://www.omg.org/docs/formal/02-06-39.pdf)
6. Sun Microsystems: Java IDL. (http://java.sun.com/products/jdk/idl/)
7. Microsoft: Microsoft interface definition language. (http://msdn.microsoft.com/library/en-us/midl/midl/midl_start_page.asp)
8. World Wide Web Consortium: Web interface definition language. (http://www.w3.org/TR/NOTE-widl)
9. Sun Microsystems: Java RMI. (http://java.sun.com/products/jdk/rmi/)
10. Sun Microsystems: Jini. (http://www.jini.org/)
11. Sun Microsystems: Enterprise JavaBeans technology. (http://java.sun.com/products/ejb/)
12. World Wide Web Consortium: Web service description language (WSDL). (http://www.w3.org/TR/wsdl)
13. Hewlett Packard: HP web services platform. (http://www.hp.com/go/espeak)
14. ebXML: Collaboration protocol profile and agreement specification. (http://www.ebxml.org/specs/ebCCP.pdf)
15. Curbera, F., Weerawarana, S., Duftler, M.J.: Network accessible service specification language: An XML language for describing network accessible services. (http://www.cs.mu.oz.au/ eas/subjects/654/nassl.pdf)
16. Web-Ontology Working Group: Web ontology language - services (OWL-S). (http://www.daml.org/services/daml-s/0.9/)
17. Martin, D.L., Cheyer, A.J., Moran, D.B.: The open agent architecture: A framework for building distributed software systems. Applied Artificial Intelligence **13** (1999) 91–128
18. McIlraith, S., Son, T.C.: Adapting golog for composition of semantic web services. In: 8th International Conference on Knowledge Representation and Reasoning (KR2002). (2002) 482–493
19. Gurevich, Y.: Evolving algebras: An attempt to discover semantics. In Rozenberg, G., Salomaa, A., eds.: Current Trends in Theoretical Computer Science. World Scientific, River Edge, NJ (1993) 266–292
20. Sycara, K., Widoff, S., Klusch, M., Lu, J.: Larks: Dynamic matchmaking among heterogeneous software agents in cyberspace. Autonomous Agents and Multi-Agent Systems **5** (2002) 173–203
21. Klein, M., König-Ries, B., Obreiter, P.: Service rings – a semantical overlay for service discovery in ad hoc networks. In: The Sixth International Workshop on Network-Based Information Systems (NBIS2003), Workshop at DEXA 2003, Prague, Czech Republic. (2003)
22. World Wide Web Consortium: XML schema part 2: Datatypes. (http://www.w3.org/TR/xmlschema-2/)

Semantic Structure Matching for Assessing Web-Service Similarity

Yiqiao Wang and Eleni Stroulia

Computer Science Department, University of Alberta, Edmonton, AB, T6G 2E8, Canada
{yiqiao,stroulia}@cs.ualberta.ca

Abstract. The web-services stack of standards is designed to support the reuse and interoperation of software components on the web. A critical step in the process of developing applications based on web services is service discovery, i.e., the identification of existing web services that can potentially be used in the context of a new web application. UDDI, the standard API for publishing web-services specifications, provides a simple browsing-by-business-category mechanism for developers to review and select published services. To support programmatic service discovery, we have developed a suite of methods that utilizes both the semantics of the identifiers of WSDL descriptions and the structure of their operations, messages and data types to assess the similarity of two WSDL files. Given only a textual description of the desired service, a semantic information-retrieval method can be used to identify and order the most similar service-description files. This step assesses the similarity of the provided description of the desired service with the available services. If a (potentially partial) specification of the desired service behavior is also available, this set of likely candidates can be further refined by a semantic structure-matching step assessing the structural similarity of the desired vs. the retrieved services and the semantic similarity of their identifier. In this paper, we describe and experimentally evaluate our suite of service-similarity assessment methods.

1 Introduction

The development of web-based applications in the service-oriented architecture style, as implied by the web-services stack of standards, relies on a set of related specifications, defining how reusable components should be specified (through the Web-Service Description Language – WSDL [15]), how they should be advertised so that they can be discovered and reused (through the Universal Description, Discovery, and Integration API – UDDI [12]), and how they should be invoked at run time (through the Simple Object Access Protocol API – SOAP [11]). A critical step in the process of reusing existing WSDL-specified components for building web-based applications is the discovery of potentially relevant components. UDDI servers are essentially catalogs of published WSDL specifications of reusable components. These catalogs are organized according to categories of business activities. Service providers advertise services by adding their WSDL specifications to the appropriate UDDI directory category. Through a well-defined API, software developers can browse the UDDI catalog by category.

This category-based service-discovery method is clearly insufficient. It is quite informal and relies, to a great extent, on the shared common-sense understanding of

M.E. Orlowska et al. (Eds.): ICSOC 2003, LNCS 2910, pp. 194–207, 2003.

the domain by publishers and consumers. It is the responsibility of the provider developer to publish the services in the appropriate UDDI category. The consumer developer must, in turn, browse the "right" category to discover the potentially relevant services. More importantly, this discovery process does not provide any support for selecting among competing alternative services that could potentially be reused; prioritization of the candidates is again the responsibility of the consumer.

In this paper, we discuss a set of WSDL similarity-assessment methods, which can be used, in conjunction with the current UDDI API, to support a more automated service-discovery process, by distinguishing among the potentially useful and the likely irrelevant services and by ordering the candidates in the first category according to their relevance to the task at hand. This method utilizes both the semantics of the identifiers of WSDL descriptions and the structures of their operations, messages and types to assess the similarity of two WSDL files. Given only a textual description of the desired service, a semantic information-retrieval method can be used to identify and order the most similar service-description files. This step assesses the similarity of the provided desired-service description, extended to include semantically similar words according to wordNet [16], with the available services. If a (potentially partial) specification of the desired service behavior is also available, this set of likely candidates can be further refined by a semantic structure-matching step assessing the structure and semantic similarity of the desired vs. the retrieved services.

The intuition underlying this method is that a plausible means of querying UDDI servers is "query by example", i.e., by providing a (potentially partial) specification of the desired service. The consumer developer may define various aspects of the desired service, such as descriptions in natural language, the namespaces of its data types and the input/output parameters of its operations, and the proposed method will return a set of candidate services with an estimate of their similarity to the provided example.

The remainder of the paper is organized as follows: section 2 discusses related work; section 3 explains in detail the design and implementation of our approach; section 4 discusses the results of our experimentation; section 5 outlines our plans for future work and concludes with a summary of our results to date.

2 Related Research

The problem of service discovery is similar to the well-studied problems of component retrieval and information retrieval. On one hand, a WSDL specification is the description of a "software component" including a description of its interface and a description of where the actual implementation exists and how it can be used. On the other, a WSDL specification usually includes a set of natural-language description of the service itself and comments on its elements. Thus, we looked at both these research areas for applicable results to the service-discovery and similarity-assessment problem.

2.1 Component Retrieval

In general, there are two categories of methods for component discovery: signature matching [8, 18] and specification matching [1, 19].

Polylith [8] proposed one of the earliest signature-matching methods for interface adaptation and interoperation. Through its NIMBLE language, coercion rules could be specified so that the parameters of the invoking module could be matched to the signature of the invoked module, including reordering, type mapping and parameter elimination. Zaremski and Wing [18] described exact and relaxed signature matching as a means for retrieving functions and modules from a software library.

Signature matching is an efficient means for component retrieval, for several reasons. Function signatures can be automatically generated from the function code. Furthermore, signature matching efficiently prunes down the functions and/or modules that do not match the query, so that more expensive and precise techniques can be used on the smaller set of remaining candidate components. However, signature matching considers only function types and ignores their behaviors; and two functions with the same signature can have completely opposite behaviors. Specification matching aims at addressing this problem by comparing software components based on formal descriptions of the semantics of their behaviors. However, because these specifications are developed independently from the module code, there is no guarantee that they correctly and completely reflect the component's behavior. Moreover, it is hard to motivate programmers to provide a formal specification for each component they write.

Zaremski and Wing [19] extended their signature-matching work with a specification-matching scheme.

WSDL [15], the Web-Services Definition Language, is an XML-based interface-definition language. It describes "services" as a set of operations implemented by a set of messages involving a given set of data types at a high level of abstraction. WSDL specifications of service-providing components are published in UDDI registries. UDDI [12] is designed as an online marketplace providing a standardized format for general business discovery. Developers can browse and query a UDDI registry using the UDDI API to identify businesses that offer services in a particular business category and/or services that are provided by a certain service provider.

WSDL service specifications do not include semantics. On the other hand, DAML-S [2] is a formal logic-based language that supports the specification of semantic information in RDF format. As part of the "semantic web" effort, it is intended as the means for specifying domain-specific semantics of ontologies. An extension of DAML-S supports service specification, including behavioral specifications of their operations; as a result, it enables discovery through specification matching, such as the method proposed in LARKS [4]. If indeed services were specified in DAML-S instead of WSDL it would be possible to formally prove that the requirements of the desired service and a discovered service do not conflict. However, there is no widespread adoption yet of DAML and DAML-S, and the high cost of formally defining of provided and required services makes this adoption unlikely. This is the underlying motivation for this research: to provide some lightweight semantic comparison of syntactic specifications in WSDL, based on the syntactic structure of the specifications and the natural-language semantics of their identifiers, comments and descriptions.

2.2 Information Retrieval

Traditional information-retrieval methods rely on textual descriptions of artifacts to assess their similarity and organize them in clusters or retrieve them in a "query-by-example" mode [3]. According to the vector-space model, documents and queries are represented as t-dimensional vectors, where t is the number of distinct words in the document; similarity assessment then becomes equivalent to vector-distance calculation.

WordNet [16] is a lexical database, inspired by current psycholinguistic theories of human lexical memory. English nouns, verbs, adjectives and adverbs are organized into synonym sets, each representing one underlying lexical concept. Relationships between conceptions such as hyponym and hypernym relations are represented as semantic pointers linking between related concepts [5, 6]. WordNet has been used in numerous natural language processing applications, hoping to ameliorate traditional information-retrieval results [7, 9, 13] with limited success.

3 The Web-Service Discovery Method

Our service-discovery method is aimed at enabling programmatic service discovery and integrates information- and component-retrieval ideas. The method assumes as input a (potentially partial) specification of the desired WSDL specification and a set of WSDL specifications of available services, such as the services advertised in UDDI. First, a traditional vector-space model information-retrieval step, enhanced with WordNet, retrieves the most similar services according to their WSDL service descriptions specified in natural language. Given the retrieved list of candidate services, a structure-matching algorithm, extended by a second WordNet method that calculates semantic distances between identifiers of WSDLs, further refines and assesses the quality of the candidate service set.

3.1 WordNet-Powered Vector-Space Model Information Retrieval

In traditional vector-space model, documents and queries are represented as T-dimensional vectors, where T is the total number of distinct words in the document collection after the preprocessing step. Preprocessing includes eliminating stop words (very commonly used words) and conflating related words to a common word stem. Each term in the vector is assigned a weight that reflects the importance of a word in the document. This value is proportional to the frequency a word appears in a document and inversely proportional to number of documents in which this word appears [10, 13]. A common term importance indicator is *tf-idf* weighting the importance of a word i in document j is as follows:

$$w_{ij} = tf_{ij}\, idf_i = tf_{ij} \log_2 (N/df_i) \quad (1)$$

In the above formula, tf_{ij} is the normalized term frequency across the entire document collection, and idf_i is the inverse document frequency of term i. N is total number of documents in the collection, and *Log* is used to dampen the effect relative to *tf*.

The WordNet-powered vector-space model extension involves the maintenance of three sub-vectors for each document and query: stems of original words in a document, stems of words' synonyms for all word senses, and stems of words' direct hypernyms, hyponyms and siblings for all word senses. All document terms' word senses are included, and therefore we bypass the problem of lacking effective automated word sense disambiguation techniques, frequently discussed in the literature.

The WSDL syntax allows textual descriptions for services, their types and operations, grouped under <documentation> tags. Given a natural language description of the desired service, we employ the WordNet-powered vector space model to retrieve published WSDL services that are most similar to the input description on the respective vectors. Corresponding sub-vectors from documents and queries are matched and we obtain three similarity scores accordingly. Different weights are assigned to sub-vector matching scores: matching scores of original word stems (first sub-vectors) are assigned twice the weight assigned to matching scores of synonyms (second sub-vectors), hypernyms, hyponyms, and siblings (third sub-vectors). A higher overall score indicates a closer similarity between the source and target specifications.

3.2 WSDL Structure Matching

A straight-forward extension of the signature-matching method to WSDL specifications involves the comparison of the operations' set offered by the services, which is based on the comparison of the structures of the operations' input and output messages, which, in turn, is based on the comparison of the data types of the objects communicated by these messages.

The overall process starts by comparing the data types involved in the two WSDL specifications. The result of this step is a matrix assessing the matching scores, i.e., the degree of similarity, of all pair-wise combinations of source and target data types. It is interesting to note here that the data types of web services specified in WSDL are XML elements; as such, they can potentially be highly complex structures.

The next step in the process is the matching of the service messages. The result of this step is a matrix assessing the matching scores of all pair-wise combinations of source and target messages. The degree to which two messages are similar is decided on the basis of how similar their parameter lists are, in terms of the data types they contain and their organization.

The third step of the process is the matching of the service operations. The result of this step is a matrix assessing the matching score of all pair-wise combinations of source and target operations. The degree to which two operations are similar is decided on the basis of how similar their input and output messages are, which has already been assessed in the previous level.

Finally, the overall score of how well the two services match is computed by identifying the pair-wise correspondence of their operations that maximizes the sum total of the matching scores of the individual pairs.

After all target WSDL specifications have been matched against the source WSDL specification, they are ordered according to their "overall matching scores": a higher score indicates a closer similarity between the source and target specifications. For each target specification, the algorithm also returns the mapping of its data types and operations to the corresponding data types and operations of the source specification as an "explanation" of its assigned match score. This algorithm is described in detail in [14].

3.3 Semantic WSDL Structure Matching

The WSDL structure-matching algorithm of section 3.2 aims at optimizing the mapping of the corresponding service structures. The semantic WSDL structure-matching algorithm is an extension to it: it also tries to find an optimal mapping between source and target service components based both on the similarity of their syntactic structures and also the semantic similarity between the identifiers of data types, operations and services to assess service similarities. The intuition behind it is that the chosen names of the types, operations, and services usually reflect the semantics of the underlying capabilities of the service.

The identifier-matching process is similar to that of the original WSDL structure matching. It starts by comparing the names of the data types (identifiers) involved in the two WSDL specifications. The result of this step is a matrix assessing the matching scores of all pair-wise combinations of source and target data-types. The next step in the process is the matching of the service operations. The result of this step is a matrix assessing the matching scores of all pair-wise combinations of source and target operations. The degree to which two operations are similar is decided on the semantic distance between operations' names and how similar their parameter lists are, in terms of the identifiers they contain. Finally, the overall score for how well the two services match is computed by matching the services' names and by identifying the pair-wise correspondence of their operations that maximizes the sum total of the matching scores of the individual pairs.

Figure 1 lists the algorithm `matchDocumentTerms` that explains the WordNet-based "cost structure" for assessing the similarity of two identifiers. If two words are identical or synonymous (regardless of words' senses), they are assigned a maximum score of 10 and 8 respectively. Otherwise, if two words are in a hierarchical semantic relation, i.e. they are hypernyms, hyponyms or siblings to each other we count the number of semantic links between these words along their shortest path in WordNet hierarchy. The identifier-similarity score between two such terms is calculated by dividing 6 by the number of links found between them. Thus, the term-similarity score is a function of the terms' semantic distance in the WordNet hierarchy: terms that are farther away from each other have smaller similarity scores than terms that are located closer to each other in WordNet. Similar to the WordNet-based information-retrieval step, word senses are not disambiguated.

```
double matchDocumentTerms (term1, term2) {
  maxScore = 10;
  if (term1 is identical to term2)
    score = maxScore;
  else if (term1 and term2 are synonymous)
    score = 8;
  else if (term1 and term2 have hierarchical relations)
    score = 6 / number of hierarchical links;
  else score =0;
  return score; }
```

Fig. 1. Matching Document Terms Using WordNet.

In the end, the semantic structure-matching score between a web service S and a query service Q, $\mathrm{Sim}_{\text{semantic-structure-matching}}(S,Q)$, is a function of its structure matching score and its identifier matching score as follows:

$$\mathrm{Sim}_{\text{semantic-structure-matching}}(S,Q) = \mathrm{Sim}_{\text{structure-matching}}(S,Q) + \mathrm{Sim}_{\text{identifier-matching}}(S,Q) \qquad (2)$$

In the above formula, $Sim_{structure\text{-}matching}(S,Q)$ and $Sim_{identifier\text{-}matching}(S,Q)$ are similarity scores calculated by the structure matching and the identifier matching method respectively. We assume that programmers follow Java-style naming conventions and use meaningful names for methods and data types. Under this assumption, all identifiers and names are broken into tokens by identifying delimiter characters such as underscores and capital letters.

4 Evaluation

To evaluate our service-discovery method as a whole and the effectiveness of its constituent elements, we had to obtain families of related specifications in order to evaluate the degree to which our algorithm can distinguish among them. We found such a collection published by XMethods [17]. The XMethods collection provided us with nineteen service descriptions from five categories: currency rate converter (three services), email address verifier (three services), stock quote finder (four services), weather information finder (four services), and DNA information searcher (five services).

In this section, we report on four sets of experiments: service discovery with WordNet-powered vector space model, discovery with structure matching, discovery with semantic structure matching, and discovery with WordNet-powered vector space model combined with semantic structure matching.

4.1 WordNet-Powered Vector-Space Model

In this experiment, we matched service descriptions specified in natural language of each service from each category (requests) against the text descriptions of all other services from all categories (candidates).

The similarity score between a given web service *S* and service requests from a given category *C* is the average of the similarity scores calculated between *S* and each request from category *C*. The candidate web services are ranked according to their similarity to the requests and the top 50% of services in the list are returned. We assume that if a web service ranks in the second half of the list, chances are that this web service is irrelevant to the request. Table 1 summarizes the results of this experiment.

We evaluate the effectiveness of our retrieval methods by calculating their precision and recall. "Precision is the proportion of retrieved documents that are relevant, and recall is the proportion of relevant documents that are retrieved" [13]. Average precision and recall for each test collection from each category of service requests are calculated and are listed in the first column of Table 1. Retrieved matching service advertisements are listed in column 2 of Table 1. They are sorted according to their similarity to requests from a given category. The WordNet-powered vector space model achieves a precision of 41.8% at 100% recall on average on this set of experiments.

Table 1. WordNet-Powered Vector Space Model on the XMethods collection

Requests	Retrieved Matching Advertisements (Category: service name)
Currency rate converter Precision: 33% Recall: 100%	Currency: CurrencyExchangeService Currency: PwspNoCentrebankCurRates Currency: Currencyws Weather: TemperatureService DNA: TxSearch Stock: StockQuotes1 Weather: WeatherService Email: advancedemailcheckService Stock: StockQuotes (2)
DNA info Searcher Precision: 55% Recall: 100%	DNA: TxSearch DNA: Fasta DNA: ClustalW DNA: Blast Email: advancedemailcheckService Email: DOTSEmailValidate DNA: SRS Currency: pwspNoCentrebankCurRates Stock: StockQuotes (1)
Email Address Verifier Precision: 33% Recall: 100%	Email: AdvancedemailcheckService Email: DOTSEmailValidate Email: ValidateEmail Stock: MBSoapService(1) Stock: MBSoapService (2) DNA: Blast Stock: StockQuotes1 Stock: StockQuotes2 Weather: getCAWeatherService
Stock Quote Finder Precision: 44% Recall: 100%	Stock: MBSoapService(2) Stock: MBSoapService (1) Stock: StockQuotes1 Stock: StockQuote2 Weather: WeatherService Weather: TemperatureService Email: DOTSEmailValidate Weather: getCAWeatherService Weather: USWeather
Weather Info Finder Precision: 44% Recall: 100%	Weather: USWeather Weather: TemperatureService Stock: StockQuotes (1) Weather: WeatherService Stock: StockQuotes (2) Weather: getCAWeatherService Currency: CurrencyExchangeService Currency: Currencyws Stock: MBSoapService (2)

4.2 Structure Matching

Experiments with structure matching were conducted in a similar manner: we matched the structure of each service from each category (requests) against the structures of all other services from all categories (candidates). Averages are calculated between service requests from each category and all candidate services. The candidate web services are ranked according to their similarity scores to the requests, and the top 70% of the list are returned. The results of this set of experiments are listed in Table 2.

Table 2. Structure Matching on the XMethods Collection

Requests	**Retrieved Matching Advertisements (Category: service name)**
Currency rate converter Precision: 14% Recall: 67%	Email: AdvancedemailcheckService Stock: StockQuote1 DNA: TxSearch, Blast, Fasta Stock: MBSoapService(1) Stock: MBSoapService (2) DNA: ClustalW, SRS Stock: StockQuote2 Email: ValidateEmail Currency: Currencyws Weather: USWeather Currency: pwspNoCentrebankCurRates
DNA info Searcher Precision: 36% Recall: 100%	DNA: Fasta Stock: MBSoapService(1) Stock: MBSoapService (2) DNA: Blast Currency: Currencyws DNA: ClustalW DNA: SRS DNA: TxSearch Email: DOTSEmailValidate Stock: StockQuote1, StockQuote2 Weather: USWeather Email: ValidateEmail Weather: WeatherService
Email Address Verifier Precision: 14% Recall: 67%	Email: DOTSEmailValidate Stock: StockQuote1 DNA: TxSearch DNA: Blast Currency: pwspNoCentrebankCurRates DNA: SRS Currency: Currencyws Stock: MBSoapService(1), Stock: MBSoapService(1) DNA: ClustalW, SRS, TxSearch Email: DOTSEmailValidate Stock: StockQuote1, StockQuote2 Weather: USWeather Email: ValidateEmail Weather: WeatherService
Stock Quote Finder Precision: 28% Recall: 100%	Email: DOTSEmailValidate DNA: Fasta, SRS, ClustalW, TxSearch Stock: MBSoapService(1) Stock: MBSoapService(2)

	Weather: USWeather DNA: Blast Stock: MBSoapService(1) Stock: MBSoapService(1) Currency: CurrencyExchangeService Currencyws, PwspNoCentrebankCurRates
Weather Info Finder Precision: 7% Recall: 25%	Email: DOTSEmailValidate Stock: MBSoapService(1) Currency: Currencyws Stock: MBSoapService(2) DNA: Blast, TxSearch Stock: MBSoapService(1) Stock: MBSoapService(2) DNA: ClustalW, Fasta, SRS Email: ValidateEmail Currency: CurrencyExchangeService Weather: USWeather

Average precision and recall are calculated for each set of queries, and on average, structure matching achieves a precision of 20% at 72% recall. Both precision and recall are considerably poor in this set of experiments because some related services have substantially different structures and some irrelevant services can often have higher matching scores because they have many spurious substructures that happen to match the query structure.

4.3 Semantic Structure Matching

In this experiment, we matched the services' structures and their chosen identifiers. The experiments were conducted in a similar manner as the experiments of sections 4.1 and 4.2 described above. Web services are ranked according to their similarity scores to the requests, and top 50% of web services on the lists are considered to be relevant to the requests and are returned to the users. The results of this set of experiments are listed in Table 3.

Semantic structure matching method achieves a precision of 35.2% at 81.8% recall on average. Please note that compare to performance of pure structure matching method, precision is improved by 15.2% from 20% and recalled is improved by 9.8% from 72%. Based on this experiment, we can infer that considering the implicit semantics of the WSDL identifiers is, in fact, enabling a more precise service matching.

4.4 WordNet-Powered Vector-Space Model and Semantic Structure Matching

Looking at the services retrieved with each query in the various experiments, we noticed that each method "picks" different types of similarity, which led us to hypothesize that their combination might be more effective than the best one of them.

To investigate this hypothesis we conducted a fourth set of experiments where WordNet-powered vector space model and semantic structure matching method are combined. The WordNet-powered vector-space model was first used on all services as described in section 4.1 to obtain relevant web services compared to the query (top 50% of the services in the ranked list). Then, semantic structure matching was applied to the pruned list of candidates as described in section 4.3. The candidate services were matched and re-ranked, and the top 50% of the services in the list were returned. Therefore, after the two-step matching and refining, only the top 25% of all web services are returned as relevant services. The results of these experiments are shown in Table 4.

Table 3. Semantic Structure Matching on the XMethods collection

Requests	**Retrieved Matching Advertisements (Category: service name)**
Currency rate converter Precision: 22% Recall: 67%	Email: DOTSEmailValidate Stock: StockQuotes (1) Weather: WeatherService Currency: Currencyws DNA: Blast, TxSearch, Fasta Stock: StockQuotes (2) Currency: pwspNoCentrebankCurRates
DNA info Searcher Precision: 55% Recall: 100%	DNA: Blast, Fasta, SRS, ClustalW, TxSearch Currency: Currencyws Stock: MBSoapService (1) Stock: MBSoapService (2) Email: DOTSEmailValidate
Email Address Verifier Precision: 22% Recall: 67%	Stock: StockQuotes (1) Email: DOTSEmailValidate Currency: pwspNoCentrebankCurRates Email: ValidateEmail Currency: Currencyws Weather: USWeather Stock: StockQuotes (2) Weather: WeatherService DNA: Blast
Stock Quote Finder Precision: 44% Recall: 100%	Email: DOTSEmailValidate Stock: MBSoapService (1) Stock: MBSoapService (2) Currency: Currencyws Stock: StockQuotes (2) Stock: StockQuotes (1) Currency: pwspNoCentrebankCurRates DNA: Blast DNA: Fasta
Weather Info Finder Precision: 33% Recall: 75%	Email: DOTSEmailValidate Stock: StockQuotes (1) Weather: USWeather Currency: Currencyws Weather: WeatherService Currency: pwspNoCentrebankCurRates Stock: StockQuotes (2) Email: ValidateEmail Weather: getCAWeatherService

Table 4. WordNet-Powered Vector Space Model and Semantic Structure Matching on the XMethods Collection

Requests	Retrieved Matching Advertisements (Category: service name)
Currency rate converter Precision: 60% Recall: 100%	Currency: CurrencyExchangeService Currency: Currencyws Stock: StockQuotes (1) Currency: pwspNoCentrebankCurRates Weather: WeatherService
DNA info Searcher Precision: 100% Recall: 100%	DNA: Fasta DNA: ClustalW DNA: TxSearch DNA: Blast DNA: SRS
Email Address Verifier Precision: 60% Recall: 100%	Email: DOTSEmailValidate Email: ValidateEmail Stock: StockQuotes (1) Email: advancedemailcheckService Stock: StockQuotes (2)
Stock Quote Finder Precision: 80% Recall: 100%	Stock: MBSoapService (2) Stock: MBSoapService (1) Email: DOTSEmailValidate Stock: StockQuotes (1) Stock: StockQuotes (2)
Weather Info Finder Precision: 60% Recall: 75%	Weather: USWeather Stock: StockQuotes (1) Weather: TemperatureService Weather: WeatherService Currency: Currencyws

On average, this retrieval method that uses both the WordNet-powered vector space model and the semantic structure matching achieves a precision of 72% at 95% recall. Compared to the performance of WordNet-powered vector space model, precision is increased by 30.2% from 41.8% and recall dropped by 5% from 100%. Both precision and recall improved significantly compared to the results obtained by semantic structure matching method alone.

5 Conclusions and Future Work

In this paper, we described a web-service discovery method that combines two WordNet-based techniques with a structure-matching algorithm leveraging the structure of the XML-based service specification in WSDL. Currently developers can only browse UDDI registries and query the advertised services by business category. This is a very blunt and imprecise service-discovery mechanism.

Our web-service discovery method is inspired by traditional information retrieval methods, signature matching methods and many experiments conducted with WordNet for component retrieval. It is designed to calculate semantic and structural similarity between a desired service and a set of advertised services. WordNet-based methods do not attempt to resolve word senses; this problem has been proven difficult by current research, but fortunately it does not apply in the case of the WSDL descriptions, comments and identifiers, which are not likely to be complete grammatical sentences. WordNet is used as a "query expansion" mechanism: it includes semantically similar words retrieved from WordNet database for all documents and queries to ameliorate information retrieval results. The structure-matching algorithm respects the structural information of data types and is flexible enough to allow relaxed matching and matching between parameters that come in different orders in parameter lists. Our web service discovery method that combines WordNet-powered vector space model with semantic structure matching constitutes an important extension to the UDDI API, because it enables a substantially more precise service-discovery process.

We have conducted various experiments to evaluate the effectiveness of our retrieval system with very positive results. In the future, we plan to extend this algorithm to exploit the full WSDL syntax. Currently, we are not considering some of the syntax WSDL offers such as minOccurs, maxOccurs that indicate minimum and maximum occurrences of data types, and some other attributes of element tags. We also plan to experiment with larger sets of web services.

Acknowledgements. The authors wish to thank Tu Hoang for his help in developing parts of these algorithms. This research was supported by an IRIS grant.

References

1. I. Cho, J. McGregor, and L. Krause. "A protocol-based approach to specifying interoperability between objects". In Proceedings of the *26th Technology of Object-Oriented Languages and Systems* (TOOLS'26), 3–07 August 1998, Santa Barbara, CA, 84–96. IEEE Press.
2. The DARPA Agent Markup Language Homepage. http://www.daml.org/
3. C. Faloutsos, and D.W. Oard. "A survey of Information Retrieval and Filtering Methods, University of Maryland". Technical Report CS-TR-3514, August 1995.
4. K. Sycara, S. Widoff, M. Klusch and J. Lu. "LARKS: Dynamic Matchmaking Among Heterogeneous Software Agents in Cyberspace". *Autonomous Agents and Multi-Agent Systems*, 5, 173–203, 2002.
5. G.A. Miller, R. Beckwith, C. Felbaum, D. Gross and K. Miller, "Introduction to WordNet: An On-line Lexical Database", International Journal of Lexicography, Vol. 3, No.4, 1990, 235–244.
6. G.A. Miller, "Nouns in WordNet: A Lexical Inheritance System", International Journal of Lexicography, Vol3, No.4, 1990, 245–264.
7. R. Mandala, T. Takenobu and T. Hozumi. "The Use of WordNet in Information Retrieval," in *Proceedings of the COLING/ACL Workshop on Usage of WordNet in Natural Language Processing Systems*, Montreal, 1998, 31–37.
8. J. Purtilo and J.M. Atlee. "Module Reuse by Interface Adaptation". Software Practice and Experience, Vol. 21, No. 6, 1991, 539–556.
9. R. Richardson and A.F. Smeaton. "Using WordNet in a knowledge-based approach to information retrieval." Dublin City University School of Computer Applications Working Paper CA-0395.

10. G. Salton, A. Wong and C.S. Yang. "A vector-space model for information retrieval", In Journal of the American Society for Information Science, Vol. 18. November 1975, 13–620. ACM Press.
11. Simple Object Access Protocol (SOAP) http://www.w3.org/TR/2003/REC-soap12-part0-20030624/
12. UDDI technical paper, http://www.uddi.org/pubs/Iru_UDDI_Technical_White_Paper.pdf
13. E. Voorhees. "Using WordNet for Text Retrieval", in C.Fellbaum (ed.), *WordNet: An Electronic Lexical Database* 1998, The MIT Press, Cambridge, MA. 1999, 285–303.
14. Y. Wang and E. Stroulia. "Flexible Interface Matching for Web-Service Discovery". In Proceedings of 4*th International Conference on Web Information Systems Engineering,* December 10th - 12th, 2003 (to appear).
15. Web Services Description Language (WSDL) (WSDL) http://www.w3.org/TR/wsdl
16. WordNet http://www.cogsci.princeton.edu/~wn/
17. XMethods homepage. http://www.xmethods.com/
18. A. M. Zaremski and J. M. Wing. "Signature Matching: a Tool for Using Software Libraries". ACM Transactions on Software Engineering and Methodology, Vol. 4 No. 2, 146–170, Apr. 1995.
19. A. M. Zaremski and J. M. Wing. "Specifications Matching of Software Components". ACM Transactions on Software Engineering and Methodology, Vol. 6, No. 4, 333–369, Oct. 1997.

Preliminary Report of Public Experiment of Semantic Service Matchmaker with UDDI Business Registry

Takahiro Kawamura[1], Jacques-Albert De Blasio[1], Tetsuo Hasegawa[1], Massimo Paolucci[2], and Katia Sycara[2]

[1] Research and Development Center, Toshiba Corp
[2] The Robotics Institute, Carnegie Mellon University

Abstract. The public experiment of the semantic service search with the public UDDI registry is shown in this paper. The UDDI is a standard registry for Web Services, but if we consider it as a search engine, the functionality is restrictive, that is, based on keyword retrieval only. Therefore, the Matchmaker was developed to enhance the UDDI search functionality by using semantics such as ontology and constraints. However, for Web Services as e-Business platform, compliance with the standard specification such as SOAP, WSDL, UDDI is the key. Thus, our goal of this experiment is to seamlessly combine semantic search with those standards, and investigate the feasibility of using semantics with Web Services. This paper firstly shows the overall architecture where the Matchmaker can be located between UDDI and service developers/users. Then, the Matchmaker and our semantic service description which can be complementary used with the standard WSDL and UDDI Data Structure are shown. Also, we illustrate some tools which generate the service description and support the use of the Matchmaker. Finally, we qualitatively evaluate this experiment on the response from business users.

1 Introduction

Web Services are considered as the core technology of e-Business platforms. The spreading of Web services in the Intranets and in the near future in the whole Internet reveals the needs of sophisticated discovery mechanisms. In the space of discovery, UDDI is emerging as the de-facto standard registry for Web services and it is proposed as the main tool for Web service discovery. However, the only discovery mechanism provided by UDDI is keyword search on the names and the features of businesses and services descriptions; unfortunately, keyword search fails to recognize the similarities and differences between the capabilities provided by Web services. Ultimately, UDDI is useful only to find information about known Web services, but it completely fail as a general Web services discovery mechanism.

To address this problem, we developed Semantic Services Matchmaker, a search engine for Web services, that enhances the discovery facilities of UDDI

M.E. Orlowska et al. (Eds.): ICSOC 2003, LNCS 2910, pp. 208–224, 2003.

to make use of semantic information. Furthermore, we initiated an experiment on a publicly available UDDI maintained by NTT-Communications, one of four official UDDI operators to evaluated the scalability and viability of our approach on a large scale[1].

The Semantic Services Matchmaker is based on the LARKS[1] algorithm, but it also borrows some ideas from the DAML-S matching algorithm[2]. Specifically,it adopts the LARKS filtering approach which uses sophisticated information retrieval mechanisms to locate Web services advertisements in UDDI even when no semantic information has been provided. To this extent, we can show the contribution and the limits of information retrieval techniques to Web services discovery, and the contribution of ontological information to increase the precision of matching.

In the rest of the paper we will discuss our approach and experiment. In section 2 we first introduce the overall architecture of this experiment; in section 3 and 4 we will introduce the Semantic Service Matchmaker and its semantic service description called Web Services Semantic Profile (WSSP). In section 5 we describe supporting tools that provide an interface to UDDI that allows semantic markup and matching. Then, in section 6, we will present an initial evaluation on the response from business users we have collected during its design and deployment phase.

2 Architecture of Public UDDI Registry and Matchmaker

The architecture of the integrated UDDI Registry and Matchmaker is shown in Fig. 1. In the architecture, the Matchmaker is inserted between the users of the matchmaker, namely users that request services and Web Services developers that advertise them, and the UDDI registry. The Matchmaker API is equivalent to the UDDI API to facilitate the users seamless connection; furthermore, the format of the results returned adopts the same format of the results returned by UDDI. The result is that the Matchmaker can be added to any UDDI registry leaving to users and developers the choice of the most preferable Web Services registry in accordance with the cost and interoperability with their already-existing systems. Fig. 2 shows the internal architecture of the Matchmaker, which will be discussed in details in section 3.

The second feature of the architecture is that it strives to be compliant with the current standard technology of Web Services such as SOAP and WSDL, since the use of any proprietary technology would reduce the advantage of using Web Services as the common e-Business platform.

[1] The Semantic Services Matchmaker has been implemented in a collaboration between Carnegie Mellon University and Toshiba Corp. The public experiment is a collaboration between Toshiba Corp. and NTT-Communications. The experiment site is at www.agent-net.com.

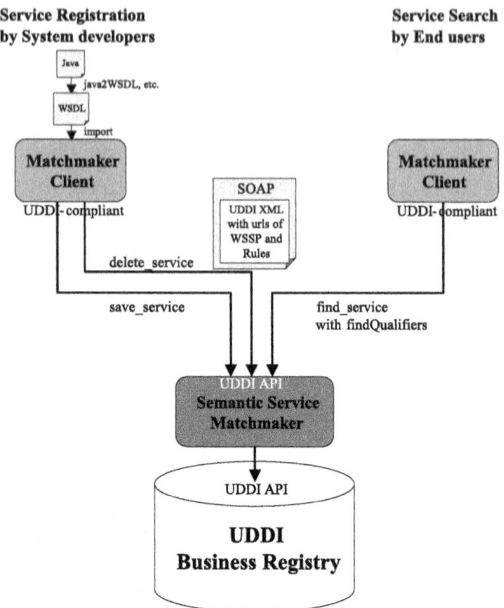

Fig. 1. Network architecture of UDDI and Matchmaker

2.1 Usage Scenario

In the rest of this section we will describe how the Matchmaker is used, and specifically we will describe service registration and search scenarios. We hope to demonstrate the contribution of the Matchmaker to the UDDI search facilities.

Registration

1. During service registration the client tools associated with the Matchmaker Client in Fig. 1, are used to generate a semantic service description from a WSDL description which has been automatically generated from the java source code. The client tools, which will be described in details in section 5, support annotation of the ontology classes in RDFS[8], DAML+OIL[9], or OWL[10] to inputs and outputs' parameters, and also the definition of rules as inputs and outputs' constraints. Of course the client may decide not to send any semantic description to the Matchmaker at all; in the latter case, the client registers as a standard UDDI client.
2. Upon receiving the registration, the Matchmaker extracts the semantic annotation. If the annotation is found, the Matchmaker stores it with all the ontologies it refers to. Finally, the Matchmaker registers the service with the UDDI registry.

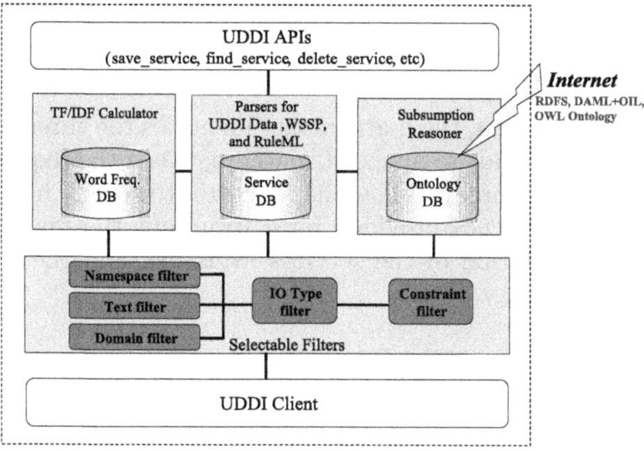

Fig. 2. Semantic Service Matchmaker

Search

1. During the service search, the client sends a search request to the Matchmaker. The search request consists of a search in UDDI augmented with a semantic annotation of the desirable service interface, consisting of all the desirable inputs' ontology classes and outputs' ontology classes. As in the case of the service registration, users can specify the inputs and outputs' constraints. Furthermore, the client may also decide to restrict his search to the requirements of a normal UDDI keyword search tool.
2. The Matchmaker checks whether or not the search request includes semantic designation like ontology classes and rules. If so, the matching engine searches for a service that is similar enough to the service requested in the registered services database. After making the matching results, the Matchmaker retrieves the detailed information of those results from the UDDI registry, then get back them to the client. Note that several search options for the Matchmaker can also be specified via UDDI APIs.

3 Semantic Service Matchmaker

Above we showed how users and programs can exploit the Matchmaker and the UDDI API to find the services that provide the capabilities that they expect. In this section, we provide the details of how the matching of capabilities is performed.

Ideally, when the requester looks for a service, the matchmaker will retrieve a service that matches exactly the service that the requester expects. In practice, it is very unlikely that such a service is available, instead the matchmaker will retrieve a service whose capabilities are *similar* to the capabilities expected by the requester. One of the challenges of matchmaking is to locate services that the requester could despite the differences from the request. Furthermore, the matchmaker should be able to characterize the distance between the request and the matches found, so that the requester can make an informed decision on which services to invoke.

To address this problem, the matchmaker identifies the three levels of matching where *exact* corresponds to an exact match between the request and the services provided. Furthermore, we allow the requester to specify how closely should the request and the matches provided be. Ultimately, the matching process is the result of the interaction of the services available, and the requirements of the requester.

Exact match is the highest degree of matching, it results when the two descriptions are equivalent.

Plug-in match results when the service provided is more general than the service requested, but in practice it can be used in place of the ideal system that the requester would like to use. To this extent the result can be "plugged in" place of the correct match. A simple example of a plug-in match is the the match between a requested service that sell books and a service that sells printed materials. Since books are printed materials chances are that the latter service can be used instead.

Relaxed match. The relaxed match has a weakest semantic interpretation: it is used to indicate the degree of similarity between the advertisement and the request.

The second aspect of our matchmaker is to provide a set of filters that help with the matching, and we allow users to decide which filters they would like to adopt at any given time. Specifically, the matching process is organized as a series of five filters. All filters are independent from each other, and each of them narrows the set of matching candidates with respect to a given filter criterion. The first three filters are meant for the relaxed match, and the last two are meant for the plug-in match (see Fig. 3). Users may select any combination of these filters at the search time, considering the trade-off between accuracy and speed of the matching process. We briefly illustrate each filter as follows. Further details are provided in Sycara et al.[1].

3.1 Namespace Filter

Pre-checking process which determines whether or not the requested service and the registered ones have at least one shared namespace (a url of an ontology file). The intersection of namespaces can be considered shared knowledge between the request and the advertisement. Therefore, only the registered services which have at least one shared namespace go into the next filter. Namespaces of default like rdf, rdfs, xsd, etc. are not considered the intersection. Of course, there is a case that the relation between two nodes of different ontology files does exist, although the distance would be relatively long. This filter and the next two filters are meant for the reduction of the computation time of the last two filters.

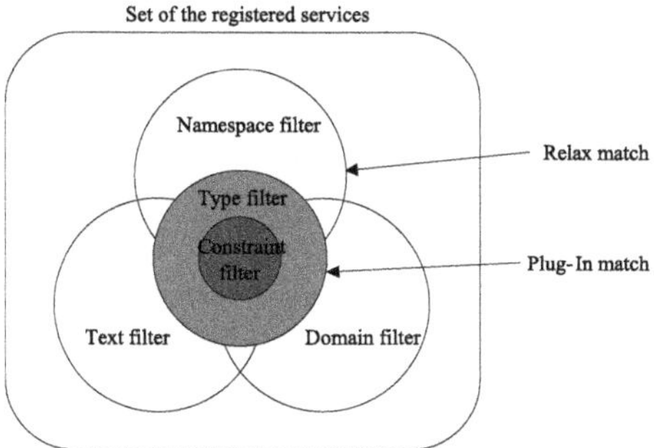

Fig. 3. Criterion of each filter

3.2 Text Filter

Pre-checking process for human-readable service explanation parts such as comment and text descriptions. It utilizes the well-known IR (Information Retrieval) technique called TF/IDF (Term Frequency Inverse Document Frequency) method. This filter help to minimize the risk to miss the services which have any relation to the requested one.

3.3 Domain Filter

Pre-checking process to check whether or not each registered service and the requested one belong to an ontology domain. The ontology domain here means a subtree in a ontology tree. To determine the subtree which two services belong to, we first we extract ontology nodes related with the service category or outputs as concepts of the services, then we select a common ancestor in the ontology tree. If the advertisement and the request are in a certain size of the subtree, the registered one passes the filter. Note that if we can find relationship such as subClassOf, sameAs between different ontology trees, we merge the trees and trace up them seamlessly.

3.4 I/O Type Filter

The Type Filter checks to see if the definitions of the input and output parameters match. In the semantic service description shown in the next section, parameter types of inputs and outputs are defined as ontology classes. A set of subtype inferencing rules mainly based on structural algorithm are used to determine in this filter.

Such a match is determined if: (see Fig. 4)

- the types and number of input/output parameters exactly matches, OR
- outputs of the registered service can be subsumed by outputs of the requested service, and the number of outputs of the registered service is greater than the number of outputs of the requested service, AND/OR

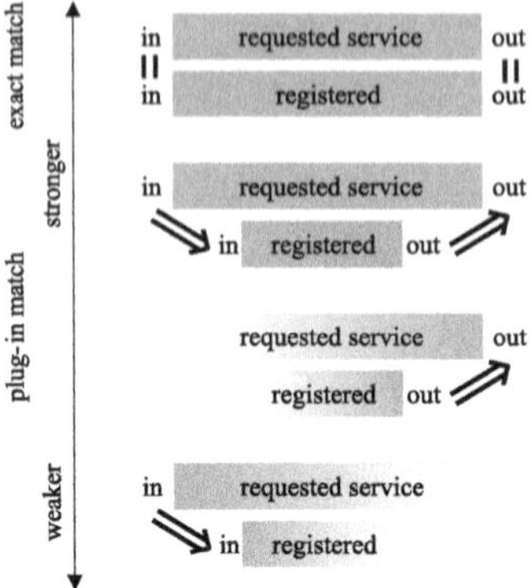

Fig. 4. Levels of plug-in match

- inputs of the requested service can be subsumed by inputs of the registered service, and the number of inputs of the requested service is greater than the number of inputs of the registered service.

If there is a mismatch in the number of parameters, then the filter attempts to pair up parameters in the registered one with those in the request, by seeking the registered one's parameters that are sub-types of the requested one's parameters.

Further, the request may not have a model of what inputs may be required, and may need to obtain this information from the returned service. To support this, inputs and inputs' constraints in the next section also match when those of the request are empty.

3.5 Constraint Filter

The responsibility of this filter is to verify whether, the subsumption relationship for each of the constraints are logically valid. The constraints filter compares the constraints to determine if the registered service is less constrained than the request. The Matchmaker computes the logical implication among constraints by using polynomial subsumption checking for Horn clauses. Matching is achieved by performing conjunctive pair-wise comparisons for the properties. In detail, the logical implication among constraints is computed using polynomial θ-subsumption checking for Horn clauses.

The constraints for inputs and outputs are defined for the request (R_I and R_O) and for each registered service (A_I and A_O). The constraints for inputs R_I is compared with A_I, and a match is determined if A_I subsumes R_I, i.e.

$$match(R_I, A_I) \Leftarrow (\forall j, \exists i : (i \in R_I) \wedge (j \in A_I) \wedge subs(j,i)) \vee R_I = \emptyset$$

where $subs(j,i)$ is true when j subsumes i. The constraints for outputs match when all the elements in R_O subsumes elements in A_O, i.e.

$$match(R_O, A_O) \Leftarrow \forall i, \exists j : (i \in R_O) \wedge (j \in A_O) \wedge subs(i,j)$$

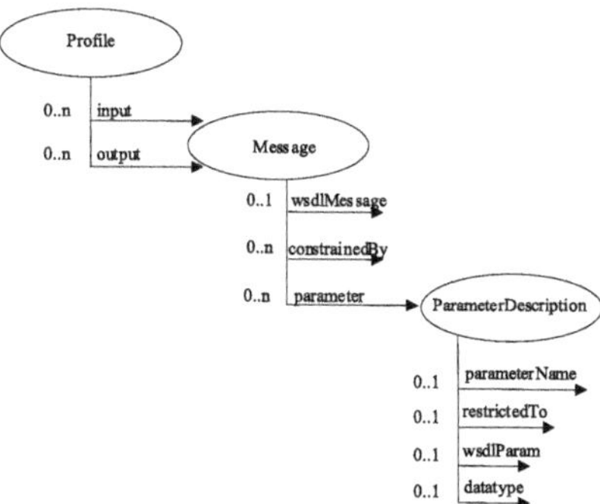

Fig. 5. Structure of WSSP

4 Semantic Service Description

In the previous section we described the matching process, and specifically we described how ontologies are used by the constraint filter. In this section, we describe the Web Service Semantic Profile (WSSP), a way to encode semantic information in WSDL that is inspired by the DAML-S Service Profile[11].

WSDL specifies the programming interface of Web service to be used at invocation time. To this account it specifies the name of the function to invoke and the type of data that the Web service expects as input or it generates as output. Data types describe how the information is formatted, but because there are arbitrarily many ways of encoding the same information in data types, they fail to express the semantics of the information that they encode. Unfortunately, semantic information is exactly what is needed to express the capabilities of Web services. The aim of the WSSP is to enrich WSDL with the semantics it needs to represent capabilities of web services.

Fig. 5 shows the structure of a WSSP, and its relation with WSDL. As in a WSDL file, we define each message and each parameter of those messages. *Parameter descriptions* store descriptions of parameters that are used to define the semantics of the parameter in the *restrictedTo* element as well as the data types of the information in the *datatype* element, as shown in the example below.

Moreover, we offer the possibility to add constraints to the inputs and outputs of the web service. Doing so we give the possibility to represent the web service more accurately, and we allow the search engine to perform a more accurate search. Constraints are added to the WSDL specification through the element *constrainedBy* which specifies the URI of a fact or rule written in an RDF-RuleML file [7].

The relation between the facts and rules and the WSSP are simple: each parameter of an input or output of the web service corresponds to a variable which can be used in facts and rules. It means that if a web service has "n" inputs parameters and "m" output parameters, the number of available variables will be "n+m". Thus we can write constraints using the inputs and outputs of

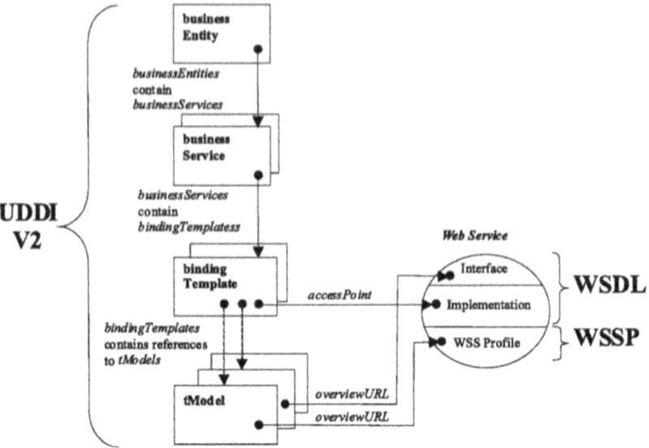

Fig. 6. Relationship between UDDI, WSDL and WSSP

the web service. Note that facts and rules are not bound to any input/output of the web service, they just uses them.

An example of an input message of a WSSP is given below. It presents examples of use of all the elements described above, and it also shows the relation to the original WSDL file through xPointer links [6].

```
<profile:input>
  <profile:message rdf:ID="1st_INPUTMessage">

    <profile:parameter>
      <profile:ParameterDescription rdf:ID="1st_INPUTMessage_Param_1">
        <profile:parameterName>Param_1</profile:parameterName>
        <profile:restrictedTo rdf:resource="http://ont.com/Onto.owl#Item1"/>
        <profile:wsdlParam>xPointer to wsdl parameter</profile:wsdlParam>
        <profile:datatype>XMLSchema.xsd#String</profile:datatype>
      </profile:ParameterDescription>
    </profile:parameter>

    <profile:constrainedBy rdf:resource="http://rule.com/rules.rdf#1"/>
    <profile:constrainedBy rdf:resource="http://rule.com/rules.rdf#2"/>

    <profile:wsdlMessage>xPointer to wsdl message</profile:wsdlMessage>

  </profile:message>
</profile:input>
```

In Fig. 6, we describe the relation between UDDI, WSDL and WSSP. A Web Service is completely described by three entities, the WSDL interface and binding (implementation) and the WSSP. This architecture provides a clear separation between how the Web Service works and what it does. Moreover, as we mention later, there is no redundancy between the data recorded in the UDDI description of the Web Service and a WSSP.

5 Supporting Tools

In this section, we introduce our client tools for the registration and search of services through an example. These tools allow human users to register Web services with the Matchmaker and UDDI, as well as search for Web services. The example we use concerns a web service that can tell a requester in how many days a given manufacturer can deliver a certain type of material (called parts in our example). This web service has first been described via a WSDL file which may have been generated automatically from Java source code. In this example, the user will first import the WSDL interface in *Matchmaker Client* and then add semantic annotations to input and output parameters using *Ontology Viewer*. Furthermore, the user adds facts and rules in order to add input constraints by using *Rule Editor*

The following is the part of the WSDL interface containing the description of the input and output messages of the web service.

```
<message name="PartsRequest">
  <part name="part" type="xsd:string"/>
  <part name="numberParts" type="xsd:int"/>
  <part name="manufacturer" type="xsd:string"/>
  <part name="country" type="xsd:string"/>
</message>

<message name="DeliveryResponse">
  <part name="deliveryDays" type="xsd:int"/>
</message>

<portType name="PartsService">
  <operation name="getQuote">
    <input message="sq:PartsRequest"/>
    <output message="sq:DeliveryResponse"/>
  </operation>
</portType>
```

5.1 Matchmaker Client

The following steps illustrates a typical use of the Matchmaker Client. Note that because the Matchmaker has the same API as the UDDI registry, the Matchmaker Client can be used as a UDDI client tool, and also other UDDI client tools can be used to register and search to the Matchmaker, but in this case they require the creation of WSSP with the appropriate semantic information.

Creation of a Business Service. The tools for the creation of the *Business Service* are shown in Fig. 7,8. To create a Business Service the user can import the WSDL file in the Matchmaker Client, completing automatically some of the fields. The user can add the ontology annotations using the Ontology Viewer, which parses ontology files written by RDFS, DAML+OIL, or OWL, then show them as graphical trees. The user can specify any ontology class to be annotated to each parameter by clicking a node in the trees (see Fig. 9). Finally, the user can add facts and rules using the Rule Editor, described in details below.

Registration of the Business Service. After creating a Business Service, the user can register it with the Matchmaker and UDDI as a consequence. Fig. 10 shows that the WSSP is created automatically as part of the registration. The WSSP is then uploaded on the Matchmaker with all the ontology files and the definitions of the rules.

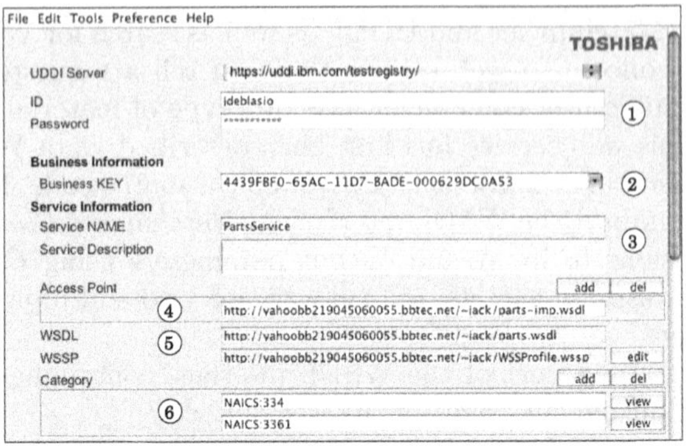

1. Information about the UDDI Server and the user's login and password
2. Business Key corresponding to the business entity for which the user wants to register this business service
3. **Auto-completed** fields after having read the WSDL file
4. URL to implementations of the web service
5. URLs to the WSDL and WSSP files (the latter must be uploaded by the user once automatically created)
6. List of categories under which the business service can be classified

Fig. 7. Service registration - part1

An example of WSSP generated by the Matchmaker Client is shown below. There one of the inputs is a `part` that is described semantically by the concept `Parts.owl#Part` and syntactically specified as a `XSD:String`. Furthermore, the example shows a set of rules that provides additional properties that we want that part to hold. As pointed out above, xPointers are used to relate the WSSP to the WSDL. The precise definition has been omitted here to make the code more readable.

```
<profile:input>
  <profile:Message rdf:ID="PartsRequest">

    <profile:parameter>
      <profile:ParameterDescription rdf:ID="PartsRequest_part">
        <profile:parameterName>part</profile:parameterName>
        <profile:restrictedTo rdf:resource="http://example.com/onto/Parts.owl#Part"/>
        <profile:wsdlParam>xPointer to this parameter in the WSDL file</profile:wsdlParam>
        <profile:datatype>http://www.w3.org/2001/XMLSchema#string</profile:datatype>
      </profile:ParameterDescription>
    </profile:parameter>

    [other input parameters...]

    <profile:constrainedBy rdf:resource=http://bb.net/rules.rdf#ManufacturerOf(Part,Acme)/>
    <profile:constrainedBy rdf:resource=http://bb.net/rules.rdf#ManufacturerOf(Toshiba,Computers)/>
    <profile:constrainedBy rdf:resource=http://bb.net/rules.rdf#CountryManufacturer(Toshiba,JAPAN)/>
    <profile:constrainedBy rdf:resource=http://bb.net/rules.rdf#ManufacturerOf(Ford,Cars)/>
    <profile:constrainedBy rdf:resource=http://bb.net/rules.rdf#CountryManufacturer(Ford,USA/>
    <profile:wsdlMessage>xPointer to this message in the WSDL file</profile:wsdlMessage>

  </profile:Message>
</profile:input>
```

Search of the business service. Finally, Fig. 11 specifies the search tools that we defined. They allow to specify the number of inputs and output of the desired service, to choose ontologies for each parameter through the Ontology Viewer, and finally, to select facts and rules with the Rule Editor.

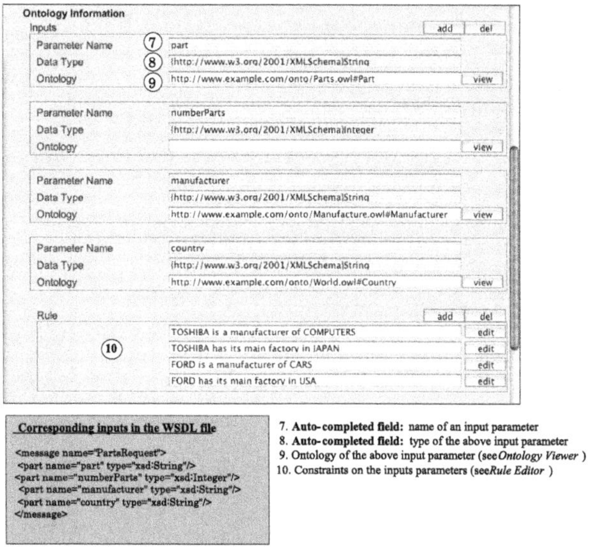

Fig. 8. Service registration - part2

5.2 Rule Editor

The writing of RuleML rules is a difficult and wordy process even for logic experts. The example of fact below, shows a very simple statement: `CountryManufacturer(Toshiba,JAPAN)` takes 16 lines of XML code to be expressed. While RuleML adds value and expressive power to WSSP, it is bound to be unusable unless we facilitate the process of creating rules. To address this problem, we developed a tool called the Rule Editor which allows anyone to easily write facts and rules, as if they were writing natural sentences.

The Rule Editor is invoked by the user by pressing the "edit" button when registering a service or searching for one. The invocation of the Rule Editor will result in the interface shown in Fig. 12 and the user will be able to easily create facts and rules. He will then choose one of the fact or rule and click on the "Send to WSMM" button. Thus doing, the id of fact or rule will appear in the "Rule" text field of the Matchmaker Client, and a RDF-RuleML file will be automatically generated.

The variables used in the facts and rules correspond to the input and output parameters of a WSDL file. Following is a part of the file generated by the Rule Editor (the part corresponds to the selected fact on the snapshot). Note the difference between how the fact is represented in the Rule Editor and how it is actually written in the RDF-RuleML file. The correspondence between the two is realized via an external file that tells the Rule Editor how to read predicates. For instance there would be, in this definition file, a line stating that the predicate "CountryManufacturer" is read "has its main factory in" and that it has two terms. This file would have been created by an expert. Eventually, creating facts

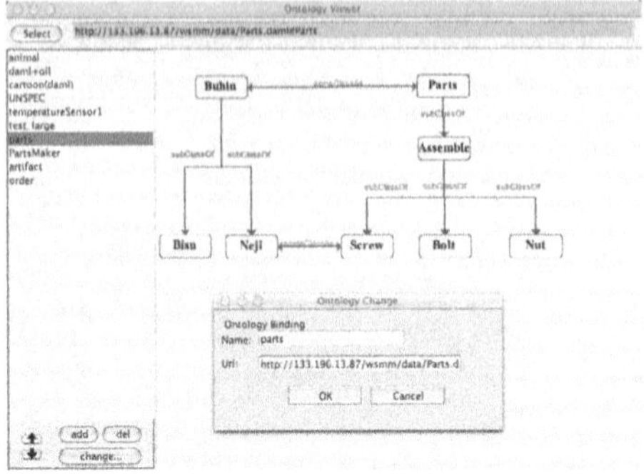

Fig. 9. Ontology Viewer

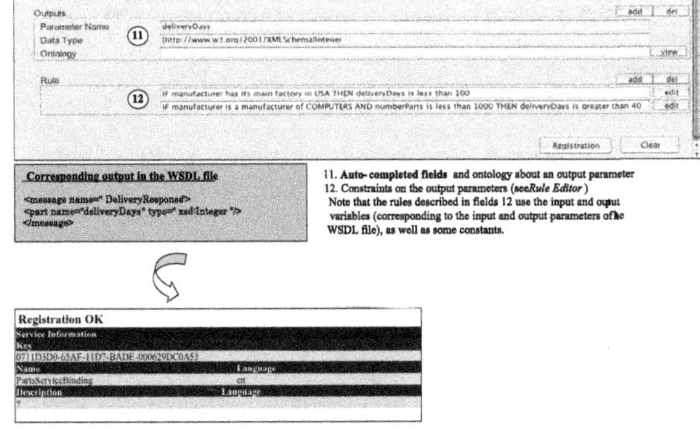

Fig. 10. Service registration - part3

and rules will become easy to any user, because writing those using our Rule Editor will be as natural as to write simple English sentences.

```
<ruleml:Fact ruleml:label="CountryManufacturer(Toshiba,JAPAN)">
  <ruleml:head>
    <ruleml:Atom ruleml:rel="http://example.com/preds/Predicates.owl#CountryManufacturer">
      <ruleml:args>
        <rdf:Seq>
          <rdf:li>
            <ruleml:Ind ruleml:name="http://example.com/onto/Manufacture.owl#TOSHIBA" />
          </rdf:li>
          <rdf:li>
            <ruleml:Ind ruleml:name="http://example.com/onto/World.owl#JAPAN" />
          </rdf:li>
        </rdf:Seq>
      </ruleml:args>
    </ruleml:Atom>
  </ruleml:head>
</ruleml:Fact>
```

Find Service Results

Services		
Service Name	Description	Owning Business
PartsServiceBinding		4439FBF0-65AC-11D7-BADE-000629DC0A53

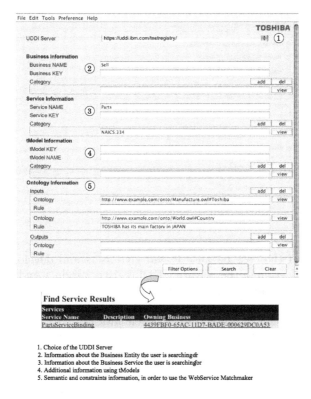

1. Choice of the UDDI Server
2. Information about the Business Entity the user is searchingfr
3. Information about the Business Service the user is searchingfor
4. Additional information using tModels
5. Semantic and constraints information, in order to use the WebService Matchmaker

Fig. 11. Service Search

6 Evaluation

The Matchmaker service described in this paper, which provide a semantically-enhanced UDDI Business Registry has started its operations only recently, therefore we can report only a qualitative evaluation of our system design.

At the design and deployment phase of this experiment, we have collected lots of VoC (Voice of Customer) from system integrators and user companies of Web Services, by using DFACE (Define-Focus-Analyze-Create-Evaluate) methodology, a version of "Design for Six Sigma" [12] developed by Stanford University.

The responses of the users in terms of requirements for Web Services are as follows. The No.1 request from both of system integrators and users is the reduction of the cost of development and administration. The second requirement is interoperability with the current systems running or selling in their companies. The third one is a track record and security in general. In term of Web Services search engine itself, the most important thing is ease of use and search speed, rather than advanced functions.

Those results made us decide to obey the standard technology as much as possible. This means not only the improvement of the interoperability, but also

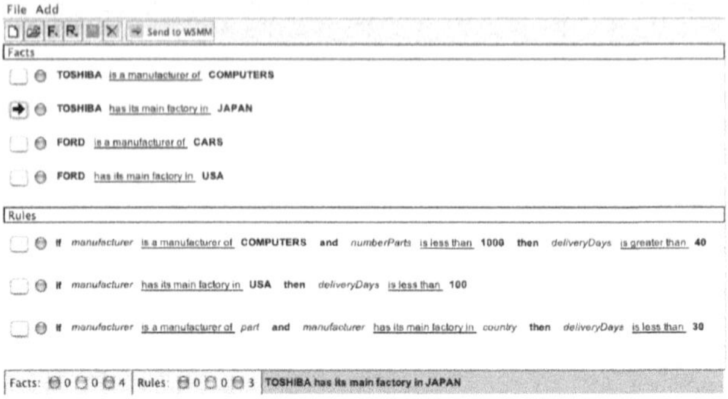

Fig. 12. Rule Editor

the reduction of the cost because it will give users and developers freedom of choice at the selection of the private UDDI registry product and the client tools. Besides, we expect this public experiment contributes to the track record. Further, we expect that client tools including the Rule Editor and the Ontology Viewer will lower the threshold of use of semantics.

Here we should note that from the point of the interoperability WSSP is a weakness of our system since it does not correspond to any existing Web service description language. However the combination of of Web Services and semantics is a kind of missing link at this time. Therefore we had to invent it as a glue. Although we adopted WSSP in this experiment, if any standard will allow the description the same contents as the WSSP in near future, we will be pleased to adopt it.

As future work, we would like to present the quantitative evaluation of this whole experiment in terms of usability, accuracy, speed, and so forth.

7 Related Work

As we mentioned above, the Matchmaker is based on the LARKS[1] and the DAML-S matchmaker[2]. Here we briefly describe other approaches of the matchmaking problem.

InfoSleuth[4] is a multi-agent system that supports information discovery and retrieval application where broker agents provide semantic brokering. Service provider agents advertise their service capabilities and constraints to the broker in LDL++, a logical deduction language developed by MCC, the InfoSleuth company. The requester agents query for the service providers to the broker in the same language. Then the broker uses constraint-based reasoning to find agents whose services match the constraints specified by the requester. In contrast, we prefer to close to Web Services standards such as WSDL and UDDI, then complement them with Semantic Web standards such as OWL and RuleML.

Horrocks et al.[5] have develped a framework for matchmaking based on Semantic Web technology like DAML-S[11]. Their matchmaker uses a DL (Descripion Logics) reasoner to match service arvertisements and requests based on the semantics of ontology-based service description. Then, the performance evaluation shows that DL reasoning technology could cope with large scale e-commerce application. We can see similarities between their matchmaker and our work, since their work is based on the LARKS to some extent. Although their DL reasoner is highly organized, we are using not only the DL technology but also the information retrieval technique for no semantic information. Beside, as with the above, our work differs from their system in the aspects of adherence to Web Services standards.

In terms of the services description language, WSSP has been greatly inspired by the work done for the DAML-S Profile[11], although our work reflects a different point of view which is one of our main goals, closer to the industry needs.

DAML-S is meant to describe everything a web service can do by combining a Service Profile, a Service Model and a Service Grounding. This approach is very powerful because all the details about a web service, from the most general down to the smallest, can be fully described. Yet, because of the relations between the different modules of DAML-S, it is difficult to use only the Service Profile without implicitly adopting the Process Model and the Grounding. On the other side, the industry is fragmented with different standards emerging, so any commitment to one technology or the other may prove very dangerous at this point. In this work we adopted the basic ideas of DAML-S, and we imported them directly in WSDL which is the minimum common denominator of all the Web services technology.

One of the goals of this search engine was to work as a semantic layer on top of UDDI. The results of a search would be a list of one or more UDDI Business Service. The solution proposed for DAML-S to work along with UDDI implied the mapping of the DAML-S Profile to a UDDI Data Structure[3]. Although this solution is elegant, we would have redundancy if we map the data of the DAML-S Profile and WSDL to the UDDI Data Structure. Thus, we decided to make our profiles "lighter" and avoid repeating descriptions between our profiles and WSDL.

8 Conclusion and Future Work

In this paper, we provides an initial report on our public experiment implementing the Semantic Service Matchmaker to expand the functionalities of the NTT-Communications public available UDDI registry. Here we described the architecture and the functionalities of the Matchmaker, and specifically the matching process. Furthermore, we provide a description of the WSSP, an extension of WSDL to describe capabilities of Web services, and the supporting tools implemented guided by business users' voice.

This is the first step toward the experiment, and that we did it on the bases on the interaction with the users and their comments. As the future works, we do need to make the quantitative evaluation after getting some amount of users' records, then tune the performance and functionality of the Matchmaker, and usability of the supporting tools. Further, although this is not our own issue, we should tackle the problem of ontology definition and management to facilitate the use of ontology.

References

1. K. Sycara, S. Widoff, M. Klusch, J. Lu, "LARKS: Dynamic Matchmaking Among Heterogeneous Software Agents in Cyberspace". In Autonomous Agents and Multi-Agent Systems, Vol.5, pp.173–203, 2002.
2. M. Paolucci, T. Kawamura, T. R. Payne, K. Sycara, "Semantic Matching of Web Services Capabilities", Proceedings of First International Semantic Web Conference (ISWC 2002), IEEE, pp. 333–347, 2002.
3. M. Paolucci, T. Kawamura, T. R. Payne, K. Sycara, "Importing the Semantic Web in UDDI", Proceedings of E-Services and the Semantic Web Workshop (ESSW 2002), 2002.
4. M. H. Nodine, J. Fowler, T. Ksiezyk, B. Perry, M. Taylor, and A. Unruh, "Active information gathering in infosleuth", International Journal of Cooperative Information Systems, pp. 3–28, 2000.
5. L. Li and I. Horrocks, "A software framework for matchmaking based on semantic web technology", Proceedings of the Twelfth International World Wide Web Conference (WWW 2003), pp. 331–339, 2003.
6. "XML Pointer Language",http://www.w3.org/TR/xptr.
7. "The Rule Markup Initiative", http://www.dfki.uni-kl.de/ruleml/.
8. "Resource Description Framework", http://www.w3.org/RDF/.
9. "DAML Language", http://www.daml.org/language/.
10. "Web-Ontology Working Group", http://www.w3.org/2001/sw/WebOnt/.
11. "DAML Services", http://www.daml.org/services/.
12. "Six Sigma Academy", http://www.6-sigma.com/.

Comparing WSDL-Based and ebXML-Based Approaches for B2B Protocol Specification

Martin Bernauer, Gerti Kappel, and Gerhard Kramler

Business Informatics Group, Vienna University of Technology, Austria
{lastname}@big.tuwien.ac.at

Abstract. When automating business processes spanning organizational boundaries, it is required to explicitly specify the interfaces of the cooperating software systems in order to achieve the desired properties of interoperability and loose coupling. So-called B2B protocols provide for the formal specification of relevant aspects of an interface, ranging from document types to transactions. Currently, there are two main approaches proposed for the specification of B2B protocols, the WSDL-based approach supporting Web Service languages, and the ebXML-based approach supporting languages defined along the ebXML project. Unfortunately, these approaches are not compatible, thus an organization wanting to engage in B2B collaboration needs to decide whether to embark on any of these new approaches, and which ones to use. This paper introduces a conceptual framework for B2B protocols, and based on this framework, a methodical comparison of the two approaches is provided, answering the questions of what the differences are and whether there are chances to achieve interoperability.

1 Introduction

The automation of business processes spanning organizational boundaries has potential. First steps towards this goal have proven highly successful, namely the use of email for communication between human agents, and the use of web applications for communication between humans and business applications published to the extranet or internet. The complete automation of business processes, however, still suffers from high implementation cost. Basically, the additional complexity is that the business applications of cooperating organizations cannot be developed independently of each other but need to be interoperable.

Interoperability of cooperating business applications which provides automation requires explicit specification of requirements and constraints on the business application's interfaces. Such specifications are referred to as B2B protocols [3], business protocols [16], public workflows [23], or conversation processes [5]. It has to be emphasized that the specification of a B2B protocol should be separated from the specifications of workflows within organizations that support the protocol, in order to facilitate loose coupling and design autonomy of the intra-organizational workflows [4,6].

M.E. Orlowska et al. (Eds.): ICSOC 2003, LNCS 2910, pp. 225–240, 2003.

A B2B protocol defines various aspects of an interface, such as the transport protocol, document types, security requirements, and transactional properties, to mention just a few. An organization playing a certain role in a collaboration has to support the protocol specifications in order to guarantee interoperability. If a protocol specification does not cover certain aspects, these have to be agreed on out of band by organizations willing to cooperate in order to achieve interoperability of their applications. Examples of widely used B2B protocols are EDIFACT, which covers only document types, and RosettaNet, which covers all of the above mentioned aspects.

Defining protocol specifications by means of formal languages – such as W3C's XML Schema for the specification of document types – is beneficial in various respects. First, it enables tool support for development tasks such as consistency checks, development of data transformations, and customization of predefined protocols in a controlled manner, thus easing the adoption of a B2B protocol by an organization. Second, interpretation of the specification allows for a generic, re-useable implementation of functions such as schema validation, messaging, and security management. Finally, formal specifications which are published on the web or in specialized repositories provide the basis for automated dynamic discovery and integration with any organization supporting a matching B2B protocol.

Currently, there are two main technologies proposed for the specification of B2B protocols. Most prominently, the Web Services idea [12] subsumes a set of specification languages, with WSDL as its core and several proposed extensions, such as BPEL4WS for the specification of behavioral aspects. Although the intended application domain of Web Services is not limited to B2B protocols, B2B is considered the most prominent one. In parallel to Web Services, the ebXML initiative[1] has developed a set of standards specifically targeted at the specification of B2B protocols. Vendor support for ebXML, however, is not as strong as for Web Services. Furthermore the ebXML-based and the WSDL-based approaches are not compatible, thus an organization wanting to engage in B2B collaboration needs to decide whether to embark on any of these new technologies, and which ones to use.

There have already been efforts in comparing ebXML and Web Services. In [3], Bussler identifies the required elements of a B2B protocol, and classifies various B2B standards using the categories "business event", "syndication", and "supporting". Languages for the specification of (aspects of) B2B protocols, such as ebXML and WSDL, are identified as supporting standards. No further evaluation of the classified B2B standards concerning the required protocol elements is provided. In [22], van der Aalst uses a comprehensive set of control flow and interaction patterns to evaluate the features of several languages proposed for the specification of processes, including BPEL4WS and workflow management products. The evaluation is focused on the control flow aspect, and does not include languages specific for B2B protocol specification. It is concluded that languages proposed by software vendors are often influenced by that vendors' product inter-

[1] `http://www.ebxml.org/`

ests, neglecting the real problems. In [18], Shapiro presents a detailed comparison of BPEL4WS, XPDL, the WfMCs proposed standard for XML-based workflow specification languages, and BPML, a language similar in scope with BPEL. The comparison focuses on the specification of executable workflows and leaves out the concepts provided by BPEL4WS and BPML for protocol specification. Similarly, our previous work [2] provides an overview of various process specification languages including WSDL-based and ebXML-based ones, but without making a clear distinction between protocol specification and implementation specification, and without specifically highlighting the differences between WSDL-based and ebXML-based approaches. The relationship of Web Services and ebXML has also been discussed in various magazine articles. For example, [10] argues that ebXML is advantageous in typical "regulated" B2B scenarios, whereas Web Services are considered adequate for more loose collaborations without formal commitments.

This paper intends to provide further insight by presenting a methodical comparison of languages focusing on protocol specification based on a framework for the classification of protocol layers and aspects. Specifically, we aim to answer the questions of what the actual differences are between WSDL-based and ebXML-based languages, and whether there are chances to achieve interoperability. In the following section, we present the framework used to guide the comparison. Section 3 gives a short overview of the languages and their relationship to our framework. The detailed comparison is given in Section 4. Section 5 concludes with a summary of the comparison and an outlook to future research.

2 Framework for Comparison

To describe and compare the capabilities of the two approaches, this section introduces a conceptual framework to provide for common terms. The framework is based on the eCo Framework [7], which provides for a general description of e-commerce systems, and on the workflow model proposed in [17], which provides for a more specific description of workflow systems.

First, the conceptual framework is based on the eCo Framework. The latter is a layered model and can be used by businesses to define and publish descriptions about their e-commerce systems. It defines seven layers, whereby the upper three layers (i.e., the "networks", "markets" and "business" layer) are not relevant for the description of a B2B protocol. The fourth layer, the *services layer*, is used to describe services by their interfaces which are provided and used by businesses. A service may be composed of sub-services and may invoke other services. These interactions between services are described at the *interactions layer*. It describes the types of interactions behind each service, and the types of messages which are exchanged during each interaction. A message type may contain several document types, which are described at the *documents layer*. Finally, the *information items layer* describes the types of information items that may be used in document types.

Each layer of the eCo Framework provides for the layer above and builds on the layer beneath. The layered architecture implies that an artefact defined at one layer is independent of any layer above. For example, a document type is defined independent of interactions or services it is used in. Thus it can be reused across interactions and services.

Second, the conceptual framework is based on the workflow model proposed by Rausch-Schott [17], which describes several aspects of workflows that workflow descriptions have to cope with. While the *functional aspect* specifies what is to be executed, i.e., the semantics of a function provided by a workflow, the *operational aspect* defines how the function is implemented. The *behavioral aspect* describes how functions can be composed, e.g., as a sequence or alternative. Concentrating on data, the *informational aspect* describes data structures and data flow between functions. The *organizational aspect* describes personal and technical resources. The *transactional aspect* deals with consistency, i.e., how transactions can be used to guarantee consistent execution of functions or whole workflows. The *causal aspect* defines why a certain B2B protocol is specified in a certain way and why it is being executed. And finally, the *historical aspect* defines which data should be logged at which point in time.

While Rausch-Schott's model is intended to describe workflows that execute within a single business, all but one aspect apply for B2B protocols as well and can thus be leveraged for their characterization. The historical aspect cannot be leveraged because it describes aspects that each participating business is responsible for separately. Since B2B protocols cross business boundaries in contrast to traditional workflows, it is necessary to introduce an additional *security aspect*. It describes confidentiality, non-repudiation, integrity, authorization, and authentication.

Table 1. Supported combinations of eCo layers and workflow aspects

	func.	org.	info.	behav.	secur.	trans.	causal	oper.
services	X	X	X	X	-	X	-	-
interactions	X	-	X	X	X	X	-	X
documents	-	-	X	-	-	-	-	-
info. items	-	-	X	-	-	-	X	-

The conceptual framework uses the layers of the eCo framework as a classification of requirements on a B2B protocol specification language, whereby each layer is refined by relevant workflow aspects. Considering relevance of combinations of aspects and layers, we consider only combinations of aspects and layers that are supported by the approaches. The respective meaning of each of these combinations has been derived from the idiosyncrasies of the ebXML-based and WSDL-based approaches and will be described along the layer-by-layer comparison of approaches in Section 4. Table 1 summarizes the supported combinations of layers and aspects.

3 Overview of Approaches

Each of the two approaches employs a set of specific languages for the specification of different parts of a B2B protocol. The languages employed in the WSDL-based approach have been selected from the various proposals made in the Web Services area. Since Web Service languages are developed by software vendors in loose cooperation, different options are available for certain specification tasks. For the purpose of the comparison, we have included those languages which we consider as having the broadest support among software vendors. The languages employed in the ebXML-based approach are those developed along the ebXML project and following efforts. The comparison is based on the most recent language specifications. This section introduces the languages employed by either approach, and how these languages relate to each other and to our conceptual framework (cf. Figure 1).

The WSDL-based approach employs XML Schema (cf. [25,26]) for the specification of information items. The documents layer is not supported. Interaction types are specified using WSDL (Web Service Description Language, cf. [24]) in combination with WSSP (Web Services Security Policy, cf. [9]), whereby WSSP complements WSDL in that it focuses on the security aspect. It should be noted that WSSP is in an initial public draft state, which exhibits inconsistencies. Nevertheless, it has been included in this comparison because it is the only option available for specifying the security aspect. Service types are specified using BPEL (Business Process Execution Language for Web Services, cf. [1]). Note that WSDL also supports specification of service types, but WSDL's concept of service type refers to software components, whereas BPEL specifies service types from a business case point of view, which is also the view taken in this paper.

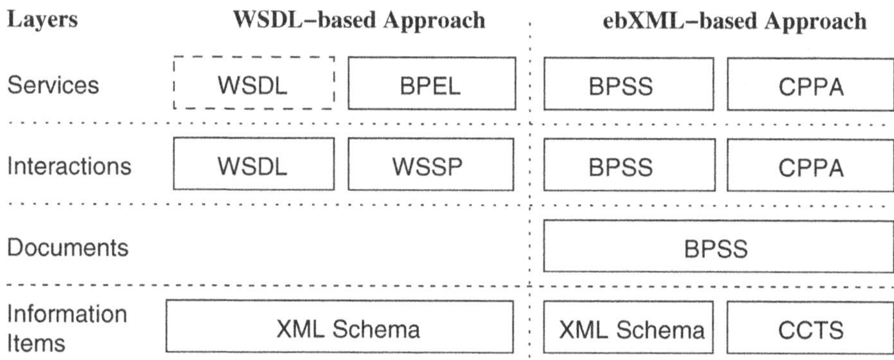

Fig. 1. Layers of the conceptual framework and supporting languages

The ebXML-based approach also employs XML Schema for the specification of information items. Furthermore, CCTS (Core Components Technical Specification, cf. [20]) defines a methodology and language for identification of information items, which can be used in the process of defining information items. Document types are specified using BPSS (Business Process Specification Schema, cf. [21]). Interaction types are specified in terms of BPSS and CPPA (Collaboration-Protocol Profile and Agreement Specification, cf. [13]). BPSS provides for the technology- and business-independent aspects, whereas CPPA is used to supplement technology and business details. In particular, CPPA can be used to overwrite certain properties of interaction types as defined with BPSS in order to adapt them to the needs of a specific business. Service types are specified using also BPSS and CPPA. Similar to the interaction layer, CPPA can be used to adapt a service type to a specific business.

4 Comparison

The comparison is performed along the layers of the eCo model. Beginning at the base layer, layer by layer and aspect by aspect we will detail the conceptual framework and analyze and compare the two approaches. The approaches are described in terms of our conceptual framework, with links to the keywords of the specific languages to provide for a better understanding. Keywords are denoted in sans serif font using the above introduced language-specific acronyms as namespace prefix (e.g., wsdl:message). Note that this comparison is performed at the level of language concepts, for an example specification expressed using both approaches it is referred to [11].

4.1 Information Items Layer

The Information Items layer specifies re-useable data types, such as address, product code, and price, independent of their use in particular documents. Aspects of workflow modeling supported in the specification of information items are the informational and the causal aspects.

Both the WSDL-based and the ebXML-based approach support XML Schema as the preferred language for the specification of information items. We will briefly review XML Schema in the light of our conceptual framework.

The Informational Aspect is concerned with the structure and semantics of information items, including refinement of information items, composition of information items, and various constraints such as cardinality.

In this respect, XML Schema provides built-in datatypes and structuring mechanisms. XML Schema's built-in datatypes are very generic and do not provide semantics specific to the needs of B2B applications. It is therefore necessary to define more specific ones. Recently, standardization efforts in the B2B area, such as OAG[2] and UBL[3], have begun to support XML Schema for the specifica-

[2] `http://www.openapplications.org/`

[3] `http://www.oasis-open.org/committees/ubl/`

tion of information items, thus such standard information items can be directly employed in a WSDL-based or ebXML-based B2B protocol specification.

The Causal Aspect is concerned with the reasons behind the design of information items, i.e., the identification of influence factors such as the requirements of a specific industry or a certain country.

XML Schema does not support the causal aspect of information item specification. However, CCTS, a part of the ebXML project, addresses this aspect. CCTS defines a methodology and language for the identification and specification of so-called core components, i.e., generic information items which are independent of any particular business context such as business process, industry, and official constraints, and thus widely reusable. To make core components usable in a specific application context, they are adapted by means of restrictions and/or extensions in order to incorporate the specific requirements. As the semantics of a specific information item can be derived from the semantics of the core component it is based upon, semantic expressiveness and interoperability is improved. CCTS does not specify a concrete schema language for core components and information items, which makes the methodology applicable to different technologies such as EDI and ebXML. Unfortunately, there is no standardized way to transform core components to XML Schema. As a possible solution to this problem, the UBL effort creates schemas in XML Schema for core components which have been derived from existing standard document types. UBL schemas can be directly used in both ebXML-based and WSDL-based protocol specifications.

4.2 Documents Layer

Documents are containers for information items and are used to carry information in the workflow within and across businesses. Only the informational aspect is supported in the specification of document types.

In the WSDL-based approach, document types are not supported at all, meaning that message types are defined directly based on information items. In the ebXML-based approach, there is some support for document types addressing the informational aspect. A document type is specified in terms of a name and the information item contained in the document (bpss:BusinessDocument). The information item may be further restricted allowing for application-specific restrictions of standard information items, e.g., the status value must be "accept" (bpss:ConditionExpression).

4.3 Interactions Layer

An interaction is a basic exchange of messages between business partners having a certain effect. Interaction types are specified in a declarative way by means of predefined constructs supporting common interaction patterns. A typical interaction pattern is request/response, e.g., one partner sends a purchase order request, and the other responds with an acknowledgement, meaning that the order is in effect. Another typical pattern is the oneway interaction, e.g., one business partner sends a shipment notification. Several workflow aspects are supported in the specification of an interaction type, namely the functional, informational, behavioral, security, transactional, and operational aspects.

In the WSDL-based approach, interactions have the semantics of remote procedure calls (wsdl:operation), i.e., the initiating partner requests some function and the responding partner performs that function and returns the result. Two kinds of interaction types are supported, namely request/response and oneway.

In the ebXML-based approach, the guiding principle behind interactions is the so-called business transaction (bpss:BusinessTransaction), i.e., a request/response kind of interaction which may create or resolve a commitment between the two involved partners. Specifically, the ebXML-based approach adheres to the metamodel for business transactions defined by UMM (UN/CEFACT Modeling Methodology, cf. [19]). UMM also defines a set of so-called analysis patterns for business transactions such as Commercial Transaction and Query/Response, which can be directly used in ebXML.

The Functional Aspect defines the intention of an interaction, i.e., its goal.

In the WSDL-based approach, the functionality of an interaction is specified only in terms of a name and whether the interaction delivers a result (request/response pattern) or not (oneway pattern).

In the ebXML-based approach, an interaction is specified in terms of a name, informal pre- and postconditions, and whether it delivers a result. Furthermore, an interaction is decomposed into the functionality at the initiating role (bpss:RequestingBusinessActivity) and at the responding role (bpss:RespondingBusinessActivity), each of which is specified by a name.

The Informational Aspect refers to the messages exchanged during an interaction. Messages are defined by a message type, which in turn specifies the documents to be included in the message.

In the WSDL-based approach, oneway interaction types comprise only one message (wsdl:input), whereas request/response interaction types comprise a request message (wsdl:input), and a number of alternative response messages (wsdl:output or one out of a set of named wsdl:fault messages). Message types are named reusable entities (wsdl:message), defined in terms of a list of named information items (wsdl:part).

In the ebXML-based approach, interaction types comprise one requesting message and optionally a number of alternative responding messages. A message type (bpss:DocumentEnvelope) is defined by a name, one primary document, which is defined by a document type, and additionally any number of named attachments, which can be defined either by a document type, by a MIME type, or left unspecified.

The Behavioral Aspect addresses the control flow during an interaction in terms of ordering message exchanges and of defining initiating and responding roles. Furthermore, timing and exceptions need to be considered. Typically, the behavior, i.e., the control flow of interactions is predefined and only limited means of customization are possible.

In the WSDL-based approach, the behavior of the oneway interaction type is asynchronous, i.e., the initiator sends a message to the receiver. Neither timing nor exceptions are relevant at this level of abstraction. The request/response interaction type is synchronous, i.e., the initiator sends a request message to the responder, who responds after processing the message with either a normal response or an exception message. It is not possible to specify any timing parameters.

In the ebXML-based approach, the behavior of interactions follows the UMM metamodel for business transactions, which defines the control flow as an enhanced request/response model. Basically, the initiator sends a message to the responder, the responder processes the request, and optionally sends back a response message thereby indicating success or failure of the interaction (bpss:isPositiveResponse). This basic model is enhanced with optional acknowledgement signals indicating receipt of the request and response messages, respectively, or indicating acceptance of the request message. Signals indicate either success or exceptional termination. A receipt acknowledgement may inform about successful schema validation (bpss:isIntelligibleCheckRequired), an acceptance acknowledgement informs about some further validation of the request message's content. Timeout values can be specified for both signalling and request processing (bpss:timeToPerform).

The Security Aspect addresses security properties of interactions, namely integrity, authenticity, and confidentiality of messages, as well as authorization and non-repudiation.

In the WSDL-based approach, only integrity, authenticity, and confidentiality of individual messages are addressed. In particular, a message type can have an attached security policy (wssp:Policy), which can specify integrity and authenticity (wssp:Integrity) and confidentiality (wssp:Confidentiality) requirements of selected parts of a message. Selecting parts of a message is done using XPath, which is very expressive but requires knowledge about the SOAP message format and processing model.

In the ebXML-based approach, the following security requirements can be specified for each document which is part of a message: integrity (bpss:isTamperProof), authenticity (bpss:isAuthenticated), and confidentiality (bpss:isConfidential). Authorization (bpss:isAuthorizationRequired) and non-repudiation (bpss:isNonRepudiationRequired and bpss:isNonRepudiationOfReceiptRequired, respectively) can be specified for the initiating role and the responding role.

The Transactional Aspect considers transactional properties of an interaction, such as atomicity and consistency, which are of particular importance in a distributed system without central control.

In the WSDL-based approach, transactional properties of an interaction cannot be specified explicitly. Although transaction support is addressed by several proposed protocols such as WS-Transaction[4] and BTP[5], the means for including them in a WSDL-based protocol specification have yet to be defined.

In the ebXML-based approach, at least the atomicity property of transactions is supported in that each interaction is considered atomic, meaning that an interaction has a defined end and in that both parties have a consistent knowledge of whether it has succeeded or failed. If it has failed, it doesn't create any commitments. It has to be mentioned that the behavior of an interaction is not sufficient to guarantee a consistent understanding about an interaction's final state, therefore a separate interaction may be necessary to notify the responder about a failure at the initiator. A detailed analysis of the differences between the ebXML behavior and two-phase distributed transaction protocols such as BTP can be found in [8]. Besides atomicity, it can be specified that an interaction must be conducted using a reliable means of communication (bpss:isGuaranteedDeliveryRequired), essentially regarding message exchanges as sub-transactions of an interaction.

The Operational Aspect considers how interactions are performed, i.e., the particular implementation-level protocols to be used for message transport and encoding, security, and transaction coordination. While in either approach some of these decisions are fix, some options can be selected in the protocol specification.

In the WSDL-based approach, several options for message transport and message encoding are available (wsdl:binding), e.g., SOAP over HTTP. Message security is realized according to WS-Security[6].

The ebXML-based approach defines its own messaging protocol [14]. It builds on SOAP and provides extensions addressing reliable messaging, message security, and others. The underlying transport protocols and message encoding can be flexibly defined, supporting both synchronous and asynchronous bindings. Message security is realized using S/MIME and XML Signature. Non-repudiation and transaction coordination are realized on top of the ebXML interaction behavior utilizing the the request/response messages and the corresponding acknowledgement signals.

4.4 Services Layer

A service is the work done by a business (the service provider) that benefits another (the service consumer). For the specification of a service type, the supported workflow aspects are the functional, organizational, behavioral, informational, and transactional ones, as discussed below.

---

[4] `http://www.ibm.com/developerworks/library/ws-transpec/`

[5] `http://www.oasis-open.org/committees/tc_home.php?wg_abbrev=business-transaction`

[6] `http://www-106.ibm.com/developerworks/webservices/library/ws-secure/`

In the WSDL-based approach, service types are *unilateral*, i.e., the service functionality, behavior, etc. are specified from the service provider's point of view. In particular, service types are specified using BPEL, which builds upon WSDL interaction types and provides for the specification of so-called abstract processes (bpel:process). BPEL also provides concepts for the specification of so-called executable processes, which define the workflow realizing a service type, however, these are out of scope of a B2B protocol.

In the ebXML-based approach, two kinds of service types are distinguished. *Bilateral* service types are restricted to exactly two roles, i.e., service provider and service consumer (bpss:BinaryCollaboration). *Multilateral* service types involving many roles can be specified as a composition of bilateral service types (bpss:MultiPartyCollaboration). Each of these two kinds of service types address all but the informational workflow aspect.

The Functional Aspect is concerned with the work provided by the service type and its functional decomposition. Regarding decomposition, a service type can be decomposed into sub-services and ultimately into interactions as defined in the interactions layer.

In the WSDL-based approach, the functionality of a service type is specified in terms of a name and the decomposition into interactions (bpel:invoke and bpel:receive/bpel:reply for used and provided functionality, respectively). Through appropriate combination of these constructs, execution dependencies between interactions can be defined in flexible ways.

In the ebXML-based approach, bilateral service types are specified in terms of a name, informal pre- and postconditions, and the decomposition into bilateral sub-services (bpss:CollaborationActivity) and interactions (bpss:BusinessTransactionActivity). Multilateral service types are specified in terms of a name and the decomposition into bilateral sub-services. Execution dependencies between interactions can be defined in both service types, in particular nesting of interactions is supported (bpss:onInitiation).

The Organizational Aspect addresses the roles of businesses involved in a service type, and the authorizations and obligations of each role. Furthermore, a role's agent selection policy defines how a particular business playing that role is identified in an actual service instance.

In the WSDL-based approach, a service type specifies one primary role (bpel:process) and a number of secondary roles (bpel:partner). Only the primary role's functional, behavioral, and informational properties can be specified explicitly, whereas the corresponding properties of secondary roles are left undefined except for the compatibility requirements imposed by their relationship with the primary role. Agent selection policies are supported by means of a specific data type (bpel:serviceReference) which can be used in conjunction with a data flow specification (bpel:assign) to define possible businesses playing a certain role, allowing to determine it dynamically at run time.

In the ebXML-based approach, bilateral service types define two roles (bpss:-Role), which are associated with the initiating and responding roles of the interactions that constitute the service (bpss:fromRole and bpss:toRole, respectively), thereby implying the authorizations and obligations of each of the two roles in terms of functional, behavioral, informational, and transactional aspects. Multilateral service types define multiple roles (bpss:BusinessPartnerRole), whereby the relationship between each pair of roles is defined in terms of a bilateral sub-service. A multilateral service type can furthermore specify the coordination obligations of a role which is involved in multiple bilateral sub-services using nesting of interactions (see functional aspect). Agent selection policies are not supported in the ebXML-based approach.

The Informational Aspect is concerned with protocol relevant data used in a service type, which is defined by variables, their data types, the data flow, and message correlation, i.e., the association of messages to service instances.

In the WSDL-based approach, data used in a service type is defined local to the primary role, in terms of variables (bpel:variable), data types (wsdl:message), the data flow between variables (bpel:assign), and the data flow between variables and interactions (bpel:inputVariable and bpel:outputVariable). Protocol relevant data is explicitly identified using XPath expressions applied to the contents of variables (bpel:property). The data flow of protocol relevant data must be completely specified, whereas the flow of other application data can be specified only partially. Message correlation is defined based on a subset of the protocol relevant data which identifies a service instance in the context of an interaction (bpel:correlationSet).

In the ebXML-based approach neither variables nor data flow can be specified. Furthermore, message correlation does not need to be defined explicitly in the service type as it is handled by the underlying run time infrastructure.

The Behavioral Aspect describes the dynamics of a service type in terms of states and the control flow between them, including conditions, timing, and exception handling.

In the WSDL-based approach, behavior of a service type is described as local to the primary role, and only the states and control flow of the primary role are explicitly defined. Behavior is specified primarily in a block-structured way using atomic and composite states. Atomic states can represent interactions and service-internal data flow. Composite states support control flow constructs such as sequence, parallelism, interruptible and triggered behavior, and cascading exception handling.

In the ebXML-based approach, the behavior of bilateral service types is defined in terms of the states and the control flow of the relationship as a whole, i.e., without taking into account that each of the role playing actors must manage its own state and control flow. The concepts provided for behavior specification are similar to those provided by UML 1.x activity diagrams, whereby the activities are defined as either interactions or sub-services. The behavior of multilateral service types is specified differently in that no global synchronized state is assumed. The behavior interrelating different sub-services is specified local to the role involved in these sub-services. In particular, the control flow between certain states of interrelated sub-services can be specified as sequential or nested (bpss:Transition, bpss:onInitiation).

The Transactional Aspect considers the transactional properties of a service type, such as atomicity, and the specific means to achieve them, such as compensation handlers.

In the WSDL-based approach, the transactional aspect is considered to some extent in that a mechanism supporting the specification of transaction compensation in open nested transactions is provided (bpel:compensationHandler). It is, however, not possible to explicitly specify the transactional properties of a service type.

In the ebXML-based approach, a simple solution based on the atomicity property of interactions is provided in that also all bilateral service types are defined as being atomic units of work, but multilateral service types do not exhibit transactional properties. Regarding compensation, no specific concepts are supported, therefore compensating behavior must be specified using control flow mechanisms. Besides atomicity, it can be specified that an interaction has legal consequences if completed successfully (bpss:isLegallyBinding), which is, in some sense, a transactional property.

5 Summary and Outlook

We have introduced a conceptual framework for the analysis of B2B protocols, based on existing frameworks from the areas of B2B protocol specification and workflow management, respectively. Using this framework, two major approaches for specifying B2B protocols, the WSDL-based approach and the ebXML-based approach, have been analyzed and compared.

The results of the comparison show that the difference between the two approaches at the base layers of the eCo framework, i.e., information items and documents, are quite small, whereas at the higher layers, i.e., interactions and services, the approaches provide different concepts.

Regarding the interactions layer, the interaction types provided by the ebXML-based approach are basically a superset of the ones provided by the WSDL-based approach. The latter ones are simple and generic, suitable for many domains and supported by common middleware technology. The interaction types provided by the ebXML-based approach, on the contrary, support declarative specification of many interaction characteristics specifically relevant to business transactions, such as timing constraints, authorization and non-repudiation, messaging reliability, and interaction atomicity. Additionally, there are operational differences as the ebXML-based approach defines its own SOAP extensions.

In the services layer there is a fundamental difference in that the WSDL-based approach primarily supports specifying the interface of a software component supporting a service, meaning that service types are specified from the point of view of individual roles, whereas the ebXML-based approach is closer related to agreements or contracts between collaborating partners, in that service types basically specify binary relationships. As a consequence, behavior specification in the ebXML-based approach is much simpler than in the WSDL-based approach since there is no need to explicitly specify the synchronization of interacting roles in terms of message send and corresponding receipt. But the WSDL-based approach, on the other hand, provides higher expressiveness and flexibility. Furthermore, the WSDL-based approach supports the specification of data flow, which is an important prerequisite for the specification of executable processes. Finally, the ebXML-based approach offers a complete but simple solution to transaction specification, whereas in the WSDL-based approach transactional properties cannot be specified as such.

Resulting from the differences, there is no direct interoperability between the WSDL-based approach and the ebXML-based approach, neither conceptually nor operationally. Considering interoperability at the interactions layer, it is basically possible to express interaction types from the WSDL-based approach in terms of the ebXML-based approach, not taking into account the implied atomicity of ebXML interactions and the operational differences. Vice versa, ebXML interaction types could be expressed using existing and/or forthcoming behavior, security, and transaction features of the WSDL-based approach (cf. Services Layer). This approach allows the combination of features in very flexible ways, e.g. one could realize a transaction which involves several interactions and spans multiple business partners, which is not possible in the ebXML-based approach. The downside is that the resulting specification is much more complex and that the semantics of ebXML's business transactions is not captured explicitly. Besides conceptual interoperability, operational interoperability could be achieved by adaptation mechanisms to translate between the different technologies, however, having conceptual interoperability as a prerequisite. Regarding interoperability at the services layer, in general it is not possible to express WSDL-based service specifications in terms of ebXML-based ones due to ebXML's lack of expressive power in the informational and behavioral aspects. Translating ebXML-based service specifications to WSDL-based ones is possible to some extent. The binary and multiparty relationships as well as the semantics of transactionality and business transactions, however, cannot be translated.

Finally, answering the question of which of the approaches to use, the ebXML-based approach is favorable for its closer alignment with the B2B domain, because it provides more specific concepts and is therefore much simpler to use while being expressive enough to cover typical B2B applications. The WSDL-based approach, on the other hand, is favorable for its stronger vendor support and tool availability. Furthermore, it is closer aligned with existing software components which need to be integrated in the implementation of a B2B protocol in an organization.

To get best of both approaches, one could use a conceptual modeling language such as UML for the design of B2B protocols independent of the idiosyncrasies of particular specification languages, and automatically generate WSDL-based and/or ebXML-based specifications out of the UML models following the model-driven architecture approach[7]. This would require to define a UML profile for B2B protocol specification and corresponding mappings to WSDL and ebXML. Such a UML profile would likely be based on the conceptual framework used in this paper, and on already existing work such as the UMM [19] and OMG's UML Profile for Enterprise Distributed Object Computing [15]. Elaborating the feasibility of these ideas, as well as completing the conceptual framework with the business and market layers of the eCo framework, is subject of ongoing work.

References

1. BEA, IBM, Microsoft, SAP, and Siebel. Business Process Execution Language for Web Services, Version 1.1. `http://ifr.sap.com/bpel4ws/BPELV1-1May52003Final.pdf`, May 2003.
2. M. Bernauer, G. Kappel, G. Kramler, and W. Retschitzegger. Specification of Interorganizational Workflows – A Comparison of Approaches. In *Proceedings of the 7th World Multiconference on Systemics, Cybernetics and Informatics (SCI 2003)*, 2003.
3. C. Bussler. B2B Protocol Standards and their Role in Semantic B2B Integration Engines. In *Bulletin of the IEEE Computer Society Technical Committee on Data Engineering*, volume 24, pages 3–11. IEEE, 2001.
4. C. Bussler. Modeling and Executing Semantic B2B Integration. In *Proceedings of the 12th Int'l Workshop on Research Issues in Data Engineering: Enginering e-Commerce/e-Business Systems (RIDE'02)*. IEEE, 2002.
5. Q. Chen, U. Dayal, and M. Hsu. Conceptual Modeling for Collaborative E-business Processes. In *Conceptual Modeling – ER 2001*, volume 2224 of *Lecture Notes in Computer Science*, pages 1–16. Springer, 2001.
6. Q. Chen and M. Hsu. CPM Revisited – An Architecture Comparison. In *On the Move to Meaningful Internet Systems 2002: CoopIS, DOA, and ODBASE*, volume 2519 of *Lecture Notes in Computer Science*, pages 72–90. Springer, 2002.
7. eCo Working Group. eCo Architecture for Electronic Commerce Interoperability. `http://eco.commerce.net/rsrc/eCoSpec.pdf`, 1999.
8. B. Haugen and T. Fletcher. Multi-Party Electronic Business Transactions, Version 1.1. `http://www.supplychainlinks.com/MultiPartyBusinessTransactions.PDF`, 2002.
9. IBM, Microsoft, RSA, and VeriSign. Web Services Security Policy Language (WS-SecurityPolicy). `http://www.verisign.com/wss/WS-SecurityPolicy.pdf`, 2002.
10. D. E. Jenz. The 'big boys' unite forces – What does it mean for you? `http://www.webservices.org/index.php/article/articleview/633/1/4/`, 2002.
11. G. Kramler. B2B Protocol Specification by Example Using WSDL and ebXML. Technical Report, `http://www.big.tuwien.ac.at/research/publications/2003/0703.pdf`, 2003.

[7] `http://www.omg.org/mda/`

12. H. Kreger. Web Services Conceptual Architecture (WSCA 1.0). http://www.ibm.com/software/solutions/webservices/pdf/WSCA.pdf, May 2001.
13. OASIS. ebXML Collaboration-Protocol Profile and Agreement Specification, Version 2.0. http://www.oasis-open.org/committees/download.php/204/ebcpp-2.0.pdf, 2002.
14. OASIS. ebXML Message Service Specification, Version 2.0. http://www.ebxml.org/specs/ebMS2.pdf, 2002.
15. OMG. UML Profile for Enterprise Distributed Object Computing Specification. OMG Adopted Specification ptc/2002-02-05, http://www.omg.org/cgi-bin/doc?ptc/2002-02-05, February 2002.
16. C. Peltz. Web services orchestration – A review of emerging technologies, tools, and standards. http://devresource.hp.com/drc/technical_white_papers/WSOrch/WS-Orchestration.pdf, 2003.
17. S. Rausch-Schott. *TriGS$_{flow}$ – Workflow Management Based on Active Object-Oriented Database Systems and Extended Transaction Mechanisms.* PhD thesis, University at Linz, 1997.
18. R. Shapiro. A Comparison of XPDL, BPML, and BPEL4WS. http://www.ebpml.org/A_Comparison_of_XPDL_and_BPML_BPEL.doc, 2002.
19. UN/CEFACT. UN/CEFACT Modeling Methodology (N090 of TMWG). http://www.unece.org/cefact/docum/download/01bp_n090.zip, 2001.
20. UN/CEFACT. ebXML Core Components Technical Specification, Version 1.90. http://xml.coverpages.org/CCTSv190-2002.pdf, 2002.
21. UN/CEFACT and OASIS. ebXML Business Process Specification Schema, Version 1.01. http://www.ebxml.org/specs/ebBPSS.pdf, May 2001.
22. W. M. P. van der Aalst. Don't go with the flow: Web services composition standards exposed. In *IEEE Intelligent Systems*. IEEE, 2003.
23. W. M. P. van der Aalst and M. Weske. The P2P Approach to Interorganizational Workflows. In *Advanced Information Systems Engineering (CAiSE 2001)*, volume 2068 of *Lecture Notes in Computer Science*. Springer, 2001.
24. W3C. Web Services Description Language (WSDL) 1.1, W3C Note. http://www.w3.org/TR/2001/NOTE-wsdl-20010315, 2001.
25. W3C. XML Schema Part 1: Structures, W3C Recommendation. http://www.w3.org/TR/xmlschema-1/, May 2001.
26. W3C. XML Schema Part 2: Datatypes, W3C Recommendation. http://www.w3.org/TR/xmlschema-2/, May 2001.

A Model-Driven Architecture for Electronic Service Management Systems

Giacomo Piccinelli[1], Wolfgang Emmerich[1], Scott Lane Williams[2], and Mary Stearns[2]

[1] Department of Computer Science, University College London, Gower Street, London, WC1E 6BT, UK
{G.Piccinelli, W.Emmerich}@cs.ucl.ac.uk

[2] HP Software and Solutions Operation, Pruneridge Avenue, Cupertino, CA 95014, USA
{scott_l_williams,mary_stearns}@hp.com

Abstract. Mainly on the wake of the Web Service initiative, electronic services are emerging as a reference model for business information technology systems. Individual applications retain core functions and technology base, but integration becomes crucial. A business service derives from the coordination of different business capabilities. The related electronic service derives from the integration of the different applications sustaining such capabilities. The effective realisation of an electronic service requires explicit modelling and active management of the relations between business capabilities and technical infrastructure. In this paper, we propose the notion of Electronic Service Management System (ESMS) as a framework for modelling and implementing electronic services. The notion of ESMS is substantiated by a workflow-oriented architecture, which we mainly derive from the experience of HP Service Composer and the DySCo (Dynamic Service Composer) research prototype. The architecture is defined in accordance with the OMG's Model-driven Architecture (MDA) principles.

1 Introduction

Electronic services are based on the convergence of the technical and the business notions of service [14,20]. On the technical side, standard and technology initiatives such as Web Services [3] provide a new delivery channel for bodies of knowledge such as the RM-ODP (Reference Model for Open Distributed Processing) [10]. On the business side, services provide an established unit of modularisation for business capabilities [4].

The challenge on the business side is to adapt business infrastructure and models to service-oriented principles. For example, re-engineering internal assets and functions as services. The challenge on the technical side is to provide a framework for electronic services that is both comprehensive and accessible. The realisation of an electronic service requires explicit modelling and active management of the relations between business capabilities and technical infrastructure.

M.E. Orlowska et al. (Eds.): ICSOC 2003, LNCS 2910, pp. 241–255, 2003.

Models must support abstractions at different levels, and the links between levels must be explicitly formalised.

In this paper, we propose the notion of Electronic Service Management System (ESMS) as a conceptual and technical framework for electronic services (Section 2). The framework (Section 5) includes a structural and operational definition of electronic service, the notion of service composition, and a blueprint for service implementation. The framework is defined in accordance with OMG's MDA (Model-driven Architecture) [6] principles, and draws upon OMG's EDOC (Enterprise Distributed Object Computing) [16] specification. The concepts proposed derive mainly from the experience of HP Service Composer (Sections 3 and 4) and the DySCo (Dynamic Service Composer) [18] research prototype. DySCo also provided an initial validation platform for electronic service modelling and implementation (Section 6). Related work is discussed in Section 7. Conclusions and future directions are discussed in Section 8.

2 Electronic Service Management

The definition of electronic service (service for shorthand) adopted for our work is that of electronic virtualisation of a business service [14]. The notion of electronic service inherits richness as well as complexity from the business notion of service. In addition, the electronic dimension introduces new issues in terms of both service content and provision.

The content of a service refers to the core capabilities enabled by the service. For example, the content of a freight service refers to the capability of moving goods from one place to the other. Provision refers to the business channel [8] between the provider and the consumer of a service. In the example, provision covers selection, product offer, pricing, and interaction processes that the freight company applies to the users. Content and provision are complementary aspects of a service. On the one side, the provision logic depends on the capabilities that the provider can support. On the other side, the capabilities made available to consumers depend on the provision logic adopted by the provider. In the example, the option of delivery tracking might be made available only to selected users. The example is based on previous research in the freight domain [13], and will be used throughout the paper.

The notion of Electronic Service Management System (ESMS) that we propose is centred on a framework for the representation of the operational logic of an electronic service, the representation of the resources involved in the content and provision of the service, and the active coordination of such resources in accordance with the operational logic of the service. An ESMS does provide a conceptual and technical infrastructure for the development and management of electronic services. For example, the ESMS can model and access the order-management system of the freight company. An ESMS does not address the business definition and engineering of the services. In the example, the ESMS would not influence the design of a new transport service. Also, an ESMS contributes to the coordination of resources involved in the content and provision of electronic services. For example, the ESMS can manage the interaction between the inventory and the order-management systems. With the exception of coordination facilities, an ESMS does not contribute new resources to be used within a service. The ultimate goal of an ESMS is to bring together resources that underpin an electronic service. The notions of workflow [5,7] and composition [14,16] are fundamental, both from a conceptual and technical perspective.

The rationale for an ESMS derives from current practices for the creation and management of electronic services (see Section 3). In the general case, service providers control resources of different types that are used in different combinations in order to produce different types of service. Different services can depend on the same resources, and the execution of one service can affect the execution of other services. For example, the same truck might be used to dispatch both perishable and non-perishable goods (compatibly with the type of package). Usage conflicts can easily occur. Moreover, different services can be related in different ways. Some services can provide complementary capabilities. In the example, a customer might need to move both perishable and non-perishable goods. Other services can instead provide alternatives for the same capability. For example, a repackaging service in combination with the transport service for non-perishable goods could provide an alternative to the transport service for perishable goods. The business knowledge developed for traditional service management must be reflected in the electronic version of a service. Presenting a provider with a coherent view of resource base, service offer, and the interdependencies between resources and services, ESMSs shorten the gap between business design and technical implementation of electronic services.

The choice of OMG's MDA as modelling technique for ESMSs reflects the need for a multi-stage approach in the development of systems for which integration is a crucial issue. Beyond communication-level protocols, the realisation of an electronic service depends upon the close integration of different applications and systems. Moreover, the dynamics of change in the resource base for a service makes the ability to adapt a fundamental requirement. The MDA provides the base for effective system integration and reengineering.

3 Case Study

The notion of electronic service management system has found inspiration as well as validation in the HP Service Composer (HPSC) [9]. The technology framework of the HPSC includes tools and infrastructure components for workflow and data modelling, workflow execution and management, back-end integration, and Web-Service lifecycle management. Most importantly, the HPSC includes a methodology for the definition and development of electronic services. The essence of the methodology is captured in the following steps:

1. **Define Public Business Processes.** The developer defines the public workflow that clients will use to interact with the service. The developer either selects an existing process definition, or defines new ones.

2. **Program Web Service Interfaces.** The developer generates the Web Services Description Language (WSDL) files, which describe the Web Services associated to the process of step one.
3. **Generate Business Objects and Data.** The developer generates or creates connections to the business objects and data that support the service.
4. **Define Internal Business Processes.** The developer defines the internal workflow specifying the operational logic for the service. For pre-existing workflows, the developer builds access points to relevant process nodes.
5. **Map Public Interfaces.** The public interfaces defined in steps one and two are mapped to back-end logic from steps three and four. As an example, a WSDL interface might be mapped to a backend component for its concrete implementation.
6. **Package the Service.** The various components and descriptor files that make up the service are combined into a deployment unit. The deployment unit can vary depending on the target platforms.
7. **Deploy the Service.** The service is deployed onto the various components of the runtime platform (e.g. application server, workflow engine, ERP– enterprise resource panning – system, Web Service infrastructure).
8. **Advertise the Services.** Once a service has been deployed, it can be offered to clients. For example, entries for the related Web Services can be added to a UDDI repository.
9. **Monitor Running Services.** Graphical tools should provide an end-to-end view of the service at instance level or as aggregates.

Aligned with industry trends such as ebXML [8] and technology trends such as Web Services, HPSC is representative of the state-of-the-art in commercial systems. As all commercial products, HPSC balances innovation with concrete and immediate applicability. From the study of the HPSC case, we derived general requirements (Section 4) for an electronic service management system. In particular, the methodology for electronic service development gave us indications about the facilities expected by an ESMS. Most important, some of the architectural choices in the HPSC provided fundamental indication on the concept of platform for an ESMS (Section 5).

4 System Requirements

The most important cluster of requirements derived from the experience with HP Service Composer concerns the granularity of business resources. An ESMS must represent the business capabilities enabled by software systems. Using RM-ODP [10] terminology, an ESMS must expose and leverage the business view of the different systems and applications sustaining an electronic service. For example, the ESMS for a freight company should expose to the service designer the customer interaction logic for the order management system. A homogeneous and coherent view on business resources is a prerequisite for the engineering of an electronic service.

Different resources must be integrated at operational, as well as communication level. Hence, the operational logic of a business resource should be explicitly modelled and actively managed. In the previous example, the order management system must be integrated with the payment system. This implies that the two systems communicate, but also that communication occurs according to a mutually acceptable process. Workflow emerges as a widely accepted model for the representation of the operational logic of business resources. Workflow also emerges as a reference model for the representation of the operational logic of an overall electronic service. In the case of workflow as well as other models and technologies, standard-based solutions are fundamental.

The distinction between resources and services is quite important. The vision of resources and services becoming indistinguishable entities sets a long-term objective. Still, an ESMS must address the peculiarities of resources as well as services (see Steps 1-5, Section 3). Accessibility, availability, control, and cost are only some of the aspects to which the distinction applies. While services and resources should be treated as different entities, an ESMS must address the inter-category relations. Resources sustain services. In the freight example, a lorry sustains the transport service. At the same time, services sustain higher-level resources. In the example, insurance services sustain the operation of the lorry. An ESMS must also address intra-category relations for services as well as resources. Services can be composed to create new services. For example, composing pure transport with packaging and progress notification can produce a new type of delivery service. Resources may also be used in composition. For example, different trailers need to be matched with a suitable truck. An ESMS must explicitly mange the various relations for services and resources.

5 MDA Model for ESMSs

The conceptual and technical framework we propose for an ESMS is defined based on OMG's MDA (Model-Driven Architecture) [6]. Both the EDOC (Enterprise Distributed Object Computing) [16] and the RM-ODP (Reference Model for Open Distributed Processing) [10] specifications constitute the conceptual foundational for ESMSs. In addition, the EDOC specification provided the template for the definition and formalisation of the ESMS model. In line with the EDOC approach, the purpose of an ESMS model is to provide a reference framework to developers of ESMS systems. In particular, the definition of a UML Profile provides immediate support for ESMS modelling and design.

After an outline of structural and operational aspects of the ESMS architecture (Section 5.1), we introduce a set of key concepts for an ESMS (Section 5.2). A metamodel [1] for ESMSs is presented in Section 5.3. The formal semantics of the proposed metamodel is discussed in Section 5.4.

5.1 Outline of the ESMS Architecture

The architectural model we propose for electronic services and related management systems is based on the definition of *business asset*. A business asset is defined as the composition of one or more business resources and services into a self-contained operational unit. For example, the composition of a lorry, a driver, and an insurance service can constitute a single asset capable of moving goods between different locations.

At the next level of aggregation, the composition and coordination of assets provide the foundation for *business capabilities*. A business capability is defined as the composition of one or more business assets in accordance with an explicitly defined business process. For example, the composition of the transportation asset with assets for packaging, loading and unloading constitute the base for a delivery capability. A business process coordinating the various assets completes the capability. One asset can contribute to the realisation of multiple capabilities. Also, different capabilities can interoperate. The interoperation logic for a *group* of capabilities emerges from the business processes of the individual capabilities. While the relation between capabilities and assets has a master-slave connotation, the interoperation between capabilities is based on a peer-to-peer approach. For example, capabilities for delivery, insurance and billing may interoperate for the fulfilment of a customer request. From a business process perspective, the difference is between the definition of a process coordinating multiple resources (capability) and the federation of multiple processes (capability group). The boundaries between assets and capabilities can vary between different business domains, as well as between different organisations in the same domain. Variability can occur also in different parts of an individual organisation.

In addition to the operational interdependencies captured by groups, business capabilities can functionally complement each other. A *cluster* captures the relation between a set of business capabilities and a specific business function or segment. For example, transport and handling capabilities for perishable goods can be aggregated into one or more clusters in the segment for perishable freights. Similarly, capabilities for accounting and payment management can be aggregated into a cluster for finance. One capability should contribute to at least one cluster. Most important, one capability can contribute to more than one cluster. Communication handling is an example of capability that is required in different business functions and segments. Relations and dependencies between clusters derive mainly from the relations and the dependencies between the capabilities contained in individual clusters. The new dimension introduced at cluster level is the distinction between content and provision (ref. Section 2). In the previous example, the cluster for perishable freights relates to the content of a fright service. The cluster for finance relates to the provision of the service.

An *electronic service* emerges from the interoperation between a specific selection of content and provision capabilities. The selection should include content-related as well as provision-related capabilities. Aspects of a service such as information and resource requirements, operational characteristics, and user interaction derive from the capabilities involved as well as the way such capabilities are set to interoperate. For example, the address for a delivery may be obtained through the interaction with a profile management capability. Alternatively, the information may be obtained by direct interaction with the user.

The realisation of a service S can be based on other services $\{S1 \ldots Sn\}$. The services Si are independent services that act as *sub-services* for S. The different Si can be provided by the organisation that implements S, or by third parties. Independently from the provider of Si, the connection with S is handled as if S were a standard user. Similarly to clusters for capabilities, services can be aggregated in *service packs*. A service pack includes services that complement each other in terms of business content. As for sub-services, a service pack can include services provided by third parties. The rationale is to present users with comprehensive solutions that leverage the product (services) of an organisation. A key difference between a composed service and a service pack lays in the responsibility for the end result. In the case of a composed service, the provider is responsible for the overall result delivered to the user. In the case of a service pack, individual providers are responsible for the results of individual services. Still, the user is responsible for the result of their combined usage.

A *service o er* is the user view on an electronic service. Service offers include elements such as price, contractual terms and conditions, interaction processes, and information on business content. Different users may be presented with different views on a service, hence with different service offers. Business roles [5] are central to business processes, hence to business capabilities and services. In concrete terms, the user view on a service derives from the *business roles* assigned to such user.

5.2 Basic Concepts for an ESMS

The concept of platform is fundamental for both the modelling and the realisation of an ESMS. Organisations have in place information systems that provide both modelling abstractions and technology infrastructure for electronic services. An ESMS must leverage abstractions of business resources and capabilities already present within an organisation. Also, the realisation of an ESMS must build on top of the technology already present in an organisation. The reference platform for an ESMS includes elements such as ERP (Enterprise Resource Planning) systems, database management systems, business process management systems, and domain-specific as well as function-specific vertical applications. Integration middleware (e.g. Web Services) already provide uniform access to the platform elements. An ESMS provides uniform abstractions and application-level integration for such elements.

Assets can be abstracted using a basic object-oriented model (e.g. the model used by Web Services [3]). Taking a progress-tracking system as an example, the system can be modelled as a Web Service that takes an order number in input and returns the number of hours before the expected delivery. The majority of existing information systems expose interfaces based on some form of object-oriented model. Further assumptions would be useful (e.g. explicit modelling of interaction flows), but in most cases unrealistic. Capabilities can be abstracted using a workflow-oriented model (e.g. the model proposed by the Workflow Management Coalition [5]). Workflow is an established formalism for the definition of business processes. Moreover, most organisations use workflow management technology.

The rationale for groups and clusters is to support the modularisation of the overall business infrastructure underpinning a service. An electronic service is defined and engineered on top of the business infrastructure provided by capabilities. Explicit modelling and active management of the relations between capabilities provide the base for modelling and managing services. In general, orchestration-oriented coordination of all the capabilities intervening in the realisation of a service is difficult to achieve. For example, explicit workflows covering end-to-end freight services would reach levels of complexity not acceptable in practice. Still, orchestration is possible and necessary for specific aspects of a service. In the freight delivery example, a workflow may coordinate order management, billing, and credit card handling capabilities to manage payments. A second workflow may coordinate the actual delivery of the goods. A third workflow may coordinate the handling of customer queries. The overall service emerges as a loose form of aggregation of such workflows. From a modelling perspective, coordination is a specific capability that can be grouped with the capabilities to be coordinated.

An ESMS requires an information base to manage all the information relevant to the operation of services. The concept of information base mainly encompasses uniform data models and access. Uniform data models and formats enable information sharing between capabilities. Uniform access enables source transparency. The realisation of an information base can imply proxy access to existing data sources, as well as database facilities. The information base can be leveraged for the realisation of loose forms of coordination between capabilities.

5.3 The ESMS Metamodel

Figure 1 captures the metamodel for an ESMS. The semantics for most of the elements in the metamodel can be derived from the discussion in the previous sections (Section 5.1 and 5.2 in particular). In addition, a formal semantics for the relation between capabilities, clusters, and services is presented in the following Section 5.4. For reasons of space, in this section we concentrate on properties, roles, rights, and responsibilities.

Properties capture different types of meta-information about capabilities. Such meta-information mainly refers to functional and non-functional requirements for a capability. For example, a property for a negotiation capability is to be usable only with a certain type of customers. A different type of property for the same capability may be the need to keep certified logs for all communications. A similar layer is defined for clusters. An example of cluster-level property is the response time to external customer requests. The relations between properties for clusters and capabilities are modelled explicitly. In particular, the emphasis is on the consistency between properties at different levels. For example, the response time specified for the cluster cannot be lower than the response time of the slowest capability.

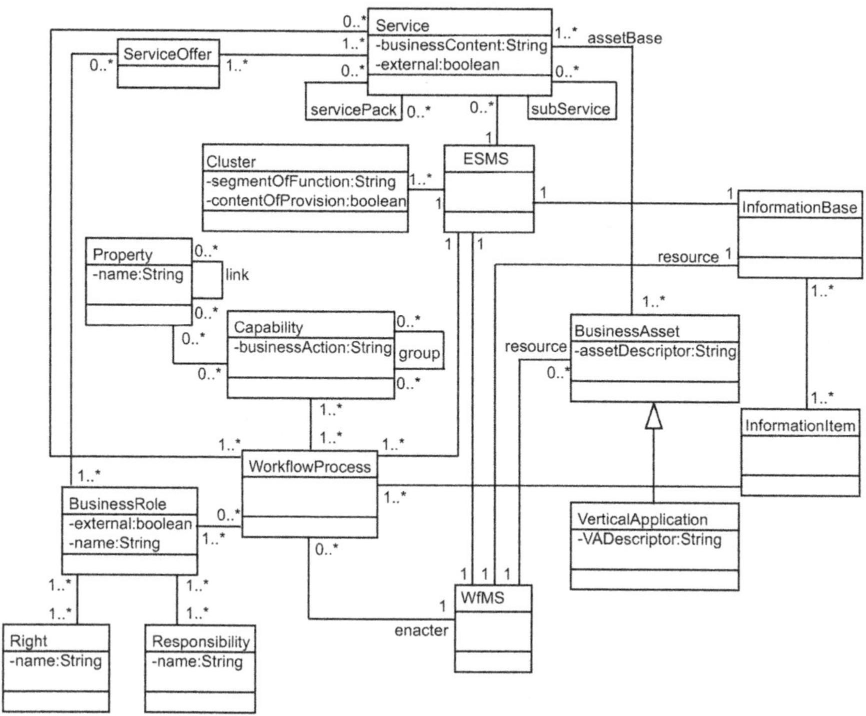

Fig. 1. Electronic Service Management System (ESMS) – Metamodel.

Rights and responsibilities are fundamental aspects for the notion of services. In an ESMS, centres of rights and responsibilities are modelled using a notion of role similar to the one used in RM-ODP [10]. The relation between roles, rights, and responsibility is subject to change over time. Such relation can be described by the following function:

$$map : Ro* \times S \rightarrow Ri* \times Re* \quad (1)$$

Given a set of roles (Ro), a set of rights (Ri), and a set of responsibilities (Re), the function connects roles to sets of rights and responsibilities. In the formula, $*$ indicates the power set of a set. S captures the notion of state, and the possibility of dynamic adaptation in the mapping. Ultimately, roles are mapped to software applications (e.g. modules of an ERP system). Rights and responsibilities are used to manage the activity of such applications (e.g. validate message flows).

5.4 Formal Semantics

A semantic characterisation of the ESMS metamodel is defined in a formal way by the Labelled Transition System (LTS) [15, 19] partially reproduced in Figure

$$IB :: CT_i \xrightarrow{\alpha} IB' :: CT_i' \qquad (CM1)\ \frac{IB :: CT_i \xrightarrow{\mu} IB' :: CT_i'}{IB :: \{CT_1 \ldots CT_i \ldots CT_N\} \xrightarrow{\mu[i]\{\}} IB' :: \{CT_1 \ldots CT_i' \ldots CT_N\}}$$

$$IB :: CT_i \xrightarrow{\alpha(s)} IB' :: CT_i'$$

$$IB :: CT_i \xrightarrow{\alpha(s,i)} IB' :: CT_i' \qquad (CMk)\ \frac{IB :: CT_i \xrightarrow{\mu} IB' :: CT_i' \quad IB :: CT_{j1} \xrightarrow{\mu^C} IB' :: CT_{j1}' \ldots IB :: CT_{jk} \xrightarrow{\mu^C} IB' :: CT_{jk}'}{IB :: \{\ldots CT_{j1} \ldots CT_i \ldots CT_{jk} \ldots\} \xrightarrow{\mu[i]\{j1,\ldots,jk\}} IB' :: \{\ldots CT_{j1}' \ldots CT_i' \ldots CT_{jk}' \ldots\}}$$

$$IB :: CL_i \xrightarrow{\beta} IB' :: CL_i' \qquad IB :: CL_i \xrightarrow{\beta(s)} IB' :: CL_i' \qquad IB :: CL_i \xrightarrow{\beta(s,i)} IB' :: CL_i'$$

$$(CLM1)\ \frac{IB :: \{CT_1 \ldots CT_i \ldots CT_N\} \xrightarrow{\mu[i]M} IB' :: \{CT_1 \ldots CT_i \ldots CT_N\}' \text{ and } \exists\, t \mid (t \in M \cup \{i\} \text{ and } t \in \{k_1, \ldots, k_v\})}{IB :: CL\,\{k_1, \ldots, k_v\} \xrightarrow{\rho(\mu)} IB' :: CL'\,\{k_1, \ldots, k_v\}}$$

$$IB :: S_s \xrightarrow{\gamma} IB' :: S_s' \qquad (S)\ \frac{IB :: \{CL_1 \ldots \ldots CL_g\} \xrightarrow{\beta(s)} IB' :: \{CL_1 \ldots \ldots CL_g\}'}{IB :: S_s\,\{i_1 \ldots i_O\} \xrightarrow{\varphi(\beta)} IB' :: S_s'\,\{i_1' \ldots i_O'\}}$$

$$IB :: S_i \xrightarrow{\gamma(i)} IB' :: S_i' \qquad (SI)\ \frac{IB :: \{CL_1 \ldots \ldots CL_g\} \xrightarrow{\beta(s,j)} IB' :: \{CL_1 \ldots \ldots CL_g\}'}{IB :: S_s\,\{i_1 \ldots i_j \ldots i_O\} \xrightarrow{\sigma(\beta)} IB' :: S_s\,\{i_1 \ldots i_j' \ldots i_O\}}$$

Fig. 2. Extract form the definition of the LTS of the ESMS. From the top down: capabilities, clusters, and services.

2. The LTS formalism provides an operational view of the ESMS, and a precise definition of the behaviour expected at different levels within the system. The focus is on the relations between capabilities, clusters, and services as described in Section 5.1.

As described in the ESMS model, a capability can be related to more than one cluster. The transition rules CM1 and CMk (Figure 2) indicate that capabilities can evolve either individually ($CM1$) or cooperatively (CMk). The evolution of a capability (from C to C') is associated with tangible results (μ). Different results can have different impact on services and service instances. Some results do not affect any specific service (α). Some results affect a service as a whole ($\alpha(s)$). Some results affect specific service instances ($\alpha(s,i)$). The results achieved cooperatively ($m[i]\{j1 \ldots jk\}$) are annotated with indications of the capabilities involved ($j1 \ldots jk$), and of the coordinating capability ($[i]$).

Clusters can evolve autonomously, but most commonly a cluster evolves as a consequence of the evolution of at least one of the capabilities it depends upon ($CLM1$). In the latter case, the result of the cluster evolution derives from the result of the related capabilities ($\rho(\mu)$). Multiple clusters can evolve as a consequence of the same evolution steps at capability level. As for the capabilities, the results produced at cluster level can have different degrees of impact on services and service instances (β, $\beta(s)$, $\beta(s,i)$). The evolution of services (S) and service instances (*SI*) is directly related to the evolution of the clusters, which implies a degree of indirection with respect to specific capabilities.

The benefits of formal semantics and the use of LTS for describing an ESMS metamodel are in terms of simulation and analysis made available by tools such as the LTSA (LTS Analyser) [15]. Initial experiments indicate that the tool is particularly useful for scenario-based validation of the metamodel. Behavioural modelling and analysis validate the adequacy of the structural aspects of an ESMS.

5.5 UML Profile

In-line with the methodology defined for the MDA, Tables 1 and 2 outline the UML profile corresponding to the ESMS metamodel. The immediate benefit of the profile is that standard UML modelling tools can by used to support the design ESMSs. In particular, tools can enforce the compliance of specific ESMS models with the overall metamodel defined in the previous sections. As an example of the structural constraints included in the profile, the following OCL (Object Constrain Language) rule captures the need for a property to be associated with a capability or a cluster:

```
context Property inv:
-- a Property must be related to at least one Cluster or Capability
self.
association.
association.
connection.
participant
->excluding(self).stereotype
->exist(name = "stripe" or name="capability")
```

The profile is defined as a single package that mainly extends (¡¡access¿¿) the package for the Core metamodel in the UML Foundation. The current version of the profile addresses the modelling of structural aspects of an ESMS. Enabling UML-based modelling of the behavioural aspects of an ESMS constitutes ongoing work.

6 Proof of Concept

The definition and characteristics of the ESMS model derive substantially from the experience of HP Service Composer. The definition takes into account both the methodology for solution development (Section 3) and the associated toolset. UML notation is used in the HPSC to enforce the separation between platform-dependent and platform-independent models of an electronic service. Workflow notation and technology is used to model and manage the business logic of a service. The HPSC framework can be directly used to refine a platform-independent model compliant with the ESMS metamodel into a more detailed

Table 1. Stereotypes for ElectronicServiceManagementSystem (UML notation: Class Diagram)

Metamodel element	Stereotype	Base Class	Parent	Tags
Business-Asset	BusinessAsset	Class	N/A	assetDescriptor
Business-Role	BusinessRole	Class	N/A	name external
Capability	Capability	Class	N/A	businessAction
InformationBase	InformationBase	Class	N/A	
InformationItem	InformationItem	Class	N/A	
Property	Property	Class	N/A	name
Right	Right	Class	N/A	name
Responsibility	Responsibility	Class	N/A	name
Service	Service	Class	N/A	external businessContent
ServiceOffer	ServiceOffer	Class	N/A	
ESMS	ESMS	Class	N/A	
Cluster	Cluster	Class	N/A	businessFunction
VerticalApplication	VerticalApplication	Class	BusinessAsset	VADescriptor
WfMS	WfMS	Class	N/A	
WorkflowProcess	WorkflowProcess	Class	N/A	

Table 2. Tagged Values for ElectronicServiceManagementSystem

Metamodel attribute	Tag	Stereotype	Type	Mult.	Default
assetDescriptor	assetDescriptor	BusinessAsset	String	1	
businessAction	businessAction	Capability	String	$1\ldots*$	
businssContent	businssContent	Service	String	$1\ldots*$	
contentOrProvision	contentOrProvision	Cluster	Boolean	1	
external	external	BusinessRole	Boolean	1	false
external	external	Service	Boolean	1	true
name	name	BusinessRole	String	1	
name	name	Property	String	1	
name	name	Right	String	1	
name	name	Responsibility	String	1	
segmentOrFunction	segmentOrFunction	Cluster	String	1	
VADescriptor	VADescriptor	VerticalApplication	String	1	

platform-independent model. The HPSC can also be used in the generation of platform-dependent models for an ESMS.

The ESMS model is also closely related to the DySCo (Dynamic Service Composer) [18] research prototype. DySCo is the result of a two-year project involving University College London (UK), the University of St. Petersburg (Russia), the University of Ferrara (Italy), the University of Hamburg (Germany), and Hewlett-Packard (UK and USA). The objective of DySCo was the development of a conceptual and technology framework for the dynamic composition of electronic services. While lacking direct support for UML, DySCo provides modelling facilities for workflows and a homogeneous execution platform for an ESMS.

The ESMS model is currently being used in the context of the EGSO (European Grid for Solar Observations) [2] project. The model-driven approach to the architecture of the service provision part of the EGSO grid is expected to address the need to integrate services based on different provision models and execution platforms. Each service provider in the EGSO grid will be equipped with an ESMS. In addition, a specific ESMS federates and manages the service provisioning capabilities of the overall EGSO grid.

7 Related Work

The Enterprise Collaboration Architecture (ECA) defined in the OMG's EDOC specification [16] provides a comprehensive framework for the modelling of enterprise systems. The ESMS architecture can be considered at the same time a vertical extension and an instance of the ECA. On the one side, an ESMS is an enterprise system that can be designed based on the ECA. On the other side, an ESMS has peculiarities that are not explicitly addressed by the ECA. With reference to the conceptual framework for the MDA [6], we envision a series of refinements (PIM PIM) before reaching the level of detail at which the ECA can be effectively used. Similar considerations apply for the Reference Model for Open Distributed Processing (RM-ODP) [10], which is also closely related with the ECA.

Most technology and conceptual frameworks for electronic services [12] focus on Web-Service-based automation of the front-end of individual services. Web Services [3,4] constitute the reference model for access to and basic orchestration of business resources. We envision Web Services playing a fundamental role in the realisation of an ESMS. Still, a more comprehensive approach is needed for the realisation and operation of business-level services. An example of the issues involved in the realisation of business-level service is HiServ's Business Port [11]. FRESCO (Foundational Research on Service Composition) [17] provides an example of second-generation framework for electronic service management. The focus of FRESCO is on the provision aspects of services.

8 Conclusions

An ESMS (Electronic Service Management System) provides the conceptual and technology framework for the aggregation and coordination of business resources towards the realisation of a complete electronic service. In particular, the realisation and operation of a service requires close integration between different systems. A model-driven approach to ESMSs helps tackling the integration issue at multiple levels. In this paper, we propose a general architecture for ESMSs. The architecture derives from the specific experience of HP Service Composer, but it is also closely related to concepts in OMG's EDOC (Enterprise Distributed Object Computing) specification and the RM-ODP (Reference Model for Open Distributed Processing). The architecture is captured as an UML-based metamodel for which a UML profile is also defined. The architectural model proposed has been applied to the DySCo (Dynamic Service Composer) research prototype, and it is currently been used in the EGSO (European Grid of Solar Observations) grid.

References

1. Booch G, Jacobson I., Rumbaugh J.: The Unified Modeling Language User Guide. Addison-Wesley, 1998.
2. Bentley R.D.: EGSO – The European Grid of Solar Observations. In Proc. European Solar Physics Meeting, ESA Publication SP-506, 2002.
3. Cerami E.: Web Services Essentials. O'Rielly and Associates, 2002.
4. Clark M. et Al.: Web Services Business Strategies and Architectures. Expert Press, 2002.
5. Fisher L. (Ed.): Workflow Handbook. Workflow Management Coalition and Future Strategy Inc., 2002.
6. Frankel D.S.: Model Driven Architecture: Applying MDA to Enterprise Computing. John Wiley and Sons, 2003.
7. Georgakopoulos D., Hornick M.F., Sheth A.P.: An Overview of Workflow Management: From Process Modeling to Workflow Automation Infrastructure. Distributed and Parallel Databases, Kluwer Academic, Vol. 3 No. 2, 1995.
8. Gibb B., Damodaran S.: ebXML: Concepts and Application. John Wiley and Sons, 2002.
9. HP: HP Service Composer User Guide. Hewlett-Packard Company, 2002.
10. ISO/IEC, ITU-T: Open Distributed Processing – Reference Model – Part 2: Foundations. ISO/IEC 10746-2. ITU-T Recommendation X.902.
11. Klueber R., Kaltenmorgen N.: eServices to integrate eBusiness with ERP systems – The case of HiServ's Business Port. In Proc. Workshop on Infrastructures for Dynamic Business-to-Business Service Outsourcing (CAISE-ISDO), 2000.
12. Kuno H.: Surveying the E-Services Technical Landscape. In Proc. Workshop on Advance Issues of E-Commerce and Web-Based Information Systems (WECWIS), IEEE, 2000.
13. Linketscher N., Child M.: Trust Issues and User Reactions to E-Services and E-Marketplaces: A Customer Survey. In Proc. DEXA Workshop on e-Negotiation, 2001.
14. Marton A., Piccinelli G., Turfin C.: Service Provision and Composition in Virtual Business Communities. In Proc. IEEE-IRDS Workshop on Electronic Commerce, Lausanne, Switzerland, 1999.
15. Magee J., Kramer J.: Concurrency: State Models and Java Programs. John Wiley and Sons, 1999.
16. OMG: UML Profile for Enterprise Distributed Object Computing Specification. OMG Final Adopted Specification ptc/02-02-05, 2002.
17. Piccinelli G., Zirpins C., Lamersdorf W.: The FRESCO Framework: An Overview. In Proc. Symposium on Applications and the Internet (SAINT), IEEE-IPSJ, 2003.
18. Piccinelli G., Mokrushin L.: Dynamic e-Service Composition in DySCo. In Proc. Workshop on Distributed Dynamic Multiservice Architecture, IEEE ICDCS-21, Phoenix, Arizona, USA, 2001.

19. Plotkin G.D.: A structural approach to operational semantics. Technical Report DAIMI-FN-19, Department of Computer Science, University of Aarhus, 1981.
20. Sillitti A., Vernazza T., Succi G.: Service Oriented Programming: a New Paradigm of Software Reuse. In Proc. of the 7th Int. Conference on Software Reuse, LNCS, 2002.

The Business Grid: Providing Transactional Business Processes via Grid Services

Frank Leymann[1] and Kai Güntzel[2]

[1] IBM Software Group, Schönaicherstr. 220, 71032 Böblingen, Germany
Leyl@de.ibm.com

[2] Fraunhofer Institut für Arbeitswirtschaft und Organisation IAO, Nobelstr. 12, 70569 Stuttgart, Germany
Kai.Guentzel@iao.fraunhofer.de

Abstract. Web Services provide a suitable technical foundation for making business processes accessible within and across enterprises. The business logic encapsulated inside Web Services often resides in already existing transactional backend-systems. However, the scope of these systems is normally limited to their domain and is not distributed across heterogeneous environments.

In this paper, we investigate the impact of the emerging Web Service technology on transactional backend-systems: Transactional context needs to propagate from activities or even business processes to services they use. Negotiations between service requestors and services on context to be propagate can be done automatically based on policies attached to the corresponding Web Service descriptions. Corresponding standards and mechanisms form the basis of a new computing and middleware paradigm: the Business Grid.

Some exemplary research work to be done to actually build the outlined Business Grid environment is sketched.

1 Introduction

Web Services can be considered as the seminal integration solution for software architecture in information technology. Nearly every software vendor and especially all major suppliers of middleware technology are supporting this new computing paradigm. Before we will explain our ideas concerning the potential of combining Web Service technology, transactional backend-systems and here especially ERP-systems and Grid environments, we will define what we understand by the term Web Service.

We describe the Service Oriented Architecture as the underpinning for Web Service technology and the necessary steps for providing and requesting Web Services which are hosted in traditional backend-systems in section 2. The problems which will arise when integrating transactional backend-systems across heterogeneous environments will be discussed and a possible solution for this challenge namely BPEL4WS (Business Process Execution Language for Web Services), WS-Transaction and WS-Coordination, the specifications for a comprehensive business process automation framework that allows companies to leverage the benefits of the Web Services architecture to create and automate business transactions will be sketched in section 3. The

M.E. Orlowska et al. (Eds.): ICSOC 2003, LNCS 2910, pp. 256–270, 2003.

Web Services Policy Framework which provides a general purpose model and corresponding syntax to describe and communicate the policies of a Web Service – a necessary feature when searching and matching Web Services with special properties – could be augmented in conjunction with WS-Coordination to achieve a transactional handshake. Therefore, WS-Policy together with WS-Coordination helps to select the correct Web Service regarding operational properties which is outlined in section 4. In chapter 5 the evolving Open Grid Services Architecture in which a Grid provides an extensible set of services that can be aggregated in various ways is shortly explained. Further on, the term Business Grid vaguely used before is specified and compared with classical Computational Grids. Classical transactional backend-systems like ERP-systems and the new concept of Business Grids are combined into a new system architecture – the effects on traditional software architectures are presented in section 6. Finally, in chapter 7, we give a short example of a Business Grid architecture which could be used to provide fined-grained SAP R/3-transactions as Grid Services. Some of these provided Grid Services are requested and selected due to operational and business properties. We will show how failures can be compensated and which precautions must be made in SAP R/3 to enable Business Grid-support. We conclude in chapter 8 with a summary and give an outlook on future research.

2 The Service Oriented Architecture and Web Services

A Web Service can be considered as a virtual software component that hides middleware idiosyncrasies like the underlying component model, invocation protocol etc. as far as possible [1]. Web Services are provided (→ publish) by Service Providers, discovered using a Service Directory (→ find) and bound dynamically by Service Requestors (→ bind).

All the action is based on standards-based protocols and formats in order that interoperability is achieved, even when the partners are using heterogeneous hard- and software. The transport medium used by this Service Oriented Architecture (SOA) is (normally) based on TCP/IP and the data exchanged by the involved partners is encoded in XML. The platform-neutral and globally available invocation mechanism for Web Services is the Simple Object Access Protocol (SOAP) [2]. Web Services can be considered as firewall-compliant remote procedure calls (RPC), since the standard transport protocol used by SOAP is HTTP. The Web Service invocation is packed in the payload of a SOAP-message (to be precise in the SOAP body of the SOAP envelope which forms the SOAP payload) and sent to a SOAP Endpoint Reference, the Service Provider.

The Basic Web Services Stack

Web Services can be discovered by browsing a Service Directory, the so called Universal Description, Discovery and Integration or for short UDDI [3]. Service Providers are populating UDDI with information about the Web Services provided by them. This information contains amongst technical descriptions (which methods can be called, what are the parameters etc.) expressed in the Web Service Description Language (WSDL) [4] information about the Service Provider himself, i.e. some background about the person providing the service. The Service Requestor selects an appropriate Web Service after querying the UDDI Business Registry (UBR) and finding a matching service. As a rule, this Web Service is called in a SOAP-message, the XML-based RPC.

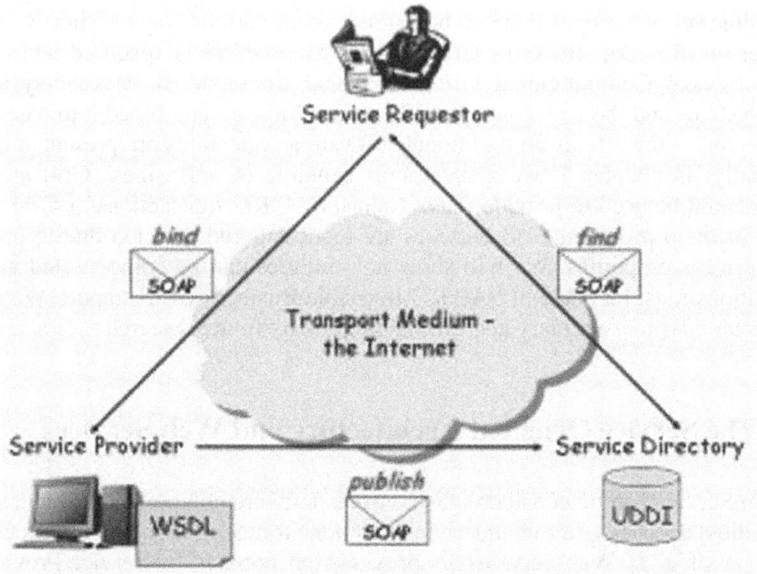

Fig. 1. The Service Oriented Architecture

Web Service Aggregation

The functions and the business logic inside the provided Web Services could be implemented when there is a need for this specific function. In fact, the business logic is often already in place and implemented on some systems, e.g. an inventory check against an inventory control system. Now, this functionality should be provided via standardized interfaces and transport protocols so that other applications can "consume" this feature in their own application without explicit stub programming as e.g. in CORBA [5]. Further on, this functionality could be provided to business partners with two positive effects: first, the business partner is checking the inventory himself before placing an order for his customer and by this reduces the internal outlays of the Service Provider and second the business partner can retrieve the information needed whenever he wants and thus becomes independent of the Service Providers office hours.

As Web Services are not for direct user-interaction as web browsers but for B2B integration we have to distinguish between "stand-alone" Web Services and Web

Services which will be aggregated into process flows. In the latter case, we have to cope with deferred failure or abort situations. This can become tricky, if the process-step performed by the Web Service is already committed, the following or adjacent step must be cancelled and therefore the Web Service must be cancelled, i.e. rolled back, too. This is a quite difficult task, when then different steps are performed in a distributed environment and locking [6] can't be assured due to costs and negative system throughput at the participating resource managers. Instead of taking the risk of inconsistencies after a failed rollback, compensation and compensation spheres [7] are an alternative solution to "classic" ACID-transactions [8].

3 Transactions and Process-Support in a Web Services World

In the real world, companies won't just consume "lonely" offered Web Services. Indeed, these software granules will be aggregated into more complex services or workflows to offer an even more sophisticated service for either internal use or to offer this encapsulated and augmented service as a new Web Service to the outside world. Anyway, the services offered will manipulate resources and these actions – whether they are short- or long-lived – should preserve the consistent state of the involved underlying systems.

In classical system-landscapes, transaction support, even across system boundaries can be achieved with transaction monitors and corresponding transaction protocols, e.g. 2PhaseCommit [9]. These concepts and techniques can't be adopted without additional assumptions or modifications to the Web Services world, on the one hand the involved transaction monitors and protocols are not known a priori when dynamically selecting a Web Service, on the other hand the selected Web Services are often integrated in higher situated workflows [10] and are therefore dependant on the outcome from long-running processes, even when the Web Service itself is a short-lived transaction.

BPEL4WS

Initially, both, IBM and Microsoft, developed their own languages for process-modelling in Web Service environments: WSFL from IBM [12] and XLANG from Microsoft [11]. But soon after that, both companies undertook an effort to combine both languages into a new standard proposal called Business Process Execution Language for Web Services (BPEL4WS) [14]. At the time this paper has been written, BPEL4WS has been published in a second release (BPEL4WS 1.1 [15]), and it has been submitted to OASIS for formal standardization.

Business processes expressed in BPEL4WS export and import functionality by using Web Service interfaces exclusively [14] and by specifying the potential execution order of operations from a collection of Web Services allows the definition of both business processes that make use of Web Services and business processes that externalize their functionality as Web Services.

This Web Service composition language builds directly on top of WSDL. An important difference between WSDL and BPEL4WS are states. WSDL is essentially stateless because the language is unaware of states between operations. The only state supported is the state between sending and receiving a message in a request-response or solicit-response operation. But only by recording the state it becomes possible what action should be taken next and thus enabling business transactions [16].

For a simple BPEL4WS example have a look at the BPEL4WS specification [14] or at the introducing article about "Business Processes in a Web Services World" [17]. As BPEL4WS is a work in progress a number of required features are absent from the current specification, for example, the actual status of a business process can't be queried.

WS-Coordination and WS-Transaction

WS-Coordination (WS-C) [18] describes an extensible framework for providing coordination protocols that coordinate the actions of distributed applications. This framework enables the involved participants to reach consistent agreement on the outcome of distributed activities. WS-C doesn't provide support for processes.

WS-Transaction (WS-Tx) [19] describes the necessary coordination types that are used with WS-C: an atomic transaction (AT) is used to coordinate activities having a short duration and executed within limited trust domains. A business activity (BA) is used to coordinate activities that are long in duration and desire to apply business logic to handle business exceptions. The long duration prohibits locking data resources to make actions tentative and hidden from other applications. Instead, actions are applied immediately and are permanent.

4 Service Arrangements with WS-Policy

Finding and selecting a matching Web Service is the first step in building a business process based on Web Services. But how to negotiate e.g. security, or transactional behaviour? For example, how can the work already done be compensated; does the backend-system providing the selected Web Service support a 2PhaseCommit or does this system work with compensation spheres instead of atomic transactions?

Transactional Handshake between Web Services

The Web Service Policy Framework (WS-Policy) provides a general purpose model and corresponding syntax to describe and communicate the policies of a Web Service [20]. The goal of WS-Policy is to provide the mechanisms needed to enable Web Service Providers to specify their policy information. This information is expressed through an XML-based structure called a policy expression and a core set of grammar elements to indicate how the contained policy assertions apply to a policy subject, i.e. the endpoint or resource to which the policy is bound. These policy information can be either associated with specific instances of services or be referenced from WSDL definitions [21]. Thus, the Service Provider can expose the conditions under which he provides the Web Service.

WS-Policy can be used to achieve a "transactional handshake" between the Service Provider and the Service Requestor. The following two figures show in a simplified manner how a Service Requestor selects in a Contracting Phase a Web Service based on certain policies. During the Binding Phase the two participants interact with a common coordinator as the activity propagates between them:

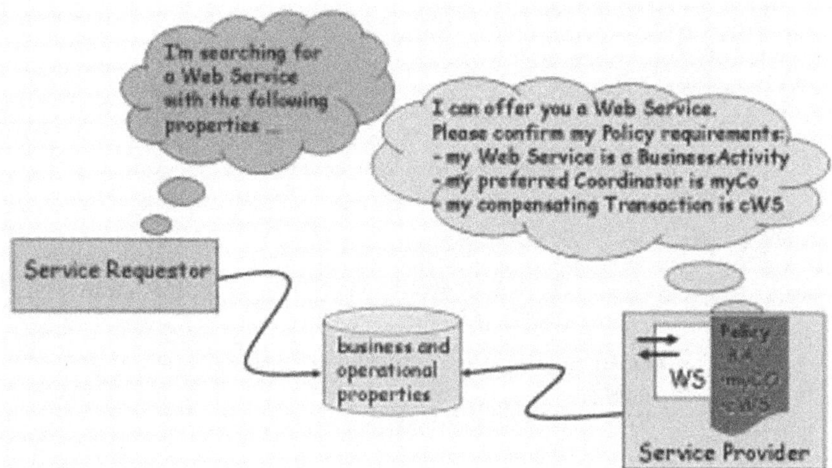

Fig. 2. Contracting Phase

(1) Due to information provided in the attached policy file, the Service Requestor knows that the requested service is a long-running BusinessActivity and therefore requests the creation of a CoordinationContext at the Activation Service ASmyCo at the specified Coordinator myCo. (2) This CoordinationContext C1 comprises a URI to the Service Provider's BusinessActivity BA. (3) In a third step, the Service Provider will then register to participate in the BusinessActivityProtocol.
Selecting a Web Service will therefore be done, first, by matching business and operational properties, e.g. the Service is performed under the control of a mission critical transaction monitor and the data produced will be stored in a relational database, and, second, by agreeing on matching policies, e.g. that in case of failures the invoked Web Service has to be compensated with a dedicated compensating Web Service offered by the same Service Provider.

5 The Business Grid

When Web Services will become more and more widespread, the consumption of the Services offered can grow up rapidly due to the standardized integration of the software granules. Inherent, Service Providers have to cope with well know problems as load balancing, dynamic selection of the most suited Service, billing techniques and Service Level Agreements [22].

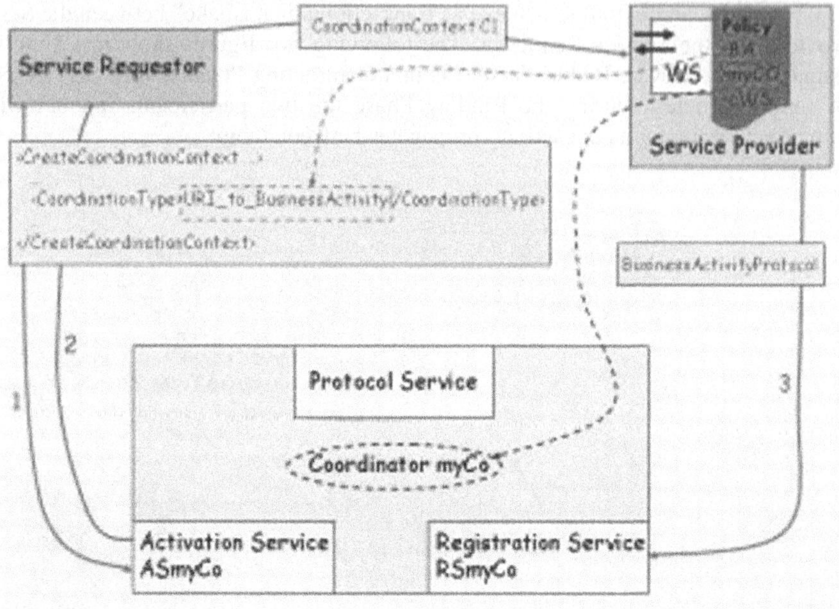

Fig. 3. Binding Phase

Service Oriented Architecture can be considered as new underpinning for a more generic Application Service Providing (ASP) model. Serving finer grained software components augmented with a standardized usage model rather than complete applications (which could be also realised with Web Services) requires to think about a scalable and service(level)-oriented middleware which will provide the necessary basic services to enable the Service Oriented Architecture even across system and enterprise domains.

Therefore it is only consequent, that researchers began to "merge" the concepts and ideas of Grid Computing with the Service Oriented Architecture and thus to adopt the Web Services Architecture [23] to the classical number crunching grid computing environment [24].

In our terminology, a Business Grid is a Grid environment with Web Services as the provided resources rather than processor time, storage area or bandwidth as it is the case with Computational Grids thus resulting in a scalable Service Oriented Architecture. Instead of a few requestors in "classical" Grid computing scenarios the number of potential service requestors in such a Business Grid environment is a priori unknown and can be enormous. There's another observation that helps distinguishing Computational Grids and Business Grids: in classic Grid environments, requestors had to cope with the issue that their software and/or their data-sets had to be split and distributed to the performing IT resources, i.e. to the resource providers in the network. When the job finished, the distributed results had to be assembled by the originating requestor. In contrast, in a Business Grid environment, the Service Requestor calls the Web Service granule over the Grid, gets his job done and continues with other tasks. The challenge in Business Grids is first to find the best Web Service for the job to be done and second to instantiate the selected Web Service by the Grid environment that the work is done as it were the only service provisioned in the Business Grid.

Service Domain

The Business Grid provides the runtime environment for provisioning Web Services across heterogeneous platforms and thus ensures the optimal utilization of resources. The selection process for a suitable Web Service is nearly the same as in a "normal" Service Oriented Architecture just that we are dealing with business and operational properties and that the Service Provider is probably not known thus resulting in a contracting phase done automatically by the environment upon the properties and the requirements.

The notion of a Service Domain [25] introduces a collection of comparable or related Web Services through a common service entry point and thus enables the selection of a specific Web Service instance not just on availability but also on the basis of Service Level Agreements (SLA) and business arrangements. Therefore, the Service Domain architecture can be described as a service sharing and aggregation model through a service entry interface [25].

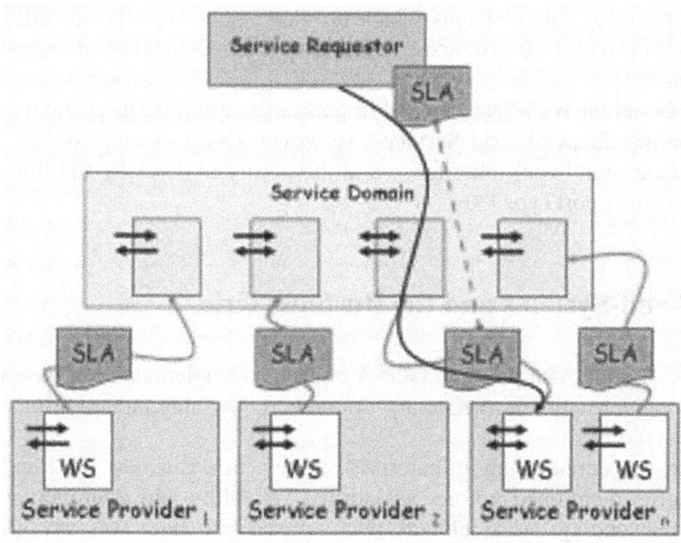

Fig. 4. A Service Domain

The conjunction of Grid technologies and Service Domains therefore forming the new concept called the Business Grid enables a new form of resource sharing and pooling of resources: in the future, whenever a company or a clerk needs some specific functionality, the user won't install an additional server component on its own server, instead he will "ask" for this functionality in the Business Grid environment he subscribed to. Then, it's up to the Service Domain to fetch the most suited service; the Business Grid has to schedule the job and to return the results to the requestor.

Open Grid Services Architecture

Several Grid technologies and toolkits are available today, such as Unicore [26] and the Open Grid Services Architecture (OGSA) [27] for instance. In what follows, we are focussing on OGSA because OGSA together with the GLOBUS Toolkit [28] is providing an infrastructure for Grid Computing that is based on a Service Oriented Architecture.

Building on concepts and technologies from both the Grid and the Web Services communities, OGSA defines a uniform exposed service semantics – the Grid Service [29]. It integrates key Grid technologies with Web Service mechanisms to create a distributed framework based around the Open Grid Services Infrastructure (OGSI) [30].

OGSI defines, in terms of WSDL interfaces and associated conventions, extensions and refinements of Web Services standards to support basic Grid behaviours. These OGSI-compliant Grid services (see figure 5) are intended to form the components of the Grid infrastructure [31]. Associated with each Grid interface is a potentially dynamic set of service data elements which provide a standard representation for information about Grid service instances, facilitating the maintenance of internal state for their lifetime [32].

OGSI is based on Web Services and in particular uses WSDL as the mechanism to describe the interfaces of Grid Services. However, OGSI extends WSDL 1.1 in two areas: interface (portType) inheritance and the ability to describe additional information elements on a portType [30].

6 Backend-Systems and the Business Grid

The Globus Toolkit, as a possible OGSA-compliant implementation base for a Business Grid, can provide the necessary framework to integrate traditional backend-systems.

However, one cannot plug an enterprise system in a Business Grid and anticipate all the benefits mentioned before: scalability, reliability and interoperability. If the concerned backend-system is already decomposed into finer software granules, i.e. Web Services, one has to look at the underlying software architecture of the affected system(s). How to cope with monitoring? Who's responsible for load-balancing: the Grid or the backend? Which system will ensure consistency after a failure of composed Web Services from different backend-systems? These questions must be answered before adjusting the affected software infrastructure.

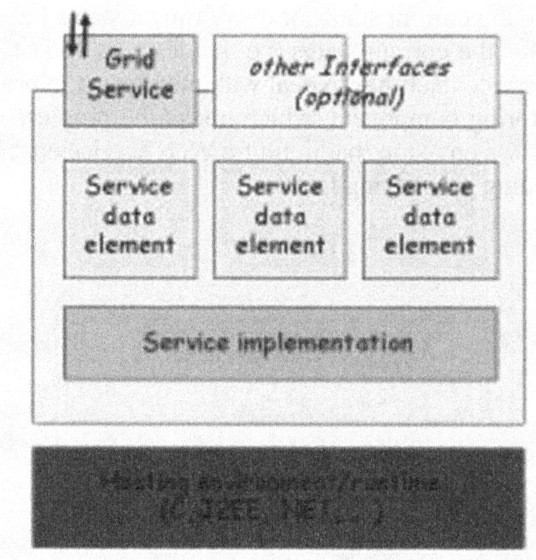

Fig. 5. OGSA Grid Service [29]

The Business Grid – Comparison with Traditional Client-Server-Computing

If we have a look at figure 6, we can observe an analogy to the classical Client-Server-Computing paradigm: a client (Service Requestor) requests a job to be done (Web Service) by a server (Service Provider). In our case, the loadbalancer moved from a dedicated server component to the Business Grid, this means that instead of reporting their actual load to their proprietary dispatching server, the Service Providers are reporting their status to the infrastructure provided by the Grid environment. If a Service Requestor asks for a specific service, the Business Grid selects as in the "classic" SOA an appropriate Service Provider, but considers besides the matching business and operational properties also system load, response time, availability and transactional behaviour.

Monitoring

Even more complicated than selecting the most suitable service and thus Service Provider amongst all services is the issue of how to deal with business processes, composed from different Web Services residing in heterogeneous backend-systems. Even if the exposed services can be triggered from the outside world, is it possible to monitor the progress of the different steps from a general perspective? In the past, research has been done on integrating workflows from existing systems in higher situated workflows [32, 33]. In the world of Web Services, status monitoring especially over different domains, is currently not supported. Therefore, workarounds have to be provided. A Service Provider can send either periodically a message to the Service

Requestor including the current status or every time a status has changed or a Service Requestor "polls" for the current status, i.e. requests an update. This is cumbersome because the Web Service itself has to deal with monitoring. Normally, every backend-system has a monitoring component, which tracks the progress of the involved processes. Nevertheless, we envision that in future Web Service enabled flow technologies facilitate corresponding monitoring features.

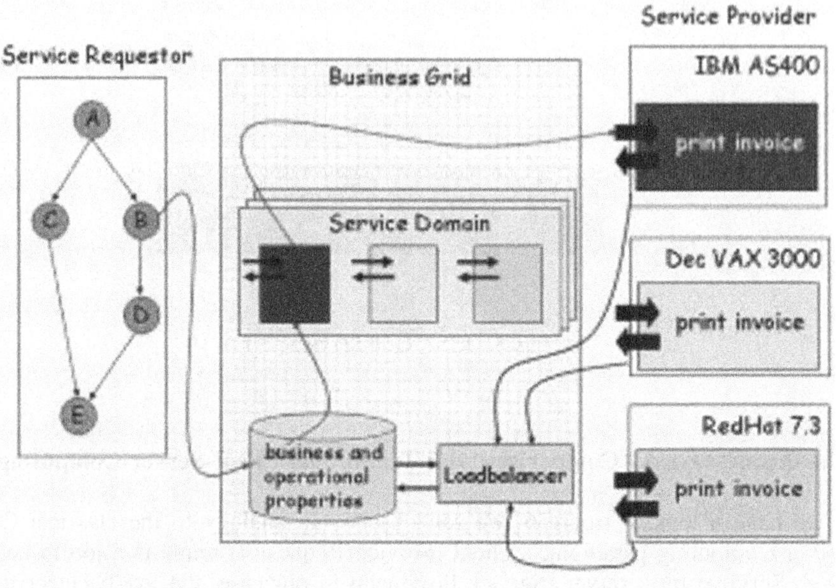

Fig. 6. Client-Server Business Grid-like

Error-Handling and Compensation

If a business process is aborted due to an application error or cancellation from the Service Requestor, already completed activities (i.e. Web Services) typically have to be undone. As mentioned in chapter 3, these Web Services often represent long running computations, and to ensure suitable performance characteristics they do not implement ACID properties. This implies that these Web Services offer compensation actions to undo transactions that they already committed in course of their processing. Since the process' activities will be bound at runtime by the Business Grid, the Business Grid has to maintain a persistent log ("compensation log") specifying pairs of activity implementations and corresponding compensating activity implementations. Often, the latter will be derived from information given in the policy-file of the activity proper.

In figure 7, the Service Requestor cancels his process. This means that the compensating activities have to be bound by the Business Grid. This is based on the information about compensating activity implementations in the compensation log. Therefore, there is no need that the Service Requestor is involved in specifying compensation actions. The Business Grid has all required information resulting in an opaque error-handling and compensation.

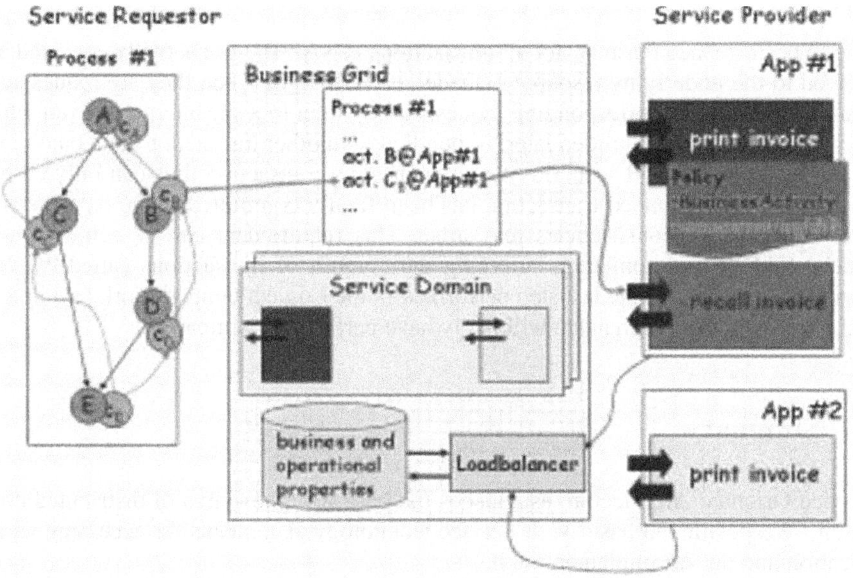

Fig. 7. Error-handling in Business Grids

7 Web Services-Based Integration of SAP R/3 in a Business Grid

SAP R/3 [34], the Enterprise Resource Planning (ERP) solution from SAP, is one of the most commonly used transactional application system for business management purposes. SAP's NetWeaver [35] Architecture makes functional components respective transactions (e.g. BAPI, RFC, IDOC) available as a Web Service.

Nevertheless it's important to understand the implications resulting from integrating SAP R/3 in a Business Grid environment. As mentioned in chapter 6, when integrating a transactional backend-system like SAP R/3 into a Business Grid, information about load and availability of the backend-system should be available to the Business Grid. In case of R/3 this information might stem from the SAP Message Server and the Dispatcher-Workprocess. Otherwise, the selection of the current load-optimized R/3 Application Server within the actual SAP R/3 environment is not possible.

SAP R/3-Transactions via Web Services

As transactions and thus the corresponding Web Services provided by SAP R/3 get long-running rather than ACID transactions, compensation must be kept in mind. Therefore, for each transaction there is a compensating one, undoing the steps as good as possible in case of an undo request. This pair of transactions can be specified in a policy attached to service description, together with the coordination type supported.

Due to performance reasons, not all transactions in SAP R/3 are actually executed and applied to the underlying resource manager at the time of when they are requested to commit. Instead the corresponding requests are written to a special queue from which they processed and committed later, or bundled with other transactions in a batch job.

In the Business Grid scenario, the compensating transaction thus can only be performed after the intended transaction has been finally committed to the database system. Otherwise, inconsistencies may arise. This requirement can be achieved with special SAP R/3-customizing, enforcing the commit of transactions called by Web Services directly after the last step performed in the Logical Unit of Work [36] in SAP R/3. However, this mechanism will likely have performance impacts.

8 Summary

Service Oriented Architecture establishes the base for a new area of distributed computing. We positioned basic Web Service technology as a means for accessing an application and not for implementing it.

The Web Services paradigm therefore enables the transition from tightly coupled applications to loosely coupled services. With the support of transactions and the composition of Web Services into processes of any degree of complexity, BPEL4WS supports orchestration of Web Services.

Contracting between Service Requestor and Service Provider regarding the preferred or even enforced Coordination Service could be realised based on attached policies. Similarly, we have argued that the compensating Web Service of a certain Web Service should published via policies too. Finally, the coordination type, i.e. the information whether the Web Service is realized via an atomic transaction or a long running business activity, for example, has to be known to enable a transactional handshake between the two parties.

Grid concepts and the evolving Open Grid Services Architecture have been briefly introduced, as well as OGSI, integrating Grid technology and Web Service technology, providing a uniform service-oriented architecture for Grid environments.

In the last section, we brought up the potential of integrating SAP R/3 with a Business Grid: every transaction or process inside SAP R/3 can be externalized as Web respective Grid Service, thus enabling a totally new integration aspect – SAP R/3-processes as loosely coupled services in higher-level workflows.

Nevertheless, integrating transactional backend-systems in Business Grids implies a clear concept how to resolve failures: compensation based recovery has to assume that activities really have been committed. Otherwise, inconsistencies will arise.

References

1. Frank Leymann: *Web Services and Business Processes*, Fraunhofer IAO Symposium Collaborative Business, Stuttgart, Germany, July 9, 2002
2. Martin Gudgin et al.: *SOAP Version 1.2 Part 1: Messaging Framework*, W3C, December 19, 2002, http://www.w3.org/TR/2002/CR-soap12-part1-20021219/
3. UDDI.org: *UDDI Version 3.0*, Published Specification, July 19, 2002, http://uddi.org/pubs/uddi-v3.00-published-20020719.pdf
4. Eric Christensen et al.: *Web Services Description Language (WSDL) 1.1*, W3C, March 15, 2001, http://www.w3.org/TR/2001/NOTE-wsdl-20010315
5. OMG: *Common Object Request Broker Architecture (CORBA)*, December 6, 2002, http://www.omg.org/technology/documents/formal/corba_iiop.htm
6. Philip A. Bernstein et al.: *Concurrency Control and Recovery in Database Systems*, Addison-Wesley, 1987
7. Frank Leymann, Dieter Roller: *Production Workflow*, Prentice Hall, 2000
8. Jim Gray, Andreas Reuter: *Transaction Processing: Concepts and Techniques*, Morgan Kaufmann Publishers, 1992
9. Philip A. Bernstein, Eric Newcomer: *Principles of Transaction Processing*, Morgan Kaufmann Publishers, 1997
10. Hans-Jörg Schek et al.: *Workflows over Workflows: Practical Experiences with the Integration of SAP R/3 Business Workflows in WISE*, in Proceedings of the Informatik '99 Workshop, Paderborn, Germany, October 1999
11. Satish Thatte: *XLANG – Web Services for Business Process Design*, Microsoft, 2001, http://www.gotdotnet.com/team/xml_wsspecs/xlang-c/default.htm
12. Frank Leymann: *Web Services Flow Language*, IBM, 2001, http://www-3.ibm.com/software/solutions/webservices/pdf/WSFL.pdf
13. Assaf Arkin et al.: *Web Service Choreography Interface (WSCI)*, BEA, Intalio, SAP, SUN, 2002, ftp://edownload:BUY_ME@ftpna2.bea.com/pub/downloads/wsci-spec-10.pdf
14. Francisco Curbera et al.: *Business Process Execution Language for Web Services (BPEL4WS) 1.0*, BEA, IBM, Microsoft, July 31, 2002, ftp://www6.software.ibm.com/software/developer/library/ws-bpel.pdf
15. Tony Andrews et al.: *Business Process Execution Language for Web Services (BPEL4WS) 1.1*, BEA, IBM, Microsoft, SAP, Siebel, March 31, 2003, ftp://www6.software.ibm.com/software/developer/library/ws-bpel11.pdf
16. Will van der Alst: *Don't go with the Flow: Web Services Composition Standards Exposed*, in Web Services: Been There, Done That?, IEEE, 2003
16. Frank Leymann, Dieter Roller: *Business Processes in a Web Services World*, IBM developerworks, August 1, 2002, http://www-106.ibm.com/developerworks/webservices/library/ws-bpelwp/
18. Felipe Cabrera et al.: *Web Services Coordination (WS-Coordination) 1.0*, BEA, IBM, Microsoft, August 9, 2002, http://www-106.ibm.com/developerworks/library/ws-coor/
19. Felipe Cabrera et al.: *Web Services Transation (WS-Transaction) 1.0*, BEA, IBM, Microsoft, August 9, 2002, http://www-106.ibm.com/developerworks/webservices/library/ws-transpec/
20. Don Box et al.: *Web Services Policy Framework (WS-Policy*, BEA, IBM, Microsoft, SAP, December 18, 2002, http://www-106.ibm.com/developerworks/webservices/library/ws-polfram/
21. Don Box et al.: Web Services Policy Attachment (WS-PolicyAttachment), BEA, IBM, Microsoft, SAP, December 18, 2002, http://www-106.ibm.com/developerworks/library/ws-polatt/
22. Alexander Keller, Heiko Ludwig: *The WSLA Framework: Specifying and Monitoring Service Level Agreements for Web Services*, IBM, May 22, 2002

23. Michael Champion et al.: *Web Services Architecture*, W3C Working Draft, November 14, 2002, http://www.w3.org/TR/2002/WD-ws-arch-20021114/
24. Ian Foster, Carl Kesselman: *The Grid: Blueprint for a New Computing Architecture*, Morgan Kaufmann Publishers, 1999
25. Yih-Shin Tan et al.: *Business Service Grid*, Part 1,2,3, IBM developerWorks, February 1, 2003, http://www-106.ibm.com/developerworks/grid/library/i-servicegrid/
26. The Unicore Forum, http://www.unicore.org
27. Ian Foster et al.: *The Physiology of the Grid: An Open Grid Services Architecture for Distributed Systems Integration*, The Global Grid Forum, the latest Version can be found at http://www.globus.org/research/papers/ogsa.pdf
28. The Globus Project, http://www.globus.org
29. Ian Foster et al.: *Grid Services for Distributed System Integration*, IEEE, 2002
30. Steve Tuecke et al.: *Open Grid Services Infrastrucutre (OGSI)*, The Global Grid Forum, the latest version can be found at http://www.ggf.org/ogsi-wg
31. Ian Foster et al.: *The Open Grid Services Architecture (OGSA)*, The Global Grid Forum, the latest version can be found at http://www.ggf.org/ogsa-wg
32. Andre Naef et al.: *Monitoring komplexer Dienste in unternehmensübergreifenden Prozessen am Beispiel von SAP R/3 Business Workflow*, in Proceedings 9. Fachtagung Datenbanksysteme in Büro, Technik und Wissenschaft, Oldenburg, Germany, March 1999
33. Crossflow: *Cross-Organizational Workflow Support in Virtual Enterprises*, ESPRIT Project 28635, http://www.crossflow.org
34. SAP AG: *SAP R/3 Enterprise*, Walldorf, Germany
35. SAP AG: *SAP NetWeaver*, Walldorf, Germany
36. SAP AG: *ADM100 SAP Web AS Administration I*, Education, Walldorf Germany

An Architectural Pattern to Extend the Interaction Model between Web-Services: The Location-Based Service Context

P. Álvarez, J.A. Bañares, and P.R. Muro-Medrano

Department Of Computer Science And Systems Engineering
University Of Zaragoza
María de Luna 1, 50018 Zaragoza (Spain)
{alvaper, banares, prmuro}@unizar.es
http://iaaa.cps.unizar.es

Abstract. Internet has succeeded as a global information system mainly because of its availability and openness, and the simplicity of its standards and protocols. However, the current use of Internet as universal middleware has clearly shown the lack of maturity of Web technology to support distributed applications, which involve communication, cooperation, and coordination. This paper proposes an architectural solution to solve these interaction restrictions. It is based on an extension of the service-oriented architectures, adding a new coordinator role that allows more flexible relationships between service providers and requestors than the provided by the client/server model. This role is inspired by the Blackboard architectural pattern and it is the conceptual basis of a Web-Coordination service able to coordinate distributed and heterogeneous applications through Internet. To prove the effectiveness of this proposal, the Web-Coordination service has been used in an highly dynamic and collaborative application context, the Location-Based Services.

Keywords: Web-service architectures, Web-service coordination, Location-based services

1 Introduction

The World Wide Web was born to provide a minimal technology for the delivery of simple multimedia hypertext documents across the Internet. For this reason, its architecture has been kept as simple as possible, with a elementary communication protocol (HTTP), a simple hypertext description language (HTML), and an addressing schema for document resources globally valid all over the Internet (URLs). Nowadays, Internet has become the de facto standard distributed platform for rapid application development by integrating network-accessible services. This new tendency has shown that the current state of Internet provides little to support the collaborative work of Web-distributed applications owing to the passive nature of the World Wide Web [7]. Therefore, it requires to

M.E. Orlowska et al. (Eds.): ICSOC 2003, LNCS 2910, pp. 271–286, 2003.

redesign the Web technology to provide enough support for building Web-based applications which involve communication, cooperation, and coordination.

These interaction restrictions are more obvious in highly dynamic and cooperative application-context, such as Location-Based Service (LBS) context. Our experiences in this context have become apparent that the integration of Web services and applications requires new interaction models more complex than the provided by the client/server model: 1) many-consumer models, 2) asynchronous models based on events, or 3) reactive models that allow to the server to have the initiative of the interaction [2]. Traditionally, these interaction requirements have been resolved using solutions based on wrapping techniques or/and middlewares. These ad-hoc solutions are hardly reusable and their results are a collection of highly coupled and cohesive services and applications. Therefore, the modern Web must be based on alternative architectural-solutions.

It is basic to understand the Web-based architectures, particularly the Service-Oriented Architectures (SOA) [10], because they encapsulate the decisions about the architectural elements and their relationships [15]. These Web architectures must be improved without changing their original capabilities to support these interaction models. The main aim of this paper is to describe an architectural solution to support more flexible relationships between Web service. It is based on an extension of the SOA model and on concepts of architectural patterns, coordination models and event-based technology.

This paper is structured like is described below. In the section 2 it is presented the architectural solution to support the required models (many-consumer, asynchronous, and reactive models). A new coordinator role has been added to the model. From a conceptual point of view, this coordinator role encapsulates a coordination model able to communicate and coordinate Web-services. This coordination model, called Linda, has been modified to be used in open and distributed environments. The coordination model and its extension are presented in the section 3. From this conceptual solution, it has been designed a Web-Coordination service to play the coordinator role in any Web-service framework built according to the SOA model. Details about its design are presented into the section 4. This coordination service has been used in the development of a LBS complete solution based on the integration of two Web-service frameworks. The suitability of the solution has been tested in an use case to improve a parcel service. Details are described in the section 6. Finally, conclusions and future work are described.

2 An Extension of the Service-Oriented Architecture

The architectural solution to support the new interaction models is based on an extension of the service-oriented architecture. As shown in figure 1, a new architectural role was added to the model to communicate and synchronize requester and provider services. This new role, called *Service Coordinator*, is inspired by the Blackboard architectural pattern [5]. It allows a collection of independent services to work cooperatively on a common data structure or blackboard using a shared vocabulary. These services communicate by putting data messages into the common structure, which can be retrieved later on by other services asking for a certain template message. The Blackboard architectural pattern determines the next process that will change the common data structure according to an opportunistic strategy.

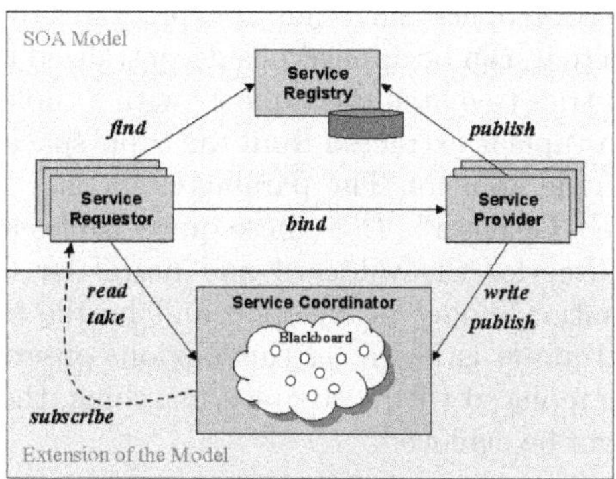

Fig. 1. Extended SOA model

This proposal provides a collection of promising features to be used in distributed and open environments:

- It allows services distributed in space to cooperate distributed in time. The cooperation is uncoupled because the writing services do not have any prior knowledge about the readers and vice versa. The interaction style is adequate enough to be used in environments where it is very important to reduce the shared knowledge between different remote entities to the minimum, such as Internet.
- Writing and reading services can cooperate without adapting or announcing themselves. It allows flexible modelling of interactions among services in highly-dynamic environments.

The key to this approach is the definition of a pure coordination model and inspired by the Blackboard pattern that it is the conceptual basis of a Web-Coordination service that plays the coordinator role. This new service must be able to coordinate distributed and heterogeneous applications through Internet supporting many data consumers and asynchronous and reactive interactions. In this way, new communication and synchronization mechanisms complement available ones. We did not consider the possibility of creating a new coordination model from scratch because there are some proposed solutions that can be used as starting points (the creation of a new model is a different goal and involves other research areas). The LINDA model was selected [9]. It is based on Generative Communication that defines a model for inter-process communication inspired by the Blackboard architectural pattern.

3 A Web-Coordination Service Based on the Linda Model

In Linda, the common data structure and messages are called tuple-space and tuples, respectively. A tuple is something as ["Gelernter", 1989], a list of untyped atomic values. The tuple space is a collection of tuples that acts as a shared memory, to which certain operations, that able processes to read and take tuples from and write them to it, can be applied in a decentralized manner. For instance, the operation in(x?) tries to match the tuple x? with a tuple in the shared space. If there is a match, a tuple is extracted from the tuple space; otherwise, it blocks until a convenient tuple appears. The parameter for in() can be a query tuple with a wildcard, like ["Gelenter", ???] (these query tuples are called templates). The match is then free for the wildcard and literal for the constants values. To use this coordination model in an open and hostile environment, it must be extended. Our proposal is based on this obvious observation: if this simple matching strategy is replaced with a complex matching, then very general kinds of interoperability can be achieved.

3.1 Linda for Open Environments

Improving data representation capability. Due to the fact that distributed processes over Internet communicate exchanging XML-encoded data, the idea of tuple has been extended to be able to represent data according to this standard format. Tuples are extended to be described by means of attribute/value pairs, like: [(author, "Gelernter"), (year, 1989)]. Although this is still an untyped setting, this bit of structure, allows recovering information from a distributed context. For the presented approach, it is important to remark that the "top-level" structure of any XML document admits the expression

```
[(att1,<val 1>),...,(attN,<val N>)],
```

but where each <val i> is structured (in particular, it may be XML-based).

Supporting reactive operations. The reading operations are blocked if no desired tuple is available in the space, which can involve long waits. An event-based approach suggests the possibility of improving the collection of operations of the tuple-space interface, adding a more reactive coordination style. Processes can subscribe their interest in receiving event notifications when other writing entities insert specific tuples into the shared space, instead of being blocked until tuples appear.

Now Linda can be used in a XML context supporting a structured matching, and providing a collection of operations that promise an interesting way to coordinate, communicate and collaborate on Internet. Besides, this structured matching can be applied to support semantic interoperability (in [1], a semantic matching for distributed heterogeneous environments has been described). Thus, if an operation in() is invoked on a different entity, where the term "author" is not used, but "creator" is used in its place, and if there is a convenient mapping between ontologies, then the request [(creator, ???), (year, 1989)] can be successfully satisfied. This kind of semantic matching is implemented through Internet, using XML as transfer format.

3.2 Using Linda to Coordinate Web-Services

Once LINDA has been extended, a Web-Coordination Service (WCS) has been designed to play the coordinator role in any Web-service framework built according to the SOA model. The WCS encapsulates the shared tuple-space, and offers the reading, writing and reactive operations of the extended Linda model as a part of its interface. These operations are accessible via ubiquitous and standard Internet protocols, such as HTTP or SOAP, and exchanged tuples are stated using standard data formats, like XML. Web-services implemented in accordance with different computation models (written in several programming languages, or running over heterogeneous hardware or software platforms), can cooperate if they share a common XML-based vocabulary. The Web Coordination service ensembles them in an orthogonal way to their heterogeneous features.

Recently, a similar solution has been presented by *IBM*, *Microsoft Corporation*, and *BEA Systems* [6]. They propose a framework to create *coordination contexts*. A coordination context provides functionality to registry: 1) Web-services and applications that require to coordinate; and 2) coordination protocols to make their coordination requirements possible. According to this proposal, Web services and applications are responsible to define the used protocols. This solution is more flexible than ours, because it is possible to create many coordination contexts using different protocols (we propose an only free-context protocol based on Linda to coordinate any Web resource). However, it ignores the complexity of defining new coordination protocols and promote the spread of ad hoc protocols.

Another similar Linda-based approach is *XSpaces* [1]. It allows the exchange of SOAP data messages across the Internet using shared spaces. The stored messages can be retrieved from spaces specifying a key associated with them, instead of using a matching strategy based on template tuples. Therefore, XSpaces demands a greater shared knowledge between remote entities than our proposal.

4 Design and Implementation of the Web-Coordination Service

In a more detailed description, the designed WCS is composed by three software components (see the figure 2):

The *XML-based Space* component encapsulates the tuple-space. Its interface provides a collection of operations for writing XML tuples into and reading them from the tuple-space, and being notified of the writing of a new XML tuple into the encapsulated space, according to the presented extension of Linda. This

[1] http://www.xmethods.net/ve2/XSpace.po

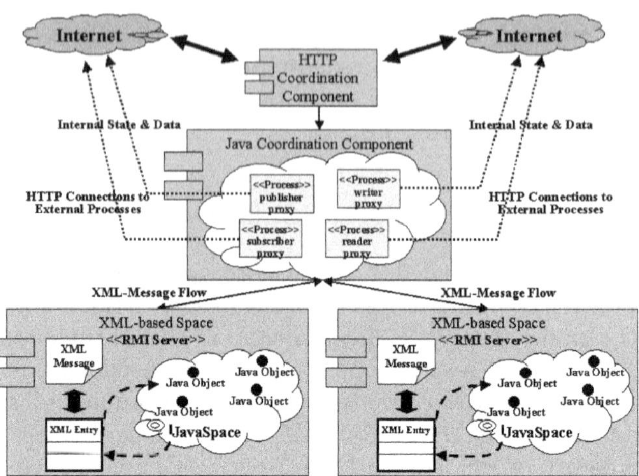

Fig. 2. Software Components of the coordination service

component has been built from *JavaSpaces* technology [8], a Java implementation of Linda, and its detailed description is the focus of this section.

On the other hand, the *Java Coordination* component is the core of the service. It has two different interfaces: the Basic Coordination Interface (BCI), which provides the collection of writing and reading operations proposed by Linda and encourages a cooperative style based on blocking readings; and the Reactive Coordination Interface (RCI), whose operations allow a process advertising its interest to generate a specific type of XML tuples, publishing the advertised XML tuples and subscribing its interest to receive XML tuples of a specific XML schema, encouraging a reactive style of cooperation among processes.

This component is a repository of agents (a computational entity which acts on behalf of other entities in a semi-autonomous fashion, and performs its tasks cooperating with other agents; the mobility and learning attributes have been excluded in this context). Every time an external Web service or application invokes a coordination operation, it is created an internal agent. These agents are able to coordinate with another agents exchanging XML tuples through XML-based spaces. Therefore, the required cooperation by external entities is executed by their respective internal agents. The result of this cooperation is communicated from agents to external entities using an event-based mechanism scalable to Internet (more details can be consulted in [2])

Finally, the *HTTP Coordination* component plays as a Web-accessible interface of the Java Coordination component, providing through its HTTP interface the same collection of operations.

4.1 Building XML-Based Spaces

According to the described design, the interactions between Web service and applications happen into the *XML-based Space* component. This component has been built using *JavaSpaces*, which provides a shared repository of Java objects and operations to read and write objets from/into it. This saves rewriting of routine code to manage tuple-spaces. Nevertheless, it was necessary to enrich *JavaSpaces* to work with XML tuples.

A generic Java object has been designed to encode any XML tuple. It is composed by structured fields to store the nodes of the XML tuple. In more detail, the generic object has two structured fields to store in ordering the tag names and values of the XML tuple. The tag name of the first node of the XML tuple is stored in the first component of the tag-name field and its value in the first component of the tag-value field, and so on. But the matching rules of *JavaSpaces* are not adequate for working with objects composed by structured fields. Objects are matched by complete fields, not within the contents of the filed. This is owing to objects are serialized for storing them into the space, and the matching between objects is made applying the equal operator on the corresponding field value. Therefore, it is required to extend the matching rules of *JavaSpaces* to support this XML-based interoperability.

To resolve these rule restrictions, the matching is made in two steps. In the first step, the matching rules of *JavaSpaces* are used. The original template is saved for the second step and a copy of it is created for being used in the first step. The tag-value field of this copy is set to null value. When it executes a read operation (provided by the *JavaSpaces* interface) using this template object, a returned object represents an XML tuple with the same XML-Schema as the template because the tag-name field is only consider for the matching. In a second step, it is invoked a particular matching method of the retrieved object, using the original template as a real parameter. This method checks that each not-null component of the template's value-field have the same value in the corresponding component of the retrieved object's value-field. If it returns true value, the retrieved object matches the template according the XML-tuple matching rules. Otherwise, the retrieved object has the same XML-Schema as the template but it does not match the template according the second matching rule for XML tuples. Following, the first step is made again until an object matches according the XML-tuple matching rules. In [4], a matching strategy in two steps is also described to exchange encrypted data among distributed processes.

It is important to realize that this matching proposal does not guarantee the semantic of Linda model because objects are retrieved from the space according to a non-deterministic strategy. For example, the first step could retrieve again and again from the space a set of objects that return false value in the second step. Nevertheless, another different object stored into *JavaSpaces* could match the template.

4.2 A Pattern to Guarantee the Semantic of the Linda Model

To resolve these semantic problems, a communication pattern has been designed which partitions the tuple-space in accordance with the XML-Schema of the stored tuples. All tuples with the same XML-Schema are stored in the same partition. A new Java object, called *Channel*, has been designed to manage a partition. Its responsibility is to guarantee the access to all the tuples stored into the partition. To achieve this aim, a channel is composed by a structured field that stores a collection of references to the tuples stored into the partition (tuples are stored as Java objects). The figure 3 shows an example of tuple-space partitioned by two different channels.

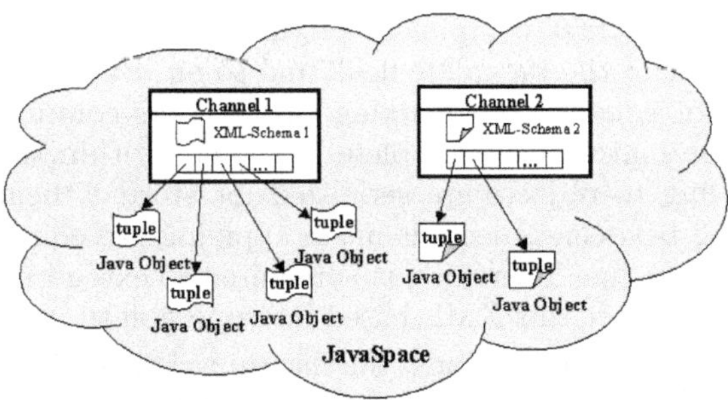

Fig. 3. Partition based on *channels* of *JavaSpaces*

When a writing operation is invoked, it is checked if there is any channel into the tuple-space that stores XML tuples with the same XML-Schema. If it exists, then the XML tuple is stored into the channel (a reference to the inserted tuple-object is saved into the channel object); or else, a new channel is created and the XML tuple is inserted into it.

On the other hand, when a reading operation is invoked, it is retrieved a copy of the channel that stores all the tuples with the same XML-Schema than the reading template. This copy is used to: 1) access all the XML-tuple objects stored into the partition; and 2) mark those XML-tuple objects that have been retrieved from the space, but they do not match the reading template. This internal strategy based on marking the checked tuples allows to retrieve an only time an XML-tuple object in the first step of the matching. If it exists a tuple into the space that matches the reading template, it will be found; or else, the reading operation will be blocked. Therefore, it is guaranteed the semantic of the reading operations of the Linda model.

The time costs involved in performing the reading operations have been evaluated for analyzing the efficiency of the proposed pattern. It is important to define a cost time categorization which represents the execution time of a Linda primitive from the user process's point of view. In this work, the categorization proposed by Bonita, a Linda implementation for distributed environment, has been used [17]. For our analysis, the most important time-cost is $T_{ReadingProcess}$,

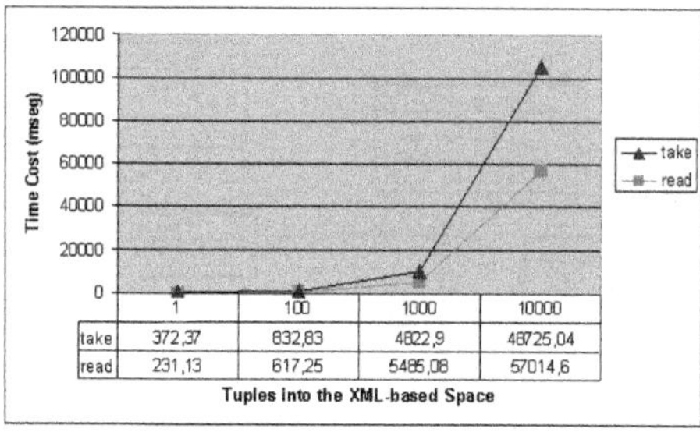

Fig. 4. Efficiency of the reading primitives

which is the time taken for the execution of a reading operation on the XML-based space finding the suitable tuple (a tuple that matches the reading template is always available into the space). To evaluate this time cost have been created partitions composed by a changeable number of tuples with the same XML-Schema, but with different content. The figure 4 shows the $T_{ReadingProcess}$ for the proposed pattern. This time cost shows a linear increase according to the number of tuples stored into the partition. As this number increases, a greater number of tuples must be checked by the matching until finding a tuple that matches the reading template. Therefore, this pattern based on channels is inefficient when the created partitions store a high number of tuples (for example, for partitions composed by more than one thousand tuples).

4.3 Partitioning Interaction Spaces to Improve the Efficiency

To improve the previously pattern, making more efficient the XML-based space, it is necessary to minimize the amount of search required for the matching. This solution must be transparent for processes that cooperate through the XML-based space, and orthogonal to the Linda model. The idea is to make an hierarchical partition of the tuple-space based on *meta-channels* and *channels* (see figure 5). A meta-channel stores all the XML tuples with the same XML-Schema. This partition level of the tuple space is created at run-time. To make more efficient the reading operations, a meta-channel is divided into one or more channels. A channel stores all the XML-tuples with a specific value into an XML-node, called *reference node*. This node must be specified at compile time (a good choice of the reference node is a determining factor to improve the efficiency; it is important to choose a node whose value is usually not-null in the reading templates).

In a more detail, a new object has been designed to manage partitions. The *Meta-channel* object is composed by a structured field able to save a collection of references to channel objects. On the other hand, the channel object has been reused from the previously pattern, and therefore, it stores a set of references to Java objects that represent XML tuples. However, an improvement has been added to control the size of the channels. It is possible to set up a maximum size of channel, storing into it the most recent XML tuples.

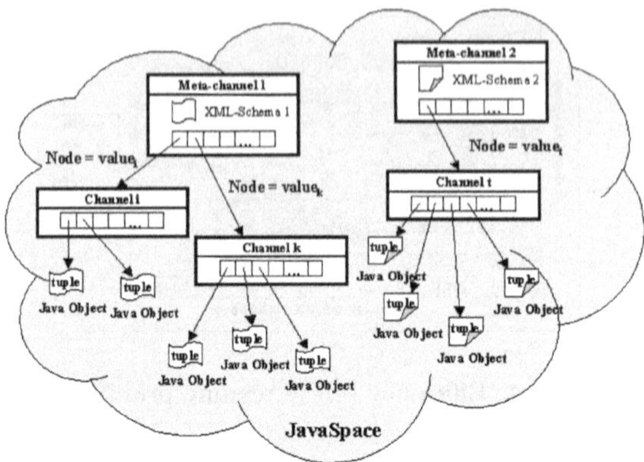

Fig. 5. Partition based on *meta-channels* and *channels*

When a writing operation is invoked, it checks if there is any meta-channel into the tuple-space that stores XML tuples with the same XML-Schema. If it exists, the tuple is inserted into the adequate channel according to the value of its reference node (if the channel does not exist, then it is created in run-time); or else, a new meta-channel and a channel indexed by the value of the tuple's reference node are created, and then, the XML tuple is inserted.

On the other hand, when a reading operations is invoked, it is retrieved a copy of the meta-channel that stores all the tuples with the same XML-Schema than the reading template. This copy is used to check if it exists into the meta-channel a channel indexed by the same value than the reading template's reference node. If it exist, a copy of the channel is retrieved and used to look up the required tuple according to the tuple-marking strategy of the pattern based on channels; or else, the reading operation will be blocked. Finally, to remark that it is possible to specify a reading template with a wildcard in the reference node. In this case, the search is applied over the meta-channel (a meta-channel is the union of all its channels) instead of being applied over a specific channel.

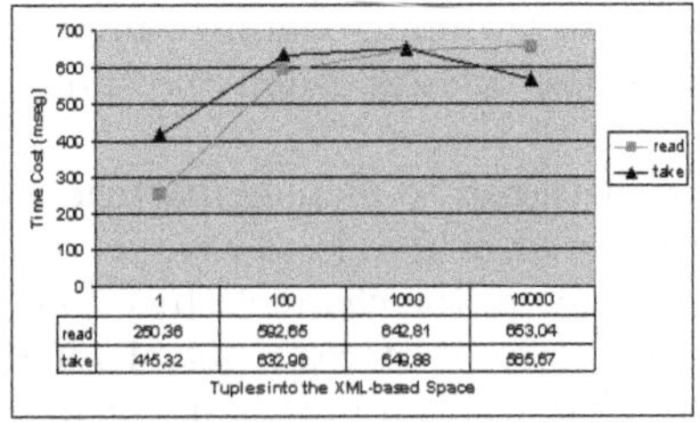

	1	100	1000	10000
read	250,36	592,65	642,81	653,04
take	416,32	632,96	649,88	565,67

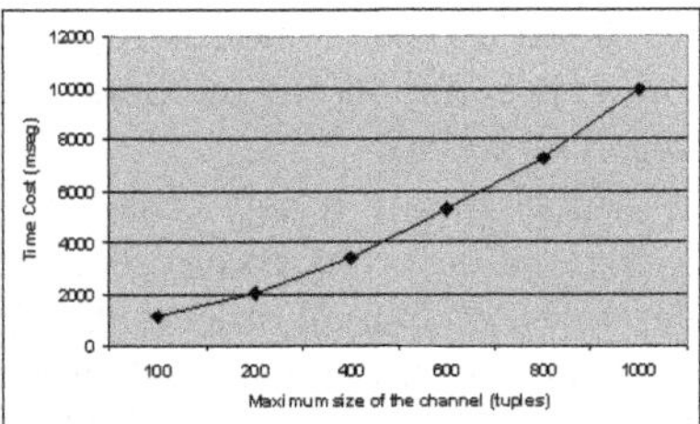

Fig. 6. Efficiency of the reading primitives making a hierarchical partition

To evaluate this new proposal, a meta-channel composed by a changeable number of channels has been created (the maximum size of a channel is one hundred XML tuples). In the figure 6, the graph on the left shows the $T_{ReadingProcess}$ for the proposal. The time cost does not show a linear increase according to the number of tuples stored into the meta-channel, because channels reduce the search space. Beside, it is important to remark that the great size of channels will be conditional on increased time cost. In the figure 6, the graph on the right shows how the size of a channel has an influence on the $T_{ReadingProcess}$.

5 The Location-Based Service Context

Geographic Information Services (GIS) and Location-based Services (LBS) are two prototypical technological contexts where many standardization initiatives have arisen. LBS extend GIS spatial processing capabilities by integrating wireless communications, location data and Internet technology [11]. In this context, two well-positioned organizations have emerged as the leaders of the LBS interoperability: LIF (Location-Interoperability Forum[2]) and OGC (Open GIS Consortium[3], and its Open Location Service Initiative (OpenLS)). Both are promoting and defining standard interfaces for a collection of wireless, Location and GIS services to provide the required LBS functionality. In more detail, LIF specifies the Mobile Location Protocol (MLP) that defines a simple but complete interface between location-data acquisition services (called, Location services) and location-based applications. On the other hand, OGC provides specifications for GIS and geoprocessing services.

OGC and LIF are aware of the necessity of integrating their standardization initiatives, but they have not reached an agreement on the integration strategy yet. In more detail, their work has focused on the definition of service interfaces, but they have ignored how to resolve the difficulty in "gluing together" these standard services. Our proposal tries to provide an architectural solution to this gap.

Starting from the work of LIF and OGC specifications we have designed two Web-service frameworks to provide LBS functionality (see figure 7). Service interfaces have been specified according to previous standards to ensure the interoperability, and are accessible via standard Internet protocols and data formats, such as SOAP, HTTP or XML. As result of this Web standard-based approach, the resulting functionality has been easily integrated into different location-dependent applications, such as a Web-enabled fleet tracking system, and a Customer Relationship Management system [3].

As it is illustrated in figure 7, the OGC-based framework is composed by three functional levels of services. The *Data Management* level is the base of the designed framework. Its services must be able of providing the necessary support for the storage and recovery of a wide variety of geodata: maps, location descriptors (street addresses, roads, place names, telephone numbers, etc.), sensor data such as immediate locations of mobile devices, or more specific data of the LBS

[2] http://www.locationforum.org/

[3] http://www.opengis.org/

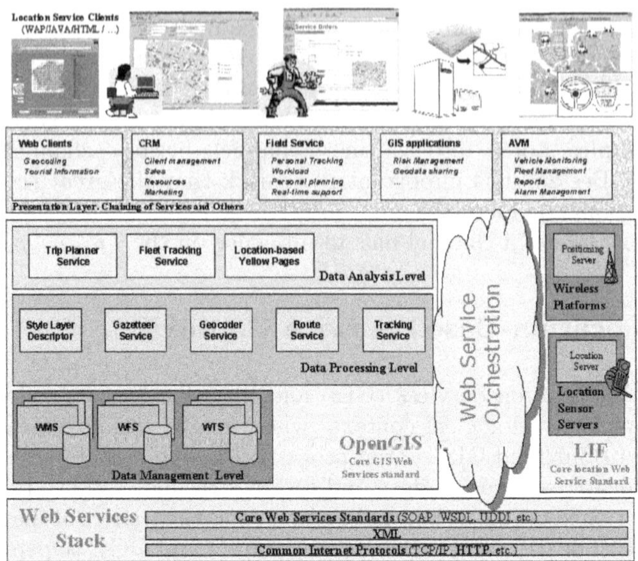

Fig. 7. Standard-based LBS framework based on LIF and OGC orchestration.

context, such as traffic conditions or road repairs. A collection of services are integrated to fulfill these requirements: Web Map Servers (WMS), able to visualize digital map on the Internet; Web Feature Servers (WFS) [12], to store geodata and execute spatial and non-spatial queries over them; and Web Traffic Servers (WTS), that provide a interface to gain access to a variety of traffic information sources. The result of a query to a WFS or WTS is a collection of GML-encoded data (an XML-based standard specified by OGC to encode geographical information [13]). These GML data can be directly visualized on the user interface of a Web-based application.

Geodata provided by these Data Management services are not usually used in an isolated way, instead they are used by the *Data Processing* services for generating more complex and elaborate data. It is interesting to have services for combining different kinds of geodata, such as maps and location descriptors; for linking many location descriptors; or for calculating structured geodata, such as ideal routes. Services of this level include geodata presentation (such as, Styled Layer Descriptor Server), utility (Gazetteers and Geocoders), and determination (Route Server). Details about them can be found in [14]. A Styled Layer Descriptor Server (SLD) visualizes the result of a WFS query over a digital map returned by the WMS, applying a visualization style specified by the service client to the displayed geodata. On the other hand, the implementation of the WFS has been utilized as the baseline for developing another geoservices [3]: Gazetteers, used to link text-based location descriptions to geographic locations; Geocoders, used to transform a textual term or code, such as an address, place name, or telephone number, into a geographic location; and Route server, used to calculate ideal routes.

Finally, the higher level of the OGC framework, called *Data Analysis* level, is composed by a collection of application services. These services are built on the lower level services and integrate their functionality into a wide variety of location-dependent Web-based applications.

Our strategy to integrate the OGC and LIF frameworks lies in the incorporation of mobile location data into the functional chain of the OGC framework. This strategy has been materialized with the design and implementation of a *Tracking service* like a WFS able to store location data of mobile entities. The mobile resources may be seen as "dynamic" features whose geographical information changes throughout the time. This decision makes possible to perform spatial queries over location data of mobile entities exploiting the OGC standard geospatial query language.

This Tracking service requires to update the stored locations collaborating with services able to acquire location data from remote mobile devices via wireless media. These acquisition services are called Location services and compose the LIF-based framework. This collaboration with the Location services is described by the MLP protocol proposed by LIF, which can be used by an Internet application to request location information from a Location Server. Although from a functional point of view the Tracking service (or Web-based application, in general) and Location services are all compatible and standards guarantee their interoperability, some orchestration problems have been identified when they cooperate through Internet such as it has been previously mentioned [2]. It is possible and easy to find solutions to them based on ad-hoc or wrapping techniques. However, the proposed WCS is a an adequate and more reusable solution to solve them as it will be illustrated in the next section.

The figure 7 shows examples of application services that uses the underlaying infrastructure: Fleet Tracking service, Trip Planner, location-based Yellow Pages, etc. A Fleet Tracking service has been developed to support the required functionality of the LBS use case presented in this paper. This service allows to make tracking tasks of mobile resources with an installed location-sensor device (such as, vehicles or employees with a mobile phone with an integrated GPS-receptor), to visualize their real-time positions, to plan a route and tracking it, or to generate operational reports. To provide these operations through its interface, it is necessary that data and geoprocessing services of lower levels collaborate among them in an adequate way as an only global system.

6 Use Case: Integration of LBS Functionality to Improve a Parcels Service

The work presented in this paper has been applied in the integration of LBS functionality into a parcel-service application to track mobile resources. Field personal, which delivers parcels carrying a radio terminal with a GPS receptor, could be on different radio coverage zones and move freely from one to another at any time. Let's suppose that due to the orographic characteristics, there are some different zones of trunking radio coverage without any link among them. It is necessary a "real time" tracking, but there is no possibility of getting the delivery men's locations continuously via radio.

The characteristics of the wireless communication media, with limited bandwidth and frequent disconnection, require a decoupled an opportunistic style of computation [16]. In our use case, we need to use the last known location, without the need to know the server that delivers this location. The proposed WCS provides the required uncoupling and provides the data in a opportunistic way.

The best solution found has been to distribute the location-data acquisition process using the deployment illustrated in figure 8. To achieve this purpose, the system has a LIF Location service to acquire location data on each coverage zone. LIF Location servers are configured in a first step (see figure 8). Remote devices send its location to the receptor that is available at the moment, depending on the coverage zone where they are. Location data received by any Location service are immediately published into the Web Coordination service (WCS). In the figure, the second step shows an example of HTTP request invoked by a Location service to write an XML-encoded location into the WCS.

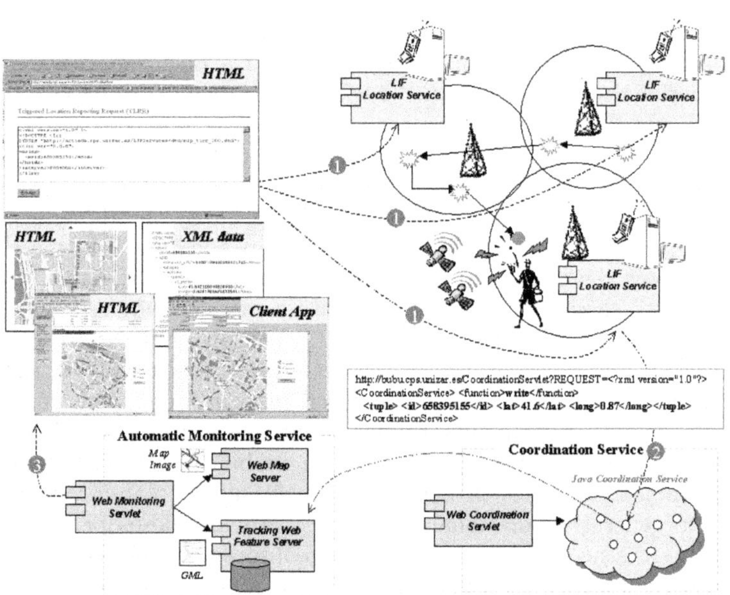

Fig. 8. Deployment architecture for tracking delivery parcels.

These location data stored into the WCS are integrated into the functional chain of the proposed framework by a Tracking service. This service is subscribed in the WCS to be notified when a new location is written into it. These notifications, third step in figure 8, trigger actions inside the Tracking service, being the most regular the updating of the field personal locations stored into its database (in this way, the last acquired and notified location is always accessible). The subscribed service receives location data without having any knowledge about the providers, and are unaware of the restrictions of the data-acquisition process.

The interface of the Tracking service provides operations to know these latest locations to make spatial or non-spatial queries. Remember that its interface has been defined according to the WFS specification. Additionally, more elaborated and filtered events can be published into the WCS taking advantage of the spatial functionality of the services. For example, the Tracking service could publish location-based events to notify that a delivery man has come into/out an irregular geographical region (department/area of a city, a province, etc.), or that it is a specific distance away from a geographical point.

Finally, with this technology it is possible to establish Web-based applications that dynamically access to network-accessible interoperable services, from simple Web browser to complex client-systems. Additionally, other services can be developed to recover the inserted locations from the WCS and to store them into local database to analyze their routes and generate operational reports. The combination of open architectures, domain standards and the ability to access a wide variety of data sources are critical for the success of this Web-based approach.

7 Conclusions and Future Work

This paper proposes an architectural solution to support new interaction models between Web services and applications. This proposal is based on the creation of a new role in the SOA model, interpreted by a Web coordination service, whose functionality is orthogonal to the computing functionality offered by the coordinated services. This coordination Web-service resolves the distributed computing difficulty in "gluing together" multiple and independent Web-services.

The key is the coordination model that defines how distributed entities collaborate. Linda has been extended to be used in open and hostile environments. This extension is based on replacing its simple matching rules with a complex matching able to support new kinds of interoperability (XML-based, semantic, etc). From this model, a Web coordination service has been designed focusing the main attention in the component that implements the interaction spaces, and how to get an efficient implementation of it. The final results has been applied in the LBS context.

Finally, open research issues are attempting to: (1) discover the real potential of the XML language to express synchronization restrictions and workflows among services; and (2) tackle with the integration of XML data and pure coordination models such as Linda and Petri Nets, solving where and how to represent coordination restrictions and XML data in a systematic way, and how to model the internal behavior of the Web-services that cooperate externally through the coordination service.

Acknowledgment. The basic technology of this work has been partially supported by the Spanish Ministry of Science and Technology through projects TIC2000-1568-C03-01, TIC2000-0048-P4-02 from the National Plan for Scientific Research.

References

1. P. Álvarez, J.A. Bañares, E. Mata, P.R. Muro-Medrano, and J. Rubio, *Generative communication with semantic matching in distributed heterogeneous environments*, Proceedings of the 9th International Workshop on Computer Aided Systems Theory. Extended Abstracts. (R. Moreno-Diaz jr., A. Quesada-Arencibia, and J.C. Rodriguez, eds.), Universidad de las Palmas de Gran Canaria, February 2003, pp. 237–239.
2. P. Álvarez, J.A. Bañares, P.R. Muro-Medrano, J. Nogueras, and F.J. Zarazaga, *Scientific engineering for distributed Java applications*, Lecture Notes in Computer Science, no. 2604, ch. A Java Coordination Tool for Web-Sercice Architectures: The Location-Based Service Context, pp. 1–14, Springer Verlag, 2003.
3. P. Álvarez, J.A. Bañares, P.R. Muro-Medrano, and F.J. Zarazaga, *Integration of location based services for field support in CRM systems*, GeoInformatics **5** (2002), no. July/August, 36–39.
4. L. Bettini and R. De Nicola, *Scientific engineering for distributed Java applications*, Lecture Notes in Computer Science, no. 2604, ch. A Java Middleware gor Guaranteeing Privacy of Distributed Tuple Spaces, pp. 175–184, Springer Verlag, 2003.
5. F. Buschmann, R. Meunier, H. Rohnert, P. Sommerlad, and M. Stal, *A system of patterns*, Wiley, 1996.
6. F. Cabrera, G. Coopeland, T. Freund, J. Klein, D. Langworthy, D. Orchand, J. Schewchuk, and T. Storey, *Web service coordination (ws-coordination)*, Tech. report, IBM & Microsoft Corporation & BEA System, September 2002.
7. P. Ciancarini, R. Tolksdorf, and F. Vitali, *Towards an interactive Web*, Submitted for publication, IEEE Internet Computing. Available in http://flp.cs.tu-berlin.de/pagespc/ieeeip/ciancarini.html, February 2003.
8. E. Freeman, S. Hupfer, and K. Arnold, *Javaspaces. principles, patterns, and practice*, Addison Wesley, 1999.
9. D. Gelernter, *Generative communication in Linda*, ACM Transactions on Programming Languages and Systems **7** (1985), no. 1, 80–112.
10. S. Graham, S. Simeonov, T. Boubez, D. Davis, G. Daniels, Y. Nakamura, and R. Neyama, *Building Web services with Java. Making sense of XML, SOAP, WSDL, and UDDI*, SAMS, 2002.
11. H. Niedzwiadek, *All businesses are in pursuit of Java location services*, Available in http://www.geojava.com/, January 2000.
12. OpenGIS Project Document 01–065, *Web feature server implementation specification (version 0.0.14)*, Tech. report, OpenGIS Consortium Inc, 2001.
13. OpenGIS Project Document 02–023r4, *Opengis geography markup language (GML) implementation specification (version 3.0)*, Tech. report, OpenGIS Consortium Inc, 2003.
14. OpenLS, *Call for participation in the open location services testbed. phase 1 (openls-1)*, Tech. report, OpenGIS Consortium Inc, 2000.
15. D. E. Perry and A. L. Wolf, *Foundations for the study of software architectures*, ACM SIGSOFT Software Engineering Notes **17** (1992), no. 4, 40–52.
16. G.P. Picco, A.L. Murphy, and G.C. Roman, *LIME: Linda meets mobility*, Proceedings of the 21st International Conference on Software Engineering (ICSE'99) (D. Garlan and J. Kramer, eds.), ACM Press, May 1999, pp. 368–377.
17. A. I. T. Rowstron and A. M. Wood, *Bonita: A set of tuple space primitives for distributed coordination*, Proceedings of the 30th Annual Hawaii International Conference on System Sciences, vol. 1, IEEE Computer Society Press, 1997, pp. 379–388.

PANDA: Specifying Policies for Automated Negotiations of Service Contracts

Henner Gimpel[1], Heiko Ludwig[2], Asit Dan[2], and Bob Kearney[2]

[1] Universität Fridericina Karlsruhe (TH), Englerstrasse 14, 76131 Karlsruhe, Germany
gimpel@iw.uni-karlsruhe.de

[2] IBM T.J. Watson Research Center, 19, Skyline Drive, Hawthorne, NY, 10025, USA
{hludwig, asit, firefly}@us.ibm.com

Abstract. The *Web and Grid services frameworks provide a promising infrastructure for cross-organizational use of online services. The use of services in large-scale and cross-organizational environments requires the negotiation of agreements that define these services. Buying at a fine granularity just when a need arises is only feasible if the costs of establishing new agreements are low. Today, negotiation is often a manual process yet many simple online services would allow full or partial automation. The PANDA approach automates decision-making and proposes to specify a negotiation policy, expressing a party's private negotiation strategy, by combining rules and utility functions. In addition, the decision-making problem can be decomposed into different aspects that can be executed by different interacting decision-makers. Using PANDA for policy specification and negotiation decision-making reduces the costs of setting up new services and contracts. Hence, the use of fine-grained on-demand services becomes feasible.*

1 Introduction

Web and Grid services facilitate on-demand use of services accessed over a network – potentially across organizational boundaries. This may lead to an environment in which services are bought at a fine granularity from a number of competing providers. Given a marketplace of providers of similar or comparable services, it also enables organizations to dynamically buy resources on the spot when additional business requires access to more capacity than available in-house. Negotiating agreements and buying services ad-hoc enables business partners to tailor their contractual bindings in regard to time varying needs and constraints. This reduces the risk of being stuck in long-term contracts that are no longer profitable.

PANDA (**P**olicy-driven **A**utomated **N**egotiation **D**ecision-making **A**pproach) facilitates automated decision-making within negotiations. It allows decomposition of intended negotiation behavior, integrates different formalisms for policy, and structures the strategic reasoning of a negotiator.

M.E. Orlowska et al. (Eds.): ICSOC 2003, LNCS 2910, pp. 287–302, 2003.

1.1 Agreements in the Web Services Domain

Relationships between organizations are defined by agreements between them. Those agreements may be implicit by accepting some fixed terms that are published by a service provider or they are made explicit in the form of a *contract* that is specifically negotiated.

Most description formats of the Web services stack are unilateral in their nature, i.e., a service provider describes properties and usage conditions of a service. This is the case, for example, for WSDL [5] and WS-Policy [4]. Unilateral descriptions are limiting because they cannot represent consensus and reciprocity. Some description formats in the context of Web services, however, represent aspects of agreements among two or more parties, such as the Business Process Execution Language (BPEL) [1] or proposed languages for service level agreements such as the Web Service Level Agreement (WSLA) language [15] and the Web Service Management Language (WSML) [19]. A draft for "Agreement-based Grid Service Management (OGSI-Agreement)" has been submitted to the Global Grid Forum [6]. As relationships between service providers and clients become more complex and more non-functional requirements such as response time guarantees must be considered, languages will be defined to express agreed relationships in contracts. In dynamic environments, those contracts will vary for each relationship and can be negotiated ad hoc.

1.2 Negotiating Agreements

Negotiations are mechanisms that increase the flexibility of possible service contracts. We use the term negotiations as comprising all exchanges of messages, such as offers and acceptance messages, between two or more parties intended to reach an agreement.

In the context of dynamically setting up service relationships, it is important to use an efficient decision-making process that reduces cost and time of the setup. Human-based negotiations are time-consuming and expensive. Hence there have been many approaches to support human decision-makers with decision support systems and negotiation support systems [14]. In addition, in some cases requiring simple decision-making, it is desirable to automate all or a part of the negotiation task of a participating party and hence to drive down the costs, and particularly time of establishing a new agreement. However, engineering negotiation applications is complex, time-consuming, and expensive. In many cases, it is not worth to implement a new negotiation application for each new negotiation task or situation.

Ideally, an employee of an organization can express the negotiation preferences as a negotiation policy that can be interpreted by a negotiation engine. A policy in the context of this paper is an explicit representation of intended behavior to be interpreted by an engine that implements the behavior. In the case of negotiations, a negotiation engine responds to offers and other communication in accordance to this specified policy. PANDA provides the expression of policies that combine utility functions and business rules.

1.3 Objective and Structure

To facilitate the automation of decision-making based on negotiation policy, the objective of this paper is to propose a mechanism an organization can use to define its preferences – PANDA. Using a combination of utility functions and rules provides a user a suitable formalism to represent preferences in a way that can be easily expressed and managed.

To this end, the remainder of the paper is structured as follows: Section 2 introduces a motivating example and discusses the specifics of negotiating services. Subsequently, expression of intended behavior is analyzed in Section 3. In Section 4 we introduce the PANDA approach that defines a model of decision-making. Section 5 illustrates the use of the presented approach based on the example. Finally, Section 6 summarizes the results, compares the approach to related work, and gives an outlook on future work.

2 Negotiation of Service Agreements

The negotiation of service agreements takes an important role in the life cycle of agreements, facilitating the creation of complex agreements in lieu of simple binding to services that are described. Parties in a potential service relationship use advertising and search functions to find each other, either directly or using an intermediary. Negotiation messages such as offers and acceptance notifications are exchanged. This may finally lead to a contract. Upon successful negotiation, each organization creates a contract implementation plan that defines how to implement a particular contract [16]. However, beyond general issues of negotiating contracts, online and Web services have some specific properties that require further analysis.

2.1 Example

To illustrate the further discussion, we use the example of a stock quote service that is offered by a service provider FastQuote that negotiates some attributes of the service for particular customers. The service is offered at an interface defined by FastQuote in a WSDL file. It exposes an operation getQuote in a binding specifying SOAP over HTTP as transport. The service is offered by FastQuote at different levels of delays of the quotes from the trading floor, 20 minutes, 5 minutes, or real time. Furthermore, on an IT level, FastQuote negotiates different levels of service regarding availability and response time at requested levels of throughput. The throughput is measured in invocations per minute. Finally, the price is open to negotiation.

FastQuote's preferences over the variety of possible contracts include a reasonable coherency between price and delay; delivering stock quotes with a shorter delay is a more valuable service and should yield higher earnings. For building up new business relationships FastQuote is willing to be more acquiescent in negotiations with first time customers.

Once an agreement is reached, FastQuote plans the deployment of the new agreement. Depending on the quality of service parameters agreed upon it plans the allocation of capacity on existing hosts or the provisioning of new hosts. The host capacity relates to the amount of memory and the number of CPU seconds required. This plan is called the contract implementation plan. The company has an algorithm that returns capacity requirements for given throughput rates and response times at a requested availability.

2.2 Service Characteristics

Services have a number of characteristics, which impose special requirements for a decision-making in the course of a negotiation. The most important are:

Non-storability denotes the fact that resources not used yesterday are worthless today [13]. The implication for marketing one's resources by providing services is that time and current resource workloads are crucial factors in decision-making. If time runs out and capacity is going to be wasted, providers will make stronger concessions.

Complexity is another service characteristic. Service contracts are usually complex due to the fact that they have many defining parameters. The complexity issue can be addressed by means of templates, utility functions, and sophisticated tactics for offer creation.

Intangibility raises problems in determining the value of a service contract because the good sold to a consumer does not equal the operating expense dedicated by the service provider. A provider has resources and uses them to yield a return on his investment. A consumer has needs and satisfies them by buying a service. The service agreement bridges the gap between provider resources and consumer needs; neither side has to be acquainted with the precise nature of the other side's concerns. The intangibility of services leads to the need of an internal transformation from a service contract to a deployment plan.

Provisioning a service instead of settlement is a feature distinguishing services from, e.g., financial products and hard goods. Many commodity trades have a settlement time, for exchanging money and goods. Services are not settled, but provisioned and consumed, which calls for a contract implementation plan accounting for the whole time span.

2.3 Negotiation Issues

A common way of analyzing negotiations is differentiating the *negotiation protocol*, comprising the rules of the encounter, the *negotiation object*, and the *decision-making model* [11]. A number of simple negotiation protocols are used for match-making and reservations without considering economic aspects. For example, SNAP (Service Negotiation and Acquisition Protocol) has been proposed for resource reservation and use in the context of the Grid [8].

The remainder of the paper focuses on direct bilateral negotiations, not involving third parties like regulators, facilitators or mediators enforcing special rules of interaction, although PANDA can be applied in that situation.

A common problem in negotiations is the *ontology problem of electronic negotiations* [20]. It deals with the common understanding of the issues among negotiating parties. One approach of solving the ontology problem is the use of templates. Templates are partially completed contracts whose attributes are filled out in the course of the negotiation. Template-based negotiations facilitate structuring of the negotiation process and understanding of resulting service contracts [18].

2.4 Requirements

The discussion in this section leads to a set of requirements to be addressed by a negotiation decision-making approach:

- The approach should impose few restrictions on the **negotiation protocol and object**.
- The policy representation should **trade off** expressiveness and ease of specification. It must allow a policy specifier to structure the policy along his or her thinking and to understand and manage real-life policies.
- The **practicality** of a negotiation system entails that a regular user should not be required to have programming skills. A negotiation is not an end in itself, but means to an end.
- **User interaction** should be possible but not mandatory. Automated decision-making is capable of speeding up the negotiation process and reducing its costs. Nevertheless, user interaction may be necessary.
- The approach must consider the **specific properties of services**, which are: non-storability, complexity, intangibility and need for provisioning.

3 Capturing Intended Behavior

Utility functions and rule-based systems are two standard methods for externalizing preferences and intended behavior. However, both approaches pose difficulties for users to express complex strategies for negotiating service agreements.

3.1 Examples of Decision Relevant Considerations

Deciding whether or not to accept an offer or to create a counter-offer may involve evaluations of many different aspects of the contract and checking many decision criteria. Below we illustrate a typical set of evaluation criteria for service offers addressed in negotiation policies:

- *Can this contract be supported?* Before accepting a new contract a provider needs to make sure it can be supported given the set of existing contracts and available resources. Answering this question may involve a detailed model of the system [6] and evaluating the expected violations with this new contract.
- *How desirable is this contract?* A highly profitable contract may be desired over an existing one even if not enough resources are available. The business may have decision criteria on terminating an existing contract not just based on profitability but many other aspects such as business reputation and customer satisfaction.

- *Will the counterparty lose interest?* A counter-offer selection can not be guided simply by maximization of profit. The business may have decision criteria on how far to deviate from a client offer or how much to concede.

For some of the above considerations the attributes of the contract template are insufficient for the decision-making process. The evaluation involves a complex estimation of one or more additional decision parameters, such as probabilistic measure of risk, resource costs and desirability of a new contract. This includes the attributes of the contract implementation plan. We refer to program components that derive these additional parameters as *estimation programs*. Both, attributes of the template and additional decision parameters can be used in utility functions and rules.

3.2 Utility Functions

Economists have been using utility functions as representation for preferences since the 19th century. A utility function maps properties related to an offer onto a single dimensional abstract utility value for an individual or an organization. The utility value is then used as a representation for the individual's preferences: alternative A is preferred to alternative B if, and only if, A's utility value is greater than B's.

In automated negotiations maximization of externalized utility functions can be used for decision-making. Hence, utility functions have to embrace four preferential aspects:

1. *Risk*[1] is a part of service negotiations mainly because of the non-storability characteristic resources might possess.
2. Complex service agreements often define multiple issues or attributes. *Multi-attribute* considerations are a well-known component of decision and negotiation analysis.
3. *Time* influences negotiations in two ways: In the short run there might be deadlines for reaching an agreement. A consumer may have a fixed time line and a provider may want to have his resource booked in advance to avoid risk. In the long run the continuity of business relations might become important.
4. *Inter-personal* elements deal with bounded self-interest, i.e. an individual's utility may depend not only on his own situation, but as well on the situation others face, examples being altruism and positional goods.

It is a well-known problem that even if an individual's preferences match a specific utility function, it is hard to externalize this function: An individual usually does not know his or her personal utility function. It has to be elicited [10, 17]. Service providers can build their utility functions by analyzing a services business model and the cost structure obtained from the IT controlling. Typical fixed costs are, e.g., the depreciation of servers. Typical variable costs are ISP bandwidth, electricity, and personnel. Consumers can derive a bigger part of their utility functions by estimating the costs of in-house provisioning and considering the benefits from service usage.

---

[1] In decision theory there is a difference between *risk* and *uncertainty*. Both terms refer to random outcomes. However, risk implies a mathematical probability measure of the outcomes, uncertainty does not. Within this paper we shall use the term *risk* to refer to either situation.

Considering the preferential elements, it is easy to imagine that one single function capturing all aspects might become complex.

FastQuote's desired price/delay coherency is an example for multi-attribute aspects within a negotiation. It can be modeled by means of a utility function, e.g., the one presented in figure 1. A higher price is better for FastQuote; consequently the function is strictly monotonic increasing in the price. The delay however determines the curvature of the function. The higher the delay, the more concave the function. This implies that for a given price the utility is higher when the delay increases.

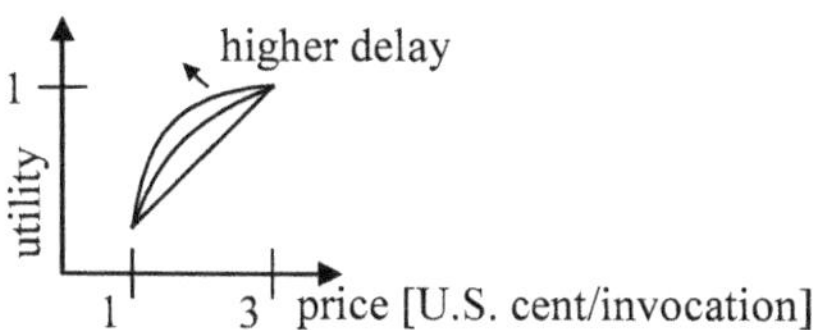

Fig. 1. Multi-attribute utility function representing FastQuote's price and delay preferences.

Integrating FastQuote's first time customer cordiality in a utility function is not straightforward. It could be done by increasing the functions dimensionality, but definition, calculation, and optimization would become far more demanding.

3.3 Rule-Driven Decision-Making

Directions for decision-making can be also represented in form of rules. There are numerous approaches for expressing business rules but no absolutely best way because one has to make a trade-off between expressive power and ease of use while ensuring automated execution. Negotiation rules have to express knowledge in a high-level machine executable language on a high degree of abstraction, which is closer to the understanding of business domain experts, who are often not educated in programming languages, than hard-coded if-then constructs. The rule corpus should be simple to modify by adding or removing single rules and execution of procedural attachments should be possible. Procedures are necessary for informational input to the rules, i.e. as sensors, and for conducting desired actions, i.e. as effectors. Some procedures might perform optimization tasks, such as implementing a trade-off heuristic for computing an adequate counteroffer.

Rule-driven strategies are integrated in some negotiation infrastructures like the ones from Su et al. [21] and Benyoucef et al. [2]. For some kinds of decisions, rules can be seen as a more human-like way of thinking than the maximization of utility, hence they are easier to elicit.

FastQuote's first time customer cordiality can be easily expressed with an if-then construct, in prose this might be: "If the customer's offer is close to FastQuote's last offer and the customer is a new customer then the offer is accepted." The price/delay coherency would be much more difficult as a rule expression, than it was in form of a utility function. The curves could be approximated by step functions defined by a sequence of rules, but a continuous function is easier to define, optimize and manage.

3.4 Mixed Policies: Externalized Negotiation Behavior

Given the advantages and drawbacks of rules and utility functions in terms of expressiveness, manageability and ease of elicitation, we propose to combine both approaches for the representation of negotiation policy. The mixed policy approach requires a model of decision-making that defines how rules relate to utility values. This includes:

- Definition of points of decision-making,
- The association of utility functions with those points, and
- The definition of objects that can be subject to rule expressions.

The PANDA approach addresses exactly these design issues and consequently helps building negotiation applications.

4 PANDA Framework

The model of decision-making is designed as an object-oriented framework. The framework decomposes the decision-making task and identifies points of decision-making, assigns different utility functions to these points, and specifies the objects that can be accessed for rule-based reasoning.

4.1 Negotiation Object and Protocol

Automated decision-making depends on the negotiation object and the protocol. In the proposed approach, the negotiation object is a contract template [16, 18], where a template comprises fixed and variable parts. The fixed ones are usually the general terms and conditions, the variable parts may either be negotiable, such as quality-of-service attributes, or non-negotiable such as the names of the parties. Variable parts may contain single values and may be restricted by ranges, enumerations of values, simple logical constraints, and inter-attribute constraints. In template-based negotiations the meaning of negotiable issues is clearly defined as parts of the template.

A negotiation protocol is a set of rules governing the interaction. The assumptions on the protocol made by the framework are fairly weak for keeping it applicable to many negotiation scenarios. The basic structure is a bilateral message exchange. The integration of an intermediary does not impose changes in the PANDA framework. Either party can start a negotiation with a *request for negotiation* indicating the template to use. Follow-up messages are of the types *accept*, *reject*, *offer*, *withdraw*, or *terminate*. The parties are neither required to alternate with sending messages nor to agree on the utilization of the decision-making framework. *Accept* leads to a contract based on the other party's last offer, *reject* to the rejection of the last offer. Offer indicates that a (partially) filled template is sent as proposed contract, *withdraw* annuls the last offer, and *terminate* ends the entire negotiation process immediately.

4.2 Decision-Maker Components

The PANDA framework's architecture is built around *decision-maker* (DM) components. The internal structure of a single DM is illustrated in figure 2. Its primary task is to combine a set of *utility functions* and processing a rule set, stored in a *XML Repository*. Rules and utility functions both have access to an *object pool*, containing data items and functions that the utility functions can evaluate and the *rule interpreter* can reason on. The object pool can, e.g., contain *estimation programs* (see 3.1), the *negotiation history* and other objects.

Rules are expressed in a high-level language specified by an XML schema. The primary goal of this language is to allow a business domain expert to specify negotiation strategies without having to deal with the programmatic implementation of the decision-making system. The implementation details of the object pool members are abstracted by means of sensors and effectors, which can then be used within rules.

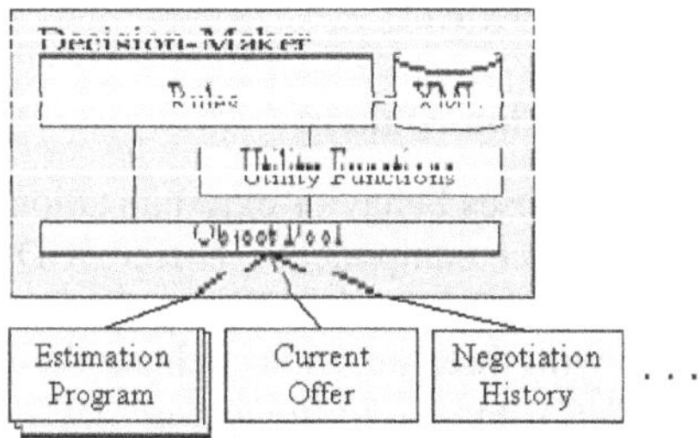

Fig. 2. Building blocks of a decision-maker component

The basic building block of a strategy is a single rule, consisting of a condition part and an action to perform, if the condition is met. A condition is a Boolean expression, composed of Boolean- and mathematical operators, constants, and so called data sources. An action is simply a series of data sources. In conditions and actions likewise a data source is build from a sensor or an effector and a list of parameters. Sensors and effectors are defined separately and map their name to the call of a procedure belonging to one of the object pool's elements. Parameters can either be constants, data sources, or objects. Following is a rudimentary rule example, including the sensor *LEVEL_OF_DISSENT* and the effector *ACCEPT_OFFER*, the definition of both is omitted.

An example rule, in prose, is: *If the level of dissent is less than 0.05 accept the counterparty's offer. The level of dissent is defined as the utility difference between the party's last offer and the counterparty's last offer.*

The same rule in the proposed XML representation:

```
<Rule>
  <Condition>
    <BooleanExp>
      <RelationExp>
        <Operator>LESS</Operator>
        <Sensor>
          <Name>LEVEL_OF_DISSENT</Name>
        </Sensor>
```

```
        <Constant>0.05</Constant>
      </RelationExp>
    </BooleanExp>
  </Condition>
  <Action>
    <Effector>
      <Name>ACCEPT_OFFER</Name>
    </Effector>
  </Action>
</Rule>
```

Rules are assembled to rule sets. A strategy can contain an arbitrary number of rule sets. The clustering of rules allows inducing control flow within the strategy interpretation. Some of the control-flow aspects are iterations over a rule set (i.e. a *while* loop), stopping a rule set's processing after a certain rule within it was fired (i.e. a *break* statement), and the unconditional processing of a rule set at the end of the strategy interpretation (i.e. a *finally* statement).

4.3 Combining Multiple Decision-Makers

The PANDA framework decomposes behavior externalization by delegating different aspects to different decision-maker components. Different DMs can then be assembled for getting the overall intended behavior. Figure 3 exemplifies FastQuote's negotiation system architecture with three decision-makers: the *negotiating agent* (NA), the *negotiation coordinator* (NC), and the *utility update* (UU).

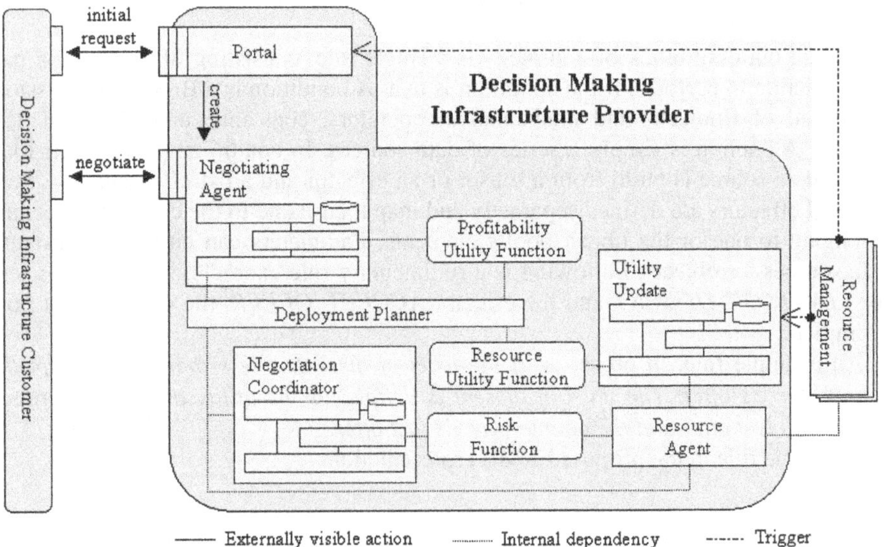

Fig. 3. Combination of decision-maker components in a single negotiation system

This configuration is appropriate for FastQuote's needs, but not mandatory within the framework. PANDA allows the combination of an arbitrary number of DMs. The UU could be needless in some scenarios; others might require additional components like, e.g., the integration of a customer relationship component. DMs can either be objects directly accessible from another DM, or they can be detached and indirectly affect others by changing their objects.

A negotiation is initiated through the *portal*, either by handling an incoming request or triggered by changes in the resource management. The portal creates a NA instance for each new interaction and endows it with information on the counterparty, the template to use, and the relevant negotiation policy and objects. In figure 3 the NA, the *deployment planner* (DP) and the *profitability utility function* (PUF) are individually instantiated for each negotiation. The other components are singletons. After creation the new NA is registered at the NC and takes control of the interaction with the counterparty.

- **Negotiating Agent (NA):** The NA is the focal point of negotiation handling and all other components within the decision-making infrastructure, except the Portal, support it by providing information on the current situation and environmental conditions. Upon reception of a message, the NA performs some administrative tasks such as checking the validity of the incoming message before proceeding to more sophisticated message handling depending on the message type. Upon reception of a termination or acceptance the procedure is straightforward: cleaning up all negotiation dependent objects and possibly canceling resource reservations, or passing the final contract on for deployment. Otherwise, the NA processes its rule corpus for producing a response message to send or for deciding to wait.

  The NA can via its object pool (partially outlined in figure 3) obtain information on all messages in the negotiation history, perform searches for utility maximizing points within offer-spaces and access counter-offer tactics such as trade-off heuristics [9] and if necessary user input. The *resource agent* (RA) establishes the interface to *resource management* and forecasting systems and is able to handle reservation and information requests. The PUF is a multi-attribute utility function, evaluating a *contract template.* Since service provisioning involves the use of resources which are often not explicitly defined in the service contract, the PUF cannot evaluate all contract attributes and has to invoke the *resource utility function* (RUF). The RUF is another multi-attribute utility function. It aggregates the resource requirements for deploying a service to a single utility value that is further processed by the PUF.
- **Negotiation Coordinator (NC):** The NC is designed to coordinate multiple NAs, as each single one of them is ignorant of its siblings and the work load risk. Each NA can invoke the NC for receiving a level of giving in, which is determined by processing the NCs rule corpus. This provides an indication on how strongly a NA should concede the counterparty. The NC can reason on status reports requested from all NAs and it has access to the *risk function* (RF). The RF is the third utility function within FastQuote's decision-making system. Unlike PUF and RUF, it doesn't consider multi-attribute aspects, but takes the work load risk into account. This enables a business domain expert to incorporate the desired level of committed resources.
- **Utility Update (UU):** The UU cannot be directly accessed from the NA, but modifies the RUF which might be volatile and depended on the resources' work loads. A sparse resource might, e.g., have more influence within the function, than an

abound one. As the individual resources' loads change over time, the RUF can adapt. The update process is triggered by a resource management system and comprises the interpretation of a utility update strategy by the UU. The strategy can use data, obtained from the RA, to change the RUF during runtime.

The **Deployment Planner (DP)** is an important component besides the three decision-makers. As figure 3 indicates, the NA consults the DP when calling the NC, RA, or indirectly the RUF. Often, the utility depends on the resources consumed, specified in the contract implementation plan, in addition to the negotiated parts of the contract. The decision-making infrastructure must map from the contract to the contract implementation plan. The DP determines resource requirements by transforming contract attributes.

The DMs and the DP described above facilitate the manageable specification of a negotiation policy comprising utility functions and rules. The PANDA framework is implemented in Java and defines the basic components as well as the control flow for decision-making in negotiations. Existing object types can be extended and additional object types can be added to decision-makers by using the mechanisms provided by Java inheritance.

5 Policy Example

The example illustrates a possible negotiation strategy of FastQuote and its potential customer NewsOnline, a personalized online newspaper. Due to a change in subscriber behavior NewsOnline has to increase its capacity in stock quotes and initiates a service negotiation with FastQuote.

5.1 FastQuote's Negotiation Policy

Besides publishing a contract template, FastQuote internally specifies a contract implementation plan and a negotiation policy: rules for the negotiating agent and the coordinator, a profitability utility function, a resource utility function, and a risk function. The following rules are not expressed via XML for space restrictions; capitalized words indicate sensors and effectors.

The rules of the NA are:

```
RuleSet:
  Rule NA1:
   if      LEVEL_OF_DISSENT < 0.05
   then    ACCEPT; break;
  Rule NA2:
   if      LEVEL_OF_DISSENT < 0.2 and NEW_CUSTOMER
   then    ACCEPT; break;
  Rule NA3:
   if      LEVEL_OF_DISSENT > 0.2
   then    FIND_TRADE_OFF_OFFER(LAST_UTILITY - 0.5*LGI);
           MAKE_OFFER; break;
  ...
End
```

The rules of the NC are:

```
RuleSet:
  ...
  Rule NC4:
   if     RISK_UTILITY < 0.65 and RISK_UTILITY > 0.5
   then   LGI = (1-RISK_UTILITY) / NUMBER_NEGS; break;
  ...
End
```

The three utility functions are jointly outlined in figure 4. RUF and PUF are both computed by evaluating the sub-functions in the leaf nodes and aggregating them by building the weighted sum. The weights are displayed at connecting edges. The RF first aggregates work load forecasts for the two resource types by taking the maximum and then maps this maximum on the interval from zero to one. 70% is the target work load that FastQuote wants to achieve.

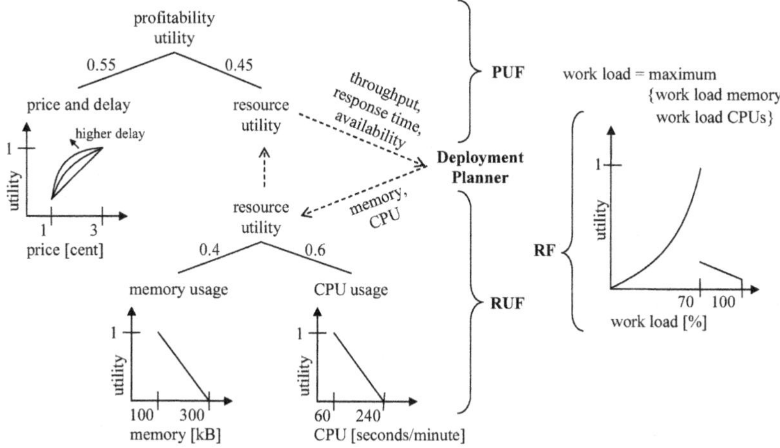

Fig. 4. Example utility function composition.

5.2 Creating a Counteroffer

Figure 5 gives a snapshot of the offers exchanged between FastQuote and NewsOnline.

Prices are given in cents per invocation, delay is zero, 5, or 20 minutes, throughput in invocations per minute, response time in seconds, and availability is either 98%, 99%, or 99.9%.

Sender	...	FastQuote	NewsOnline	FastQuote	...
Message No.		5	6	7	
Price		2.4	1.5	2.3	
Delay		0	0	0	
Throughput		400-600	800	600	
Response time		≥ 3	≤ 3	3	
Availability		99%	99.9%	99.9%	

Fig. 5. Example of an offer sequence during a multi-attribute service negotiation.

The creation of FastQuote's offer number 7 goes as follows: FastQuote's NA receives message 6, approves it as valid offer, and the starts processing its rule corpus containing a single rule set. Rule NA1 invokes the sensor LEVEL_OF_DISSENT, which computes the utility difference of offers 5 and 6. Computing utility values involves invoking the PUF, which passes the attributes throughput, response time, and availability on to the DP. The DP maps these three attributes to resource requirements and calls the RUF. The resulting utility values might, e.g., be 0.78 and 0.54 respectively. As a result the level of dissent is 0.24. Rule NA1 does not fire, neither does NA2.

Rule NA3 fires and the effector FIND_TRADE_OFF_OFFER invokes a method in the object pool for calculating a reasonable counteroffer. The calculation comprises searching for a contract which utility value equals at least the one given as a parameter and which is close to NewsOnline's last offer. The closeness makes it likely to be acceptable by NewsOnline. The parameter, i.e. the desired utility value, is calculated by integrating the coordinator via the sensor LGI, i.e. the level of giving in.

The coordinator consults the RA, receives work load forecasts of 60% for memory and 53% for CPUs, and aggregates them by taking the maximum. The corresponding RISK_UTILITY value of 0.64 is derived from the risk function and used during rule processing. Rule NC4 is the first rule to fire and the sensor NUMBER_NEGS simply counts the number of ongoing negotiations for services affecting either memory or CPUs. Currently their might be three negotiations, including the one with NewsOnline. The level of giving in is hence set to 0.12.

LAST_UTILITY is currently the utility value of offer 5, i.e. 0.78; therefore the parameter of the FIND_TRADE_OFF_OFFER effector is 0.72. Rule NA3 sets the type of message 7 to *offer*. It is not yet send at this point, as following rules might change either the offer's attribute values, or the message type, e.g., to *accept* or *terminate*. However the break statement in NA3 exits the single rule set. The NA identifies a valid message type and filled out template and sends message 7 to NewsOnline.

6 Conclusion and Future Work

The Policy-driven Automated Negotiation Decision-making Approach (PANDA) proposes a novel mechanism for the specification of a party's negotiation policy, i.e. the private specification that guides the analysis of offers and creation of responses. In the context of fine-granular Web services that are to be bound and integrated into composite Web services across domain boundaries, organizations need to automate the negotiation process for new service usage as far as possible to make a service-based business model viable. To enable automated negotiations it is important that organizations can specify their negotiation policies in a concise and easy way.

PANDA enables the representation of a negotiation policy based on the novel combination of utility functions and rules. This policy is executed by decision-maker components within the PANDA framework. The combination of multiple decision-makers facilitates the decomposition of the policy. Using this approach, a specifier can divide the decision problem into manageable units according to his or her understanding. Different aspects of the decision problem such as profitability of an offer and resource situation can be specified separately for different decision-makers and can refer to each other. Using this approach, PANDA allows the specification of sophisticated negotiation behavior in a manageable way.

The approach is agnostic to specific negotiation protocols, although a particular specifier must understand them. PANDA has a template-based approach to represent the negotiation object and can deal with arbitrary service contracts. The high-level rule language helps keeping programming requirements low. In addition, the framework facilitates the involvement of users in the decision-making process, if necessary. The example shows how to use PANDA in a Web services context and hence addresses the specific needs of service negotiations.

Related work has been published on various aspects of negotiations, decision-making and rules, as discussed in the paper. Particularly relevant are the following contributions: The negotiation server by Su et al. uses rules to describe how to relax constraints defining acceptable offers in the course of the negotiation [21]. Cost-benefit analysis is used to choose between multiple acceptable offers. While no suitable offers are found, this approach does not benefit from the use of utility functions to guide the negotiation process. The complexity of utility functions and contract implementation plans is addressed by Boutilier et al. [3]. This approach is used for collaborative resource allocation within an organization and does not address negotiations across organizational boundaries.

Future work will address the specification of utility functions in an externalized representation. Also, the framework extensions are planned to implement a library of common object pool elements such as estimation programs. Furthermore, users would benefit from a policy editor that supports the creation of specifications. Work is being conducted to connect the negotiation framework to an automated deployment function in the Grid context. Finally, an experimental evaluation of the mixed policy approach is necessary.

References

1. T. Andrews, F. Curbera, H. Dholakia, Y. Goland, J. Klein, F. Leymann, K. Liu, D. Roller, D. Smith, S. Thatte, I. Trickovic, S. Weerawarana: *Business Process Execution Language for Web Services, Version 1.1.* 2003.
2. M. Benyoucef, H. Alj, K.Levy, R. Keller: A Rule-Driven Approach for Defining the Behavior of Negotiating Software Agents. *Proceedings of the Fourth International Conference on Distributed Communities on the Web.* Sydney, 2002.
3. C. Boutilier, R. Das, J.O. Kephart, G. Tesauro, W.E. Walsh: Cooperative Negotiation in Autonomic Systems using Incremental Utility Elicitation. *Proceedings of Nineteenth Conference on Uncertainty in Artificial Intelligence (UAI 2003).* Acapulco, 2003.
4. D. Box, F. Curbera, M. Hondo, C. Kaler, D. Langworthy, A. Nadalin, N. Nagaratnam, M. Nottingham, C. van Riegen, J. Shewchuk: *Web Services Policy Framework (WS-Policy), Version 1.1.* 2003.
5. R. Chinici, M. Gudgin, J-J. Moreau, S. Weerawarana: *Web Services Description Language (WSDL), Version 1.2, Part 1: Core Language.* W3C Working Draft, 2003.
6. C. Crawford, A. Dan: eModel: Addressing the Need for a Flexible Modeling Framework in Autonomic Computing. *IEEE/ACM International Symposium on Modeling, Analysis and Simulation of Computer and Telecommunications Systems (MASCOTS 2002).* Fort Worth, 2002.

7. K. Czajkowski, A. Dan, J. Rofrano, S. Tuecke, M. Xu (eds.): *Agreement-based Grid Service Management (OGSI-Agreement), Version 0.* 2003.
8. K. Czajkowski, I. Foster, C. Kesselman, V. Sander, S. Tuecke: SNAP: A Protocol for Negotiation of Service Level Agreements and Coordinated Resource Management in Distributed Systems. *Job Scheduling Strategies for Parallel Processing: 8th International Workshop (JSSPP 2002).* Edinburgh, 2002.
9. P. Faratin: *Automated Service Negotiation between Autonomous Computational Agents.* Ph.D. Dissertation. University of London, 2000.
10. Y. Guo, J.P. Müller, C. Weinhardt: Learning User Preferences for Multi-attribute Negotiation: An Evolutionary Approach. *Multi-Agent Systems and Application III, Proceedings of the 3rd Int./Central and Eastern European Conference on Multi-Agent Systems (CEEMAS 2003).* Prague, 2003.
11. N.R. Jennings, P. Faratin, A.R. Lomuscio, S. Parsons, C. Sierra, M. Wooldridge: Automated Negotiation: Prospects, Methods and Challenges. *International Journal of Group Decision and Negotiation.* 10 (2), 2001.
12. A. Keller, H. Ludwig: The WSLA Framework: Specifying and Monitoring Service Level Agreements for Web Services. Accepted for publication in: *Journal of Network and Systems Management, Special Issue on "E-Business Management".* 11 (1), 2003.
13. C. Kenyon, G. Cheliotis: Architecture Requirements for Commercializing Grid Resources. *11th IEEE International Symposium on High Performance Distributed Computing (HPDC'02).* Edinburgh, 2002.
14. G. Lo, G.E. Kersten: Negotiation in Electronic Commerce: Integrating Negotiation Support and Software Agent Technologies. *Proceedings of the 29th Atlantic Schools of Business Conference.* Halifax, 1999.
15. H. Ludwig, A. Keller, A. Dan, R. King: A Service Level Agreement Language for Dynamic Electronic Services. *Proceedings of WECWIS 2002*, Newport Beach, 2002.
16. H. Ludwig: A Conceptual Framework for Electronic Contract Automation. *IBM Research Report*, RC 22608. New York, 2002.
17. H. Raiffa, J. Richardson, D. Metcalfe: *Negotiation Analysis.* The Belknap Press of Harvard University Press, Cambridge, 2003.
18. D.M. Reeves, M.P. Wellman, B.N. Grosof, H.Y. Chan: Automated Negotiation from Declarative Contract Descriptions. *Computational Intelligence*, 18, 482–500, 2002.
19. A. Sahai, A. Durante, V. Machiraju: Towards Automated SLA Management for Web Services. *Hewlett-Packard Research Report HPL-2001-310 (R.1).* Palo Alto, 2002.
20. M. Ströbel: *Engineering electronic negotiations*, Kluwer Academic Publishers, New York, 2002.
21. S.Y.W. Su, C. Huang, J. Hammer: A Replicable Web-based Negotiation Server for E-Commerce. *Proceedings of the Thirty-Third Hawaii International Conference on System Sciences (HICSS-33).* Maui, 2000.

Model Checking Correctness Properties of Electronic Contracts

Ellis Solaiman, Carlos Molina-Jimenez, and Santosh Shrivastava

School of Computing Science, University of Newcastle upon Tyne,
Newcastle upon Tyne, NE1 7RU, England
{Ellis.Solaiman,Carlos.Molina,Santosh.Shrivastava}@ncl.ac.uk

Abstract. Converting a conventional contract into an electronic equivalent is not trivial. The difficulties are caused by the ambiguities that the original human-oriented text is likely to contain. In order to detect and remove these ambiguities the contract needs to be described in a mathematically precise notation before the description can be subjected to rigorous analysis. This paper identifies and discusses a list of correctness requirements that a typical executable business contract should satisfy. Next the paper shows how relevant parts of standard conventional contracts can be described by means of Finite State Machines (FSMs). Such a description can then be subjected to model checking. The paper demonstrates this using Promela language and the Spin validator.

Keywords: Contract, electronic contract, finite state machine, contract representation, contract enforcement, model-checking, validation, correctness requirements, safety and liveness properties.

1 Introduction

A *conventional contract* is a paper document written in English or other natural language that stipulates that two or more signatory parties agree to observe the clauses stipulated in the document. An *executable contract (x-contract)* is the electronic version of a conventional contract that can be enacted by a contract management system to enforce what the English text contract stipulates. The purpose of both conventional and electronic contracts is the same: enforcement of the rights and obligations of the contracting parties. However, there is a crucial difference between the two kinds of contract. A conventional contract is human oriented. Thus, it is likely to contain ambiguities in the text that are detected and interpreted by humans when the contract is performed; whereas an x-contract is computer oriented; consequently, it tolerates no inconsistencies. According to our findings, contract inconsistencies can be categorized into two groups. (i) Internal enterprise policies that conflict with contract clauses. (ii) Inconsistencies in the clauses of the contract. In our view, and to gain in simplicity, these two issues can be treated separately. In this paper we address the second issue.

We have observed that inconsistencies in the clauses of conventional contracts are normal rather than exceptional, for this reason the logical consistency of a conven-

M.E. Orlowska et al. (Eds.): ICSOC 2003, LNCS 2910, pp. 303–318, 2003.

tional contract should be proven by some means before implementing it as an executable contract.

The question that we attempt to answer in this paper is what are the correctness requirements that a typical contract should satisfy and how can they be validated? The paper is organised as follows: In Section 2 we discuss the differences between our approach to validating contracts and related research work. In Section 3, we provide a list of what we consider the most common correctness requirements for business contracts and classify them into conventional safety and liveness properties. In Section 4 we briefly discuss our contract model which is based on finite state machines. In Section 5 we illustrate with examples how Spin can be used for validating correctness requirements. Finally, we draw some conclusions in Section 6.

2 Related Work

In this section we will summarise the essential ideas behind three works that we consider to be close to the research work of this paper.

In the work of Milosevic et. al. [1] [2] a contract is informally defined as a set of policy statements that specify constraints in terms of permissions, prohibitions and obligations for roles involved in the contract. A role (precisely, a role player) is an entity (for example a human being, machine, program, etc.) that can perform an action. Formally, each policy statement is specified in deontic logic constraints [3].Thus each deontic constraint precisely defines the permissions, prohibitions, obligations, actions, and temporal and non-temporal conditions that a role needs to fulfil to satisfy an expected behaviour.

For example, a constraint can formally specify that, "Bob is obliged to deliver a box of chocolates to Alice's desk every weekday except on Wednesdays for three years, between 9 and 9:15 am, commencing on the 1st of Jan 2004". The expressiveness of deontic notation allows the contract designer to verify temporal and deontic inconsistencies in the contract. The authors of this approach argue that it is possible to build verification software to visually show that, Bob's obligations do not overlap or conflict. Such verification mechanisms would easily detect a conflicting situation where Bob has to deliver a box of chocolates to Alice's desk and to Claire's who works miles away from Alice's desk. Similarly, the verifier would detect that Bob is not obliged and prohibited to deliver chocolates to Alice during the same period of time.

Another research work of relevance to ours is the EDEE system. EDEE provides a framework for representing, storing and enforcing business contracts [4]. In EDEE a contract is informally conceived as a set of provisions. In legal parlance, a provision is an arrangement in a legal document, thus in EDEE a provision specifies an obligation, prohibition, privilege or power (rights). An example of a provision is "Alice is obliged to pay Bob 20 cents before 1st Jan 2004". Central to EDEE is the concept of occurrence. An occurrence is a time-delimited relationship between entities. It can be regarded as a participant-occurrence-role triple that contain the name of the participants of the occurrence, the name of the occurrence and the name of the roles involved in the occurrence. An example of an occurrence that involves Alice (the payer) and Bob (the payee) is "Alice is paying Bob 20 cents on 31st Dec 2003." The formal specification of a contract in EDEE is obtained by translating the set of informal provisions derived from the clauses of the contract into a set of formal occurrences. Another basic concept in EDEE is query. A query is a request for items satisfying certain criteria (for example, "Payments performed by Alice before 31st Dec 2003"). At implementation level, the occurrences representing the contract provisions are stored together with queries and new occurrences in an occurrence store in SQL views.

Business operations invoked by the contractual parties are seen as occurrences intercepted and passed through the occurrence store where they are analysed to see if they satisfy the contractual occurrences associated with the operations. EDEE has been provided with some means for detecting contract inconsistencies. To detect overlap between queries (a set of occurrences being both prohibited and permitted, a set of occurrences being obliged and prohibited, etc.) the authors of EDEE rely on a locally implemented coverage-checking algorithms.

Of relevance to our research is also the Ponder language [5]. Ponder is a declarative language that permits the specification of policies for managing a distributed system or contractual service level agreements between business partners. Ponder specifies policies in terms of obligations, permissions and prohibitions and provides means for defining roles and relationships. To detect and prevent policy conflicts such as conflict for a given resource or overlapping of duties, Ponder's notation permits the specification of semantic constraints that limit the applicability of a given policy in accordance with person playing the role, time, or state of the system.

A common pattern of the related works discussed above is that all of them rely on elaborate logical notations that include temporal constraints and role players in their parameters. The expectation is that this notation should be able to specify arbitrarily complex business contracts and detect all kind of inconsistencies. This generality is certainly desirable; however, because of the complexity of the problem it might be rather ambitious. We believe that a modular approach is more realistic for detecting contract ambiguities. For that to be possible, we need to be able to identify and isolate the different sources of possible inconsistencies in business contracts.

In our business model [6] enterprises that engage in contractual relationships are autonomous and wish to remain autonomous after signing a contract. Thus a signing enterprise has its own resources and local policies. In our view each contracting enterprise is a black box where private business processes represented as finite state machines, workflows or similar automaton, run. A private business process interacts with its external environment through the contract from time to time to influence the course of the shared business process. Thus, a contract is a mechanism that is conceptually located in the middle of the interacting enterprises to intercept all the contractual operations that the parties try to perform. Intercepted operations are accepted or rejected in accordance with the contract clauses and role players' authentication.

From this perspective, we can identify two fairly independent sources of contract inconsistencies:

- Internal enterprise policies conflicting with contractual clauses.
- Inconsistencies in the clauses of the contract.

It is our view that these two issues should be treated separately rather than encumbering a contract model with excessive notation (details, concepts and information) that might be extremely difficult to validate. Such a separation is not considered in the work discussed above. In this paper we address only the second issue, that is, we are concerned only with the cooperative behaviour of business enterprises and not their internal structure.

Our approach is to represent business interactions as finite state machines. Use of finite state machines for representing such interactions has been proposed for Web services (Web service conversation language, WSCL [7]). We note that inter-organisation business interactions, PIPs (partner interaction processes) as specified in Rosettanet industrial consortium [8] can also be represented as finite state machines.

In our business model each contracting enterprise has the privilege and responsibility of verifying that its internal policies do not conflict with the clauses of the contract. Similarly, each enterprise exercises its independence to choose the roles players that would invoke operations on the contract and provide them with a proper contract role player certificate (a cryptographic key for example). Consequently, it is the responsibility of each enterprise to prevent inconsistencies with role players such as duty overlapping, duty separation, etc.

In our contract model we intentionally leave the notion of role players out of the game. However, we assume they are authenticated by the contract management system before they are allowed to perform operations of the FSMs. It can be argued that our FSM model is less expressive in comparison with the related works discussed above. However we believe that its expressiveness is good enough for modeling a wide variety of business interactions. Our model is simple. Thanks to this simplicity we can rely on widely used of-the-shelf model checkers like Spin [9] to validate general safety and liveness properties of contracts, relatively easily. We have to admit that so far he have modeled static contracts (contracts whose clauses do not change once the contract is signed), it remains to be seen whether we can use the same paradigm for describing complex contracts where the clauses change and the signing parties join and leave while the contract is in execution. This is a topic for further research.

3 Common Correctness Requirements

Knowing the correctness requirements of an x-contract at design time is crucial as an x-contract can be proven correct only with respect to a specific list of correctness requirements. It is sensible to think, that different contract users would be interested in being assured of the correctness of different parts of a given contract. On the other hand, the parts of a contract that more likely contain logical inconsistencies vary from contract to contract. Because of this, it is too ambitious to intend to identify a complete list of correctness requirements for business contracts. However, it is possible to provide a list of fairly standard correctness requirements and to generalise them. The list provided below, is the result of analyzing several traditional business contracts. Hopefully, this generalisation will help designers of x-contracts reason about correctness requirements of x-contracts in terms of conventional and well understood terminology such as correct termination, deadlocks, etc. In the following list CR stands for correctness requirement:

CR1: Correct commencement: An x-contract should start its execution in a well-defined initial state on a specific date or when something happens. This correctness requirement is a special case and cannot be guaranteed by the x-contract itself but by the human being or system (software or hardware) that triggers the execution of the x-contract.

CR2: **Correct termination:** An x-contract should reach a well-defined termination state on a specific date or when something happens. For example, the x-contract terminates on the 31st of Dec 2005 or the x-contract terminates when the purchaser delivers 500 cars.

CR3: **Attainability**: Each and every state within an x-contract should be attainable, i.e. executable at least in one of the execution paths of the x-contract.

CR4: **Freedom from deadlocks:** An x-contract should never enter a situation in which no further progress is possible. For example, an x-contract should not make a supplier wait for a payment before sending an item to the purchaser while the purchaser is waiting for the item before sending the payment to the supplier.

CR5: **Partial correctness:** If an x-contract begins its execution with a precondition true then, the x-contract will never terminate (normally or abnormally) with the precondition false, regardless of the path followed by the x-contract from the initial to its final state. For example, if the amount of money borrowed by a customer from a bank is *Debt= 0* at the beginning of the x-contract, the x-contract cannot be closed unless *Debt=0.*

CR6: **Invariant:** If an x-contract begins its execution with a precondition true then, the precondition should remain true for the whole duration of the contract. A slight variation of this correctness requirement would be a requirement that the precondition remains true only or at least during certain parts of the execution of the x-contract. To mention an example we can think that an x-contract between a banker and a customer stipulates that the amount of money borrowed by the customer should never exceed the customer's credit limit.

CR7: **Occurrence or accessibility:** A given activity should be performed by an x-contract at least once no matter what execution path the x-contract performs. A slight variation of this requirement is one that demands that a certain activity should be performed infinitely often. For example, an x-contract between a bank and a customer should guarantee that the customer will receive bank statements at least once a month.

CR8: **Precedence:** An x-contract can perform a certain activity only if a given condition is satisfied. For example, the lend period of a book in the possession of a student should not be extended unless the waiting list for the book is empty.

CR9: **Absence of livelocks:** The execution of an x-contract should not loop infinitely through a sequence of steps that has been identified as undesirable, presumably because the sequence produces undesirable output or no output at all. For example, an x-contract between an auctioneer and a group of bidders should not allow one of the bidders to place his bids infinitely often and leave the rest of the bidders bid-starving. This correctness requirement is also known as *fairness* or *absence of individual starvation.*

CR10: **Responsiveness:** The request for a service will be answered before a finite amount of time. For example, an x-contract should guarantee that a buyer responds to every offer from a client in less than five days.

CR11: **Absence of unsolicited responses**: An x-contract should not allow a contractual party to send unsolicited responses. For example, an x-contract between a banker and a customer should not allow the banker to send unsolicited advertisement to the customer.

3.1 Model-Based Validation of Correctness Requirements

Model-based validation is widely used for validating correctness requirements. This approach relies on the use of software tools that are known as model checkers. The core idea behind this approach is to use model-checking algorithms to determine [Spin-Book-chapter11], whether the contract model (a finite state transition system) satisfies a list of correctness requirements. The correctness requirements are specified as safety and liveness properties translated into temporal logics or regular expressions. We discuss safety and liveness properties thoroughly in the Section 3.2. Model-based validation is a compromise between bare-eye inspection and mathematical proof and works well for distributed applications of moderate complexity. For this reason from here on we will focus our discussion on model-based validation and leave bare-eye inspection and mathematical proof aside.

3.2 Safety and Liveness Properties

Informally we can define safety and liveness properties as follows: a *property* is a quality of a programme that holds true for every possible execution of the program. Properties are expressed as statements. A *safety property* is a statement that claims that something will not happen. In other words, a safety property is a claim that a programme will never perform a given activity (for example, send $message_j$ before $message_i$) presumably, because the activity is bad, that is, undesirable. Similarly, a *liveness property* is a statement that claims that something will eventually happen. In other words, a liveness property dictates that a programme will eventually perform a given activity (for example, send the sequence of messages $message_i$, $message_j$, $message_k$), presumably because the activity is good and desirable.

On the ground of our own experience with x-contract validation we argue that most, if not all, correctness requirements of traditional business contracts can be readily expressed either as safety or liveness properties. With the intention of giving the designer of an electronic contract some guidance about the kind of correctness requirement he/she is faced with, we will classify into safety and liveness properties the list of typical correctness requirements of electronic business contracts provided in Section 3:

- Safety properties: attainability, partial correctness, invariant, deadlocks, precedence, absence of unsolicited responses.
- Liveness properties: correct termination, occurrence, livelocks, responsiveness.

We are aware that it has been shown that not all correctness requirements can be readily classified as either safety or liveness property [10]. Fortunately, it has been formally proven that any correctness property can be represented as the intersection of a safety property and a liveness property [11]. The idea behind our approach is that a complex correctness requirement demanded by a signing party can always be expressed as a combination of a number of the basic correctness requirements listed in Section 3.

4 Representation of Contracts by Means of FSMs

A contract can be represented as a set of FSMs, one for each of the contracting parties that interact with each other. Conceptually, we can assume that a FSM is located within each contracting party and that these FSMs communicate with each other through communication channels. Each entry in a contract is called a *term* or a *clause*. The clauses of a contract stipulate how the signing parties are expected to behave. In other words, they list the rights and obligations of each signing party. The rights and obligations stipulated in a contract can be abstracted and grouped into a set of Rights (R) and a set of Obligations (O). The sets R and O can be mapped into the events and the operations that the x-contract involves.

Fig. 1, shows the graphical representation of x-contracts we use in this paper, where *e* and *o* stand for event and operation, respectively (a null operation will be represented by ε). Thus *e* are business events, and *o* are business operations.

Any event can be triggered by a decision taken internally within the enterprise in which the event is to be performed (for example the purchaser exercising the right of deciding to send a purchase order), or by an operation performed externally within another enterprise (for example when the supplier wants to offer a new item to the purchaser).

The lines between the finite state machines in Fig. 1 indicate events being triggered by external operations. For example the event *p* was triggered at the purchaser's side when the Supplier exercised the right of performing operation *O1*.

The supplier's FSM will allow the supplier to execute only the operations he has the right to execute and nothing else. Likewise, the FSM enforces the supplier to execute the operations he has the obligation to execute. The purchaser's FSM works in a similar way.

For more details on representing contracts as FSMs, we refer the reader to [6].

5 Validation of Correctness Requirements with Spin

Spin is a model checker that has gained a wide acceptance. Spin validates safety and liveness properties of models coded in the Pomela modelling language. The Spin toolkit is freely available, and includes a simulator and a validator.

5.1 Spin Verification Tools

Spin comes with a graphical user interface called XSpin which can be used to edit Promela code, and to run the simulator and the validator.

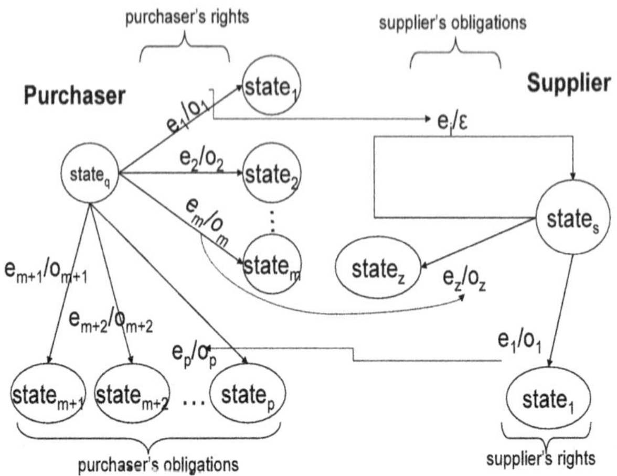

Fig. 1. Contractual rights and obligations represented with FSMs.

The Spin Simulator

The Simulator runs through a single sequence of reachable states (path or routes) of the model coded in Promela. The designer can choose a specific path for the simulator to run through, or can leave the simulator to run through a random path. The simulator will test a specific path for some safety correctness requirements; freedom from deadlocks (CR4), unspecified receptions (which covers CR11), and unattainable states (CR3).

The Spin Validator

The Validator is used for validating the correctness requirements of *Promela* code (the verification model). It generates and inspects all the states and paths of the system that are reachable from the initial state. The Spin validator lists a number of correctness properties that the designer can choose from to validate the correctness of its model. Spin's correctness properties are very similar to the contractual correctness requirements that we listed in Section 3. Consequently we have found that Spin's validator can be used to successfully validate contract correctness requirements.

To validate a contract model, we run the validator against each of the desired correctness requirements. The validator will highlight any paths through the model that have errors. The designer can then use the Simulator to run through the erroneous path, and trace the point at which the error originated.

In this section, we present an example of a contract (Fig. 2) for the supply of e-goods between a *Supplier* and a *Purchaser.* The contract at a first glance looks correct. We will use Spin to verify whether the contract satisfies some of the correctness requirements listed in Section 3, and therefore discovering any inconsistencies within the contract.

The contract clauses that we would like to verify are the following:

2. Offer

2.1 The supplier may use his discretion to send offers to the purchaser.

2.2 The purchaser is entitled to accept or reject the offer, but he shall notify his decision to the supplier.

3 Commencement and completion

3.1 The contract shall start immediately upon signature.

3.2 The purchaser and the supplier shall terminate the x-contract immediately after reaching a deal for buying an item.

This deed of agreement is entered into as of the effective date identified below.
Between
[Name] of [Address] (To be known as the (Supplier)), and [Name] of [Address] (To be knows as the (Purchaser)).
Whereas
(Supplier) desires to enter into an agreement to supply (Purchaser) with [Item].
Now it is hereby agreed that (Supplier) and (Purchaser) shall enter into an agreement subject to the following terms and conditions:
1. Definitions and Interpretations
1.1 Price, Dollars or $ is a reference to the currency of the [Country].
1.2 All information (purchase order, payment, notifications, etc.), is to be sent electronically.
1.3 This agreement is governed by [Country] law and the parties hereby agree to submit to the jurisdiction of the Courts of the [Country] with respect to this agreement.
2. Offer
2.1 The supplier may use his discretion to send offers to the purchaser.
2.3 The purchaser is entitled to accept or reject the offer, but he shall notify his decision to the supplier.
3. Commencement and completion
3.1 The contract shall start immediately upon signature.
3.2 The purchaser and the supplier shall terminate the x-contract immediately after reaching a deal for buying an item.
4. Disputes
4.1 (Supplier) and (Purchaser) ***shall*** *attempt to settle all disputes, claims or controversies arising under or in connection with the agreement through consultation and negotiations in good faith and a spirit of mutual cooperation.*
4.2(Supplier) and (Purchaser) ***shall*** *provide electronic evidences about breaches of the e-contract.*
4.3 This method of determination of any dispute is without prejudice to the right of any party to have the matter judicially determined by a [Country] Court of competent jurisdiction.
5 Amendment
5.1 This agreement ***may*** *only be amended in writing signed by or on behalf of both parties.*
E-SIGNATURES
In witness whereof (Supplier) and (Purchaser) have caused this agreement to be entered into by their duly authorized representatives as of the effective date written below.
Effective date of this agreement: [day] of [month] [year]

[E-signature]	*[E-signature]*
[Person]	*[Person]*
[Role]	*[Role]*

E-address for Notices:

[E-address]	*[E-address]*

Fig. 2. A contract between a purchaser and a supplier for the purchase of goods.

From these contract clauses, we can extract the sets of rights and obligations for the Purchaser and the Supplier and express them in terms of operations for FSMs. The sets of rights and obligations stipulated in this contract look as follows:

Purchaser's rights:

R_1^P : SendAccepted -- right to accept offers.

R_2^P : SendRejected -- right to reject offers.

Purchaser's obligations:

O_1^P : StartEcontract -- obligation to start the x-contract.

O_2^P : SendAccepted or SendRejected -- obligation to reply to offers.

O_3^P : EndEcontract -- obligation to terminate the x-contract.

Supplier's rights:

R_1^s : SendOffer -- right to send offers.

Supplier's obligations:

O_1^S : StartEcontract -- obligation to start the x-contract.

O_2^S : EndEcontract -- obligation to terminate the x-contract.

Fig. 3 shows how the sets R and O are mapped into FSMs.

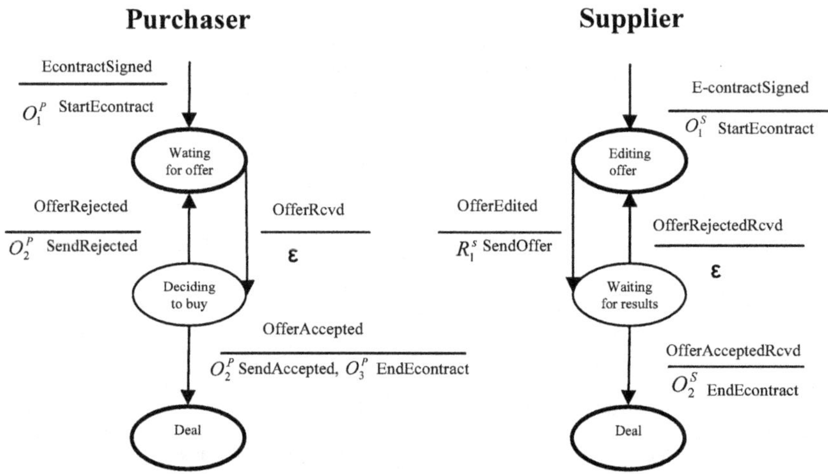

Fig. 3. Representation of a contract for the purchase of goods, with FSMs.

To validate our contract clauses we have to convert the FSM shown into the modeling language *Promela* first. The result of this conversion is shown in Fig. 4.

5.2 X-Contract Verification

Safety Properties

Safety properties can be categorized into, *general* safety properties that must hold true for any x-contract (CR3: Attainability, CR4: Freedom from deadlocks, CR11: Absence of unsolicited responses), and *specific* safety properties that must hold true only if so required by the contracting parties for the specific requirements of a certain x-contract (CR5: Partial correctness, CR6: Invariant, and CR8: Precedence).

Running the Spin validator under its default settings will check for *general* safety properties. Validation of the remaining *specific* safety properties can be done by inserting "Assertions" within the Promela code. Running the Spin validator under its default settings gives us the results shown in Fig. 5.

```
/*Verification Model for the Contract Finite State Machines*/
/*in their initial ambiguous state*/

#define            MA  20 /*Maximum acceptable offer*/
#define OA   1 /*Offer accepted */
#define OR   0 /*Offer rejected*/

mtype = {Offer, Response}
chan S2P = [1] of {mtype, int};
chan P2S = [1] of {mtype, byte};

proctype Supplier() /***Suppliers FSM***/
{
 int offerValue;
 byte responseValue; /*OA or OR*/
 SupEContractSigned:
 EditingOffer:
if
   :: offerValue = 30; /* An offer that is too high > MA*/
   :: offerValue = 20; /* < MA */
   :: offerValue = 10; /* < MA */
 fi;
 if
   :: S2P!Offer(offerValue) -> goto WaitingForResults;
   :: skip /*Taking into account the possiblity that*/
 fi;    /*the supplier might not send anything */
 WaitingForResults:
 P2S ? Response(responseValue);
 if
   :: (responseValue == OR) -> goto EditingOffer;
   :: (responseValue == OA) -> goto Deal;
fi;
 Deal:
 printf("\n\n Supplier: Deal \n\n");
 end:
 printf("\n\n Supplier: End \n\n");
}

proctype Purchaser() /***Purchasers FSM***/
{
 int offerValue;
 PurEContractSigned:
 WaitingForOffer:
 S2P ? Offer(offerValue) ->
 DecidingToBuy:
 if
   ::(offerValue>MA)-> P2S!Response(OR);
       goto WaitingForOffer;
   :: else -> P2S ! Response (OA); goto Deal;
 fi;
 Deal:
 printf("\n\n Purchaser: Deal\n\n");
 end:
 printf("\n\n Purchaser: End\n\n");
}

init
{
 run Supplier();
 run Purchaser();
}
```

Fig. 4. A contract coded in Promela.

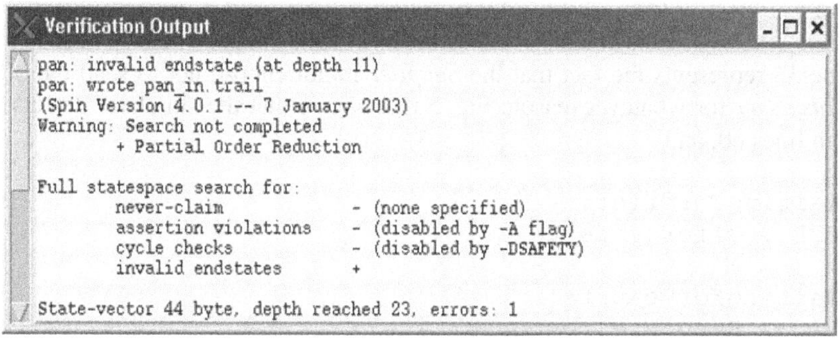

```
Verification Output
pan: invalid endstate (at depth 11)
pan: wrote pan_in.trail
(Spin Version 4.0.1 -- 7 January 2003)
Warning: Search not completed
        + Partial Order Reduction

Full statespace search for:
        never-claim            - (none specified)
        assertion violations   - (disabled by -A flag)
        cycle checks           - (disabled by -DSAFETY)
        invalid endstates      +

State-vector 44 byte, depth reached 23, errors: 1
```

Fig. 5. Output of the Spin validator.

Spin has detected an error in our verification model. "*invalid endstate (at depth 11)*". The fourth line in Fig. 5 indicates that the Spin validator stops the verification process before completion because it detects an error in the model. XSpin saves the path where the error is detected. To trace the point at which the error occurred we can instruct XSpin to run the simulator through the offending path. The results of this simulation are shown in Fig. 6.

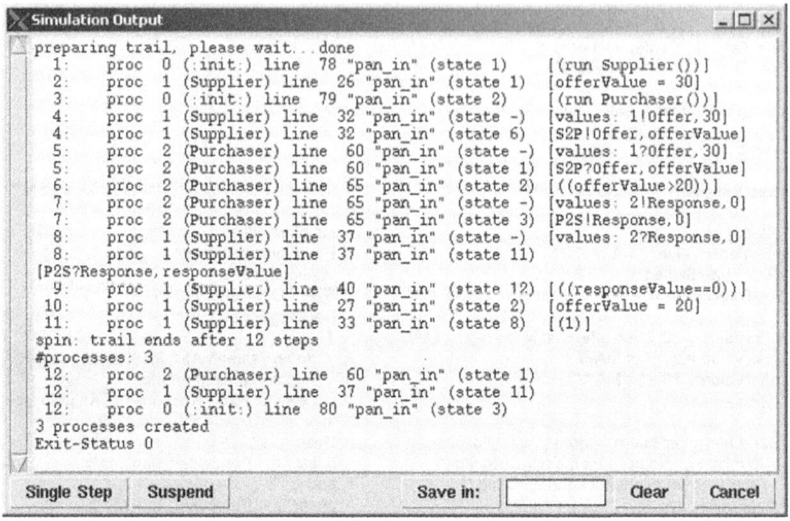

```
Simulation Output
preparing trail, please wait...done
  1:    proc  0 (:init:) line  78 "pan_in" (state 1)     [(run Supplier())]
  2:    proc  1 (Supplier) line  26 "pan_in" (state 1)   [offerValue = 30]
  3:    proc  0 (:init:) line  79 "pan_in" (state 2)     [(run Purchaser())]
  4:    proc  1 (Supplier) line  32 "pan_in" (state -)   [values: 1!Offer,30]
  4:    proc  1 (Supplier) line  32 "pan_in" (state 6)   [S2P!Offer,offerValue]
  5:    proc  2 (Purchaser) line  60 "pan_in" (state -) [values: 1?Offer,30]
  5:    proc  2 (Purchaser) line  60 "pan_in" (state 1) [S2P?Offer,offerValue]
  6:    proc  2 (Purchaser) line  65 "pan_in" (state 2) [((offerValue>20))]
  7:    proc  2 (Purchaser) line  65 "pan_in" (state -) [values: 2!Response,0]
  7:    proc  2 (Purchaser) line  65 "pan_in" (state 3) [P2S!Response,0]
  8:    proc  1 (Supplier) line  37 "pan_in" (state -)   [values: 2?Response,0]
  8:    proc  1 (Supplier) line  37 "pan_in" (state 11)
[P2S?Response,responseValue]
  9:    proc  1 (Supplier) line  40 "pan_in" (state 12) [((responseValue==0))]
 10:    proc  1 (Supplier) line  27 "pan_in" (state 2)   [offerValue = 20]
 11:    proc  1 (Supplier) line  33 "pan_in" (state 8)   [(1)]
spin: trail ends after 12 steps
#processes: 3
 12:    proc  2 (Purchaser) line  60 "pan_in" (state 1)
 12:    proc  1 (Supplier) line  37 "pan_in" (state 11)
 12:    proc  0 (:init:) line  80 "pan_in" (state 3)
3 processes created
Exit-Status 0

Single Step   Suspend          Save in:          Clear   Cancel
```

Fig. 6. Spin output showing and erroneous path.

After step 10, the Supplier was expected to send an offer to the Purchaser, but the Simulator does not show this occurring. A closer look at step 11 reveals that the trail ended after the simulator went through line 33 of the *Promela* verification model:

```
31  if
32  :: S2P!Offer(offerValue) -> goto WaitingForResults;
33  :: skip /*Taking into account the possibility that*/
34  fi;       /*the supplier might not send anything */
```

Line 33 represents the fact that the *Supplier* might choose not to send the offer to the *Purchaser* for whatever reason. Fig. 5 also shows that the simulator detects problems in lines 60, and 37:

```
59 WaitingForOffer:
60 S2P ? Offer(offerValue) ->

36 WaitingForResults:
37 P2S ? Response(responseValue);
```

No *offerValue* was received by the *Purchaser* process, and subsequently, no *responseValue* was received by the *Supplier* process. The finite state machines of the *Supplier* and the *Purchaser* fall into a deadlock situation.

A possible solution to avoid this undesirable situation is to make use of the *Promela "timeout"* statement. This statement allows a process to abort and not wait indefinitely for a condition that can no longer become true such as the one we just encountered:

```
WaitingForOffer:
if
  ::S2P ? Offer(offerValue)
  ::timeout -> goto end
fi;
```

We can run the validator as many times as necessary, and after ensuring the correctness of the *general* safety requirement, we can use the validator to check for some *specific* safety correctness requirements. For example, we would like to check that the invariant "The price offered by the *Supplier* should not be accepted by the Purchaser if the price exceeds an agreed price *P*" holds (see CR6 in Section 3). To guarantee this invariant we can insert an assertion of the form *assert(offerValue<=P)* at the required check points in the verification model. We then set and run the validator to check for assertions. The validator does not signal any errors, so we know that the invariant we specified holds true.

Liveness Properties

Unlike safety properties, there are no *general* liveness properties. All liveness properties are *specific* to the requirements of the contracting parties depending on the purposes of a specific contract. To validate liveness properties (correct termination, occurrence or accessibility, livelocks, responsiveness) we can insert specifically designed labels such as "accept" labels that check for livelocks, "progress" labels that check for progress states, and temporal claims, in the Promela code.

As an example, in our x-contract we would not desire a situation where the supplier infinitely often makes undesirable offers. That is we do not want livelock (CR9) in the x-contract. We can insert an accept label in line 20 as follows:

```
17  EditingOffer:
18  if
19    :: offerValue = 30;
20 acceptOfferTooHigh: skip  /* An offer that is too
                                         high > MA*/
21    :: offerValue = 20; /* < MA */
22    :: offerValue = 10; /* < MA */
23  fi;
```

We can now set the validator verification parameters to detect "livelock". The output results show that the search stops after detecting an error. A simulator run would show that the problem occurs after the Supplier makes an offer with *offerValue=30*. The output shows that we have an undesirable situation where the *Supplier* can make unacceptable offers infinitely. There are many possible solutions to this problem, one would be for example to limit the Supplier to *N<=10* offers.

Following testing the x-contract model against the desired correctness properties, and removal of detected ambiguities, the verification model and therefore the x-contract must be modified accordingly. For our example, the finite state machines are modified as can be seen in Fig. 7.

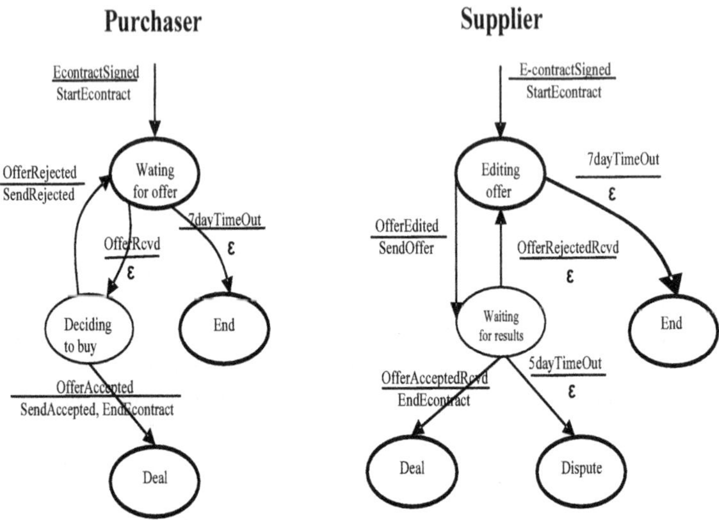

Fig. 7. Representation of a contract with FSMs (revised version of Fig. 3).

After the corresponding modifications the contract clauses look as follows:

2 Offer

2.1 The supplier may use his discretion to send offers to the purchaser.

2.2 If no offer is sent within seven days after the signature of the x-contract, or after the latest rejected offer, the x-contract shall be terminated.

2.3 The purchaser is entitled to accept or reject the offer, but he shall notify his decision to the supplier within five days after the receipt of the offer.

3 Commencement and completion

3.1 The contract shall start immediately upon signature.

3.2 The purchaser and the supplier shall terminate the x-contract immediately after reaching a deal for buying an item.

Complex Correctness Requirements

A very useful facility provided by Spin is the verification of "temporal claims". Temporal claims can be used to express complex correctness requirements. This facility is very useful as transactions between parties to a contract may need to run in a certain sequence, and/or under certain conditions.

As a separate example let us consider the Promela code of Fig. 8 which describes a complaint handling state machine. We want the validator to check the requirement that a complaint about the quality of the goods must not be sent by the *Purchaser* before the goods are received from the *Supplier*. The verification model to express possible scenarios is shown in Fig. 8.

In *XSpin*, verification of temporal claims is done using the Linear Temporal Logic (LTL) Manager. We are claiming the following: It is invariantly true that following the placement of an order a complaint should not be received before the order is received. This is expressed in Linear Temporal Logic as follows:
[] (placeOrder -> !complaintRecd U orderRecd).

We can enter this formula into the LTL Manager (Fig. 8) and then run the validator. As expected, the validator detects that our claim is false. As it can be proved with the validator, it is enough to remove the lines in the Promela model that gives the Purchaser the option to complain before receiving the order, to make our claim hold true.

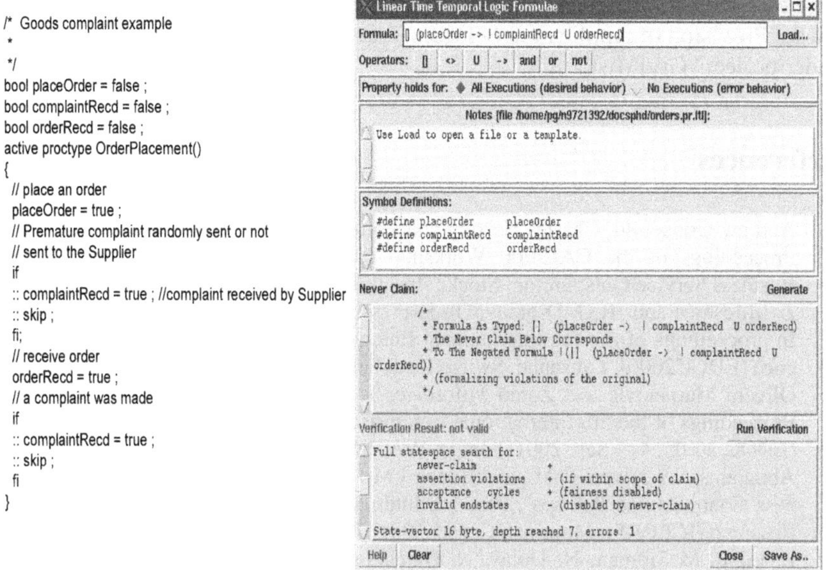

Fig. 8. Use of the LTP property manager for validating a temporal claim in a Promela model.

6 Conclusions and Further Work

This paper contains some of the results we have obtained from our work on modeling business contracts. Our thesis is that contracts are complex systems that involve contractual and private policies. Contractual policies regulate the interaction between the trading enterprises, whereas private policies regulate the interaction between the members of a trading enterprise and the contract. To simplify the problem, we propose to study the two kinds of policies separately. Thus in this paper we focused on contractual policies. We argue that conventional business contracts normally contain ambiguities that should be detected and eliminated before converting the contract into its electronic equivalent. To help the validator of an electronic contract, we provide a list of correctness requirements that most traditional business contracts should satisfy.

The list is not exhaustive but illustrative. To put contract correctness in the context of traditional program correctness, we mapped the list of contract correctness requirements into conventional safety and liveness properties. We also argue that FSMs are a suitable formal notation for describing conventional contracts and show how a contract described by means of FSMs can be validated using standard and readily available model checkers such as Spin. To support our arguments we illustrate the validation of two simple contracts. More complex examples are discussed in [12].

Acknowledgements. This work is part-funded by the UK EPSRC under grant GR/N35953/01: "Information Co-ordination and Sharing in Virtual Environments"; by the European Union under Project IST-2001-34069: "TAPAS (Trusted and QoS-Aware Provision of Application Services)"; and by the UK DTI e-Science programme under project "GridMist".

References

1. Andrew Goodchild, Charles Herring and Zoran Milosevic, Business Contract for B2B, In Proceedings of the CAISE00 Workshop on Infrastructure for Dynamic Business-to-Business Service Outsourcing; Stockholm, June 5–6, 2000.
2. Z. Milosevic and R.G. Dromey, On Expressing and Monitoring Behaviour in Contracts, In proceedings of the 6th International Enterprise Distributed Object Computing Conference (EDOC2000), Lausanne, Switzerland, Sep. 17–20, 2002.
3. Olivera Marjanovic and Zoran Milosevic, Towards Formal Modeling of e-Contracts, In Proceedings of the 5th International Enterprise Distributed Object Computing Conference (EDOC 2001), 4–7 Sep. 2001, Seattle, WA, USA, IEEE Computer Society 2001.
4. Abrahams A.S., Eyers D.M., and Bacon J.M. "Mechanical Consistency Analysis for Business Contracts and Policies". Proc 5th International Conference on Electronic Commerce Research (ICECR5), Montreal, Canada, 23–27 October 2002.
5. E. Lupu, M Sloman, N. Dulay, N. Damianou, Ponder: Realising Enterprise Viewpoint Concepts, In proceedings of the 4th International Enterprise Distributed Object Computing Conference (EDOC2000), Makuhari, Japan, 25–28 Sep. 2000.
6. Carlos Molina-Jimenez, Santosh Shrivastava, Ellis Solaiman and John Warne, "Contract Representation for Run-time Monitoring and Enforcement", Proc. IEEE Int. Conf. on E-Commerce (CEC-2003), Newport Beach, California, June 2003.
7. Web Service Conversation Language (WSCL) 1.0 (http://www.w3.org/TR/wscl10/).
8. Rosettanet implementation framework: core specification, V2, Jan 2000. http://rosettanet.org.
9. Gerard J. Holzmann, The Model Checker Spin, IEEE Transactions on Software Engineering, Vol. 23, N. 5, May, 1997.
10. Gleb Naumovich and Lori A. Clarke, Classifying Properties: An Alternative to the Safety-Liveness Classification, In Proceedings of the Eighth International Symposium on the Fundations of Software Engineering, Nov. 2000.
11. B. Alpern and F.B. Schneider, Defining liveness, Information Processing Letters, Vol. 21, N. 4, Oct, 1985.
12. Ellis Solaiman, University of Newcastle upon Tyne, PhD Theses (In preparation).

Supporting Dynamic Changes in Web Service Environments

Mohammad Salman Akram, Brahim Medjahed, and Athman Bouguettaya

Department of Computer Science, Virginia Tech
7054 Haycock Road, Falls Church VA 22043, USA
{salman,brahim,athman}@vt.edu

Abstract. The Web has become the universal medium for publishing and using of Web accessible services called *Web services*. The widespread adoption of XML standards including WSDL, SOAP, and UDDI has spurred an intense research activity to deal with issues related to Web services. One of the most important issues is the management of changes that occur in Web service environments. Web services operate in a highly dynamic environment where changes can be initiated to adapt to evolving business climates. All changes performed to Web services must be efficiently propagated to ensure global consistency. In this paper, we combine *Web services*, *ontologies*, and *agents* to cater for the management of changes in Web services. We address the challenging issues of *detection*, *propagation*, and *reaction* to both *internal* and *external* changes to Web services.

1 Introduction

The role of the Web is shifting from a distributed information storage to a world wide service provider. This shift is being propelled by the current work on Web service standards, both in industry and academia. A Web service is a set of related functionalities that can be programmatically invoked through the Web [1]. The Web service framework facilitates dynamic and efficient methods of interactions on the Web. Web services are poised to be the foundation of the envisioned service oriented architecture [2].

The Web service model involves three types of participants: *requester*, *provider*, and *registry* [3]. In a simple scenario, the service provider first publishes its WSDL (Web Service Description Language) description in a UDDI (Universal Description, Discovery, and Integration) [4]. A service requester then searches the UDDI for a Web service that matches a given criteria. If the search is successful (i.e. one or more service providers are located), the service requester invokes the service provider using SOAP (Simple Object Access Protocol) messaging. This depicts a simplified model of service request processing. The ultimate goal of Web services is to serve as independent components in loosely coupled systems such as electronic marketplaces (or e-marketplaces) [5] and Web based Virtual Enterprises [6]. These systems typically process requests that target more than one Web service. Service requests in these systems become significantly more

M.E. Orlowska et al. (Eds.): ICSOC 2003, LNCS 2910, pp. 319–334, 2003.

dynamic and complex as the number of target services increases [7]. The success of fulfilling such service requests relies on dealing with the *volatile* and highly *dynamic* nature of Web services. Additionally, the service request must interact with an *exploratory* service space for locating Web services. We characterize the Web service environment by the following features:

- **Exploratory:** Exploratory refers to the *nondeterministic* process of identifying Web services necessary for a given request. Web services are *a priori* unknown and may only be determined dynamically, i.e., after the need for the service is established. It is not required that the interacting entities be cognizant of each other prior to interaction.
- **Volatile:** Volatility implies that a Web service answering a request at any given time may not be available to answer the same request at a later time. Once provider services are selected, it is possible that those services may be inaccessible before or during the execution of a request.
- **Dynamic:** Web services have highly dynamic content. The *content* of a Web service refers to the information it provides through its operations (e.g., the price of a given stock. This content may change frequently and unpredictably. Furthermore, changes may occur while requests are being processed and affect the overall execution of a request.

In this paper, we describe an architecture that supports requests over exploratory, volatile, and highly dynamic Web services. We propose the use of *ontologies* to select services from an exploratory service space [8,9,10]. We employ *agents* to deal with Web service volatility and dynamism. This will be accomplished by managing change to Web services [6]. Our approach is illustrated using an electronic stock market. In this example, we simulate user requests to buy, sell, and inquire about stocks of one or more companies. The environment where these requests are executed is characterized by three features: (i) Web services that provide interaction with stock markets are *a priori* unknown, (ii) Web services are volatile and their availability is uncertain, and (iii) the content (e.g. stock prices) of the Web services is highly dynamic (i.e., changes very frequently).

The paper is organized as follows: In Section 2, we propose a model for dynamic service requests. Section 3 is a detailed description of the proposed conceptual architecture. In Section 4, we present the implementation of this architecture within the context of an electronic stock market. We provide related work in section 5. Finally, we provide some concluding remarks in Section 6.

2 A Model for Dynamic Web Service Change Management

Servicing requests is a challenging issue when targeting environments consisting of volatile and dynamic Web services. The execution of service requests must be supported by the (i) discovery and selection of Web services in an exploratory service space and (ii) an environment that adapts to changes to Web services. Changes to Web services may be internal or external. *Internal* change refers the dynamic nature of Web service content. Internal change includes change in the information provided by a Web service. *External* change refers to the volatility of the Web service. This type of change includes the unavailability of a service and its operations during the execution of a request. The problem of supporting dynamic service requests has two facets:

- **Web service discovery and selection:** An important step in the process of answering a service request is to discover and select Web services with appropriate functionality. A request may involve several distributed and remote services that are determined on the fly (i.e., at run-time). Service discovery and selection may be initiated when the request is first issued or it may be a result of change. The challenge is to dynamically and efficiently discover the appropriate services for a given request within an acceptable response time.
- **Adapting to Web service changes:** Any request dependent on a Web service must deal with the issue of change management. *Change management* is the timely detection, propagation, and reaction to both internal and external changes. *Detection* is the method of identifying a change that is of interest to the system. *Propagation* requires that all interested system components be informed of those changes. *Reaction* is initiating a compensatory process in response to a change.

2.1 Service Request Specification

The service space in our proposed model consists of a set of remote Web services registered with a global service registry. Each Web service provides some stock market functionality through its operations. In particular, it provides information about the stocks available in that market and the ability to trade them. In our scenario, Web services provide access to stock markets located in New York (NYSE), London (FTSE), Paris (CAC), and Tokyo (TSE). Each Web service specializes in one or more stock categories. Examples of categories include bookstore, Internet service provider (ISP), and travel.

A *service request* is a list of atomic (sequential and concurrent) orders. Each *order* is defined by the order type (`type`), stock identifier (`stockID`), stock category (`stockCatg`), stock market (`stockMarket`), acceptable price (`price`), number of shares (`quantity`), and the duration of the order (`time`). A request may consist of one or more of these orders. Furthermore, a single order may be divided into one or more execution threads. An *execution thread* is an instance of an order interacting with a single Web service. Formally, a request may be represented by any expression generated by the following language:

```
Req ::=   Req ; Req |
          Req || Req |
          Order
```

Where:

- ";" denotes a set of two orders that must take place in the given sequence
- "||" denotes the concurrent (i.e., parallel) execution of two orders
- *Order* is defined as the 7-uple:
  `(type, stockID, stockCatg, stockMarket, price, numShares, time)`

Example:

```
Req1:    { ("sell", AMZN, Bookstore, NYSE, $21, 500, 00:30) ||
           ("sell", YHOO, ISP, NYSE, $19, 350, 00:30) ;
           ("buy", NTC, Computer, CAC, $16.5, 950, 01:00) }
```

The previous request translates to concurrently attempt to sell 500 shares of *Amazon.com* (AMZN) at a price not less than \$21 and 350 shares of *Yahoo!* (YHOO) at a price not less than \$19 per share. The orders should be repeatedly attempted until they are terminated by (i) a successful execution or (ii) the thirty minute time limit (whichever comes first). If and only if the two previous orders succeed, then attempt to buy 950 shares of *Intel Corporation* (NTC) at a price not more than \$16.5 per share. This order would be attempted for a one hour interval.

Req_1 provides an example of "buy" and "sell" order types. A user may also issue an "inquiry" request that asks for information about a particular stock or a stock category. Req_2 is an example of a request that inquires about the values of all the stocks in the *ISP* category at the NYSE. The inquiry will continue for a period of one hour. The highest and lowest prices of each stock in the *ISP* category will be reported to the user.

```
Req2:    { ("inquiry", *, ISP, NYSE, *, *, 01:00) }
```

The asterix (*) represents an undefined value for the corresponding attribute. For example, the first asterix implies that the `stockID` is unknown. The use of asterix in service requests introduces flexibility and dynamism in user requirements. Service request may also target multiple stock markets. Req_3 illustrates a situation where a user is searching for the stock market that currently offers NTC shares at \$16 or lower. Notice that the asterix in the time attribute denotes immediate execution of the request.

```
Req3:    { ("inquiry", NTC, *, *, $16, 220, *) }
```

The examples above indicate that simple user requests may become extremely complex at processing time. Figure 1 displays the process of resolving a service request. The diamonds indicate the stages in request processing. Solid arrows describe the control flow between stages. Dotted arrows represent the access and update of service descriptions. All requests issued by the user are first parsed to validate the format of the request. A parsed request is decomposed into atomic orders, if needed. For example, Req_1 illustrates situations where a request is translated into three orders. Each order is evaluated to determine the required

Web services. For instance, Req_3 implies inquiry for NTC stocks in all available services. In this case, the order will be divided into several execution threads with each thread mapping to a single Web service. After service invocation, the request enters the change management stage. If the execution is successful, a response is generated and sent back to the user. In the next subsection, we describe the use of ontologies for the service selection stage.

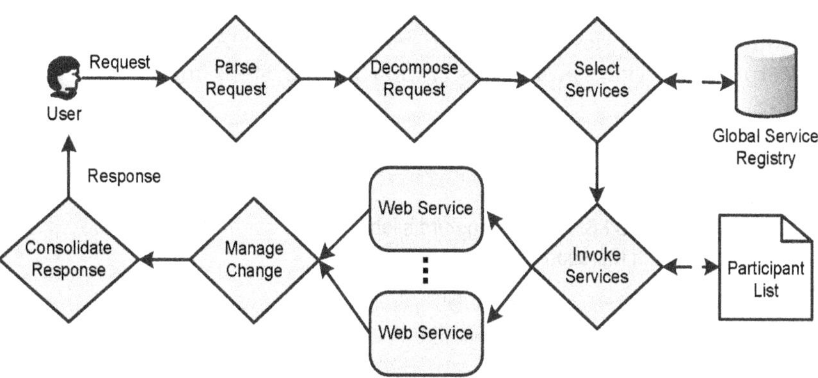

Fig. 1. Request Processing

2.2 Using Ontologies for Locating Web Services

The problem of discovering and selecting the services necessary to answer requests is particularly challenging in the dynamic Web context. Discovering appropriate Web services dynamically is essential to answering a service request (Figure 1). Our approach to the problem is based on the idea of organizing Web services into ontologies. An *ontology* describes a coherent slice of the service space, i.e., a collection of Web services that share the same domain of interest [11]. In our stock market example, the category of a Web service defines its domain of interest. For example, services that deal with AMZN stocks may belong to a *bookstore* ontology.

DAML-S (DARPA Agent Markup Language for Web services) provides the ability to organize Web services into ontologies [12]. DAML-S divides service descriptions into the service profile, model, and grounding. The service *pro le* provides a high level description of a Web service. It expresses required input of the service and the output the service will provide to the requester. The service *model* defines the operations and their execution flow in the Web service. Service *grounding* provides a mapping between DAML-S and the WSDL standard and describes how the service may actually be invoked.

The service profile provides sufficient information for discovery. It is divided into a description of the service, the functionalities, and the functional attributes.

The *description* provides human understandable information about the Web service. For example, a description includes the name of the service and its textual description. A *functionality* in DAML-S describes properties like input, output, precondition, effect, etc. The *functional attributes* provide information such as response time and costs [13,12].

To understand how DAML-S may be used in our solution, let us refer to our stock market example. Stock markets generally involve many categories of businesses. Each Web service may belong to one or more categories. We define these different categories for our Web services using DAML-S. Figure 2 depicts an excerpt of a service profile description for our stock market example using DAML-S.

```
(1) <daml:Class rdf:ID="NYSE">
(2)   <rdfs:label>NewYorkStockExchange</rdfs:label>
(3)   <rdfs:subClassOf rdf:resource="&service;"/>
(4) <daml:Class>

(5) <rdf:Property rdf:ID="Bookstore">
(6)   <rdfs:label>Bookstore</rdfs:label>
(7)   <rdfs:subPropertyOf rdf:resource="&profile;serviceCategory"/>
(8)   <rdfs:domain rdf:resource="&service;serviceProfile"/>
(9)   <rdfs:range rdf:resource="&daml;#Thing"/>
(10) </rdf:Property>

(11) <rdf:Property rdf:ID="Travel">
(12)   <rdfs:label>Travel</rdfs:label>
(13)   <rdfs:subPropertyOf rdf:resource="&profile;serviceCategory"/>
(14)   <rdfs:domain rdf:resource="&service;serviceProfile"/>
(15)   <rdfs:range rdf:resource="&daml;#Thing"/>
(16) </rdf:Property>

(17) <rdf:Property rdf:ID="ISP">
(18)   <rdfs:label>ISP</rdfs:label>
(19)   <rdfs:subPropertyOf rdf:resource="&profile;serviceCategory"/>
(20)   <rdfs:domain rdf:resource="&service;serviceProfile"/>
(21)   <rdfs:range rdf:resource="&daml;#Thing"/>
(22) </rdf:Property>
```

Fig. 2. DAML-S Description

This description is for the Web service that provides interactions with NYSE. Lines 1-4 present the human understandable description of the service profile. It defines the class name (NYSE) and also indicates that the class is a *service*. The remaining lines define categories of the service. In this case, the Web service belongs to three categories. Lines 5-10 define a service property that implies the Web service deals with stocks in the bookstore category. Lines 11-16 indicate the Web service belongs to the travel ontology. Finally, lines 17-22 describe the Web service's membership in the ISP category.

Web services needed to answer a request are discovered using descriptions provided in DAML-S registries. The selection criteria for the service is first extracted from the order. For example, Req_2 needs all Web services from the *ISP* category that provide services for NYSE. In this case, a search is initiated in the DAML-S registry for a class name that matches "NYSE". If such a class name is located, the search will continue to check the properties of the Web service. The service property must match *ISP*. The fulfillment of these steps indicate that a Web service has been located successfully. After a service has been located, it may be invoked by using the service *grounding* in DAML-S and its mapping to WSDL [12].

Individual services may join or leave the formed ontologies at their own discretion. An overlap of two ontologies implies that a service provides information that is of interest to both ontological domains. For example, the intersection between the two ontologies *bookstore* and *ISP* may contain services that are involved in both types of companies.

2.3 Managing Changes

Requests targeting service providers require mechanisms to *detect*, *propagate*, and *react* to changes in the provider services. Changes to Web services can be planned or unexpected. They may occur in several forms. We classify the changes that need to be managed in a request as:

- **External:** External change primarily refers to temporary or permanent unavailability of a service or its operations. This unavailability may occur before or during the execution of the request. It may be a result of a network failure, service relocation, request overload, operation rename, etc. In this case, the request needs to be rolled back and an alternate service must be selected to fulfill the request.
- **Internal:** Any change in the content of a Web service may need to be detected to fulfill a request constraint. In our example of stock markets, the values for stocks change very frequently. Important (financial) consequences may result if the mechanism handling change management fails to react promptly to fluctuations in the markets. These reactions may only be required if the change reaches a certain threshold [14].

Consider the following request:

Req_4: { ("buy", AMZN, *, *, *, 150, 00:15) }

Req_4 translates into an order to buy 150 shares of AMZN (from any market) with the lowest price in the interval of fifteen minutes. Assume that while the system is executing this order at NYSE (because the lowest price for AMZN was quoted there), a change occurred at CAC that made AMZN's price fall below its price at New York. To react to this change and fulfill the user's constraint (i.e., buying at the lowest price), the execution of purchase order at NYSE must be aborted and performed at CAC. In the previous example, the replacement was not the result of a failure but, rather, the result of a constraint violation. Using the same request, let us assume that while a service request is executing at the CAC Web service, a network failure occurs and the service becomes unavailable. In order to fulfill the request, the execution at the respective CAC Web service needs to be rolled back and an alternate service (that meets given constraints) should be invoked.

The examples illustrate a need for change management in a Web service environment. Change management consists of detection, propagation, and reaction to changes. Our approach to solving this problem is based on using agents that play the role of *monitors* and *noti ers* [15,6]. These agents are background processes that monitor the participant Web services for relevant changes (e.g. changes in stock price, unavailability of Web service) and notify entities concerned with the change.

Change detection: Change detection is the awareness that a change has occurred and the subsequent identification of its cause. It deals with changes that occur (i) before a provider service is invoked and (ii) during execution of a Web service. For changes that occur before service invocation, we employ change detection through soft states [16]. *Soft states* is a method used to maintain membership of entities in a loosely coupled system. This method requires that a member periodically send "refresh" messages to renew its membership. These messages are sent to a node that maintains the membership list.

In our case, the provider Web services are members or participants in the loosely coupled system. The membership information is stored in the *participant list*. A participant list is generated for every request. Agents act as intermediaries between the participant list and the Web services. They also maintain the participant list by updating the list at time of change. An participating Web service is assigned to each agent that monitors changes in the status of that service. This agent periodically verifies the availability of the service and its operations, and the contents of the Web service [14]. To verify changes in the availability of a service, the agent will send "alive" messages to the Web service. If the Web service responds, the service is assumed to be available. However, if a response message is not received from the Web service within an acceptable time limit, the service is considered as unavailable.

Changes to operations are detected by retrieving the service descriptions from the UDDI. Any change to a service operation (e.g., rename, change of parameters, etc.) implies that the change was made explicitly by the Web service programmers. This justifies our assumption that the Web service description in the UDDI will be appropriately updated after an operation change. Change in content of a Web service requires the assigned agent to repeatedly invoke an operation that provides the respective content. Let us take the example where a service request is inquiring for the price of AMZN stocks in the next half hour.

The agent will invoke the operation in regular intervals (e.g., thirty seconds) and compare output values with values provided in the previous invocation.

Change that occurs during an interaction with a Web service is detected by the failure of service invocation. The reason of the failure is identified by the agent that manages the particular Web service. The technique for identifying the cause consists of change detection through the process mentioned above. For all changes that are detected, the agent uses appropriate mechanisms for propagation and reaction as explained below.

Change propagation: We use the participant list to propagate changes in the system. The participant list contains references to all Web services that have been selected to answer the service request (i.e. that are part of the system). Agents will update the participant list in case of any external change. The update involves the removal of the service reference stored in the participant list. Since a service reference must be present in the participant list before it can be invoked, the removal of service reference terminates the membership of that service. If an internal change (i.e. change in the data provided) is detected, the data used for response consolidation is updated to reflect the change.

Reaction to changes: Reaction to change depends on the (i) type of change and (ii) availability of alternate services. In case of an external change, an alternate service must be selected to fulfill the user request. The service selection stage is initiated and provided with the description of the required service. If an appropriate service does not exist (or cannot be located), the request must be canceled. However, if an alternate service is selected successfully, it is registered with the participant list and request processing is resumed. In the event of an internal change (e.g. change in stock prices), the previous data will be replaced with the current response.

Change management algorithm: Figure 3 displays an algorithm that describes the change management process. The algorithm takes two parameters: `request_time` and `participant_list`. `request_time` is the `time` attribute extracted from the order. `participant_list` contains the list of all Web services that are currently participating in the system. The algorithm executes for the duration of the request. The algorithm starts by verifying the availability of each Web service by sending alive messages to the Web services in the the `participant_list`. If a Web service is not available, it is removed from the `participant_list` and an alternate service is selected. Second, the algorithm requires checking for changes in operations. The respective agent retrieves the current description of each Web service from the global service registry and compares it with the description in the system. If the description has changed, the agent removes the service description from the `participant_list` and selects an alternate service. Finally, the agent compares the contents returned by the Web service with the contents of the previous response. If the agent detects any change, the response must be reconsolidated.

```
Input: request_time, participant_list
{
 time = request_time
 while (request_time != 0)
 {
  for each Web Service WS in participant_list
  {
   send alive message to WS
   if not alive then
   {
    remove WS from participant_list
    call (Service_Selection (service_description (WS)))
   break
   }

   global_description = WS service_description from global_service_registry
   if service_description (WS) not equals global_description
   {
    remove WS from participant_list
    call (Service_Selection (service_description (WS)))
   break
   }
   current_data = invoke WS.operation
   if current_data not equals previous_data
   {
    call (Response_Consolidation (current_Data))
    break
   }
  }
  decrement time
 }
}
```

Fig. 3. Change Management Algorithm

3 Proposed Architecture

The architecture proposed to support dynamic service requests is illustrated through the electronic stock market example. A Graphical User Interface (GUI) is used to interact with the user. A *request broker* serves as an intermediary between the GUI and the participant Web services. The concept of a request broker is very similar to a stock broker in a stock market and it serves as an integral part of our architecture.

In our proposed architecture, the GUI allows users to specify and submit their requests (Figure 4). It supports both short-lived requests (e.g., inquiry about the current value of a given stock) and long-lived requests (e.g., inquiry about the lowest value of a given stock in one hour). The GUI is also responsible for parsing and validating requests and sending them to the Request Broker. The Request Broker (RB) implements the remaining stages of request processing (Figure 1). Specifically, it performs decomposition, service selection, service invocation, change management, and response consolidation.

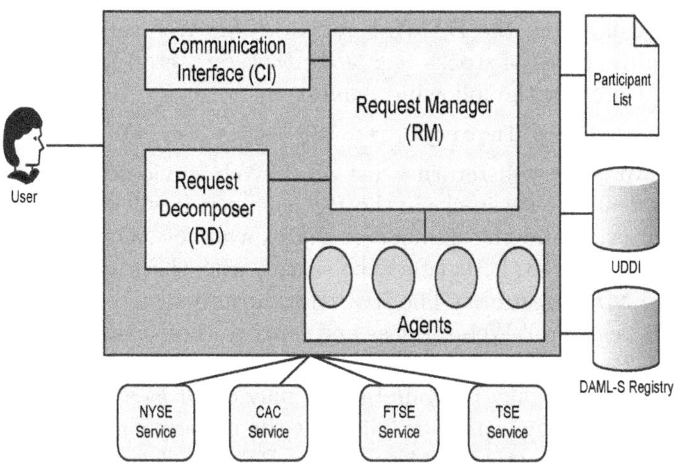

Fig. 4. Architecture

Every user is assigned a single instance of the RB. Communication between RBs and the various registered Web services takes place using the SOAP standard (Simple Object Access Protocol). Each Web service corresponds to one stock market (e.g. NYSE) and provides information about the stocks associated with the stock market. In the remainder of this section, we first elaborate on the functionality of the RB with reference to our stock market example and then present the internal components of the RB.

3.1 Request Broker Functionality

Request Brokers are the intermediaries between the GUI and service providers. Each RB deals with requests from one particular user. In essence, the RB is responsible for four major functions:

- **Request Decomposition:** When an RB receives a request from the user (via GUI), it translates that request into one or more orders. These orders are further broken down into execution threads that invoke operations at the underlying Web services or *participants*. Consider the following request:

  $\texttt{Req}_5$: { ("inquiry", AMZN, *, *, *, *, *) }

  When the RB receives the order corresponding to this request, it generates multiple SOAP messages, each invoking a Web service that represents stock markets dealing with *AMZN* stocks.

- **Service Selection:** Once the order has been translated, the RB needs to select the Web services that are required to fulfill the order. The RB will search the UDDI registry if the name of the stock (AMZN) and the stock market (e.g. NYSE) is explicitly provided. If a stock category is provided, the RB will search the DAML-S registries for Web services that deal with the required types of stocks (e.g. *ISP*, *bookstore*, etc.) in the specified stock market. Consider the following request:

  $\texttt{Req}_6$: { ("inquiry", *, ISP, *, *, *, *) }

  The above order will return a list of all Web services that represent stock markets dealing with stocks in the *ISP* category. It will also return the lowest available price and the number of shares available. Once a Web service is selected by the RB, it registers the service with the *Participants list*.
- **Change Management:** The RB must capture *signi cant* changes that occur in its registered Web services and react to these changes. It also updates its local *Participants list* when a service joins or leaves the system. *Join* and *Leave* events may be voluntary or may occur as a result of transient or permanent reconfiguration or failure at the underlying communication middleware. When reacting to changes, the RB may decide to abort a pending operation (i.e., submitted but not committed or aborted yet) and re-submit it to another participant that has become more suitable for that particular operation.
- **Response Consolidation:** A request that is broken into several orders and execution threads needs to be consolidated before the response is sent back to the user. For example, a request may require buying a number of shares at the lowest possible price. For these orders, the RB collects the results of all execution threads and selects the thread that produces the lowest price result.

3.2 Request Broker Components

User requests are processed by the Request Broker module. This module: (i) handles communication between the GUI and the underlying layers of the system, (ii) decomposes the requests into execution threads and dispatches each thread to the appropriate Web service, (iii) manages changes in the system, (iv) and consolidates a response for the user. The RB has five components:

- **Communication Interface (CI):** The CI is responsible for secure communication between the GUI and the underlying Web services. To communicate with the RB, the GUI first establishes a secure channel with the CI. The CI is responsible for encrypting and decrypting messages to and from the GUI. The CI also has the task of formatting messages using SOAP standard for communications with the Web services. The CI removes the SOAP envelopes from response messages from the Web services.
- **Request Decomposer (RD):** This component decomposes the request into a list of (sequential and parallel) orders. For example, if the user sends

a request to search for the lowest price for a certain stock, the RD will decompose the request into atomic orders for every stock market currently in the system. In this process, the RD also determines the participant Web services that will be used to fulfill this request. If the RD does not find any participant for the order (e.g., no relevant Web service is currently available), it informs the *Request Manager* which, in turn, aborts the execution of the order and notifies the user.

- **Request Manager (RM):** The RM is in charge of receiving requests from the Communication Interface and sending them to the Request Decomposer. It receives atomic orders and a list of recommended Web services determined by the Request Decomposer. These orders are then dispatched via the Communication Interface to the appropriate Web service. The RM monitors the execution of all orders sent to the Web services. When the execution of *all* the orders terminates and the respective results are collected from the participating Web services, the RM generates an aggregate result and verifies if the service request was *safe*.
  A service request's commitment is safe if and only if:
  - *None* of its orders have been interrupted as a result of the reception by the RM of a notification message.
  - All of its orders have been committed.

  If the order is safe, the RM consolidated the response and sends it to the GUI via the Communication Interface. If the RM cannot commit an order within a system-set time, the RM aborts *all* the execution threads of the order. The RM will also not commit an order if it receives an *abort* message from one or more participating Web services. It then aborts *all* the relevant threads executing at the participants and sends a notification to the Request Decomposer to select another service(s).
- **Notifying Agents (NA):** Notifying agents are processes specialized in monitoring changes in a distributed environment and propagating these changes to entities that need to be notified of these changes. Their goal is to detect, propagate, and initiate reactive processes to changes. They respond to both internal and external change. For all pending orders (i.e., not committed yet), the Request Manager creates one Notifying Agent. This agents periodically send queries to the associated Web service and if there is a change, it notifies the Request Manager.

4 Implementation

The architecture described in the previous section is implemented within a pilot stock market application. The implementation uses state-of-the-art database technologies including Oracle, Informix, and DB2. It also uses Web service technologies, RMI, and database API (JDBC). Mobile agents (implemented using IBM Aglets) are used to detect changes in the system. Web services are described using WSDL and DAML-S. Example of Web services include, NYSE, CAC, FTSE, and TSE services. Each service accesses a backend database to provide the request service.

We generate WSDL descriptions using *Axis s Java2WSDL* utility provided in the *IBM Web Services Toolkit*. These descriptions are published in a UDDI. We implement the UDDI with *Systinet s WASP UDDI Standard 3.1*. *Cloudscape 4.0* database is used to create the registry for the UDDI. Communication between Web services are encapsulated in SOAP envelopes. *Apache SOAP* provides the tools necessary for deploying SOAP messaging.

To simulate the price fluctuation in stock markets, we use a *Stock Market Simulator*. This simulator is a multi-thread Java application. It has four threads, each thread invokes an operation from different types of Web services. The operation updates the *Bid* and *Ask* prices of the stocks in a Web service database every ten seconds. At each update time, the stocks and their update price are randomly selected. Changes in stock prices do not exceed 5%. To make the simulation more realistic, Java threads are used to synchronize the price changes of stocks.

For external changes, we are implementing a simulator function that will randomly change Web service descriptions. Specifically, it changes the status of operation availability in our local UDDI. By removing the description of a service operation, we indicate that the operation is no longer available. Changes are also randomly initiated in the DAML-S registry. We change the category (property) of the Web service to indicate a change in service domain.

The Request Broker is the integral part of our application. It accesses the UDDI and DAML-S registries to select appropriate services. Once services are discovered, its operations are invoked through *SOAP Binding Stub*. The stub is implemented with Apache SOAP API. All messages in the applications are monitored by the agents to determine change.

Users access the system through a Graphical User Interface (GUI). The system's GUI was developed using Java 2/Swing. It consists of two panels. The left panel displays the requests input by the user. The right panel displays all the information returned by the system (e.g., request execution results, registration and authorization information). Users may access the system from any Internet host. All information transfers between the GUI and the Communication Module of the Request Broker occur using a secure TCP connection.

5 Related Work

Web services are slated to be an active research area. We overview some of the research on Web services that is closely related to our work. WebBIS proposes composition and change management for services on the Web [6]. It focuses on the issues of detection, propagation, and reaction to change in service communities. WebBIS uses *ECA rules* and *change operations* to enable change management. WebBIS, however, lacks the support of change management for within the Web service standards. XLANG implements exception handling and transaction rollback by initiating a *compensation* process [17]. This compensation process attempts to "undo" the effects of an incomplete business transaction. This concepts relates to our approach of reacting to change. XLANG does not support our approach of detection and propagation of changes. It only handles reaction through compensation. eFlow uses the notion of *process template* to model composite services [18]. Composers need to browse the *process library* to search for process templates of interest. Furthermore, they need to manually handle interactions and change management between component services when defining composite services.

Commercial platforms are increasingly targeting Web services [19]. *Microsoft*'s *.NET* enables service composition through *Biztalk Orchestration* tools which use XLANG [20]. *IBM*'s *WebSphere* supports key Web service standards [21]. *IONA*'s *Orbix E2A* includes the *Orbix E2A Web Services Integration Platform* [22]. It provides a set of tools for business integration using Web service standards. Developers create Web services from existing applications, including EJBs and CORBA objects. *Sun ONE* (*Sun Open Net Environment*) is a platform for Web services developed by *Sun* [23]. *Sun* began its Web services efforts only recently. Most of these commercial platforms deal with service composition. Changes after composition need to be managed manually. To the best of our knowledge, they provide little or no support for dynamically dealing with changes to services.

6 Conclusion

We proposed in this paper an architecture that supports change management in Web service environments. We describe a generic algorithm for change management in Web service environments. The proposed architecture is based on two key ideas: (i) using ontologies to organize and efficiently select Web services, and (ii) using agents as a mechanism to manage change within the information space.

Acknowledgment. This research is supported by the National Science Foundation under grant 9983249-EIA and a grant from the Commonwealth Information Security Center (CISC).

References

1. Tsur, S., Abiteboul, S., Agrawal, R., Dayal, U., Klein, J., Weikum, G.: Are Web Services the Next Revolution in e-Commerce? (Panel). In: VLDB Conf., Rome, Italy (2001) 614–617
2. Medjahed, B., Benatallah, B., Bouguettaya, A., Ngu, A., Elmagarmid, A.: Business-to-Business Interactions: Issues and Enabling Technologies. The VLDB Journal **12** (2003) 59–85
3. Gottschalk, K., Graham, S., Kreger, H., Snell, J.: Introduction to the Web Services Architecture. IBM Systems Journal **41** (2002)
4. Curbera, F., Duftler, M., Khalaf, R., Nagy, W., Mukhi, N., Weerawarana, S.: Unraveling the Web Services Web: An Introduction to SOAP, WSDL, and UDDI. IEEE Internet Computing **6** (2002)

5. Feldman, S.: Electronic Marketplaces. IEEE Internet Computing (2000)
6. Benatallah, B., Medjahed, B., Bouguettaya, A., Elmagarmid, A., Beard, J.: Composing and Maintaining Web-based Virtual Enterprises. First VLDB Workshop on Technologies for E-Services (2000)
7. Papazoglou, M., Aiello, M., Pistore, M., Yang, J.: Planning for Requests against Web Services. IEEE Data Engineering Bulletin **25** (2002)
8. McIlraith, S.A., Martin, D.L.: Bringing Semantics to Web Services. IEEE Intelligent Systems (2003)
9. McIlraith, S.A., Son, T.C., Zeng, H.: Semantic Web Services. IEEE Intelligent Systems (2001)
10. Medjahed, B., Bouguettaya, A., Elmagarmid, A.K.: Composing Web Services on the Semantic Web. VLDB Journal **to appear** (2003)
11. Ouzzani, M., Benatallah, B., Bouguettaya, A.: Ontological Approach for Information Discovery in Internet Databases. Distributed and Parallel Databases **8** (2000)
12. Ankolekar, A., Burstein, M., Hobbs, J.R., Lassila, O., Martin, D., McDermott, D., McIlraith, S.A., Narayanan, S., Paolucci, M., Payne, T., Sycara, K.: DAML-S: Semantic Markup for Web Services, (http://www.daml.org/services/pub-archive.html)
13. Payne, T.R., Paolucci, M., Sycara, K.: Advertising and Matching DAML-S Service Descriptions. In: International Semantic Web Working Symposium, California, USA (2001)
14. Deolasee, P., Katkar, A., Panchbudhe, A., Ramamritham, K., Shenoy, P.: Adaptive Push-Pull: Disseminating Dynamic Web Data. IEEE Transactions on Computers **51** (2002)
15. Maes, P., Guttman, R.H., Moukas, A.G.: Agents that Buy and Sell. Communications of the ACM **42** (1999) 81–91
16. McCanne, S.R.S.: A model, analysis, and protocol framework for soft state-based communication. Proceedings of the conference on Applications, technologies, architectures, and protocols for computer communication (1999)
17. Thatte, S.: XLANG, http://www.gotdotnet.com/team/xml_wsspecs/xlang-c/. (2001)
18. Casati, F., Ilnicki, S., Jin, L., Krishnamoorthy, V., Shan, M.C.: Adaptive and Dynamic Service Composition in eFlow. In: CAiSE Conf., Stockholm, Sweden (2000) 13–31
19. Vaughan-Nichols, S.J.: Web Services: Beyond the Hype. IEEE Computer **35** (2002) 18–21
20. Microsoft: .NET, http://www.microsoft.com/net. (2002)
21. IBM: WebSphere, http://www-3.ibm.com/software/infol/websphere. (2003)
22. IONA: Orbix E2A, http://www.iona.com. (2003)
23. Sun: Sun ONE, http://wwws.sun.com. (2003)

Planning and Monitoring the Execution of Web Service Requests

Alexander Lazovik[1,2], Marco Aiello[1], and Mike Papazoglou[1,3]

[1] Department of Information and Telecommunication Technologies
University of Trento
Via Sommarive, 14, 38050 Trento, Italy
{lazovik,aiellom}@dit.unitn.it

[2] ITC-IRST
Via Sommarive, 18, 38050 Trento, Italy

[3] Infolab
Tilburg University
PO Box 90153, NL-5000 LE, The Netherlands
mikep@uvt.nl

Abstract. Interaction with web services enabled marketplaces would be greatly facilitated if users were given a high level service request language to express their goals in complex business domains. This could be achieved by using a planning framework which monitors the execution of planned goals against predefined standard business processes and interacts with the user to achieve goal satisfaction.
We present a planning architecture that accepts high level requests, expressed in XSRL (Xml Service Request Language). The planning framework is based on the principle of interleaving planning and execution. This is accomplished on the basis of refinement and revision as new service-related information is gathered from UDDI and web services instances, and as execution circumstances necessitate change. The system interacts with the user whenever confirmation or verification is needed.

1 Introduction

Service oriented computing (SOC) is rapidly becoming the prominent paradigm for distributed computing and electronic business applications. SOC allows for service providers and service application developers to construct value-added services by combining existing services that are resident on the Web. To achieve this, firstly, web services must be described in terms of the standard web service definition language WSDL (`http://www.w3.org/TR/wsdl`) and subsequently must be inter-linked to express how collections of web services work jointly to realize more complex functionalities typified by business processes. A new web service can be defined in terms of compositions of existing (constituent) services on the basis of the standard Business Process Execution Language for Web Services (BPEL4WS or BPEL for short,

M.E. Orlowska et al. (Eds.): ICSOC 2003, LNCS 2910, pp. 335–350, 2003.

`http://www-106.ibm.com/developerworks/library/ws-bpel/`). BPEL models the actual behavior of a participant in a business interaction as well as the visible message exchange behavior of each of the parties involved in the business protocol. A BPEL process is defined "in the abstract" by referencing and inter-linking `portTypes` specified in the WSDL definitions of the web services involved in a process. A BPEL process is a reusable definition that can be deployed in different ways and in different scenarios, while maintaining a uniform application-level behavior across all of them. Service compositions in BPEL are described in such a way (e.g., WSDL over UDDI) that allows automated discovery and offers request matching on service descriptions.

In many situations it is desirable to empower a user to gain explicit control over the execution of BPEL expressions and dynamically change the nature of the web service interactions conducted with a particular business partner depending on the state of the process. Consider for example the case of a traveler deciding to change their hotel reservation to take advantage of an unexpectedly lowly priced weekend offer. Users may need to change message property values in the midst of a computation, e.g., update their holiday budget based on ticket, hotel prices and availability, evaluate different behavioral alternatives or scenarios during a computation and change their course of action dynamically, or revisit different execution paths based on non-deterministic message property values that result from the invocation of services involved in a process. This implies that BPEL execution must be made adaptable at run-time to meet the changing needs of users and businesses. Obviously, BPEL specifications do not allow for the flexibility required to react swiftly to unforeseen circumstances or opportunities as choices are predefined and statically bound in BPEL programs. To meet such requirements serious re-coding efforts are needed every time that there is need for even a slight deviation.

Such advanced functionality can only be supported by a service request language and its appropriate run-time support environment to allow users to express their needs on the basis of the characteristics and functionality of standard business processes whose services are found in UDDI registries. A service request language provides for a formal means of describing desired service attributes and functionality, including temporal and non-temporal constraints between services, service scheduling preferences, alternative options and so on.

Our research work concentrates on developing a service request language for XML-based web services that contains a set of appropriate constructs for expressing requests and constraints over requests as well as scheduling operators. We have named this language XSRL for XML Service Request Language [1, 9]. XSRL expresses a request against standard processes defined in a vertical domain, e.g., e-travel, and returns a set of documents as the result of executing the request, e.g., by sending a end-to-end holiday packages (documents). The user requests generate a plan based on a standard business process that invokes a series of web services and interacts with the user to satisfy her/his request.

The remainder of the paper is organized as follows. In Section 2 an example in the traveling domain which runs throughout the paper is presented. The architecture of the proposed framework is illustrated in Section 3, in particular, we define the planning domain (3.1), we present an example of domain (3.2), we introduce an enhanced syntax and semantics for XSRL (3.3) and provide algorithms for satisfying XSRL requests (3.4). In Section 4 we exemplify the functionality of the architecture on the running example. The paper is concluded by a summary and brief overview of related work.

2 Organizing a Trip

Suppose a user is planning a one night trip to Paris and is interested in a number of possibilities in connection with this trip. These include making a hotel reservation in Paris, avoiding to travel by train, if possible, and spending an overall amount not greater than 300 euros for the whole package. Further, the user prefers to spend less than 100 euros for a hotel room but, if this is not possible, he may be willing to spend no more than 200 euros for that room. The user wants to pay under the condition that he receives a confirmation for the entire package. Of course, the user would also need to specify dates for his trip and night stay in Paris. This will not be considered in this example as it provides no additional explanation of the ideas behind the presented system. The wishes of the user have not much meaning unless they are matched against a standard business process in the e-travel domain. What the user requires is a business process description that prescribes how to interact with an e-travel marketplace infrastructure such as travel agents, hotel services and so on.

Nowadays standard business descriptions and terminology descriptions are given in XML schemas, e.g., for the automotive industry, travel industry, chemical industry and so on (`http://xml.coverpages.org/xmlApplications.html`) we expect that in the near future abstract definitions of such business process will be given in BPEL or similar service orchestration languages.

A snippet of a simple hypothetical standard business process for reserving a trip in the e-travel domain is given in Figure 1. This process is called a business domain and is modeled as a state transition diagram, that is, every node represents a state in which the process can be, while labeled arcs indicate how the process changes state. Actors involved in the process are shown at the top of the diagram. The actors include the user, a travel agency, a hotel service, an air service, a train service and a payment service.

The process is initiated by the user contacting a travel agency, hence, (1) is the initial state. The state is changed to (2) by requesting a quote from an hotel (action a_1). The dashed arcs represent web service responses, in particular arc a_2 brings the system in the state (3). The execution continues along these lines by traversing the paths in the state transition diagram until we reach state (14). In this state a confirmation of an hotel and of a flight or train is given by the travel agency and the user is prompted for acceptance of the travel package (13).

The state transition diagram is non-deterministic. This is illustrated, for instance, in state (4). In this state the user has accepted the hotel room price but is faced with two possible outcomes, one that a room is not available (where

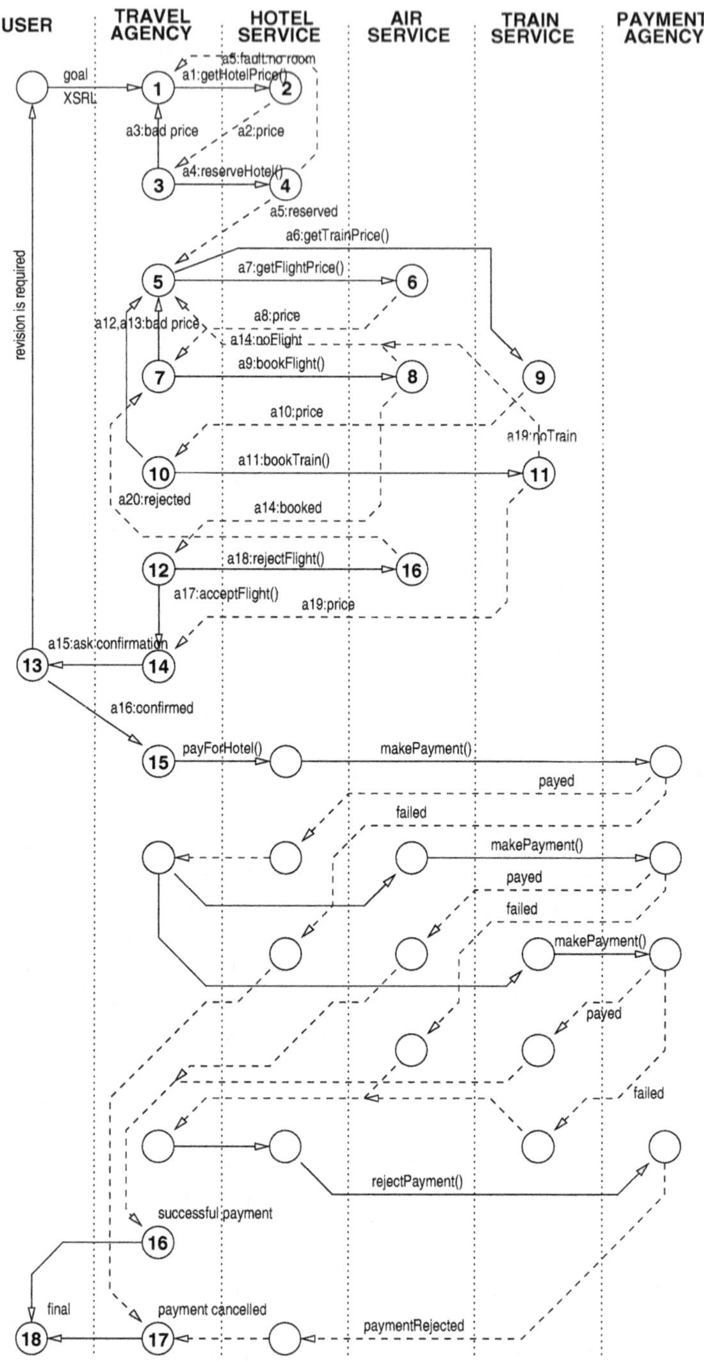

Fig. 1. Am e-travel business domain.

the system transits back to state (1)) and the other where a room reservation is made (state (5)).

The lower part of the business process models the payment of the travel package.

3 The XSRL Framework

The planning architecture proposed is based on the notion of interleaving planning and execution. The framework receives a request from the user and tries to fulfill it against a standard business process, assuming that it is syntactically correct. The standard business process can be specified in the abstract in BPEL and we assume that is represented graphically by the state transition diagram given in Figure 1. The framework returns a failure if the request cannot be satisfied in the given business process under the current run-time circumstances, e.g., ticket dates or hotel prices are not available. During execution the system interacts with UDDI to find suitable service providers, in a web service enabled marketplace, and with the user to ask confirmation or request additional information, if necessary.

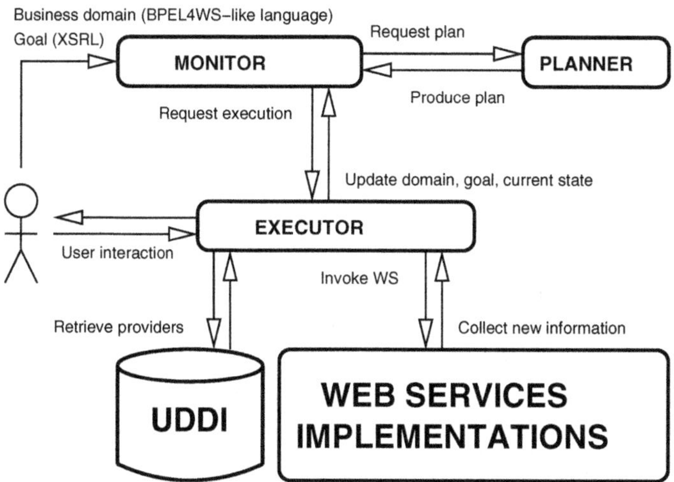

Fig. 2. High-level XSRL architecture.

The planning framework, shown in Figure 2, comprises four interacting components: monitor, planner, executor, and run-time support environment.

Figure 2 illustrates the user issuing a request to the system expressed against a business process (domain). The *monitor* manages the overall process of the interleaved planning and execution. First, it requests the *planner* to construct a plan. Subsequently the planner either produces a plan or returns a failure (if the request is not correctly specified). The *executor* processes the plan provided by the planner by invoking the corresponding web services. It is also responsible for finding a set of web service *providers* for a particular service in the *UDDI* registry. The executor may contact the user for confirmation if user interaction is demanded by the business process. The executor does not always execute an entire plan. It rather executes it in steps. It may gather new information, e.g., hotel rates, from the environment (UDDI) and inform the monitor, which in turn may request a new plan to be generated in the light of the information obtained. The executor updates the monitor regarding the status of the execution when re-planning is potentially needed or when it terminates the execution of a plan.

3.1 Planning Domain

To perform automatic planning and execution, it is necessary to formally define the domain under which the system acts. Although such a formalization can potentially be extracted from a BPEL definition, BPEL cannot be used directly as, among the other things, it lacks formal semantics. Thus, we use BPEL and extrapolate from it state-transition systems enriched with web service domain operators and constructs.

State-transition systems are the basis of most AI planning systems and form the core of our formalization. In particular, we use a representation able to represent non-determinisms and the potential absence of information of the environment (incomplete information).

Definition 1 (Planning domain). *A* non-deterministic web services planning domain *is a tuple* $\mathbf{D} =< \mathcal{S}, Var, Act, R, P, Out, Tr, Role_{Act}, Role_P >$*, where:*

- $\mathcal{S}$ *is the set of* states *which represent the states of the business process state-transition system.*
- Var *is the* variable space *generated by the the Cartesian product of a number of arbitrary domains such as the integers, the real numbers and boolean values. Further, we de ne the rst k elements of the variable space as* knowledge variables.
- Act *is the set of* actions *that can be performed in the transition system.*
- R *is a set of* service roles *associated with actions.*
- P *is a set of* service providers *identi ed by their URI.*
- Out *is a set of* output types *representing the possible response message types from services.*
- $Tr : \mathcal{S} \times Act \times Out \to \mathcal{S}$ *is the* transition function. *The generic element of this relation* $Tr(s_i, a, o_a) = s_j$ *represents the transition from state* s_i *to state* s_j *by means of action* a *with output type* o_a*. An action* a *is called* deterministic *in a state* s *if* $\exists s' \forall o \in Out \; Tr(s, a, o) = s'$.
- $Role_{Act} : Act \to R$ *is the* role association *function which relates actions to service roles.*
- $Role_P : R \to 2^P$ *is the* role assignment function *that associates every provider to a role in the process.*

To assign meaning to the elements of the transition relation we use semantic rules. A semantic rule is an arbitrary function $f : Act \times Var \times Out \rightarrow Var$. Finally, we say that an action $a \in Act$ is *knowledge gathering* (or a *sensing*) action if it affects at least one knowledge variable. Formally, knowledge variables are associated with actions and output types as follows $\forall o \in Out$ $(\exists i \leq k : f(a, v, o)_i \neq v_i)$ where $f()_i$ represents the restriction of the function i to the i-th element and the first k elements of $v \in Var$ are knowledge variables.

The concept behind the presented formalization of the planning domain is that a given business process is, at any instant, in a state from which a number of actions can be performed to move to a new state. Roles, which represent service interfaces, are associated to actions and implemented by service providers.

3.2 A Domain Instance

To provide more intuition for the planning domain just presented, we formalize the upper half of the traveling business process in Figure 1 in accordance with Definition 1 integrating information where necessary. In fact, Definition 1 has a number of additional features with respect to the figure. In particular, in the figure the set variables, the set of service providers, the role assignment function and the semantic rules are not represented.

There are fourteen states $\mathcal{S} = \{1, 2, \ldots, 14\}$ in the upper half of the figure. The set of variables Var is $\{hotelReserved, hotelPrice, location, trainBooked, trainPrice, flightBooked, flightPrice, confirmed, money\}$, among which one distinguishes the boolean variables ($hotelReserved$, $trainBooked$, $flightBooked$, $confirmed$), from the real variables ($hotelPrice$, $trainPrice$, $flightPrice$, $money$), and a variable representing location names ($location$). In the set of variables a subset is defined to be of knowledge variables. In the example, we define $hotelPrice$, $trainPrice$, $flightPrice$ to be knowledge variables. There are also nineteen actions that can be performed in the domain $Act = \{a_1, \ldots, a_{19}\}$.

Four roles are involved in the process $R = \{hotel, air, travel\text{-}agency, train\}$ and the $Role_{Act}$ relation associates to each of them the following actions: *hotel* has $\{a_1, a_2, a_4, a_5\}$ associated, *travel-agency* has $\{a_3, a_{12}, a_{13}, a_{15}, a_{16}, a_{17}\}$, *air* has $\{a_7, a_8, a_9, a_{14}, a_{18}, a_{20}\}$, and *train* has the set of actions $\{a_6, a_{10}, a_{11}, a_{19}\}$ associated. The set of actual service providers for this services obtained by contacting the UDDI could be $Hilton$ and $BestWestern$ for the *hotel* role, $BritishArways$, $Virgin$ for *air* role, *ClubMed* for the travel agency and $TrenItalia$ for the train role. The set of output messages is $Out = \{normal, NoRoomFault, NoSeatOnFlight, NoSeatOnTrain\}$.

Finally, the transition function is given by the set of labeled arcs in the figure, for example, $Tr(4, a_5, normal) = 5$, $Tr(4, a_5, NoRoomFault) = 1$ represent that the action a_5 with a *normal* output brings the system into state 5, while the state 1 is reached with the $NoRoomFault$ message. Semantic rules are associated with all actions. The rules for actions *Act* follow:

- $a_2, normal$: $hotelPrice = result$
- $a_3, normal$: $hotelPrice = 0$

- a_5, *normal*: $money+ = hotelPrice; hotelReserved = true$
- a_5, $NoRoomFault$: $hotelPrice = 0$
- a_8, *normal*: $flightPrice = result$
- a_{10}, *normal*: $trainPrice = result$
- a_{12}, *normal*: $trainPrice = 0$
- a_{13}, *normal*: $flightPrice = 0$
- a_{14}, *normal*: $money+ = flightPrice; flightBooked = true$
- a_{16}, *normal*: $confirmed = true$
- a_{19}, *normal*: $money+ = trainPrice; trainBooked = true$
- a_{20}, *normal*: $money- = flightPrice; flightBooked = false$

For instance, the semantic rule for action a_5 with a *normal* output message increments the value of the *money* variable with the price of the reserved hotel and sets the *hotelReserved* variable to true. While the same action with an $NoRoomFault$ output message yields the reseting of hotel price to zero.

The domain could easily be enriched with further details. For example, one might consider reservation dates, flight numbers and so on. To take this into account one only needs to define additional variables that store this information and enrich the semantic rules attached to the actions in order to update these variables during execution. This is not illustrated in this paper for space reasons.

3.3 XSRL

XSRL (Xml Service Request Language) was first introduced in [1,9] as a request language for compositions of web services in the context of off-line planning that is not interleaving planning and execution. This paper provides an extension of XSRL dealing with the interleaving of planning and execution. The improved XSRL syntax is defined as follows:

```
xsrl        <- '<XSRL>' goal '</XSRL>'
goal        <- proposition | and | then | vital |
               optional | atomic | vital-maint | optional-maint
achieve-all    <- '<ACHIEVE-ALL>' +goal '</ACHIEVE-ALL>'
then           <- '<BEFORE>' goal '</BEFORE><THEN>' goal '</THEN>
prefer         <- '<PREFER>' goal '</PREFER><TO>' goal '</TO>'
vital          <- '<VITAL>' proposition '</VITAL>'
optional       <- '<OPTIONAL>' proposition  '</OPTIONAL>'
atomic         <- '<ATOMIC>' proposition '</ATOMIC>'
vital-maint    <- '<VITAL-MAINT>' proposition '</VITAL-MAINT>'
optional-maint <- '<OPTIONAL-MAINT>' proposition '</OPTIONAL-MAINT>'
proposition    <- '<CONST ATT="true|false">' |  var  |
                  '<AND>' +proposition '</AND>' |
                  '<OR>' +proposition '</OR>' |
                  '<NOT>' proposition '</NOT>' |
                  '<GREATER>' var '</GREATER><THAN>' rval '</THAN>' |
                  '<LESS>' var '</LESS><THAN>' rval '</THAN>' |
                  '<EQUAL>' var rval '</EQUAL>'
var            <- a..zA..Z[rval]
rval           <- +a..zA..Z0..9.
```

Before dealing with the details of the semantics of XSRL constructs, we provide their intuitive meaning. The atomic objects of the language are propositions, that is, boolean combination of linear inequalities and boolean propositions. These can be either true or not in any given state. Propositions are further combined by sequencing operators to form goals. The sequencing operators are: achieve-all, then, prefer. `<ACHIEVE-ALL> +goal </ACHIEVE-ALL>` succeeds when all subgoals defined inside the tag `<ACHIEVE-ALL>` are satisfied, it fails otherwise. `<BEFORE> goal1 </BEFORE><THEN> goal2 </THEN>` is satisfied, if `goal1` is satisfied and, from the state where `goal1` is satisfied, `goal2` is also satisfied, it fails otherwise. `<PREFER> goal1 </PREFER><TO> goal2 </TO>` succeeds if `goal1` is satisfiable, if not then it succeeds if `goal2` is satisfiable, it fails if both `goal1` and `goal2` are unsatisfiable. `<ACHIEVE-ALL>` provides a way of collecting goals that have all to be satisfied, the operator `<THEN>` is a way of sequencing goals, while `<PREFER>` enables the user to express user preferences over goals. Note that by nesting preference statements, one may give a total order over a number of sub-goals.

A number of operators take propositions as arguments. These are used to express 'how' to satisfy the propositions. `<VITAL> proposition </VITAL>` is satisfied if there exists a state satisfying `proposition` which is reachable from any future state, it fails otherwise. `<OPTIONAL> proposition </OPTIONAL>` is always satisfied as a goal. Its meaning is that, if there exists a reachable state satisfying `proposition`, then this state must be reached, otherwise the goal is ignored. `<ATOMIC> proposition </ATOMIC>` means that `proposition` should be reached from the current state despite non-determinism of the domain. If there is no such path to a satisfaction state, it fails. Note the requirements of this operator are stronger than the `<VITAL>` operator. The `<VITAL>` operator does not guarantee satisfaction of the goal if the execution of the plan is always non-deterministically taking the 'wrong' path, this means that non-deterministic action executions always bring the system in a state different from the one in which the final goal is achieved. `<VITAL-MAINT> proposition </VITAL-MAINT>` is satisfied if for all states in the execution path `proposition` is true. If there is a state in which `proposition` is not true, then it fails. `<OPTIONAL-MAINT>` is analogous to the previous one, but as a goal it does not fail if such a path does not exist.

To provide the formal semantics of XSRL, we adapt the definitions of plan and of execution structure from [5]. We additionally define the notion of booleanization. A plan is defined as a sequence of actions executed in given context.

Definition 2 (Plan). *A* plan *for a domain D is a tuple $\pi = \langle C, c_0, action, ctxt\rangle$ where*

- *C is a set of contexts,*
- *$c_0 \in C$ is the initial context,*
- *$action : \mathcal{S} \times C \to Act$ is the action function,*
- *$ctxt : \mathcal{S} \times C \times \mathcal{S} \to C$ is the context function*

XSRL in addition to dealing with boolean variables used in typical goal languages, such as the one proposed in [10], deals with variables that range over domains like reals, integers, and so on. To allow for this we introduce the notion of 'booleanization'. The idea behind booleanization is that constraints expressed in the goal over domains ranging over variables are treated as boolean propositions. For example, consider the expression *money* < 100 with an integer variable *money*. After booleanization this becomes a boolean proposition that can be either true or false.

Definition 3 (Booleanization). *The booleanization of a domain* $\mathbf{D}$ *with respect to a goal* g *is a tuple* $BD = \langle S', Prop, Act, R, P, Out, Tr', Role_{Act}, Role_P \rangle$ *derived from the original domain* $\mathbf{D}$ *in the following way. The set of variables* Var *is replaced by the set of boolean proposition* $Prop$ *according to the following rule:*

- *all boolean variables in* Var *are also in* P,
- *all linear constraints appearing in* g *are added as boolean propositions in* P,
- *all variables in* Var *that do not appear in* g *are omitted in* P.

The set of states and transition function are changed to t the above introduction of boolean propositions.

An execution structure of a plan over a booleanized domain for a given goal, represents the possible ways a plan can execute and is essential to determine the reachability of a given goal from a particular state.

Definition 4 (Execution Structure). *The execution structure of plan* π *in the booleanization of domain* D *with respect to goal* g *from state* s_0 *is the structure* $K = \langle S, R, L \rangle$, *where*

- $S = \{(s, c) : action(s, c)$ *is de ned* $\}$ *is the set of states of the execution structure,*
- $R = \{((s, c), (s', c')) : if\, \exists (s, c) \rightarrow (s', c')$ *and* $ctxt(s, c, s') = c'\}$ *is the relation*
- $L(s, c) = \{b \in P\}$,

The execution structure of a plan in a domain represents how the domain is traversed by the plan. Before defining the notion of goal satisfaction, we need to introduce a few elements of notation. We use the symbol σ to denote *nite paths.* S denotes the set of all states in the execution structure K. Given a set Σ of finite paths, the set of minimal paths in Σ is defined as $min\{\Sigma\} = \{\sigma \in \Sigma : \forall \sigma' < \sigma \implies \sigma' \notin \Sigma\}$. Given a goal g, $S_g(s)$ represents the the set of finite paths that lead to the satisfaction of goal g from state s, while $F_g(s)$ represents the set of finite paths that lead to a failure. A state s' is said to be *reachable* from the state s if there exists a path starting from s and leading to s'. A plan is denoted by π.

The notion of goal satisfaction $K, s \models g$ is defined in terms of the set of failure states for the goal g on the execution structure K derived from a booleanized domain with starting state s as follows

$$K, s \models g \text{ iff } F_g(s) = \emptyset$$

The set of failure states $F_g(s)$ for a goal g from a state s is defined inductively in the following way:

p
: $S(s) = \{(s)\}$, $F(s) = \emptyset$, that is, $p \in L(s)$ for all proposition letters p of the booleanized domain, otherwise $S(s) = \emptyset$, $F(s) = \{(s)\}$

$\neg p, p_1 \wedge p_2, p_1 \vee p_1$
: not p, p_1 and p_1, p_1 or p_1

achieve-all $g_1..g_n$
: $S(s) = min\{\sigma : \exists\sigma_1 \leq \sigma\ \sigma_1 \in S_{g_1}(s) \wedge \ldots \wedge \exists\sigma_n \leq \sigma\ \sigma_n \in S_{g_n}(s)\}$
: $F(s) = min\{F_{g_1}(s) \cup \ldots \cup F_{g_n}(s)\}$

before g_1 **then** g_2
: $S(s) = \{\sigma_1;\sigma_2 : \sigma_1 \in S_{g_1}(s) \wedge \sigma_2 \in S_{g_2}(last(\sigma_1))\}$
: $F(s) = \{\sigma_1 : \sigma_1 \in F_{g_1}(s)\} \cup \{\sigma_1;\sigma_2 : \sigma_1 \in S_{g_1}(s) \wedge \sigma_2 \in F_{g_2}(last(\sigma_1))\}$

prefer g_1 **to** g_2
: $S(s) = \{\sigma_1 : \sigma_1 \in S_{g_1}(s)\} \cup \{\sigma_1;\sigma_2 : \sigma_1 \in F_{g_1}(s) \wedge \sigma_2 \in S_{g_2}(last(\sigma_1))\}$
: $F(s) = \{\sigma_1;\sigma_2 : \sigma_1 \in F_{g_1}(s) \wedge \sigma_2 \in F_{g_2}(last(\sigma_1))\}$

atomic p
: if there is some infinite path ρ such that $\forall s' \in \rho\ s' \not\models p$ then $S(s) = \emptyset$, $F(s) = \{s\}$, otherwise: $S(s) = min\{\sigma : first(\sigma) = s \wedge last(\sigma) \models p\}$, $F(s) = \emptyset$

vital p
: $S(s) = min\{\sigma : first(\sigma) = s \wedge last(\sigma) \models p\}$
: $F(s) = min\{\sigma : first(\sigma) = s \wedge \forall s' \in \sigma\ s' \not\models p \wedge \forall\sigma' \geq \sigma\ last(\sigma') \not\models p\}$

optional p
- if $\exists\pi : \pi, s \models vital\ p$, otherwise
- if $\forall\pi' \neq \pi : \pi', s \not\models vital\ p$

optional-maint p
- if $\exists\pi : \pi, s \models vital\ maint\ p$, otherwise
- if $\forall\pi' \neq \pi : \pi', s \not\models vital\ maint\ p$

vital-maint p
: if $K, s' \models p$ holds for all states s' reachable from s then $S(s) = \emptyset$, $F(s) = \emptyset$, otherwise $S(s) = \emptyset$, $F(s) = \{s\}$

The satisfaction of a goal has thus been defined in terms of whether a goal can fail or not during execution.

3.4 Interleaving Planning and Execution

The architecture presented in Figure 2 divides the framework into three main functional units: a monitor, a planner and an executor. In this section we provide three algorithms for each of these units.

The *monitor* (Algorithm 1) is responsible of invoking the planner, recovering from failure and invoking the execution of plans. Starting with a domain, an initial state and an XSRL goal, it invokes the planner requesting the synthesizing of a plan. Then monitor analyzes the plan. An empty plan means that the goal has been reached and the request has been successfully met. If the planner returns failure, i.e., the goal cannot be satisfied under the current execution context, then it attempts to change a provider. `chooseNewProvider` contacts

Algorithm 1 monitor(domain d, state s, goal g)

```
π = plan(d, s, g)
if π = ∅ then
  return success
else
  if π = failure then
    if chooseNewProvider then
      d' = updateDomain(d)
      return monitor (d', s, g)
    else
      return failure
    end if
  end if
  (d', s', g') = execute(π, d, s, g)
  return monitor (d', s', g')
end if
```

the executor module which has a list of possible providers for services and keeps track of which providers have been considering during the execution of the plan. If a new provider can be assigned, the execution proceeds, otherwise the monitor returns failure. Finally, if a non-empty plan has been produced, the plan is passed on to the executor by invoking the `execute` function. This function returns an updated domain, current state and the new XSRL goal for which one needs to continue the monitoring.

The *executor* (Algorithm 2) starts from a plan, a domain, an initial state and an XSRL goal. It iterates by attempting the execution of all the actions of the input plan. The `firstAction` of the plan is stored in the variable a and then removed from the plan. If this action requires interaction with a web service, then one needs to seek for a provider for that action. The construct *role* stores the role associated with the current action. If the executor has not assigned a provider for that role during the execution so far, then the UDDI is contacted to ask for providers for the given role. A provider is chosen from the list of possible providers using some heuristic function (the first provider, the one for which there are good references, etc.). If, on the other hand, a provider has already been assigned to a role, then we must continue executing the following actions assigned to the role with the same provider. Once the provider has been identified, the provider is invoked with action a and the possible return messages are stored in the `message` variable. The next step is that of updating the domain, the current state and the goal by the effects of having executed the action. This step is necessary as the execution of the action may have brought the system in a new state, it may have changed the values of some variables and it may have satisfied subgoals of the current goal. If the action has been a knowledge gathering action, we have acquired new information and we want to return the current status to the monitor in order to perform re-planning, otherwise we reiterate the cycle by looking at the following action of the plan.

Algorithm 2 execute(plan π, domain d, state s, goal g)

```
repeat
  a = firstAction(π)
  π = π − a
  if webServiceAction(a) then
    role = Rol_Act(a)
    if noProviderForRole(role) then
      providersList = contactUDDI(role)
      provider = chooseProvider(providersList)
    else
      provider = previouslyChosenProvider(role)
    end if
    message = invoke(a, provider)
  end if
  (d', s', g') = update(d, s, g, a, message)
  if isKnowledgeGathering(a) then
    return (d', s', g')
  end if
until π = ∅
return (d', s', g')
```

Algorithm 3 plan(domain d, state s, goal g)

```
domain_bool = booleanize(d)
goal_bool = booleanize(g)
return MBPplan(domain_bool, s, goal_bool)
```

The *planner* function (Algorithm 3) is very short as it relies on an existing planner (MBP, [2,5]). MBP is a model based planner which, given a domain description and a goal, synthesizes a plan for the given goal or returns failure if a plan does not exist. This reduction, called booleanization, takes all linear constraints over non boolean variables and turns them into boolean propositions which are true, false or undefined in the current state of the domain. The same reduction is necessary for the goal. The planner returns a sequence of actions for 'reaching' the booleanized goal. We do not give the full details of booleanization here, but simply explain the basic concept behind it.

(i) The booleanized domain is as the original one except that instead of the set of variables we have a set of proposition letters (specified by the rules below).

(ii) Non boolean linear constraints in the goal are transformed into boolean propositions. Note that two distinct propositions (e.g., $price < 10$ and $price > 5$) are introduced to take into account two constraints on the same variable.

(iii) The truth of the propositions is established on the domain by starting from the current state, looking at the current values of the variables and moving along the actions using semantic rules to establish the truth of propositions. In case of conflicting values for a proposition in a state (e.g., the case of two actions with different semantic rules entering in the same state), the state is divided into two states and then the propagation proceeds independently.

4 Executing a Sample XSRL Request

To exemplify the concepts behind the algorithms just presented, we provide a sample XSRL request run against the domain introduced in Section 2.

To illustrate the execution of g on the domain d of Figure 1 using the algorithms of Section 3.4, we write the XSRL request omitting XML tags as follows (refer to [6] for more detailed example):

achieve-all
  before
    achieve-all
      prefer vital-maint $hotelPrice < 100$ **to vital-maint** $hotelPrice < 200$
      optional-maint $\neg trainBooked$
      vital $confirmed \ \wedge \ location = \text{``}Paris\text{''} \ \wedge \ hotelReserved$
  then
    atomic $final$
  vital-maint $price < 300$

This XSRL request is executed as follows: Algorithm 1 is invoked on the domain d in Section 3.2 with initial state $s = 1$ and the defined goal g. The first step is to invoke the planner of Algorithm 3 with (d, s, g). As there exists a plan for the booleanized version of (d, s, g) the planner returns a plan π with initial actions a_1, a_2, a_4. Subsequently, the execute function (Algorithm 2) is invoked on (π, d, s, g). The first action is a_1=`getHotelPrice`. The role associated with the action a_1 is 'hotel service'. Since this is the first action UDDI will be contacted to get a list of providers associated with this role. We suppose to get a list with two providers 'Hilton' and 'BestWestern' and further that the first one is chosen. Subsequently, the service is invoked. The update of the domain moves the current state to 2. Since a_1 is not a knowledge gathering action, execution of the plan continues. Following this the execution proceeds by considering the role of a_2=`price` which is again 'hotel service'. Note that this action modifies the knowledge variable price as the interaction with the hotel provider will return a price value. Since we have already chosen the provider 'Hilton' for the hotel service role, we continue with it and store in `message` the price of, say, 150 euros. Next, the domain, goal and current state are updated accordingly. In particular, the new state is 3 and the goal is unchanged. Since the action is a knowledge gathering one, the executor returns the control to the monitor specifying the updated domain, current state, and goal. The monitor function invokes the planner on the new current state 3. Again a plan exists because, even if the cost of the hotel is more than the 100 preferred value it is still less than 200 euros. The initial sequence of actions of the new plan is now $a_4, a_5, (a_7$ or $a_1)$. Interleaving of planning and execution proceeds analogously as in the previous points by executing the action a_4=`reserveHotel`.

The next action a_5 in the plan is non-deterministic, i.e., both states 1 and 5 could be reached with this action. Let us assume that we have received a confirmation message from the provider 'Hilton' and the current state is therefore 5. The following actions request a flight price and reserve a seat in an analogous manner assuming that the cheapest flight provider 'Virgin' is chosen with a ticket price of, say, 200 euros. The choice of 'Virgin' is achieved if the heuristic behind the `chooseProvider` function in Algorithm 2 orders the providers by offered prices. The planner will produce a new plan whose next action is a_6=`getTrainPrice` since the flight action will be retracted as the `vital-maint` goal of spending less than 300 euros is violated. Suppose that the price returned by a train provider is of 140 euros. The execution of the plan proceeds smoothly until we reach state 14. The following action is asking the user for confirmation before payment. If it is accepted, the new state is 15 and the goal is updated by considering the subgoal after the `then` statement. The last subgoal of `atomic` final is achieved as there the final state 18 is always reachable from the current state 15.

5 Summary

AI planning provides a sound framework for developing a web services request language and for synthesizing correct plans for it. Based on this premise we have developed a framework for planning and monitoring the execution of web service requests against standardized business processes. The requests are expressed in the XSRL language and are processed by a framework which interleaves planning and execution in order to dynamically adapt to the opportunities offered by available web services and to the preferences of users. The request language results in the generation of executable plans describing both the sequence of plan actions to be undertaken in order to satisfy a request and the necessary information essential to develop each planned action.

From the AI planning perspective, our work is primarily based on planning as model checking under non-determinism for extended goals [10,5] using the MBP planner [2]. Extensions toward interleaving planning and execution in the above context are reported in [3]. The latter work emphasizes on state explosion problems rather than information gathering, furthermore, it does not handle numeric values. Various authors have emphasized the importance of planning for web services [4,7,8]. In particular, Knoblock et al. [4] use a form of template planning based on hierarchical task networks and constraint satisfaction, in [7] regression planning is used, while in [8] the Golog planner is used to automatically compose semantically described service. Our approach differs from these recently proposed planning approaches for web services in that it is based on non-deterministic planning whereas most of the previously cited approaches focus on gathering information, on applying deterministic planning techniques, on using precompiled plans or on assuming rich semantic annotations of services.

We have defined the full semantics of XSRL in terms of execution structures and we have provided algorithms that satisfy XSRL requests based on UDDI supplied information and information gathered from web service interactions.

Preliminary experiments with MBP planner have been conducted to illustrate the feasibility of the approach. In the next phase of experiments we will implement the algorithms described in the paper to test the proposed framework.

An issue for future investigation is the interaction of the system with UDDI registries. In particular, UDDI could be enhanced by providing better support for provider selection, e.g., based on service quality characteristics. This has an impact, among other things, on the `chooseProvider` function. From the point of view of planning, there are several aspects that need to be addressed. For example, the current version of the planner does not keep track of previous computations or "remember" history and patterns of interactions.

References

1. M. Aiello, M. Papazoglou, J. Yang, M. Carman, M. Pistore, L. Serafini, and P. Traverso. A request language for web-services based on planning and constraint satisfaction. In *VLDB Workshop on Technologies for E-Services (TES02)*, 2002.
2. P. Bertoli, A. Cimatti, M. Pistore, M. Roveri, and P. Traverso. MBP: A Model Based Planner. In *Proc. IJCAI'01 Workshop on Planning under Uncertainty and Incomplete Information*, 2001.
3. P. Bertoli, A. Cimatti, and P. Traverso. Interleaving Execution and Planning via Symbolic Model Checking. In *Proc. of ICAPS'03 Workshop on Planning under Uncertainty and Incomplete Information*, 2003.
4. C. A. Knoblock, S. Minton, J. L. Ambite, M. Muslea, J. Oh, , and M. Frank. Mixed-initiative, multi-source information assistants. In *Proceedings of the World Wide Web Conference*, 2001.
5. U. Dal Lago, M. Pistore, and P. Traverso. Planning with a language for extended goals. In *18th National Conference on Artificial Intelligence (AAAI-02)*, 2002.
6. A. Lazovik, M. Aiello, and M. Papazoglou. Planning and monitoring the execution of web service requests. Technical Report DIT-03-049, University of Trento, 2003.
7. D. McDermott. Estimated-regression planning for interactions with Web Services. In *6th Int. Conf. on AI Planning and Scheduling.* AAAI Press, 2002.
8. S. McIlraith and T. C. Son. Adapting Golog for composition of semantic web-services. In D. Fensel, F. Giunchiglia, D. McGuinness, and M. Williams, editors, *Conf. on principles of Knowledge Representation (KR)*, 2002.
9. M. Papazoglou, M. Aiello, M. Pistore, and J. Yang. Planning for requests against web services. *IEEE Data Engineering Bulletin*, 25(4):41–46, 2002.
10. M. Pistore and P. Traverso. Planning as model checking for extended goals in non-deterministic domains. In *Proc. 7th International Joint Conference on Artificial Intelligence (IJCAI-01)*, 2001.

WS-Workspace: Workspace Versioning for Web Services

Garret Swart

Computer Science Department
University College Cork
Cork, Ireland
g.swart@cs.ucc.ie.

Abstract. When using web services to perform complex data manipulations, users and administrators need control over how their changes are managed and seen by other clients of the service. This includes support for undo of changes, batch publishing of many changes, 'what if' analysis, the collaboration of several people in making and approving a complex change, workspace based access control, and the auditing and tracking of changes. We propose taking the workspace versioning model, used extensively in CAD and CASE products, and using it to augment web services in a backward compatible way based on the WS-Coordination protocol. The resulting protocol, which we call WS-Workspace, facilitates the writing of web services that support applications with undo, collaboration, and auditing.

1 Introduction

The evolution of data access in web services is following a path that traditional web applications have already evolved along. At the dawn of the web, web applications filled their first niche as information navigators, they then adapted to meet the needs of commerce by developing order entry capability, and now, as the web is being used as a delivery vehicle for applications of all types, web applications are struggling to meet the needs of more general online data authoring and manipulation.

Web Services are going through a distributed version of this same evolution. The first applications for web services were oriented towards distributed information access, allowing applications like comparison-shopping, contacting many product sources to find the lowest price; information portals, collecting information from a variety of information sources and presenting them in the same web page (e.g. [13]); and application integration (e.g. [20]), integrating application functionality from various vendors onto a provider's web site. Evolving standards provide support for these uses of web services.

Distributed order-entry web services are in development, allowing the reliable and secure placing and accepting of orders, allowing both horizontally distributed applications, such as booking an itinerary on a variety of carriers and hotels, and vertically distributed applications, such as automatically matching incoming inventory to out

M.E. Orlowska et al. (Eds.): ICSOC 2003, LNCS 2910, pp. 351–366, 2003.

going orders. These applications require coordination between the services to ensure that partial updates are not committed. For example, to make sure that a partial itinerary is not booked or that an order for additional inventory is not confirmed before the order for the finished product is confirmed. Proposals such as WS-Transaction protocol [7] are addressing these issues.

The next stage of web service evolution is to allow for more general online authoring and manipulation of data. Complex data types and web-based maintenance of these values are becoming more common in server-based applications as the complexity and richness of data maintained by web applications is increasing. System architects would like to use web services for applications with complex authoring needs such as:

- Resource scheduling: Defining resources, constraints, resource classes, and resource demands and allowing the authoring and editing of schedules, either automatically or manually.
- Work-flow management: Defining processes and flows and maintaining the state of orders, inventories, claims, or sales calls.
- Catalogue maintenance: Authoring online catalogues of all types, for example a school's class offerings, a mail order firm's product offerings, or a service company's service offerings.
- Business Rules maintenance: Online authoring of rules that determine how a system works, e.g. how it determines pricing, which products to present to the customer, how to deal with delinquent customers, or how the work flow should be routed.
- Online content authoring: From Web Logs to Photo Albums to RFP preparation, users are authoring complex entities constructed from many components.

In each case, the objects being authored are complex, have interactions with other objects and the changes need to be tested by humans before they are published widely. Only the last example is a traditional authoring application, however, taking an authoring point of view on all these applications can make understanding the problem and its solution easier. Note that in each case a particular user update may require changes made to data that is accessed through many different web services and stored on many different underlying data stores.

Web services underlying such applications would benefit from facilities for:

- Batched Publishing: The ability for a caller to specify that the changes being made should be held until the entire batch is completed and then published as a unit for the other callers of the service.
- 'What if' analysis: The authoring of a possible future state so that it can be analyzed to determine whether the effort should be rolled back or continued. A cautious management team may want to see a complete picture of a future state before any steps in that direction are taken.
- Undo: The ability for a caller that has just made a change to issue a subsequent undo request that would undo the last change.
- Collaborative Workspaces: The ability for a caller to make an update in a workspace that may be shared and further modified by a select group of other users.

- Controlled Update: The ability for management to define processes for changing certain data, e.g. all changes must first be tested by QA, approved by marketing and signed off by legal before being published on a public site, and making sure that the web services manipulating the data, enforce those rules.
- Auditing: The ability to see what changes were made and who made them.
- Coordinated Update: The ability to combine changes made through different web services into one perceived global change to the system state.

Most web services, and in fact most web applications, do not offer any of these facilities today. Commonly, each valid update a caller performs using a web service is immediately committed to the database to be seen by all other callers of the web service. Undo is usually nonexistent: once an update is performed, the previous state has been lost. Programmers implement auditing on a piecemeal basis. Sharing work in progress is not a concept in most web services.

In a separate paper

We propose to make the web services world ready for complex object authoring by introducing the concept of workspace versioning to web services and the data that they manipulate. Workspace versioning has been used extensively in the CASE [12] and CAD industry but it is not generally used in server based applications. This extension builds on the WS-Coordination extension [6]. It allows changes made by a web service invocation to create new versions of the updated objects that are part of a particular workspace.

In this paper we are discussing the versioning of the data being manipulated by a web service, not the versioning, compatibility issues or configuration of the web service implementation or its WSDL interface. That is a separate problem that is not addressed in this paper.

Existing work in making versioned updates via the web has been done primarily in the context of content and source management. WebDAV [11, 14] provides a protocol to allow documents to be versioned and published. The Wiki repository [30] allows documents to be added and updated using a web interface. Commercial content management systems like Interwoven [0] and Vignette [29] provide interfaces for updating objects living in a virtual versioned file system.

Traditional CAD and CASE systems are now also allowing access to their systems via the web, very commonly for viewing and sometimes for update.

2 Workspace Versioning Concepts

There is a rich literature and practice in versioning, especially for object and document systems [8, 10, 17, 18, 26]. Here we generalize and formalize the traditional versioning concepts so that they can be applied to arbitrary data objects.

Data Store: A set of data items. This may be a file system, a relational database, an object store or an ERP system. The operations that may be issued on a data store and the data items that it supports depend on the type of the data store and the APIs that it supports. A single web service may use many data stores and a single data store may be used by many web services.

Transactional data store: A data store that supports transactions. To facilitate transactions that span data stores, data stores typically register themselves as resource managers with a transaction manager as they are accessed by a transaction. The data store is then invoked as the transaction manager coordinates a rollback or a commit of the transaction [1, 9, 21, 22].

Data item: A uniquely identified item of data present in a data store. This may be a row in a relational store, an object in an object store, a file in a file store, or an account in an ERP system. A data item may have a complex value with many properties associated with it, including references to other data items. Each data item is assumed to get a unique identity when the data item is first created and for that identity never to change even as changes are made to the value of the item. In this way the item's identity is distinct from a mutable primary key in a relational database or a file name in file system.

Data item version: A value of a data item to be made visible in a particular context. More formally it is a node in an acyclic directed graph associated with the data item, each node in the graph is labeled with a sequence of operations that were used to create that version. The value of each version is the result of applying that sequence of operations. Applying an operation to an existing data item version creates a new version with an arc between the old version and the new one. The original version is called the predecessor and the resulting version is called the successor. The new version is labelled with the new operation appended to its predecessor's label. Since operations may be applied to any version of a data item, a version may have many successors. The version of a data item that results when a **delete** operation is applied has a special value that precludes any additional operations being applied to it. An **insert** operation creates a new data item with a single version node.

Versioned data item: A data item that may have more than one version in its data store. Not all versions of a data item must remain accessible, only those that can be accessed by active workspaces.

Common ancestor: The first common version that may be reached by following back through the predecessors of two versions of the same data item. Since all data items start as a single version, created by the **insert** operation, any two versions of the same data item must have a common ancestor.

Data item merge: An operation on two versions of the same data item resulting in a new data item version created by merging the operations applied to each version since their common ancestor. The resulting data item version has both data item versions as its predecessors. The semantics of the merge operation depends on the data store and the data item; some merges can be done automatically by the data store – when the operations applied to each version since their common ancestor commute – while others require program or even human intervention to resolve. Merges that cannot be resolved automatically are called merge conflicts. The merge operation itself must be commutative and the merge of a version with any of its ancestors or itself, results in the same version. That is, given two versions x and y of the same object with common ancestor z, then

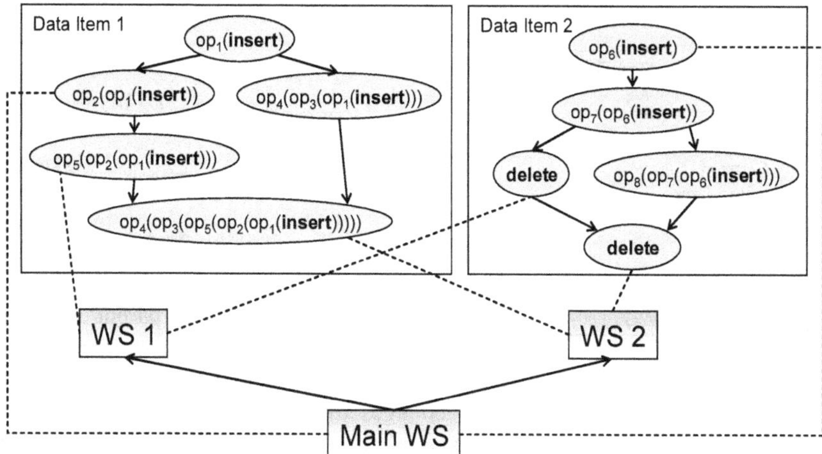

Fig. 1. Illustration of three workspaces and two data items. Each workspace contains a version of each data item. The versions of each data item form a directed graph rooted an initial insert operation. Two merge operations are also illustrated on the left showing how commutative operations are merged, and on the right, how a delete operation might take precedence

$$\mathbf{merge}(x,y) = \mathbf{merge}(y,x)$$
$$\mathbf{merge}(x, z) = x$$
$$\mathbf{merge}(y,z) = y$$

Versioned Data Store: A data store that holds versioned data items.

Workspace: A partial function from the set of data items to the corresponding data item versions. The range represents the data items that are available in the workspace. The range defines the values that are operated on by transactions executing in the context of this workspace. For example, above in Fig. 1, the domain of WS1 is the set consisting of data item 1 and data item 2 while the range is the data item version labeled "$op_5(op_2(op_1(\text{insert})))$" associated with data item 1 and the deleted value associated with data item 2.

Update: A set of operations to apply to a workspace atomically. More formally it is a partial function from the set of data items to a sequence of operations that is to be applied to that data item. An update is applied to a workspace by applying the operation sequences to the corresponding data item versions from that workspace, creating new successor versions, and updating the range of the workspace to include those new versions in place of the old versions. If an operation is an **insert**, then a new data item is added to the domain of the workspace. Data store consistency constraints should be checked in each workspace as operations are applied.

If W_i is the version of data item i inside workspace W and **domain**(W) is the set of data items which have versions in W, and U is the update whose value for data item i

is U_i, then the range of the workspace W' that results from applying the update U to W is

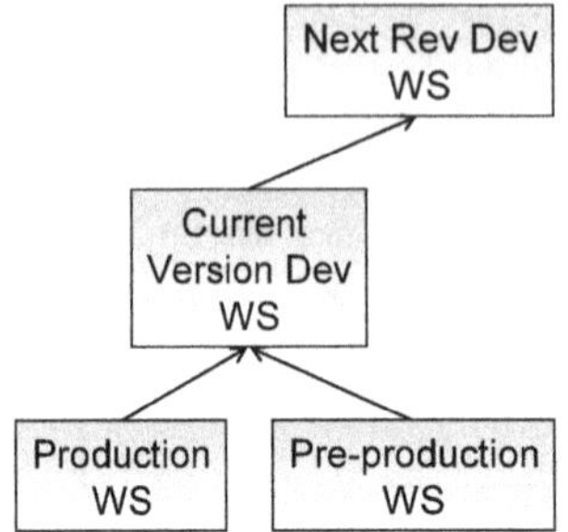

Fig. 2. Workspace Relationships.

$$\bigcup_{i \in \mathbf{domain}(W) \cap \mathbf{domain}(U)} U_i(W_i)$$
$$\cup \bigcup_{i \in \mathbf{domain}(U) - \mathbf{domain}(W)} U_i(\mathbf{insert})$$
$$\cup \bigcup_{i \in \mathbf{domain}(W) - \mathbf{domain}(U)} W_i$$

Workspace Branch: A child workspace created by making a copy of an existing parent workspace. Changes in the child or the parent workspace do not affect each other. This is used to create a context for making changes that are not seen by users of other workspaces. It can also be used to implement what some version management systems call a snapshot or a label. Workspaces are generally named to allow them to be more easily referenced by users.

Workspace Merge: The workspace that results from computing the union of the data item merges of the data item versions from one workspace with the corresponding data item versions from a second workspace and any data item versions from either workspace which do not have corresponding versions in the other. The range of the merge is of workspaces S and T is:

$$\bigcup_{i \in \mathbf{domain}(S) \cap \mathbf{domain}(T)} \mathbf{merge}(S_i, T_i)$$
$$\cup \bigcup_{i \in \mathbf{domain}(S) - \mathbf{domain}(T)} S_i$$
$$\cup \bigcup_{i \in \mathbf{domain}(T) - \mathbf{domain}(S)} T_i$$

The merged workspace typically replaces one of the original workspace when the merge is performed in the context of that workspace. The merged workspace should be verified to satisfy all of the data store's consistency constraints. A workspace merge replacing the parent workspace is typically used as the commit mechanism in a version based long running transaction system. Such a merge would be successful only if there were no conflicts in any of the individual item merges.

Check out: An exclusive lock held by a child workspace on a data item version inside of the parent workspace. A check out lock is acquired to preclude the introduction of any successor version of the version in the parent. The lock is typically released when the child merges into the parent workspace. To reduce the chance of merge conflicts on a change, one should acquire a check out lock for the affected objects in all the workspaces where merges are anticipated. Note that this does not preclude parallel activity when that activity is localized in a portion of the workspace tree unaffected by the check out lock.

Main Workspace: A distinguished primordial workspace that is the parent to all other workspaces. Note that the version of the data items in the main workspace is sometimes called the 'current' version of a data item.

In practice a more complex strategy with several distinguished workspaces is generally used. For example, an enterprise may maintain a production workspace being used by customers, a pre-production workspace getting final approval from management, a development workspace holding the latest integrated version of the current web site, and another development workspace with a partially integrated next release of the web site. This is illustrated in Fig. 2.

3 Workspace Versioning

Orthogonal versioning refers to the process of taking an existing data access API and turning it into a versioned data access API while supporting the original API and defining the default behaviour so that version unaware applications will still behave naturally. This was the approach that was taken when Microsoft Repository was upgraded from the version-less Version 1 to the version and workspace supporting Version 2 [3] and argued for independently in a manuscript by [19]. It was also a guiding principle used more recently in defining the semantics in the Oracle Workspace Manager [23].

We extend the notion of orthogonal versioning to say that versioning should not only be orthogonal to the applications, but should be orthogonal to the web service protocol being extended.

Rather than taking each web service protocol and independently extending it with its own notion of versioning; we use the notion of a coordinator from the WS-Coordination proposal and extend it to manage versioning and workspaces across all web services using a single extension. In the calling language, ideally, the workspace coordinator context is bound to the thread, allowing the workspace to be an implicit parameter to the web services' language level access API.

The advantages of this approach are:

1. Workspaces and undo can span many web services.
2. Having a single versioning approach for all web services reduces the conceptual load on the programmer.
3. A layered coordination protocol means that web service definitions do not need to change extensively when versioning is supported; they just have to refer to the WS-Workspace coordination protocol.

The first advantage is very important as in many applications a single user perceivable change is made up of many updates to many different web services. Just as traditional distributed transactions and WS-Transaction services allow for short lived transactions to extend beyond a single data store, so too long lived transactions and workspaces can be extended to span several data stores. These data sources might include relational databases, object layers on top of relational databases, Enterprise Resource Planning (ERP) systems, and content management systems. An example may include a workspace that contains both changes to a site's content, stored in a

Table 1. Version Aware Applications and Web Services.

	Version Aware Web Service	Unversioned Web Service
Version Aware Application	Application specifies workspace	Special code needed
Version Oblivious Application	Use distin-guished workspace	Use current state

content management system, and corresponding changes to a site's database to refer to that content. Having a workspace containing related changes in several data stores that can be merged into a production workspace in an atomic action is a new and powerful capability.

In addition to having version aware and version oblivious applications, an application may access versioned and unversioned web services. Consider all four cases illustrated in Table 1.

A version aware application using a version aware set of web services will specify the workspace to use and issue any needed branch and merge operations it needs. A version oblivious application using a version aware set of data stores will need to execute in the environment of some workspace, the obvious one being the workspace distinguished by the service or configured when the application is deployed. A more complex case is when a version aware application is using an unversioned data store. In this case the application is expecting certain semantics that the data store may not provide. This is analogous to a transactional program using a data store that does not provide transactions, e.g. a traditional file system. It can be done, but it has to be done carefully.

Extending an existing application for versioning can be quite simple. For example, an existing web application might store the logged in user in its session state. A versioned extension of that application might be configured to also store a workspace context in its session state. To minimally Workspace enable the application, only one new UI element may be required: A form to trigger the session's workspace to be merged into the main application workspace – a long running transaction commit.

4 Workspace Versioning Application Protocol

A sample application protocol for workspace versioning is described below. This protocol extends the coordination protocol similar to the way that the WS-Transaction extends the WS-Coordination protocol for the atomic transaction (AT) and business transaction (BT) protocols.

The operations defined below are the basics needed to meet the requirements of the web server applications that are the primary target of this effort. Many more entry

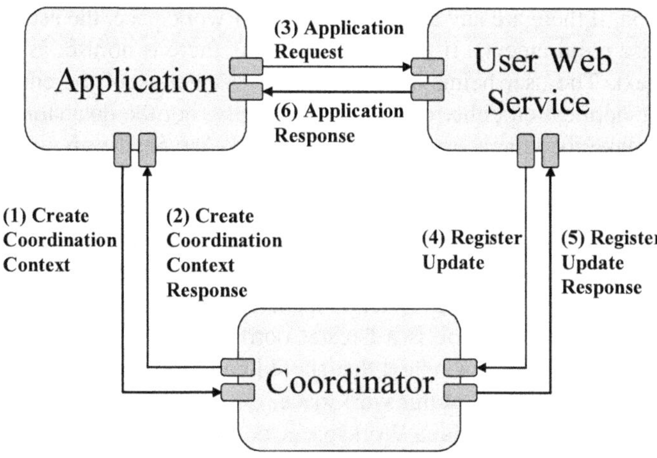

Fig. 3. Making an update to a Workspace through a Web Service

points could be defined for more complex environments, e.g. allowing data to automatically be updated between workspaces, automatic version check out options, merging between sibling workspaces, more flexible schemes for backing out committed operations, or creation of subsetted or time based workspaces. Note that the 'Application' in these illustrations may not be a web server application but may be any process capable of initiating web service calls.

The names of these operations and messages are relative to the base URL, for which we tentatively propose:

```
http://schemas.cs.ucc.ie/ws/2003/06/wsws
```

The coordination protocol provides for the creation and return of a CoordinationContext type, the propagation of that type on calls made to other services, and the registration of services by clients to receive notifications when certain user level operations are executed.

The following operations are operations of the Workspace Coordinator's Activation service. This port type is for use by applications to manipulate the workspace. The communication pattern is for making an update is illustrated in Fig. 3.

- CreateCoordinationContext Operation: When called to create a context with the wsws coordination type, it either creates a new workspace or looks up an old workspace depending on the arguments. The CreateCoordinationContext message includes the following elements:
  - WorkspaceName: The name of the workspace to be created or modified
  - ParentWorkspace: The optional name of the parent for the new workspace. If the WorkspaceName is new and this is not given, the new Workspace will be a child of the application default workspace.
  - User: The optional user name of the user performing the operation. This user is to be associated with any update made using this Context for auditing or undo.

In addition, if there are any access rules for this workspace, the user will have to meet those requirements. If the user is missing, there is no user associated with the context. The user being set here is a representation of the end user that is using the application either directly or indirectly, not the data store user that is used to make the connection to the data store. A typical web application runs using a single data store user per data store even while providing service to thousands of authenticated end users. The recipient of this operation may trust that its caller has already authenticated this user. Alternately the user name may be replaced with a signed delegation so that the coordinator knows that the end user has authorized the caller to act on its behalf.

The response to this operation is a CreateCoordinationContextResponse message that contains a CoordinationContext that should be sent passed on to all operations that are to act in the context of this workspace.

- Refresh Operation: Called with a WorkspaceCoordinationContext. Merges updates from the parent workspace into this workspace. Responds with a Refresh Response message which contains a ConflictList if there were any conflicts, that is, data items that were changed both in the parent and this workspace since the last successful Refresh. Data item versions that could not be merged are left unchanged in this workspace. While conflicts remain unresolved, the workspace may be in an invalid state and must not be published.
- GetConflicts Operation: Called with a WorkspaceCoordinationContext. Responds with the list of unresolved conflicts in this workspace, similar to that returned by Refresh Operation. Conflicts are created by the Refresh operation, above, and are resolved using the resolve operation below.
- Publish Operation: Called with a WorkspaceCoordinationContext. Merges this workspace into the parent workspace and returns a Publish Response message. If there are any conflicts, the operation fails making no updates to the parent workspace. If this happens, the client should perform the Refresh operation, resolve the conflicts, and then invoke Publish again.
- Undo Operation: Undoes the last update that was performed by this user in this workspace. If the user was not set as part of this WorkspaceCoordinationContext, it will undo the last update committed by any user in this workspace. If there were any subsequent incompatible changes to those objects, a ConflictList is returned as part of the response and the objects are left unchanged [24]. The undo operation never undoes an undo; it instead undoes the previous committed update. Use the Redo operation below, to undo an undo. Note that the changes instigated by the Undo and Redo must be committed before any other client can see them. This operation may also fail due to the data for the user's last operation being unavailable.
- Redo Operation: Undoes the effects of the last Undo operation done by this user in this workspace. Returns any conflicts caused by changes made to this workspace by other users that conflict with changes that the redo wants to perform. If there is any such conflicts, the Redo operation fails having made no changes. Note that undo and redo are most effective if they are done in a workspace that is private to a single user, as in that case no conflicts will ever arise.

A ConflictList object contains a list of data item Conflict elements. Each Conflict element contains a set of WorkspaceCoordinationContexts that when included with a web service request to read the given data item, allow all three versions of the conflicted object to be read, the parent version, the child version, and the ancestor version.

In addition the Conflict element provides a port reference to a service end point implementing the ConflictResolution port type. This port type provides an operation for marking the conflict as resolved.

- Resolve Operation: Marks this conflict as being resolved. This should normally be called after making any needed updates to the conflicted data item version in this Workspace.

5 Workspace Coordination Protocols

In addition to the application level protocols, additional port types are needed to allow the web services performing updates to communicate with the coordinator, to register their updates with the coordinator and to be called back in response to the high level application operations. A publish operation is illustrated in Fig. 4.

For this purpose we define the following port types. The Workspace Register port type supports the following operations:

- Register Update Operation: A specialization of the Coordinator Register Operation to allow an update made by a web service to be registered. The message includes a port reference to a port implementing the Update Manipulation port type. This information is used to implement the application level Undo and Redo operations. The Register Update message can contain arbitrary service specific elements that are also recorded, to identify the update and to make undo and redo of the update more efficient. The Register Update operation should either be made as part of an atomic transaction along with the actual update operation, or it should be done before the update and the implementation of the registered Undo Operation should be able to deal with the fact that the update may not actually have been performed.
- Register Data Store: A specialization of the Coordinator Register Operation to allow a data store used by a web service to be registered. The message includes a port reference to a port implementing the Data Store port type. The coordinator maintains stably the set of data stores used by the workspace so that they can be invoked to implement workspace level operations.

The Data Store protocol contains an operation for each of the Workspace wide application operations. In each case, these operations do the operation, but only on the subset of the data items residing on this data store.

- Refresh Operation: Merges updates from the parent workspace in this data store into this workspace. Returns a list of conflicts which the coordinator unions with the result of the Update operations on the other data sources.
- Get Conflicts Operation: Returns all conflicts in this workspace in this data store. The coordinator unions the result of this operation over all data stores registerd for the workspace.
- Publish Operation: Merges the changes made in this workspace onto its parent's workspace.

The Update Manipulation protocol has operations corresponding to the Undo operations and is used by the coordinator to perform user level undo operations. Note that the Register Undo operation

- Undo Operation: Undoes the indicated operation. Takes as an argument the Register Update operation that was used to log this event. If the Register Update and the actual update were not done as atomic transactions, then the implementation of this operation has to be ready
- Redo Operation: Redoes the indicated operation. Takes as an argument the Register Update operation that is to be redone. This operation can only be executed after an Undo Operation with the same argument has been executed in this workspace, or a workspace branched from it.

6 Relationships with the WS-Transaction Protocols

The WS-Transaction protocol [7] provides two sets of protocols, a tightly coupled protocol for atomic transactions and a less tightly coupled protocol for coordinating business activities. The workspace protocol proposed here lies halfway between these two protocols, matching the tightly structured format of the atomic transaction

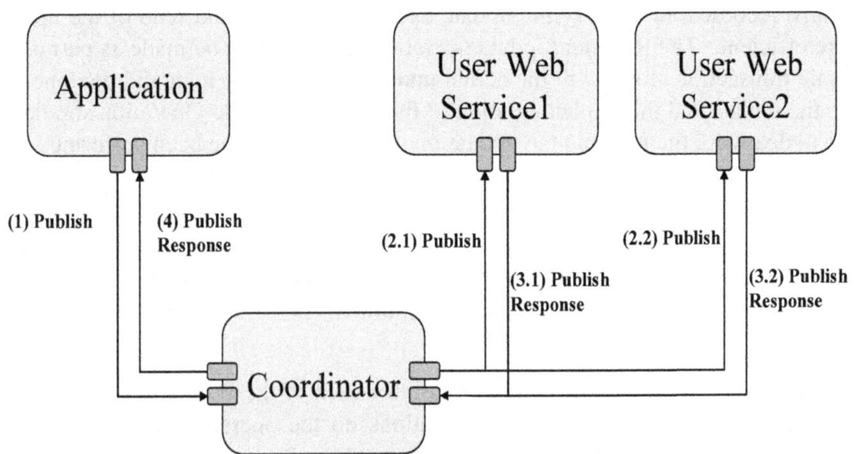

Fig. 4. Performing a publish operation

protocols, but supporting the long running, lock-free activities of the business activity protocol.

The three protocols solve different problems and are complementary. For example, one could layer the workspace protocols on top of the atomic transaction protocol. Each atomic transaction could then be used to bracket a set of changes, perhaps from different data stores, that make up a workspace update. This allows the scope of an update to be defined by the application rather than by each web service. This allows the notion of an update and thus of undo to be defined in an application specific, rather that service specific, way.

Similarly the business activity approach can be used to specify the required workflow to be used in publishing a set of changes made in a workspace, or to specify a compensation to be performed when undoing an update in a particular workspace that refers to data that is stored in an unversioned data store.

For certain data, architects will have to decide whether to model a particular user action as a compensateable update in the primary workspace, or as a regular change in a secondary workspace. The decision will typically hinge on visibility. The update in the secondary workspace will be effectively hidden, while the update in the primary workspace will be seen by all, even though it may later be undone by a business-process compensation.

Consider putting together an academic department's schedule of classes for next year. For some time the users might consider themselves to be in authoring mode and would be happy for there to be no actual rooms or instructors assigned to schedule. However at some point, the users want to start collecting real rooms and get approval for hiring additional instructors. By that point the itinerary would need to be published to a primary workspace shared by all of the departments and by the facilities department, which is responsible for assigning classrooms, and the finance department, which is responsible for approving budgets. Of course the academic department may continue to make changes to the schedule even after it has had classrooms assigned and job requisitions approved. In this case, the changes may invalidate the work done by the other department and may need to trigger business process actions, automated or otherwise, to reassign the resources.

7 Management Protocols

In addition to the protocols needed to implement the application level functionality, versioning systems have need of management protocols to support:

- Version browsing: Viewing the version tree of a particular data item.
- Auditing: Finding all the updates performed by a given user or in a specific time period.
- Workspace Access Control: In addition to having access control on individual data items, there can be access control on workspaces. Sometimes the access control on a workspace may override the access control on an individual data item. For example, a marketing researcher may not have write permission into the discount rules in the production workspace, but the researcher may have write permission

into these rules in a development workspace. Often a workspace may be locked so that no one can make any changes so that a particular snapshot of the environment may be saved

- Workspace browsing: Browsing and pruning workspaces. Unused workspaces can tie up lots of storage unnecessarily.
- Cache rule manipulation: Infrequently accessed data item versions may be represented by deltas from some base versions, so fast access means that these versions need to be cached.

8 Future Work

The author is evaluating this protocol and interfacing it with data stores that already implement workspace versioning. The implementation of the coordination protocol is similar to that of a transaction manager in its integration with the data stores. Versioned data stores that support the workspace model include Oracle's relational Workspace Manager [23], Microsoft's Repository object store [2, 3], and IBM's Clearcase file store [25], as well as various research efforts [19, 27].

While undoubtedly there will be many issues that will arise during the implementation of the system, the most interesting question to be answered is the usefulness of the distributed workspace model to application programmers. Just as the proof of a pudding is in the eating, the proof of a new data model is in the using. For this reason we will also be building several significant applications where the authoring, collaboration and data manipulation component are important. Applications and scenarios we are considering include:

- Catalogue and business rules maintenance in an e-commerce system. This example is examined in more detail in [28]. It involves a team building the autumn catalogue for an e-commerce system: inserting new content in the content management system, new products in the product database, new business rules in the rule system, and new accounts in the ERP system. The catalogue is constructed in a set of private workspaces and then merged into the main workspace on the 'go live' date.
- Work-flow maintenance. In this example, we devise a simple data driven system for routing and approving insurance claims. We then postulate that a revised claim processing workflow is to be implemented, tested and deployed. This change in policy is implemented by a member of the IT staff who tests it on a set of fake claims. The claims processing manager, after seeing who the new system in a mock up environment, agrees to try use it for all new claims initiated in the Seattle office, while existing claims and claims initiated in other offices continue to use the old policy. Eventually, after some tweaking and an ill advised change made to the Seattle test environment and then undone, the new workflow is released to the whole company.

Since this paper was written, the WS-CAF [4, 5] protocols have been introduced to complete with the WS-Coordination protocol discussed here. It appears that this work is largely independent of the underlying coordination framework and that WS-Workspace can be built on top of either framework.

9 Conclusion

As web services evolve to handle more complex problems, they will also need to support the authoring of more complex data. This will drive user requests for web services that can support full featured authoring environments for their data including features like

- Undo
- Batch Publishing
- Collaboration
- Auditing and Change Tracking

While it is possible for each web service to implement these notions in its own separate way, a coordination protocol allows the same approach to be used for all versioned web services and allows for workspaces and updates to span many different web services and their associated data stores.

We have introduced a coordination protocol that allows a simple way of manipulating workspaces and an application protocol that allows web services to allow their callers to control their workspace environment. The WS-Workspace protocol takes the lessons learned from configuration management in CASE and CAD products and makes it available to business applications by allowing the integration of disparate web services into a uniform workspace model.

References

1. BEA Tuxedo ATMI, http://e-docs.bea.com/tuxedo/tux80/interm/atmi.htm
2. Bergstraesser, T., P.A. Bernstein, S. Pal, D. Shutt, "Versions and Workspaces in Microsoft Repository," Proc. SIGMOD 99, pp. 532–533.
3. Bernstein, P.A., T. Bergstraesser, J. Carlson, S. Pal, P. Sanders, D. Shutt, "Microsoft Repository Version 2 and the Open Information Model," Information Systems 24(2), 1999, pp. 71–98.
4. Bunting, Doug, et al., Web Services Composite Application Framework (WS-CAF). July 2003. http://developers.sun.com/techtopics/webservices/wscaf/primer.pdf
5. Bunting, Doug, et al., Web Services Transaction Management (WS-TXM). July 2003. http://developers.sun.com/techtopics/webservices/wscaf/wstxm.pdf
6. Cabrera, Felipe, et al., Web Services Coordination (WS-Coordination). August 2002. http://www.ibm.com/developerworks/library/ws-coor
7. Cabrera, Felipe, et al., Web Services Transaction (WS-Transaction). Aug 2002. http://www.ibm.com/developerworks/library/ws-transpec/
8. Cellary, W., and J. Rykowski, "Multiversion Databases - Support for Software Engineering." Proc. of the 2nd World Conference on Integrated Design and Process Technology, pp. 415–420, Austin, Texas, 1996
9. Cheung, Susan, and Vlada Matena, Java Transaction API (JTA), Version 1.0.1, Sun Microsystems Inc., April 1999
10. Chou, Hong-Tai, Won Kim. "A Unifying Framework for Version Control in a CAD Environment." VLDB 1986: 336–344

11. Clamm, G., J. Amsden, T. Ellison, C. Kaler, J. Whitehad, Versioning Extensions to WebDAV (Web Distributed Authoring and Versioning). March 2002. RFC 3253. http://www.ietf.org/rfc/rfc3253.txt
12. Dart, Susan, Spectrum of Functionality in Configuration Management Systems, CMU/SEI-90-TR11.
13. Diaz, Angel Luis, Peter Fischer, Carsten Leue, Thomas Schaeck, Web Services for Remote Portals (WSRP). http://www.ibm.com/developerworks/library/ws-wsrp/
14. Goland, Y., J. Whitehead, A. Faizi, S. Carter, D. Jenson, HTTP Extensions for Distributed Authoring – WEBDAV, RFC 2518. February 1999. http://www.ietf.org/rfc/rfc2518.txt
15. Interwoven Inc., TeamSite 5.5, http://www.interwoven.com
16. Jomier, G., W. Cellary, The Database Version Approach, Networking and Information Systems Journal, Hermes Science Publishing 2000, Vol. 3, pp. 177–214, January 2000
17. Katz, R.H. "Toward a Unified Framework for Version Modeling in Engineering Databases," ACM Computing Surveys 22, 4 (Dec. '90).
18. Klahold, Peter, Gunter Schlageter and Wolfgang Wilkes, A General Model for Version Management in Databases, VLDB'86 Twelfth International Conference on Very Large Data Bases, August 25-28, 1986, Kyoto, Japan
19. Marquez, A., Orthogonal Object Versioning in an ODMG compliant Persistent Java, Department of Computer Science, Australian National University, http://www.cs.adelaide.edu.au/~idea/idea7/PDFs/marquez.pdf
20. Microsoft Corporation, Microsoft Mappoint WebService. http://www.microsoft.com/mappoint/net/
21. Microsoft Corporation, Microsoft Transaction Server. http://www.microsoft.com/com/tech/MTS.asp
22. The Open Group, Distributed TP: The XA Specification, C193 UK ISBN 1-872630-24-3, February 1992
23. Oracle Corp. Oracle Workspace Manager, http://technet.oracle.com/products/workspace_mgr/content.html
24. Prakash, A. and Knister, M.J., "A Framework for Undoing Actions in Collaborative Systems," ACM Trans. on Computer-Human Interaction, Vol. 1, No. 4, pp. 295–330, Dec. 1994.
25. Rational Software. Rational Clearcase. http://www.rational.com/products/clearcase
26. Sciore, E., "Versioning and Configuration Management in an Object-Oriented Data Model," VLDB Journal 3, 1994, pp. 77–106
27. Soules, Craig A.N.. Garth R. Goodson, John D. Strunk, Gregory R. Ganger. Metadata Efficiency in a Comprehensive Versioning File System, May 2002 CMU-CS-02-145 School of Computer Science Carnegie Mellon University
28. Swart, Garret, Collaboration and Undo: The Web Workspace Paradigm, Fourth International Conference on Web Information Systems Engineering, 2003.
29. Vignette Inc., Vignette V7, http://www.vignette.com
30. WikiWeb, Web Based Collaboration Tools. http://www.wikiweb.com/

Secure Service Provision in Ad Hoc Networks

Radu Handorean and Gruia-Catalin Roman

Department of Computer Science and Engineering
Washington University in St. Louis
Campus Box 1045, One Brookings Drive
St. Louis, MO 63130-4899, USA
{radu.handorean, roman}@wustl.edu

Abstract. Ad hoc networks are formed opportunistically as mobile devices come within wireless communication range of each other. Since individual devices are typically subject to severe resource limitations, it is both possible and desirable for a device to enhance its functionality by taking advantage (in a cooperative manner) of capabilities available on other devices. Service provision refers to the process by which devices advertise their willingness to offer specific services and discover other services. This paper describes a service provision model designed specifically for use in ad hoc settings. Security policies governing service accessibility can be specified at the application level while secure communication among devices is ensured by the implementation.

1 Introduction

Advances in portable computing and wireless technology are opening up exciting possibilities for the future of mobile networking. The opportunity for applications to exploit an ever-increasing range of resources is expanding rapidly. Any application or device can advertise and provide services, turning the network into a global service repository. As portable devices become cheaper and more powerful, their number is expected to grow significantly in the coming years. At the same time, the ability to offer highly specialized capabilities by means of devices directly connected to the network turns such devices into service providers. In such an environment the interest in and reliance upon particular services changes over time. In part, this is because devices having limited capabilities exhibit a growing dependence on services provided by others. Expressive and dependable means are required to support service discovery. Such environments demand the ability to obtain support for the task at hand only when needed.

Traditionally, a host sought help from another by means of client-server interactions. It is customary to assume that the client knows the address of the server that supports the service it needs, has the code necessary to access the server, and knows the communication protocol the server expects. While this type of interaction between remote components still dominates distributed computing, new strategies have emerged to allow servers to advertise services, and clients to lookup and access them without explicit knowledge of the network structure and

M.E. Orlowska et al. (Eds.): ICSOC 2003, LNCS 2910, pp. 367–383, 2003.

communication details. These discovery-based techniques are growing in importance, as services become ubiquitous. The high level of abstraction characterizing these techniques frees the client from handling the communication protocol.

To accomplish this, services may be discovered at runtime and may be accessed through customized proxies. A proxy abstracts away the network from the client by offering a high-level interface specialized for service exploitation while hiding the proxy's interface to the server. Services are advertised by publishing a profile containing attributes and capabilities useful when searching for a service and for proper service invocation. Clients search for services using templates generated according to their momentary needs. These templates must be matched by the advertised profiles. Services use a service registry to advertise their availability and clients use the same registry to search for services they need. This approach offers an unprecedented degree of run-time flexibility.

Mobile ad hoc networks are opportunistically formed structures that change in response to the movement of physically mobile hosts running potentially mobile code. New wireless technologies allow devices to freely join and leave networks, form communities, and exchange data and services at will, without the need for any infrastructure setup and system administration.

A major challenge in ad hoc networking is frequent disconnection among hosts which often leads to data inconsistency in centralized service registries. Since this may affect the structure of the network and the availability of services, this paper seeks to provide service registries that guarantee the consistency of their content, i.e., information about the service availability is updated atomically with respect to configuration changes.

Architectures based on centralized lookup directories are no longer suitable. Mobile ad hoc computing cannot rely on any fixed infrastructure. The interactions among devices are peer-to-peer and entail no external infrastructure support. Since nodes are mobile, the network topology may change rapidly and unpredictably over time. The network is decentralized and all activities, including topology discovery and message delivery must be carried out by the nodes themselves. The network structure at any moment depends on the available direct connectivity between mobile devices (unless ad hoc routing is used, i.e., nodes route packets among nodes that cannot reach each other directly).

As flexibility and ease of access to resources increases, so do the possibilities to tamper with various parts of a distributed application. This represents yet another major challenge to service provision in ad hoc settings. In open systems, where the network access is not controlled at the physical level, there is a special need for security mechanisms that facilitate safe interactions among remote components of a distributed application and guarantee the identity of processes that offer or use resources over the network. The advertisement of a service must be protected from unauthorized removal, replacement, or use.

The goal of this paper is to extend the applicability of these kinds of techniques to ad hoc mobility. The reminder of the paper is organized as follows. Section 2 introduces the service model, security mechanisms, and the challenges of the ad hoc networking environment. Section 3 presents our model for secure service provision. Section 4 describes the implementation of the model. Section 5 presents a test application developed using our model. Section 6 discusses related work. Section 7 concludes the paper.

2 Secure Service Provision

The service model is composed of three components: services, clients and a discovery technology. Services provide functionality to clients. Clients use services. The registration feature enables services to publish their capabilities and clients to find and use needed services. As a result of a successful lookup, a client may receive a piece of code that actually implements the service or facilitates the communication to the server offering the service. Part of the quality of a service being offered by a server is the security guarantees the server offers to potential clients. Among them is the guarantee that the service cannot be faked by an intruder and that the usage of the service is safe for the client (e.g., it does not reveal personal information about the client to the external world).

In a stationary setting, where all hosts access a wired (and therefore reliable) network, a server can be set up to run the service repository. All service providers can advertise their offers on this server and clients can connect to this server to search for the services they need. Security issues are easy to deal with since the applications can rely on central databases containing information about users, passwords, credentials and capabilities. Trust management in a distributed system operating in a stationary setting is easier when applications can always rely on the presence of a (server) service ready to authenticate offers and requests.

In the ad hoc network case, both the discovery techniques and security considerations face new challenges. A simple transition of old software to new settings does not suffice. Service discovery protocols that rely on centralized service registries are prone to malfunctions, as described in Figure 1a: if the node hosting the service registry suddenly becomes unavailable, the entire advertising and lookup of services becomes paralyzed even if the nodes representing a service and a potential client remain connected. The goal is to make these two nodes communicate in a peer to peer fashion. Furthermore, because of frequent disconnections, the service registry should reflect changes affecting service availability in a timely fashion. Services that are no longer reachable should not be available for discovery. In Figure 1b we present a scenario that can happen in Jini [1,2], where the advertisement of a service is still available in the lookup table until its lease expires, even though the provider of the service is no longer reachable.

From the security point of view, in the ad hoc network case, when two devices come in contact, identifying the other party is not as easy as asking a trusted third party to verify the other's identity. While an authentication server may be available from time to time, the design of the applications cannot rely on this for their proper functioning. There is no guarantee that an authentication service is available at a given point in time or that it will become available any time soon. The two nodes will need to take steps to protect themselves. This leads to special safety measures that have to be taken both by clients and servers to ensure proper secure interaction in the ad hoc setting.

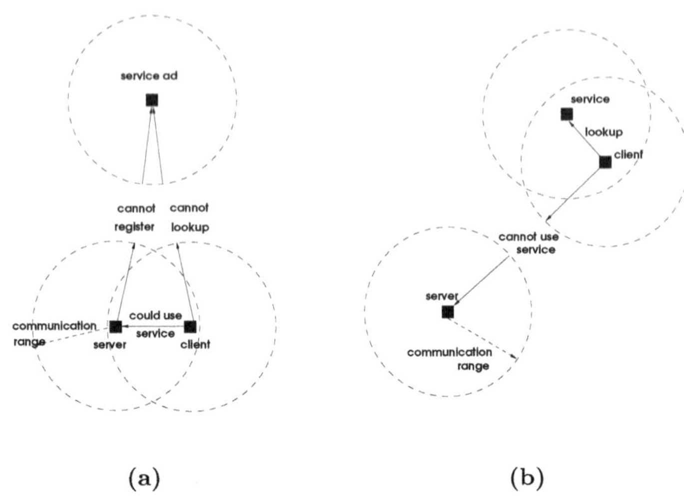

Fig. 1. Ad hoc environment challenges. **(a)** The client could use the service but cannot discover it. **(b)** The client discovers a service that is no longer reachable.

A new design solution is needed, one suited specifically for ad hoc networks. In a model addressing these issues, all nodes should be simple users or providers of services. The system should not depend on the behavior of a single node for service discovery or secure interactions. The new challenge is to permit users and programs to be as effective as possible in this environment of uncertain connectivity, without changing their manner of operation (i.e., by preserving the semantics of interaction) while still offering security guarantees. The advertising and lookup of services in this setting need a lightweight model that supports direct communication and offers a higher degree of decoupling. A consistent, distributed, and simple implementation of the service registry is the key to the solution, along with a simple approach to trust management. Security enforcement is needed to protect the easily accessible service registries from tampering or unauthorized usage and the new model should address this issue to the maximum extent possible under the additional constraints imposed by ad hoc networking.

3 Secure Service Provision in Ad Hoc Settings

The new model, inspired by the service provision ideas described above, seeks to address challenges raised by the ad hoc environment while offering a reasonable level of security. Active entities are logically separated into service providers (servers) and service users (clients). Both clients and servers may be mobile agents able to migrate among reachable hosts. Hosts themselves are physically mobile and form ad hoc networks as connections are established and break down.

A service is the functionality offered by a program or a hardware device to other programs or hardware devices that need it at run time. In our model, the interface to the service is provided by a software object (proxy), that can be transferred over a network to the user of the service. The proxy will represent the service locally to the client. This distinguishes the approach from techniques where a client is expected to know a priori how to contact a specific server (i.e., its IP address and port number) and was expected also to handle all the communication details (i.e., the client was responsible for managing the communication protocol used by each server). The communication details between the proxy and the implementation of the service (i.e., the protocol being used, the handling of disconnections while work is in progress) are outside the client's area of concern. In some cases, the proxy can implement the entire service itself.

This approach is similar to Jini [1,2], which uses proxy objects and the RMI protocol to hide the communication details from the user of the service, and UPnP [3], which uses the SOAP [4] protocol to access objects remotely (the implementation of the service which runs on a different host). Models that do not aim to hide these details from the user of a service include SLP [5] and Bluetooth's SDP (Service Discovery Protocol) [6].

A service provider is any host that offers services over the network. Such a server registers (advertises) a service by publishing a profile that contains the capabilities of the service and attributes describing these capabilities, so as to allow clients to discover and use the services properly. Along with the profile, the server provides the service proxy. The server has the possibility to deregister a service previously advertised. This does not necessarily involve the termination of the service. Clients that are in process of using the service may be allowed to terminate their jobs in progress, depending on the implementation of the service.

A client searches for services using a template that defines what the needed service should do. The template contains attributes to request a certain level of quality. If a service profile satisfying all client's requirements is available (i.e., the advertised profile of the service is a superset of the client's template and the attributes advertised by the server meet the client's criteria), the service proxy, which is part of the service's profile, is returned to the client. This proxy handles the communication with the server offering the service. Location information can be considered a special attribute of the service's advertisement (if specified by server) but it is not required in order to discover the service requested by the client, i.e., the client does not *need* to know where the implementation of a service is running in order to discover the service, but can use the information as part of the quality of service evaluation. This information can map to a physical location (e.g., for a printer it is more important where it is physically located than what IP address it has) or to a logical location (e.g., for encryption services the client *may* care if the server is within its domain).

The registration, deregistration, and lookup processes take place in service registries. Service registries are identified by name. They are local to each agent (client or server) and are shared among agents that created service registries with the same name when the hosts they are running on are connected or when they run on the same host. Service registries shared by different agents under the same name form a single, federated service registry. After sharing its local service registry, each agent accesses the federated service registry as if it were local. The transient sharing of the service registries makes the update of their content transparent to disconnection and always consistent with respect to connectivity (Figure 2). Service availability is always consistent with advertisement availability and is based on (possibly multi-hop) connectivity among hosts.

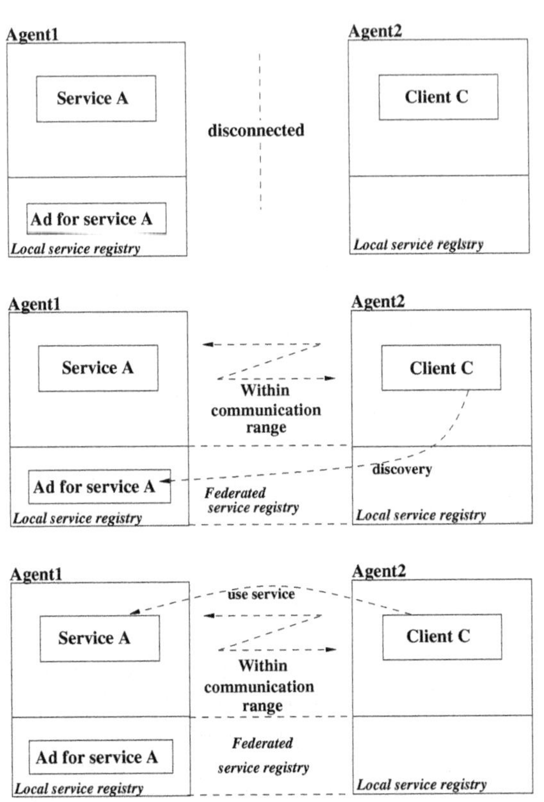

Fig. 2. Federated service registry access.

The model supports multiple servers (each server can offer multiple services), multiple clients, and multiple service registries. Clients and servers can interact via a service registry if they both have a local service registry with the same name. The model supports code and host mobility. This means that hosts can move in physical space and clients and servers can represent mobile code able to migrate anywhere in the network. Upon migration of a client or server the local service registries will migrate with them and will be re-shared from the new location. The availability of services is consistently taken care of by the nature of the service registries. Any connection and disconnection is atomically reflected in the visible content of the federated service registry. While the migration is in progress, the migrating agent is temporarily unavailable to the community. Once at destination, the agent restarts execution. Migration may not always be possible (e.g., if the service needs a piece of hardware on the host where it is currently running), may be restricted to a subset of the connected hosts (those that have the hardware needed by a service), or may not be restricted at all. A client's migration may be restricted by the type of services it is using at the moment of migration. Those services may support resuming service utilization at the new location or may require the service to be restarted. The programmer of a service has to take all these details into consideration. The designer of the proxy-server communication protocol may have to take into account possible disconnections (due to physical movement, logical migration, or communication failures).

The system provides a default public service registry, that can be used to advertise and lookup general services. Any server can create a new service registry. Any service registry, except for the default, can be password protected. The password is used to encrypt the clear name so that it won't be accessible except to those who can generate the same encrypted name from the correct clear name and the correct password. If a password is associated with a service registry, that password will secure all the transfers between remote hosts, associated with that service registry (i.e., any message carrying a query or the result of a query will be encrypted with the password that protects the registry involving that query). The use of different names and passwords enables creation of multiple (protected and/or unprotected) administrative domains where servers can publish services and clients can look them up, grouped by common interest or access rights. The same applies to clients, i.e., the clients also create a service registry locally for search purposes; a search operation will span all service registries with the same name, local to servers within communication range.

This default registry can be used by agents to advertise or verify the existence of a particular service registry. For example, all sorting services can be grouped in a public registry called "Sorting Services". Each agent looking for a painting service can look in the default, public registry and see if there's any note of a registry grouping painting services. Similarly a server trying to advertise a service will check for the note in the public registry. If such a pointer is found, the server can go use the same registry. If the pointer is not there, the server can assume it is the first one to offer such a service and create the note itself.

Given the variety of data present in a repository and the multitude of users accessing it at any moment, often, the protection has to be extended to a finer grained level than the entire registry. The ad for a service can be marked read-only by its provider protecting it with a remove-password. This will prevent unauthorized (accidental or fraudulent) removal of the service ad as well as the replacement of the ad with a fake one. Additionally, each ad can be protected by a read-password, different from the password that protects the entire registry. This will enable a service provider to protect services its in a highly individualized manner.

The transient sharing of service repositories supported by the system eliminates single points of failure scenarios. By simply disconnecting from a party (e.g., a conference room printer), the stability of a system (e.g., a PDA) is not affected and interactions with other devices continue to function normally (e.g., PDAs from the same conference room having a wider communication range than the printer). Services are discovered solely on the basis of connectivity among devices (producers and consumers).

4 Implementation

The implementation of the new model is based on LIME [7], an adaptation of the Linda [8] coordination model to the ad hoc networking setting. LIME's transient tuple space sharing together with the security features newly added to the original model provide a natural starting point for our implementation. LIME's implementation does not depend of whether ad hoc routing is used or not, only the notion of host connectivity is affected. The model we described works in the same way whether ad hoc routing is used or not.

4.1 Implementation Infrastructure: LIME

The LIME middleware supports the development of applications exhibiting physical mobility of hosts and logical mobility of agents. An agent is the basic building block for the mobile application, a software component that may reside permanently on a host or may move from one host to another connected host, hence the name *agent.* Hosts serve as containers for agents and run local versions of LIME. As suggested earlier, LIME extends the coordination model of Linda in significant ways. First, the globally accessed persistent tuple space of Linda is replaced in LIME by transient sharing of identically named tuple spaces belonging to agents that are part of the same group, i.e., reside on hosts that are mutually accessible over the ad hoc network. Other LIME extensions to Linda include location specific operations, transparent tuple migration, and the ability to react to the presence of tuples in tuple spaces.

Transparent Context Maintenance. The model underlying LIME accomplishes the shift from a fixed global context to a dynamically changing one by distributing the single Linda tuple space across multiple tuple spaces, each local to an agent, and by introducing rules for transient sharing of the individual tuple spaces based on naming and connectivity; LIME allows an agent to structure its holdings across multiple tuple spaces each being shared only with other identically named tuple spaces local to other agents within the group. Group membership is controlled by connectivity among hosts. Sharing of multiple tuple spaces results in the formation of a virtual global data structure called a federated tuple space. The content of a federated tuple space is the union of the contents of the contributing tuple spaces. Access to the federated tuple space is accomplished by simply accessing the API for the local tuple space.

Basic access to the tuple space takes place using traditional Linda primitives: **out** takes a tuple t and places it into a tuple space; **in** takes as parameter a template p and blocks until a tuple matching the template is written to the tuple space at which point **in** removes the tuple and returns its contents; **rd** is similar to **in** but does not remove the tuple. Details of the matching mechanism will be explained later. LIME offers also non-blocking versions of **in** and **rd** in the form of probe variants of the same operations (e.g., **inp**, **rdp**). In general, non-blocking operations return a matching tuple (if one is available) and null otherwise. Both blocking and non-blocking extensions designed to handle entire groups of tuples matching the same template are also included in LIME.

A tuple is an ordered list of fields. Each field has a type and a value. A template is an ordered list of fields that can contain type designators (*formals*) or explicit values (*actual*). A tuple and a template match if both contain the same number of fields and each corresponding pair of fields matches. Initially, two field-level matching policies were available (1) Exact type matching: the field in the template is a formal and its type is the same as the type of the object in the corresponding tuple field and (2) exact value matching, the template field provides an actual that will match exactly the type and the value of the corresponding field in the tuple. We've added a third one: (3) polymorphic matching: the field in the template can be a formal whose type is a supertype of the corresponding object in the tuple. This yields the highest degree of flexibility, since the Java Object class (or the Java Serializable interface for objects that travel across the network) works as a wildcard. We also added the possibility for a tuple to specify what type of matching must be used for each field (e.g., a tuple may require the template to provide the exact value for the first field).

Controlling Context Awareness. A read-only tuple space called the `LimeSystemTupleSpace` provides an agent with a view of the overall system configuration. Its tuples contain information about the mobile agents present in the community, physical hosts they execute on, and tuple spaces created for coordination. Standard tuple space operations on `LimeSystemTupleSpace` allow an agent to respond to the arrival and departure of other agents and hosts. Furthermore, LIME provides fine-grained control over the context on which an agent chooses to operate by extending its operations with tuple location parameters that define projections of the federated tuple space.

Reacting to Changes in Context. LIME extends the basic Linda tuple space with the notion of *reaction*. A reaction $\mathcal{R}(s, p)$ is defined by a code fragment s that specifies the actions to be executed when a tuple matching the template p is found in the tuple space. Blocking operations are not allowed in s, as they could prevent the program from ever terminating.

In LIME, reactions come in two forms: *strong reactions* and *weak reactions*. Strong reactions execute atomically with the writing of the tuple that enables them. They must be restricted to a host or agent because the requirements of atomicity would entail a distributed transaction encompassing multiple hosts for every tuple space operation. LIME also provides the notion of *weak reaction*. The difference is that the execution of s does not happen atomically with the detection of a tuple matching p, but it is guaranteed to take place eventually (if connectivity is preserved). This eliminates the need for a distributed transaction and allows this type of reaction to execute over the federated tuple space.

4.2 Security Support Implementation

The security extensions we had to introduce to Lime in order to support secure service provision and other secure interactions were designed so as to have minimal impact over the programming interface offered to the developer. The extensions take password(s) as extra parameter(s) in calls that handle protected targets (i.e., tuples and tuple spaces). Secure inter-host communication is automatically turned on by the usage of secure tuple spaces, therefore it has no impact on the programmer interface.

For encryption we use the 3DES private key encryption algorithm (the keys are generated internally in a deterministic fashion from the provided passwords). The data being encrypted represents messages passed between hosts and not data that has to be stored safely. We assume that Java language protection mechanisms are robust enough (e.g., a *private* member of an object cannot be accessed by any other object). We do not address physical level attacks like wireless signal jamming. The architecture overview is shown in Figure 3.

Password Protected Tuple Spaces. The name of the tuple space is the key to gaining access to the information in that tuple space. To protect the information means to protect the name of the tuple space. Changes are required to ensure that extracting the name of a protected tuple space from `LimeSystemTupleSpace` will no longer provide enough information for an agent to create a tuple space with the same name and share it with other agents thus gaining unauthorized access to information.

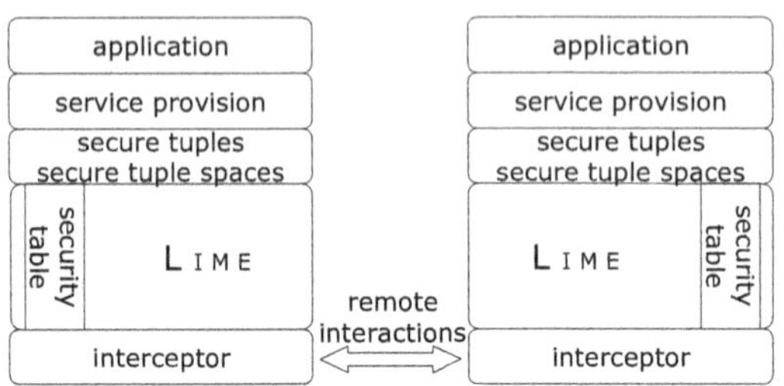

Fig. 3. Architecture overview.

The tuple space name (clear or encrypted) will be prefixed by a differentiator: letter "U" for unencrypted or "S" for secure tuple space. The tuple space called "blue" is different from the tuple space called "blue" and protected with password "pwd" (the latter will actually have the internal name $K_{pwd}(blue)$). They can coexist but no sharing takes place. The prefixes ensure that a tuple space cannot be created incorrectly. Since they are internally added, they cannot be manipulated by agents. This will prevent an attacker from successfully creating a protected tuple space after inspecting the content of `LimeSystemTupleSpace`.

The constructor call (Figure 4) is the only place where the agent explicitly uses the password. Once the agent has the handle to the tuple space, it does not need the password anymore. A tuple space operation can only be called by the LIME agent that created it. Even if the handle of a tuple space is obtained correctly by an agent, it cannot be transferred and used by another agent. Thus, a tuple space password is not needed for tuple space access operations.

The encrypted name of a protected tuple space and the password that protects it are also important for inter-host communication. This is why the redesigned LIME server has a **SecurityTable** that stores entries of the form [encrypted name, password]. This **SecurityTable** is a very important target that has to be protected. Since this paper does not address the Java security model, we assume this model is secure enough for our research.

SecureLimeTupleSpace(java.lang.String name, java.lang.String password)
— creates a new secure tuple space using the public tuple space name and the password. This call places an entry in the **SecurityTable** mapping the encrypted name to the password.

Fig. 4. The call that creates a secure tuple space.

Tuple Level Protection. To implement password-protected tuples, every tuple space operation will add to the end of the user specified fields (if any) three fields: the read-password, the remove-password and the name of the operation that uses that tuple or template (e.g., "rd" for any type of read operation or reaction, "in" for any type of remove operation—these two apply to templates—and "out" for any type of write operation—this will differentiate the tuple from templates, since they both are instances of the same Tuple class). The fields containing passwords are subject to the exact value matching policy. These fields are not explicitly available to the programmer for direct manipulation but are used by methods calls used to manipulate tuples.

The tuple content is not encrypted. The access control is realized by filtering tuples based on the three security fields. The filtering happens during the matching process between the template used by an operation that tries to access a tuple in the tuple space and the tuple(s) already in the tuple space. It is important to note that the matching of the three fields added to the end of the tuples/templates is slightly altered to accommodate common sense scenarios like: the tuple has both a read-password and a remove-password and the template provided by a read operation has the remove-password and not the read-password. We consider normal for this operation to succeed because if someone has the password to remove a tuple, he/she should also be able to read the tuple (note that removing a tuple returns the tuple to the process and doesn't just erase it from the tuple space, therefore this will not produce a security breach). Another example is the case when a tuple has a read-password but no remove-password. A remove kind of tuple space operation will need to provide the tuple's read-password as the template's remove-password for the operation to succeed. The reason is that if the user needs a password only to read the tuple, he/she will need a password to remove the tuple and therefore the read-password will protect the tuple from removal. If the tuple has a different, non-null remove-password, the mechanism described above does not work anymore.

lts.out(ITuple tuple, char[] readPwd, char[] removePwd)
— writes a tuple to the tuple space and protects it against reading and/or removing. Any combination of the two passwords is permitted.

lts.rd(ITuple template, char[] readPwd)
— reads a tuple from the tuple space if the tuple and the template match (and the correct password is provided).

lts.in(ITuple template, char[] removePwd)
— removes a tuple from the tuple space if the tuple and the template match (and the correct password is provided).

Fig. 5. The tuple space interaction operations.

Communication Level Protection. When an agent executes an operation that extends beyond the current host, an interceptor catches it, analyzes the tuple space that the message refers to (the name of the tuple space is always present in the message that travels across hosts) and takes the appropriate action. The use of the interceptor pattern [9] is natural for this case, when we add security to a system that in its initial design did not address this issue. It also offers great flexibility with respect to the choice of encryption protocol.

The interceptor checks whether the tuple space name in the outgoing message is in the `SecurityTable`. If the message refers to an unprotected tuple space, the interceptor lets it pass through unchanged. If the tuple space is a secure one, the interceptor will extract from the table the password that corresponds to that tuple space and will use it to encrypt the message. The interceptor creates a packet that contains the encrypted message and the encrypted name of the tuple space the message refers to and forwards this packet to the destinations. On the recipient's side, actions happen symmetrically. The returned results are handled similarly.

Note that using protected tuples in unprotected tuple spaces leads to these tuples/templates being shipped between hosts unencrypted and thus vulnerable to eavesdropping. Once an attacker captures a packet and extracts the passwords clearly written in the tuple, he will be able to remove these tuples. Unprotected tuple spaces do not provide any security guarantees for protected tuples when communication across hosts is involved.

4.3 Service Model Implementation

The implementation consists of a new LIME agent class, **`ServiceAwareAgent`**. This is because LIME restricts the tuple space access to a LIME agent, the one that created it. The programmer will need to extend the **`ServiceAwareAgent`** class and implement its **`run()`** method. The new agent will inherit from **`ServiceAwareAgent`** the functionality it needs to manipulate service ads (Figure 6).

A service repository is created around a LIME tuple space, with or without a password (which makes it public or protected). Each client/server can create multiple service registries and receives handles to each of them. The handles will be used when registering, deregistering of searching for services.

A service is advertised as a tuple in the specified service registry (or in the default public service registry) together with a profile (the **Profile** class is a container for pairs [interface, attributes], where the attributes describe the associated interface which the service implements). When the service is advertised, it will be assigned by the system a unique service identifier (`sid`), if not specified by the server (i.e., it is advertised for the first time). This `sid` will be used for removing the advertisement when no longer needed.

When searching for a service, a client can specify the `sid` if it had previously used the service. This is the easiest way to rediscover a service. If the client does not have the `sid` for the needed service or if the service identified by the sid is no longer available, the search has to be performed using the service description. The client will provide a profile pattern for the service it needs. The tuple matching mechanism will return tuples that represent services whose profiles match the request made by the client (i.e., implement all the interfaces the client requested and the values of the advertised attributes match the values requested by the client). The result is a wrapper (the **Service** class) which contains the proxy

```
public ServiceAwareAgent()
    — creates a new ServiceAwareAgent.
public abstract void run()
    — abstract method that defines the agent's behavior and has to be
      implemented by the programmer in the class that extends ServiceAwareAgent.
public String[] listPublicRegistries()
    — returns the list of the names of all public registries currently available.
protected ServiceRegistry createServiceRegistry(String name, char[] pwd)
    — creates a new service registry protected with password pwd, if specified. If pwd
      is null the service registry will be unprotected.
public ServiceID registerService(ServiceRegistry sr, ServiceID sid,
      Serializable proxy, Profile prof, char[] upwd, char[] rpwd)
    — registers a new service in the specified service registry.
public void deregisterService(ServiceRegistry sr, ServiceID sid, char[] pwd)
    — deregisters the service identified by 'sid', if all conditions are met.
public Service findService(ServiceRegistry sr, ServiceID sid,
      Profile prof, char[] pwd)
    — searches for a service that corresponds to the description.
```

Fig. 6. ServiceAwareAgent's public interface.

object and the sid of the service. The security requirements must be met in both cases (i.e., when using a sid and when using the entire profile).

Service deregistration translates to removing the tuple carrying the service advertisement from the corresponding service registry, i.e., the corresponding tuple space. The agent trying to deregister the service must have the service `sid` and password (if applicable). The passwords that protect a service translate to read-password and remove-password in the LIME secure tuple space access.

5 Sample Application

The framework presented in this paper was first evaluated in a test application (Figure 7) that allows a car driving down a highway to make an electronic payment to an approaching tollbooth. As the car approaches and discovers the tollbooth, it receives the proxy object for the payment service, the list of prices, pays by credit card, and continues its trip without stopping. The proxy completes the payment when arriving at the exit tollbooth. Meanwhile the proxy obtained from the car the distance it travelled (also computable from the two tollbooths positions), the type of car (sedans, SUVs and trucks have different prices), and the driver's credit card number from his/her PDA.

The car has an agent specialized in automatic payments (toll roads, parking, etc.). All these charge points are configured to establish contact with vehicle agents in a predefined, unprotected tuple space, called "payments". The agent in the car is continuously looking for payment services. Near the tollbooth, the car discovers the payment service, retrieves the proxy object and "launches" the service, displaying the proxy's GUI on a screen inside the car.

The tollbooth advertises the service in a read-only tuple. However an attacker can be nearby and advertise using a read-only tuple, in the same "payments" tuple space, another proxy object that claims to handle the toll payment. The car agent has to decide now which of the two services to use. One possibility is for the car to specifically read the service from tollbooth's local tuple space. This implies that the car agent knows how to use location parameters to limit the service query to the tollbooth part of the tuple space. While this is doable for the daily drive from home to office and back (assuming the same route), on a long journey this can get complicated. The configuration time can be much longer than a regular cash payment. In this second case, once the proxy object is "launched" on the car's computer, it can connect to the tollbooth and light up a visual signal to indicate it can communicate with the tollbooth. A proxy retrieved from an attacker will not be able to interact with the tollbooth. Short range wireless communication is another trick that can help at the physical level.

Since the car can read the tuple **from** the tollbooth, the vulnerability is to read a tuple put there by an attacker. The car agent will have to verify that the tuple is read-only (i.e., by failing in an attempt to remove it). The reader is reminded that the read-only tuple could not have been placed there by anybody else since such tuples cannot migrate.

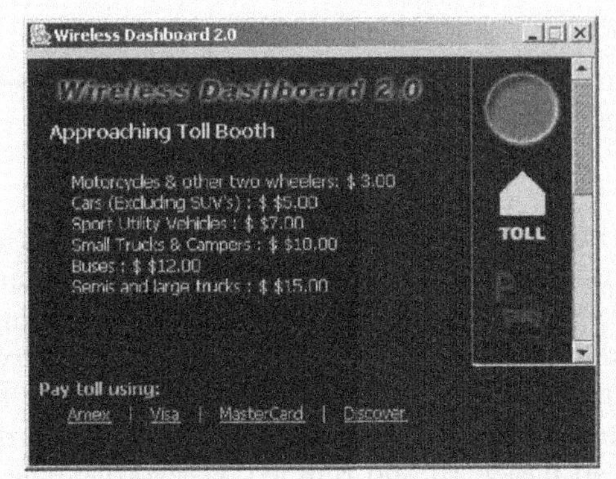

Fig. 7. Automatic toll payment is one of the features offered by a simulated wireless dashboard application.

While on the highway on the way to the exit point, the service GUI displays the price for the current type of car and the list of credit cards the proxy retrieved from the driver's PDA (or from the software running on car's computer). The driver can choose which one to use and this completes the interaction with the toll proxy. Note that for the daily route from home to the office (for example), most of the actions can be automated. The driver could be prompted only if there is a change in price. The driver can also designate a default credit card for this type of payments, etc.

When leaving the highway, the proxy displays the distance driven and the price, and sends the payment information to the tollbooth, issues an electronic receipt and then terminates execution. The proxy-tollbooth interaction is carried out via a protected tuple space and then using a private, raw socket protocol.

The application shows how transient tuple space sharing between the car and the tollbooth makes the payment service available to the car and how security mechanisms employed by the infrastructure help establish a safe interaction between the two parties. The effort invested to deliver this application sums to less than 300 lines of Java code, not including the GUI.

6 Related Work

The discovery technique constitutes the main difference among various existing implementations of the service discovery model. Sun Microsystems developed Jini [1,2]. It uses as a service registry lookup tables managed by special services called lookup services. These tables may contain executable code in addition to information describing the service. A Jini community cannot work without at least one lookup service. IETF offers the Service Location Protocol [10] where directory agents implement the service registry. They store service profiles and the location of the service but no code. The discovery of services involves first locating these directory agents. If no directory agent is available, clients may multicast requests for services and servers may multicast advertisements of their services. The most common service types use, by default, the service templates standardized by Internet Assigned Numbering Authority (IANA). Microsoft proposed Universal Plug'n'Play [3], which uses the Simple Service Discovery Protocol [11]. This protocol relies upon centralized directory services for registration and lookup. If no such proxy is available, SSDP uses multicast to announce new services or to ask for services. The advertisement contains a Universal Resource Identifier (URI) that leads to an XML description of the service. This description is accessible only after the service has been already discovered through a lookup service. The novelty of this model is the auto configuration capability based on DHCP or AutoIP. The Salutation project [5] uses a relatively centralized service registry called Salutation Manager (SLM). There may be several such managers available, but the clients and servers can establish contact only via these SLMs. The advantage of this approach is the fact that these SLMs can have different transport protocols underneath, unlike the above-mentioned models that assume an IP transport layer. To realize this, Salutation uses transport-dependent modules, called Transport Managers that broadcast internally, helping SLMs from different transport media interact with each other. In [12], the authors address the nomadic computing case from the point of view of the flexibility of the service advertisement and lookup matching.

Security issues are addressed in [13] which discusses threats and protection mechanisms for distributed systems. A capability-based security system is presented in [14]. The authentication mechanism is similar to ours, in that the capabilities can be verified locally, as opposed to an access control list approach where a central server is needed (e.g., Lampson's access matrix[15]). In[16] the authors describe an infrastructure for secure service discovery which offers privacy and authentication at the expense of a loaded infrastructure and centralized architecture allowing single points of failure. [17] addresses proxy-based security protocols for mobile devices, but also relies on a relatively centralized architecture for accomplishing some key tasks. Security is accomplished by adapting SPKI/SDSI [18,19] for proxy-server and/or proxy-proxy interactions. In [20] the authors use public keys as authentication certificates for Jini services, manually managed in local databases as initial trust relationships. In Service Location Protocol, authentication is done using public key encryption and having trust relationships between directory agents and service agents defined by the network administrator [21]. Decentralized trust management issues are also addressed in

KeyNote [22]. The authors describe an infrastructure that binds keys to the authorization to perform specific tasks rather than to names. KeyNote was inspired by PolicyMaker [23] and supports local control of trust relationships thus eliminating the need for certifying authorities.

7 Conclusions

In this paper we presented a technique that allows for consistent service advertisement and discovery in ad hoc networks. Key is the fact that service registry updates are atomic with respect to changes in service availability due to mobility and disconnections. We also described security features that can provide for safe service advertisement and utilization in ad hoc networks. The model presented provides the necessary support for safe distribution of public keys in ad hoc networks. Once this mechanism is in place, it enables the development of algorithms for establishing session keys or simply the distribution of secret keys.

Acknowledgements. This research was supported in part by the National Science Foundation under Grant No. CCR-9970939 and the Office of Naval Research under MURI research contract N00014-02-1-0715. Any opinions, findings, and conclusions or recommendations expressed in this paper are those of the authors and do not necessarily reflect the views of the research sponsors. The authors would also like to thank Rohan Sen for his contribution in the implementation and testing.

References

1. Sun Microsystems: Jini technology core platform specification (2000)
2. Edwards, K.: Core JINI. Prentice Hall (1999)
3. Microsoft Corporation: Universal plug and play forum. (http://www.upnp.org)
4. W3C: Simple object access protocol (soap). (http://www.w3.org/TR/SOAP)
5. Salutation Consortium: Salutation specifications. (http://www.salutation.org)
6. SIG, B.: Bluetooth specification. (https://www.bluetooth.org/foundry/ specification/document/specification)
7. Murphy, A., Picco, G., Roman, G.C.: LIME: A middleware for physical and logical mobility. In: Proceedings of the 21st International Conference on Distributed Computing Systems. (2001) 524–533
8. Gelernter, D.: Generative communication in Linda. ACM Transactions on Programming Languages and Systems **7** (1985) 80–112
9. Schmidt, D., Stal, M., Rohnert, H., Buschmann, F.: Pattern Oriented Software Architecture. Volume 2. John Wiley & Sons, Ltd. (1999)
10. Guttman, E.: Service location protocol: Automatic discovery of IP network services. IEEE Internet Computing **4** (1999) 71–80
11. Goland, Y., Cai, T., Leach, P., Gu, Y., Microsoft Corporation, Albright, S., Hewlett-Packard Company: Simple service discovery protocol/1.0: Operating without an arbiter. http://www.upnp.org/download/draft_cai_ssdp_v1_03.txt (2001)
12. Jacob, B.: Service discovery: Access to local resources in a nomadic environment. In: OOPSLA '96 Workshop on Object Replication and Mobile Computing. (1996)

13. Hubaux, J.P., Buttyan, L., Capkun, S.: The quest for security in mobile ad hoc networks. (In: ACM MobiHOC 2001 Symposium)
14. Gong, L.: A secure identity-based capability system. In: Proceedings of the IEEE Symposium on Security and Privacy. (1989) 56–63
15. Lampson, B.: Protection. In: 5th Princeton Conf. on Information Sciences and Systems. Volume ACM Operating Systems Rev. 8. (1971) 18–24
16. Czerwinski, S.E., Zhao, B.Y., Hodes, T.D., Joseph, A.D., Katz, R.H.: An architecture for a secure service discovery service. In: Mobile Computing and Networking. (1999) 24–35
17. Burnside, M., Clarke, D., Mills, T., Devadas, S., Rivest, R.: Proxy-based security protocols in networked mobile devices. In: Proceedings of Selected Areas in Cryptography. (2002)
18. Ellison, C., Frantz, B., Lampson, B., Rivest, R., Thomas, B., Ylonen, T.: Simple public key certificates. Internet Draft http://world.std.com/cme/spki.txt (1999)
19. Rivest, R.L., Lampson, B.: Sdsi – a simple distributed security infrastructure. (Presented at CRYPTO'96 Rumpsession (http://citeseer.nj.nec.com/ rivest96sdsi.html))
20. Eronen, P., Lehtinen, J., Zitting, J., Nikander, P.: Extending jini with decentralized trust management. In: The Third IEEE Conference on Open Architectures and Network Programming (OPENARCH). (2000)
21. Vettorello, M., Bettstetter, C., Schwingenschlgl, C.: Some notes on security in the service location protocol version 2 (slpv2). In: Proc. Workshop on Ad hoc Communications, in conjunction with 7th European Conference on Computer Supported Cooperative Work (ECSCW'01). (2001)
22. Blaze, M., Feigenbaum, J., Keromytis, A.D.: Keynote: Trust management for public-key infrastructures. In LNCS, S., ed.: Security Protocols International Workshop. Volume 1550. (1998) 59–63
23. Blaze, M., Feigenbaum, J., Lacy, J.: Decentralized trust management. In Press, I.C.S., ed.: 17th Symposium on Security and Privacys. (1996) 164–173

Single Sign-On in Service-Oriented Computing

Kurt Geihs[1], Robert Kalcklösch[1], and Andreas Grode[2]

[1] Intelligent Networks and Management of Distributed Systems
Berlin University of Technology, D-10587 Berlin
{geihs, rkalckloesch}@ivs.tu-berlin.de
[2] DIN IT Service GmbH
Burggrafenstr. 6
D-10787 Berlin
andreas.grode@dinits.de

Abstract. Support for Single Sign-On (SSO) is a frequently voiced requirement for Service-Oriented Computing. We discuss SSO strategies and approaches, their requirements and constraints. The two most prominent approaches in this field are presented, i.e. Microsoft Passport and Liberty Alliance. Because implementations of Liberty were not widely available and in order to understand the conceptual implications and practical requirements of SSO we have built our own SSO solution. Its modular and flexible design is compatible with the Liberty specifications. The prototype reveals valuable insights into SSO design and operations.

Keywords: Service oriented computing, security, service authentication, single sign on

1 Introduction

Service-oriented Computing and Web Services are critical ingredients in making the Internet a universal platform for electronic commerce [1]. The new technology supports a loosely coupled collaboration style for business to business and business to consumer scenarios. New technical challenges and requirements arise primarily from the inherent autonomy of actors as well as the heterogeneity of components. Clearly, security concerns are uttermost important in such an open environment. On the one hand we need effective security mechanisms to protect the individual business assets. On the other hand we clearly want to lower the inconvenience hurdles for using the new application potential.

The authentication of a service user to a service provider is one area where this dilemma is evident: While one has to acknowledge the autonomy of services to choose their own authentication mechanism, one should also avoid inefficient and insecure repetitions of service sign-on procedures. Password proliferation is a frequent consequence of multi-service environments. It often leads to violations of security policies and thus weakens the security. Ideally, service users want to sign on to "the distributed system" only once, just like the user of an operating system logs on to a computer once and may then use the different operating

M.E. Orlowska et al. (Eds.): ICSOC 2003, LNCS 2910, pp. 384–394, 2003.

system services. An SSO mechanism should not only provide the necessary level of security but also should be easy to use and should work for arbitrary service types.

This paper addresses Single Sign-On (SSO) strategies for service-oriented computing environments. Solving the SSO problem is much harder in such environments due to the inherent distribution and heterogeneity as well as the autonomy and independence of the involved actors.

The paper is structured as follows. In Section 2 we analyse the SSO requirements and constraints, and we provice a classification of SSO approaches. Section 3 discusses the two most prominent approaches for SSO in Service-Oriented Computing, i.e. Microsoft Passport and Liberty Alliance. Because implementations of Liberty were not widely available and in order to understand the conceptual implications and practical requirements of SSO we have built our own SSO solution. Section 4 describes our prototype system and reports on the lessons learnt. Section 5 concludes the paper and points to further work.

2 Single Sign On

A SSO system enables users to access multiple services or computer platforms after being authenticated just once [12]. This does not mean that a SSO system unifies the account information (e.g., username and password) for all services, even if this is a popular interpretation for many people. Instead, it hides the account information for the participating services behind only one account. Thus, the user logs on to the SSO system once and the system manages the logins for the specific services the user chooses to work with. Especially, the system does not automatically perform a login for the user at all services managed by the SSO system. A login takes place only at those services that the user chooses to work with. The SSO system has to maintain a list of username-password pairs for the services. Obviously, this list is a remunerative target for an attacker. If an attacker gains access to the SSO system he therefore has access to all participating applications. This is also true, if an attacker gets the account information from a specific user. With this information he is able to access all services the genuine user is allowed to access.

Consequently, security is a major aspect of a SSO system. The accounting information has to be stored in a secure way, ensuring that only the owner has access to it. Also, the login to participating services must take place in a secure way.

There exist three major mechanisms for user authentication. First, user and service share a not commonly known secret (e.g., a password) which is bound to a special identity. The second mechanism involves some material token, including personal characteristics (e.g., a driving license or a magnetic card). The third one is a variation of the token, whereby the token is a biometric attribute (e.g., the fingerprint or the signature). The main point is that no mechanism is per se better than the other. A carefully chosen password which is changed regularly may be better than a token which can be easily faked. Thus, not only the mechanism itself, but also the behavior of the user contributes to the level of security of the authentication.

Although an authentication maps a network identity to a real life person, it is not necessary that all services behind a Single Sign-On know exactly with whom they are dealing. Thus, a SSO system should support pseudonymity in a way, that the user can decide, based on the specific needs of an application, to which extend he is willing to reveal his identity. However, it must be ensured that at least at one point the mapping between the pseudonym and the real identity can take place. Pseudonymity is an issue especially in the European Community with its strong privacy policies.

2.1 Cooperative vs. Non-cooperative SSO

Basically, there exist two different approaches for SSO: cooperative and non-cooperative SSO. In a cooperative SSO system the participating services know about the SSO system. SSO is not transparent for the services in this case. Normally, the services have to be modified, at least regarding the login procedure, to cope with the requirements of the cooperative SSO system. Through cooperation among themselves the services are able to build a network, where a user, once successfully logged in, could move from one service to another, without further login procedures. Also, it is possible to link the different identities together building a group of services and enriching each others services.

The alternative is non-cooperative SSO. In this approach the participating services do not know about the SSO system. This is no contradiction, if one looks at the desired behavior of a Single Sign-On mechanism. It should group together services and offer the user a single authentication point to login to all services. Such a system could be a local application at the user-side or a server-side proxy, managed and operated by an administrator who manages the login on behalf of the user. This can be fully transparent to the involved services. Obviously, not all services may be suited to be unified in such a way. There are several requirements they have to match. The usage of standardized techniques for the authentication is the major requirement. If the service provider is using proprietary software for the authentication, the provider of the Single Sign-On may not be able to map his account information to the desired procedure. Also, the service entry point and the authentication procedure should be stable and not change to often, as this would lead to an increasing effort in keeping the SSO up-to-date.

A rather straightforward approach to build such a non-cooperative SSO is conceivable for the World Wide Web. User login can be handled by an appropriately enhanced proxy such that the SSO is transparent for the services. Assuming that the login procedure for a service is known, it can be automated through an intercepting proxy that provides the authentication information automatically to the service. The proxy retrieves the authentication data from e.g. a configuration file set up by the system administrator. Thus, after the login to the proxy, the login to the services is hidden from the user.

3 Related Work

Today, for Web-based service environments two major approaches to SSO exist: Microsoft Passport and Liberty Alliance. Both systems are based on the cooperative SSO model. Their differences lie in the architectural structure. Passport is using a centralized approach, where only one entity (e.g. Microsoft) is able to authenticate a user. In contrast to that Liberty is designed to operate in a decentralized way. There may be many (cooperating) entities, that are allowed to authenticate a user. Both approaches are described briefly in the next sections.

A good taxonomy for SSO systems is given in [10], where the authors try to categorize different SSO approaches.

3.1 Microsoft Passport

The main objective of Passport [8] is the centralized storage of account information in order to simplify the login procedures and thus to ease the eCommerce activities of registered partner applications. Therefore, the Passport Server manages the authentication of users and only transmits a unique user identifier to the services.

Both the user and the service provider have to register themselves on the Microsoft Passport Server in order to use this SSO service. As part of the registration a service provider has to provide Microsoft with information about his safety guidelines and the offered service, and he has to comply with the technical requirements of Passport. Microsoft then assigns a unique ID to this service provider and transmits it to the provider together with a symmetric key, which is used for the encrypted communication between Passport and the provider. The encryption is done by a software provided by Microsoft, which has to be installed on the server side.

The users register with a valid email address and a password. The email address is used to transmit a confirmation mail which therefore checks the validity of the address. After that the user gets assigned a Passport Unique Identifier (PUID). Subsequently, this PUID is used to identify the user in all participating applications. It is a perfect pseudonym which does not reveal any links to the original user. As it is not told to the user, the user account is the valid email address.

The sequence chart of a successful login is depicted in figure 1. After initiating the login process on the webpage of a service provider the user will be redirected to a Passport server. There, the actual login form is created and the user performs the login. For the transmission of the user data a ssl connection is used. If the provided pair of username and password is valid, the server sends a redirect to the service provider and places some cookies on the users computer. These cookies are encrypted using 3DES and contain among other information the PUID of the user. With this PUID the service provider is able to identify the user and can thus be sure that the user has successfully logged in to the Passport server.

If the user now wants to use another Passport-enabled service he just needs to push the "login with Passport"-Button on the according web-site. With the following redirect the already existing Passport-cookie will be sent to a Passport server. Instead of creating the login form, the server now checks the cookie and, if it is valid, acts like after a successful login depicted in figure 1.

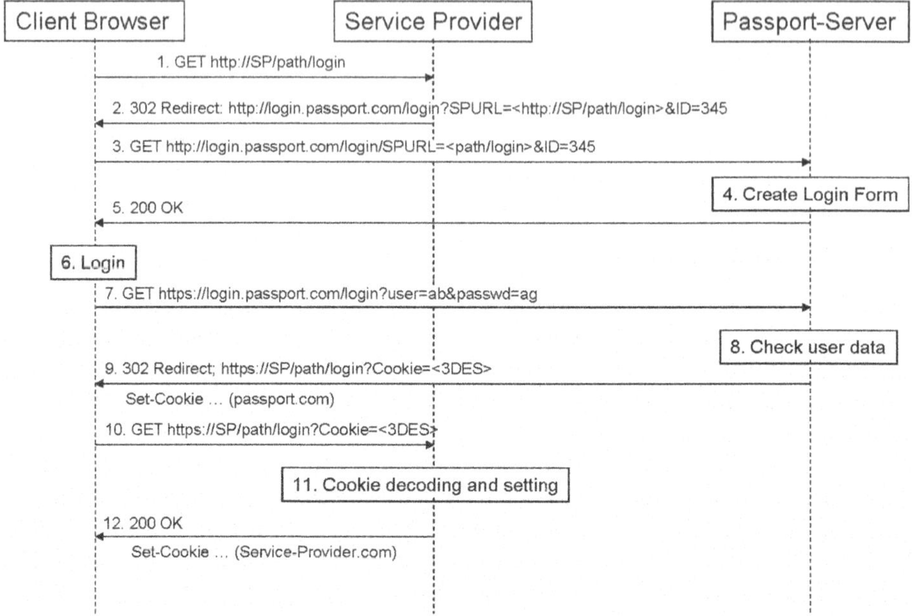

Fig. 1. Passport Single Sign-On Protocol

3.2 Project Liberty

The Liberty Alliance was founded to set up a SSO standard which should lead to different interoperable products from different vendors. The main objective is the coupling of multiple user identities distributed over cooperative service providers. The standard aims to support all popular operating systems, programming languages, and network structures [7] and is designed to ensure the compability and security between Liberty-aware applications [11]. As this was a new standard, no Liberty-aware applications existed in a productive environment when we started our work. Only a reference implementation from SUN [13] had been released. Today, there are several Liberty-enabled products[1].

The benefits for the users are given mainly through three points. First of all, Liberty allows the coupling of identities a user has for different service providers without announcing these to other providers. Within this group the user is able

[1] http://www.projectliberty.org/resources/enabled.html

to stretch a single login for one provider to all coupled providers leading to a single sign-on. Also, a single log-out is possible where a user logs out of all participating providers simultaneously.

A special service provider in the sense of Liberty is the Identity Provider (IP). It offers the management of user accounts for other service providers and users. Additionally, it offers authentication mechanisms. The Liberty standard does not prescribe any particular authentication mechanism. The choice of mechanisms is up to the Identity Providers. Naturally, a service provider could demand a specific method for the authentication as a minimum requirement for a successful login.

The SSO protocol used by Liberty is depicted in figure 2. After navigating to a service provider, the user chooses one of the proposed Identity Providers, that a service provider is willing to work with. The user is then redirected to that IP. Contained within the redirect is a defined XML structure (*AuthRequest*) which controls the behavior of the IP for that specific service provider and user. If the user is not yet logged in to the IP, he has to login first. After the successful authentication the user is redirected to the service provider. This redirect contains a SAML artifact with a random number. SAML is an XML-based framework for exchanging authentication and authorization information [9]. The random number in the SAML artifact serves as a handle for the service provider to access information about the user. After decoding the artifact, typically the service provider issues a SOAP-Request to the IP to fetch this information. In the SOAP-Response an authentication assertion is included, which holds the information. Among other things it includes the user ID. With this the service provider is now able to identify the user.

A group of service providers can build a so-called "Circle of Trust" in which a user, once authenticated can move easily from one service to another. Thus, the user can choose from a list provided by the service provider to which other provider within this circle he wants to go. By clicking of the according link, his profile is sent to the new provider. If the authentication level is acceptable for the new provider, that means, that the authentication mechanism chosen by the original provider meet his own security requirements, the user is automatically logged in without the need for any other interaction.

4 SSO Prototype

In order to study the practical requirements and limitations of SSO in a WWW environment, we have built our own prototype SSO system. In particular, we were looking for a general and comprehensive, but nevertheless easy to use and easy to administer solution. We aimed at a non-cooperative SSO system that does not require modification of the participating target services. Thus, it should transparently maintain individual passwords for each service.

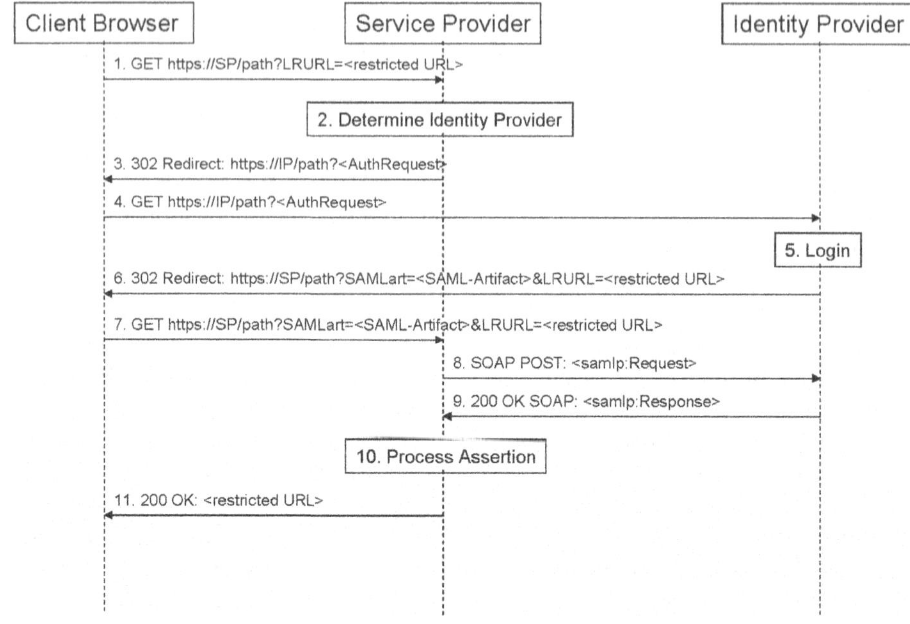

Fig. 2. Liberty Single Sign-On Protocol

4.1 Overview

The implemented SSO system provides an non-cooperative SSO service, where remote, protected web-applications are encapsulated through a "normal" protected intermediate SSO service. The different services do not need to know each other and do not get any information about the users outside of their scope. The service-internal implementation and authentication mechanisms continue to function as before. Therefore, the web applications are still usable even without the SSO server. The SSO server himself stores information about each user and his credentials for each of the participating web application. A proxy server in between the user's browser and the service is the key component. The desired content is proxied to the user's http-client (browser). Hence, no direct connection between remote service and user browser will be established. To prevent the browser from connecting to the remote server directly by following an absolutely addressed link, every tag with embedded hyperlink attributes has to be changed (transcoded) to "point" to the SSO-Server, preserving the information which remote document should be fetched. The SSO-Server therefore acts as a *transcoding reverse proxy* or *transcoding surrogate* . Different authentication mechanisms, access restrictions and session-tracking techniques may be employed and are hidden from the user, who only needs to authenticate to the SSO server using one authentication scheme.

This approach of creating a SSO service is rather simple. By the modular design of the chosen components, which are created with open source software only, integration of additional remote services with different protection schemes (such as HTTP authentication or cookies) is relatively straightforward. If needed, new transcoding rules have to implemented and added to the transcoding surrogate. In addition, configuration data needs to be included for accessing the desired URLs of the remote services.

The main objective of this first implementation was to provide a lightweight and extendable prototype of a SSO server which can be installed and configured easily. Extensions for a comfortable user and configuration management have to be created separately. As an administrator for a specific SSO server knows best, which applications are participating and what their configuration possibilities are, the development of a sophisticated configuration interface would be up to him. Naturally, a simple and generic interface could be provided as a starting point.

Because of the danger that the SSO service might become a single point of failure for many encapsulated services, the design payed careful attention to availability concerns for the SSO server. For example, configuration and user management is decoupled from the internal transcoding engine. This rather static information is stored in a separate database with internal redundancy in a central or distributed architecture. These "helper applications" are accessed via a defined API and are independent from the implementation of the SSO server itself, which can be installed on a couple of servers to provide redundancy and a higher availability.

4.2 Implementation

As mentioned above the implementation of the SSO server is built with open source software only. The main component is the well known and popular Apache HTTP Server [2]. One of its benefits besides stability and usability is its modular design which supports the integration of modules from third parties in a rather straightforward way. In our implementation we use mainly the Perl module to extend the Apache API with Perl applications inside the HTTP server. The development of the Apache module which drives the SSO server is done in the Perl programming language with all well-known benefits for writing web applications and the big number of available Perl modules from CPAN [3]. In the scope of the SSO server the Apache HTTP server is used to provide the framework for HTTP(S) transactions. It acts as a container for the reverse proxy (the so called *surrogate*) with the internal rewriting engine. All communication activities (proxy functions) and the transcoding of HTML documents is done with the Perl modules `LWP` [2] and `HTML::Parser` [3] and their derivates within the developed module `Apache::Transcode`. The Apache HTTP server can be used in conjunction with `mod-ssl`, which lets the HTTP server act as a HTTPS server

[2] http://www.cpan.org/modules/by-module/LWP

[3] http://www.cpan.org/modules/by-module/HTML

by the use of OPENSSL, the open source implementation of the SSLv3/TLS 1.0 [5,4] specification. HTTPS is needed for confidential communication between the SSO server and the user's browser. It also allows the use of client-side SSL certificates for user authentication. All data which has to be kept across multiple HTTP transactions is stored outside the scope of the server application with use of DBI [4], the database abstraction layer for Perl, available from CPAN [3].

4.3 Discussion

In our prototype implementation we have shown that SSO is possible in a way that it is transparent for service providers. So far, this is working only for sites built out of plain HTML, whereat it does not matter if the content is generated dynamically or served from static files. Hence, more work has to be done to integrate more sophisticated web techniques. Especially DHTML pages require careful examination to guarantee that the user is not leaving the SSO server during his session by accident.

Another subtle problem is the copyright issue. Although the service provider does not know about the SSO system it is necessary to inform him and to get his permission for the participation of his site, because the contents of the web pages are under the copyright of the providers. A cooperation between the service providers and the SSO service seems to be advisable here. In order to alleviate the copyright problem, our SSO server would be suited best for an Intranet, where many services with different authentication schemes are provided.

Another point is, that in heterogeneous environments where different HTTP-based applications, using different approaches for the authentication and administration of users, already exist, it could be difficult to migrate at once to a centralized directory-based approach using for example LDAP as the underlying protocol. Nevertheless, this technique does not implement SSO out of the box. It just provides the simplification to use only one account for every application, but the login itself has still to be done for each application. To address this problem, as mentioned before, it is possible to automate the login process in two ways: Firstly, on the client side, where a central database could be used as many popular commercial SSO solutions do, or secondly on the server side with the described SSO server.

Several points remain open at this stage of our investigations. First of all, the system is only a prototype. Especially, the reliability and the scalability of the system are issues we have to take a closer look at. For a productive system we will also need to study more carefully the efficiency and the resource requirements of our transcoding algorithms.

As the design of the prototype SSO server is quite modular, the current authentication mechanism in the proxy could be easily exchanged. For example, it could be replaced by a call to a Liberty Identity Provider. This would make the participating services Liberty-aware, regardless of their own capabilities and without changing their implementation.

---

[4] http://www.cpan.org/modules/by-module/DBI

To gain more experiences and to further improve our implementation, it is envisaged to use the SSO server inside the Intranet of the DIN IT Service GmbH, to group multiple document management systems (DMS) of the same vendor. Therefore, the prototype is now used for local testing with one DMS.

5 Conclusion and Outlook

In future Service-Oriented Computing environments service users in B2B and B2C scenarios need to sign on frequently to many different independent services. Each service may have its own authentication procedure. Without support for SSO, service users are forced to handle as many authentication credentials and procedures as there are accessed services. Clearly, the more services a user navigates, the greater the likelihood of user errors and thus compromised security. With a properly configured SSO system, once authenticated the user has immediate and convenient access to a number of services.

In this paper we have analysed the requirements and constraints of SSO for web environments. Furthermore, we have presented a prototype SSO system that works according to the non-cooperative model as a proxy that is transparent to the service applications. The prototype demonstrates that SSO support can be implemented effectively based on transcoding HTTP requests. No changes are required for services in order to participate. Consequently, our prototype solution works with arbitrary web-based services.

The future of SSO for Web Services and Service-Oriented Computing is not clear today. While the need for SSO has been clearly identified and expressed by many people, it is questionable whether and how fast users will overcome their scepticism and will trust another service component that has full control over the user's credentials and decides about very sensitive authentication activities. Microsoft's Passport has faced a lot of headwind already [6]. The Liberty Alliance undertakes great efforts to gain more acceptance. For e-commerce over the web, SSO remains one of the great technical and personal challenges.

References

1. *Communications of the ACM*, 46(6), June 2003.
2. Apache Software Foundation. www.apache.org.
3. CPAN. Comprehensive Perl Archive Network. www.cpan.org.
4. T. Dierks and C. Allen. The TLS Protocol Version 1.0. January 1999.
5. Alan O. Freier, Philip Karlton, and Paul C. Kocher. The SSL Protocol Version 3.0. November 1996.
6. David P. Kormann and Aviel D. Rubin. Risks of the Passport Single Signon Protocol. *Computer Networks, Elsevier Science Press*, 33:51–58, 2000.
7. Liberty Alliance. Liberty Architecture Overview Version 1.1. January 2003.
8. Microsoft. Microsoft .NET Passport Review Guide. March 2003.
9. OASIS. Assertions and Protocol for the OASIS Security Assertion Markup Language (SAML) v1.1. July 2003.

10. Andreas Pashalidis and Chris J. Mitchell. A Taxonomy of Single Sign-On Systems. In *The Eighth Australasian Conference on Information Security and Privacy (ACISP 2003)*, volume 2727 of *LNCS*. Springer, January 2003.
11. Birgit Pfitzmann. Privacy in Enterprise Identity Federation - Policies for Liberty Single Signon. Dresden, December 2003. 3rd Workshop on Privacy Enhancing Technologies (PET 2003), Springer.
12. R. Shirey. RFC: 2828: Internet Security Glossary. May 2000.
13. SUN. Interoperability Prototype for Liberty. 2002.

Tracking Service Availability in Long Running Business Activities

Werner Vogels

Dept. of Computer Science, Cornell University, Upson Hall, Ithaca, NY 14853
vogels@cs.cornell.edu

Abstract. An important factor in the successful deployment of federated web services-based business activities will be the ability to guarantee reliable distributed operation and execution under scalable conditions. For example advanced failure management is essential for any reliable distributed operation but especially for the target areas of web service architectures, where the activities can be constructed out of services located at different enterprises, and are accessed over heterogeneous networks topologies. In this paper we describe the first technologies and implementations coming out of the Obduro project, which has as a goal to apply the results of scalability and reliability research to global scalable service oriented architectures. We present technology developed for failure and availability tracking of processes involved in long running business activities within a web services coordination framework. The Service Tracker, Coordination Service and related development toolkits are available for public usage.

1 Introduction

One of the driving forces behind the emerge of service oriented computing is the desire to use services architectures to construct complex, federated activities. When composing a business activity out of services that are heavily distributed a strong need arises to provide guarantees about the reliability and availability of the components that make up the activity. In the same context one wants to ensure that the aggregated service can handle failures of the individual services gracefully. To provide these advanced guarantees, the web service architectures can draw from the experiences of two decades of advanced middleware systems development, which had similar reliability goals, albeit at a smaller scale and in less heterogeneous settings.

Some first steps in providing an interoperable framework for distributed message oriented services have been set with the security, routing, coordination and transaction specifications [2,3]. Together with the reliable messaging specifications these will provide the first building blocks for constructing simple forms of federated web services based activities. Although these specifications do a reasonable job in laying the ground work for the interaction between the various services and the guarantees that can be achieved by making all of the distributed

M.E. Orlowska et al. (Eds.): ICSOC 2003, LNCS 2910, pp. 395–408, 2003.

operations explicit, they are remarkably vague with respect to failure scenarios and failure handling.

The issue of failure management becomes especially important when we are considering long running business activities in federated setting. These activities are often the aggregate of several distributed services, and some may have running times of several hours. For this class of systems it becomes essential to provide the activity composer with the right tools to track the availability of the individual services and to provide mechanisms for service selection to support various styles of compensating actions in the case of failures. Long running activities need to deal with more complex failure scenarios than those that can be implemented using simple atomic transactions. For example a failure of a crucial service may need to be compensated by trying to use an alternative supplier or a replica service, before deciding on the rollback of the overall activity.

In the context of the *obduro* project we are developing a range of support tools for managing complex federated service execution. One of basic tools necessary to construct more complex activities is the Service Tracker, which is used to address the need for failure management of especially longer running activities.

The distributed systems core of the Service Tracking system has two fundamental components: failure detection and membership information dissemination. A variety of algorithms for both components has been developed over the years, but mainly for research systems, while industrial systems in general have resorted to simple heartbeat, time-out and flooding schemes [4,6,8,10,13, 14,15]. The prototype of the service tracking engine developed for this project is extremely well suited for cases where robustness and scalability are important. The prototype is based on epidemic techniques, and the a-synchronous and autonomous properties of this system make it simple to implement and operate.

Failure detection can also be used as the building block to simplify the implementation of other essential distributed systems services such as *consensus* [5]. Consensus is used when a set of processes need to agree upon the outcome of an operation. Many consensus protocols require knowledge about which processes are involved in the execution of the protocol to establish a notion of majority, quorums, etc. Even though some protocols such as Paxos [11,12] do not use failure detectors in their specification, the implementation of these protocols is greatly simplified by their use.

This paper is organized as follows: section 2 provides a brief overview of the research context in which the tracker has been developed. In section 3 the Service Tracker framework and the interface are described, while section 4 gives the details on the Epidemic Service Tracker. Section 5 contains some implementation details and thoughts on future work.

An earlier, preliminary description of the Service Tracker was distributed under the title *ws-membership*.

2 The Obduro Project

In the Obduro[1] Project we are applying our experiences in building reliable distributed systems to the services oriented architectures. The web service architectures provide us with an opportunity to design robust distributed systems that are highly scalable. We have long been arguing that the scalability of distributed systems has been severely hindered by hiding the distributed aspects of the services behind a transparent single address-space interface. The "software as a *distributed* service" approach will allows us to build distributed systems more reliably than in the past [18].

In the recent years our research group has shifted its focus to the reliability problems triggered by the increasing scale of distributed systems and the failure of traditional systems to provide robust operation under influence of scale. In the Obduro project we will continue to exploit technologies such as epidemic communication and state-management to provide frameworks for building scalable, autonomous web services in federated setting.

The project focuses on deliverables in 4 areas:

1. Development of advanced distributed services in the context of the web services Coordination framework. These services will include a failure management service, a consensus service and a lightweight distributed state-sharing engine.
2. Development of high-performance server technology for web service routing, routing to transport mapping, content based routing and service selection. This technology specifically targets high-performance enterprise cluster environments.
3. Integration of reliability and other advanced distributed systems services into coordination and choreography engines.
4. Development of a framework for global event dissemination and event management for real-time enterprise applications. This development will particularly focus on global scalable reliable event systems based on a publish/subscribe paradigm. [17]

The work described in this paper comes out of the first area. The Service Tracker is an essential tool in managing service availability and is a building block for other, more complex distributed services.

3 A Service Tracking Framework

Based on our experiences with building a variety of distributed systems and applications, we realize that there is no single service tracking or membership service implementation that serves the needs of all (reliable) distributed systems. Some may require high accuracy while others need aggressive fail-over, where again others may require distributed agreement before failures are reported.

[1] Obduro is latin for *to last long, to be hard, persist, endure, last, hold out*

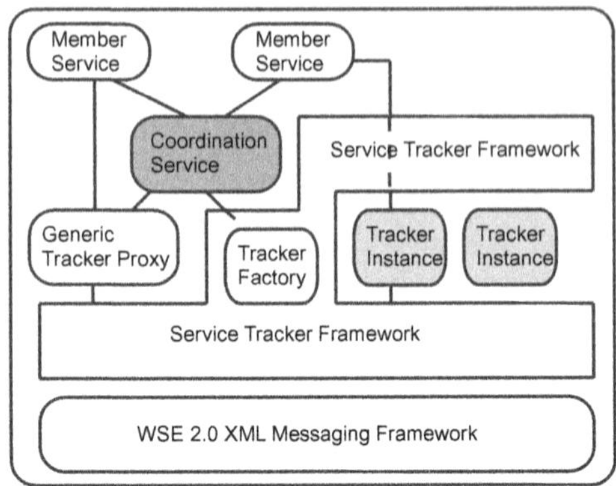

Fig. 1. Some of the components involved in Service Tracking

World wide failure detection requires different protocols than clustered systems in a datacenter. In the Obduro project we have implemented a prototype base on epidemic techniques that is particularly well suited for environments where robustness and scalability under adverse conditions is important. We expect to develop additional prototypes that target will different deployments.

These different implementations are developed using the Service Tracking Framework and have a single Service Tracking interface in common which services use to register themselves and service monitors can use to track the registered member services. The Service Tracking Framework, which relies on the Obduro Coordination Toolkit, provides the membership developer with basic classes that abstract the interaction of the tracking engine with member services and proxies.

The Service Tracking Interface is designed according the Activation/Registration pattern prescribed by the *ws-coordination* specification. The main task for the Coordination Service in this setting is to route the activation and registration requests to the appropriate component factory or instance multiplexer based on *CoordinationType* and *CoordinationContext* which are specified as parameters in the service requests

There are five roles modeled in the Service Tracking system:

- *Coordination Service.* Receives the activation and registration requests and routes these to the Service Tracking Framework. Its functionality is described in the *ws-coordination* specification.
- *Service Tracker.* Provides failure detection of registered web services and disseminates membership information. The actual implementation depends on the tracker type selected.
- *Member Service.* A software component that has registered itself for failure detection, either directly with a Service Tracker instance or through a Tracker Proxy. If the service registers itself with Service Tracker or with the Generic Tracker Proxy, it must implement its part of the tracker interrogation protocol.

- *Tracker Proxy.* A software component that is interposed between a member service and the Service Tracker for reasons of efficiency or accuracy. The proxy can be a dedicated component that uses specialized techniques to monitor member services such as a process monitor or an application server management module [19]. A generic version of the Tracker Proxy is implemented in the Service Tracker Framework for use by the Coordination Service in case a registration request is accepted for which no earlier activation action was taken at this Coordinator.
- *Services Monitor.* This service registers itself with the Service Tracker to receive changes to the membership state. While traditionally this functionality was combined with the Member Service role, e.g. registering as a member meant receiving membership updates; in this setting this functionality is decoupled. This allows for example the failure monitor of a BPEL4WS activity to register for membership updates with being part of the membership itself. In this usage example the individual member services have no use for the membership information as any compensating actions for service failure are initiated by the failure monitor.

The process of activation and registration will make the relation between these roles clearer.

3.1 Activation and Registration

The Coordination Service provides a 2-step access to Service Tracking. In the first step a participant in the activity, such as a member service or a activity monitor, *activates* the tracking system by sending a *CreateCoordinationContext* request to the Coordination service with the CoordinationType set to the following uri:

http://ws.cs.cornell.edu/schemas/2002/11/cucsts.

This will instantiate a Service Tracker at the coordination site using optional configuration parameters in the extensibility elements of the request. The operation will return a *CoordinationContext* to the requestor which includes information for other Service Tracker instances to join in the protocol.

If the activation is requested with an existing *CoordinationContext* as a parameter, the Coordination Service actives the Service Tracker, which joins the other Tracker instances activated with the same context. For example the Epidemic Service Tracker uses the information in the context to contact an already activated Service Tracker instance to bootstrap the current membership list. The new instance will add information about itself to the context, such that future activations at other coordinators have alternative Service Trackers to bootstrap from.

When the Service Tracker instances are activated at the Coordinators, the set of Trackers is established that will monitor each other. However if no *registration* request reaches a particular Tracker instance within the time-to-live period specified in the context, that instance will de-activate and will voluntarily leave the Tracker membership. The service membership list remains empty until Member Service instances are registered.

A service instance will request to be added to the membership through the *RequestMemberService* action. Parameters to the request include a URI uniquely identifying the Member Service instance, a *CoordinationContext* that represents the set of Service Trackers collaborating in the membership tracking and a port-reference on which the service is willing to accept *MemberProbe* interrogation messages. In the response to the request the service will receive a port-reference at the Service Tracker to which it can send its *MemberAlive* interrogation responses and the *MemberLeaves* notification when the service wants to exit the membership gracefully.

A second possibility for a service to be added to the membership is through interposing a Tracker Proxy. As described earlier such a proxy can be a dedicated software module that uses specialized techniques to monitor the service. Also a generic Tracker proxy is interposed by a Coordination service in response to a *RequestMemberService* request when no Service Tracker was previously activated at this Coordinator for the specified CoordinationContext.

Proxies register with a Service Tracker instance through the *RegisterTrackerProxy* request which contains a port-reference at the proxy to which *ProxyProbe* interrogation messages will be send and the unique id the service provided to the proxy. A proxy can register itself multiple times for different services using the same port reference. The response to the proxy contains the port-reference at the Service Tracker to which the proxy can send its *ProxyAlive* message as well as *MemberLeaves* and *MemberFailed* messages when a Member Service connected to a proxy fails. The proxy interrogation sequence is used to keep track of the health of the proxy service, if the proxy is determined to have failed; all associated services will be marked failed in the membership. How a dedicated proxy determines the health of a service is outside of the scope of this paper, but the generic proxy uses the regular *MemberProbe/MemberAlive* interrogation sequence.

A Services Monitor registers using the *RegisterServicesMonitor* request, which includes a port-reference on which the monitor wants to receive the *MembershipUpdate* messages. A membership update includes at minimum a list of the currently active Member Services, but can be extended with information on Members Services that have left gracefully or recently joined, that have failed or are suspected to have failed.

To ensure that no false information is spread about the health of the Member Services, the Service Tracker, proxies, members and monitors all use the ws-security services to sign their messages.

4 The Epidemic Service Tracker

The basic Service Tracking engine implemented for the Obduro Project is based on a gossip-style failure detector, which was first described in [13]. This proba-

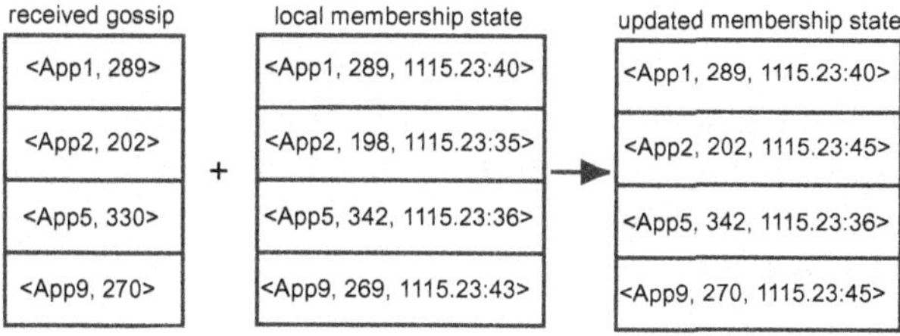

Fig. 2. Example heartbeat counter state merge

bilistic approach to failure detection was the basis for the design of the membership services in the Galaxy federated cluster management system [16] and in Astrolabe [14] which is an ultra-scalable state maintenance system. This prototype is based on experiences with the failure detection modules in those systems.

The Service Tracker is based on epidemic state maintenance techniques which provide an excellent foundation for constructing loosely coupled, a-synchronous, autonomous distributed components. The guarantees offered by the service are of the 'eventual consistency' category. For a member tracking service this means that if at any given moment one takes a snapshot of the overall system not all participants may have an identical membership list, but that eventually, if no other external events happen (members join, leave or fail), all participants will have the same state.

Additional advantages of using epidemic techniques for the tracking service are

- The strong mathematical underpinnings of the epidemic techniques allows us to calculate the probability of making a mistake (e.g. declaring a participant failed while it has not) based on the chosen communication parameters. One can adjust these parameters at cost of accuracy or increased communication
- The communication techniques used to exchange membership state among the participants are *highly robust*. Message loss or participant failures have only limited impact on the performance, and only then in terms of latency until all participants have received the updated state. When using epidemic techniques, it is not necessary to receive state directly from a participant, but this information can arrived through other participants.
- The membership information exchange between participants is implemented as a purely *a-synchronous* action. A participant will send a digest of its state to another participant without expecting that participant to take any action or to provide a response. The communication is really of the form *re-and-forget*, which contributes to the scalability of the service architecture. In large scale federation settings one can expect very heterogeneous participant capabilities, in terms of processing and network access, and relaxing the synchronous nature of the system will enable us to deal with this heterogeneity more efficiently.
- Participants are able to reach decisions *autonomously* about failures of other participants. No additional communication such as an agreement protocol is

needed as the decision can be based on a combination of local timestamps and the configuration parameter of the epidemic protocol. Basically if the state related to a remote participant has not changed for a time-period based on the gossip interval and number of members, which a certain probability one can state that none of the participants has received any communication from this participant.

These robustness and scalability properties make this approach to failure detection and membership management attractive to use in a large federated environments.

There are some disadvantages to using epidemic failure detection. The protocol in itself can become inefficient, as the size of the messages exchanged grows with the number of participants. A number of optimizations have been developed using adaptive and hierarchical techniques, allowing the protocol to scale better. The prototype implementation targets small to medium membership sizes up to 50 – 100 participants, for which it is not necessary to implement these optimizations. A second disadvantage is that the protocol does not deal very well with massive concurrent participant failures, which temporarily influences the accuracy of the detection mechanisms, although we have not seen any other light-weight membership modules that do much better.

The detection of failed participants is very accurate, but is often configured rather conservative. In other settings where we have used epidemic membership management and where a more aggressive approach was needed we added a layer of interrogation style probing modules to enabling early suspicions of failures.

4.1 Operational Details

The Epidemic Service Tracker (EST) is based on the principles developed in the context of the Xerox Clearinghouse project [7]. In epidemic protocols a participant forwards its local information to randomly chosen participants. In Clearinghouse this protocol was used to resolve inconsistencies between distributed directories, in EST the protocol is used to find out which participants are still 'gossiping'.

The basic operation of the protocol is rather simple: each participant maintains a list of known peers, including itself, with each entry at least holding the identification of the remote participant, a timestamp and a single integer dubbed the *heartbeat counter*. Periodically, based on protocol configuration, the participant will increment its own heartbeat counter and randomly select a peer from the membership list to send a message containing the all the <address, heartbeat> tuples it has in its membership list. Upon receipt of a message, a participant will merge the information from the message with its local membership list by adapting those tuples that have the highest heartbeat counter values. For each member for which it adopted a new heartbeat value, it will update the timestamp value in the entry. See Figure 2 for an example.

If a participant's entry has not been updated based on the configured failure period, it is declared to have failed and associated monitors are notified. The

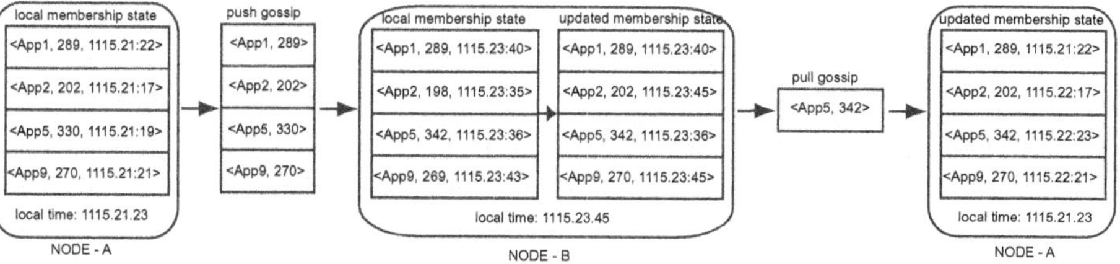

Fig. 3. Example *push-pull* style epidemic exchange of the heartbeat counters. Node-A gossips to Node-B a digest of its membership state. Node B, after merging the update with its local state returns a message to Node-A with the state that it knows is newer. As shown in the figure there is no need for the local clocks to be synchronized, all actions based on time are on local clock values.

failure period is selected such that the probability of an erroneous detection is below a certain threshold, and is directly related to the gossip communication interval. For a detailed analysis of the failure detection protocol and the relation between the probability of a mistake and the detection time see [13].

The EST prototype departs from the original model by implementing a *push-pull* model for its communication instead of the *push* used in the original design. In this model the receiving participant will, if it detects that is has entries in its membership table that are newer (e.g. have higher heartbeat counter values), send a message back to the original sender with those tuples for which it has newer values. The push-pull model has a dramatically better dissemination performance than the push model, especially in those cases where the local state at the participants change frequently, which is the case in our system. See figure 3 for an example of a push-pull operation.

4.2 Service Membership

The membership protocol operates between instances of the Service Tracker, and the failure detection described in the previous section detects failures of other Service Tracker instances. The membership however describes Member Services, and multiple such services can be registered with a single Service Tracker instance.

To implement the Member Service membership, the membership list is extended to include a list of Member Services registered with each Service Tracker instance, and this information is included in the gossip messages between the Service Trackers. Each Tracker instance can thus construct the complete list of all Member Services associated with the CoordinationContext. If a Service Tracker instance fails, all the associated Member Services are marked as failed.

If a Service Tracker determines that a Member Service has failed, either through the repeated failure of an interrogation sequence or through the *MemberFailed* indication of a Tracker Proxy, the service is marked as failed in the membership list. Other instances will receive this information through the epidemic spread of the membership information.

The information per participant send in the gossip messages is organized in five sets of Member Services:

1. Members. This is the list of the Member Service URIs that are registered and are active. This information set includes a logical timestamp (the value of the local heartbeat counter) indicating when the set was last updated.
2. *Joined.* A list of Member Services that have recently registered, with each the logical timestamp of the moment of registration. These members also appear in the *Members* set, but are included separately to ease the parsing of large membership lists. Members are removed from this list based on the epidemic protocol configuration, and all the participants will have seen the join with high probability.
3. *Left.* When a Member Service gracefully exits, it should send a *MemberLeaves* indication to the Service Tracker it has registered with. This will remove the member from the *Members* list and places it in the *Left* set, annotated with the logical timestamp.
4. *Failed.* After a member has been detected as failed it is removed from the *Members* set and placed in this set, annotated with the logical timestamp.
5. *Suspected.* An option at Activation time is to specify a threshold that would mark a member as suspected, before it is marked failed. As soon a Member Service or a Service Tracker is suspected to have failed; the related members can be placed in the *Suspected* set without that they are removed form the *Members* list. This allows the protocol to be configured to be very conservative in marking members as failed, but to be more aggressive in indicating whether a member is problematic.

4.3 Optimizing Concurrent Activations

The implementation of the Epidemic Service Tracker optimizes the case of multiple activations of the protocol. If multiple protocol instances are created at a Coordination Service instance (e.g. they have a different CoordinationContext), and there is an overlap between the participants in the protocol, the different instances will share a common epidemic communication engine. This will ensure that no unnecessary communication will take place, by avoiding duplicate gossiping. It also allows smaller member groups to benefit from the increased robustness of using a larger number of epidemic communication engines.

A second optimization implemented for tracking large but stable service groups is to gossip only a digest of the membership information instead of the complete membership lists. In this case a participant will only gossip about last logical timestamp the *Members* list was updated. If a participant receives a message with a newer logical timestamp, it can request a full membership from the sender of the gossip message or from the participant for which the updated timestamp was received.

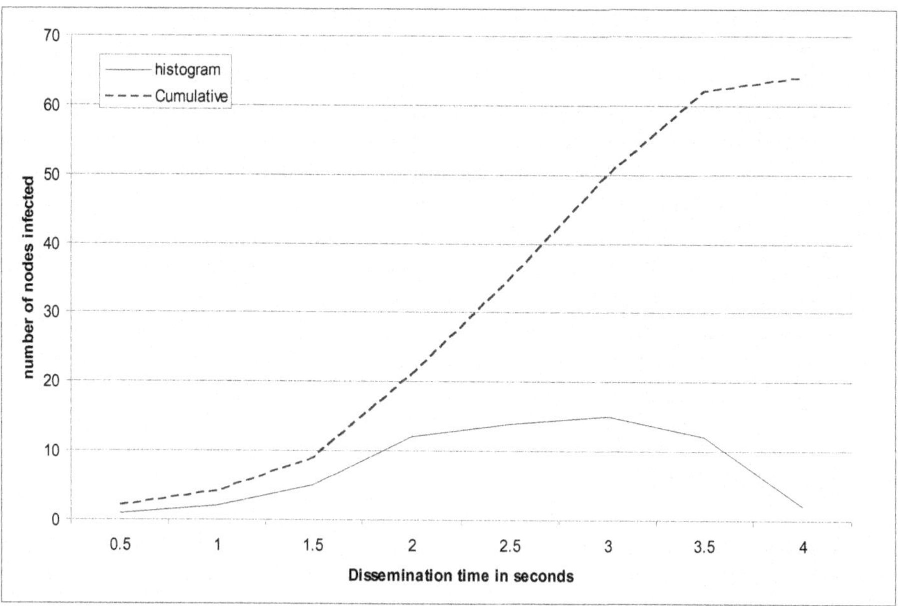

Fig. 4. Dissemination of membership information using epidemic techniques with 64 nodes with a 1 second gossip interval

5 Implemenation

The Coordination Service and Service Tracker Framework, and the Epidemic Service Tracker are implemented using functionality from Obduro Toolkit which in its part is based on the Microsoft WSE 2.0 XML Messaging Framework. A simple process monitor implementing the Tracking Proxy protocol has also been implemented.

The Service Tracker deploys 3 types of failure detection:

1. *Member Services* - through the *MemberProbe* interrogation protocol.
2. *Tracking Proxies* – through the *ProxyProbe* interrogation protocol.
3. *Service Trackers* – through the epidemic protocols.

It is a best practice to run as few remote Member and Proxy probes as possible. Running an instance of the Service Tracker on the same node as the Member Services or the Tracker Proxy will allow the probe protocols not to be subjected to network message loss, avoiding the need for a reliable transport, which improves the efficiency and accuracy of the probe protocol. The robustness of the inter- Service Tracker failure detection is not impacted by moderate message loss rate or even transient high loss rates.

In general a Service Tracker will use a separate dissemination channel to send membership updates to other participants in the membership protocol. In the case of the Epidemic Service Tracker we have chosen to include this information in the gossip messages. The advantages of this choice are that there is no need for additional communication primitives which in general needs to be a form of a reliable multicast protocol, or a brute force flooding technique. Adding a scalable reliable multicast would increase the complexity of the system while reliable flooding has scalability limitations. The epidemic dissemination of the membership information has the best of both worlds, it provide a flooding of the information, but in a very scalable, controlled and robust manner.

A disadvantage of the choice to piggy back the information on the gossiping of the heartbeats is that it disseminates rather slowly throughout the network. As can be seen in figure 4, in a setup with 64 instances of the Service Tracker it takes more than 4 seconds for the information to spread to all the nodes if these nodes only gossip once per second.

6 Related Work

We are not aware of any tracking or membership service, in research or production, which particularly targets long running business activities in service oriented architectures. We are also not aware of any public implementation of the Coordination Service/Framework that allows for dynamic management of new Coordination types.

There is a large body of work on failure detectors for different types of distributed systems, from reliable process group communication to large scale grids and from real-time factory floor settings to multi-level failure detection for clusters [4,6,8,9,10,13,14,15,19]. We expect that some of those implementations will also find their application in the web services world and we hope that our Coordination Serviceand Service Tracker Frameworks can be used to simplify the implementation and use of those systems.

An earlier preliminary description of the Service Tracker was distributed under the title *ws-membership*.

7 Future Work

This is only the first step in the development of a range of technologies as noted in section 2. One of the first follow-up tasks is to investigate how we can integrate the Service Tracker into the execution environment of system that use BPEL4WS as a driver

The software distribution of the Obduro Toolkit, the Coordination Service, the Service Tracker Framework and the Epidemic Service Tracker is slated for pubic availability in the fall of 2003.

Acknowledgements. This work is supported by a grant from Microsoft Research and by funding from DARPA under AFRL contract F30602-99-1-0532 and AFOSR/MURI contract F49620-02-1-0233.

References

1. Birman, K., and van Renesse, R., Software for reliable networks, Scientific American, 274, 5, pp. 64–69, May 1996.
2. Cabrera, F., Copeland, G.,Cox, B., Freund, T., Klein, J., Storey, T., Thatte, S., Web Services Transaction (ws-transaction), 2002, http://www.ibm.com/developerworks/library/ws-transpec/
3. Cabrera, F., Copeland, Freund, T., Klein, J.,Langworthy, D., Orchard, D., Shewchuk, J., and Storey, T., Web Services Coordination (ws-coordination), 2002, http://www.ibm.com/developerworks/library/ws-coor/
4. Chandra T.D. and Toueg S., Unreliable failure detectors for reliable distributed systems. Journal of the ACM , 43(2), pp:225–267, March 1996.
5. Chandra, T.D., Hadzilacos, V., and Toueg, S., The Weakest Failure Detector for Solving Consensus Proceedings pf the. 11th annual ACM Symposium on Principles of Distributed Computing, pages 147–158, 1992
6. Das, A., Gupta, I., Motivala, A., SWIM: Scalable Weakly-consistent Infection-style Process Group Membership Protocol, in Proceedings. of The International Conference on Dependable Systems and Networks (DSN 02), Washington DC, pp. 303–312, June, 2002
7. Demers, D. Greene, C. Hauser, W. Irish, and J. Larson. Epidemic algorithms for replicated database maintenance, in Proceedings. 6th Annual ACM Symp. Principles of Distributed Computing (PODC '87), pages 1–12, 1987
8. Felber, P., Defago, X., Guerraoui, R., and Oser, P., Failure detectors as first class objects, in Proceedings. of the 9th IEEE Int'l Symp. on Distributed Objects and Applications(DOA'99), pages 132–141, Sep. 1999.
9. Fetzer, C., Raynal, M., and Tronel, F., An adaptive failure detection protocol, in Proceedings. of the 8th IEEE Pacific Rim Symp. on Dependable Computing(PRDC-8), 2001.
10. Gupta, I., Chandra, T.D., and Goldszmidt, G., On Scalable and Efficient Distributed Failure Detectors, in Proceedings of the 20th Symposium on Principles of Distributed Computing (PODC 2001), Newport, RI, August, 2001.
11. Lamport, L., The Part-Time Parliament, ACM Transactions on Computer Systems 16, 2 (May 1998), 133–169.
12. Lampson B.W., How to build a highly available system using consensus, in Proceedings of 10th Int. Workshop on Distributed Algorithms, pp:9–11, Bologna, Italy, (October 1996).
13. Renesse, van R. Minsky, Y., and Hayden, M., A gossip-style failure detection service", in Proceedingc. of Middleware'98, pages 55–70. IFIP, September 1998.
14. Renesse, van R. Birman, K., and Vogels, W., Astrolabe, A Robust and Scalable Technology for DIstributed System Monitoring, Management and Data Mining ACM Tranactions on Computer Systems, Volume 21, Issue 2, pages 164–206, May 2003.
15. Stelling, P., Foster, I., Kesselman, C., Lee, C., and von Laszewski, G., A fault detection service for wide area distributed computations, in Proceedings. of the 7th IEEE Symp. On High Performance Distributed Computing, pages 268–278, July 1998.
16. Vogels W., and Dumitriu, D., An Overview of the Galaxy Management Framework for Scalable Enterprise Cluster Computing, in the Proceedings of the IEEE International Conference on Cluster Computing: Cluster-2000, Chemnitz, Germany, December 2000

17. Vogels, W., Technology Challenges for the Global Real-Time Enterprise, in the Proceedings of the International Workshop on Future Directions in Distributed Computing, Bertinoro, Italy, June 2002.
18. Vogels, W., van Renesse R., and Birman, K., Six Misconceptions about Reliable Distributed Computing, Proceedings of the 8th ACM SIGOPS European Workshop, Sintra, Portugal, September 1998.
19. Vogels, W., World-Wide Failures, in the Proceedings of the 1996 ACM SIGOPS Workshop, Connemora, Ireland, September 1996.

A Broker Architecture for Integrating Data Using a Web Services Environment

K.H. Bennett[1], N.E. Gold[2], P.J. Layzell[2], F. Zhu[1], O.P. Brereton[3], D. Budgen[3], J. Keane[2], I. Kotsiopoulos[2], M. Turner[3], J. Xu[1], O. Almilaji[2], J.C. Chen[2], and A. Owrak[2]

[1] Department of Computer Science, University of Durham, Durham, UK, DH1 3LE
{keith.bennett, jie.xu, fujun.zhu}@durham.ac.uk
[2] Department of Computation, UMIST, Manchester, UK, M60 1QD
{nicolas.gold, paul.layzell}@co.umist.ac.uk
[3]Department of Computer Science, Keele University, Keele, UK, ST5 5BG
{d.budgen, o.p.brereton}@cs.keele.ac.uk

Abstract. The web service protocol stack provides capabilities for loosely integrating software services but does not provide the higher level support needed for rapid evolution. An experimental system is described for integrating the data from autonomous organizations within the UK health service domain. The results of this experiment have confirmed the need for an integration layer on top of the web service stack to provide the required higher level functionality. In this paper, we summarise our progress to date, and highlight several key research issues of general concern to the web services field, which have emerged from our prototype system. These are set in a general context of providing better ways to provide a service-based model to IT users.

1 Introduction

The web service protocol stack (SOAP, WSDL etc) provides capabilities for loosely integrating software services. Currently, such protocols are limited to providing communication and basic synchronization between services but do not support the higher-level functionality needed to enable dynamic and ultra-late binding of services to form software applications on demand to a specific set of requirements. Over the last decade, we have been investigating ways to produce highly-evolvable software, resulting in a service-oriented approach to software construction. This approach requires far more than the current web service protocol stack provides, specifically, an integration layer allowing the interpretation of requirements, negotiation of terms, conditions and price, service failure management (including warranty and redress) and management of the service supply chain. These issues were identified in early prototype implementations [8] and have been re-confirmed by our experience of building the prototype described here. The issues we identify provide a roadmap for the development of the web service stack.

M.E. Orlowska et al. (Eds.): ICSOC 2003, LNCS 2910, pp. 409–422, 2003.

2 Background to Our Research: "Software as a Service"

In the 1990s, the Pennine Research Group (software engineers from the universities of Durham, Keele and UMIST) together with members of the British Telecom Research Laboratories undertook a project to consider the future of software over a ten year timespan. The main findings [8, 9, 10] are expressed in terms of six key themes. Our approach was to address software from a user perspective, and a summary major conclusion was that the cost of ownership needs to be reduced. For example, users were very unhappy with having to evolve, install, and support software (whether bespoke or shrink wrapped). These disadvantages arise because software is owned, whereas most users simply require the results from using the software.

Our conclusion was that software needs to move from being supply-side led to demand-side led; in other words, software becomes something that is used, not owned. The choice of competitive services within a marketplace is up to the user (or their applications) based on qualities such as cost, warranty and performance. We coined the term "software as a service" to describe this (see www.service-oriented.com). A service-based model is one in which one or more services are configured to meet a specific set of requirements at a point in time, executed and disengaged [10]. This view is an example of a demand-led software market in which software possession and ownership is separated from its use. This allows alternative services to be substituted between each use of a system, allowing much richer finer-grained flexibility. The data becomes available on demand and as available without perturbing the operational systems.

We identified the importance of indirection and ultra-late binding (at the point of need) in a large-scale distributed system to support this model. This is necessary but not sufficient. As a simple example, a service application on machine A, wishing to use a service on machine B, will need to pay for it, and in doing so expect some obligations in return (such as quality of service, warranty, and performance). Binding to such information will need to be automatic, without human assistance. Typically, agreement of such costs will require negotiation between parties. Thus software as a service involves issues far wider than the simple late binding of services using standard protocols. Many of the new problems occur in this area, which we call "terms and conditions".

Such terms and conditions arise because service based software is being used in a business environment. It is unrealistic to expect or require that software engineers invent a whole new environment for doing business according to a whole range of business models. Instead we expect that existing models will be used, of which there is of course a vast experience acquired over thousands of years. The contribution will therefore be to understand how these existing solutions are adapted, represented and used in the programmatic interfaces offered by service based software. Solutions are expected to be interdisciplinary, and a group, ISEN, has been set up to foster research (www.service-oriented.com/isen/).

During this research, a significant development in web services technology took place, which has become part of the enabling technology baseline by which part of our vision for future software could be realised.

Shirky [6] suggests that web services address application program inter-operability. The most general form involves binding complex programs together from pieces anywhere in the world. General inter-operability has been tried before, but with partial success, for example DCOM, Corba, and RMI. With these systems, both the client and server have to load the system; with web services, the idea is to know nothing about the "other end" other than what can be communicated via standard protocols. So WSDL allows the description of a service so that a call for it can be assembled and invoked from elsewhere. In order to communicate data in a system independent way, XML is used. A UDDI registry allows service vendors to offer services, and users to locate and call them using WSDL descriptions published along with service identification information.

However, these web service technologies are really only the first part of the solution to more flexible software. At the end of the initial phase of work, our conclusion was that for web services to be widely used, a good technical solution alone is insufficient. A major factor in the widespread acceptance of service-based approaches is to provide an architectural layer beyond the existing web service technology which provides added-value in terms of a service supply-chain, a services market and appropriate levels of trust, confidence and importantly, security [11, 12]. Such a layer can be regarded as an *integration* layer in a services technology stack.

Software has previously been developed, delivered and maintained as a product. The internet is stimulating interest in software which is instead delivered and used on demand, because this potentially allows faster and more flexible evolution to meet changing business needs; there is a much looser coupling with a service based approach between business requirements and software solution. However, actually implementing this is far more complex than technical considerations alone would suggest. For example, service based software needs to be identified and then selected; this may well require negotiation within a market [7]. The consumer application will need to have confidence that the service performs as described, and if not, means of redress are available. Fundamentally, the service model will fail if there is a lack of trust between vendors and users. Our overall research is therefore directly concerned with these *wider* problems.

To test our research findings and to scope the requirements for an integration layer in the web services stack, we have undertaken a prototype implementation of web services, addressing a real life problem. We choose, as the prototype application domain, the issue of *integrated health care data*. This was a highly appropriate case study because it combines the need for flexible software (functionality) with issues of independent, heterogeneous data sources (data) which similarly need the type of ultra-late binding required by the system's functionality.

3 The Experimental System

3.1 Application Domain

We aim to support decision-making processes where multimodal information is drawn from a set of heterogeneous, autonomous agencies. The domain of health and social care has been chosen as it offers practical examples of all the problems for which we seek technical solutions.

The UK approach is basically imposed, top down, large IT systems which encompass all the contributing organisations, ranging from general medical practitioners, through acute hospitals, and include specialist services such as pathology. Additionally in the UK, the social services are included, because of the desired aim to produce "seamless" service for the hospital patient who is then discharged to the care of local social services.

One approach is *data warehousing* [1] where operational data sources are collected into a large, centralised data store. This 'filing cabinet' approach has the disadvantages of data duplication, and update issues. Further complications arise when the underlying data is 'owned' by different organisations and is confidential. Large-scale fully integrated IT systems have failed repeatedly to provide solutions possibly because these systems were difficult to construct, manage, and evolve. Therefore, in a rapidly evolving environment alternative solutions have been proposed to enable adaptation to continuous change and maintenance of the trustworthy requirements related to ownership of confidential data, whilst enabling the global view of the distributed data sources.

Primary care practices, hospitals, mental health trusts and community health services are independent organisations, each with their own information systems and with strict rules about who may access information. Treatment of a patient will however require access to *all* records relevant to the case. Our aim is to explore the integration of data from many sources, given its often heterogeneous nature, for example, in terms of such aspects as format, semantics, meaning, importance, quality, ownership, cost and ethical control.

When information is created, modified, and stored independently, its integration requires run-time binding on demand. In human-centred management of information, this role is often performed by a human broker (such as a travel agent), who is able to integrate information on demand. In this project, we are employing a similar model, and the purpose of IBHIS (Integration Broker for Heterogeneous Information Sources) is to create an *information broker service* that will support the reliable integration of information held and managed by heterogeneous autonomous agencies. The potential for this approach can be found in many domains as well as healthcare (travel, military command & control, entertainment etc.). The project is being evaluated through the development of a series of prototype brokers and proof-of-concept healthcare demonstrators.

Brokerage, where distributed, heterogeneous data sources act as a global resource for the purposes of querying associations between and within sources, allows existing data sources to continue operational activity on their data and to retain ownership of that data. Brokerage builds on both information integration and interoperability in order to provide mediation to resolve impedance at multiple levels [2].

Potential advantages of a broker approach against fully integrated systems include:

–Supports *multiple, independent* data sources

–Handles *syntactic, semantic* and *system heterogeneity*

–Deals with *globally distributed information*

–Provides a *pathway* towards discovery and access of new information resources with the minimum of human intervention.

The broker seeks to give the user a customised, virtual picture of key information, when and where it is needed, using with permission data from autonomous systems.

There are different approaches to the problem of integration of heterogeneous information sources depending on various constraints such autonomy, security, level of integration, performance etc. Agent based systems, knowledge-based information brokers, web information retrieval and brokering systems and Federated Database Systems are all different implementations of the mediated approach. A detailed survey of such systems is published by Paton et al. [3].

Several mediated systems or information brokers have been applied in the health domain. WebFINDIT [4] is targeted at medical research in hospitals. Syanpses and SynEx [5] provide integrated views of patient data from heterogeneous, distributed information systems using the federated approach.

The health service is a highly complex domain, and for the purposes of our project, it was decided to focus on three key research areas:

1. The extent to which broker architectures can support the integration of heterogeneous data to given a single view of data for a patient.
2. How security and privacy should be addressed within a strong ethical context. Such properties have to be provided with a very strong audit function.
3. To what extent the evolution of health service IT can be supported.

In order to gain a good understanding and model of the domain, extensive activities have been undertaken involving health service professionals; these are not reported here.

3.2 Architecture

Our approach uses a three stage experiment, of which we report in detail on stage (a) which has been implemented:

a) a federated schema approach using a passive broker with data access services.
b) a service based approach using a passive broker.
c) a service based approach using an active broker.

A "passive" broker seeks information on demand and offers a customised view of data. An "active" broker notifies the user of key changes. Our basic concept is that the user queries IBHIS, and IBHIS interrogates 'local' data access services, and coalesces results. Initially, this is based on statically-bound set-up knowledge of data sources where the frequency of change may be critical; IBHIS uses a traditional federated schema solution to integration. In the next version, this will be replaced by a broker which itself is a service and can dynamically locate and bind data sources which are not compile time fixed. The architecture of the first IBHIS broker is an amalgamation of FDBMs, ontology use, and service-based software

The service-based model is realised in the first phase architecture by using web services and open standards and protocols such as Java, SOAP, WSDL and UDDI. At the same time, the global view of the distributed data is achieved by the creation of one or more federated schemas according to the user requirements. Data source registration and schema integration are essentially assumed to occur 'once-and-for-all' at set-up time. Within the Health and Social care domain this is adequate as a prototype; the possibility of data sources becoming unavailable during periods is catered for. IBHIS currently operates within and between a relatively small number of data sources, all of which hold 'real' data. In a more realistic model, it is necessary to design a supply chain, where a hierarchical structure is used, and the potential for one of the data sources itself to an IBHIS operating in a neighbouring health or social care authority. In our experiments, only artificial data about imaginary patients is used.

This notion of a 'meta-IBHIS' lends itself potentially to a scalable architecture, but the efficacy of this model across many hundreds of data sources is an area of investigation.

The users of the IBHIS broker are provided with transparent access to the heterogeneous, distributed data access services once the set-up phase is complete. During the set-up, the registration of the users and the underlying data services takes place. The system (or federation) administrator constructs the federated schema and resolves all the semantic differences. The data recorded or created during the system set-up are passed using XML to the Operational System. The architecture of the IBHIS broker is described below and in Fig. 1.

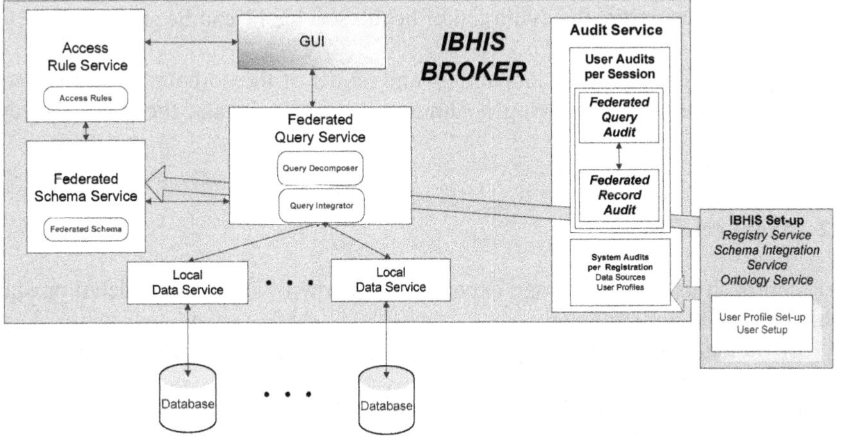

Fig. 1. The IBHIS Broker

3.3 Operational System

The aim of the operational system is to acquire a query from the user, identify access rights, locate the appropriate information sources and return the results to the user. In order to provide this functionality, the operational system consists of five communicating web services and a user interface. The web services interact according to the following model [13]:

- A data access service advertises its WSDL definition into a UDDI registry which in our case is integrated in the registry service.
- The client looks up the service's definition in the registry.

- The client uses information from the WSDL definition to send messages or requests directly to the service via SOAP.

Access Rule Service (ARS). The ARS is responsible for the initial user authentication and subsequent authorisation. Within the architecture, the ARS is primarily concerned with authorising access to the available data access services. Authorisation to other system resources is performed by the services themselves.

The initial authentication is based around usernames and encrypted passwords. The user logs onto the front-end, which in turn passes the user's credentials to the ARS. The current solution uses role based access control, where each role has its set of access rights. Much research has been conducted into Role Based Access Control (RBAC), and specifically into how it can be applied within the Health domain. However, this work has indicated that RBAC alone was too inflexible and generalised for use within the system architecture and so a more complex set of user-based access rules were developed. These, along with the access rights for the corresponding role, are used to form a user profile. In conjunction with the Federated Schema Service, the user profile identifies which aspects of the federated schema the user is authorised to view.

Federated Schema Service (FSS) and Query Service (FQS). The Federated Schema Service (FSS) keeps the federated schema and all the mappings between the export schema and the federated schema. The FSS is consulted by the Federated Query Service during the query decomposition and integration process.

The Federated Schema and the corresponding mappings to the Export Schemas are created during the set-up of the IBHIS broker.

The FQS is comprised of two sub-modules:

- *Query Decomposer:* decomposes the federated query into a set of local queries; this is done in consultation with the FSS.
- *Query Integrator:* receives the set of local results from the data access services and it integrates them into a federated record.

The FQS sends the federated query and the federated record to the audit service; this is comprised of two sub-modules which keep track of every action of IBHIS that needs to be recreated or audited in the future.

- *User Audit* (per session): holds information such as: user log-in date, time, IP, logout, sequence of federated queries, of federated record, of sessions, etc.
- *System Audit* (per Registration): holds information about data source (e.g. registration date and time, intervals of availability, etc) and user setup.

Data Access Service (DAS). The DAS is constructed using web services, but unlike typical web services, the DAS are data intensive and are responsible for providing data from their respective sources. The broker administrator implements and describes the service using WSDL and the Web Services Policy Framework [14] and also provide the consumer of the service (the FQS) with the following information:

- The data that the DAS provides, and its format
- The domain and functionality related to the data,

- The security requirements for using the service
- Other non-functional characteristics, including quality of service, and cost

The administrator then publishes the description file into the registry service, for discovery at run-time by the IBHIS operational system. For example, the DASs themselves may be programmed using different languages, and may access data sources produced by different vendors or may run on different operating systems, but the DASs provide a unified way to access the data. This is essential in the UK health services where data sources derive from many autonomous organisations, and use a range of different technologies.

When the FQS decomposes the federated query into a set of local queries, the FQS uses the registry service to look for a corresponding DAS that provides the required data outputs for each sub-query. It then uses the DAS description to bind with the data service, which accesses the data source owned by, for example, a local hospital.

A detailed study of suitable implementation tools and environments was undertaken. We are currently using Sun's Java 2 Platform, Enterprise Edition (J2EE) and IBM's Websphere.

The experimental system comprises three databases holding data about imaginary patients:
–Basic Patient Information (Keele)
–Treatment History (Manchester)
–Further Appointments (Durham)
There are three users with different authorisation levels according to their role.

This first prototype has achieved the following: a substantial application has been built using web services. Familiarity has been gained with web services toolsets and environments, providing reassurance on the technology. Extensive understanding of a highly complex domain has been achieved. The basic idea of a broker has been implemented.

This prototype has been useful in re-confirming our identification of the major problems which are discussed further in the next section.

4 Discussion and Results

4.1 Architectural Issues

The prototype implementation represents one particular approach on a spectrum of static binding to very late dynamic binding. A federated schema structure was employed, built on component data access services at three sites. This showed that creating such a high level schema manually from several data access services was feasible, provided that the number of data access services is small, and the data access services do not change often. If the approach is to be scaled up, manual integration of the federated schema (at design time), based on rapidly changing component data access services is not viable. A clear research problem is to understand better the trade-offs in achieving late binding (on demand) of data.

4.2 Web Service Protocols

As far as possible, the prototype employed standard web services protocols. The use of SOAP was successful. The prototype used RPC protocols for client-server interaction. This proved simple to implement, and offered good performance for simple calls. On the other hand, it enforced rigid data typing and binding. In retrospect, the use of document access protocols would have allowed a query to the data access service to be constructed dynamically. The RPC mechanism forced us to use artificial methods of parameter transmission using packed strings instead of arrays (hence requiring an overhead to pack, and then parse).

We also found that the tight coupling inherent in RPC calls caused severe problems during the development of the prototype, as service interfaces changed rapidly. It is not likely that RPC will provide an adequate mechanism for inter-program service calls in the face of rapid evolution. Our prototype was able to cope because we specified the service interfaces in advance. This is a serious restriction, and in subsequent prototypes we will abandon this and experiment with document messaging.

4.3 Registry

In the prototype, a UDDI registry was not used; as a result, the broker needed to know about component data access services and interfaces at design time, although it still enabled particular data access services to be located and bound in at run time (given that the broker has a built-in extensive knowledge of the services). Clearly this does not allow new data access services to be added easily, or permit changes to existing services. A priority in the next prototype is the addition of a full UDDI type registry for the support of dynamic data access services. This is a significant research problem, as most web service experiments are concerned with providing executable code as a service, not data. For example, it is not clear if the interface to the data access service should be procedural (perhaps including in the service some business logic); an alternative is to provide an interface based on SQL.

4.4 Web Services Description

We used WSDL exclusively to describe our web services. This was sufficient to define adequate descriptions for the prototype, but we do not feel it will be sufficient to describe the full functional and non-functional attributes necessary for a realistic service oriented approach. In particular, it does not provide an adequate level of description of security, versioning, quality of service, and costs. More generally in the health service environment, we see that ontology-base approaches will be essential to map between the various schemes of terminology in use; certainly, the keyword type access of UDDI will be insufficient.

4.5 Development Issues

The three distributed data access services were programmed using different concepts, at three different sites, on heterogeneous platforms, and based on different data base management systems.
The project used IBM's Websphere for the prototype. The services constructed met the aim of platform and language independence, and we are confident that (following experiments with GLUE, a second development environment) that implementation independence should be readily achievable.
We found that Websphere (V5) provided the facilities to implement, test and deploy web services. The ability automatically to generate WSDL, SOAP and XML saved much time. The Concurrent Versions System supported version control for development distributed across three sites.

4.6 Summary

The use of an integrated development environment saved considerable time, though there was an inevitable overhead in familiarisation. Otherwise, two central issues have emerged from our prototype:

1. Potentially, web services can benefit from very late binding in order to construct, on the fly, a system which is required by the user. On the other hand, the achievement of dynamic binding is beyond the capabilities of current protocols. The trade-offs and capabilities on this spectrum of static through to ultra-late binding need further experimentation and deeper understanding.

2. Much work on web services has concentrated on functional provision. It is clear that additional problems of description, performance, scale, privacy and level of abstraction arise with services which focus on data.

5 Wider Issues

Our experience with the IBHIS project has additionally confirmed that many of the wider issues in service-based software that we have identified in previous work [8, 9, 10] exist for data-oriented service integration as much as for functional service integration. This section describes these in more detail.

5.1 Supply Chain Formation and Management

The potential issues about supply chain management have been recognised in component-based software engineering (CBSE) environments. However, most of the solutions suggested are largely confined to using repositories or documents to indicate component attributes [15, 16, 17, 18]. Such solutions favour stable user requirements which are unlike the rapidly changing nature of the user requirements in IBHIS environments. On the other hand, web services only address the technological issues of the problem caused by heterogeneity among enterprise applications, middleware, and components. Web services do not solve the problem of rapidly changing requirements and the vast dynamics in supply chains (essentially recursive use of web services) caused by requirement changes.

In a service environment, software services will be procured and assembled from sub-services or components along supply chains. Therefore, optimising such supply chains is essential. One question emerges: are the supply chains visible for all participants in order to extend optimisation and coordination? A negotiation description language (NDL) provides part of the answer to this question. Information stored in automatic negotiations along supply chains can be very useful for other participants to adjust their own activities for the purpose of optimising the whole performance of supply chains. So far NDL is specific to one-to-one negotiation situations [7, 19]. By expanding the scope of NDL to many-to-many negotiations, participants can simultaneously obtain information about other suppliers and react accordingly. More importantly, the information exchanged in negotiations can cover both technical conformance and other legal, commercial aspects. Such information will determine the success of online marketplaces in service environments. Successful negotiation results guarantee not only the conformance of technical requirements but also the agreement and fulfillment across various non-functional issues such as prices, terms and conditions.

The central theme of our current research in this area is to combine the aspects of many-to-many negotiations in NDL and optimize them using techniques such as Quality Function Deployment [20]. With this approach, a user can go to the marketplace to post requests for software services and have needs satisfied. Service providers in the supply chain responsible for the request can procure, assemble, and deliver their promised service according to agreed price, time duration, or other kinds of technical or contractual conformances. This approach could allow service providers to manage their service offerings and the according supply chains in an efficient and viable way.

5.2 Service Quality Assessment

A new process is needed to address the issue of software quality. This would form a *just-in-time* audit agent rapidly to assess the quality of individual software services prior to system composition. Such a process would need to satisfy all of the usual characteristics that exist within product quality evaluation, whilst addressing the specific needs that are essential to the delivery of services. Furthermore, the development of such a process will allow system brokers and consumers to identify the important quality features that are relevant to their needs prior to system composition. We are developing an automated tool, capable of performing quality assessments on the fly.

We are concerned with two aspects of quality. The first focuses on what attributes and characteristics of quality can be identified within our “software as a service” model. The second addresses the measurement of these quality characteristics with the aim of allowing automatic compatibility assessments of services to take place.

Selecting the 'best' service is a complex decision process for clients. The process requires a large number of quality characteristics to be simultaneously measured and evaluated. Many of these are related to one another thus may conflict insofar as improvement in one often results in decline of another (e.g. as usability increases, security may decrease).

We have devised a quality model linked to the International Standard for Software Product Evaluation ISO-9126 (see [21]). The model aims to support the automated evaluation of services prior to service composition.

5.3 Minimising Composition Time

One factor crucial to the success of our model is the speedy composition and delivery of services to the customer. Two major factors are:

1. *Searching time*: the time spent on the process of screening the marketplace to find the required service's components.

2. *Composition time*: the estimated time spent on assembling the combination of selected components. Composition can be defined as the binding of many services into new service that is expected to satisfy the user requirements and be ready to run. Based on that, the composition phase of producing service-based software could be seen as equivalent to the design phase in traditional software engineering.

In our current composition model, the selection of a service's components will depend on the behaviour or functions required while the form or style of the composition will rely on the communication. Thus, the style of the composition which will be carried out will consider only the communication (interface, connectors, data and the relationships) specified between the service's components. No knowledge of the internal structure of the service's components is used to derive the composition.

5.4 Comprehending Service-Based Systems

Another aspect of our work is looking at mechanisms, information, and processes for handling software failure in a service-oriented architecture. This work is at an early stage but thus far we have only theoretical discussions of how such a failure might be comprehended.

6 Conclusion

We have described the first stage of an implementation of a service based solution to integrating heterogeneous independent databases, using a broker architecture. The IBM Websphere and J2EE systems have been used as the testbed. We have been able to draw wider conclusions about the appropriateness of our approach for larger scale systems which include both data and functional services. In terms of the three research questions posed in 1.1, we have implemented a solution to the first two used web services. We have not yet addressed the third issue (evolution) and this is now the focus of our research.

Acknowledgements. The authors would like to thank all members of the IBHIS project and the Pennine Group for their valuable contributions to this paper. The financial support of EPSRC through the DIM programme is acknowledged.

References

1. Widom, J., Research problems in data warehousing, Proceedings of 4th International Conference on Information and Knowledge Management, (1995)
2. Kashyap, V. and Sheth, A., Information brokering across heterogeneous digital data: a metadata-based approach. Boston; London: Kluwer Academic (2000)
3. Paton, N.W., Goble, C.A., and Bechhofer, S., Knowledge based information integration systems, Information and Software Technology, Vol. 42, No. 5 (2000) 299–312
4. Bouguettaya, A., Benatallah, B., Ouzzani, M., and Hendra, L., WEBFINDIT: An architecture and system for querying web databases, IEEE Internet Computing, vol. 3, No. 4 (1999) 30–41
5. Grimson, J., Stephens, G., Jung, B., Grimson, W., Berry, D., and Pardon, S., Sharing health-care records over the Internet, IEEE Internet Computing, Vol. 5, No. 3 (2001) 49–58
6. Shirky, C., Web services and context horizons. IEEE Computer, September, Vol.35, No. 9 (2002) 98–100
7. Layzell, P. J. and A. Elfatatry, Negotiating in Service Oriented Environments. Comm. ACM. (to appear).
8. Bennett, K. H., Gold, N. E., Munro, M., Xu, J., Layzell, P. J., Budgen, D., Brereton, O. P. and Mehandjiev, N. Prototype Implementations of an Architectural Model for Service-Based Flexible Software. Proc. Thirty-Fifth Hawaii International Conference on System Sciences (HICSS-35), edited by Ralph H. Sprague, Jr. Published by IEEE Computer Society, CA, ISBN 0-7695-1435-9 (2002)
9. Bennett, K. H., Layzell, P. J., Budgen, D., Brereton, O. P., Macaulay, L., Munro, M., Service-Based Software: The Future for Flexible Software, IEEE APSEC2000, The Asia-Pacific Software Engineering Conference, 5–8 December 2000, Singapore, IEEE Computer Society Press (2000)
10. Brereton, P., Budgen, D., Bennett, K.H., Munro, M., Layzell, P.J., and Macaulay, L.A., The Future of Software: Defining the Research Agenda, Communications of the ACM, Vol. 42, No. 12 (1999)
11. Yang, E.Y., Xu, J., and Bennett, K.H., A fault-tolerant approach to secure information retrieval, in Proc. 21st IEEE International Symposium on Reliable Distributed Systems, Osaka, Oct. (2002)
12. Yang, E.Y., Xu, J., and Bennett, K.H., Private information retrieval in the presence of malicious faults, in Proc. 26th IEEE International Conference on Computer Software and Applications (COMPSAC2002), Oxford, Aug. (2002)
13. Vinoski, S., Web services interaction models, part 1: Current practice, IEEE Internet Computing, vol. 6, No. 3, (2002) 89–91
14. IBM, Microsoft, BEA, SAP, Web Services Policy Framework, http://www-106.ibm.com/developerworks/library/ws-polfram/, 10 March (2003)
15. Bachman, F., Bass, L., Buhman, C., Comella-Dorda, S., Long. F., Robert, J., Seacord. R, and Wallnau, K., Volume II: Technical Concepts of Component-Based Software Engineering, Technical Report, May, Software Engineering Institute, Carnegie Mellon University (2003) (CMU/SEI-2000-TR-008)
16. Iribarne, L.; Troya, J.M.; Vallecillo, A., Trading for COTS components in open environments, Euromicro Conference, 2001. Proceedings. 27th, 4–6 Sept (2001) 30–37

17. Ncube, C. and Maiden, N.A., Acquiring COTS software selection requirements, IEEE Software, Vol. 15, No. 2, Mar-Apr (1998) 46–56
18. Seacord, R., Mundie, D., and Boonsiri, S., K-BACEE: A Knowledge-Based Automated Component Ensemble Evaluation Tool, Technical Note, Software Engineering Institute, Carnegie Mellon, December (2000) (CMU/SEI-2000-TN-015)
19. Elfatary, Ahmed, Service Oriented Software: A Negotiation Perspective, PhD thesis, Department of Computation, UMIST, UK (2003)
20. Akao, Yoji, Quality Function Deployment: Integrating Customer Requirements into Product Design, translated by Mazur, G..H. and Japan Business Consultants, Cambridge, MA. (1990)
21. ISO/IEC 9126–1 Information Technology – Software Product Quality Part 1: Quality Model, International Standards Organisation (1998)

Design and Implementation of the Multilingual Product Retrieval Agent through XML and the Semantic Networks in EC *

Yoo-Jin Moon [1], Kijoon Choi [1], Kyongho Min [2], Wan Pyong Kim [1], Youngho Hwang [3], Pankoo Kim [4], and Youngse Mun [5]

[1] MIS Department, Hankuk University of Foreign Studies
270 Imun-dong Tongdaemun-Gu
Seoul 130-791, Korea
yjmoonmis@hanmail.net, kjnch@orgio.net, wan100@chollian.net

[2] School of Computer and Information Sciences
Auckland University of Technology
Auckland 1020, New Zealand
kyongho.min@aut.ac.nz

[3] Kunsan University, Kunsan, Cheonbuk 573-701, Korea

[4] Chosun University, Kwangju 506-741, Korea

[5] Korea National Defense University, Seoul 122-875, Korea
yhwang@kunsan.ac.kr, pkkim@chosun.ac.kr

Abstract. Retrieval for products is an important task for e-commerce, since it represents an interface of the customer contact to e-commerce. And e-commerce should provide customers with easily accessible processes in searching. Especially, the product information on the World Wide Web needs integration and standardization to keep the pace of rapid expansion with wide reachable ranges. International standards on product catalogs are converging on UNSPSC (Universal Standard Products and Services Classification). With adoption of this standard, we designed the architecture of a multilingual product retrieval agent. The architecture is based on the central repository model of product catalog management with a distributed updating process. It also includes the perspectives of buyers and suppliers. In addition, the consistency and version management of product information are controlled by UNSPSC. The multilingual product names are resolved by semantic networks, a thesaurus, and product name ontology, which enable the present architecture to be expanded to the Semantic Web applications.

1 Introduction

One prerequisite to facilitate web-based e-commerce is a technological infrastructure. The technological infrastructure has several layers, which include network protocols,

* This work was supported by Korea Research Foundation Grant (KRF-2002-041-B00166).

M.E. Orlowska et al. (Eds.): ICSOC 2003, LNCS 2910, pp. 423–433, 2003.

application architecture, and business process technologies. Recently many researchers move toward issues of the application architecture. The architecture issues address the impending problems without losing flexibility and potential appropriation. A key process of the architecture issues is a product search or a retrieval service for potential buyers in Internet. From the buyers' point of view, the searching process on the World Wide Web is tightly related with efficiency of the electronic transactions.

A classification system of the product plays a key role in developing a solution of product retrieval using a standard framework in e-commerce [1]. Thus, it is important to standardize e-catalogs of the product classification system. In reality, each industry develops its e-catalogs independently. Therefore, we need to integrate product information across industries and languages for a globalized e-commerce environment. The complexities of language translation and product information representation are mixed in web-based e-commerce sites. And endeavors to solve these complexities lead to Semantic Web implementation in e-commerce. The advance of integration technologies and mechanisms based on the world wide web paved the way to design a multilingual product retrieval agent with a semantic processing capability. We propose the architecture of the multilingual product retrieval agent, based on the Semantic Web, that tackles the complexities of the language translation and the product information representation.

2 Literature Review

To process product information in Internet for e-commerce we need to develop XML-based knowledge representation [2]. Self-describing features of XML trigger an integration problem among web-based documents [3]. Each developer may use a different set of XML tags and structures, which results in the chaos of semantic interpretations. This limitation of XML invokes Semantic Web activities [4]. The Semantic Web can give a formal structure to the web-based documents, and enables software agents to automate semantic processing on behalf of users.

XML has definite limits on semantic representation of the structure in a consistent way [5]. So it may be used for an integration mechanism at the conceptual level for the product retrieval agent. Therefore, we need a Semantic Web technology to deal with various product information and a multilingual problem involved in globalized e-commerce environments, even when we use the e-catalogs [6], [7].

RDF (Resource Description Framework) is a cornerstone of the Semantic Web, in which the RDF represents semantic relations by subjects, predicates, and objects [8], [9]. The RDF provides minimal consistency without losing flexibility, and it delegates domain-dependent representation to ontologies [10], [11]. Some part of the ontology is contained in an e-catalog system [7]. The Semantic Web will enable the computer-operated WWW data to be automated, integrated, and reused [12], [13].

Ontology is used for knowledge representation of facts or states defined by entities and their relationships. The ontology is an enabler of Semantic Web technologies [14]. The ontology provides relevant domain knowledge for RDF [15], [16], which has relational structures among resources, properties, and values. The well-defined ontology on the relevant domain is a prerequisite for semantic applications in e-commerce [17].

Semantic networks represent hypernyms of word senses in the form of isa-hierarchy. WordNet [18] is an English semantic network based on a psycholinguistic theory. It represents lexical concept in the form of isa-hierarchy of each word sense. Synonym sets (synsets) is a set of lexical concepts of English nouns, adverbs, adjectives, and verbs. Each synset represents one underlying lexical concept. This paper refers to WordNet for nouns as a knowledge base to disambiguate word senses in English product names.

The semantic network of Korean nouns, called Korean Noun Networks (KNN) [19], has been built in the form of ISA hierarchy. The ISA hierarchy consists of a node and an edge. The node represents synonym sets composed of Korean nouns and English WordNet. The edge represent hypernymous relations between the nodes. In this paper, KNN are utilized to automatically extract the sets of hyponymous concepts. This paper refers KNN as a knowledge base to disambiguate word senses in Korean product names.

There are many kinds of agents for e-commerce, for example, agents for recommendation, agents for negotiation, agents for comparison shopping, agents for e-catalog management, and etc. The agents proposed in this paper have common characteristics with those for recommendation and comparison shopping. The agents for recommendation need to meet the conditions as follows. First, acquisition of users' information should follow the semantic relationships of web-based documents or contents. Second, the agents have to show flexible responses to changes in web site contents. Third, they need to accommodate, incrementally and persistently, the change of a user's requirement. Fourth, they should have a natural user interface. Fifthly, they need implicit methods to draw user requirements. Finally, they should allow continuous learning for performance enhancements. With these features enabled, we need a distributed agent managing product codes used in e-catalogs [6].

Standardization can contribute to reduce the development cost [1], and to facilitate interoperability between heterogeneous systems [20]. Several propositions about standardization have been published within interoperable B2B business frameworks. Most frameworks are based on XML and Table 1 summarizes the most popular standardized frameworks such as BizTalk by Micoroft, RossettaNet by IBM and Intel, ebXML by UN/CEFACT and OASIS.

Table 1. General Characteristics of E-commerce Frameworks

Framework	Structure	Applicable Industry	Major Groups
ebXML	horizontal	General	OASIS, UN/CEFACT
RossetaNet	vertical	IT/EC/SM	IBM, Intel, and other commercial corp.'s
BizTalk	horizontal	General	Microsoft
eCo	horizontal	General	CommerceNet

There are two kinds of product code for e-commerce: a product classification code and a product identification code. The product classification code enables categorical searches by grouping similar products, and the product identification code matches a specific product to a code. An UNSPSC (Universal Standard Products and Services Classification) code system has been developed especially for e-commerce. It is the one of the best code systems for alignment of diverse systems in distributed environments. The characteristics of the UNSPSC code system are as follows. First, it fits for e-commerce, ERP, spending analysis, and etc. Second, product categories are adjustable to most industries. Third, the classification is detailed and publicly accessible without restriction.

A central repository model is for the alignment of e-catalog storages by ebXML and UDDI (Universal Description, Discovery and Integration) technologies. There are other e-catalog alignment models such as the single server model, the virtual catalog model, and the mediator model.

3 Design of a Multilingual Product Retrieval Agent

The architecture utilizes the central repository model for e-catalog management. The central repository model is a pull model that the users register their product codes voluntarily, and the repository maintains the catalog information providing access to anyone. We used UNSPSC (Universal Standard Products and Services Classification) as a product code system that provides consistent digit-based universal product, and service codes across language variants.

The proposed architecture reflects both buyers' and suppliers' perspectives in product information integration. Structures built in the directories of product information may be maintained individually. The digit-based product code system gives the consistency across different mechanisms involved.

Ambiguity and uncertainty of product names, that are caused by synonyms, homonyms, and polysemys, can be processed for product names by a semantic network, a thesaurus, and an ontology dictionary of product names. Fig. 1 illustrates examples of the synonyms which will be processed by the semantic network of each language. Fig. 2 illustrates examples of a pair of homonyms and a pair of polysemys which will be processed for a convenient user interface by the ontology dictionary and the thesaurus for products, from the viewpoint of buyers and suppliers. Referencing the thesaurus may provide relevant terms and concepts, but it can not provide semantic differences in computer-operable ways. So, the ontology dictionary of product names is introduced for differentiation of polysemys illustrated as in Fig. 2.

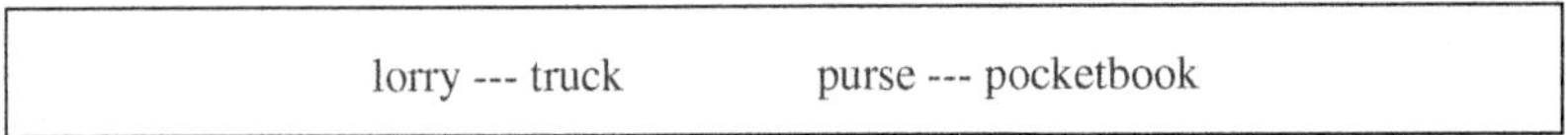

Fig. 1. Examples of Synonyms in Product Names

foil -> sheet metal,	foil -> fencing sword
bonnet -> hat,	bonnet -> protective covering (ex. a part of car)

Fig. 2. Examples of Homonyms and Polysemys in Product Names

RDF is a representation of metadata for resources [19], [20]. Generally, it applies to information on web sites. Ontology on product information may be integrated with RDF modelings to facilitate product retrieval on the web sites. In Fig. 3, 'Shoes' is represented by a RDF graph. The UNSPSC code of Shoes is 53111600: 53 for a segment, 11 for a family, 16 for a class, 00 for a commodity. Table 2 shows the composition of the UNSPSC codes of 'Shoes', 'Men's Shoes', 'Women's Shoes', and 'Skate Shoes'.

Table 2. Examples of UNSPSC Codes for Products

Product	Segment	Family	Class	Commodity
Shoes	53	11	16	00
Men's Shoes	53	11	16	01
Women's Shoes	53	11	16	02
Skate Shoes	49	15	16	02

Properties or predicates can be used to represent the relational property of product information as illustrated in Fig. 3. In this example productCode_Of is a predicate element. It may also be represented as an object.

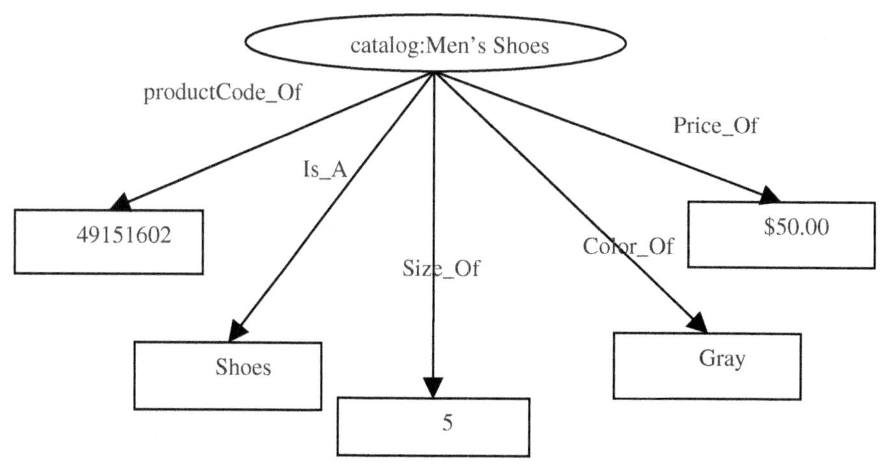

Fig. 3. An Example of Properties of Men's Shoes in a RDF Graph

Fig. 4 shows an example of RDF representation of properties of Men's Shoes in Fig. 3.

```
<RDF xmlns:a="http://mislab.hufs.ac.kr/catalog#">
<rdf:Description ID="Men's Shoes">
   <a:Price_Of>$50.00</a:Price_Of>
   <a:Color_Of>Gray</a:Color_Of>
   <a:Size_Of>5</a:Size_Of>
   <a:Is_A>Shoes</a:Is_A>
   </rdf:Description>
</rdf:RDF>
```

Fig. 4. RDF Representation of Properties of Men's Shoes

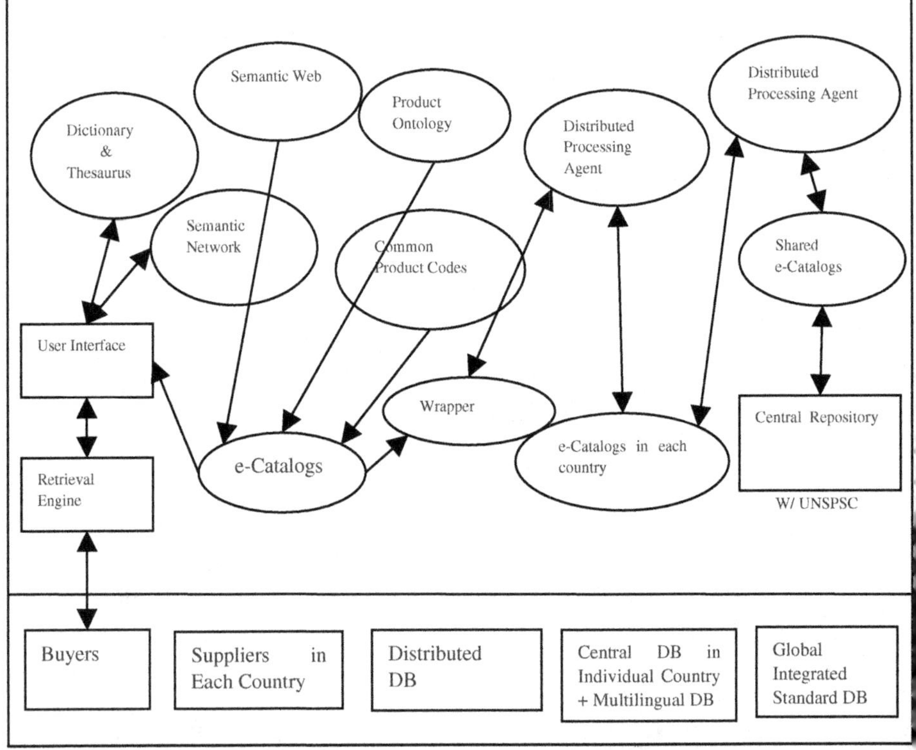

Fig. 5. Architecture of A Product Retrieval Agent

Fig. 5 illustrates the architecture in which our proposed retrieval agent works. The main characteristics of the proposed product retrieval agent are as follows:

- Knowledge bases: a common product code (UNSPSC), product ontology, common e-catalogs, a bilingual dictionary, multilingual semantic networks, and a thesaurus
- Perspectives: buyers' and merchants' perspectives
- Management model of e-catalogs: a central repository model with distributed processing environments
- Level or range: buyers, merchants, suppliers, product information processing procedures in each country, globally integrated standard catalogs

In this paper we used the semantic network to resolve ambiguities caused by synonyms, homonyms, and polysemys in the system implementation. The architecture covers overall interactions among components involved in product retrieval processes. The architecture is based on the central repository model of e-catalog management using globally integrated standardization of product information. The central repository model is an alignment model for industry e-catalog storages using ebXML and UDDI. And the classification structures are to be implemented in XML, specifically in Semantic Web.

Data consistency is maintained by 8-digit (optionally 10-digit) coded UNSPSC. The UNSPSC code system is well suited for external interoperability of product information, and is specifically developed for electronic commerce. The problems of a static product code system can be alleviated by the semantic networks, that support a semantic-based retrieval process from the buyers' perspective.

4 Implementation of the Agent for Product Retrieval

In this chapter, we describe the main implementation algorithms of ambiguous product names, which are not included in the UNSPSC code system for convenient multilingual product retrieval processes. And we define several functions of the algorithms related to the multilingual product retrieval agent, as follows:

- UNSPSC(user): a set of UNSPSC list translated into a_language used by a user;
- UNSPSC_CODE(pn): a UNSPSC code of pn (i.e. product_names) in UNSPSC list;
- SYNSET(pn): a set of synset of pn extracted from semantic networks;
- HYPERNYM(pn): an ordered list of pn's hypernyms extracted from an ontology dictionary;
- HYPONYM(pn): an ordered list of pn's hyponyms extracted from an ontology dictionary;
- SEMANTIC_NETWORKS(user): a set of semantic networks built by the user's language;
- THESAURUS(user): a set of thesaurus for product names written in language used by the user;
- RELATED(pn): an ordered list of a product name related to pn in the thesaurus;
- TRANSLATED(pn): translated pn into English using a bilingual dictionary;

An algorithm retrieving synonyms of product names selects a product name and its code from the UNSPSC code system in each language, using the semantic networks and the ontology dictionary of product names.

```
RetrievalForSynonyms(pn, user)   :
{Input of pn(a product name) from the user};
if pn is found in UNSPSC(user)
   then return the UNSPSC code
   else if SEMANTIC_NETWORKS(user) is not found
           then { pn = TRANSLATED(pn);  user=English;}
        EndIf;
EndIf;
find SYNSET(pn) from SEMANTIC_NETWORKS(user);
if  SYNSET(pn) is null   then exit();
for each i in SYNSET(pn) {
  if  i  is found in UNSPSC(user)
      then return  i &UNSPSC_CODE(i);
  for each j in HYPONYM(i) from SEMANTIC_NETWORKS(user)
    if   j is found in UNSPSC(user)
         then display i&j;
  for each k in HYPERNYM(i) fromSEMANTIC_NETWORKS(user)
    if  k is found in UNSPSC(user) then display  i & k;
}EndFor

Let the user select what he wants to retrieve from the
displayed lists;

if the user selects one item,
then return the item and UNSPSC_CODE(item);
EndRetrievalForSynonyms
```

An algorithm retrieving homonyms of product names selects the product name and its code from the UNSPSC code system using the ontology dictionary of product names.

```
RetrievalForHomoyms(pn, user)   :
{Input of pn(a product name) from the user};
If pn is found in UNSPSC(user) more than once
   then find all pairs of pn & UNSPSC_CODE(pn)
   else exit();
EndIf;
for  each i in all pairs of pn & UNSPSC_CODE(pn) {
     find  HYPERNYM(i)  from an ontology dictionary;
     display i & HYPERNYM(i);
}EndFor
```

```
Let the user select what he wants to retrieve from the
displayed lists;

if the user selects one item,
then return the item and UNSPSC_CODE(item);
EndRetrievalForHomonyms
```

An algorithm that retrieves polysemys of product names selects the product name and its code from the UNSPSC code system using the ontology dictionary and the thesaurus of product names.

```
RetrievalForPolysemys(pn, user)  :
{Input of pn(a product name) from the user};
If pn is found in the entry of  THESAURUS(user)  more
than once
  then find all pairs of pn & UNSPSC_CODE( RELATED(pn))
  else exit();
EndIf;
for each i in pairs of pn & UNSPSC_CODE(RELATED(pn))
   display i & RELATED(i);

Let the user select what he wants to retrieve from the
displayed lists;

if the user selects one item,
then return the item and UNSPSC_CODE(item);
EndRetrievalForPolysemys
```

The suggested algorithms were tested for the agents of keyword-based product retrieval. If the retrieved product name exists in the UNSPSC code system in either English or other languages, the agent returns the exact UNSPSC code number. Then the product retrieval is considered to be performed successfully.

Experiments show that 21 out of 24 synonyms of the product names have succeeded in product retrieval, and that 20 out of 20 homonyms of the product names have succeeded in product retrieval. Synonyms of the product names trigger failure in product retrieval when they do not exist in the semantic network. Polysemys of PN (product names) trigger failure in product retrieval when they are coined words.

5 Conclusion

The interoperability can be assured by developing XML-based e-catalogs on products. E-catalogs can represent structured product information, but may not be used to integrate heterogeneous product information for efficient buyers' product searches. Recently proposed semantic web mechanisms, presented in RDF graphs, provide new opportunities for web product retrieval. The keyword-based retrieval is efficient as long as the product information is well structured and organized. But when the product information is displayed across many online shopping malls, especially when it is described in different languages with different cultural backgrounds, buyers' product retrieval needs language translation of the product information disambiguated in a specific context. We presented a RDF modeling case that resolved semantic problems in the representation of product information and across the boundaries of the language domain.

With adoption of the UNSPSC code system, we designed and implemented an architecture for the multilingual product retrieval agent. The architecture was based on the central repository model of product catalog management with distributed updating processes. It also included the perspectives of buyers and suppliers. And the consistency and version management of product information were controlled by the UNSPSC code system. The ambiguities of multilingual product names were resolved by the semantic network, the thesaurus, and the ontology dictionary of product names. The suggested algorithm would be applied to multilingual product retrieval in any language, as long as there exists its bilingual dictionary or its semantic network.

Classification standards representing products in electronic commerce require researches on design and implementation issues to validate the industrial guidelines involved in the standard-setting procedures. The UNSPSC code system should be standardized in the product code system and in the integration of product information across the industries.

Future works are, firstly, to update synonym sets of the semantic networks for convenient interfaces, and to update coined words in the UNSPSC system and the semantic networks. Secondly, the product names in the UNSPSC system should be completed with cooperation of suppliers and venders. Thirdly, each country should keep its own UNSPSC system translated into its language.

References

1. Zhao, Y.: Develop the Ontology for Internet Commerce by Reusing Existing Standards. Proceedings of International Workshop on Semantic Web Foundations and Application Technologies. (2003)
2. Anutariya, C., Wuwongse, V., and Akama, K.: XML Declarative Description with Negative Constraints. Proceedings of International Workshop on Semantic Web Foundations and Application Technologies. (2003)
3. Choi, M. Y., and Joo, K. S.: A Unified Design Methodology based on Extended Entity-Relationship Model for XML Applications. 2nd International Conference on Computer and Information Science (ICIS 2002). (2002) 136–141
4. Fu, Fengli, Song, Y., and Kim, Y.: XML and Bioinformatics. 2nd International Conference on Computer and Information Science. (2002) 147–152
5. Chao-Min, C.: Reengineering Information Systems with XML. Information Systems Management, Vol.17:4. (2000) 40–54

6. Baron, J. P., Shaw, M. J., and Bailey Jr., A. D.: Web-based E-catalog Systems in B2B Procurement. Communications of the ACM, Vol.43:5. (2000) 93–100
7. Stanoevska-Slabeva, K., and Schmid, B.: Internet Electronic Product Catalogs: An Approach Beyond Simple Keywords and Multimedia. Computer Networks, Vol.32. (2000) 701–715
8. Fensel, D., Hendler, J., Lieberman, H., and Wahlster, W.: Spinning the Semantic Web. MIT Press (2003)
9. Geroimenko, V., and Chen, C.: Visualizing the Semantic Web. Springer-Verlag (2003)
10. W3C: Resource Description Framework(RDF) Model and Syntax Specification. (1999)
11. W3C: Resource Description Framework(RDF) Schema Specification 1.0. (2000)
12. Berners-Lee, T.: The Semantic Web. Scientific American (2001)
13. Berners-Lee, T.: Weaving the Web. HarperCollins (2000)
14. Desmontils, E., and Jacquin, C.: Indexing a Web Site with a Terminology Oriented Ontology. (http://www.semanticweb.org/SWWS/program/full/paper5.pdf). (2003)
15. Broekstra, J., Klein, M., Decker, S., Fensel, D., van Harmelen, F., and Horrocks, I.: Enabling Knowledge Representation on the Web by Extending RDF Schema. Computer Networks, Vol.39. (2002) 609–634
16. Horrocks, I., and Hendler, J.: The Semantic Web - ISWC 2002. Springer-Verlag (2002)
17. Gruber, T. R.: A Translation Approach to Portable Ontology Specifications. Knowledge Systems Laboratory Technical Report KSL 92–71. Knowledge Systems Laboratory, Stanford University (1993)
18. Miller, G. A. , Beckwith, R., Fellbaum, C., Gross, D., and Miller, K.: Introduction to WordNet : An On-line Lexical Database. in Five Papers on WordNet, CSL Report. Cognitive Science Laboratory, Princeton University (1993)
19. Moon, Y.: Construction of Semantic Networks for the Language Information Processing. Proc. of International Symposium on Advanced Intelligent Systems. (2001) 42–46
20. Jhingran, A. D., and Pirahesh, M. N.: Information Integration: A Research Agenda. IBM Systems Journal, Vol.41:4. (2002) 555–562
21. Cruz, I. F.: Final Report of NSF Sponsored Workshop, International Semantic Web Working Symposium (SWWS). (2001) (http://www.semanticweb.org/SWWS/report/swws-report.pdf).

SpaceGlue: Linking Spaces for Adaptive and Situational Service Location

Tomoko Itao[1], Satoshi Tanaka[1], and Tatsuya Suda[2,3]*

[1] NTT Network Innovation Laboratories
3-9-11 Midori-cho, Musashino-shi,Tokyo, 180-8585 Japan
{tomoko, satoshi}@ma.onlab.ntt.co.jp
[2] Department of Information and Computer Science
University of California, Irvine
Irvine, CA 92697-3425 USA
suda@ics.uci.edu

Abstract. We propose and describe a networking technology called SpaceGlue for locating, communicating with, and interacting with services/people in a ubiquitous computing environment. In SpaceGlue, service components are embedded in a local communication area called a *ubiquitous space* and collaboratively provide an application. A user can locate desired service components offered in the local space by sending a query within the space. To allow users to discover service components that match their preferences in remote spaces, SpaceGlue dynamically links or "glues" together different spaces based on relationships among spaces that are estimated from the behavior history of many users. For example, if many users often visit a cafe and theater on the same day, these two spaces creates bonds to each other, reflecting the strong relationship among them. This lets users in the theater discover services in the cafe. We propose an algorithm for manipulating bonds to enable adaptive service location. We designed and implemented SpaceGlue using a distributed service platform called Ja-Net and showed that SpaceGlue is useful for adaptively locating services through simulation.

1 Introduction

The recent expansion of wireless network coverage opens the door to ubiquitous computing applications — diverse service components will be embedded in the user's physical environment and integrated seamlessly with the user's local activities. We call such a service environment a *ubiquitous space* (hereafter, space). In these spaces, service components are more or less tied to real-world entity such as people, places (e.g., school, cafe and theater), environments (e.g.,

* A part of Tatsuya Suda's research presented in this paper was supported by the National Science Foundation through grants ANI-0083074 and ANI-9903427, by DARPA through Grant MDA972-99-1-0007, by AFOSR through Grant MURI F49620-00-1-0330, and by grants from the University of California MICRO Program and Nippon Telegraph and Telephone Corporation (NTT).

M.E. Orlowska et al. (Eds.): ICSOC 2003, LNCS 2910, pp. 434–450, 2003.

temperature, humidity and air), things (e.g., furniture, food and plants), and information shared by people. Thus, ubiquitous spaces and their applications are situational and tend to exhibit strong locality. End users (hereafter, users) travel among multiple spaces and receive services that are offered locally in a space. Although navigating users through spaces and services that meet their needs is important, due to the magnitude and dynamism of spaces, estimating and suggesting spaces and services that best support users is not straightforward. To achieve this, an infrastructure for spaces must be capable of (1) collecting and analyzing pieces of information that are derived from real-world users' activities, (2) discovering useful rules (e.g., characteristic user behavior patterns) based on which services can be customized, (3) delivering resulting services to users' computing environments.

SpaceGlue is a technology for adaptively linking or "gluing" two spaces based on user behavior patterns to adaptively locate, communicate with, and interact with groups of services/people in different spaces. SpaceGlue dynamically creates/adjusts logical links called "bonds" between two spaces by estimating important relationships among spaces by collecting and analyzing users' behavior history information. Spaces tied with strong bonds are closely related and encouraged to collaborate with each other to jointly provide services to users. This promotes efficient user navigation among spaces and services that meet their preferences.

In this paper, we describe the model, design, and implementation of SpaceGlue. We implemented SpaceGlue using a distributed service platform called Ja-Net, which is characterized by autonomous service components and a relationship mechanism to dynamically establish logical links between service components. The adaptation capability of SpaceGlue is evaluated through simulation.

2 Model and Algorithms of SpaceGlue

2.1 Model of Service Location

A space is a unit of physical area such as a cafe, theater, or bookstore where wireless communication is available. PCs, PDAs, and mobile phones are nodes in a space. Each space defines a multicast group where all nodes in the space belong to the multicast group.

Various service components are provided and running on nodes. Different spaces may provide different service components in the context of each space. For example, a cafe waiter service, which takes an order and serves a cup of coffee to a customer, may be provided at a cafe while a movie trailer service, which delivers a movie content to customers, in a theater.

In SpaceGlue, a space is represented by a service component called a "space agent (SA)" where nodes that run SAs can communicate via the Internet. SAs dynamically create bonds with one or more partner SAs reflecting behavior patterns of many users (See Figure 1). For example, if the majority of users visit and buy something at a cafe and gift shop in the same day, SAs in the cafe and gift shop create bonds with each other. A bond can be thought of as an information cache that SA maintains for each of its partner SA. Its attributes include name, pointer to the partner, and strength that indicates the usefulness of the partner. Each SA creates a bond for each of its partners.

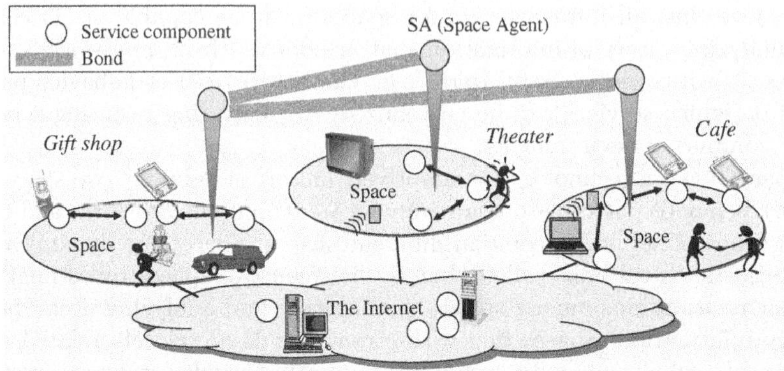

Fig. 1. Ubiquitous spaces are dynamically linked by bonds.

In SpaceGlue, a service component is known by its *advertisement* that includes a metadata description of the service it offers such as name and type and interface information to access the service. Each service component registers its advertisement with a local SA. SA maintains a list of advertisements (called a *local advertisement list*). To share local advertisements with other spaces in a meaningful manner, an SA sends its local advertisement list to remote SAs to which it has a bond. The receiver SA registers the received advertisement list (called a *remote advertisement list*) along with the sender SA's name.

To locate a service, a user first sends a query to its local SA, specifying advertisement attributes if necessary. Upon receipt of a query, the SA first examines its local advertisement list and then examines its remote advertisement lists. Remote advertisements are sorted in descending order of the bond strength and examined until a maximum of M remote advertisements match the query. Finally, the SA replies to the user with a list of advertisements that matched the query. When a user receives an advertisement for a remote space and wishes to receive the service, the user moves to the space before receiving the service.

2.2 Bonding Algorithm

In SpaceGlue, as bonds are developed, advertisements propagate on a bond network. The bond strengths are dynamically adjusted, which enables spaces to always offer relevant advertisements reflecting behavior patterns of many users. This happens in the following manner.

Adding history. In SpaceGlue, each user maintains two types of history: *Information History (IH)* and *Action History (AH)*. A record of IH and AH is a key-value pair where the key is the name of a space that sent advertisements to a user and the value is a list of names of remote spaces that have a bond with the space specified as a key and whose advertisements were sent to the user via the space.

- IH is intended to record all advertisements that a user has ever received and that may have influenced the user's actions. When a user receives a query reply with a set of advertisements from a local space, a new record is added to the user's IH.
- AH is intended to record user actions that actually took place. When a user sends a request to an advertised service, a new record is added to AH. The name of the space that offers the requested service is set as a key along with a list of names of spaces whose advertisements were sent to the user via the space as a value.

For example, in Figure 2, suppose that a user visits spaces S_1, S_5, S_8, and S_9 and receives advertisements about remote spaces S_2 and S_4 (at S_1), S_2 and S_8 (at S_5), S_5, S_7 and S_9 (at S_8), and S_6 and S_8 (at S_9). At this point, records with keys with S_1, S_5, S_8, and S_9 are added to the user's IH. Suppose also that the user requested services that are offered by S_5 and S_9. Two records with keys S_5 and S_9 are added to the user's AH.

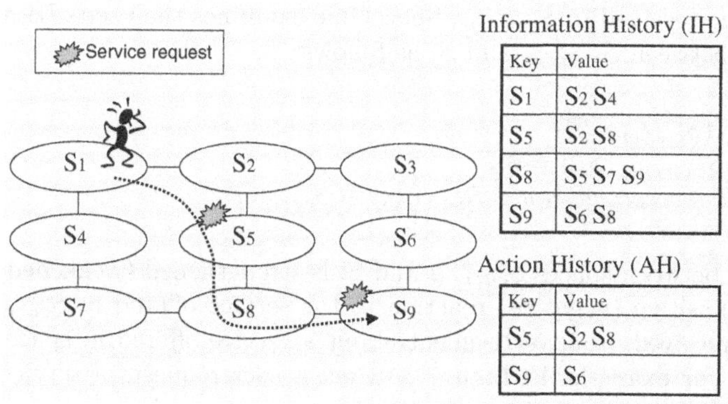

Fig. 2. Examples of information and action histories of user X, who visited spaces S_1, S_5, S_8, and S_9 and requested services at S_5 and S_9.

Let us denote the maximum length of IH as N_{IH} and that of AH as N_{AH}. In our algorithm, the minimum values of N_{IH} and N_{AH} are 2 and 1. When the history exceeds the maximum length, the oldest record is deleted first.

User evaluation. When a user makes a query and receives advertisements in a space, the user evaluates them based on the level of satisfaction for each advertisement in one of three ways: (1) *positive*: a user requests an advertised service (moves to the space if the advertisement is forwarded from a remote space), (2) *neutral*: simply ignores or closes advertisements, and (3) *negative*: explicitly rejects the advertisement. Upon receiving such indication of satisfaction level, SAs create/adjust bonds among SAs by looking at the history of individual user behaviors (See Section 2.2).

Creating glue. Assume that a user is currently in space $S_{current}$. Let us denote the i th key (space) in the user's AH as space S_i. When a user requests a service in $S_{current}$ (i.e., positive reaction), SpaceGlue examines the user's AH and creates a bond between $S_{current}$ and S_i as follows:

$$\begin{aligned} &\quad create\ (S_{current},\ S_i) \\ &if\ \ bond\ (S_{current},\ S_i) = \emptyset \\ &where\ \ AH\ \ni\ record(key = S_i) \end{aligned}$$

For example, in Figure 2, when a user who had once requested a service in S_5 requests a service in S_9, a bond is created between S_9 and S_5.

Adjusting bond strengths. Assume that a user is currently in space $S_{current}$. Let us denote the i th key (space) in the user's IH as space S_i. When a user in $S_{current}$ indicates positive, neutral, or negative reaction to an advertisement that he/she received in $S_{current}$, SpaceGlue examines the user's IH and updates the bond between $S_{current}$ and S_i as follows:

$$\begin{aligned} &\quad update\ (S_{current}, S_i) \\ &if\ \ bond\ (S_{current},\ S_i)! = \emptyset \\ &where\ \ IH\ \ni\ record(key = S_i,\ value \ni S_{current}) \end{aligned}$$

Bonds between spaces $S_{current}$ and S_i is strengthened (weakened) if the user indicates positive (negative) reaction to the service offered in $S_{current}$ and the user had received an advertisement about a service offered in space $S_{current}$ in space S_i. For example, in Figure 2, when a user requests a service in S_9 and indicates positive satisfaction, the bond between S_9 and S_8 is strengthened.

2.3 AdAppli: An Example Service Scenario

In this section, we illustrate a realistic application scenario using SpaceGlue. The application is called *AdAppli* (Advertisement Application). In the scenario, we assume a shopping mall complex with several shops. Each shop corresponds to a space and runs an SA on a shop PC. A number of customers visit the mall, spend time shopping, and then leave. We assume that many of the people who visit the mall carry a PDA, and they run user agents representing themselves. Each shop stores a single advertisement about the shop's merchandise (in a local advertisement list). It also stores advertisements of other shops that are linked with glue (in a remote advertisement list). Customers who visit a shop can retrieve these advertisements by sending a query. In AdAppli, the content of advertisements retrieved in a shop adapts to typical shopping sequences of a crowd of customers (users) as described below.

Trends generated in user preferences. In AdAppli, we consider the following assumptions about customer preferences: Different customers may have different preferences for types of shops and merchandise, and each of them buys merchandise that matches his/her preferences. Although different customers have different preferences, we assumed that the differences were small, and partly overlapped. This results in a non-uniform distribution of customer preference for merchandise, i.e., trends in the preferences of the crowd in the mall. We further assumed that although customers constantly come and go in the mall, the types of shops and merchandise that they prefer do not change significantly over a certain time period.

History management. In AdAppli, shops in the shopping mall create and acquire IH and AH as follows.

- A shop sends advertisements to the PDAs of customers in the shop. By looking at advertisements on user's PDA, shop SA knows which advertisements the customer have ever received (i.e., the IH of the customer).
- A shop issues a coupon that is available at all shops in the shopping mall to a customer who bought something in the shop. By looking at coupons on user's PDA, shop SA knows which shop the customer made purchses at (i.e., the AH of the customer).

User satisfaction level. In AdAppli, the level of user's satisfaction is mapped to the user's actions as follows:

- User buys merchandise by looking at an advertisement, which indicates that the user is *positive* about the advertisement.
- User simply ignores or closes an advertisement, which indicates that the user is *neutral* about the advertisement.
- User explicitly indicates that he/she dislikes the advertisement, which indicates that the user is *negative* about the advertisement.

User navigation process. Assume that bonds have not yet been established among shop SAs and that user navigation based on SpaceGlue happens in the following manner.

When customer A first arrives at the mall, she does not go in any specific direction but enters shops at random. When customer A arrives at a cafe, for example, the cafe's CE displays its own advertisement which contains information about its merchandise (e.g., the shop's coffee menu) on customer A's PDA.

Customer A may buy merchandise (e.g., a cup of coffee) if it matches her preferences. When this happens, the cafe's SA issues her with a coupon which she may use when she next buys something at another shop.

When she leaves the shop and moves to the next shop at random (e.g., gift shop) in the mall, the shop's SA displays its own advertisement on her PDA. This time, customer A may buy a gift using the coupon issued at the cafe. When the gift shop's SA receives the coupon, it attempts to create a bond with the cafe's SA. This will cause the gift shop's SA and cafe's SA to display each others advertisements on customer PDAs. Thus, when a new customer arrives at the cafe, ads of the cafe and the gift shop will be displayed on her PDA, and vice versa.

In AdAppli, a number of different customers visit different shops, based on which shop SAs have established bonds and the bond strengths are adjusted according to customers' shopping pattern. Through these bonds, shop SAs can guide customers through the mall by having their partners show their advertisements to potential customers. Without these bonds, customers would have to move randomly between shops.

3 Design and Implementation of SpaceGlue on Ja-Net

We implemented SpaceGlue for the AdAppli scenario using the Jack-in-the-Net Architecture (Ja-Net) [1][2][3] that enables adaptive service creation/provision. In Ja-Net, application services are implemented by a group of autonomous service components (i.e., agents) called *cyber-entities* (CEs). Each CE implements one or more service components and follows simple behavioral rules (such as migration, replication, energy exchange, death, and relationship establishment with other CEs). They autonomously form organizations to collectively provide higher services by establishing relationships with several other CEs. Ja-Net platform software provides a runtime environment for CEs called ACERE (ACE Runtime Environment) and APIs to manipulate relationships among CEs, such as creating, deleting, and updating relationships, and selecting CEs based on attributes of CEs or their relationships. Thus, the bonding algorithm of SpaceGlue can be easily implemented based on the relationship mechanism of Ja-Net.

3.1 System Overview

Figure 3 shows a system overview of SpaceGlue. Shops 1 and 2 are defined as spaces. PCs that run SAs of shops 1 and 2 are connected to the same network via Ethernet. We used a notebook PC instead of PDA as a user's terminal on which a user CE is running. Each shop is coupled with an IEEE802.11b access point allowing wireless communication with users' notebook PCs. Although the coverage of multicast messages in Shops 1 and 2 overlaps, multicast messages are distinguished by the MAC address of access points that are piggybacked on each message. A user carries a notebook PC and can move between Shops 1 and

2. A daemon process is running on the user's notebook PC to monitor the link status and notify the Ja-Net platform software whether the link is up or down.

The shop and user GUI windows which are shown on the shop's PC and user's notebook PC are also shown in Figure 3. On the user's notebook PC, an advertisement is shown along with buttons "buy", "close", and a checkbox "don't like". If the user selects "buy" button, it is interpreted as a positive reaction. If the user marks the checkbox and selects any button, it is interpreted as a negative reaction. Otherwise, it is interpreted as a neutral reaction.

The bond strength is adjusted by

$$S = \frac{P}{T}, \tag{1}$$

where P is the number of positive reactions and T is the number of positive or negative reactions that the Shop CE received from users when it sends the advertisement of a partner Shop CE. The initial value of strength is set to 1.

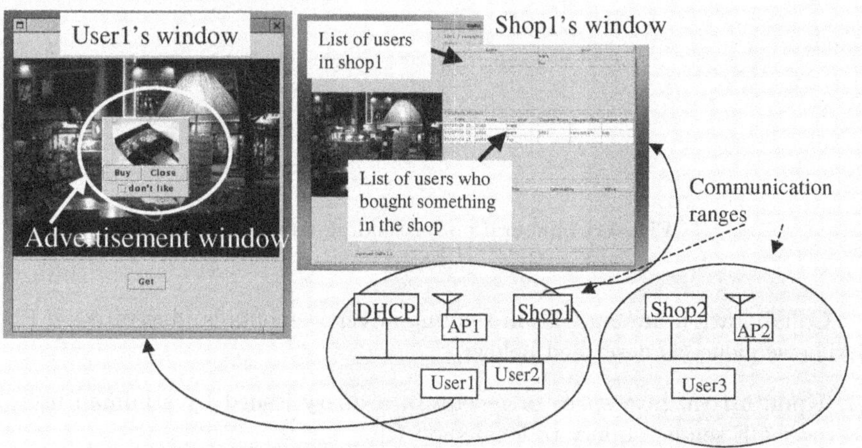

Fig. 3. Configuration of GUI windows on shop's PC and user's notebook PCs.

3.2 Collaboration

Shop SA and users are implemented as CEs (i.e., *Shop CE* and *User CE*). In addition, we implemented the following two functions/information content as CEs to enable active collaboration.

- *Advertisement CE* carries an advertisement of a Shop CE and definition of GUI components (such as buttons and panels) to display on the user's notebook PC.

- *UserTerminal CE* controls the GUI of the user's notebook PC such as displaying advertisements and inputting user commands.

In our design, IH and AH are represented by Advertisement CEs and coupons that a User CE has. By looking at the Advertisement CEs on a user's notebook PC, a Shop CE knows the IH of the user. Similarly, by looking at coupons carried by a User CE, Shop CE knows the AH of the user. Note that coupon information includes the name of the coupon's originator SA. Note also that our implementation is designed for IH and AH with history lengths of 2 and 1, respectively.

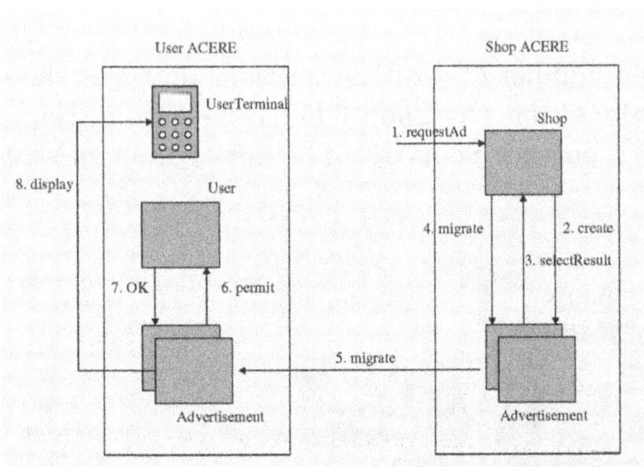

Fig. 4. Collaboration for sending advertisements

Collaboration among CEs in sending advertisements is illustrated in Figure 4. The sequence is described below:

1. Upon arrival in a space or receipt of a query issued by a human user, the user CE sends a query to local shop CE.
2. The shop CE creates an Advertisement CE.
3. The ID of the Advertisement CE is reported to the shop CE via selectResult event.
4. The shop CE sends a migration request to the Advertisement CE.
5. The Advertisement CE migrates to the user CE's ACERE. (adding IH)
6. The Advertisement CE asks permission to display its content on the display.
7. The user CE gives permission.
8. The Advertisement CE sends request to a UserTerminal CE to display its content on the display.

Collaboration among CEs for relationship (bond) creation is illustrated in Figure 5. The sequence is described below:

1. A human user buys merchandise (clicks the "buy" button of an advertisement), which is reported to the User CE.

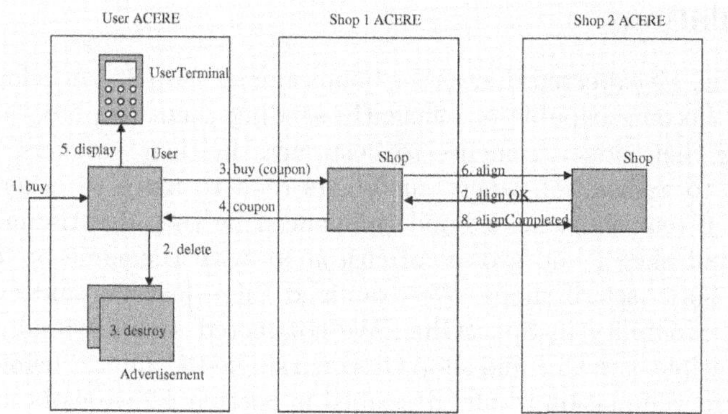

Fig. 5. Collaboration for creating glue (relationships)

2. The User CE deletes the Advertisement CE.
3. The User CE informs Shop1 CE of the purchase. A coupon issued by Shop2 CE at a previous purchase is sent to Shop1 CE along with the message.
4. The Shop 1 CE issues a coupon and sends the information to the User CE. (adding AH)
5. The User CE displays on the user's notebook PC that it has received a coupon.
6. By looking at the coupon information sent by the User CE, Shop1 CE asks Shop2 CE to create a bond.
7. Shop2 CE agrees and creates a bond with Shop1 CE.
8. Shop1 CE creates a bond with Shop2 CE.

3.3 System Measurement

The program sizes of Shop CE, User CE, Advertisement CE, and UserTerminal CE are 222, 52, 282, and 194 KB, respectively. The Ja-Net platform software is 388 KB. The number and size of messages sent among CEs during the sequence described in Section 3.2 (i.e., sending advertisements from Shop CE to user and creating glue between Shop CEs) is shown in Table 1. Ja-Net messages are 4.5 times the number of SpaceGlue messages.

Table 1. Messages sent while a user is in a shop

Message	Num. messages	Total message size	Average message size
Ja-Net	9	37 KB	14 KB (for migration), 1.3 KB (excluding migration)
SpaceGlue	2	6 KB	3.3 KB

4 Simulations

In SpaceGlue, we expected that as the bonds among shop SAs develop, some shop SAs would become capable of efficiently sending them to potential customers by showing their advertisements to customers in their partners' shops. This would lead to a situation where customers tend to move to other shops with which the current shop has a bond (influenced by the advertisements received in the current shop), and groups of customers with the same preference move among the same set of shops. We examined these features and evaluated the adaptation capability in SpaceGlue. We conducted several simulations by (1) running multiple user CEs and shop CEs on a single PC and (2) using a simulator of SpaceGlue. Simulation results described in Section 4.2 were obtained through (1) and those in Sections 4.3, 4.4, and 4.5 through (2). Note that in (1), User CEs automatically simulate human shopping activity, i.e., visiting shops, buying something, and evaluating advertisements. Note also that (2) yielded equivalent results to (1).

4.1 Simulation Definitions

Customer preferences. In the simulation, each shop had an ad keyword representing the shop and its merchandise. Each user had a set of five distinct ad keywords out of M ad keywords in its preference keywords. Customers bought merchandise if the ad keyword of target shop matched one of their preference keywords at the probability of P_P (this is called the *Purchase Probability*, i.e., the likelihood that the user will buy merchandise).

Significance in trends in customer preferences. We used mutual information [4] to measure the significance of trends generated by customer preferences in the shopping mall. The calculation of mutual information was based on the co-occurrence of an ad keywords pair in the preference keyword of all customers, and is defined as follows:

$$I(A;B) = \sum_{A,B} P(a,b) log \frac{P(a,b)}{P(a)P(b)}, \qquad (2)$$

where $P(a,b)$ is the probability of co-occurrence of two *ad keywords* in the preference keywords for all customers, a and b, and $P(a)$ and $P(b)$ are the probability of the single occurrence of an ad keyword a and b in the preference keywords for all customers, respectively. The greater the MI value is, the more significant the trends in customer preferences are.

To determine how the preferences of a group of customers affect the performance of AdAppli, we prepared two preference keyword sets with different MI levels: MAX, $High(H)$, $Low(L)$, and MIN where MAX and MIN were maximum and minimum mutual information, respectively. Figure 6 shows an example of ad keywords occurring (depicted as 1–36 on the x axis) in preference keywords when $MI = MAX$ (i.e., the most significant trends in the preferences of the crowd).

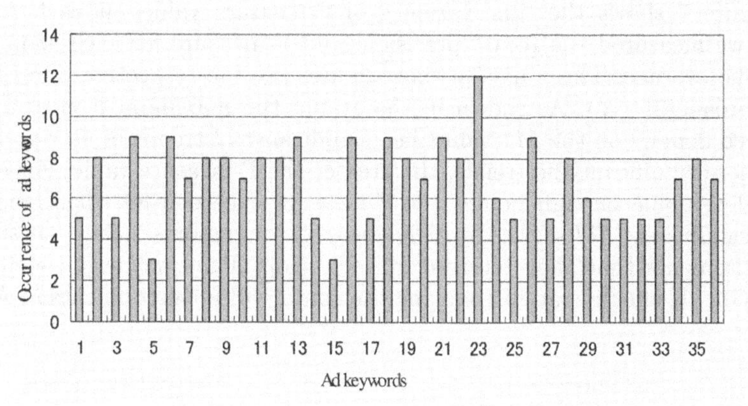

Fig. 6. Example of preference keywords occurring with $MI = MAX$.

Evaluation measure. The *Recall* and *Precision* of each Shop CE are defined as:

$$Recall = \frac{C}{T} \cdot 100, \quad \text{and} \tag{3}$$

$$Precision = \frac{C}{H} \cdot 100, \tag{4}$$

where C is the number of potential customers for a given shop (i.e., User CEs that have the ad keyword of the Shop CE in their preference keywords) that the Shop CE sent its ad to, T is the total number of the given shop's potential customers, and H is the total number of customers that the Shop CE sent its ad to. C and H were obtained by examining the value of user reactions received by a given shop during five periods when ads were broadcast. C is the number of users' positive or neutral reactions and H is the total number of users' reactions. Recall and precision tend to have a trade-off relationship, but we need to achieve both high recall and precision.

To evaluate the adaptation capability of SpaceGlue, we used the *F-measure* [4] which combines recall and precision in a single efficiency measure (the harmonic mean of precision and recall), which is given by

$$F\text{−}measure = \frac{2 \cdot Recall \cdot Precision}{Recall + Precision} \cdot 100 \tag{5}$$

4.2 Adaptation Capability of SpaceGlue

In our simulation, we ran 36 Shop CEs and 50 User CEs. Each User CE had five distinct ad keywords out of 36 ad keywords in its preference keywords. *Purchase probability* P_p was set to 0.7 for all user CEs. Initially, User CEs were randomly placed in one of the 36 shops. Each shop CE periodically broadcast a set of ads N times. For each shop CE, the time for broadcasting ads was set to 90 seconds.

Figure 7 shows the time variance of F-measure values at each MI level. Here, we measured the recall, precision, and F-measure for each shop CE and took the average. The x axis in those figures are the respective times that ads were broadcast (N). As shown in the graph, the maximum F-measure values achieved depend on the MI value, i.e., significance of trends in user preferences. The more significant the trends, the greater the F-measure value. For example, after developing enough bonds, the F-measure exceeded 80 when trends were most significant ($MI = MAX$). That is, 80% of customers were satisfied with advertisements that they received at each shop. Thus, we may conclude that SpaceGlue is effective at customizing the content of advertisements in AdAppli.

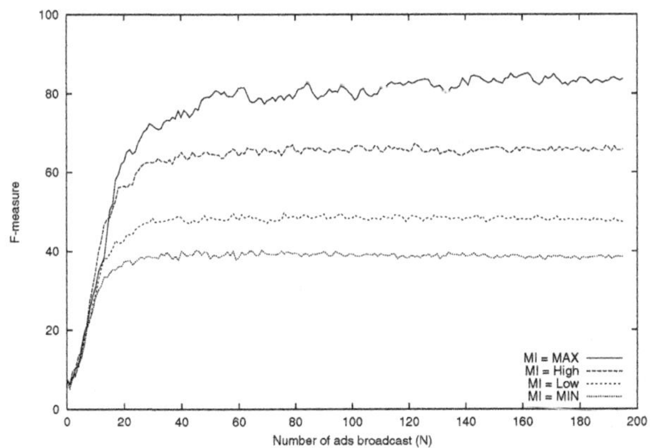

Fig. 7. F-measures with $MI = MAX, H, L, MIN$.

Figure 8 shows the time variance of the number of bonds that shop CEs created at $MI = MAX$ where the x axis in these figures is the respective times that ads were broadcast (N). The number of bonds increased in the beginning as time progressed and saturated after $N = 140$. Note that when the F-measure value exceeded 80 for the first time at $N = 52$, the number of bonds was 4.2, which was less than the maximum number of bonds created during the simulation (5.5). That is, a subset of total bonds may be sufficient to achieve the optimal F-measure.

4.3 Impact of Glue

In order to examine the impact of glue, we compared the F-measure values in the following three cases: (1) SpaceGlue, (2) Flooding, (3) No glue. In (1) "SpaceGlue", shop CEs sent advertisements using SpaceGlue technology. In (2) "Flooding", each and every shop CE sent advertisements of all other shops to customers in their shops. Thus, customers received 36 advertisements because there were 36 shops in the mall. In (3) "No glue", a shop CE sent a single

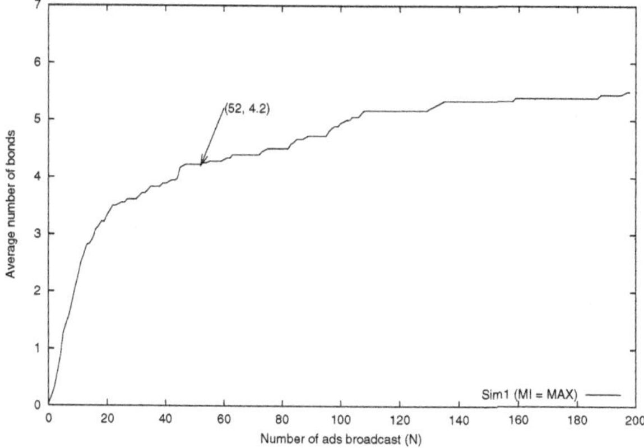

Fig. 8. Number of bonds with $MI = MAX$.

advertisement of its own to customers in the shop. Thus, customers move among shops at random.

The results are shown in Figure 9 where the time variance of F-measure in cases (1)–(3) are shown. Case "Flooding" and "No glue" achieved almost constant F-measure (about 23 and 5, respectively) throughout the simulation. Although "Flooding" achieved a better F-measure during the first 14 time periods, "SpaceGlue" overtook it once it developed bonds. The F-measure of "Flooding" is inferior to "SpaceGlue" because "Flooding" always achieves poor precision. In contrast, by adaptively selecting a subset of advertisements that match customer preferences, "SpaceGlue" achieves good precision. Thus, SpaceGlue achieves adaptability by its bonding technique.

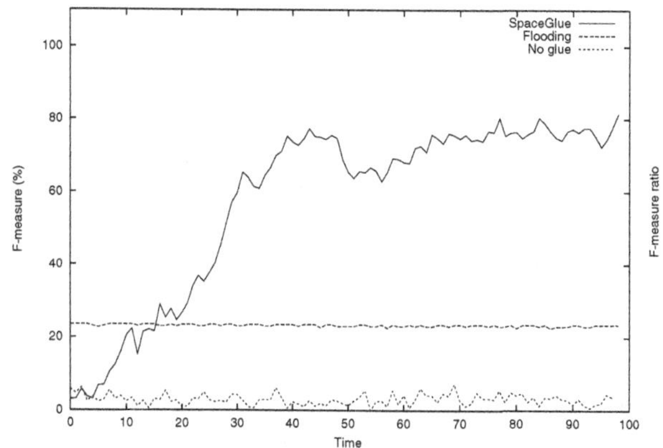

Fig. 9. F-measure comparison among SpaceGlue and flooding modes with $MI = MAX$.

4.4 Impact of History Length

To examine the impact of history lengths of IH and AH, we measured the average F-measure during 100 time periods with different history lengths in comparison. We compared the history length combinations of (IH, AH) where IH = 2, 4, 8 and AH = 1, 2, 4, 8. Figure 10 shows the results. The (IH, AH) = (4, 4) achieved the maximum F-measure on average (67) and was thus most appropriate. Note that (IH, AH) = (8, 8), which exhibited the maximum history length, achieved only 57. Thus, we may say that there is an optimal combination of history lengths of IH and AH. Examining such optimal history lengths through simulation is important in SpaceGlue.

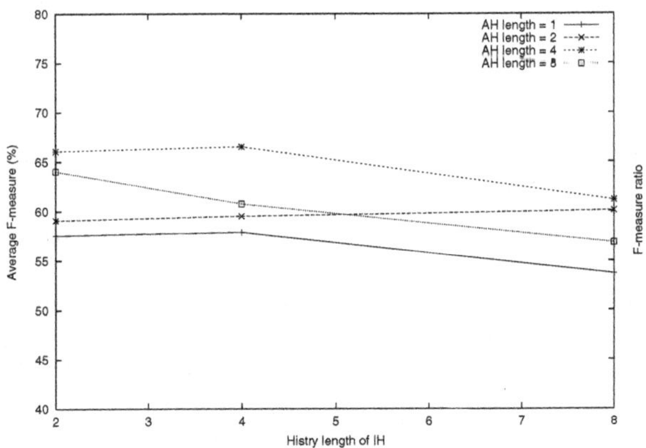

Fig. 10. Impact of history lengths on F-measures (average) with $MI = MAX$.

4.5 Scalability of SpaceGlue

Figure 11 shows average F-measure during 1000 time periods with different numbers of shops and customers; (shop, customers) = (36, 50), (100, 150), and (400, 600). The x axis shows the number of shops (36, 100, 400). The line labeled "SpaceGlue" shows the average F-measure achieved using SpaceGlue. The line labeled "No glue" shows the average F-measure achieved without glue (no bond). The line labeled "SpaceGlue/No glue ratio" shows the ratio of average F-measure of "SpaceGlue" and "No glue". Although the F-measure values of "SpaceGlue" and "No glue" decreased as the number of shops increased, the ratio of F-measure between "SpaceGlue" and "No glue" increased. That is, SpaceGlue is effective at maintaining adaptability in a scalable manner.

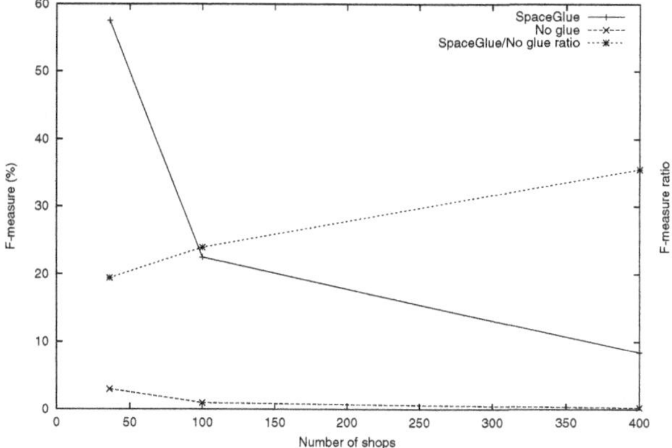

Fig. 11. Impact of the number of shops and customers with $MI = MAX$.

5 Related Work

The concept of SpaceGlue is similar to the association rule of data mining[6] although their mechanisms are different. Data mining is based on a centralized architecture where all the information is accumulated in a central database because the data mining algorithm requires entire sets of information as input. Unlike data mining, SpaceGlue is designed based on a distributed architecture where the bonding algorithm is implemented by each SA and processed based on local interactions among SAs. Thus, SpaceGlue requires no central administration. In addition, SpaceGlue provides a total environment for adaptive service provision: implementing, delivering, analyzing, and customizing services are all-in-one while data mining systems are operated separately from service systems. Thus, SpaceGlue is more portable and easy to deploy.

Although the current SpaceGlue only considers bonds between two CEs, further improvement of estimation should be possible if it considers topological information of bond networks. PageRank[7] provides a method of ranking network nodes based on the topology of hyperlinks between web pages. However, calculating PageRank requires topology data for each and every pair of web pages as input, which is difficult in the dynamic environment assumed in SpaceGlue where bonds are dynamically created/adjusted based on user activities. Thus, application of PageRank to SpaceGlue requires a distributed mechanism to calculate PageRank.

6 Conclusion

SpaceGlue is a technology for adaptively linking or "gluing" ubiquitous spaces to adaptively locate, communicate with, and interact with groups of services/people in different ubiquitous spaces. We are investigating SpaceGlye for mobile phone networks. For this, a lightweight version of Ja-Net platform software is necessary.

Various applications can be designed using SpaceGlue, including (1) Situational marketing: shop owners in a shopping mall identify potential customers based on their behavior patterns and send commercial advertisements that match their preferences at the right place and time, (2) Community creation: IM chatters can search for groups of users with related interests based on the association degree between spaces, and (3) Collaborative services: services in two related spaces may jointly provide a higher-level service to create new services. We will design and implement such applications to empirically verify that SpaceGlue is useful for building ubiquitous computing applications.

References

1. T. Itao, T. Nakamura and M. Matsuo, T. Suda, and T. Aoyama, "Service Emergence based on Relationship among Self-Organizing Entities," Proc. of the IEEE SAINT2002, Nara, Japan, Jan. 2002. (Best Paper)
2. T. Itao, T. Nakamura, M. Matsuo, T. Suda, and T. Aoyama, "Adaptive Creation of Network Applications in the Jack-in-the-Net Architecture," Proc. of the IFIP Networking 2002, Pisa, Italy, May 2002.
3. T. Suda, T. Itao, and M. Matsuo, "The Bio-Networking Architecture: A Biologically Inspired Approach to the Design of Scalable, Adaptive, and Survivable/Adaptable Network Applications," to appear, Internet as a Large Complex System, the Santa Fe Institute Book Series, Oxford University Press.
4. C. J. Van Rijsbergen, "Information Retrieval", 2nd edition, Butterworths, London, 1979.
5. Web services web site, http://www.webervices.org/
6. R. Agrawal, T. Imielinski, and A. Swami, "Mining Association Rules between Sets of Items in Large Databases," Proc. of SIGMOD, pp. 207–216, 1993.
7. PageRank web site, L. Page, S. Brin, R. Motwani, and T. Winograd, "The PageRank Citation Ranking: Bringing Order to the Web," Stanford Digital Library Technologies, Working Paper 1999–0120, 1998.

Organizing Service-Oriented Peer Collaborations

Asif Akram and Omer F. Rana

Department of Computer Science
Cardiff University, UK
{A.Akram, O.F.Rana}@cs.cf.ac.uk

Abstract. Locating suitable resources within a Peer-2-Peer (P2P) system is a computationally intensive process, with no guarantee of quality and suitability of the discovered resources. An alternative approach is to categorise peers based on the services they provide – leading to the interaction of peers with common goals to form societies/communities. Organization of peers in different communities is suggested to be useful for efficient resource discovery. The concept of communities is explored with reference to questions such as: why communities are desired? How they are formed? How communities work and interact? What are different possible types of communities and their overall behaviour? What are the advantages of community formation? The communities are adaptive in nature and evolve based on changes in their operating environment – such as changes in neighbouring communities. We suggest the benefit of this approach for resource discovery, and use a JXTA prototype to illustrate the concepts. The particular focus of this paper is to explore different types of organizational structures in the context of software provision in the context of service communities.

1 Introduction

Emerging distributed computing paradigms, such as Grid Computing [2], comprise of resources which may freely join and leave the system – and are said to constitute a "Virtual Organisation". Identifying how such an organization should be structured is an important part of developing more useful and efficient collaborations. Such Virtual Organizations already exist in both science and engineering projects – whereby a collection of scientists come together to solve a single large problem. In the High Energy Physics domain (such as the D0 project [15]), many groups and institutions come together for collaborative problem solving. Identifying a service-based infrastructure, which makes use of Grid technologies, is therefore important to support multi-disciplinary science in the future.

There is no reliable way to discover such dynamic peers and resources, making it impossible to have updated information about all available resources. However, without such information resource discovery becomes a time-consuming process and imposes an overhead on network access [1]. As the number of peers grow, the rate of possible interactions among peers increase exponentially. It is not scaleable to interact with all peers to discover appropriate resources, and all peers are unlikely to have information about all other peers. Restricting interaction within a set of peers is a key factor to scale the resource discovery problem. Peers can be categorised based on criteria such as the type of service, quality of service, etc. Any initial cost in categorising resources can provide benefits for discovering preferable resources

M.E. Orlowska et al. (Eds.): ICSOC 2003, LNCS 2910, pp. 451–466, 2003.

without a large discovery cost subsequently – thereby leading to the development of "communities". A community of autonomous peers, or community of communities, or even hybrid community, can exploit the scaling effects and benefit from the presence of other communities [3]. Further enhancements in the discovery of resources are possible if "similar-minded" communities i.e. communities offering similar services/resources or have similar resource requirements share their knowledge of a distributed environment [6]. Thus, the discovery problem of resources is scaled to known similar-minded communities where the probability of resource availability is likely to be high.

The concept of communities is very similar to interactions between different departments at a University. For instance, a lecturer can be a member of different faculties e.g. a mathematics lecturer teaching calculus to computer science students. This analogy helps us to define two terms, *Expertise* and *Interest* [4], [5]. Expertise of a peer is the basic service provided by that peer and Interest of a peer is the service/services provided by other peers which are supportive to its main service. In this example, a mathematics lecturer is an expert in mathematics and may not have any interest in computer science. If another department introduces a new calculus module, for instance, then instead of contacting all university lecturers (peers) individually it is preferable to contact the mathematics department (community) – as this improves the possibility of locating an appropriate peer capable of offering such a service. A common problem in Grid Computing is what Davis and Smith refer to as the "connection problem" [7], where peers need to find other suitable peers to co-operate with, assist, or interact with. "Focused Addressing" [8] is one solution to the connection problem where requests are sent to particular subset of peers, believed to assist the requesting peer. Communities in Grid Computing exploit the concept of societies. Similar-minded peers who either have similar expertise or interest in each other's expertise form societies. In societies or communities, the interests of individuals are protected, whilst allowing them to interact with each other for common benefits. It is a concept similar to the producer and consumer paradigm; if a producer does not market its service/s in a proper way, then the consumer may not be able to locate the producer.

The development of communities should allow similar-minded peers to be combined/grouped. Furthermore, the process of community formation should be automatic, and enable individual peers to benefit from joining one or more communities. One may assume each peer to be selfish, and only interested in the services they require and be in a position to be easily discovered by clients. If both conditions are not met then individual autonomous peers may not have any incentive in joining a community. Peers themselves are not loyal to communities but benefit from being in a community in accordance with their personal goals, thus creating a social network, which is self-supportive in nature.

2 Communities

Individual peers, although selfish, are expected to interact with each other in some way. Co-operation of one form or another therefore becomes essential. Each peer prefers to be in an environment where it may be easily discovered by a suitable client.

and can locate other peers with minimum efforts, thus enhancing its utility. Utility of peer is its effectiveness for other community members, and activeness within the community. Hence the more useful a peer to the objectives of the group, and the more activities it performs, the higher will be its utility. We assume there is some incentive for each peer to be discovered by others – perhaps based on some pay-off (or reward). In a Grid system, this could be to enable a peer to maximize its resource utilization. Peers providing different services, even with different service attribute i.e. quality of service, reliability, etc may be grouped together based on attributes such as type of services, resources and domains [6]. Similar-minded peers are grouped together to form communities; these communities can be treated as autonomous units in Grid Computing. It is proposed that a Grid environment is a collection of autonomous communities, which are dynamic in nature, as peers may join and leave at any time. Different peers either providing similar services/resources or interested in any particular services/resources interact with each other to form communities. Peers collaborating with each other to form a community should have one special peer acting as a community manager – we call this the Service Peer. Each community has one Service Peer with dual responsibility of not only managing the member peers but also keeping track of other communities with which they interact on behalf of member peers. A Service Peer is similar to an ordinary peer with respect to service/s and resource/s but with few additional responsibilities, the concept is similar to peers in JXTA where a peer can have additional responsibility of rendezvous peer [11]. Interaction between communities to discover new resources/services is only through the Service Peers. Direct interactions between peers for discovery of resources are prevented to restrict message traffic across communities [9].

3 Community Formation

Each Service Peer is an empty community which is automatically created when Service Peer is created. Service Peer may also offer specialist services, such as file sharing, content management service etc. along with different management services (section 6). A Service Peer manages a membership policy based on its expertise, and one that restricts the entry of other peers into a community. If no such expertise is held, then the membership policy is decided by the expertise of the first peer that joins the community. A new peer first tries to discover the Service Peer which may have interest in its capabilities/services. If the interests of a Service Peer are different, the new peer is referred to other Service Peer/s, or the new peer tries to locate alternative Service Peer/s with compatible interests (if the contacted Service Peer has not responded). A Service Peer and all peers registered with it constitute a community. A Service Peer manages all peers within the community and interacts with neighbouring Service Peers on the behalf of its member peers. A Service Peer therefore encodes the combined capability offered by all peers within its community. A Service Peer is essential for the bootstrapping of a new peer, as it supports a new peer to discover enough network resources to sustain itself. We make the following assumptions, which may be treated as the limitations of the system, but these assumptions will be justified latter:

1. More than one community exists in the system at a time.
2. Neither every peer nor its Service Peer know about every other peer or Service Peer, nor does any peer or Service Peer require complete information about all other peers or Service Peers.
3. It is appropriate to group peers on the basis of common attributes [6] i.e. type of service, domain, quality of service, into communities or clusters. Any given peer might be in more than one community or cluster simultaneously, depending on the services it is providing.
4. Each community has expertise depending on the type of services offered by member peers, but it can have different interests from member peers. Expertise and interests are two different things and should be kept separate [4], [5].
5. Each peer is impartial to any other peer, and only interested in the services the other peer provides.
6. A Service Peer may share information with other peers with different expertise, depending upon the nature of its interest. It is not necessary for only Service Peers with common interest to communicate with each other.
7. It is possible to prioritise Service Peer interests and expertise, such that we can say that a particular interest or expertise of Service Peer A is more like Service Peer B than Service Peer C.
8. Each community has at least one Service Peer.
9. A community can be created in a way similar to a JXTA Group with certain expertise and interests without any member peer/s.

4 Type of Communities

Individual autonomous peers have expertise and interests in specific resource/s. Based on these expertise and interests, peers are grouped together, but expertise and interests are not the only criteria for categorizing peers. Communities/societies can be of different types i.e. Competing Communities and Co-Operative Communities. We outline aspects of these different types of communities, and how they help structure a P2P system.

4.1 Competing Community

In a Competing Community all peers have the same expertise and to some extent member peers are providing the same service/s – although some service attributes may vary. Similarity in expertise may develop competition amongst member peers, as member peers have to compete with each other to get selected by a client. The competition is mainly for attributes which are not shared by peers like service quality, cost and hardware resources available [6]. Overall, these types of communities will result in competition and improved quality of services within the community. This concept is similar to what happens in human societies. For instance, different hardware manufacturers advertising in the same news media for the same product. Such manufacturers should differentiate themselves in some way to be selected by a buyer. A Competing Community may have two types of Service Peers: (i) a *Service-Oriented Service Peer, and a* (ii) *Non Service-Oriented* Service Peer. A *Service-*

Oriented Service Peer manages all member peers for completion of any single request/service. If any one peer fails to complete the assigned task, then a *Service-Oriented Service Peer* can assign that responsibility to another available peer within the community (Figure 1a and 1b), and this change will be transparent to the client application.

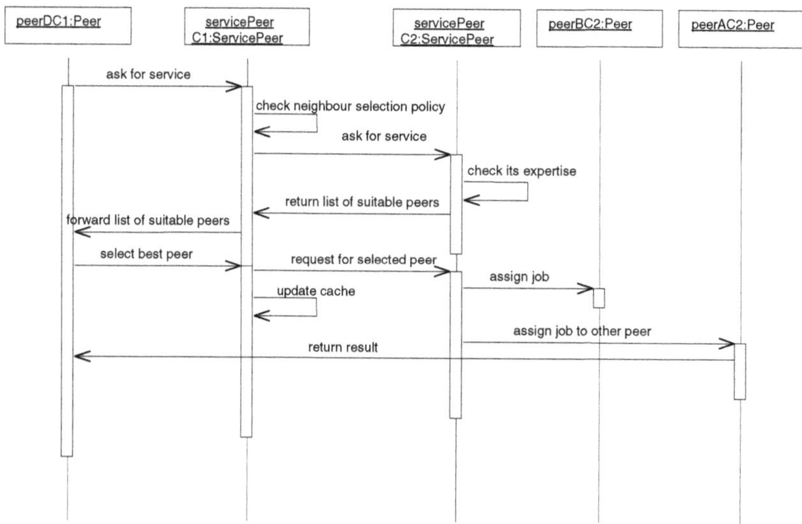

Fig. 1a. Sequence Diagram for Service-Oriented Service Peer in Competing Community

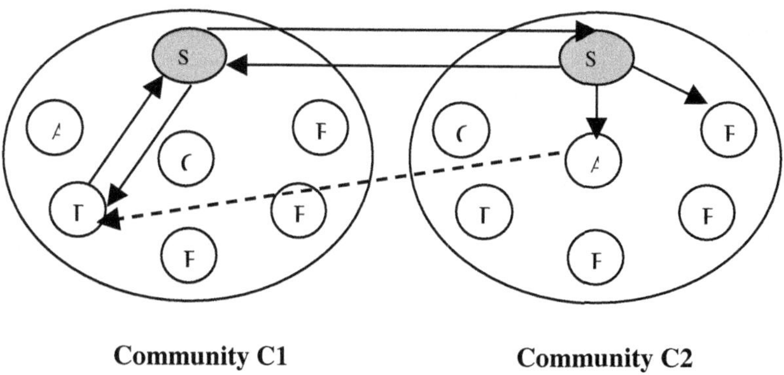

Fig. 1b. Peer A of C2 completing the task on failure of peer B of C2 in Service Oriented Competing Community

A Non Service-Oriented Service Peer in a competing community will not interfere with a client application and the service provider peer. From Figure 1, a Service Peer of community C2 informs Service Peer of community C1 about the unavailability of peer B.C2. The Service Peer of community C1 must now contact another community (such as C3) for the completion of the request, while peer D.C1 will remain unaware of the whole process of discovery and will only receive the new list of potential peers for selection. Figure 2 illustrates the failure of one peer in a Competing Community with *Non Service-Oriented* Service Peer.

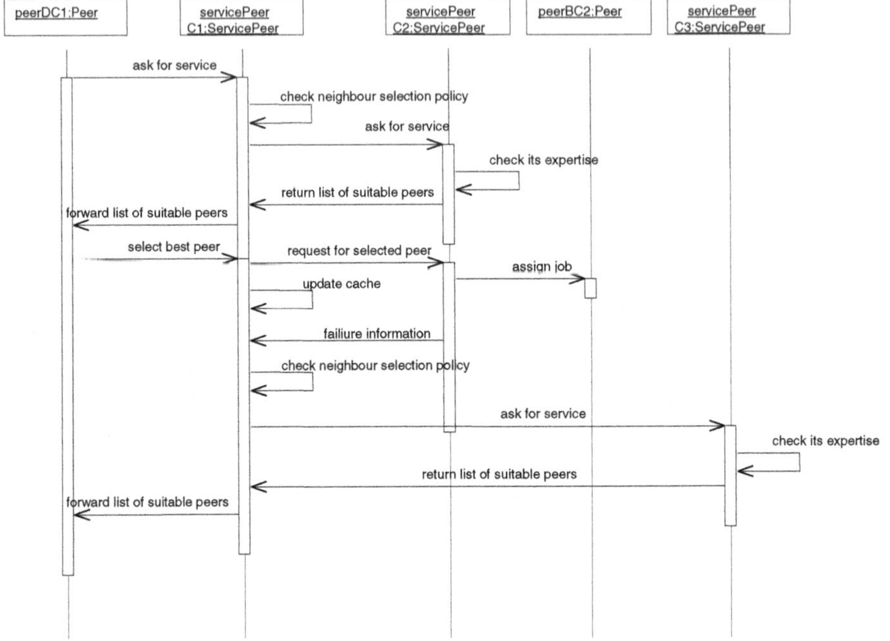

Fig. 2. Sequence Diagram for Non Service-Oriented Service Peer in Competing Community

Regardless of the type of Service Peer an individual community has, the overall result is less resource consumption in discovery for new resources. A Service Peer utilises a neighbour selection policy based on the expertise and interests [6] of other Service Peers it interacts with. It is more efficient for a Service Peer to maintain a neighbour selection policy instead of individual peers in the community, as a single policy is applicable to all peers, each member peer can be restricted by that single policy and each member peer can also benefit from the previous interactions of a Service Peer.

4.2 Co-operative Community

In Co-Operative communities all peers provide different services i.e. have different expertise, but have interests in the expertise of member peers. Each peer within such a community is providing a limited set of services, which may not be utilised individually, but along with services and resources of other member peers within the same community. As an analogy to electronic markets, a motherboard manufacturer needs other manufacturers to supply CPU, Hard Disk, Memory Card and VGA Card etc to be viable. In such communities, each peer is dependent on at least one other member peer which may be dependent on the service of any third member peer. Hence, when one peer is selected by a client, then there is a better possibility of selecting another member peer. This mutual co-operation is suitable for those peers which provide very simple and basic services, thus each peer directly or indirectly support the service of other member peers in the Co-Operative Community.

A Co-Operative Community has a few advantages, as a single community is providing the complete service using different member peers. Hence, a client may not have to discover different resources for accomplishing a single task - which means efficient discovery and less interaction with different communities. The effectiveness of Co-Operating communities is however dependent on the co-ordination of individual peers.

A Co-Operative community may also have a: (i) a *Service-Oriented Service Peer (SOSP),* and a (ii) *Non Service-Oriented* Service Peer *(NSOSP).* A service provided by a Co-Operative Community is divided into different independent phases which must be co-ordinates into a workflow. Each individual member peer works on a particular phase of the client application, and returns its results to either a Service-Oriented Service Peer or directly to another member peer responsible for the next phase. In the case of a Non Service-Oriented Service Peer, this does not make any difference as long as interactions are within the community. Involvement of a Service Peer *(Service Peer Oriented Community)* after each phase is essential when different peers can accomplish a particular phase to enable selection of the most appropriate peer within the community. To reduce traffic within a community, each member peer may know about the sequence of phases and peers involved, and only transfer the final outcome to the Service Peer, as illustrated in the scenario in Figure 3.

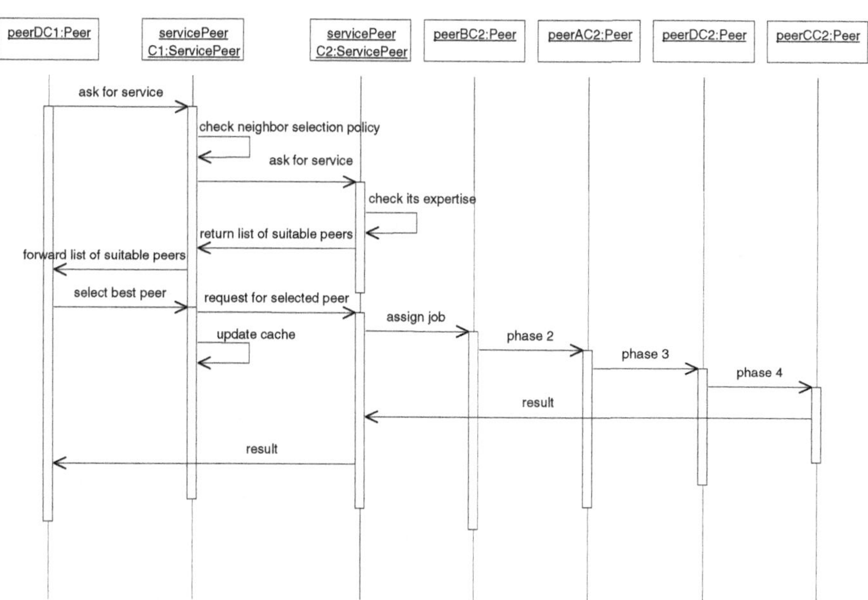

Fig. 3. Sequence Diagram for Service-Oriented Service Peer in Co-Operative Community

4.3 Goal Oriented Community

Another type of community is one which has a collection of peers to achieve a particular goal. In this community, a Service Peer is required to accomplish a user-defined goal related to its expertise. Based on its goal function, a Service Peer searches for ordinary peers and on locating appropriate peers it invites them for limited membership. Membership in such a community is only allowed to accomplish the assigned task – and membership of the community is terminated on task completion. These communities are a strict type of Co-Operative Communities, in which peers interact with each other in a pre-defined sequence dependent on the context of the service/s. Goal-oriented communities may also be important in self-organising systems, whereby the interaction between member peers is not pre-defined, but the services required are. In such instances, member peers may interact with each other in arbitrary ways to achieve a given end result.

4.4 Ad Hoc Community

Here, peers may be in different communities regardless of the nature of those communities, but still work together as a team. In ad hoc communities peers interact directly with each other without interference and involvement of a Service Peer. Two peers belonging to different communities providing two different but supporting services form the basis of an ad hoc community, as long as both concerned communities have agreed to use each other's service. This is an exceptional community in which involvement of Service Peer is very limited and member peers in ad hoc communities are more independent.

4.5 Domain-Oriented Community

Such a community is formed by linking together similar-minded organisations and institutions, instead of the services they provide, such as academic communities, research communities, and open-source communities. Hence these communities are domain-oriented rather than service-oriented. A typical Domain-Oriented Community is quite diverse in nature and cannot be categorised on the basis of the provided services. Furthermore, peers in these communities may not have interest in each other. Communities such as these can be restricted to a particular geographical location, specific organisations etc. The importance of such communities is that they enable common mechanisms to view common problems that a given community is likely to encounter. It is possible for members of the community to solve the same types of problems in common ways – using different types of services.

5 Architecture of a Community

The architecture of communities should be simple and supportive to the main purpose of their formation. Each type of community has a similar architecture, with one Service Peer, which manages the whole community. A Service Peer is similar to an ordinary peer with respect to the services and resources it provides, but with additional management services (such as a rendezvous peer in JXTA [11]). Each peer must be a member of one or more communities.

5.1 Discovery and Membership

A newly created peer tries to locate Service Peers in a Grid environment by using a Service Peer discovery message sent on the network (provided the local network supports broadcasting or multicasting). Alternatively, a newly created peer may only send a message to one Service Peer, which then either responds directly or refers the message onwards. If a peer is interested in joining a particular community, it sends a request to the Service Peer for that community. It is not necessary that each Service Peer which receives the discovery message will reply, and even a reply does not imply the acceptance of membership. A peer will act solely to maximize its long-term utility, so during membership of particular community, peer will take discounted estimate of future rewards into considerations [9] (to decide whether to remain in the community).

5.2 Individual and Collective Interests

Each member peer has a unique interest which varies from peer to peer. This interest is based on the type of service(s) that the peer provides. A Service Peer is responsible for intercommunity interactions, and must reflect the interests of all member peers within a community. A Service Peer must therefore summarise the interests of a community by combining interests of each of its members into a list. This is currently achieved by listing all the services that are being offered by each member peer within the community.

5.3 Internal Rating of Members

A Service Peer rates member peers according to their activeness (number of times a successful service has been provided), the type(s) of expertise they have, the quality of service they offer, etc. This internal rating mechanism is mostly general, but each Service Peer may have different criteria based on its local policies. A Service Peer selects the best available member peer/s as a result of a request for any service from a client, based on the expertise provided by the community. On selection of any member peer by a client, the Service Peer will increment the internal rating of the member peer. The most active peers will have the maximum rating; if any member peer is unavailable, overloaded or not responding for a long time, then the Service Peer will not select it for subsequent recommendations. A similar rating mechanism is used for Service Peers of external communities, and used in supporting query referral [5]. Regardless of the type of community, each peer aims to maximise its rating over a particular period. Non-availability of service/s from any peer will also affect the overall ranking of the peer.

5.4 Multiple Memberships

Individual peers can be members of different communities, and the selection and membership of a community is based on the expertise and different interests of each individual peer. Membership for a new peer is completely dependent upon the type of service offered, organizational domain of peer, quality and completeness of service and finally the expertise and interest of community. As the internal rating of the peer increases, it will have a better chance to move to other communities where its services are likely to be in a higher demand. The internal rating provided by a Service Peer may also be a criterion that a particular peer may wish to make known; hence, each peer tries to be active in all communities for which it has valid membership. Membership of many communities can drastically affect the internal ratings of a peer, as a peer has limited resources. However, if a particular community does not get a large number of requests, then the services offered by a member peer may not get utilized properly. Consequently, in communities where the number of requests is not that significant, it is in the interest of a service providing peer to belong to multiple simultaneous communities to increase its utilization. Membership policy for each joined community will be different based on the type and expertise of that particular community.

5.5 External Ratings of Communities

Service Peers maintain information of member peers and a restricted set of other communities; this interest is governed by the expertise and interest of each Service Peer. Based on interactions with other communities, a Service Peer records external ratings of other Service Peers, and this rating is considered during future interactions [5]. Each community has its own rating of other communities as each one has its own expertise and interests. The higher the rating, the more compatible it is with other community [10]. The rating of communities can be used as a measure to identify communities which are likely to be more effective when working together. Based on a policy, a Service Peer may not reveal such rating to other Service Peers.

5.6 Virtual Community of Communities

It is desired that each community should have a list of characteristics i.e. expertise, interest of other communities known to it. A Service Peer will try to match the characteristics of different communities known to it, and the characteristics it has about itself, to form a virtual community of communities [5]. This virtual community of communities is based on the perspective of the Service Peer, as other communities will have their own virtual community of communities with entirely different participating communities [4]. For instance, a Service Peer of community A has a Service Peer of community B in its list of Service Peers (i.e. virtual community of communities) based on similar, but it is not necessary that Service Peer of community A is also in the virtual community of Service Peer of community B. Service Peer of community A and B have some common characteristics, and these may be important for Service Peer of community A but not for Service Peer of community B. The nature of these communities change over time based on the changes in their membership. Neighbor selection [10] is influenced by the commonalities in characteristics i.e. expertise and interests and external rating of the community.

5.7 Information Sharing

Service Peers frequently exchange their contents with other communities in its virtual community of communities, but there is no guarantee that two Service Peers from different communities have the same view. Such content may also include ratings of other communities, thereby indicating the suitability of such external communities to host particular types of resources/services. As each community has different neighbors due to its different expertise and interests, this exchange of information may help identify many other communities which may provide useful expertise, to varying extents of usefulness. Normally, a Service Peer will interact with other Service Peers (communities) which have similar expertise and interests. A Service Peer updates its virtual community based on the (dynamic) ratings of other Service Peers – and records this for a lease duration – a limited period after which it tries to re-build its acquaintance list. Each Service Peer maintains a list which contains the names and contents from the last r Service Peers (communities) that this Service Peer has communicated with [4], [6].

5.8 Learning and Adaptivity

Peers are free to join and leave communities, and may join different communities of different types. This makes tracking of peers a difficult job for the Service Peer. A peer will act solely to maximize its long-term utility during membership [14]. After a certain time period each peer will primarily aim to be in a community or communities where it has maximum rewards. The system reaches equilibrium over time, provided the environment does not change significantly, and the internal and external rankings of the communities will not change significantly as new peers are added. Achievement of stability in the system is an important objective in the long run. However, this is also dependant on the rate of change of the environment within which the communities exist. A dynamic operating environment is likely to prevent the system stabilising, as new members may be added/removed from the system rapidly, and the services offered by the members may also change in unpredictable ways. Communities are much more consistent in nature. They provide this consistency by giving membership only to "similar-minded" peers – based on their expertise and interests.

6 Common Services in Communities

Each community requires a set of common services to function adequately. These common services generally offer management capability to enable individual members of a community to function well. Communities require different services to manage the interests of individual autonomous peers.

Different types of communities requires different common services, and these may be offered by a Service Peer i.e. Application Server with specialist middleware, or separate peers providing management services i.e. Application Server using middleware from different vendors [12]. A Service Peer works as a gatekeeper and manages all services residing on different peers within a community, and every message from/to another community passes through it (except in the case of an Ad Hoc community). Communities must support one or more of the following services:

1. **Security Manager Service:** Focuses on the requirements for supporting authentication, authorization, accounting, and auditing of access to and services provided by the community.

2. **Scheduling Service:** Schedules responsibilities to different peers, and monitors different phases of job execution.
3. **Transaction Manager Service:** Ensures the dynamic (or static) load balancing within the community to maximize throughput when required.
4. **Concurrency Controller Service:** Co-ordinates two or more peers providing the same service to the same client.
5. **Resource Monitoring Service:** Monitors use of internal resources among member peers within the community and external network resources for inter community interactions. Such monitoring may be supported through specialist tools that are available on hosting platforms for particular peers.
6. **Performance Controller Service:** Responsible for finding non-overloaded peers to maintain a given Quality of Service. Hence, monitors the performance and activity of internal resources for better external rating of the community. May work in liaison with the Resource Monitoring Service.
7. **Policy Manager Service:** Implements the policy for a specific type of community i.e. membership policy, neighbour selection policy, internal rating policy, inter-community interaction policy.
8. **Networked Information Discovery and Referral Services:** Manages the external rating, availability, quality and expertise of neighbouring communities and discovers communities of interest.

Different communities' offers different services and Table 1 shows the essential services offered by different communities. It is clear from Table 1 that each community doesn't have all services.

Table 1. Comparison among different communities based on type of components required

Community Type	Security Manager	Scheduler	Transaction Manager	Concurrency Controller	Resource Monitor	Performance Controller	Policy Implementer
Co-operative NSO	X		X			X	X
Co-operative SO	X	X	X		X		
Competing SO	X	X	X	X	X	X	X
Competing NSO	X				X		X
Goal Oriented	X	X	X		X		X
Ad Hoc	X					X	
Domain Oriented	X				X		X

7 Comparison of Different Communities

Each type of community has advantages or disadvantages and there is no easy way of comparing them and requires different components for optimized performance. Below is the comparison of different types of communities based on factors like resources overhead, reliability etc. Table 2 compares different communities with respect to use of different additional resources.

Table 2. Comparison of different communities based on required components

Community Type	External Interactions	Internal Interactions	Network Resources Required	No. of Components	Efficient Resource Usage	Service Replication	Reliability
Co-operative NSO	Min	Avg.	Min	Avg.	Max	Avg.	Avg.
Co-operative SO	Min	Max	Min	Max.	Max.	Avg.	Max
Competing SO	Min	Avg.	Min	Max	Max.	Max.	Max.
Competing NSO	Avg.	Min	Avg.	Avg.	Avg.	Max.	Avg.
Goal Oriented	Avg.	Avg.	Max.	Avg.	Avg.	Min.	Avg.
Ad Hoc	Max.	Min.	Max.	Min.	Avg.	Min.	Min.
Domain Oriented	Avg.	NA	Avg.	Min.	NA	Avg.	NA

8 A Prototype System

For simulation purposes we have implemented a prototype using JXTA. We provide an option for creating Groups and Peers along with their properties, as shown in Figures 4a and 4b. This description is used to specify membership criteria. When a Peer applies for membership, its description is matched with the description of the group.

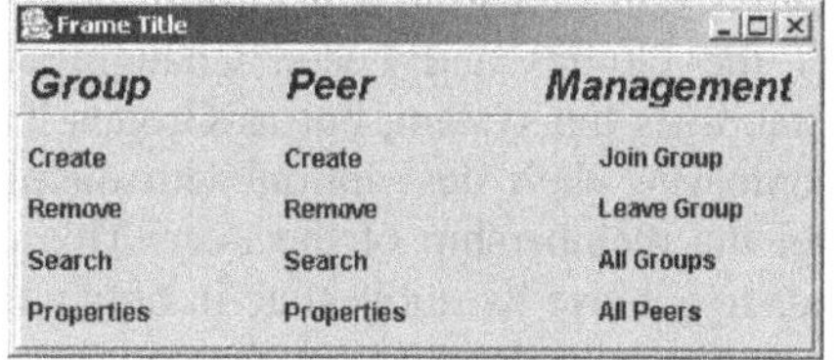

Fig. 4a. Main Menu

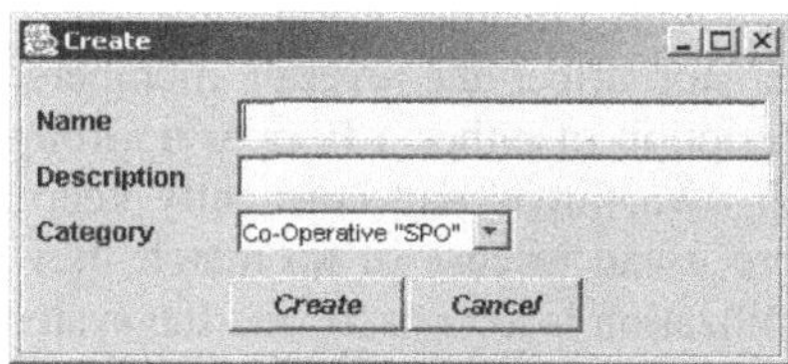

Fig. 4b. GUI to create Group

Each JXTA Group is created with a randomly generated External Rating. A Group assigns randomly generated Internal Rating to all of its members at the time of membership. Each JXTA Group has a sorted list of its member Peers and each Peer has a sorted list of Groups to which it belongs. Peers apply for membership based on a high external rating of a JXTA Group. A JXTA Group grants membership based on overall rating of Peer (average of (IR of Peer * ER of Group)) and description of Peer. At any time a Group can have five members and any Peer can be a member of three different Groups. Peers can be added in different Groups using the interface but membership will be awarded based on the selection criteria of that specific Group.

Similarly, any Peer can resign from a Group at any time. Graphical User Interface for adding and removing Peer/s from Group/s is shown in Fig. 5a and member peers of Group Computer Science in Fig. 5b.

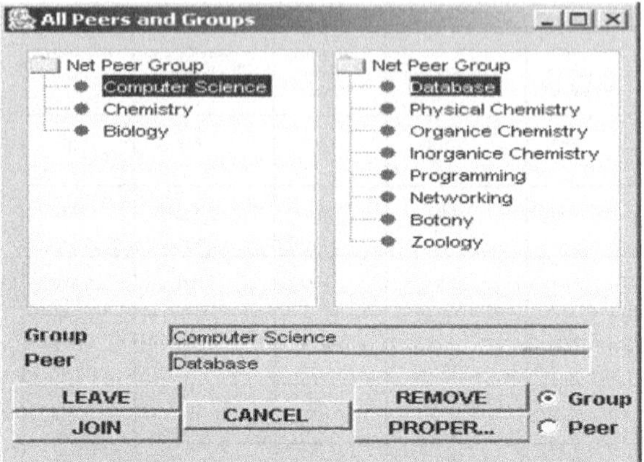

Fig. 5a. GUI for managing Group/s

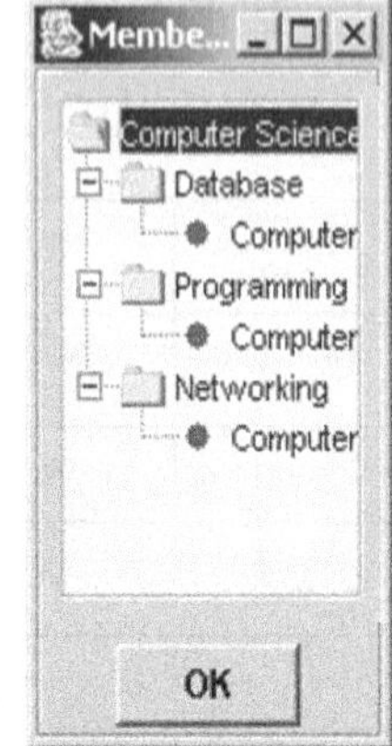

Fig. 5b. Members of Group

Each Peer has its own thread and after a certain time interval it discovers new Groups from the local cache of the JXTA environment and applies for membership. Peers will apply for membership to only that Group which has a high External Rating, as compared to the Group/s to which it already belongs. Peers keep on looking for the best Group and on discovering any suitable Group resign from the lowest rated Group. Similarly, each Group prefers to have highly rated Peers and on the membership of any new highly rated Peer cancels the membership of existing Peer with lowest rating. Result of this simulation was quite encouraging and as expected in the beginning the system has Groups and Peers attached without any uniform pattern but with the passage of time the system achieved stability and Groups with high rating have highly rated peers. Once the whole system is stable creating new Groups or Peers does not affect the overall membership of the Groups and Peers. Changing the description of either a Peer or a Group de-stabilizes the system, but as Groups have their own thread and constantly keep on comparing their description with member Peers – and in case of no match they cancel the membership of the Peer. This de-stabilization is temporary and the system tends to achieve its stable state in only a few iterations. Number of iterations to achieve stable state depends on the rating of a Group or a Peer, higher the rating of a Peer or a Group quicker the stabilization is achieved.

For each Group and Peer structured document is created which has description and rating of the peer. This structured document is used for creating credentials for the Peer, which is required to authenticate the Peer by a Group at the time of membership. During experimentation there are mainly three activities going on which are following:

1. Search of new Groups by Peers
2. Request for membership to those Groups
3. Membership acceptance by the Group

In the beginning all three activities are quite frequent as a new Peer applies for membership without any specific selection but with the passage of time Peer becomes more selective and apply for the membership to only those Groups which have higher rating than member Group with minimum rating. Similarly with the passage of time the Groups also become more selective in accepting the membership. As system becomes more stable there is even decline in the request for membership from Peers although this is true only for Peers with high ranking as they are already in highly ranked Groups but for Peers with low ranking the process of discovery of new Group always follow the membership request. It is noticed that Peers with high ranking end up in the Groups with higher ranking and Peers with low ranking end up in the Groups with low ranking, from which it is concluded that ranking of Group is indication of the member Peers ranking. In the simulation Peers are not caching any type of information about Groups with failed membership and thus keep on applying for the membership on each discovery of that Group but if Peers start caching the information of failed applications then there will be much more reduction in membership applications.

Each type of Group has it own membership policy which is implemented by corresponding java class extending net.jxta.membership.MembershipService. This java class has core membership methods i.e. apply(…), join(…) and resign(), which implements the membership policy of specific type of Group and update the member Peers for the corresponding Group. Membership policy of each type of Group can be easily changed by modifying the membership logic in apply(…) & join(…).

9 Conclusion and Summary

We present the concept of categorizing peers in communities on the basis of their expertise and interests. Social networks are a natural way for people to go about seeking information. Organizing peers in one form or another makes the discovery of resources efficient, whilst minimizing computational overheads. Categorizing the peers in communities is simple, open and easy to implement, and the initial overhead of developing communities pays-off latter at the time of resource discovery. Communities are more stable, and stability increases with the passage of time, have a simple learning time and are more adaptive to operate in a dynamic environment. We have proposed the external and internal rating for communities and peers respectively which may be used to support a given Quality of Service, effective participation of autonomous peers and better interaction among communities and member peers. Finally, we discuss the different services required to manage the group and requirements of the member peers. A JXTA implementation of a prototype system is discussed to describe the salient features of our approach. A key theme of this work is to determine how communities should be structured to support resource discovery, and how particular roles within a community can be used to determine interactions between participants within a community, and those between participants across community. This work extends techniques and results discussed in [14].

References

1. Karl Aberer: P-Grid: A Self-Organizing Access Structure for P2P Information Systems, Proceedings of the Sixth International Conference on Cooperative Information Systems (CoopIS 2001), 2001
2. S. R. H. Joseph, "Adaptive Routing in Distributed Decentralized Systems" http://www.neurogrid.net/publications/publications.html (2001)
3. Bin Yu, Mahadevan Venkatraman and Munindar P. Singh: 'An Adaptive Social Network for Information Access: Theoretical and Experimental Results', *Journal of the Applied Artificial Intelligence*, Volume 17, Number 1, (2003) 21–38
4. Leonard Foner. Yenta: 'A multi-agent, referral-based matchmaking system'. In *Proceedings of the 1st International Conference on Autonomous Agents*, (1997) 301–307.
5. Bin Yu and Munindar P. Singh: 'Searching Social Networks', *Proceedings of Second International Joint Conference on Autonomous Agents and Multi-Agent Systems*, 2003, to appear.
6. Leonard Foner: *'Clustering and Information Sharing in an Ecology of Cooperating Agents, or How to Gossip without Spilling the Beans'*, Conference on Computers, Freedom and Privacy, 1995
7. Davis, R. and R. G. Smith: 'Negotiation as a Metaphor fro Distributed Problem Solving'. Artificial Intelligence (1983) 20, 63–109
8. Parunak, H. V. D.: 'Distributed Artificial Intelligence', Chapt. Manufacturing Experionce With the Contract Net, pp. 285–310, Research Notes in Artificial Intelligence. Los Altos, CA: Morgan Kaufmann Publishers, 1987
9. Christopher H. Brooks and Edmund H. Durfee: 'Congregation Formation in Multiagent Systems'. to apear in *The Journal of Autonomous Agents and Multiagent Systems*, early 2003
10. Pinar Yolum, Munindar P. Singh: *'Emergent Properties of Referral System'* Second International Joint Conference on Autonomous Agents and Multi-Agent Systems, 2003, to appear
11. Li Gong, "Project JXTA: A Technology Overview" http://www.jxta.org/project/www/docs/jxtaview_01nov02.pdf , October 2002
12. RFC 2768, "Middleware components" http://www.ietf.org/rfc/rfc2768.txt?number=2768
13. Mike Carew, "Anatomy of Components" http://www.middleware.net/components/articles/anatomy.html. ComponentFocus
14. Steven Lynden and Omer Rana, "Coordinated Learning to support Resource Management in Computational Grids" Second International Conference on Peer-to-Peer Computing, (2002) 81–89
15. FermiLab, "The DZero Project". See Web site at: http://www-d0.fnal.gov/

Service-Based Distributed Querying on the Grid

M. Nedim Alpdemir[1], Arijit Mukherjee[2], Norman W. Paton[1], Paul Watson[2], Alvaro A.A. Fernandes[1], Anastasios Gounaris[1], and Jim Smith[2]

[1] Department of Computer Science
University of Manchester
Oxford Road, Manchester M13 9PL
United Kingdom

[2] School of Computing Science
University of Newcastle upon Tyne
Newcastle upon Tyne NE1 7RU
United Kingdom

Abstract. Service-based approaches (such as Web Services and the Open Grid Services Architecture) have gained considerable attention recently for supporting distributed application development in e-business and e-science. The emergence of a service-oriented view of hardware and software resources raises the question as to how database management systems and technologies can best be deployed or adapted for use in such an environment. This paper explores one aspect of service-based computing and data management, viz., how to integrate query processing technology with a service-based Grid. The paper describes in detail the design and implementation of a service-based distributed query processor for the Grid. The query processor is service-based in two orthogonal senses: firstly, it supports querying over data storage and analysis resources that are made available as services, and, secondly, its internal architecture factors out as services the functionalities related to the construction of distributed query plans on the one hand, and to their execution over the Grid on the other. The resulting system both provides a declarative approach to service orchestration in the Grid, and demonstrates how query processing can benefit from dynamic access to computational resources on the Grid.

1 Introduction

The Grid is an emerging infrastructure that supports the discovery, access and use of distributed computational resources [7]. Its name comes by analogy with the electrical power grid, in that the intention is that computational resources (by analogy with power generators) should be able to be accessed on demand, with the location and ownership of the resources being orthogonal to their manner of use. Although the Grid was originally devised principally to support scientific applications, the functionalities associated with middlewares, such as Globus [www.globus.org] and Unicore [www.unicore.de], are potentially relevant to applications from many domains, in particular those with demanding, but unpredictable, computational requirements. For the most part, Grid middlewares

M.E. Orlowska et al. (Eds.): ICSOC 2003, LNCS 2910, pp. 467–482, 2003.

abstract over platform or protocol-specific mechanisms for authentication, file access, data movement, application invocation, etc., and allow dynamic deployment of applications on diverse hardware and software platforms.

In parallel with the development of Grid computing, *Web Services* (WSs) [9] have gained widespread acceptance as a way of providing language and platform-independent mechanisms for describing, discovering, invoking and orchestrating collections of networked computational services. For the most part, WSs are static, in that specific services are deployed, described and advertised with human intervention, and with fixed computational capabilities.

The principal strengths of Web and Grid services thus seem to be complementary, with WSs focusing on platform-neutral description, discovery and invocation, and Grid services focusing on the dynamic discovery and efficient use of distributed computational resources. This complementarity of Web and Grid Services has given rise to the proposed Open Grid Services Architecture (OGSA) [6,18], which makes the functionality of *Grid Services* (GSs) available through WS interfaces. The Open Grid Services Infrastructure (OGSI) is the base infrastructure underlying the OGSA. It allows the dynamic creation of service instances on computational resources that are discovered and allocated as, and when, they are needed. The OGSI is currently undergoing a standardisation process through the Global Grid Forum [www.gridforum.org].

Although the initial emphasis in Grid computing was on file-based data storage [15], the importance of structured data management to typical Grid applications is becoming widely recognised, and several proposals have been made for the development of Grid-enabled database services (e.g., Spitfire [1], OGSA-DAI [www.ogsa-dai.org.uk]). To simplify somewhat, a Grid-enabled database service is a programmatic interface to a database that uses one or more GSs (e.g., for authentication or data transport).

The provision of facilities that support application development is relevant to both GSs and WSs. For example, in the Grid setting, applications can use GSs through toolkits, or Grid-enabled versions of parallel programming libraries such as MPI [5]. In the WS setting, tools exist to support the generation of client stubs (e.g., AXIS [www.apache.org]), but, more ambitiously, XML-based workflow languages have been developed to orchestrate WSs, of which BPEL4WS [www.ibm.com/developerworks/library/ws-bpel] is perhaps the most mature. However, all of these approaches are essentially procedural in their nature, and place significant responsibility on programmers to specify the most appropriate order of execution for a collection of service requests and to obtain adequate resources for the execution of computationally demanding applications. Furthermore, support for large-scale processing of structured data is minimal.

This paper argues that distributed query processing (DQP) can provide effective declarative support for service orchestration, and describes an approach to service-based DQP on the Grid that:

1. supports queries over *Grid Database Service* (GDSs) and over other services available on the Grid, thereby combining data access with analysis;
2. uses the facilities of the OGSA to dynamically obtain the resources necessary for efficient evaluation of a distributed query;

3. adapts techniques from parallel databases to provide implicit parallelism for complex data-intensive requests; and
4. uses the emerging standard for GDSs to provide consistent access to database metadata and to interact with databases on the Grid.

As well as using the emerging GDS standard, the Grid distributed query processor described in this paper is itself a GDS, and thus can be discovered and invoked in the same way as other GDSs. Thus, the Grid stands to benefit from DQP, through the provision of facilities for declarative request formulation that complement existing approaches to service orchestration. Furthermore, a complementary claim is that DQP stands to benefit from GSs, since they facilitate dynamic discovery and allocation of computational resources, as required to support computationally demanding database operations (such as joins), and implicit parallelism for complex analyses.

The remainder of this paper is structured as follows. Section 2 describes how GSs evolved from WSs. Section 3 motivates and describes current efforts to provide high-level database access services in the Grid. Section 4 contains the technical contributions of the paper, viz., a detailed description of how a DQP engine can be realised that uses Grid services both as architectural components in the design of the engine itself and as nodes in distributed query execution plans. The engine described has been implemented for first public release in July 2003 and is referred to as **OGSA-DQP**. Section 5 draws contrasts with other work on distributed query processing. Finally, Section 6 states some conclusions.

2 Grid Services

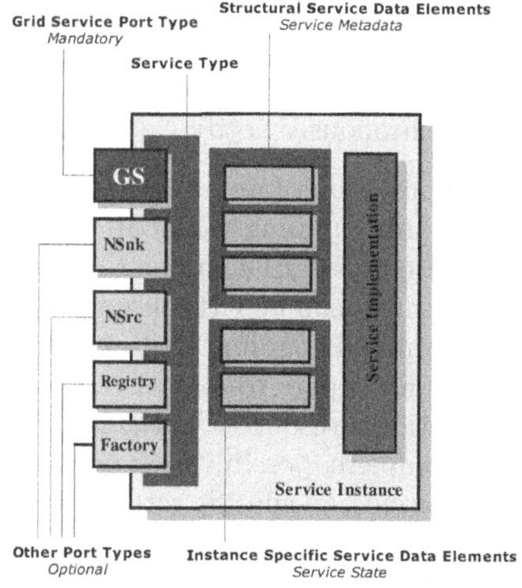

Fig. 1. Internal Structure of a GS

Among the drivers for the evolution to service-based architectures are the networking infrastructure now available, of course, and, more importantly, the emergence, in both e-business and e-science, of a cooperation model referred to as a *virtual organisation* [7]. The service-based approach seems to many a good solution to the problem of modelling a virtual organisation as a distributed system. GSs build upon and extend the service-oriented architecture and technologies first proposed for WSs [9]. Figure 1 shows the structure of a GS instance. WSs cannot be created dynamically and are stateless from the viewpoint of the requester. The Grid community has sought to address these limitations, thereby responding to the needs of applications in the high performance distributed computing area where dynamic allocation of highly shared, powerful resources is essential.

Thus, the OGSA [6,18] proposes interfaces for GSs that, unlike WSs, can be instantiated dynamically by a call to their factory and are stateful.

A GS must define a `Grid Service` port type, and may define optional port types, such as `Notification Sink` (NSnk) and `Notification Source` (NSrc) in Figure 1, as discussed below. Associated with a GS is a potentially dynamic set of *Service Data Elements* (SDEs). An SDE is a named and typed XML element that is used to represent information about GS instances, thereby opening the way for the discovery and management of potentially dynamic GS instance state.

The OGSA specifies the following functionalities:

- **Registration and Discovery** – A standard interface is defined for registering information about GS instances with registry services. A GS that also implements the `Registry` port type becomes a *Grid Service Registry* (GSR). The `findServiceData` operation can be used to query registry metadata.
- **Dynamic Service Creation** – One of the most important characteristics of the OGSA is its acknowledgement of the need to create and manage new GS instances dynamically. A `Factory` port type is defined (with the expected semantics) to achieve this. Once created, a GS instance is denotable by a globally unique *Grid Service Handle* (GSH).
- **Lifetime Management** – Because GSs can be created dynamically, they need to be disposed of. The `GS` port type defines operations for managing the lifetime of a GS instance and for reclaiming services and state associated with failed operations. The OGSA adopts soft-state protocols that enable the host itself to discard a GS instance if the stream of keep-alive messages that reaffirm the need for it to be retained dries up.
- **Notification** – Common abstractions and service interfaces for subscription to, and delivery of, event notifications are supported through the notification sink and source port types, so that dynamic, distributed GSs can asynchronously notify each other of relevant changes to their state.

The provision of an infrastructure with the properties above is an important step towards fulfilling the goal of supporting virtual organisations. Concretely, this goal requires that, among other tasks, the access to, and management of, Grid resources can be virtualised. By virtualised is meant, roughly, that the levels of cohesion and coupling that obtain among application components are such as to allow developers to express the needs of a virtual organisation for data and computational resources at the grain of complete, possibly federated, databases, and of complete, possibly orchestrated, applications. Initiatives to provide value-adding services in specific settings are being pursued, e.g., security, or transport. Of particular importance for the work presented in this paper, are the data access and integration services discussed in Section 3.

3 Grid Database Services

While query processing technology is characterised by high levels of cohesion coupling it to applications has often required special attention. This need has occurred at several granularities, from programs to distributed systems.

The service-based approach to data access and integration offers very low levels of coupling (because of its high-level consistent interfaces) at a very coarse granularity (e.g., that of a, possibly federated, database system). From this fact stem challenges and opportunities as this and the remaining sections show.

The main objective of the OGSA-DAI initiative is to build upon the OGSA infrastructure to deliver added-value, high-level data management functionality for the Grid. OGSA-DAI components are either *data access components* or *data integration components*. The former give access to stored collections of structured data managed by database management systems implementing standard data models. The latter provide facilities for combining or transforming data from multiple data access components in order to present some integrated or derived view of the data. The DQP system introduced in this paper is an example of a data integration component providing combination facilities. OGSA-DAI extends GSs with the following services and port types:

- A *Grid Data Service Registry* (GDSR) is a facility for the publication of GDSs. Services are registered with a GDSR via a `registerService` operation. The data that is used to describe a service for registration is generally a subset of the SDEs exposed by the GDS. Registered services (and their capabilities) can be found using a `findServiceData` call. A GDSR is also capable of reporting registered service changes to service instances that have subscribed for this via a `subscribe` call.
- A *Grid Data Service Factory* (GDSF) is configurable to create GDS instances tailored to specific requests. A `createService` operation is passed configuration information for the requested GS instance, including database management system location, database and query language.
- The `Grid Data Service` (GDS) port type is the core contribution of OGSA-DAI. It accepts a request (as an XML document) which instructs the GDS instance to interact with a database to create, retrieve, update or delete data. The primary operation in the `GDS` port type is `perform`, through which a request can be passed to the GDS (e.g., for an SQL query to be evaluated).
- The `Grid Data Transport` (GDT) port type enables data transport between GDSs and between client processes and GDSs. It is used by the GDS to satisfy delivery requests and allows data to be pushed or pulled through `putData` and `getData` calls, respectively. The `GDT` port type is crucial for efficient and reliable data transport when large data volumes prevail.

Figure 2 illustrates the interaction of these services and port types in a typical scenario. Circled numbers (written inside parentheses in running text) denote the position of an interaction in a sequence. Solid arrows denote invocation. Dashed ones, instantiation. (1) A GDSF registers itself with one or more registries (possibly a virtual organisation registry) as part of its initialisation procedure. (2) A client discovers the GDSF by issuing a `findServiceData` request to the GDSR. (3) The client uses the GDSF to create a GDS instance. (4) The client submits queries using the `perform` call in the GDS port type. (5) The results of the query are then delivered by the GDS instance to the consumer (assumed in Figure 2, for illustration purposes, to be different from the client).

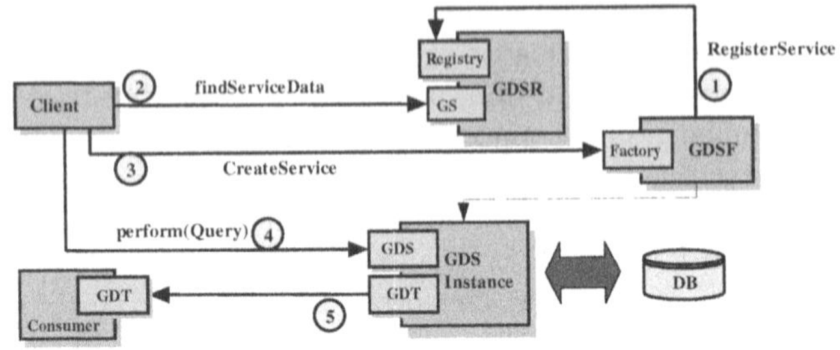

Fig. 2. OGSA-DAI Service Interactions

The current OGSA-DAI software (V 2.5) is layered on top of the OGSI reference implementation (initially known as OGSI) released as Globus Toolkit 3 (Beta) in June 2003. Both are available under open source licenses, from [www.globus.org/ogsa] and [www.ogsa-dai.org.uk].

4 A Service-Based DQP Architecture

This section describes a query processing framework in which query compilation, optimisation and evaluation are viewed (and implemented) as invocations of OGSA-compliant GSs. Moreover, both the execution nodes and the data nodes of the distributed query execution plans are OGSA-compliant GSs. Benefits include the following: (i) Grid services can be used to identify lightly loaded resources that are suitable for query evaluation and to allocate query evaluators on these nodes; (ii) Grid security supports single sign-on for remote resources, simplifying authentication for distributed execution; (iii) since source databases and intermediate evaluators support consistent interfaces for data delivery, the design of the query processing framework is simplified; (iv) consistent resource discovery and allocation mechanisms can be used for both data sources and analysis tools accessed from a query.

The query processing framework presented in this section extends the OGSA and OGSA-DAI with two new services (and their corresponding factories):

- A `Grid Distributed Query Service` (GDQS) extends the GDS interface. When a GDQS is set up, it interacts with the appropriate registries to obtain the metadata and computational resource information that it needs to compile, optimise, partition and schedule distributed query execution plans over multiple execution nodes in the Grid. The implementation of the GDQS builds on our previous work on the Polar* distributed query processor for the Grid [17] by encapsulating its compilation and optimisation functionality.
- A `Grid Query Evaluation Service` (GQES) also extends the GDS interface. Each GQES instance is an execution node in the distributed query plans alluded to above. It is in charge of a partition of the query execution plan assigned to it by a GDQS. It implements a physical algebra over GDSs (encapsulated within which lie the actual data sources whose schemas were imported during GDQS set-up).

Figure 3 provides an overview of the interactions during the instantiation and set-up of a GDQS as well as those that take place when a query is received and processed. Conventions are as for Figure 2, with dotted arrows labelled by dark-background sequence numbers denoting interactions that take place in the set-up phase, which occurs only once in the lifetime of the GDQS instance. Solid arrows denote interactions that take place when a query is submitted. The 3-dot sequence in Figure 3 can, as usual, be read as 'and so on, up to'.

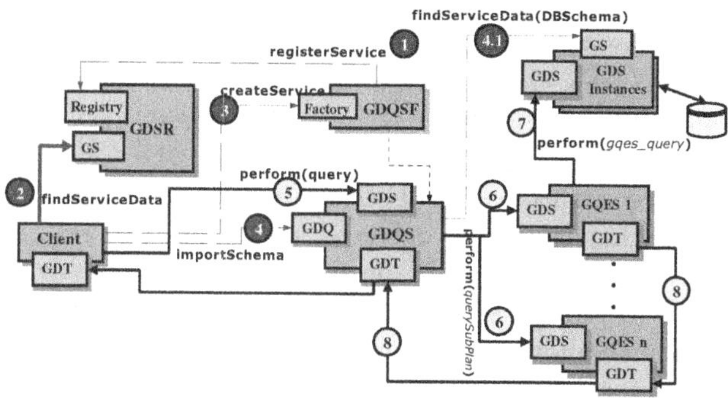

Fig. 3. GDQS Interactions: Set-Up and Querying

Note that since the GDQS is OGSA-DAI compliant, interactions (1) to (3) are the same as those illustrated in Figure 2. The fourth interaction is specific to a GDQS (and hence justifies the additional GDQ port type). It allows the GDQS to import logical and physical schemas of the participating data sources as well as information about computational resources into the metadata dictionary used by the query compiler and optimiser.

After importing the schemas of the participating data source, the client can submit queries (5) via the GDS port type using a `perform` call. This call is compiled and optimised into a distributed query execution plan, the partitions of which are scheduled for execution at different GQESs. The GDQS then uses this information to create GQES instances on their designated execution nodes (and these could be, potentially, anywhere in the Grid) and hands over to each (6) the plan partition assigned to it (as described in more detail in Section 4.2). This is what allows the DQP framework described in this paper to benefit from (implicitly) parallel evaluation even as the uniform service-based interfaces hide most of the low-level complexity necessary to achieve this. Finally, (some of the) GQES instances interact (7) with other GDS instances to obtain data, after which the results start to propagate (8) across GQES instances and, eventually, back to the client via the GDT port type.

```
select p.proteinId, blast(p.sequence)
from   p in protein, t in proteinTerm
where  t.termId = 'GO:0008372' and
       p.proteinId = t.proteinId
```

Fig. 4. Example Query

In the remainder of the paper, the characteristic query in Figure 4 is used to illustrate issues and challenges and to describe the solutions to them that this paper contributes. The setting is that of the ODMG [2] data model and its associated query language, OQL. This query returns, for each protein annotated with the GO term 'GO:0008372' (i.e., unknown cellular component), those proteins that are similar to it. Assume that (as in [17]) the `protein` and `proteinTerm` extents are retrieved from two databases, respectively: the Genome Information Management System (GIMS) [img.cs.man.ac.uk/gims] and the Gene Ontology (GO) [www.geneontology.org], each running under (separate) MySQL relational database management systems. The query also calls the BLAST sequence similarity program [www.ncbi.nlm.nih.gov/BLAST/], which, given a protein sequence, returns a set of structures containing protein IDs and similarity scores. Note that the query retrieves data from two relational databases, and invokes an external application on the join results.

A service-based approach to processing this query over a distributed environment allows the query optimiser to choose from multiple providers (in the safe knowledge that most heterogeneities are encapsulated behind uniform interfaces), and to spawn multiple copies of a query-algebraic operator to exploit parallelism. In the example query, for instance, the optimiser could choose between different GO and GIMS databases, different BLAST services, and different nodes for running GQES instances[1]. Moreover, a DQP engine built upon GSs can offer better long-term assurances of efficiency because dynamic service discovery, creation and configuration allow it to take advantage of a constantly changing resource pool which would be troublesome for other approaches.

4.1 Setting Up a Distributed Query Service

The GDQS service type (i.e., the collection of port types it supports) implements two port types from the OGSA, viz., `GS` and `NSnk`, and two from OGSA-DAI, viz., `GDS` and `GDT`. To these, it adds a **`Grid Distributed Query`** (GDQ) port type that allows source schemas to be imported. Note that currently schema integration and conflict resolution are not carried out in the wake of schema import. However, a collection of GDSs characterizes a class of queries over which a global model can be specified (e.g., using a global-as-view approach). On top of these building blocks, one can build schema-integration services, potentially also implementing GDS port types.

The steps involved in identifying and accessing the participating data sources depend on the lifetime model applied to GDS instances that wrap those data sources. We assume that the GDS instances are created per-client and can handle multiple queries but are still relatively short-lived entities. This model is also applicable to the lifetime of the GDQS instance. Note that other approaches to lifetime management are possible, each having particular advantages and disadvantages. For instance, the GDQS could be implemented to serve multiple queries from multiple users for a long period of time.

In that case the cost of setting up the system would be minimal, at the expense of somewhat increased complexity in handling query requests because of the need to manage multiple simultaneous requests and the need to manage resource allocation for the corresponding interactions. On the other hand the GDQS instance could be designed to be a per-query, short-lived entity, in

[1] The first release of **OGSA-DQP** does not support this facility because of limited functionality in the OGSI implementation it builds upon.

which case, the cost of setting up the system would constitute a considerable proportion of the total lifetime of the instance. The approach adopted for our particular implementation (i.e. an instance per-user that is capable of responding to multiple requests), avoids the complexity of multi-user interactions while ensuring that the cost of system set-up phase is not the dominating one. We also assume that the client knows enough about the data sources to discover the GDS factories for them, and to hand over their GSHs to the GDQS. The GDQS can then request that those GDS instances be created (thereby obtaining control over the lifetimes of the GDS instances), and imports their schemas. This model balances the responsibilities of the client and those of the GDQS by assigning instance creation and lifetime management to the latter, while leaving identification and discovery of the data sources to the former. Figure 5 shows the detailed interaction sequence before and during an `importSchema` call. Notation is as in Figure 2.

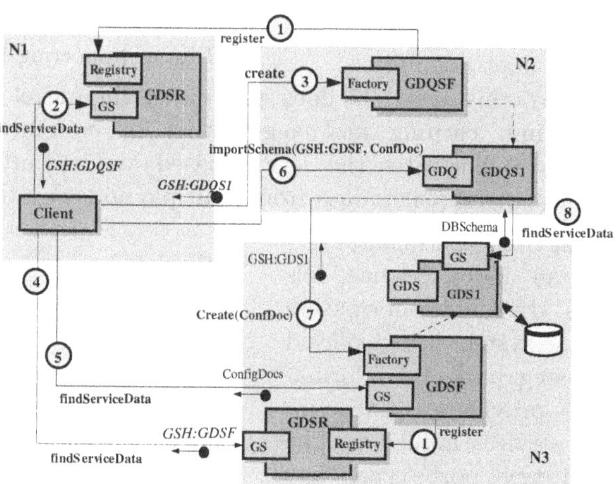

Fig. 5. Importing Service Metadata

(1) reflects the default behaviour for a GDSF of registering itself upon activation. In the figure, the client starts by discovering (2) a GDQS factory and creating from it (3) a GDQS instance *GDQS*1. Note that typically, there would be a public (or a virtual organisation wide) registry already known to the client, where GDQS Factory has already been registered. The service registration and discovery schemes adopted for GDQS are fully compatible with those of OGSA and OGSA-DAI [18]. The client then discovers (4) a GDS Factory for a particular data source, obtains (5) a configuration document by querying the GDSF), and passes (6) the handle *GSH:GDSF* of this factory and the configuration document to *GDQS*1 via an `importSchema` call. The GDQS instance creates (7) a GDS instance *GDS*1 using the factory handle and the configuration document provided by the client, and obtains (8) the database schema of the data source wrapped by that GDS.

It is also necessary to import metadata about external services (e.g., BLAST, in the example query) that are required to participate in the queries the GDQS supports. The participation of an external service occurs when the service is called from within the OQL query. For instance, in the example query, the call to the BLAST sequence similarity algorithm. As the service is described by a

WSDL document, **importSchema** obtains the latter and incorporates the data types and operation definitions into the metadata collection.

It is also important for the GDQS to collect sufficient data about the available computational resources on the Grid to enable the optimiser to schedule the distribution of the plan partitions as efficiently as possible. Although the current OGSA reference implementation does not fully support this need, it does provide a high-level **Index Service**, to enable collecting, caching and aggregating of computational resource metadata. Figure 6 illustrates the service-based architecture that enables a GDQS to collect resource metadata from multiple nodes on the Grid.

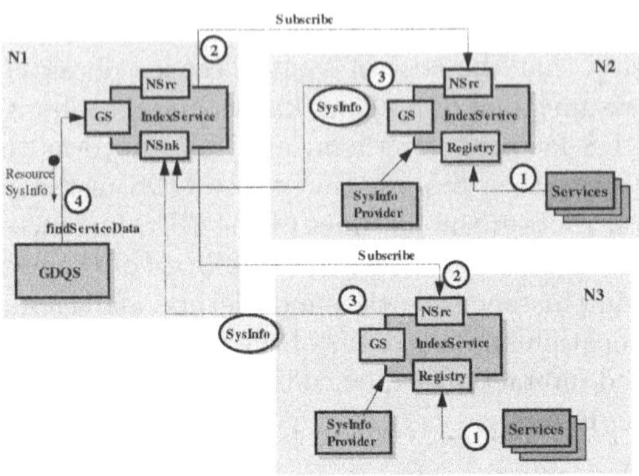

Fig. 6. Importing Resource Metadata

In this experimental setup, an index service collects dynamic information on the system it is deployed in using back-end information providers. Since index services implement the **Registry** port type, any service can be published (1) using them. The GDQS identifies a central index service as its server for caching and aggregating metadata, and causes (2) it to subscribe to other distributed index services.

```
<GridNodeInfo
  hostsDataSource="1" hostsService="0"
  hasEvaluatorFactory="1">
  <nodeID>mach1.cs.man.ac.uk</nodeID>
  <CPUSpeedMHz>1400</CPUSpeedMHz>
  <CPULoadPercentage>10</CPULoadPercentage>
  <connectionSpeedMBperSec>1.0</connectionSpeedMBperSec>
  <hostedDataSource
    GDSFactoryHandle
    ="http://x.cs.man.ac.uk/ogsa/services/GDSFactory"
  <evaluatorFactory>
    http://x.cs.man.ac.uk/ogsa/services/EvaluatorFactory
  </evaluatorFactory>
</GridNodeInfo> <GridNodeInfo
  hostsDataSource="0" hostsService="1"
  hasEvaluatorFactory="0">
  <nodeID>mach1.ebi.co.uk</nodeID>
  <CPUSpeedMHz>1000</CPUSpeedMHz>
  <CPULoadPercentage>95</CPULoadPercentage>
  <connectionSpeedMBperSec>2.0</connectionSpeedMBperSec>
  <hostedService>
    http://www.ebi.ac.uk/.../AxisServlet/urn:spoofblast
  </hostedService>
</GridNodeInfo>
```

Fig. 7. Computational Resource Metadata

The remote index services send (3) notification messages at specified periods whose payload is resource metadata in a format determined by the back-end information provider. The GDQS can use (4) a **findServiceData** call to obtain the aggregated information as SDEs from its server. Note that one would expect the index service hierarchy to have been set up as part of a virtual organisation's infrastructure, since the identification of Grid nodes that constitute the organisation's resource pool is beyond the operational scope of the GDQS. The GDQS captures computational resource metadata for all machines hosting a schema it has imported.

The XML fragment in Figure 7 shows the canonical form in which computational resource metadata is maintained within the GDQS. Each `GridNodeInfo` element in the fragment contains information such as the CPU speed, CPU load (as a percentage), the network bandwidth, the address of the GDSF (if there exists one) that wraps the data source hosted in that particular node, and the URLs of hosted services. Once a GDQS is set up as described, it is ready to accept queries against the schemas and resources that it ranges over. The XML fragment in Figure 8 shows, for the example query, the document that is passed as the parameter of the `perform()` call. The query request document consists of a header specifying the document name, the document version and the GSH of the originator service; and a body conveying the OQL query and indicating how results are to be delivered.

```
<GridDataServiceRequest>
 <Header>
    <RequestName>Example 1</RequestName>
    <Version>
        <Config>config</Config>
        <RequestEnvironment>
            environment
        </RequestEnvironment>
    </Version>
    <Originator>GSH of Originator</Originator>
  </Header>
  <Body>
        <Statement name="xyz"
            dataResource="MyDataResource">
            select p.proteinId, blast(p.sequence)
            from   p in protein, t in proteinTerm
            where  t.termId='GO:0008372' and
                   p.proteinId=t.proteinId
        </Statement>
        <Delivery name="delivery">
            <Mechanism type="bulk"/>
            <Mode type="full"/>
            <From>xyz</From>
            <To>response</To>
        </Delivery>
        <Execute name="execute">xyz</Execute>
  </Body>
</GridDataServiceRequest>
```

Fig. 8. Query as a GDS Request Document

Due to lack of space, details about the compilation and optimisation are omitted. They can be found in [17]. Figure 9 depicts the execution plan produced by the compiler/optimiser. Three partitions (i.e., the dashed regions) have been decided upon whose intersections are marked by the exchange operators used to bind them, as explained below. Note that the partition containing the potentially expensive the BLAST operation_call has been scheduled to run on two of the four nodes N1-N4 harnessed for executing the query.

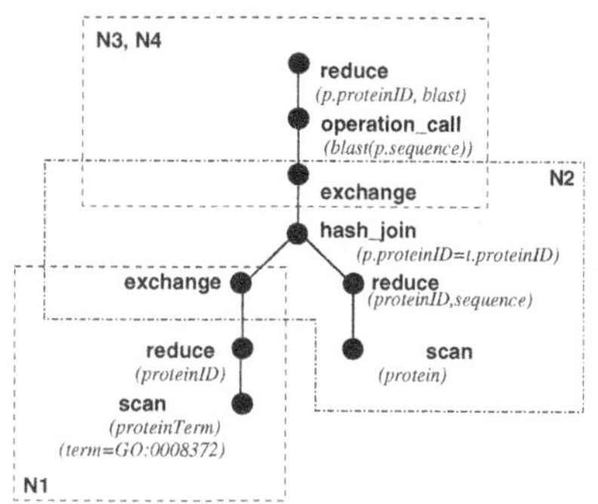

Fig. 9. Distributed Query Plan

4.2 Evaluating Distributed Plans

Evaluator functionality is exposed via GQES instances that implement the GS, GDS and GDT port types from the OGSA and OGSA-DAI.

The GDQS creates as many GQESs instances as stipulated in the distributed query plan constructed by the compiler (see Figure 9). The GDQS had already obtained a handle on each GDS that contributes to the evaluation of a partition, as illustrated in Figure 5.

Each partition, along with the GDS handles it needs, is mapped to XML and sent to be evaluated by the GQES instance it is assigned to.

For the example query, this gives rise to the GS interaction diagram in Figure 10. Conventions are as in previous figures. The GQESs that scan stores, viz., N1 and N2, are instantiated in different hosts. Conditions at N2 (e.g., available memory) are such as to justify the GDQS having decided on using, say, a hash_join, assigning it to N2. For the BLAST operation_call, the GDQS saw benefits in parallelising it over two GQESs N3 and N4.

The GDQS receives the request (1) and compiles it into a distributed query plan, each partition of which is assigned to one or more execution nodes. Each execution node corresponds to a GQES instance which is created by the GDQS (2). The GDQS then dispatches (3), as an XML document, each plan partition to its designated GQES instance. Upon receiving its plan partitions, each GQES instance initiates its evaluation.

The overall behaviour of a GQES instance is as follows. Execution is a data flow computation using an iterator model [10], with each operator implementing an {open(), next(), close()} interface. Each GQES starts executing its partition independently by calling open() on the topmost operator, so introducing parallelism between partitions. Every GQES instance that has an exchange leaf[2] is fed data by the GQES instance executing the partition whose root is

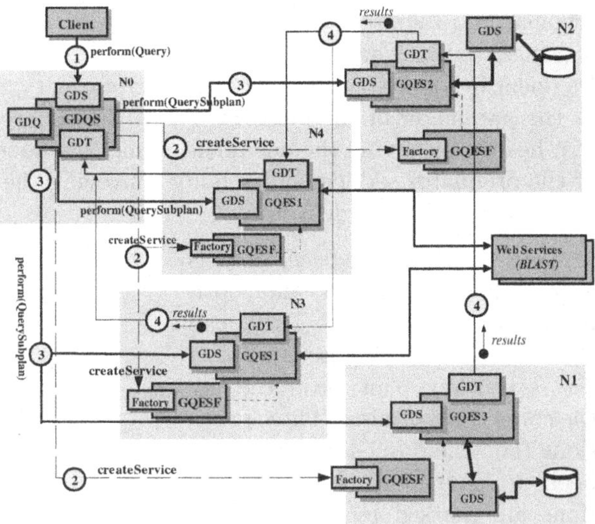

Fig. 10. GQES Instances and Query Partitions

[2] An exchange operator [10] encapsulates control flow, data distribution and inter-process communication

the corresponding exchange. Data flows from the GQES instances that execute partitions containing operators whose semantics requires access to stores.

Within each GQES instance, the initialisation procedure starts when an open() call reaches the topmost operator. This call propagates down the operator tree from parent to children at every level until it reaches the leaf operators. Then, interaction with other GDSs occurs. The handle for each such GDS will have been planted by the GDQS in the XML document passed to each GQES instance that needs it. For example, in node N2 (in Figure 10, but see also Figure 9), when this stream of open() calls reaches a, say, scan operator (see Figure 9), it causes the N2 GQES to interact with the GDS instance on N2, whereby data becomes ready to flow upwards from the protein extent in the GDS through which the GIMS database is accessed. Following the open(), a stream of next() calls again propagates from the topmost operator down to the leaf operators. When a next() call reaches a leaf, the standing-by GDS begins responding with tuples, and data flows upward.

Taking as example, again, node N2 in Figure 10, its topmost operator is an exchange, which, as alluded to, encapsulates inter-evaluator interaction semantics. Its effect is to cause tuples to flow (4) across this GQES instance's boundary and along the inter-GQES channels. When an eof is received in response to a next(), the flow is over and a close() is called, leading to clean up and dynamic resource de-allocation Eventually, all operators have been closed, at which point that GQES instance has fulfilled its purpose. Across all GQES instances, results propagate up the tree, and exchanges ship (4) them to their destination.

5 Related Work

The distributed nature of Grid applications means that services to support coordinated use of Grid resources are important, and considerable attention has been given to functionalities for managing data derivation (e.g., [8]) and replication (e.g., [3]). However, such higher-level Grid data management functionalities are still targeted principally at file-based data, and the only previous work on distributed query processing in a Grid setting is the Polar* proposal from the authors [17]. Polar* differs from the approach presented in this paper in that it is not service-based; in Polar*, Grid middleware is accessed using a Grid-enabled version of MPI [5]. The absence of the service-based context in Polar* means that connection to external databases and computational services is much less seamless than in the OGSA setting.

In the Web Services setting, structured data representations, at least in the form of XML Schemas, have been much more prominent from the start. In addition, vendors have been quick to integrate Web Service and data management products (e.g. [13,16]). However, we know of only one previous proposal for querying over collections of Web Services, viz. that of SkyQuery [14], which applies the classical wrapper-mediator architecture in a service-based setting. SkyQuery deploys WSs at each database store for handling metadata, performing queries, and cross matching partial results. However, the SkyQuery proposal is less ambitious than that presented here, in a number of respects: (i) the only services that contribute to query evaluation are the data sources – there is no dynamic discovery and allocation of evaluators, for example, to support evaluation of large joins; (ii) the execution plan generated by the optimiser is a straightforward pipeline – there is no partitioned parallelism; and (iii) the query language supported is specialised for use with astronomical queries, and seems to assume that database nodes contain horizontal partitions of the overall database – there seem not to be generic facilities for joining data from multiple nodes, for example. Thus SkyQuery is an important early demonstration of the viability of Web Services for supporting distributed query processing, but it lacks dynamic allocation of resources to match the needs of specific requests. This latter feature is central to the ethos of the Grid, in which computational resources are made shareable, and thus can be deployed flexibly to support changing user needs and system loads.

How does the work presented here compare with other work on DQP, as surveyed in [12]? The principal differences derive from the context in which queries are executed. The aim of the current proposal is essentially the same as that of the developers of systems such as Garlic [11] and Kleisli [4], i.e., to support declarative query formulation over distributed data stores and analysis tools. However, the development of service-based Grids provides certain opportunities for the developers of DQP systems that were more elusive before. For example, Web Services promise to make available comprehensive discovery and access facilities for distributed resources that ease their integration into federated architectures. We note that no custom-built wrappers were developed to support the bioinformatics application illustrated in this paper – generic Grid Database Services were used to access the databases, and existing BLAST Web Services were used to perform sequence comparisons. This contrasts with both Garlic and Kleisli, where custom wrappers are constructed for interfacing the query engine to the external resources. Furthermore, we observe that the resources used to evaluate the example query were obtained dynamically, based on the anticipated needs of the request. Had the request required substantially greater resources to run efficiently, these would have been allocated from those available on the Grid. This contrasts with both Garlic and Kleisli, where query evaluation is shared between the central query evaluator and the source wrappers, with no dynamic resource discovery. Thus, although many characteristics of existing DQP systems carry over largely unchanged to the service-based setting, various features of relevance to DQP deployment and development are significantly affected by service-based architectures.

6 Conclusions

Web Services, in particular in conjunction with the resource access and management facilities of Grid computing, show considerable promise as an infrastructure over which distributed applications in e-business and e-science can be developed. However, to date, the emphasis has been on the development of core middleware functionalities, such as for service description, discovery and access. Extensions to support the coordinated use of such services, for example using distributed transactions or workflow languages are still under development. This paper seeks to contribute to the corpus of work on higher-level services by demonstrating how techniques from distributed query processing can be deployed in a service-based Grid. The proposal is service-based in two respects:

- Queries are written with respect to and evaluated over distributed resources discovered and accessed using emerging Web Services and Grid Services standards. This is important because it is as yet far from clear how best to orchestrate collections of Web and Grid Services. Although it is likely that workflow languages will have a prominent role, DQP offers system-supported optimisation of declarative requests with implicit parallelism, a combination that should yield significant programmer productivity and performance benefits for large-scale, data intensive applications. As such, we believe that service-based architectures stand to benefit significantly from DQP. The proposal made in this paper is much the most comprehensive to date for a distributed query processor that acts over services.
- The query processor has been designed and implemented as a collection of cooperating services, using the facilities of the OGSA to dynamically discover, access and use computational resources to support query compilation and evaluation. This is important because although the OGSA has found widespread support within the academic and industrial Grid community, there are as yet few examples of higher-level services developed over the OGSA. This proposal can be seen to provide important validation of OGSA facilities for developing higher-level services. Furthermore, it has been shown how the combination of dynamic computational resource discovery and allocation can be used to match the requirements of a distributed query to the resources available in a heterogeneous distributed environment. As such, we believe that DQP stands to benefit significantly from the availability of service based grids. The proposal made in this paper is much the most comprehensive to date for a distributed query processor that uses grid services in its implementation.

The proposal described in this paper has been prototyped. The resulting software, referred to as **OGSA-DQP**, is scheduled for public release from [www.ogsa-dai.org.uk] in July 2003.

Acknowledgements. The work reported in this paper has been supported by the UK e-Science Programme through the OGSA-DAI project and the myGrid project, and by the UK EPSRC grant GR/R51797/01. We are grateful for that support. The ideas in this paper have benefited greatly from, and build upon, our collaboration with colleagues, from IBM, Oracle, the UK National e-Science Centre and the Edinburgh Parallel Computing Centre, in the OGSA-DAI project.

References

1. W. H. Bell, D. Bosio, W. Hoschek, P. Kunszt, G. McCance, and M. Silander. Project Spitfire - Towards Grid Web Service Databases. In *Global Grid Forum 5*, 2002.
2. R. G. G. Cattell and D. K. Barry. *The Object Database Standard: ODMG 3.0*. Morgan Kaufmann, 2000.
3. A. Chervenak, E. Deelman, I. Foster, L. Guy, W. Hoschek, A. Iamnitchi, C. Kesselman, P. Kunszt, M. Ripenu, B. Schwartzkopf, H. Stocking, K. Stockinger, and B. Tierney. Giggle: A Framework for Constructing Scaleable Replica Location Services. In *Proc. Supercomputing*. IEEE Press, 2002.
4. S. B. Davidson, J. Crabtree, B. P. Brunk, J. Schug, V. Tannen, G. C. Overton, and C. J. Stoeckert. K2/Kleisli and GUS: Experiments in Integrated Access to Genomic Data Sources. *IBM Systems Journal*, 40(2):512–531, 2001.
5. I. Foster and N. Karonis. A Grid-Enabled MPI: Message Passing in Heterogeneous Distributed Computing Systems. In *Proc. Supercomputing*. IEEE Press, 1998.
6. I. Foster, C. Kesselman, J. M. Nick, and S. Tuecke. Grid Services for Distributed System Integration. *IEEE Computer*, 35(6):37–46, 2002.
7. I. Foster, C. Kesselman, and S. Tuecke. The Anatomy of the Grid: Enabling Scalable Virtual Organizations. *Int. J. Supercomputer Applications*, 15(3), 2001.
8. I. Foster, J. Voeckler, M. Wilde, and Y. Zhao. The Virtual Data Grid: A New Model and Architecture for Data-Intensive Collaboration. In *Proc. CIDR*, 2003.
9. K. Gottschalk, S. Graham, H. Kreger, and J. Snell. Introduction to Web Services Architecture. *IBM Sys. Journal*, 41(2):170–177, 2002.
10. G. Graefe. Encapsulation of Parallelism in the Volcano Query Processing System. In *Proc. SIGMOD*, pages 102–111, 1990.
11. V. Josifovski, P. Schwarz, L. Haas, and E. Lin. Garlic: A New Flavor of Federated Query Processing for DB2. In *Proc. SIGMOD*, pages 524–532, 2002.
12. D. Kossmann. The State of the Art in Distributed Query Processing. *ACM Computing Surveys*, 32(4):422–469, 2000.
13. S. Malaika, C. Nelin, R. Qu, B. Reinwald, and D. C. Wolfson. DB2 and Web Services. *IBM Systems Journal*, 41(4):666–685, 2002.
14. T. Malik, A. S. Szalay, T. Budavari, and A. R. Thakar. SkyQuery: A Web Service Approach to Federate Databases. In *Proc. CIDR*, 2003.
15. R. W. Moore, C. Baru, R. Marciano, A. Rajasekar, and M. Wan. Data-Intensive Computing. In I. Foster and C. Kesselman, editors, *The Grid: Blueprint for a New Computing Infrastrcuture*, chapter 5, pages 105–129. Morgan Kaufmann, 1999.
16. R. M. Riordan, editor. *Microsoft ADO.NET Step by Step*. Microsoft Press, 2002.
17. J. Smith, A. Gounaris, P. Watson, N. W. Paton, A. A. A. Fernandes, and R. Sakellariou. Distributed Query Processing on the Grid. In *Proc. Grid Computing 2002*, pages 279–290. Springer, LNCS 2536, 2002.
18. S. Tuecke, K. Czajkowski, I. Foster, J. Frey, S. Graham, C. Kesselman, T. Maquire, T.Sandholm, D.Snelling, and P.Vanderbilt. Open Grid Service Infrastructure (OGSI). Technical report, OGSI-WG, Global Grid Forum, 2003. Version 1.0.

Peer–to–Peer Process Execution with OSIRIS

Christoph Schuler[1], Roger Weber[1], Heiko Schuldt[2], and Hans-J. Schek[1]

[1] Swiss Federal Institute of Technology (ETH),
CH–8092 Zurich, {schuler,weber,schek}@inf.ethz.ch
[2] University for Health Informatics and Technology Tyrol (UMIT),
A-6020 Innsbruck, heiko.schuldt@umit.at

Abstract. Standards like SOAP, WSDL, and UDDI facilitate the proliferation of services. Based on these technologies, processes are a means to combine services to applications and to provide new value-added services. For large information systems, a centralized process engine is no longer appropriate due to limited scalability. Instead, in this paper, we propose a distributed and decentralized process engine that routes process instances directly from one node to the next ones. Such a Peer-to-Peer Process Execution (P^3E) promises good scalability characteristics since it is able to dynamically balance the load of processes and services among all available service providers. Therefore, navigation costs only accumulate on nodes that are directly involved in the execution. However, this requires sophisticated strategies for the replication of meta information for P^3E. Especially, replication mechanisms should avoid frequent accesses to global information repositories. In our system called OSIRIS (*Open Service Infrastructure for Reliable and Integrated Process Support*), we deploy a clever publish/subscribe based replication scheme together with freshness predicates to significantly reduce replication costs. This way, OSIRIS can support process-based applications in a dynamically evolving system without limiting scalability and correctness. First experiments have shown very promising results with respect to scalability.

1 Introduction

Modern technologies like XML, SOAP, and WSDL provide a simple yet powerful means to publish information services and to access services. The platform independent definitions of these technologies further simplify the composition of services to offer new value added services [5]. One way to achieve this goal is to define transactional processes [20] over web services. Such processes compose web service calls in an application-specific invocation order –by defining control and data flow– together with transactional guarantees. Each activity of a process corresponds to the invocation of a (web) service. Programming using processes is referred to as "programming in the large" or "mega programming" [24]. Essentially, processes are again (higher-level) web services, i.e., they are accessible via SOAP (Simple Object Access Protocol) [21] and described by a WSDL (Web Service Description Language) [26] document such that other users can easily integrate them into even larger processes.

M.E. Orlowska et al. (Eds.): ICSOC 2003, LNCS 2910, pp. 483–498, 2003.

Processes impose several vital requirements to the underlying infrastructure. In terms of failure handling, the traditional "all-or-nothing" semantics of atomicity is too restrictive and should be generalized. Process specification must allow for several contingency strategies to handle failures at the application level. Essentially, it is the task of an infrastructure to guarantee correctness even in case of network or software failures. Although not all applications require concurrency control, an infrastructure should be able to coordinate the access to shared resources in case it is needed.

Usually, several semantically equivalent web services are available at different places. An infrastructure for processes must be able to equally distribute the load over all web service providers. Similarly, we want to optimize process executions by taking costs and expected execution times. To this end, the infrastructure should bind services dynamically at execution time rather than at process definition time. This decoupling provides a high degree of flexibility since new providers and services are seamlessly integrated (following the ideas of autonomic computing [25]).

Finally, the system has to provide a high degree of scalability in terms of the number of service providers and the number of concurrent processes.

1.1 Survey of Existing Infrastructures

Recently, various *frameworks* supporting the invocation of web services have been proposed. Microsoft's .NET [14], for example, allows to integrate web service calls into applications. However, since each web service call is considered independently, .NET does not provide execution guarantees for complete applications. Moreover, application developers must link services at build-time and there is no support for dynamic service selection at run-time. Therefore, the task of balancing the load among all available service providers is shifted from the infrastructure to the applications.

Work ow management systems are the traditional infrastructures for process support. Systems like IBM's MQSeries Workflow [13] support the integration of web service calls into workflow processes. Usually, these systems offer well-engineered execution guarantees, especially in terms of failure handling. However, they lack a flexible binding of service calls at run-time and, thus, are not able to optimally distribute the overall load among all service providers at run-time. Since these systems follow a centralized architecture consisting of dedicated workflow engine(s), their scalability is limited.

In contrast, *grid* infrastructures [7] offer optimal support for load balancing. Essentially, the infrastructure maintains the available resources of a grid and assigns tasks to the least loaded nodes. In addition, it is even possible to install new services in the grid in case a bottleneck is detected. However, these systems lack a sophisticated support for combining several service calls into processes. This is because they act more like a UDDI repository (Uniform Description and Discovery Interface) [1] focusing on optimal routing of service requests.

1.2 OSIRIS at a Glance

In this paper, we describe an new architecture for distributed and decentralized process management system. OSIRIS, short for **O**pen **S**ervice **I**nfrastructure for **R**eliable and **I**ntegrated process **S**upport, combines the benefits of several existing infrastructures, namely: i.) discovery and invocation of web services from frameworks like .NET, ii.) process support and execution guarantees from workflow management systems, iii.) late binding of service calls and load balancing from grid infrastructures, and, finally, iv.) Peer-to-Peer Processes Execution (P^3E) in analogy to peer-to-peer file systems. An interesting characteristic of P^3E in OSIRIS is that process navigation costs only accumulate on nodes of the community that are directly involved in the execution of a process. Especially, there is no central component in charge with process execution. Therefore, and in contrast to a centralized process engine, P^3E bears the potential to scale well with the number of concurrent processes and the number of service providers. First experiments based on the OSIRIS system verify this behavior.

To enable P^3E, nodes require global meta information about service providers and the load of their hosts. The approach of OSIRIS is to maintain meta information in global repositories, and to distribute the information to the nodes. Thereby, replication of meta information runs completely independent of process execution, i.e., P^3E always considers only local replicas of meta information. To reduce the amount of update messages in the system, nodes subscribe only for parts of the meta information. If meta data changes, only nodes having subscribed for this piece of information receive an update (*publish/subscribe replication*). Moreover, we relax the freshness of local replicas. For instance, nodes require load information to balance the load of service requests among all available providers. Since load information is highly dynamic, consistent replication would be very expensive. Consequently, OSIRIS only guarantees that the nodes' local copies of a piece of global meta information fulfill some freshness constraints (i.e., the difference to the correct load value never exceeds 10%).

The focus of this paper is on the presentation of the main concepts of OSIRIS and the verification of its high scalability capabilities by first performance evaluations. The latter very well supports our belief that the shift from centralized process management to decentralized solutions will boost large scale information systems. Especially, P^3E has the potential to scale well with the number of concurrent processes and the number of nodes connected to the community.

1.3 Organization

The remainder of this paper describes our approach in more detail. Section 2 and 3 describe the basic concepts and the implementation of OSIRIS, respectively. In section 4, we present fist results of a performance evaluation on the basis of the OSIRIS system. Section 5 summarizes related work, and Section 6 concludes.

2 Peer–to–Peer Process Execution

In this section, we first shortly describe the *hyperdatabase* concept which is the basis for the infrastructure we have built. Then, we present the OSIRIS system as an implementation of a hyperdatabase in more detail.

2.1 The Hyperdatabase Concept

In short, a hyperdatabase (HDB) [17,16,18] provides transactional guarantees for processes over distributed components using existing services. The HDB provides sophisticated routing strategies to dynamically choose among the available providers. And finally, a hyperdatabase does not follow a monolithic system architecture but consists of an additional thin software layer, a so-called *hyperdatabase layer* (HDB layer). The HDB layer resides on every node of the community and extends existing layers like the TCP/IP stack with process related functionality. In terms of routing of requests, a service is called by only specifying its type. The HDB layer then maps the service type to a real network address taking the list of available service providers and the current load of their hosts into account. As such, the HDB layer abstracts from service routing much like TCP/IP abstracts from data packet routing. Moreover, while the TCP/IP protocol guarantees correct transfer of bytes, the HDB layer guarantees the correct shipment of process instances.

Of course, a hyperdatabase requires that each service provider locally installs an additional software layer. Ideally, this layer comes together with the operating system much like the TCP/IP stack does (comparable to the .NET framework). For the time being, the community of service providers is split into two parts: on the hand side, there are providers that cooperate and have the HDB layer installed on their hosts. On the other hand side, we can incorporate external providers via proxy components. A proxy runs the HDB layer and forwards all service invocations to an appropriate external provider. Hence, providers can join the community even without installing the HDB layer.

2.2 Architecture of OSIRIS

The architecture of OSIRIS consists of two parts: firstly, each node runs an HDB layer that is responsible for the execution of processes, routing of service requests, and failure handling. The main emphasis of our design was to avoid any central component for process navigation. Rather, the execution of a process instance involves only nodes that provide a service for that process (see the process flow in Figure 1). To do so, each HDB layer requires global meta information, e.g., about service providers and their current load. This leads to the second part of our architecture: additional global repositories maintain the global meta information about the nodes in the community (cf. middle box in Figure 1). Each HDB layer contains replica of those pieces of meta information it needs to fulfill its tasks.

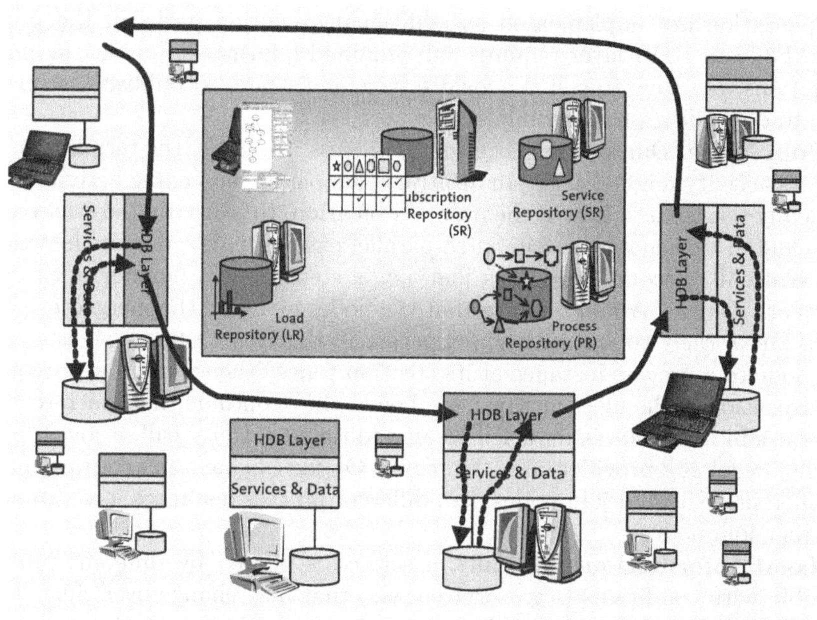

Fig. 1. Peer-to-peer process execution

It is important to distinguish between the task of process execution and the tasks of meta data replication. Process execution in OSIRIS follows a true peer-to-peer approach touching only nodes that provide a service for the process, and accessing meta information only locally. Meta data replication, on the other hand, is based on a hierarchical organization with central repositories (but distributed over a set of nodes), and clients (= HDB layers) replicating from them. Process execution and meta data replication run independent of each other.

Subscription Information. Usually, several providers offer semantically equivalent services. To simplify the discovery of services, OSIRIS deploys a publish and subscribe (pub/sub) mechanism for service invocations: a service provider subscribes for the *execution of its services* at a global service repository (similar to a UDDI repository). If a client requests a service, it publishes this request with the service type as the topic, and the HDB layer selects and invokes one of the available services. In OSIRIS, this means that a process instance is migrated by publishing the instance data with the service topics of subsequent steps. Of course, there is no central pub/sub component routing publications. Rather, each HDB layer holds local replicas of the global subscription lists and migrates process instances in a peer-to-peer way, i.e., plays the role of a pub/sub broker .

Required Process Information. A service invocation may lead to two result states: success or failure. In case of a success, the current execution path is followed. Otherwise, an alternative path is executed, possibly compensating some of the previous activities (partial roll back). Note that alternatives and compensation are implemented as additional execution paths in the process. With P^{3}E, an HDB layer requires only minimal information about the process definitions, i.e., how to call the local service and whom to publish the instance data to depending on the result state.

Join Node. During the execution of process instances, the termination of a process activity might trigger an arbitrary number of succeeding activities. This is usually termed as a fork of the process execution. In a distributed environment like OSIRIS, this enables a true intra-parallel execution of a process instance. A fork is usually accompanied by a join, i.e., a step where a number of execution paths are merged. A join requires that the nodes along all the merged execution paths know *where* to join with *which* paths. To this end, OSIRIS assigns a unique join node to a process instance at its creation time. Whenever a join is required, the execution paths meet at this node before they continue their path together. Since a join in OSIRIS is modeled as an additional activity call, a join typically will not occur at a provider node. Moreover, OSIRIS can have an arbitrary number of different dedicated join nodes, i.e., different process instances have (possibly) different join nodes.

Load Information. Typically, a service is offered by different providers possibly with conditions (e.g., service costs) that may change over time. Therefore, the HDB layer selects services at runtime to optimize the throughput and response times of processes. As a consequence, the HDB layers require load information about nodes offering those service types that potentially may receive process instance data from this HDB layer.

2.3 Replication Management

So far, we did not yet address how global meta information is distributed among the nodes of the OSIRIS system. Obviously, we have to avoid that nodes request information from a central repository each time the information is needed. On the other hand, full and consistent replication may be too costly, e.g., the distribution of load information in a peer-to-peer manner would lead to $O(n^2)$ messages for n components. Our solution exploits the following characteristics:

- Updates on certain pieces of information are infrequent, e.g., process definitions or subscription lists of service providers.
- Nodes only require parts of the global information, e.g., only information about processes that may run at the node.
- Changes on the global information are not always critical, e.g., if the load of a node slightly changes, its new load does not need to be published.

Pub/Sub Replication. The basic idea of our replication scheme is based on publish/subscribe techniques: the primary copy of the data resides at a single node, i.e., a global repository. OSIRIS stores such information in a semi-structured representation (an XML document). Then, each client that wants to replicate data first has to subscribe for the document. As a result of this subscription the repository publishes the current state of the XML document. Whenever the primary copy changes, the repository publishes corresponding update messages to all subscribed clients. Such an update message comprises only the minimal information needed to update the clients versions to the current state.

Partial Replication. Replicating the entire XML document is not optimal if clients only require small pieces of the document. For instance, the HDB layer does not need the entire process definition to execute the current step of an instance. Another example comprises subscription information and load information: consider a large process with a service B immediately following a service A along one of the execution paths. A node running service A only must know about providers and load data of nodes running service B, but not about those offering other services for that process. In general, the HDB layer only requires a small subset of the global information. Hence, instead of subscribing for the entire XML document, a node subscribes only for a portion of it by passing an XPath expression with the subscription.

Freshness Predicates. Replication often demands that the primary copy and all replicas are consistent, i.e., they contain the same data. For some global information, this requirement is vital (e.g., process definitions). For other pieces of global meta information like subscription lists and load information, this requirement is far too strong. Consider for instance subscription lists: as long as the replicated version is *su ciently* close to the primary copy, the HDB layer is still able to route process instances appropriately. Another example is load information: if the load of a service only marginally changes, we do not have to propagate these updates to all clients. Our generic approach allows to add a so-called *freshness predicates* to the subscription. These predicates define under what circumstances changes on the primary copy have to be published.

3 The Prototype System

In addition to the two components of hyperdatabases for process support, i.e., the hyperdatabase layer that is installed on every node of the community and core services that globally provide basic functionality required for the process management, the OSIRIS prototype also consists of O'GRAPE (OSIRIS GRAphical Process Editor) [22], an additional tool to graphically model and define processes. OSIRIS has been implemented over the past two years and is currently being applied to support process executions in the context of a virtual campus and a large scale image retrieval engine. In order to give a rough impression of the complexity of OSIRIS, the basic infrastructure together with services for the two applications consists of about 300'000 lines of code.

3.1 The Hyperdatabase Layer

The local hyperdatabase layer. consists of number of plug-able modules, i.e., we can adapt the system to the needs of the application. For instance, if concurrency control is not important (non-critical application or no conflicts between service invocations), we may omit the module from the local software layer. In the following, we concentrate on the description of the most interesting modules:

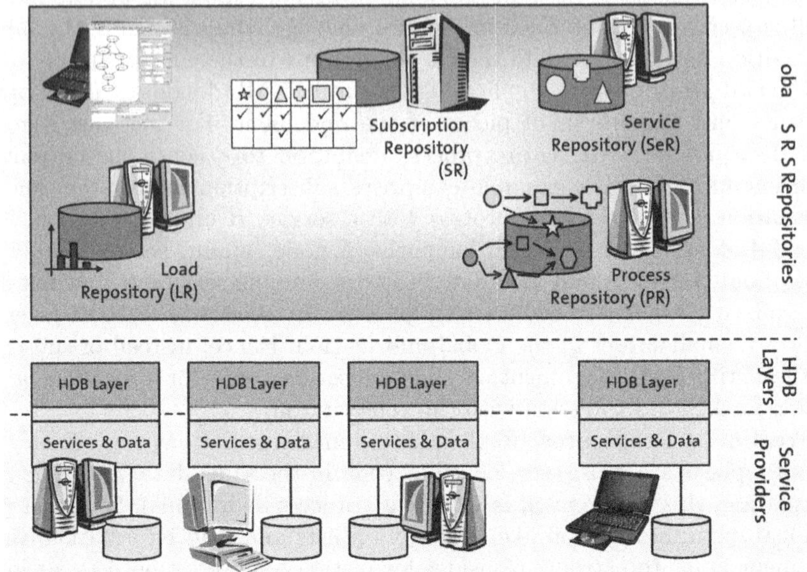

Fig. 2. OSIRIS architecture overview

- **Replication Manager.** This module provides the basic replication services as described in Section 2.3. The replication manager may take the roles of both server and client, i.e., it replicates information from remote sources and it maintains information for remote clients.
- **Process Manager.** Whenever a process instance enters the HDB layer, the process manager requests the corresponding process definition from the replication manager, and calls the specified service locally. After a service call, the process manager determines the services to be called next. For each service, it migrates the process instance to a suitable service provider for subsequent steps via the communication module. Since process definition is replicated at HDB layer, a process instance consists of a reference to the process definition, the name of the current activity, and all global process instance data.
- **Communication.** The communication module resolves pub/sub addressing and deploys the load balancing module to determine an optimal provider among the list of subscribed nodes. Communication is message-based and asynchronous. The transfer of a message between two nodes is based on a 2PC protocol over persistent queues[1]. Since the number of messages is typically quite large, we use priority queues to boost important messages.
- **Publish Subscribe Routing.** The implementation of the pub/sub module is rather simple due to the deployment of the replication manager. The

[1] Note that there are only two participants in this distributed transaction. Hence, the protocol is rather simple.

pub/sub module replicates subscription lists from the global Subscription Repository. To resolve a pub/sub address, it simply returns the list corresponding to the topic.

- **Load Balancing.** In our implementation, the load balancer chooses the provider that is able to work off the next execution unit at the earliest point in time[2]. For that purpose, the Load Balancing module replicates data from the global Load Repository via the Replication Manager. Since load information is not so critical, we use less strict freshness predicates as in the case of the pub/sub module and the Process Manager.
- **Service Manager.** The service module builds a bridge between the OSIRIS system and the local service providers. At startup time, the service manager registers all local services at the global Subscription Repository. If needed, the service manager may download new releases of service software from the Service Repository. Furthermore, the service manager keeps track of the load of all local services and publishes this information to global load repositories.
- **Concurrency Control.** The task of this module is to provide functionality for globally synchronizing process instances. This is needed in cases where concurrent process instances access shared resources and if there is a flow of information between these instances. Unlike many workflow management systems where this task is delegated to the applications, OSIRIS makes concurrency control transparent to the processes.

3.2 Core Services

The core services of OSIRIS are essential to run process in a peer-to-peer manner. Four core services maintain global repositories from which the HDB layer replicate. A further service is dedicated to concurrency control. In addition to these core services, our current prototype runs more than 100 application-specific services, mainly to support image retrieval and the virtual campus application.

- **Subscription Repository** (SR) manages a list of all services offered by the providers in the OSIRIS–community. This service is comparable to a name server in a common TCP/IP network infrastructure. Note that, in contrast to related pub/sub approaches, the subscription repository provides no routing functionality. Rather, each local component routes process instances in a peer-to-peer manner to the targeting system.
- **Service Repository** (SER) holds the interface definitions for all services available in the system. In addition, it holds executables (software) for a subset of services to support on demand installation of hot-spot services. If the load of a service type becomes large, OSIRIS can decide to install additional instances of this service type to enhance throughput.

---

[2] It is simple to extend this notion with more complex costs functions. For that purpose, we can exchange the load balancing module with a more sophisticated one.

- **Process Repository** (PR) holds the global definitions of all processes of the community. This service decomposes process definition to *execution units* [3] consisting of pairs of subsequent activities.
- **Load Repository** (LR) organizes and manages the load of service providers in the system. Significant changes in queue status of providers are propagated to corresponding components.
- **Concurrency Control** (CC) When a request for the invocation of a service is sent to the local HDB layer, it is forwarded to a global concurrency control service. There, correct synchronization is guaranteed by applying protocols at the process level [19]. However, an important optimization is done at the local HDB layer: before forwarding a request to the global CC service, it is first checked whether this invocation may have side-effects on other service invocations (i.e., whether potential conflicts exist). This dramatically reduces the overhead of concurrency control as it is commonly observed that conflicts at the level of service invocations are rather rare.

Note that the repositories do not require a centralized implementation. For instance, OSIRIS can contain a large number of process repositories. These repositories may exchange and coordinate their contents, and may serve as a repository for a limited number of nodes. If the number of nodes increase, we simply can add more repositories. To decrease the load on the other repositories, we may partition the communities into disjunctive sets of nodes. For each partition, a dedicated subscription, service and load repository is available. From time to time, these repositories exchange information and publish changes of remote partitions to the members of their own partition.

3.3 Failure Handling

OSIRIS handles failures at various levels. Firstly, *network failures* might occur when a node of the community is currently not available. If the address was determined from a subscription list, we choose an alternative address from that list (via load balancing) and continue with invoking the new service instance. If no alternatives exist or all alternatives fail, we suspend the message until new entries for the list arrive from the replication module.

Software failures denote that a service or the local HDB layer fails. If a service crashes, the local HDB layer immediately restarts the failed service and re-submits the requests the service was handling at the point in time of its failure (we do so with persistent queues). If the local HDB layer crashes (or the host on which it is running), the user (a watchdog or a reboot) must restart the software. OSIRIS then recovers by consulting the content of the local persistent queue and logging tables, subscribes all local services at the subscription repository, and re-starts the processing of the queue entries from their last persistent

[3] An execution unit is a part of a global process definition that holds all information needed to handle activity data flow, call a local service. In addition, preprocessed information about next activities are needed to determine the subsequent service calls.

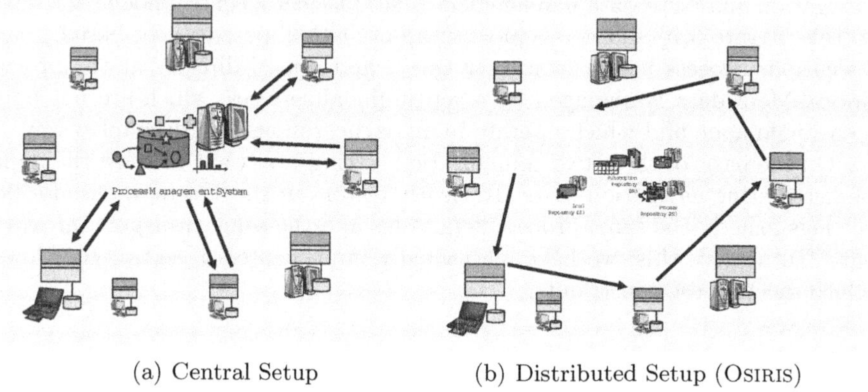

(a) Central Setup (b) Distributed Setup (OSIRIS)

Fig. 3. System configuration settings in performance evaluations

state. Moreover, the HDB layer must check the state of message transfers at time of the crash. Depending on the log information from the 2PC protocol, messages are re-sent or locally removed.

Finally, OSIRIS also deals with *application failures*, i.e., a service request results in an error. However, OSIRIS can not handle this case of failures automatically. Rather, the application developer must resolve such failures at process definition time. For that purpose, our process model provides alternative paths that are followed if a service fails, and compensation steps and roll back steps which are executed to undo former side effects of a service invocation. Essentially, the application developer is responsible for a correct failure handling at the application level. If correctly done, OSIRIS guarantees that a process will terminate in a well defined state even in case of lower-level failures.

4 Measurements

In this section, we provide the results of first performance evaluations based on the OSIRIS system. The goal of these evaluations is to verify the high potential of the P^3E paradigm compared to a traditional centralized process engine, especially in terms of scalability.

4.1 Measurements Setup

We consider process execution on top of a set of distributed services. These services are installed on several provider nodes. The goal is to set up a simple configuration in order to measure the scalability of the navigation concept of OSIRIS. Figure 3(a) shows the centralized configuration. A dedicated process management node calls services of distributed service providers in a traditional request/reply style. This system configuration represents a state-of-the art process management system executing (web) service-based processes. Both process navigation and meta data management takes place at a central node. In contrast to this, Figure 3(b) shows a typical setup of OSIRIS' peer-to-peer-based process execution. Process instances are navigated and routed directly at the provider nodes. Meta data is managed by a set of global services, which are not bound to a single node and which operate in an asynchronous and decoupled way.

On the basis of these two configuration settings, we want to show the impact of distributing navigation costs. To clearly factor out the effects, we use for both settings exactly the same process definitions and the same transport infrastructure. To achieve this, we have additionally implemented a central coordinator which meets these constraints.

4.2 Preliminary Results

In the following, we illustrate preliminary experiments to measure the pure navigation costs of process instances. For that purpose, we have used a process (consisting of three activities, i.e., three different service invocations) with no actual payload, i.e., the service calls just return after invocation. This way, it possible to only measure the overhead of process management. In addition to the centralized and distributed execution scheme, our experiments further consider two different service binding paradigms. In the first setting (denoted as *3 x nodes*), the process engine does not use late service binding load balancing, i.e., services are hard-coded into the process definitions much like in a .NET application. In a second setting (denoted as *20 Nodes*), late binding and load balancing are available and the complete cluster of service providers is used.

Figure 4.2 illustrate first results with varying numbers of concurrent processes. In each experiment, we started a number (from 200 to 10,000) of processes at the start time and measured the total time to work off all process instances. This time divided by the number of processes approximates the mean overhead of process navigation for a single process instance. With a centralized process engine, there is no big difference whether late service binding and load balancing are turned on or off (upper two graphs in the plot). The main reason for this behavior is the fact that the central engine is not able to work off processes fast enough and to route them to the service providers. As a result, most processes are "endlessly" delayed in the engine's internal queue for navigation (although more than 10 threads were concurrently handling entries in the queue). CPU monitoring of the involved nodes exhibited that the coordinator node was fully loaded (CPU load at 100%) while the nodes of the service providers were idle over long phases of the run.

Decentralized process management, on the other hand, significantly improves process throughput. Even more interestingly, average navigation costs remain constant over the entire range of the number of concurrent process instances. With late binding and load balancing enabled, distributed process management always leads to navigation costs of around 50 ms per process regardless of the number of concurrent processes (from 200 up to 10,000). Without late binding and load balancing, our distributed approach also suffers from extensively long queues at the three service providers utilized by the process (with our approach

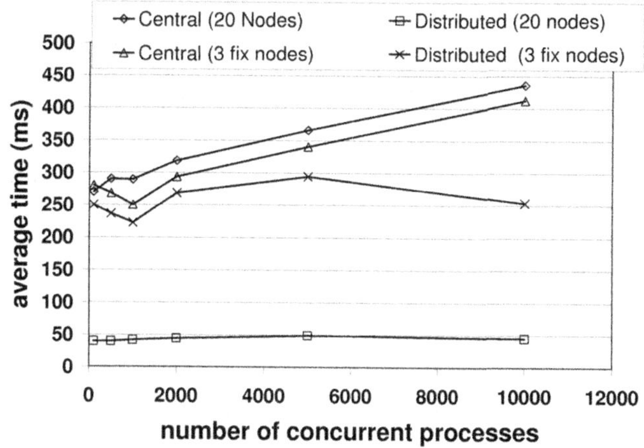

Fig. 4. Overall Process Navigation Time

in OSIRIS, they have to execute all navigation steps). But in contrast to the centralized approach, these three service providers are able to work off the process instance much faster than the central coordinator.

Based on these first experiments, we conclude that process navigation is much cheaper in a distributed environment and that a distributed process management system scales much better to larger workloads than a central coordinator. However, the advantage of decentralized process execution only pays off in combination with late binding and load balancing of service invocations. In order to further investigate the different performance characteristics of centralized and decentralized process execution, we are currently defining a benchmark for process management system.

5 Related Work

An important feature of the OSIRIS system is that process execution takes place in a peer-to-peer way without involving a centralized component. This is in sharp contrast to state-of-the-art process support system like MQSeries Workflow [13], BizTalk [12], etc. Although these systems allow process instances to be shipped between different distributed process engines, services within processes are nevertheless invoked from one single engine at a time in a request/response style. Yet, the peer-to-peer execution of OSIRIS requires that a middleware layer is installed on every participating component resp. service provider. This is very similar to frameworks like .NET [14] or CORBA [3]. However, the local middleware layers within these frameworks only support the invocation of single services without the possibility of combining services to higher level applications.

One crucial requirement for the peer-to-peer execution is that meta information has to be distributed between the local middleware layers with dedicated freshness guarantees. Pure peer–to–peer file sharing approaches like FastTrack [6] or Gnutella [9] use (optimized) flooding algorithms to distribute meta data within the complete system. OSIRIS, in contrast, applies publish/subscribe techniques. Essentially, this allows for a fine-grained treatment of different meta data and to apply individual freshness guarantees.

Self-adaptability to a dynamically changing environment is another core aspect of the OSIRIS system. Essentially, this means that prior to each service invocation, a decision is needed to determine the provider of an actual service invocation. Several process management systems use publish/subscribe techniques for this purpose (Dayal et al. [4] provide a detailed overview of these systems). However, conventional implementations of publish/subscribe techniques either require a centralized publish/subscribe broker or use broadcast technologies. In contrast, OSIRIS uses neither of them. This is possible since each local hyperdatabase layer is equipped with a publish/subscribe broker that is able to correctly handle local events and to route service invocations. While service discovery is shielded in OSIRIS by the clever replication of meta information, other systems like eFlow [2] or CrossFlow [10] have to explicitly provide support for service discovery. In terms of self-adaptability, OSIRIS reacts on changes of the overall configuration (e.g., new service providers) by implicit feedback loops [23]. In addition, following the idea of service grids [7], active changes of the overall configuration are also possible by the installation of new service instances. In medical information systems, even instances of long-running patient treatment processes have to be continuously migrated to the most recent process description so as to provide up-to-date treatment knowledge. Therefore, systems like ADEPT$_{flex}$ [15] have to deal with instance evolution. Such mechanisms are however orthogonal to OSIRIS and could be seamlessly integrated to additionally enable this kind of dynamic changes.

6 Conclusions and Future Work

In order to provide an infrastructure for processes execution that is, at the same time, flexible, highly scalable, and that is able to dynamically adapt to changing environments, OSIRIS combines several concepts. First, this includes support for the discovery and invocation of web services by using established protocols like SOAP and WSDL. Second, several service calls can be combined to processes. To this end, OSIRIS is extended by O'GRAPE, a graphical modeling tool for processes. Moreover, OSIRIS provides dedicated transactional execution guarantees for process instances. Third, flexibility and dynamic adaptation is realized by supporting late binding strategies for service invocations. This allows to dynamically chose among the available service providers and to apply sophisticated load balancing techniques. Finally, by applying clever replication algorithms for meta data, OSIRIS supports executions of process instances in a peer-to-peer style. Due to this peer-to-peer execution, a centralized process engine is avoided. As a consequence, OSIRIS is optimized for achieving a high degree of scalability both in terms of the number of process instances in the system an in terms of the number of service providers. First evaluations presented in this paper have shown promising results.

In order to extend these first performance evaluations, we have recently started with the specification of a fair benchmark (similar to the one presented in [8]) that allows to compare the decentralized OSIRIS prototype with a rather conventional centralized process engine. Such a possible benchmark setup consists of large number of cluster nodes acting as service providers (to this end, the 128 node Xibalba cluster of ETH Zürich will be exploited). These providers offer a different set of services. In here, it is an important task to find a balance between services that are location-dependent (i.e., that are only available with dedicated providers) or location independent services which can be installed at any node in case of a bottleneck. Hence, a benchmark application should be a well-balanced mix of data-centric services accessing, for instance, database repositories and computationally intensive services. The latter are usually location independent and can be replicated on demand. In addition to basic benchmark specifications like numbers and types of processes, this will also contain a specification on the fluctuation and dynamic behavior of available service providers in the overall system. Evaluations based on this benchmark are performed within a joint project –together with the IBM labs– that has recently been settled.

Finally, in order to provide a truly peer-to-peer execution even in the presence of services with a large number of conflicts, the current global concurrency control service will be replaced by a distributed implementation. Although concurrency control is a problem that requires a global solution, we have started to investigate a decentralized implementation that replaces synchronization at a global component with communication between the individual HDB layers [11].

Acknowledgement. We thank Frank Leymann for constructive comments and many stimulating discussions.

References

1. Ariba, IBM, and Microsoft. UDDI Technical White Paper. `http://www.uddi.org`.
2. F. Casati, S. Ilnicki, L. Jin, V. Krishnamoorthy, and M. Shan. Adaptive and Dynamic Service Composition in eFlow. In *Proc. Conf. on Advanced Information Systems Engineering*, Stockholm, 2000.
3. CORBA – Common Object Request Broker Architecture. `http://www.omg.org/`.
4. U. Dayal, M. Hsu, and R. Ladin. Business process coordination: State of the art, trends, and open issues. In *Proceedings of 27th International Conference on Very Large Data Bases, Roma, Italy*, September 2001.
5. M. Schmid F. Leymann, D. Roller. Web services and business process management. *IBM Systems Journal*, 41(2):198–211, 2002.
6. FastTrack – P2P Technology. `http://www.fasttrack.nu`.
7. I. Foster, C. Kesselmann, J. Nick, and S. Tuecke. The Physiology of the Grid: An Open Grid Services Architecture for Distributed Systems Integration. `http://www.gridforum.org/ogsi-wg/`.

8. M. Gillmann, R. Mindermann, and G. Weikum. Benchmarking and configuration of workflow management systems. In *Cooperative Information Systems, 7th International Conference, CoopIS 2000, Eilat, Israel, September 6-8, 2000, Proceedings*, pages 186–197, 2000.
9. Gnutella RFC. `http://rfc-gnutella.sourceforge.net`.
10. P. Grefen, K. Aberer, H. Ludwig, and Y. Hoffner. CrossFlow: Cross–Organizational Workflow Management for Service Outsourcing in Dynamic Virtual Enterprises. *IEEE Data Engineering Bulletin*, 24:52–57, 2001.
11. K. Haller and H. Schuldt. Consistent Process Execution in Peer-to-Peer Information Systems. In *Proceedings of the 15th Conference on Advanced Information Systems Engineering (CAiSE 2003)*, pages 289–307, Klagenfurt/Velden, Austria, 2003. Springer LNCS, Vol. 2681.
12. B. Metha, M. Levy, G. Meredith, T. Andrews, B. Beckman, J. Klein, and A. Mital. Biztalk Server 2000 Business Process Orchestration. In *IEEE Data Engineering Bulletin 24(1)*, 2001.
13. IBM MQSeries Workflow. `http://www.ibm.com/software/ts/mqseries/workflow/`.
14. Microsoft .NET. `http://www.microsoft.com/net/`.
15. M. Reichert and P. Dadam. ADEPT$_{\text{flex}}$ — Supporting Dynamic Changes of Workflows without Losing Control. *Journal of Intelligent Information Systems*, 10(2):93–129, March 1998.
16. H.-J. Schek, K. Böhm, T. Grabs, U. Röhm, H. Schuldt, and R. Weber. Hyperdatabases. In *Proceedings of the 1st International Conference on Web Information Systems Engineering (WISE'00)*, pages 14–23, Hong Kong, China, June 2000.
17. H.-J. Schek, H. Schuldt, C. Schuler, and R. Weber. Infrastructure for information spaces. In *Proceedings of Advances in Databases and Information Systems, 6th East European Conference, ADBIS 2002*, volume 2435 of *Lecture Notes in Computer Science*, pages 23–36, Bratislava, Slovakia, September 2002. Springer.
18. H.-J. Schek, H. Schuldt, and R. Weber. Hyperdatabases – Infrastructure for the Information Space. In *Proceedings of the 6th IFIP 2.6 Working Conference on Visual Database Systems (VDB'02)*, Brisbane, Australia, May 2002.
19. H. Schuldt. Process Locking: A Protocol based on Ordered Shared Locks for the Execution of Transactional Processes. In *Proceedings of the 20th ACM Symposium on Principles of Database Systems (PODS'01)*, pages 289–300, Santa Barbara, California, USA, May 2001. ACM Press.
20. H. Schuldt, G. Alonso, C. Beeri, and H.-J. Schek. Atomicity and Isolation for Transactional Processes. *ACM TODS*, 27(1), March 2002.
21. SOAP – Simple Object Access Protocol. `http://www.w3.org/TR/SOAP/`.
22. R. Weber, C. Schuler, H. Schuldt, H.-J. Schek, and P. Neukomm. WebService Composition with O'GRAPE and OSIRIS. In *Proc. of 29rd International Conference on Very Large Data Bases*, Berlin, Germany, September 2003.
23. G. Weikum, A. Mönkeberg, C. Hasse, and P. Zabback. Self-tuning Database Technology and Information Services: from Wishful Thinking to Viable Engineering. In *PProceedings of 28th International Conference on Very Large Data Bases*, pages 20–31, Hong Kong, China, August 2002.
24. G. Wiederhold, P. Wegner, and S. Ceri. Towards Megaprogramming. *Communications of the ACM*, 35(11):89–99, November 1992.
25. I. Wladawsky-Berger. Advancing the Internet into the Future. Talk at the *International Conference Shaping the Information Society in Europe 2002*, April 2002. `http://www.ibm.com/de/entwicklung/academia/index.html`.
26. WSDL – Web Service Description Language. `http://www.w3.org/TR/wsdl/`.

Disconnected Operation Service in Mobile Grid Computing*

Sang-Min Park, Young-Bae Ko, and Jai-Hoon Kim

Graduate School of Information and Communication
Ajou University, South Korea
{smpark, youngko, jaikim}@ajou.ac.kr

Abstract. In this paper, we discuss on the extension of grid computing systems in mobile computing environments, where mobile devices can be effectively incorporated into the grid either as service recipients or as more valuable service providers. First, based on the present grid architecture, we try to figure out what would be the newly required services in such a mobile/grid integrated architecture. There are a number of challenging issues when taking mobile environment into account, such as intermittent connectivity, device heterogeneity, and weak security. Among these issues to solve, we particularly focus on a disconnected operation problem in this paper since mobile resources are prone to frequent disconnections due to their confined communication range and device mobility. We develop a new job scheduling algorithm for mobile grid system and evaluate it by various methods such as mathematical analysis, simulation, and prototype implementation.

1 Introduction

A grid computing system [1] is a large-scaled distributed system, designed for effectively solving very complicated scientific or commercial problems such as gene analysis, drug design, and climate simulations. In the grid, the computing resources are autonomously managed at different locations in a distributed manner. They are aggregated through a global Internet-wide network, forming a computational grid, by which a huge workload can be run and completed with more improved performance in terms of computation speed and throughput. Mobile computing [2] is another distinct paradigm of traditional distributed systems, considering mobility, portability and wireless communications. The recent advances in wireless communication technologies and portable mobile appliances make more number of people be eligible to

* This work is supported by a grant of the International Mobile Telecommunications 2000 R&D Project, Ministry of Information & Communication in South Korea, by grant No. R05-2003-000-10607-0 from Korea Science & Engineering Foundation, by grant No. (R01-2003-000-10794-0) from the Basic Research Program of the Korea Science & Engineering Foundation, and by ITA Professorship for Visiting Faculty Positions in Korea (International Joint Research Project) by Ministry of Information & Communication in South Korea.

M.E. Orlowska et al. (Eds.): ICSOC 2003, LNCS 2910, pp. 499–513, 2003.

access information services through a shared network infrastructure (e.g., Internet) with their own mobile computing devices, regardless of their physical location.

The current grid architecture and algorithms do not take into account the mobile computing environment since mobile devices have not been seriously considered as valid computing resources or interfaces in grid communities. It has been just recently given attention to integrate these two emerging techniques of mobile and grid computing –for example, in [3,4], although they do not elaborate on how the mobile devices may be incorporated in the current grid architecture. In our view of the mobile grid computing integration, there are two possible roles of mobile devices in grid. First, mobile devices can be used as interfaces to the grid. Thus, a mobile device can initiate the use of grid resources, monitor the jobs being executed remotely, and take any results from the grid. Secondly and more interestingly, mobile devices can be assumed to participate in grid as computing resource providers, not just service recipients. We believe that recent advancement of technologies on mobile devices and wireless communications make this scenario more feasible.

Of course, clearly, many issues become the challenges when we consider mobile devices as one of grid computing resources or interfaces. Some examples of limitations that possibly hinder the integration are relatively poor local resources (in terms of computation speed, memory), battery constraints, unreliable connectivity status, weak security and so on. These limitations and constraints should be dealt with accordingly before mobile grid integration is fully enabled. We present several technical issues of mobile grid system in the first part of this paper. However, among those arise, we particularly focus on a dynamic nature of device connectivity and develop a new scheduling algorithm that provides reliable performance in a mobile grid system where the devices are prone to frequent disconnections.

2 Related Works

One of the most critical characteristics of the mobile grid system is the intermittent connectivity of mobile devices. We can find similar situations in Peer-to-Peer computing area. In general, P2P system consists of huge number of computing devices and they can act either as a client or a server. In P2P, each machine's CPU cycles, storages, and contents can be shared in order to broaden their resource limitations [5,6,7,8]. SETI@home project [7] provides a successful story that large P2P system can be effectively used for high performance applications by aggregating cycles of desktop PCs. In a P2P System, users are free to join and leave the network and one study showed that a node remained in a connection state only for 28% of time on average [6]. These frequent disconnections of the node degrade the computing performance significantly and providing the redundancy of workloads is the way used to compensate the deficiency [8]. In other words, the same work unit is disseminated into some number of nodes and the first result generated by the most reliable and the fast node is received. However, this strategy of redundancy cannot be applied in mobile grid systems. While the redundancy guarantees the improvement of performance, it also wastes the resources greatly. Although the strategy can be successfully applied in P2P systems where resources are abundant, relatively small number of nodes and high sensitivity of resource dissipation in mobile grid system will not allow large number of duplication of work units. In this paper, we present different approach to deal with performance degradation. We propose a new scheduling algorithm that takes into account of the intermittent connectivity of mobile nodes.

Since grid consists of several number of autonomously managed local resources (MPPs, clusters, and workstations), the scheduling paradigm would fall into two categories, global and local scheduling. Various global scheduling algorithms have been operational such as application-level scheduling [9], high-throughput scheduling [10], economy-based scheduling [11], and data-centric scheduling [12]. Once the grid job is scheduled and submitted by global scheduler, it is scheduled again by local resource managers like PBS [13], LSF [14], and Condor [10]. First-in, first-out is the most prominent scheduling policy in the local managers, yet more sophisticated algorithms are provided within the specific managers. The scheduling algorithm that we present in this paper would be classified in local scheduling since the scheduling decision is only applicable to local mobile resources.

3 Two Roles of Mobile Devices in Mobile Grid Computing

In this section, we present possible architecture of the mobile grid system and several technical issues that are to be dealt with in further researches. We depict an expected view of mobile grid system in Figure 1.

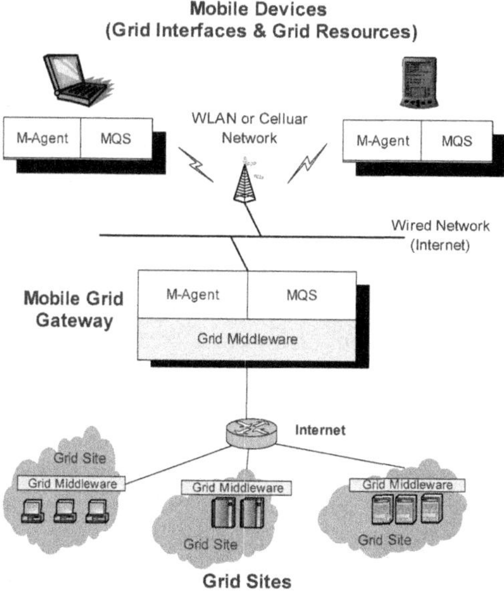

Fig. 1. Mobile Grid System

As illustrated in the Figure, the grid system is divided into three parts: static grid sites, a group of mobile devices, and a gateway interconnecting static and mobile resources. Mobile devices are wirelessly connected to Internet through a wireless LAN or a long-range cellular network like GSM and CDMA. Note that, in the figure, grid middleware, e.g., Globus [15], is installed on the gateway to provide interoperability between the virtual mobile grid site and other static grid sites. Also note that such a middleware layer is not necessary to be in a mobile device itself. This is important because our model does not require a heavy grid middleware, like Globus, to be installed on the thin mobile device. Newly added grid components realizing mobile grid computing are comprised of M-Agent (Mobile Agent), and MQS (Mobile Queuing Server). They are both on the gateway and mobile device side.

3.1 Mobile Interface Role to Grid

Mobile devices are exposed to frequent disconnections from the network. Also the mobile system itself is unreliable. Hence, it is not a good idea for the mobile devices to interact with static grid sites directly. Simply imagine that the mobile devices are suddenly disconnected during the data exchange with grid sites. Sometimes, the jobs running on grid sites need interactions with mobile user while mobile user is not in the connection state. Thus, a reliable static system should perform job submission, monitoring, cancellation, and completion process on behalf of the mobile user. In our architecture, M-Agent on the gateway performs that role of agent for the unreliable mobile devices. The M-Agent may perform two key roles as follows:

- **Adapting to various interfaces of mobile devices:** M-Agent on mobile device interacts with the mobile user, that is, the mobile user submits, monitors the grid job, and observes the results, through M-Agent. Various kinds of mobile devices have different appearances. While laptop has similar interfaces with PCs, interfaces of PDA or Handheld device is far from that of PC's. They have smaller displays, no keyboards, etc. Hence, the interface of M-Agent on mobile device should adapt to the specific class of mobile devices while sustaining the same functionality.
- **Reliable job management:** The mobile device has several constraints. The most serious problem is that its availability is unreliable due to intermittent connectivity or limited battery life problems. Thus, it is not a good approach to manage the running job directly from the mobile device. In order to solve problems induced by unreliable availability, we propose an object, **Job-Proxy**. When a mobile user submits a job through M-Agent, the M-Agent on gateway creates a Job-Proxy which performs job related tasks according to the received information from the mobile user. If the M-Agent detects an error with mobile devices, Job-Proxy becomes operational and starts to monitor executing job on the grid sites. If some interactions between the executing job and mobile user are needed (e.g., when an additional input data should be given) the Job-Proxy performs the interaction on behalf of the mobile user, based on the information received from the mobile user beforehand. When the grid job is completed, the result from the job is temporarily stored on the Job-Proxy. If the mobile device is in a good condition to receive the results, it immediately relays the result data. Otherwise, it waits until the mobile device becomes ready for receiving the result data. The mobile user may set the time-out duration of the Job-Proxy, i.e., the

running job in static grid sites will be canceled after a certain amount of time and all the resources in gateway allocated for the Job-Proxy is freed. This is because the mobile user may not be able to explicitly request cancellation of the job although running job is not needed anymore. If we do not cancel the job automatically, sustaining job execution unnecessarily consumes resources in both static grid sites and the mobile grid gateway.

3.2 The Service Provider Role to Grid

We present another aspect of mobile grid system that supports the integration mobile devices as grid resources. Even though, currently, both long-range access technologies (GSM and CDMA) and short-range connectivity (WLAN) is available, we assume that the WLAN is provided as a wireless medium for the mobile grid system. This is because not only does the wireless LAN guarantee much faster data transfer rate (11Mbps for the IEEE 802.11b), but also it is easier to control with respect to number of nodes, security concerns, and network administrations. In addition to them, WLAN is the most favored method of wireless communication for computing devices (laptops and PDAs), while the cellular networks are still dominantly used for voice communications. Except that the computing nodes are not connected through physical lines, the mobile grid system becomes similar to the conventional high performance clusters.

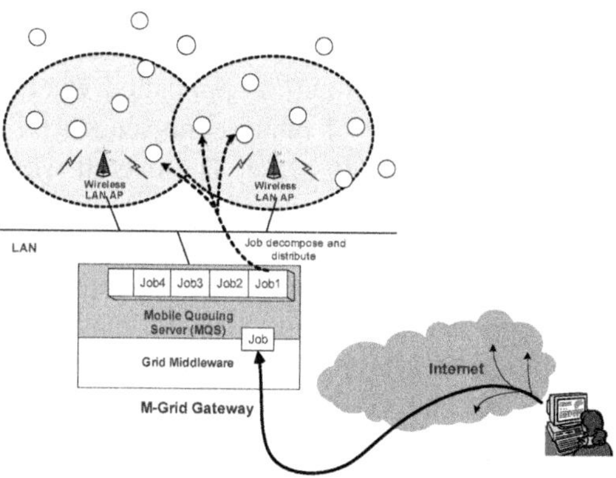

Fig. 2. Mobile resource provision to Grid using MQS

As shown by Figure 2, MQS (Mobile Queuing Server) on the gateway is a core component for the integration. The grid user submits jobs to several grid sites, and one of the grid sites performing the job is comprised of mobile devices. The group of mobile devices in the mobile grid system is viewed as a single virtual machine having several computing nodes. The virtual composing is provided by MQS in our architecture. When the job is submitted to this mobile grid site, the grid middleware (e.g., Globus) on the gateway relays the job information such as executable file location, input parameters and the location to store output files, to the MQS. Basic functions of MQS are similar to the conventional Job Queuing systems such as PBS, LSF, and NQE [16]. In addition to the basic job queuing functions, MQS cares the heterogeneity and unreliability of mobile nodes in order to hide unique characteristics of them. The mobile resources are viewed as a reliable single machine like the one in static grid site so that the grid job initiator can make use of them without further complex considerations. Followings are detailed explanation of services MQS should provide. Except for the scheduling issue, we leave these services as future research topics.

- **Fault Tolerant Service:** Unlike job queuing service in static systems, availability of resources changes dynamically in mobile grid system. The node may suddenly disappear due to disconnections or exhausted power, thus MQS should carefully monitor the status of mobile nodes. Fault tolerant services should be provided by MQS so that the unreliability of mobile node does not decrease the performance much. Time out strategy which re-submits the job when the result is not received in a determined time limit would be one of the viable approaches.
- **Hiding Platform Heterogeneity:** One of the most complex problems to deal with in mobile grid system is the hardware and OS heterogeneity. Large portion of laptop PC's are operated in Microsoft Windows, while, currently, most grid applications are running on Unix-based platforms. When we take the PDA and Handheld devices into account, the problem becomes more serious. Enforcing the care of heterogeneity to grid programmer would not be feasible, thus the MQS should hide the heterogeneity of individual mobile device.
- **Job Decomposing Service:** The job may contain many workloads. As an example, if we assume the job is Bioinformatics application which analyzes the gene sequences, the job will be composed of many gene sequences to be analyzed. A sequence is viewed as a workload in this case. The overall workloads in a job can be processed by a single node in a static grid site within a reasonable time unit. However, a single mobile node may not process the same amount of workloads in a reasonable time due to its resource limitation and unreliability, thus the workloads in a job should be decomposed and distributed to several mobile nodes according to their performance and reliability. MQS needs information about the application's workload composition to perform the job decomposing service, and this information can be provided by job initiator.
- **Job Scheduling:** In a static grid environment, job scheduling policy on a grid site is generally based on a simple FCFS (First Come, First Served). In some systems, it is based on the computing capability, i.e., when the job arrives at a grid site, the job is distributed to the node which is likely to compute it within the shortest time. Reliability of computing node is not a first-class concern for the job scheduling in the static grid environment. However, if the mobile environment is taken into account we should carefully consider the inherent unreliability of mobile devices in order to make optimal scheduling decision. We cover this scheduling issue in the following section 4.

4 The Proposed Job Scheduling Algorithm

Among various challenging issues like energy sensitivity and weak security, we concentrate on the unreliable connectivity of mobile environment hereafter. Frequent disconnections of mobile node affect the job performance significantly. Job scheduling is made based on the expected execution time on various mobile nodes. When there is available mobile node, job (workload) is extracted from the job queue and delivered to the mobile node with related input data. After completing job execution on a mobile node, job output is returned to the MQS (Mobile Queuing Server) and the mobile node performs next job. Figure 3 represents the job execution process performed on the mobile node. Since Master-Worker style applications, whose tasks can be scheduled independently of one another, are preferred form of applications in grid [10,11,17], the job on the mobile node does not need communication during its execution. However, the mobile node should be in connection state during input and output data transfer. If the mobile node is not in the connection state, MQS waits for its reconnection. Figure 4 shows the state transition diagram of a mobile node. State C and D denotes the connection state (C) and disconnection state (D), respectively. λ is the disconnection rate, and μ is the reconnection rate of the mobile node, which are governed by Poisson process.

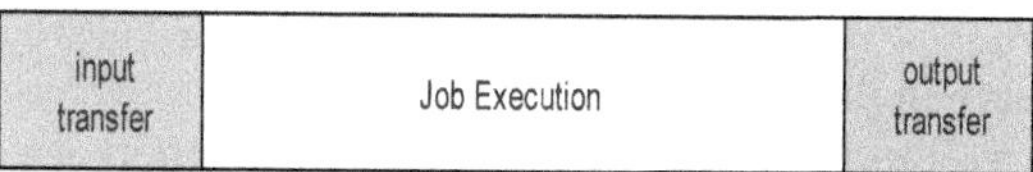

Fig. 3. Job execution process on a mobile node

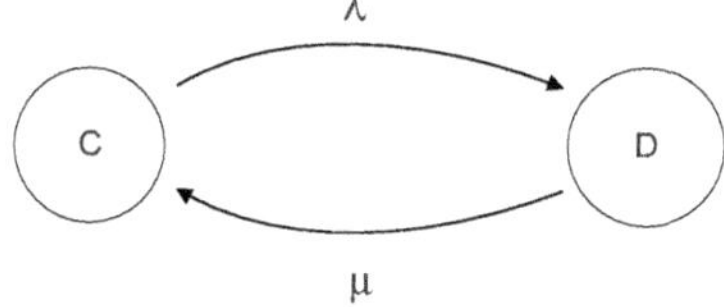

Fig. 4. State transition diagram of mobile node

When a number of jobs arrive at the MQS, or a number of workloads are decomposed from a single job, the MQS selects certain mobile nodes which perform the jobs. In a static grid environment, we achieve improving performance as the number of participating computing nodes grows. However, the rule changes when the mobile devices participate in the computing. Links of some mobile nodes are unreliable, that is, they are likely to be in the disconnection state for a long time while others are not. The unreliable mobile nodes may decrease the overall job execution performance because the MQS should wait for the reconnection of any disconnected node in order to complete the jobs. We should determine whether it is better to include a mobile node in the computing or not. Followings are the analysis to determine the participating nodes which result in the best job performance.

We consider all the mobile nodes (i.e., member nodes) as the potential participants in the computing whether they are initially in the connection state or not, at the time of job distribution. Followings are the analysis to obtain the expected time to execute a job on the mobile nodes.

Let $f_c(t)$ and $f_d(t)$ denotes the expected time required to transfer the data (input and output) of t time unit (data transfer requires t time unit without disconnection) when the mobile node is initially in the connection state and disconnection state, respectively. Let P_C and P_D be the probability of being in connection state and disconnection state, respectively. We can obtain following equations from state transitions shown in Figure 4:

$$P_C + P_D = 1$$
$$-\lambda P_C + \mu P_D = 0$$

We can compute P_C and P_D as follows:

$$P_C = \frac{\mu}{\mu + \lambda}, \qquad P_D = \frac{\lambda}{\mu + \lambda}$$

Then, $C(t,\varepsilon) = f_c(t+\varepsilon) - f_c(t)$ is the time required to perform ε time units of data transfer starting from time t when the mobile node is initially in the connection state. We can compute $C(t,\varepsilon)$ for two cases as follows:

- No disconnection occurs during ε (probability is $e^{-\lambda\varepsilon}$): ε time units are required to transfer the data.
- A disconnection occurs during ε (probability is $1-e^{-\lambda\varepsilon}$): $\frac{1}{\mu}$ time units are expected to stay in disconnection state.

ε time units are required for data transfer and $\frac{1}{\mu}$ time units are required on average for waiting for reconnection. Hence, we can obtain $C(t,\varepsilon)$ as follows:

$$C(t,\varepsilon) = f_c(t+\varepsilon) - f_c(t)$$
$$= e^{-\lambda\varepsilon}\varepsilon + (1-e^{-\lambda\varepsilon})\left(\varepsilon + \frac{1}{\mu}\right)$$

To compute $f_c(t)$:

$$\frac{\partial f(t)}{\partial t} = \lim_{\varepsilon \to 0} \frac{f(t+\varepsilon) - f(t)}{\varepsilon}$$
$$= \lim_{\varepsilon \to 0} \frac{e^{-\lambda\varepsilon}\varepsilon + (1-e^{-\lambda\varepsilon})\left(\varepsilon + \frac{1}{\mu}\right)}{\varepsilon} = \frac{\lambda}{\mu} + 1$$

Thus, we obtain expected time required to transfer the data of t time unit connection (data transfer requires t time unit without disconnection) when the mobile node is initially in connection state as follows:

$$f_c(t) = \left(\frac{\lambda}{\mu} + 1\right) t$$

Expected time required to transfer the data of t time unit connection when the mobile node is initially in disconnection state are obtained as follows (In addition, $\frac{1}{\mu}$ time units are required for reconnection on average.):

$$\begin{aligned} f_d(t) &= \frac{1}{\mu} + f_c(t) \\ &= \frac{1}{\mu} + \left(\frac{\lambda}{\mu} + 1\right)t \end{aligned}$$

The average expected data transfer time, $f(t)$, is,

$$\begin{aligned} f(t) &= P_c \cdot f_c(t) + P_D \cdot f_d(t) \\ &= \frac{\mu}{\lambda+\mu} \cdot \left(\frac{\lambda}{\mu}+1\right)t + \frac{\lambda}{\lambda+\mu} \cdot \left\{\frac{1}{\mu} + \left(\frac{\lambda}{\mu}+1\right)t\right\} \end{aligned}$$

If $f(t)$ is a function of t, λ, and μ,

$$f(t,\lambda,\mu) = \left(\frac{\lambda}{\mu}+1\right)t + \frac{\lambda}{\lambda+\mu} \cdot \frac{1}{\mu}$$

Let t_{job}, t_{in} and t_{out} denotes job processing time on a mobile node, expected time required to transfer the input data to mobile node, and expected time required to transfer the output data from mobile node, respectively. The response time of single job execution on a mobile node i can be represented as follows:

$$g_i(t_{in}, t_{job}, t_{out}) = f_i(t_{in}) + t_{job} + f_i(t_{out}) \quad \text{......} \quad (1)$$

Figure 5 shows the algorithm to select the participating mobile nodes in the computing. In step 3 and 4, nodes are listed in an increasing order of response time using equation (1). In step 5, $g_i - g_{i-1}$ means expected additional waiting time, caused by including i^{th} node, after $(i-1)^{th}$ node return the result, while $\frac{W_{total}}{i-1} - \frac{W_{total}}{i}$ means the expected reduced execution time achieved by including i^{th} node in the computing. Thus, i^{th} node is included if it turns out to reduce overall response time comparing to including up to $(i-1)^{th}$ node.

Figure 6 demonstrates the effects of the algorithm. As we include more nodes in the grid computing, each node performs fewer amounts of jobs, thus job processing time per mobile node decreases. However, as we include more nodes, the worst node is likely to be in disconnection state long and it causes increased waiting delay for input and output data transfer. Thus, it is needed to find the optimal number of participating nodes from tradeoff between deficiency and efficiency.

Step 1. N := number of mobile nodes in the mobile grid resource pool.
Step 2. W_{total} := total execution time of jobs to be processed.
Step 3. Obtain the expected response time of all mobile nodes using the equation (1).
Step 4. List the mobile nodes in increasing order of response time.
Step 5. *FOR (i=N; i>1; i--)*

$$if\left[-(g_i-g_{i-1})+\left(\frac{W_{total}}{i-1}-\frac{W_{total}}{i}\right)>0\right]$$

break;

Step 6. Distributes the jobs to the nodes up to i^{th} in the list

Fig. 5. Job scheduling algorithm for the mobile grid system

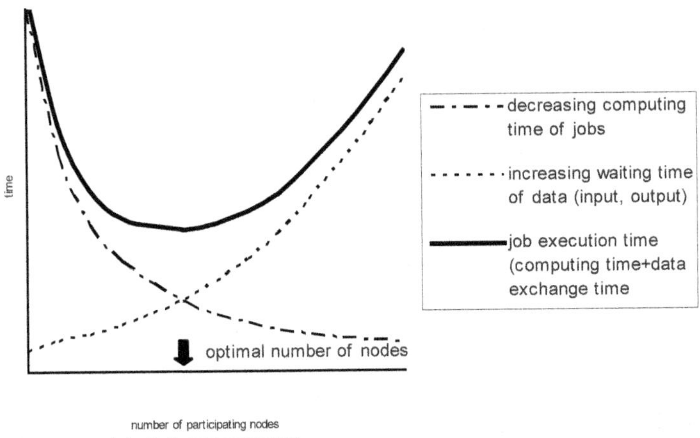

Fig. 6. Benefits and losses from increasing the participating nodes to the computing

5 Performance Evaluation

We evaluate the proposed job scheduling algorithm using mathematical analysis, simulations and experiments on the implemented prototype. We implement simple job queuing system as prototype of MQS. In the prototype, unreliable connectivity of mobile node is considered as usual behavior. Mobile nodes are repeatedly connected to and disconnected from the master system (MQS). When an available node appears (idle mobile node becomes connection state), the first job in the queue is distributed to the node and executed regardless of node's further connection state. After the job is completed, the node sends result data to master if it's in connection state, while it waits for the reconnection to the master when it's in disconnection state (e.g., out of communication range).

We assume that each mobile node in the mobile grid system has different value of λ (disconnection rate) and μ (reconnection rate). We generate the λ and μ value (uniformly random) of each mobile node between the fixed minimum and maximum of λ and μ. By differentiating the maximum and minimum value of λ and μ, we assume various mobile environments. We consider four different mobile environments with the low and high rates of disconnection (λ) and reconnection (μ). Assumed environments are stable (low λ, low μ), unstable (high λ, high μ), highly connective (low λ, high μ), and highly disconnective (high λ, low μ), as classified in [18]. The maximum and minimum value of λ and μ representing the environments are presented in Table 1.

Table 1. Assumed mobile environments

Mobile environments	Max λ	Min λ	Max μ	Min μ
Stable	0.003	0.001	0.003	0.001
Highly disconnective	0.027	0.009	0.003	0.001
Unstable	0.027	0.009	0.027	0.009
Highly connective	0.003	0.001	0.027	0.009

Table 2. Experimental environment

Mobile Node Specification (10 Nodes)	CPU	P4 1.6 GHz
	Memory	256 MB
	Network Connection	802.11b wireless LAN
Application	Blast (Bioinformatics)	
Workload amount	Number of protein sequences needed for 1000 seconds of processing	
Network disconnection & reconnection	Exponentially random value with respect to the λ and μ of mobile node	
Data	Input	Decomposed protein sequences (5 KB/*number of nodes*)
	Output	Information achieved from protein (200 KB/*number of nodes*)

Table 3. Parameters for mathematical analysis and simulations

W_{total} (total execution time of jobs)	N (Number of participating nodes)	t_{in} (time required for transferring input data)	t_{out} (time required for transferring output data
1000 sec.	10 nodes	1 sec.	1 sec.

In the simulation, the disconnection and reconnection of a mobile node is governed by Poisson process with the rate of λ and μ, respectively. We perform experiments on the implemented prototype. The experimental environment is presented in Table 2. We adopt a Bioinformatics application, Blast [19], for the experiments. Blast is the gene sequence analysis application comparing newly found protein sequences with well known sequence database and predicts the structure and functions of the newly found one. It needs very intensive processing cycles, thus grid is utilized for executing Blast in many Bioinformatics and grid projects. In the experiments, we analyze a number of sequences which need total 1,000 seconds to process on a single node. The sequences are divided according to the number of participating nodes, and then distributed to the nodes. We manually configured the disconnection and reconnection of mobile nodes in an exponentially random value with respect to the λ and μ in Table 1. Upon receiving the protein sequences and job related information (input data), the mobile nodes execute Blast and return the information about the protein (output data) to the master. Table 3 describes parameters used in the mathematical analysis and simulations. The parameters correspond to the experimental environment presented in Table 2.

Figure 7 describes the analytical results for four different mobile environments based on the analysis in previous section.

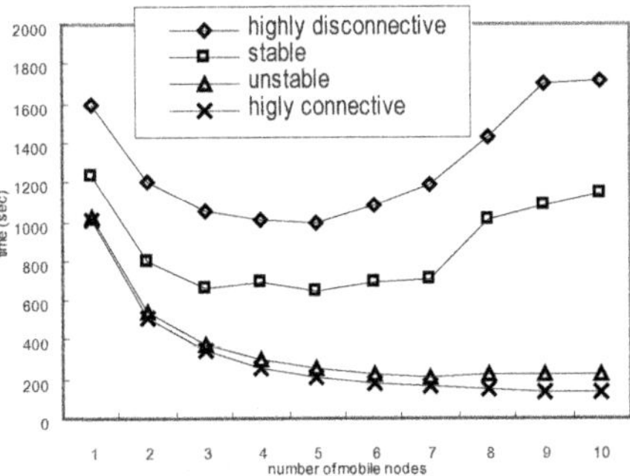

Fig. 7. Job execution time in four mobile environments (by mathematical analysis)

We use the turnaround time, which is the time required to complete a batch of tasks, as a performance metric. The x-axis represents the number of participating nodes to compute the jobs. The nodes are arranged in increasing order of expected response time (i.e., the first node is the best one). The y-axis is the turn around time. The turnaround time in highly disconnective environments is the longest among all, and that in highly connective environment is the shortest. The result in unstable environment is comparable to the highly connective case, and result of stable environment is in the middle of them. In unstable and highly connective environments, the mobile nodes remains in disconnected state shortly, thus short time period is consumed to wait to transfer the input and output data to and from the disconnected mobile nodes. On the other hand, longer time is needed to transfer the input and output data in highly disconnective, and stable environments.

As the number of participating nodes increases, the turnaround time in stable and highly disconnective environment decreases until including the nodes close to the critical point. However, it does not decrease any more as the number of participating nodes grows; instead it increases. Consequently, including nodes more than the x value of the critical point makes the turnaround time grow. Thus, the number of participating nodes should be limited to the x value of the critical point. The results from unstable and highly connective environment show different aspect. The turnaround time decreases steadily in these environments. This is because the nodes are not in the disconnection state for a long time so that having more nodes participate to the computing always produces better performance. Yet, the critical point may appear as the number of nodes grows.

Along with the analytical result, we demonstrate the simulation and experimental results of each assumed environment in Figures 8-11. In Figure 8 and 9, you can see that the turnaround time of job could be the shortest when participating node is limited to a certain number. The number of nodes which produces the best performance in real experiment is very close to the optimal number (pointed by an arrow) determined by mathematical analysis and simulation which are based on the proposed scheduling algorithm. In Figure 10 and 11, results of experiments, simulation and mathematical analysis show that including all available nodes produces the best performance. The reason is the same to the case of above analytical result.

To sum up, we are able to assure that the proposed job scheduling algorithm is a viable approach to adapt in mobile environment where links are prone to frequent disconnections, especially when mobile nodes remain in disconnection state for longer duration.

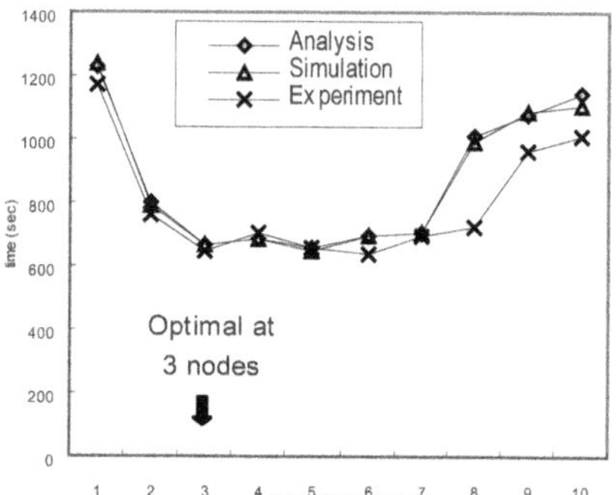

Fig. 8. Job execution time in a stable environment (By analysis, optimal number of nodes is 3)

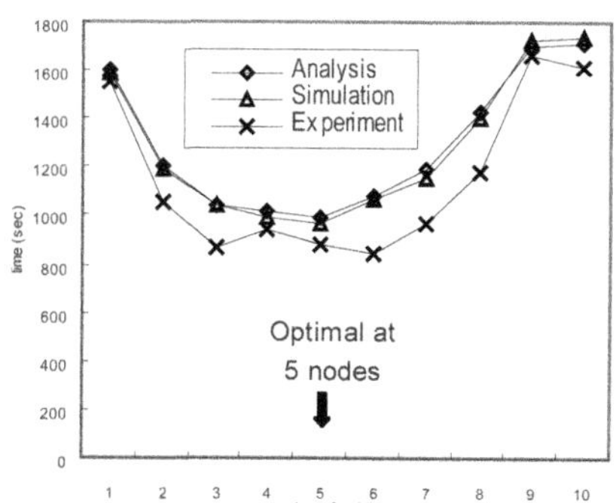

Fig. 9. Job execution time in a highly disconnective environment (By analysis, optimal number of nodes is 5)

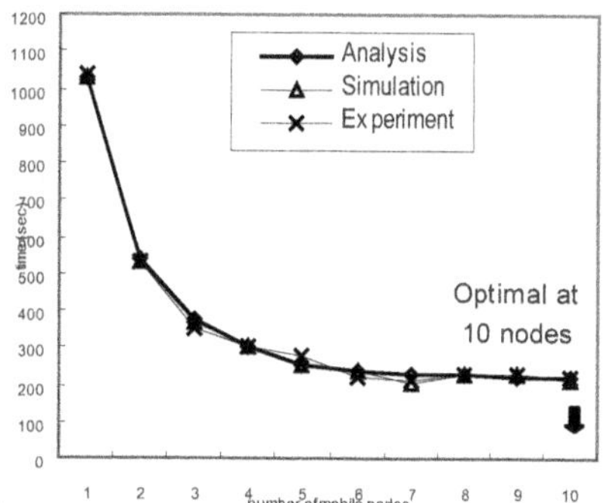

Fig. 10. Job execution time in an unstable environment (By analysis, optimal number of nodes is 10)

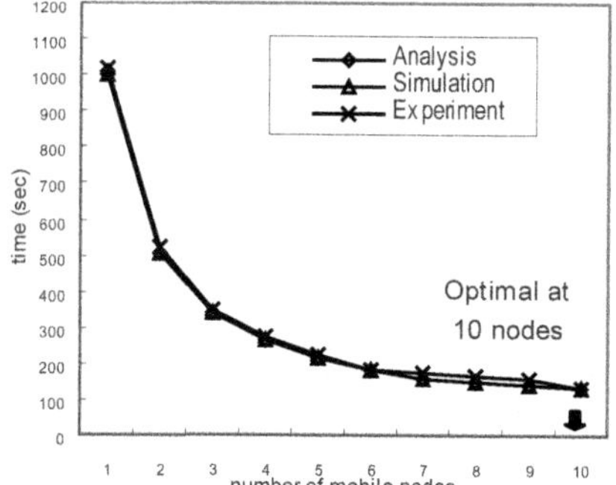

Fig. 11. Job execution time in a highly connective environment (By analysis, optimal number of nodes is 10)

6 Conclusion and Future Works

In this paper, we discuss on the issue of integrating mobile devices into grid. We propose our own view of the mobile/grid integrated system where a gateway links the static grid sites to the group of mobile devices, thus mobile users can make use of static grid resources, and also provide their mobile devices as grid resources. We present the newly emerging technical issues for realizing this mobile grid system, and particularly focus on the job scheduling algorithm to achieve more reliable performance.

We elaborate overcoming an unreliable connectivity of mobile environment thorough proposed scheduling algorithm in this paper. However, there are still challenging problems such as limited energy, device heterogeneity, security, and so on. We will tackle on these issues in future works and develop a prototype of mobile grid system.

References

[1] I. Foster, C. Kesselman and S. Tuecke. "The Anatomy of the Grid: Enabling Scalable Virtual Organizations," International J. Supercomputer Applications, 15(3), 2001.

[2] M. Satyanarayanan. "Fundamental Challenges in Mobile Computing," In Proceedings of the fifteenth annual ACM Symposium on Principles of Distributed Computing, Philadelphia, Pennsylvania, 1996.

[3] T. Phan, L. Huang, and C. Dulan. "Challenge: Integrating Mobile Wireless Devices Into the Computational Grid," In Proceedings of the 8th ACM International Conference on Mobile Computing and Networking (MobiCom '02), September 25–27, 2002, in Atlanta, GA.

[4] Clarke, Brian and Marty Humphrey. "Beyond the 'Device as Portal': Meeting the Requirements of Wireless and Mobile Devices in the Legion Grid Computing System," In Proceedings of the Parallel and Distributed Computing Issues in Wireless Networks and Mobile Computing at the International Parallel and Distributed Processing Symposium. IEEE Press, 2002.

[5] Jonathan Ledlie, Jeff Shneidman, Margo Seltzer, John Huth. "Scooped, Again," Proceedings of Second International Workshop on Peer-to-Peer Systems (IPTPS'03), 20–21 February 2003 in Berkeley, CA, USA.

[6] Bryce Wilcox-O'Hearn. "Experiences Deploying a Large-Scale Emergent Network," Proceedings of Second International Workshop on Peer-to-Peer Systems (IPTPS'02), 7–8 March 2002 in Cambridge, MA, USA.

[7] SETI@home. http://setiathome.ssl.berkeley.edu, March 2001.

[8] Derrick Kondo, Henri Casanova, Eric Wing, Francine Berman. "Models and Scheduling Mechanisms for Global Computing Applications," Proceedings of IPDPS 2002, April 15-19, 2002, Fort Lauderdale, California

[9] F. Berman and R. Wolski. "The AppLes project: A status report," Proceedings of the 8th NEC Research Symposium, Berlin, Germany, May 1997.

[10] The Condor Project. http://www.cs.wisc.edu/condor

[11] D. Abramson, J. Giddy, I. Foster, and L. Kotler. "High Performance Parametric Modeling with Nimrod/G: Killer Application for the Global Grid?," In Proceedings of the International Parallel and Distributed Processing Symposium, May 2000.

[12] Sang-Min Park and Jai-Hoon Kim. "Chameleon: A Resource Scheduler in a Data Grid Environment," 2003 IEEE/ACM International Symposium on Cluster Computing and the Grid (CCGRID'2003), Tokyo, Japan, May 2003.

[13] OpenPBS. http://www.openpbs.org

[14] LSF. http://www.platform.com/products/LSF/

[15] The Globus Project. http://www.globus.org

[16] K. Czajkowski, I. Foster, N. Karonis, C. Kesselman, S. Martin, W. Smith, S. Tuecke. "A Resource Management Architecture for Metacomputing Systems," Proc. IPPS/SPDP '98 Workshop on Job Scheduling Strategies for Parallel Processing, pg. 62–82, 1998.

[17] J.-P Goux, S. Kulkarni, J. T. Linderoth, and M. E. Yoder. "An Enabling Framework for Master-Worker Applications on the Computational Grid," Proceedings of the Ninth IEEE International Symposium on High Performance Distributed Computing, 2000.

[18] S. Radhakrishnan, N. S. V. Rao G. Racherla, C. N. Sekharan, and S. G. Batsell, "DST - a routing protocol for ad hoc networks using distributed spanning trees," IEEE Wireless Communications and Networking Conference, pp. 100–104, 1999.

[19] Cynthia Gibas. "Developing Bioinformatics Computer Skills," O'REILLY, April 2001.

A Policy Propagation Model Using Mobile Agents in Large-Scale Distributed Network Environments

Tae-Kyung Kim[1], Dong-Young Lee[1], Ok-Hwan Byeon[2], and T.M. Chung[1]

[1]Internet Management Technology Laboratory[1],
School of Information and Communication Engineering,
Sungkyunkwan University,
Chunchun-dong 300, Jangan-gu, Suwon, Kyunggi-do,
Republic of Korea
{tkkim,dylee}@rtlab.skku.ac.kr, tmchung@ece.skku.ac.kr
[2]Korea Institute of Science and Technology Information
ohbyeon@kisti.re.kr

Abstract. With the growing number of attacks on network infrastructures, we need better techniques to detect and prevent these attacks. Each security system in the distributed network requires different security rules to protect from these attacks efficiently. So the propagation of security rules is needed. Therefore, we introduce mobile agents that propagate security rules by constantly moving around the Internet as a solution to propagation of security rules. This paper describes a new approach for propagation of security rules in large-scale networks, in which mobile agent mechanisms are used. To evaluate the proposed approach, we simulated a policy propagation model using a NS-2 (Network Simulator). Our new approach presents advantages in terms of spreading rules rapidly and increasing scalability.

1 Introduction

Significant progress has been made in the improvement of computer system security. However, attacks and invasions of this kind involving computers have become frequent. Thus, security has become a key word for most companies worldwide. Intrusion detection is defined [22] as, "The problem of identifying individuals who are using a computer system without authorization and those who have legitimate access to the system but are abusing their privileges." Intrusion-detection systems aim at detecting attacks against computer systems and networks. Approaches to detecting intrusions can be broadly classified into two categories: Anomaly Detection and Misuse Detection. Misuse detection is best suited for reliably detecting known use patterns. Misuse detection systems can detect many or all known attack patterns, but they are of little use for as yet unknown attack methods. Therefore, it is required to keep security rules up to date with new vulnerabilities and environments and distributed systems are increasingly requiring differentiated policies that govern individual and collective behavior of entities in the system. A centralized approach for managing heterogeneous intrusion detection systems has some problems. For example, managing heterogeneous systems individually requires too much work and

M.E. Orlowska et al. (Eds.): ICSOC 2003, LNCS 2910, pp. 514–526, 2003.

high cost in large-scale distributed networks. Therefore, we suggested a policy propagation model for a large-scale distributed network using mobile agents. The large-scale distributed network is divided into several security zones, and one mobile agent is assigned to one security zone to propagate security rules. Each IDS in a security zone doesn't have to contain all kinds of security rules but it must have locally specialized security rules to protect systems. The priority of each security rule is different in each IDS according to its operation. Therefore, the procedure of checking the conflict of security rules is necessary when the IDS receive the security rules from the mobile agent.

Before designing the mobile agent-based rule propagation method, we investigated patterns of the intrusion detection rules. The intrusion detection rules can be divided into two systems: A forward-chaining rule-based system and a backward-chaining rule-based system [6]. A forward-chaining rule-based system is data-driven: each fact asserted may satisfy the conditions under which new facts or conclusions are derived. Alternatively, backward-chaining rule-based systems employ the reverse strategy; starting from a proposed hypothesis they proceed to collect supportive evidence. Our proposed system uses the forward-chaining rule-based system.

This paper mainly describes a dynamic agent-based rule propagation model for improving efficiency of negotiation between mobile agents and intrusion detection systems. In section 2, some related works and a mobile agent description are shown. In section 3, the design of a mobile agent-based security rule propagation and negotiation model is clarified. In section 4, the policy propagation model is simulated with respect to time. Section 5, this paper is summarized.

2 Related Works

In this section, we overview the mobile agent and briefly describe the characteristics of typical agent-based intrusion detection systems (IDSs) – EMERALD, AAFID, IA-NSM, and IDA.

2.1 Overview of Mobile Agent

A mobile agent is a kind of independent program which can migrate from one node to another node in a distributed network by itself. Unlike the traditional distributed techniques such as the Client-Server model and Code on Demand model, a mobile agent has advantages as follows:

- proper use of existing resources to fulfill user's assignment
- debase network traffic
- balance network load
- support fault-tolerance
- support mobile user
- support customized services

A mobile agent has its own lifecycle - creating, halting, executing, service searching, arriving at a new host, migrating, returning to the original host and terminating. We use this agent technology in misuse intrusion detection systems to spread the rule containing the intrusion information. A mobile agent consists of three parts: resource, function and rule information. Figure 1 shows the component of a mobile agent [2].

The resource section contains the hardware resource, computing environment, and encrypted hash value. The computing environment means the serialized state of the agent is encoded in the method part. The encrypted hash value is used to check the integrity of the agent. The function part includes the control module, communication module, and method. The control module controls all functions of the mobile agent including authentication and authorization. The communication module provides a secure communication channel between the agent and IDS.

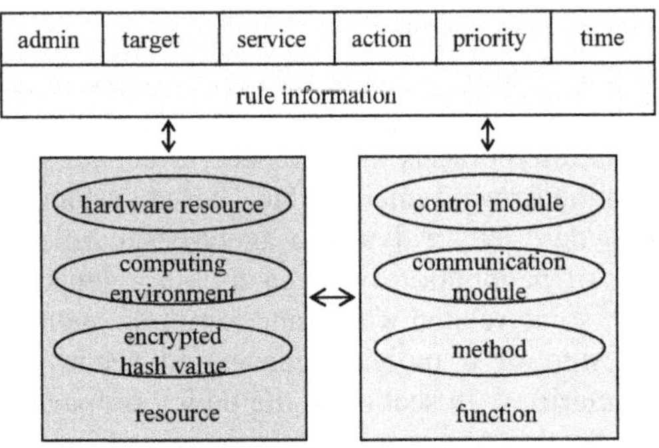

Fig. 1. Constitution of mobile Agent

A method module includes a concrete computing code and program [2]. Rule information in the agent is composed of six elements: administrator, target, service, action, priority, and time information. 'Admin' is the operator who makes the intrusion detection rule; 'target' shows the object that needs to be protected from attacks; 'service' shows which service is controlled by the intrusion detection rule; 'action' describes the action that is performed to the target; 'priority' means the order of rules; 'time' shows the generation time of security rules. Mobile agents offer a new paradigm for distributed system environments, but there are two kinds of security issues specific to a mobile agent [2, 16]: Misuse of hosts by mobile agents, misuse of mobile agents by hosts and other mobile agents. A mobile agent can abuse the information, software, hardware, or resources of a host computer. Also, a mobile agent can be destroyed, stolen from, subverted, and trapped by other mobile agents and host computers.

We have suggested a security model that provides safety from a malicious agent and a malicious host. Encrypted hash values guarantee the integrity of the mobile agent and protect unauthorized modification of the mobile agent. A trusted third party authenticates a mobile agent and host mutually. When conflict occurs between the rules of a mobile agent and those of IDS, negotiation of security rules occurs between mobile agent and IDS to solve the conflict of security rules. The use of rule adapter prevents the mobile agent and IDS from the misuse of mobile agent and IDS. Thus this system is protected from the activities of malicious agents and malicious hosts.

2.2 The Characteristics of the Typical Agent-Based IDSs

Agent technology has been applied in a variety of fields, particularly in artificial intelligence, distributed systems, software engineering and electronic commerce. Generally, an agent can be defined as a software program that can execute a complex task on behalf of the user [7]. Some authors have proposed the use of autonomous agents to construct non-monolithic intrusion detection systems [8, 9, 10]. The capacity of some autonomous agents to maintain specific information of their application domains, in this case security, confers great flexibility on these agents and hence, on the entire system. The characteristics of typical agent-based IDS are follows:

- **EMERALD**

The SRI(Stanford Research Institute) EMERALD(Event Monitoring Enabling Response to Autonomous Live Disturbance) project addresses the problems of network intrusion via TCP/IP data streams. Network surveillance monitors observe local area network traffic and submit analysis reports to an enterprise monitor, which correlates the reports. EMERALD seems to concentrate the intelligence in a central system and does not incorporate any agent technology [11, 12, 13].

- **AAFID**

The Autonomous Agents for Intrusion Detection (AAFID) project at Purdue University is based on independent entities called autonomous agents that perform distributed data collection and analysis. AAFID employs a hierarchy of agents. At the root of the hierarchy are monitors, which provide global command and control and analyze information flowing from lower level nodes. At the leaves, agents collect event information. The agents reside on special purpose agent platforms, called transceivers. Transceivers perform command and control of locally running agents and analyze and reduce the information received from the agents. Transceivers feed processed information onto monitors. Agents seem to be static once they are deployed to a transceiver, but are replaceable through reconfiguration [14, 19].

- **IA-NSM**

The Intelligent Agents for Network Security Management (IA-NSM) Project for Intrusion Detection using intelligent agent technology provides flexible integration of a multi-agent system in a classically- networked environment to enhance its protection level against inherent attacks [15].

- **IDA**

The Intrusion Detection Agent (IDA) system relies on mobile agents to trace intruders among the various hosts involved in an intrusion. IDA works by focusing on specific events that may relate to intrusions, referred to as "Marks Left by Suspected Intruder (MLSI)." If an MLSI is found, IDA gathers information related to the MLSI, analyzes the information, and decides whether or not an intrusion has occurred. The system follows a hierarchical structure, with a central manager at the root and a variety of agents at the leaves [19].

As previously mentioned, many research labs are currently working on applying agents to intrusion detection. Other works in this field are encouraging, as well. However, among all these efforts, there was no mobile agent-based rule propagation and negotiation model for intrusion detection system. In this paper, we present the model of the Mobile Agent-based Rules propagation and negotiation System (MARS) for the IDS in the large-scale distributed network environments. In MARS, the mobile agents are used as carriers, especially negotiating with other intrusion detection systems about security rules. And also, we simulate the efficiency of rule propagation model using NS-2 simulator.

3 The Design and Propagation Rules of MARS

3.1 The Design of MARS

This section describes the design details of the mobile agent-based rule propagation and negotiation system and clarifies the objectives in designing a MARS. We set up the following goals:

- Propagation rules in dynamic and distributed environments
- Security of the mobile agent-based rule propagation system
- Authentication of the mobile agent
- Negotiation of security rules between mobile agent and intrusion detection system

As shown in Figure 2, if integrated security managers managing the intrusion detection system find a new attack, they enter information about the new attacks into the security management client. Then the information is transmitted to the security management server. The security management server generates a security policy about new attacks and sends the security rule to the total policy database. The Agent Generator generates a mobile agent, which contains the security policy about new attacks. Then the mobile agent migrates to the assigned security zone through the Internet, and moves dynamically in the security zone to propagate the intrusion detection rule.

When managing heterogeneous IDSs in security domains, it is difficult to guarantee integrity for IDS policies. Breaking the integrity of IDS policies result in serious problems for network security. It also requires more efforts, and costs and managing distributed policies of network IDSs for security managers. Most IDS products currently support remote management to solve above problems. With remote management functionality, a security manager is able to manage multiple IDSs at one location. But, in many cases, remote management tools are limited to the same IDS products (or IDS products developed by one vendor). Therefore, to manage heterogeneous IDSs in a large-scale distributed network at a low cost, we have designed the MARS.

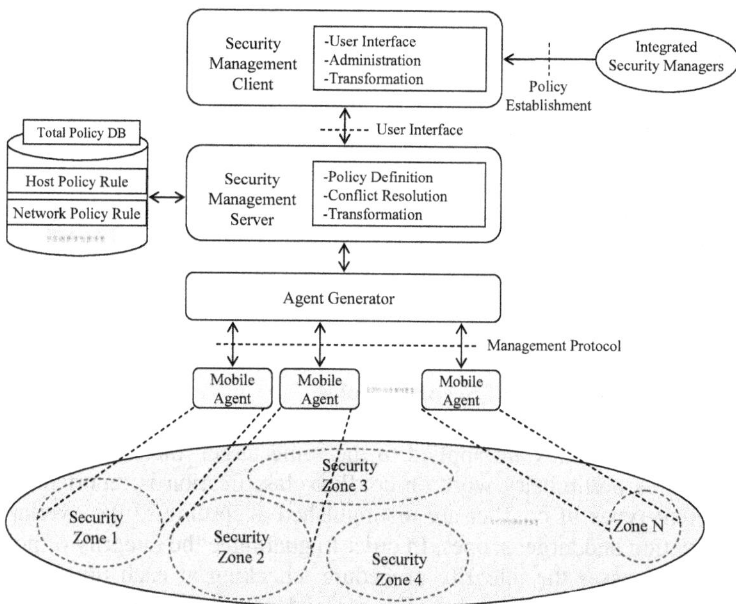

Fig. 2. Conceptual architecture of MARS

In this paper, we focus on the mobile agent having security rules and the ability of negotiation to propagate security rules to the heterogeneous IDSs in large-scale network environments. The conceptual architecture of mobile-agent based rule propagation is shown in Figure 3. The Rule adapter communicates with mobile agents and makes decisions as to whether the rule is necessary to the intrusion detection system. A trusted third party is an authentication server that authenticates the mobile agent.

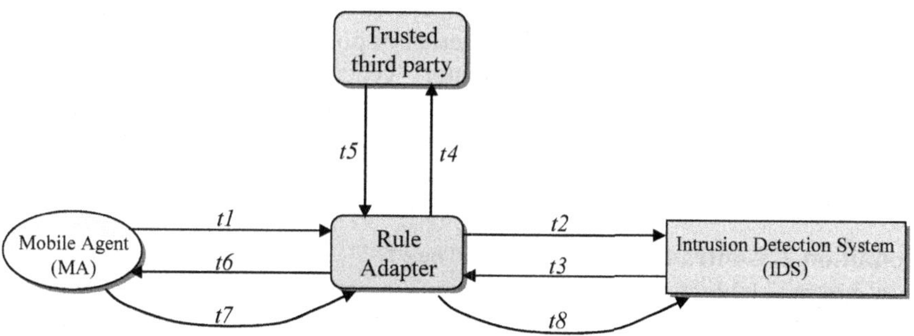

Fig. 3. Conceptual Architecture of rule propagation

When a mobile agent arrives at the rule adapter(*t1*), The Rule adapter checks the policy conflict(*t2*). If there is no conflict between the rules of the mobile agent and the rules of the intrusion detection system(*t3*), then the rule adapter authenticates the mobile agent using the trusted thirty party(*t4-t6*). And the rule adapter checks the integrity of the rule using the hash value in the mobile agent(*t7*). Finally, the rule having the information about the new attack is added to the rules of the intrusion detection system(*t8*). When there is a conflict between the rules of the agent and of intrusion detection systems, the negotiation procedure is processed to solve the conflict problems. Therefore, the rule adapter serves as a mediator in negotiations between the mobile agent and the IDS. Also we use XML as message exchange schemes among mobile agent and IDS. As stated in [20], this scheme supports increasing scalability and simplicity to propagate security policy to the different IDSs in security zones of large scale network environments.

3.2 Negotiation Procedure of Security Rules

Whenever several policies are applied to the same target, there is potential conflict between them. A preliminary work on conflict classification is reported in [3, 4, 5] where different types of conflict are distinguished according to the overlaps among the subject, action and target scopes. In order to guarantee the integrity of policies, the rule adapter processes the integrity procedure, checking at each time when mobile agents propagate the security rules. The rule adapter performs the integrity check procedure under the following three conditions. If any of these conditions are satisfied, we can consider there is a policy conflict.

The primary function of the rule adapter is detecting and resolving policy conflicts. The policy of IDS, P(x), is defined by the existing policy(old) and the newly propagated policy(new). A policy P(x) consists of policy Target T(x), Service S(x) and the action of policy A(x). That is, P(new) and P(old) are defined as follows [1]:

$$P(new) = \{T(new), S(new), A(new)\},\ P(old) = \{T(old), S(old), A(old)\}$$

Condition 1. Equivalence; P(old) = P(new)

An equivalent policy conflict occurs when two policies have the same values of policy target T(x), service S(x) and the action of policy A(x). This can be resolved by the user levels – security administrator, general user. For example, security administrator has 1-level rights, system manager has 2-level rights, and general user has 9-level rights. The policy with the highest admin level is applied when two or more policies conflict.

Condition 2. Contradiction; P(old) ↔ P(new)

A contradictable policy conflict occurs when both positive and negative policies of the same kind (i.e. permit policies or deny policies) exist. This conflict is very serious because there are no means of deciding whether the action is to be permitted or denied. A contradictable policy conflict can be resolved by user level, priority of policy, and the time of rule creation in rule information. The classification of contradiction conflict is shown in Table 1.

Table 1. Classification of contradiction conflicts

T(x); Target	S(x); Service	A(x); Action
T(old) = T(new)	S(old) = S(new)	A(new) = Positive_Action A(old) = Negative_Action
		A(new) = Negative_Action A(old) = Positive_Action
T(old) ≠ T(new)		A(new) = Positive_Action A(old) = Negative_Action
		A(new) = Negative_Action A(old) = Positive_Action

Condition 3. Inclusion; $\{P(old) \supset P(new) \vee P(old) \subset P(new)\} \wedge \{p(old) \leftrightarrow P(new)\}$

Examples of inclusive policy conflict are shown in table 2. This policy conflict occurs when the inclusive relationship with contradictable relationship between existing policy P(old) and newly requested policy P(new) exist. This can be resolved by user level, priority of policy, and the time in rule information.

Table 2. Classification of inclusive policy conflicts

T(x); Target	S(x); Service	A(x); Action
T(old) = T(new)	S(new) ⊂ S(old)	A(new) = Positive_Action A(old) = Negative_Action
		A(new) = Negative_Action A(old) = Positive_Action
	S(new) ⊃ S(old)	A(new) = Positive_Action A(old) = Negative_Action
		A(new) = Negative_Action A(old) = Positive_Action
T(old) ≠ T(new)	S(new) ⊂ S(old)	A(new) = Positive_Action A(old) = Negative_Action
		A(new) = Negative_Action A(old) = Positive_Action
	S(new) ⊃ S(old)	A(new) = Positive_Action A(old) = Netative_Action
		A(new) = Negative_Action A(old) = Positive_Action

To solve the above problems, rule adapter compares the value of admin level, priority, and time in rule information between P(old) and P(new). At first, rule adapter compares the level of admin who generate the security rule. Each admin has different rights. The policy with the highest admin level is applied when two or more policies conflict. If the rule information has the same admin, then rule adapter checks the priority of each security rule. The rule having the higher priority is adapted. If two security rules have the same priority and the same admin, the rule adapter checks the time in rule information. The newly generated security rule has higher priority than the old one. The comparison process is shown in Figure 4.

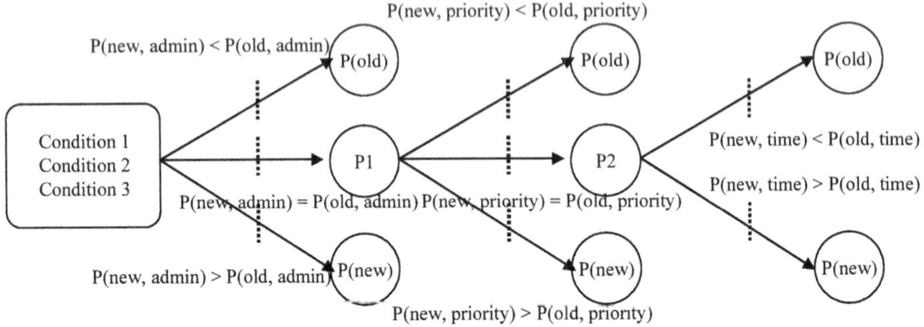

Fig. 4. The comparison process of security rules

4 Simulation Results

According to [21], delay time is the most necessary to users to handle the application. To evaluate our model with respect to time, we used the NS-2 (Network Simulator). NS-2 is an open-source simulation tool that runs on Linux. It is a discreet event simulator targeted at networking research and provides substantial support for simulation of routing, multicast protocols and IP protocols, such as UDP, TCP, RTP and SRM over wired and wireless (local and satellite) networks [17].

Figure 5 shows the network topology used in simulation. In (a), mobile agent moves from one IDS to another IDS to propagate the security rule whereas in (b), centralized manager transport security rules to each IDS. MARS is designed to use in a large-scale network environment and propagate the security rule to heterogeneous IDSs. Therefore, MARS use XML as message exchange schemes [20] and divide the large-scale network into several security zones to manage and assign a mobile agent. But in this simulation, we suppose that IDSs are homogeneous products developed from same vendor because the rule exchange schemes using XML(eXtensible Markup Language) are only possible in MARS. In figure 5, (a) means a security zone of MARS.

Parameters used in this simulation are like this: security rule is propagated to six IDSs; a TTP (Trusted Third Party) is used; Network bandwidth is 10Mbps; the distance from one IDS to another IDS are different respectively as shown in Figure 5; the size of rule files is 4.5kbyte.

The goal of the simulations was to evaluate our MARS approach against the centralized rule propagation IDS approach with respect to time. Delay can be estimated as follows [18]:

-Delay = Propagation delay + Transmission delay + Queuing delay
-Propagation delay = Distance / 2.3 $\times$ *10*^{8} *(in a cable)*
-Transmission delay = Size / Bandwidth

We didn't consider the queuing delay in this simulation. Figure 6 shows the elapsed transmission time of mobile agent and rule files used in the simulation. The results show that MARS is more efficient than centralized IDS method.

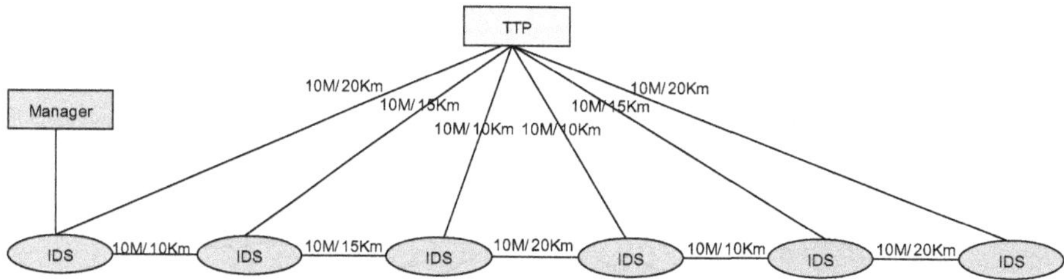

(a) The simulation topology of MARS

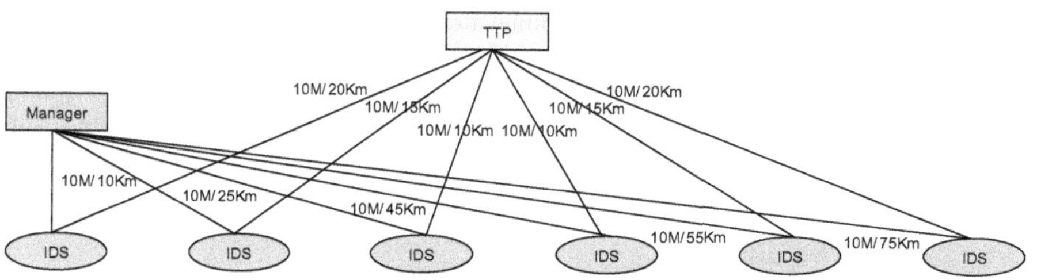

(b) The simulation topology of centralized approach

Fig. 5. Simulation topology

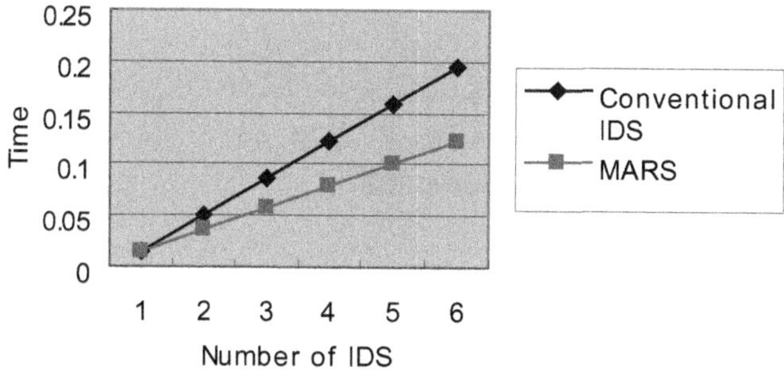

Fig. 6. Transmission elapsed time of Centralized approach and MARS

Also, we simulated this method using the tree topology. Tree topology combines characteristics of linear bus and star topologies. It consists of groups of star-configured computers connected to a linear bus backbone cable.

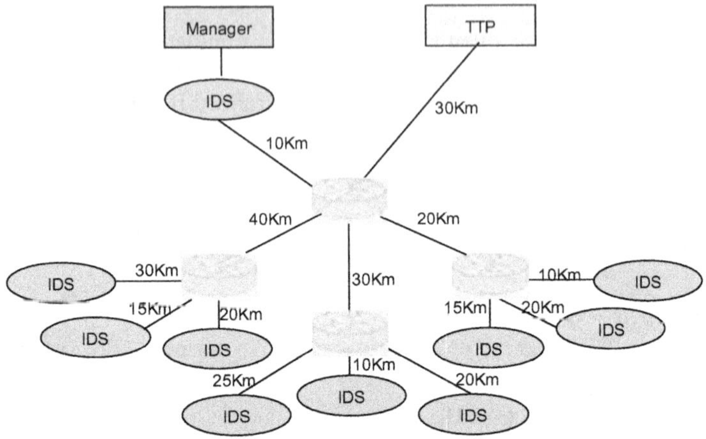

Fig. 7. Tree Simulation topology

Parameters used in this simulation were the same as above conditions. Figure 8 shows the elapsed transmission time of mobile agent and rule files. Also, the results of this simulation showed that the method of MARS was more efficient than that of centralized IDS.

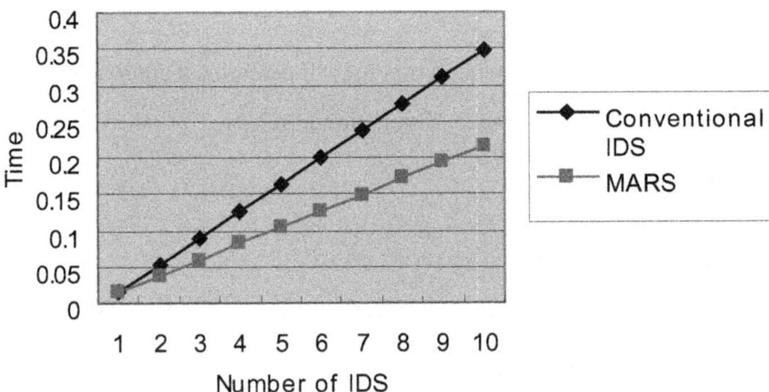

Fig. 8. Transmission elapsed time of Centralized approach and MARS in Tree topology

5 Conclusion and Future Works

With the growing number of attacks on network infrastructures, we need better techniques to detect and prevent these attacks. To protect networks from intrusion and attacks, many security systems have been developed such as firewalls and intrusion detection systems. These days, we have large-scaled networks and various security systems. To protect systems from attacks efficiently, the propagation and negotiation of security rules are required.

The goal of this research was to suggest a more proactive mobile agent-based rule propagation and negotiation model. The mobile agent can move around the IDSs within the divided security zone and quickly propagate the security rules using the XML message exchange scheme. And the mobile agent can negotiate with IDS to select, reject, upload and download the security rules. Also, mutual authentication among mobile agent, trust third party, and IDS was suggested to establish identity and maintain its own security context. And the results of the simulation show that MARS take less time than the conventional IDS to propagate the security rules. Therefore, MARS can present advantages in terms of spreading rules rapidly and increasing scalability.

In future work, we plan to improve the functions of the mobile agent so as to cooperate with other security systems about security policies and intrusion detection.

References

1. Dong-Young Lee, Dong-Soo Kim, Tae-Kyung Kim, Tai M. Chung, "Centralized Approach for Managing Heterogeneous Firewalls in Distributed Network Environments," WISA2002, Aug. 2002.
2. L. Qi, L. Yu. "Mobile agent-based security model for distributed system," Systems, Man, and Cybernetics, 2001 IEEE International Conference, 2001.
3. J. Moffett, Morris S. Sloman, "Policy Conflict Analysis in Distributed System Management," Journal of Organizational Computing, Vol.4, No.1, pp.1–22, 1994.
4. Emil C. Lupu, Morris Sloman, "Conflicts in Policy-Based Distributed Systems Management," Journal of IEEE Transaction on Software Engineering, Vol. 25. No.6, pp.852–869, 1999.
5. E. Lupu, M. Sloman, "Conflict Analysis for Management Policies," International Symposium on Integrated Network Management IM'97, pp.430–443, 1997.
6. U. Lindqvist and P. A. Porras. Detecting computer and network misuse through the Production-Based Expert System Toolset (PBEST) In Proceedings of the 1999 Symposium on Security and Privacy, Oakland, California, May 1999.
7. H. S. Nwana. Software Agents: an Overview. Knowledge Engineering Review, 1996.
8. M. Crosbie and G. H. Spafford. Defending a Computer System using Autonomous Agents. Technical Report No. 95–022, Dept. of Comp. Sciences, Purdue University, March 1996.
9. M. Crosbie, and E. H. Spafford. "Active Defense of a Computer System using Autonomous Agents," Technical Report CSD-TR-95-008, Department of Computer Sciences, Purdue University, 1995.
10. Balasubramaniyan, Jai, J. O. Garcia-Fernandez, E. H. Spafford, and D. Zamboni. An Architecture for Intrusion Detection using Autonomous Agents. Department of Computer Sciences, Purdue University; Coast TR 98-05; 1998.
11. G. G. Helmer, J. S. K. Wong, V. Honavar, and L. Miller. Intelligent agents for intrusion detection. In Proceedings, IEEE Information Technology Conference, pages 121–124, Syracuse, NY, September 1998.

12. A. Porras and P. G. Neumann. EMERALD: Event Monitoring Enabling Responses to Anomalous Live Disturbances. In Proceedings of the National Information Systems Security Conference, Oct 1997.
13. A. Porras and A. Valdes. "Live Traffic Analysis of TCP/IP Gateways," Networks and Distributed Systems Security Symposium, March 1998.
14. B. Jai, J. O. Garcia-Fernandez, E. H. Spafford, and D. Zamboni. An Architecture for Intrusion Detection using Autonomous Agents. Department of Computer Sciences, Purdue University; Coast TR 98-05; 1998.
15. K. Boudaoud, H. Labiod, R. Boutaba, Z. Guessoum. Network security management with intelligent agents. Network Operations and Management Symposium, 2000. NOMS 2000.
16. S. Greenberg, C. Byington, T. Holding, G. Harper, "Mobile Agents and Security," IEEE Communications Magazine, July 1998.
17. NS network simulator. http://www-mash.cs.berkeley.edu/ns.
18. L. Peterson and B. Davie. Computer Networks: A Systems Approach. Morgan Kaufman, 2000. 2nd Edition.
19. W. Jansen, P. Mell, T. Karygiannis, D. Marks, Applying Mobile Agents to Intrusion Detection and Response, October 1999.
20. Kwang H. Kim, Tae-Kyung Kim, Dong S. Kim, Tai M. Chung, "The Design of XML-based Internet Security Integrated System Architecture", International Conference on Computational Science 2003 (ICCS 2003), June 2003.
21. NSF CISE Grand Challenge in e-Science Workshop Report, http://www.evl.uic.edu /activity/NSF/index.html, Jan 24, 2002.
22. B. Mukherjee, T. L. Heberlein and K. N. Levitt. "Network Intrusion Detection," IEEE Network, May/June 1994.

Location-Based Services in Ubiquitous Computing Environments

Ichiro Satoh

National Institute of Informatics
2-1-2 Hitotsubashi, Chiyoda-ku, Tokyo 101-8430, Japan
Tel: +81-3-4212-2546
Fax: +81-3-3556-1916
ichiro@nii.ac.jp

Abstract. This paper presents a framework for providing dynamically deployable services in ubiquitous computing settings. The framework attaches physical entities and spaces with application-specific services to support and annotate them. By using RFID-based tracking systems, it detects the locations of physical entities, such as people or things, and deploys services bound to the entities at proper computing devices near the locations of the entities. It enables location-based services to be implemented as mobile agents and operated at stationary or mobile computing devices, which are at appropriate locations, even if the services do not have any location-information. The paper also describes a prototype implementation of the framework and several practical applications.

1 Introduction

As Mark Weiser envisioned [20], a goal of ubiquitous computing is to provide various services by making multiple computers available throughout the physical environment, but, in effect, making them invisible to the user. Another goal of ubiquitous computing is for it to integrate the physical world with cyberspace. Actually, perceptual technologies have made it possible to detect the presence or positions of people and any other object we care to think about. Context-awareness, in particular user-awareness and location-awareness, is becoming an essential feature of services that assist our everyday lives in ubiquitous computing environments.

However, ubiquitous computing devices are not suitable for providing multiple-purpose and personalized services, because most devices tend to have limited storage and processing capacity and are thus incapable of internally maintaining a variety of software and profile databases on the users. In fact, although there have been many attempts to develop location-based services thus far, most existing location-based systems have inherently focused on particular services, such as user navigation for visualizing locations on maps and information providing the information relevant to the user's current location. As a result, it is difficult for these systems to support other services for which they were not initially designed. Furthermore, they are often implemented in an ad-hoc manner with centralized management. Therefore, they cannot dynamically reconfigure themselves when new services are needed.

M.E. Orlowska et al. (Eds.): ICSOC 2003, LNCS 2910, pp. 527–542, 2003.

This paper presents a framework for deploying and operating location-based applications to solve these problems and this is based on two key ideas. The first is to introduce mobile agent technology as a mechanism to dynamically deploy services. Since many computing devices in ubiquitous computing environments only have limited resources, they cannot provide all services required due to limited computational resources, even if they are at suitable locations. Therefore, the framework provides an infrastructure for dynamically deploying service-provider agents to support services at computers that need the services. The second idea is to separate application-specific services from the infrastructure. Since each mobile agent is a programmable entity, the framework enables application-specific services, including user interfaces and application logic, to be implemented within mobile agents. Using mobile agents makes the framework independent of any applications, because application-specific services are implemented within mobile agents instead of the infrastructure. Since the infrastructure is responsible for automatically deploying mobile agents at appropriate computers, they can provide their services without any location-information.

In the remainder of this paper, we briefly review related work (Section 2), describe our design goals (Section 3), the design of our framework, called *SpatialAgent*, (Section 4), and an implementation of the framework (Section 5). We describe some experiences we had with several applications, which we used the framework to develop (Section 6). We provide a summary and discuss some future issues (Section 7).

2 Background

There have been many attempts to develop and operate location-based services. Existing services can be classified into two types of approaches.

The first is to make computing devices move with the user. It often assumes that such devices are attached to positioning systems, such as Global Positioning Systems (GPS) receivers. For example, HP's Cooltown project [7] is an infrastructure for bridging people, places, and things in the physical world with web resources that are used to store information about them. It allow users to access resources via browsers running on handheld computing devices. All the services available in the Cooltown system are constrained by limitations with web browsers and HTTP. Stuttgart University's NEXUS project [5] provides a platform that supports location-aware applications for mobile users with handheld devices, like the Cooltown project. Unlike our approach, however both projects are not suitable for supporting mobile users from stationary computers distributed in a smart environment.

The second approach assumes that a space is equipped with tracking systems which establish the location of physical entities, including people and objects, within it so that application-specific services can be provided at appropriate computers. Cambridge University's Sentient Computing project [4] provides a location-aware platform using infrared-based or ultrasonic-based locating systems in a building. Using the VNC system [12], the platform can track the movement of a tagged entity, such as individuals and things, so that the graphical user interfaces of the user's applications follow the user while he/she is moving around. Since the applications must be executed in remote servers, the platform may have non-negligible interactive latency between the servers and host the user accesses locally. Recently, a CORBA-based middleware, called LocARE, has been proposed [10]. The middleware can move CORBA objects to hosts according to the location of tagged objects. Although the project provides similar functionality to that of our framework, its management is centralized and it is difficult to dynamically reconfigure the platform when sensors are added to or removed from the environment.

Microsoft's EasyLiving project [2] provides context-aware spaces, with a particular focus on the home and office. A computer-vision approach is used to track users within the spaces. Both the projects assume that locating sensors have initially been allocated in the room, and it is difficult to dynamically configure the platform when sensors are added to or removed from the environment, whereas our framework permits sensors to be mobile and scatteredly throughout the space.

ETH has developed an event-based architecture for managing RFID tags [13]. Like our framework, the architecture can link physical objects with software entities, called virtual counterparts. However, the goal of the architecture is to develop software frameworks that ease the development of particular applications rather than a general framework for supporting various applications. Although a ubiquitous computing environment is a distributed system whose computing devices may be dynamically added to and removed from the system, the architecture is managed by a centralized server, whereas our framework is essentially managed in a plug-and-play manner. Moreover, since the architecture cannot migrate its software entities among ubiquitous computing devices, it cannot effectively support moving objects in the physical world, unlike our framework.

We presented an early prototype of the present framework in a previous paper [17] and this was just an infrastructure for allowing Java-based agents to follow moving users through locating systems and did not encapsulate application-specific tasks into mobile agents, unlike the framework presented in this paper. Also, since the previous system did not support sensor mobility, it could not support all spatial linkages (Figure 1), whereas the framework presented in this paper was designed to be based on RFID-based sensors and it therefore permitted the mobility of sensors as well as physical entities, such as people, objects, and computing devices. We will also present an extension of the framework with the ability of managing various location sensors other than RFID-based sensors in an upcoming paper [18].

3 Approach

The goal of the framework presented in this paper is to provide a general infrastructure for supporting multiple location-aware and personalized services in ubiquitous computing environments.

3.1 Dynamically Deployable Services

Various kinds of infrastructures have been used to construct and manage location-aware services. However, such infrastructures have mostly focused either on a particular application or on a specific sensor technology. By separating application-specific services from infrastructures, our framework provides a general infrastructure for location-aware services and enables application-specific services to be implemented as mobile agents.

Each mobile agent can travel from computer to computer under its own control. When a mobile agent moves to another computer, not only the code but also the state of the agent is transferred to the destination. After arriving at a computer, agents can still continue their processes and access the resource provided by the computer as long as long as the security mechanisms of the computer permit this. Mobile agent technology also has the following advantages in ubiquitous and mobile computing settings:

- Each mobile agent can dynamically be deployed at and locally executed within computers near the position of the user. As a result, the agent can directly interact with the user, where RPC-based approaches, which other existing approaches are often based on, must have network latency between computers and remote servers. It also can directly access various equipment, which belong to that device as long as security mechanisms permit this.
- After arriving at its destination, a mobile agent can continue working without losing the results of working, e.g., the content of instance variables in the agent's program, at the source computers. Thus, the technology enables us to easily build follow-me applications [4].
- Mobile agents can help to conserve the limited resources of computing devices, since each agent only needs to be present at the devices while they are required to offer the services provided by that agent. Mobile agents also have the potential to mask disconnections in some cases. Once a mobile agent is completely transferred to a new location, it can continue its execution at the new location, even when the new location is disconnected from the source location.

3.2 Location Sensing Systems

This framework offers a location-aware system in which spatial regions can be determined within a few square feet, that distinguishes between one or more portions of a room or building. Existing location-based services are typically tailored to a particular type of tracking or positioning technology, such as GPS. The current implementation of the framework uses RFID technology as an alternate approach to locate objects. This is because RFID technologies are expected to be widely used in product distribution and inventory management and tags will placed on many low-cost items, including cans and books in the near future. An RFID system consists of RF (radio frequency) readers (so-called sensors or receivers), which detect the presence of small RF transmitters, often called *tags*. Advances in wireless technology enable passive RFID tags to be scanned over a few meters. For example, the Auto-ID center [1] and its sponsors are working to develop flexible tags and readers operated at ultra-high frequency (915 MHz in the US and 868 MHz in the EU). It expects that RFID tags will cost around 5 cents when produced in bulk and RFID readers around a hundred dollar in volume. The framework assumes that physical entities, including people, computing devices, and places will be equipped with RFID tags so that they are entities that are automatically locatable.

3.3 Architecture

The framework consists of three parts: (1) location information servers, called LISs, (2) mobile agents, and (3) agent hosts. The first provides a layer of indirection between the underlying RFID locating sensing systems and mobile agents. Each LIS manages more than one RFID reader and provides the agents with up-to-date information on the identifiers of RFID tags, which are present in the specific places its readers cover instead of on tags in the whole space. The second offers application-specific services, which are attached to physical entities and places, as collections of mobile agents. The third is a computing device that can execute mobile agent-based applications and issue specific events to the agents running in it when RFID readers detect the movement of the physical entities and places that the agents are bound to.

When an LIS detects a moving tag, it notifies mobile agents attached to it about the network addresses and capabilities of the candidate hosts that are near its location. Each of these agents selects one host from the candidate agent hosts recommended by the LIS and migrate to the selected host. The capabilities of a candidate host do not always satisfy all the requirements of an agent. Each agent does not need to have to know any information about the network addresses and locations of devices, which it may migrate to. This framework assumes that each agent itself should decide, on the basis of to its own configuration policy, whether or not it will migrate itself to the destination and adapt itself to the destination's capabilities.

Our final goal is widespread building-wide and city-wide deployment. It is almost impossible to deploy and administer a system in a scalable way when all of the control and management functions are centralized. LISs are individually connected to other servers in a peer-to-peer manner and exchange information with one another. LISs and agent hosts may be mobile and frequently shut down. The framework permits each LIS to run independently of the other LISs and it offers an automatic mechanism to register agent hosts and RFID readers. The mechanism requires agent hosts to be equipped with tags so that they are locatable.

3.4 Narrowing the Gap between Physical and Logical Mobilities

This framework can inform mobile agents attached to tags about their appropriate destinations according to the current positions of the tags. It supports three types of linkages between a physical entity such as a person, thing, or place, and one or more mobile agents as we can see in Figure 1.

- In the first linkage, a moving entity carries more than one tagged agent host and a space contains a place-bound RFID tag and readers. When the RFID reader detects the presence of a tag that is bound to one of the agent hosts, the framework instructs the agents that are attached to the tagged place to migrate to the visiting agent hosts to offer the location-based services the place has as we can see in Figure 1 (a).
- In the second linkage, tagged agent hosts and RFID readers are allocated. When a tagged moving entity enters the coverage area of one of the readers, the framework instructs the agents that are attached to the entity to migrate to the agent hosts within the same coverage area to offer the entity-dependent services the entity has as we can see in Figure 1 (b).
- In the third linkage, an entity carries an RFID reader and more than one agent host and a space contains more than one place-bound tag. When the entity moves to a nearby place-bound tag and the reader detects the presence of the tag within its

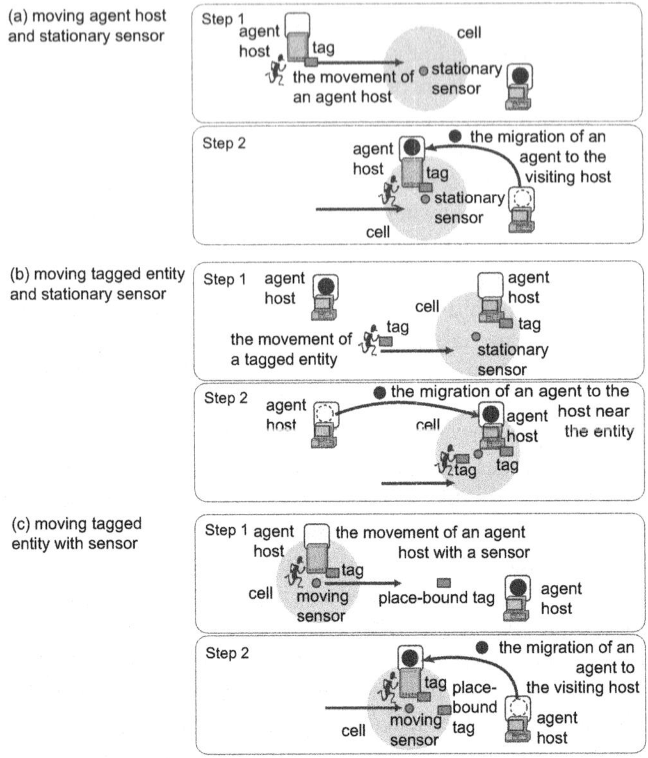

Fig. 1. Three linkages between physical and logical entities

coverage area, the framework instructs the agents that are attached to the tagged place to migrate to the visiting agent hosts to offer the location-dependent services the place has, as shown as we can see in Figure 1 (c).

Note that our framework does not have to distinguish between mobile and stationary computing devices and between mobile and stationary location-sensing systems.

4 Design

This section presents the design for the SpatialAgent framework and describes a prototype implementation of the framework. Figure 2 outlines the basic structure of the framework.

4.1 Location Information Server

LISs are responsible for managing location sensing systems and recommending agent devices at which the agents provide their services. They can run on a stationary or mobile computer and provide all LISs that can run on a stationary or mobile computer and that have the following functionalities:

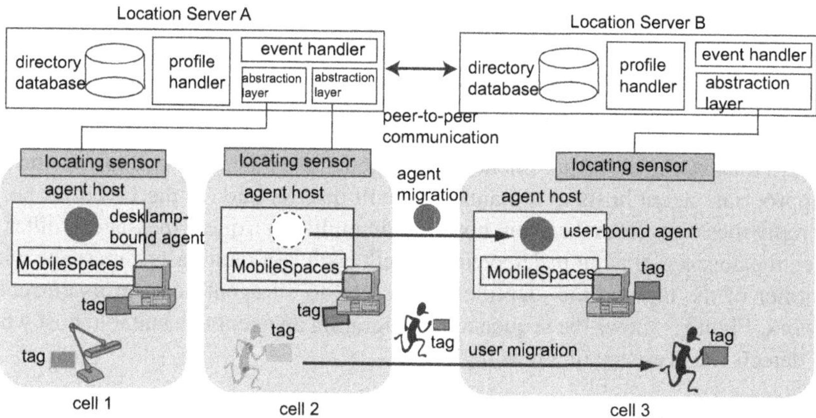

Fig. 2. Architecture of SpatialAgent Framework

RFID-based location model. This framework represents the locations of objects with a symbolic names to specifying the sensing ranges of RFID readers, instead of geographical models. Each LIS manages more than one RFID reader that detects the presence of tags and maintains up-to-date information on the identities of those that are within the zone of coverage. This is achieved by polling the readers or receiving events issued by the readers. An LIS does not require any knowledge on other LISs, but it needs to be able to exchange its information with others through multicast communication. To hide the differences between the underlying locating systems, each LIS maps low-level positional information from the other LISs into information in a symbolic model of location. An LIS represents an entity's location in symbolic terms of the RFID reader's unique identifier that detects the entity's tag. We call each RFID reader's coverage a *cell*, as in the models of location reported by several other researchers [9]. Multiple RFID readers in the framework do not have to be neatly distributed in spaces such as rooms or buildings to completely cover the spaces; instead, they can be placed near more than one agent host and the reader coverage can overlap.

Location management. Each LIS is responsible for discovering mobile agents bound to tags within its cells. Each maintains a database in which it stores information about each of the agent hosts and each of the mobile agents attached to a tagged entity or place. When an LIS detects a new tag in a cell, the LIS multicasts a query that contains the identity of the new tag and its own network address to all the agent hosts in its current sub-network. It then waits for reply messages from the agent hosts. Here, there are two possible cases: the tag may be attached to an agent host or the tag may be attached to a person, place, or thing other than an agent host.

- In the first case, the newly arriving agent host will send its network address and device profile to the LIS; the profile describes the capabilities of the agent host, e.g., input devices and screen size. After receiving a reply message, the LIS stores the profile in its database and forwards the profile to all agent hosts within the cell.

– In the second case, agent hosts that have agents tied to the tag will send their network addresses and the requirements of acceptable agents to the LIS; requirements for each agent specify the capabilities of the agent hosts that the agent can visit and perform its services at.

The LIS then stores the requirements of the agents in its database and moves the agents to appropriate agent hosts in a manner we will discuss later. If the LIS does not have any reply messages from the agent hosts, it can multicast a query message to other LISs. When the absence of a tag is detected in a cell, each LIS multicasts a message with the identifier of the tag and the identifier of the cell to all agent hosts in its current sub-network. Figure 3 shows the sequence for migrating an agent to a suitable host when an LIS detects the presence of a new tag.

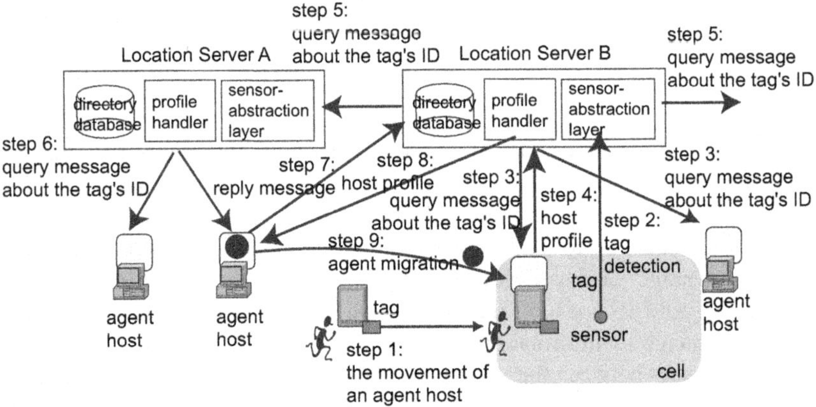

Fig. 3. Agent discovery and deployment

Spatial-dependent deployment of agents. We will now explain how the framework deploys agents at suitable agent hosts. When an LIS detects the movement of a tag attached to a person or thing to a cell, it searches its database for agent hosts that are present in the current cell of the tag. It also selects candidate destinations from the set of agent hosts within the cell, according to their respective capabilities. The framework offers a language based on CC/PP (composite capability/preference profiles) [21]. The language is used to describe the capabilities of agent hosts and the requirements of mobile agents in an XML notation. For example, a description contains information on the following properties of a computing device: vendor and model class of the device (i.e, PC, PDA, or phone), its screen size, the number of colors, CPU, memory, input devices, secondary storage, and the presence/absence of loudspeakers. The framework also allows each agent to specify the preferable capabilities of agent hosts that it may visit as well as the minimal capabilities in a CC/PP-based notation. Each LIS is able to determine whether or not the device profile of each agent host satisfies the requirements of an agent by symbolically matching and quantitatively comparing properties.

The LIS then unicasts a navigation message to each of the agents that are bound to the tagged entities or places, where the message specifies the profiles of those agent hosts that are present in the cell and satisfy the requirements of the agent. The agents are then able to autonomously migrate to the appropriate hosts. When there are multiple candidate destinations, each of the agents that is tied to a tag must select one destination based on the profiles of the destinations. When one or more cells geographically overlap, a tag may be in multiple cells at the same time and agents tied to that tag may then receive candidate destinations from multiple LISs. However, since the message includes the network address of the LIS, the agents can explicitly ask it about the cell ranges. Our goal is to provide physical entities and places with computational functionality from locations that are near them. Therefore, if there are no appropriate agent hosts in any of the cells at which a tag is present but there are some agent hosts in other cells, the current implementation of our framework forces agents tied to the tag to move to hosts in different cells.

4.2 Mobile Agent-Based Service-Provider

The framework encapsulates application-specific services into mobile agents so that it is independent of any applications and can support multiple services. In the appendix of this paper, each mobile agent is constructed as a collection of Java objects and is equipped with the identifier of the tag to which it is attached.[1] Each is a self-contained program and is able to communicate with other agents. An agent that is attached to a user always internally maintains that user's personal information and carries all its internal information to other hosts. A mobile agent may also have one or more graphical user interfaces for interaction with its users. When such an agent moves to other hosts, it can easily adjust its windows to the new host's screen by using the compound document framework for the MobileSpaces system that was presented in our previous paper [15].

4.3 Agent Host

Each agent host must be equipped with a tag. It has two forms of functionality: one for advertising its capabilities and the other for executing and migrating mobile agents. The current implementation assumes that LISs and agent hosts can be directly connected through a wired LAN such as Ethernet or a wireless LAN such as IEEE802.11b. When a host receives a query message with the identifier of a newly arriving tag from an LIS, it replies with one of the following three responses: (i) if the identifier in the message is identical to the identifier of the tag to which it is attached, it returns profile information on its capabilities to the LIS; (ii) if one of the agents running on it is tied to the tag, it returns its network address and the requirements of the agent; and (iii) if neither of the above cases applies, it ignores the message.

The current implementation of this framework is based on a Java-based mobile agent system called MobileSpaces [14].[2] Each MobileSpaces runtime system is built on the

[1] Appendix describes programming interfaces of agents.

[2] The framework itself is independent of the MobileSpaces mobile agent system and can thus work with other Java-based mobile agent systems.

Java virtual machine, which conceals differences between the platform architecture of the source and destination hosts, such as the operating system and hardware. Each of the runtime systems moves agents to other agent hosts over a TCP/IP connection. The runtime system governs all the agents inside it and maintains the life-cycle state of each agent. When the life-cycle state of an agent changes, e.g., when it is created, terminates, or migrates to another host, the runtime system issues specific events to the agent. This is because the agent may have to acquire various resources or release them, such as files, windows, or sockets, which it had previously captured. When a notification on the presence or absence of a tag is received from a LIS, the runtime system dispatches specific events to the agents that are tied to that tag and these run inside it.

5 Implementation

The framework presented in this paper was implemented in Sun's Java Developer Kit, version 1.1 or later versions, including Personal Java. This section discusses some features of the current implementation.

5.1 Management of Locating Systems

The current implementation supports four commercial RFID systems: RF Code's Spider system, Alien Technology's 915Mhz RFID-tag system, Philips' I-Code system, and Hitachi's mu-chip system. The first system provides active RF-tags, which periodically emit an RF-beacon that conveys their unique identifier (every second) via 305 MHz-radio pulse. The system allows us to explicitly control the omnidirectional range of each of the RF readers to read tags within a range of 1 to 20 meters. The Alien Technology system provides passive RFID-tags and its readers periodically scan for present tags within a range of 3 meters by sending a short 915 MHz-RF pulse and waiting for answers from the tags. The Philips and Hitachi RFID systems are passive RFID tag systems that can sense the presence of tags within a range of a few centimeters. Although there are many differences between the four, the framework abstracts these.

5.2 Performance Evaluation

Although the current implementation of the framework was not built for performance we measured the cost of migrating a 3-Kbytes agent (zip-compressed) from a source host to the destination host recommended by the LIS. This experiment was conducted with two LISs and two agent hosts, each of which was running on one of four computers (Pentium III-1GHz with Windows 2000 and JDK 1.4), which were directly connected via an IEEE802.11b wireless network. The latency of an agent's migration to the destination after the LIS had detected the presence of the agent's tag was 410 msec and the cost o agent migration between two hosts over a TCP connection was 42 msec. The latency included the cost of the following processes: UDP-multicasting of the tags' identifier from the LIS to the source host, TCP-transmission of the agent's requirements from th source host to the LIS, TCP-transmission of a candidate destination from the LIS t the source host, marshaling the agent, migrating the agent from the source host to the destination host, unmarshaling the agent, and security verification. We believe that this latency is acceptable for a location-aware system used in a room or building.

5.3 Security and Privacy

Security is essential in mobile agent computing. The framework can be built on many Java-based mobile agent systems with the Java virtual machine. Therefore, it can directly use the security mechanism of the underlying mobile agent system. The Java virtual machine can explicitly restrict agents so that they can only access specified resources to protect hosts from malicious agents. To protect against the passing of malicious agents between agent hosts, the MobileSpaces system supports a Kerberos-based authentication mechanism for agent migration. It authenticates users without exposing their passwords on the network and generates secret encryption keys that can selectively be shared between mutually suspicious parties.

The framework only maintains per-user profile information within those agents that are bound to the user. It promotes the movement of such agents to appropriate hosts near the user in response to his/her movement. Since agents carry their users' profile information within them, they must protect such private information while they are moving over a network.[3] The MobileSpaces system can transform agents into an encrypted form before migrating them over the network and decrypt them after they arrive at their destinations. Moreover, since each mobile agent is just a programmable entity, it can explicitly encrypt its particular inner fields and migrate itself with the fields along with its own cryptographic procedure, except for its secret keys.

6 Applications

This section presents several typical location-based and personalized services that were developed through the framework. Note that these services can be executed at the same time, since the framework itself is independent of any application-specific services and each service is implemented within mobile agents.

6.1 Location-Bound Universal Remote Controller

The first example corresponds to Figure 1 (a) and allows us to use a PDA to remotely control nearby electric lights in a room. Each light was equipped with a tag and was within the range covered by an RFID reader in the room. We controlled power outlets for lights through a commercial protocol called X10. In both approaches described here, the lights were controlled by switching their power sources on or off according to the X10 protocol. In this system, place-bound controller agents, which can communicate with X10-base servers to switch lights on or off, are attached to locations with room lights. Each user has a tagged PDA, which supports the agent host with WindowsCE and

[3] The framework itself cannot protect agents from malicious hosts, because this problem is beyond the scope of this paper.

wireless LAN interface. When a user with a PDA visits a cell that contains a light, the framework moves a controller agent to the agent host of the visiting PDA. The agent, now running on the PDA, displays a graphical user interface to control the light. When the user leaves that location, the agent automatically closes its user interface and returns to its home host.

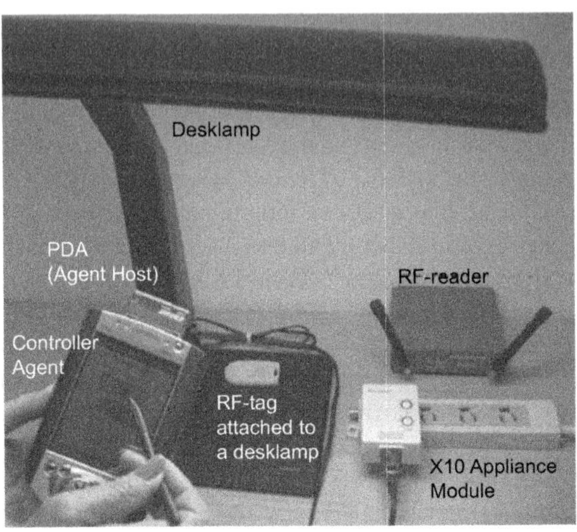

Fig. 4. Controlling desk lamp from PDA

6.2 Mobile Personal Assistance

The second example corresponds to Figure 1 (b) and offers a user assistant agent that follows its user and maintains profile information about him/her inside itself, so that he/she can always assist the agent in a personalized manner anywhere. Suppose that a user has a 915MHz-RFID tag and is moving on front of a restaurant, which offers an RFID reader and an agent host with a touch-screen. When the tagged user enters inside the coverage area of the reader, the framework enables his/her assistant agents to move to the agent host near his/her current location. After arriving at the host, the agent accesses a database provided in the restaurant to obtain a menu from the restaurant. [4] It then selects appropriate meal candidates from the menu according to his/her profile information such as favorite foods and recent experiences, stored inside it. It next displays only the list of selected meals on the screen of its current agent host in a personalized manner for him/her. Figure 5 shows that a user's assistant agent runs on the agent host of the restaurant and seamlessly embeds a list of pictures, names, and prices of selected meal candidates with buttons for ordering them into its graphical user interface. Since a mobile agent is a program entity, we can easily define a more intelligent assistant agent.

[4] The current implementation of the database maintains some information about each available food, such as name and price, in an XML-based entry.

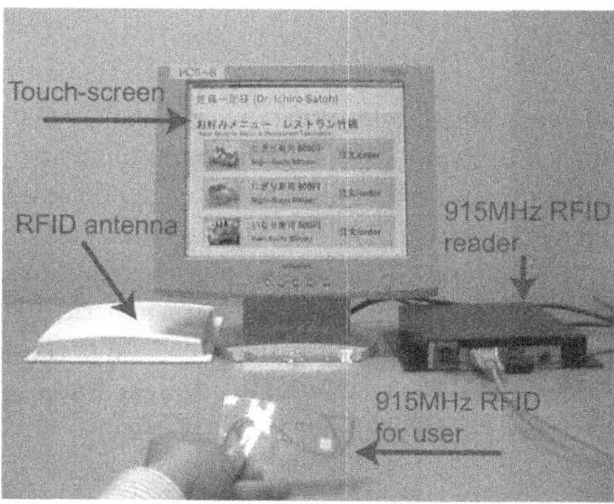

Fig. 5. Screenshot of follow-me user assistant agent for selecting its user's favorite sushi from the menu database of a restaurant that the user is in front of

6.3 User Navigation System

We developed a user navigation system that assists visitors to a building. Several researchers have reported on other similar systems [3,5]. In our system, tags are distributed to several places within a building, such as its ceilings, floors, and walls. As we can see from Figure 1 (c), each visitor carries a wireless-LAN enabled tablet PC, which is equipped with an RFID reader to detect tags, and includes an LIS and an agent host. The system initially deploys place-bound agents to invisible computers within the building. When a tagged position is located by a cell of the moving RFID reader, the LIS running on the visitor's tablet PC detects the presence of the tag. The LIS detects the place-bound agent that is tied to the tag. It then instructs the agent to migrate to its agent host and provide the agent's location-dependent services at the host. The system enables more than one agent tied to a place to move to the table PC. The agents then return to their home computers and other agents, which are tied to another place, may move to the tablet PC. Figure 6 shows a place-bound agent to display a map of its surrounding area on the screen of a tablet PC.

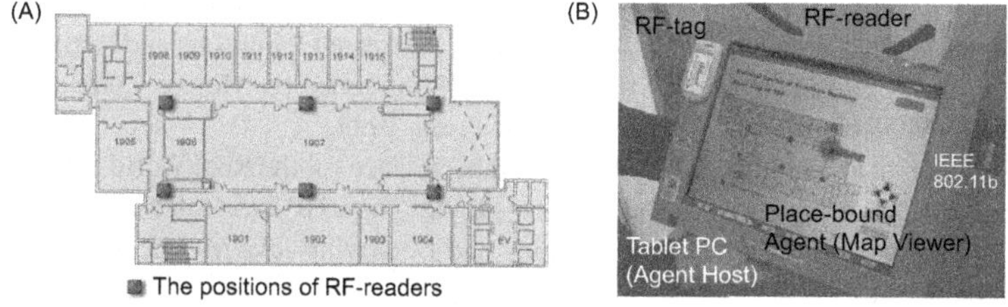

Fig. 6. (A) Positions of RF-tags in floor (B) and screen-shot of map-viewer agent running on table PC

7 Conclusion

We presented a framework for the development and management of location-aware applications in mobile and ubiquitous computing environments. The framework provides people, places, and things with mobile agents to support and annotate them. Using location-tracking systems, the framework can migrate mobile agents to stationary or mobile computers near the locations of the people, places, and things to which the agents are attached. The framework is decentralized and it is a generic platform independent of any higher-level applications and locating systems and supports stationary and mobile computing devices in a unified manner. We also designed and implemented a prototype system of the framework and demonstrated its effectiveness in several practical applications.

However, there are further issues that need to be resolved. Since the framework presented is general-purpose, we would need to apply it to specific applications in future work, as well as the three applications presented in this paper. The location model of the framework was designed for operating real location-sensing systems in ubiquitous computing environments. We plan to design a more elegant and flexible world model that represents the locations of people, things, and places in the real world by incorporating existing spatial database technologies.

References

1. Auto-ID center: http://www.autoidcenter.org/main.asp
2. B. L. Brumitt, B. Meyers, J. Krumm, A. Kern, S. Shafer: EasyLiving: Technologies for Intelligent Environments, Proceedings of International Symposium on Handheld and Ubiquitous Computing, pp. 12–27, 2000.
3. K. Cheverst, N. Davis, K. Mitchell, and A. Friday: Experiences of Developing and Deploying a Context-Aware Tourist Guide: The GUIDE Project, Proceedings of Conference on Mobile Computing and Networking (MOBICOM'2000), pp. 20–31, ACM Press, 2000.
4. A. Harter, A. Hopper, P. Steggeles, A. Ward, and P. Webster: The Anatomy of a Context-Aware Application, Proceedings of Conference on Mobile Computing and Networking (MOBICOM'99), pp. 59–68, ACM Press, 1999.
5. F. Hohl, U. Kubach, A. Leonhardi, K. Rothermel, and M. Schwehm: Next Century Challenges: Nexus – An Open Global Infrastructure for Spatial-Aware Applications, Proceedings of Conference on Mobile Computing and Networking (MOBICOM'99), pp. 249–255, ACM Press, 1999).
6. K. Kangas and J. Roning: Using Code Mobility to Create Ubiquitous and Active Augmented Reality in Mobile Computing, Proceedings of Conference on Mobile Computing and Networking (MOBICOM'99), pp. 48–58, ACM Press, 1999.
7. T. Kindberg, et al: People, Places, Things: Web Presence for the Real World, Technical Report HPL-2000-16, Internet and Mobile Systems Laboratory, HP Laboratories, 2000.
8. B. D. Lange and M. Oshima: Programming and Deploying Java Mobile Agents with Aglets, Addison-Wesley, 1998.
9. U. Leonhardt, and J. Magee: Towards a General Location Service for Mobile Environments, Proceedings of IEEE Workshop on Services in Distributed and Networked Environments, pp. 43–50, IEEE Computer Society, 1996.

10. D. Lopez de Ipina and S. Lo: LocALE: a Location-Aware Lifecycle Environment for Ubiquitous Computing, Proceedings of Conference on Information Networking (ICOIN-15), IEEE Computer Society, 2001.
11. N. Minar, M. Gray, O. Roup, R. Krikorian, and P. Maes: Hive: Distributed agents for networking things, Proceedings of Symposium on Agent Systems and Applications / Symposium on Mobile Agents (ASA/MA'99), IEEE Computer Society, 2000.
12. T. Richardson, Q, Stafford-Fraser, K. Wood, A. Hopper: Virtual Network Computing, IEEE Internet Computing, Vol. 2, No. 1, 1998.
13. K. Romer, T. Schoch, F. Mattern, and T. Dubendorfer: Smart Identification Frameworks for Ubiquitous Computing Applications, IEEE International Conference on Pervasive Computing and Communications (PerCom'03), pp.253–262, IEEE Computer Society, March 2003.
14. I. Satoh: MobileSpaces: A Framework for Building Adaptive Distributed Applications Using a Hierarchical Mobile Agent System, Proceedings of International Conference on Distributed Computing Systems (ICDCS'2000), pp. 161–168, IEEE Computer Society, 2000.
15. I. Satoh: MobiDoc: A Framework for Building Mobile Compound Documents from Hierarchical Mobile Agents, Proceedings of Symposium on Agent Systems and Applications / Symposium on Mobile Agents (ASA/MA'2000), LNCS, Vol. 1882, pp. 113–125, Springer, September 2000.
16. I. Satoh: Flying Emulator: Rapid Building and Testing of Networked Applications for Mobile Computers, Proceedings of International Conference on Mobile Agents (MA'01), LNCS, Vol. 2240, pp. 103–118, Springer, December 2001.
17. I. Satoh: Physical Mobility and Logical Mobility in Ubiquitous Computing Environments, Proceedings of International Conference on Mobile Agents (MA'02), LNCS, Vol. 2535, pp. 186–202, Springer, October 2002.
18. I. Satoh: Linking Physical Worlds to Logical Worlds with Mobile Agents, Proceedings of International Conference on Mobile Data Management (MDM 2004), IEEE Computer Society, January 2004.
19. R. Want, A. Hopper, A. Falcao, and J. Gibbons: The Active Badge Location System, ACM Transactions on Information Systems, vol.10, no.1, pp. 91–102 ACM Press, 1992.
20. M. Weiser: The Computer for the 21st Century, Scientific American, pp. 94–104, September, 1991.
21. World Wide Web Consortium (W3C): Composite Capability/Preference Profiles (CC/PP), http://www.w3.org/TR/NOTE-CCPP, 1999.

Appendix: Service Provider Programs

This section explains the programming interface for service providers, which are implemented as mobile agents. Every agent program must be an instance of a subclass of the abstract class `TaggedAgent` as follows:

```
class TaggedAgent extends Agent implements Serializable {
  void go(URL url) throws NoSuchHostException { ... }
  void duplicate() throws IllegalAccessException { ... }
  void destroy() { ... }
  void setTagIdentifier(TagIdentifier tid) { ... }
  void setAgentProfile(AgentProfile apf) { ... }
  URL getCurrentHost() { ... }
  boolean isConformableHost(HostProfile hfs) { ... }
  CellProfile getCellProfile(CellIdentifier cid)
    throws NoSuchCellException { ... }
  ....
}
```

Let us explain some of the methods defined in the `TaggedAgent` class. An agent executes the `go(URL url)` method to move to the destination host specified as the `url` by its runtime system. The `duplicate()` method creates a copy of the agent, including its code and instance variables. The `setTagIdentifier` method ties the agent to the identity of the tag specified as `tid`. Each agent can specify a requirement that its destination hosts must satisfy by invoking the `setAgentProfile()` method, with the requirement specified as `apf`. The class has a service method named `isConformableHost()`, which the agent uses to decide whether or not the capabilities of the agent hosts specified as an instance of the `HostProfile` class satisfy the requirements of the agent. Also, the `getCellProfile()` method allows an agent to investigate the measurable range and types of RFID readers specified as `cid`.[5]

Each agent can subscribe to the types of events they are interested in and have more than one listener object that implements a specific listener interface to hook certain events. The following program is the definition of a lister object for receiving events issued before or after changes in its life-cycle state or movements of its tag.

```
interface TaggedAgentListener extends AgentEventListener {
  // invoked after creation at url
  void agentCreated(URL url);
  // invoked before termination
  void agentDestroying();
  // invoked before migrating to dst
  void agentDispatching(URL dst);
  // invoked after arrived at dst
  void agentArrived(URL dst);
  // invoked after the tag arrived at another cell
  void tagArrived(HostProfile[] apfs, CellIdentifier cid);
  // invoked after the tag left rom the current cell
  void tagLeft(CellIdentifier cid);
  // invoked after an agent host arrived at the current cell
  void hostArrived(AgentProfile apfs, CellIdentifier cid);
  ....
}
```

The above interface specifies the fundamental methods that are invoked by the runtime system when agents are created, destroyed, or migrate to another agent host. If a tagged entity or place is detected for the first time, the agent associated with that object or place has to be instantiated and then its `agentCreated()` method is invoked. Also, the `tagArrived()` callback method is invoked after the tag to which the agent is bound has entered another cell, to obtain the device profiles of agent hosts that are present in the new cell. The `tagLeft()` method is invoked after the tag is no longer in a cell for a specified period of time. The `agentDispatching()` method is invoked before the agent migrates to another host and the `agentArrived()` method is invoked after the agent arrives at the destination.

[5] The identifier of each RFID reader can be represented in a string format so that the framework can easily manage various RFID systems even when the identifiers of readers in these systems are different.

Service Oriented Internet*

Jaideep Chandrashekar[1], Zhi-Li Zhang[1], Zhenhai Duan[1], and Y. Thomas Hou[2]

[1] University of Minnesota, Minneapolis, MN 55455, USA,
{jaideepc,zhzhang,duan}@cs.umn.edu
[2] Virginia Tech, Blacksburg, VA 24061, USA,
thou@vt.edu

Abstract. Effective service delivery capabilities are critical to the transformation of the Internet into a viable commercial infrastructure. At the present time, the architecture of the Internet is inadequately equipped to provide these capabilities. Traditionally, overlay networks have been proposed as a means of providing rich functionality at the upper layers. However, they suffer from their own drawbacks and do not constitute a perfect solution. In this paper, we propose a novel, overlay based *Service Oriented Internet* architecture that is meant to serve as a *flexible, unifying and scalable* platform for delivering services over the Internet. As part of this architecture, we introduce a new two-level addressing scheme and an associated *service layer.* We also describe the functionality of the new network elements that are introduced, namely *service gateway* and *service point-of-presence*, and subsequently discuss algorithms that are responsible for distributing *service reachability* across the overlay framework. We also present a few examples of application services that benefit significantly when deployed on our architecture.

1 Introduction

Over the last decade, the unanticipated popularity of applications such as the World Wide Web and E-mail has transformed the Internet into the *de facto* global information infrastructure that underlies much of today's commercial, social and cultural activities. People rely on the Internet for a variety of services essential to their daily lives, ranging from communications and information access to e-commerce and entertainment. Because of this, many new requirements of Internet services are more critical and urgent than ever before. These requirements include service *availability* and *reliability* (i.e., "always-on" services), *quality* and *security.* In spite of this, the Internet is still essentially a "best-effort" entity with end-to-end connectivity being its only service offering. In its present form, this architecture cannot adequately support the requirements of emerging services. Various *ad-hoc* mechanisms have been proposed and deployed to address these different issues. Examples include the deployment of CDNs (content distribution networks) and the widespread use of Network Address Translation. However, it is important to realize

* This work was supported in part by the National Science Foundation under the grants ANI-0073819, ITR-0085824, and CAREER Award NCR-9734428. Any opinions, findings, and conclusions or recommendations expressed in this paper are those of the authors and do not necessarily reflect the views of the National Science Foundation

M.E. Orlowska et al. (Eds.): ICSOC 2003, LNCS 2910, pp. 543–558, 2003.

that *ad-hoc* solutions are by nature temporary short term measures – they do not address the underlying problem, and in some instances simply shift the bottlenecks elsewhere.

In this paper, we describe a new architecture — the "Service Oriented Internet" or SOI, which can be described as an *efficient, generic and unifying framework* for enabling the deployment of new services. In the design of the SOI architecture, we introduce three key abstractions: (1) the notion of a *service cloud*, which is a collection of service entities that are deployed by a service provider. The simplest example would be a cooperating hierarchy of web proxy servers; (2) a new *two-level, location-independent* addressing scheme; and (3) a new abstract service layer that is used for forwarding packets to the appropriate service endpoints.

The main contributions of this paper are two-fold. We first present a critique of the current Internet architecture, highlighting obstacles in supporting future requirements of applications and services. Secondly, we outline an architectural framework that addresses these obstacles. We would like to think of our architecture as an evolutionary guideline that would enable the Internet to become a viable platform for the delivery of services. Specifically, the proposed architecture provides support for newer applications with service requirements beyond what can be currently realized. The architecture also introduces an economic framework which could be used to provide QoS support for applications that require it.

2 Service Oriented Internet

In recent times, *overlay networks* have emerged as an effective way to implement functionality which otherwise would require significant change at the IP layer. Such networks are appealing because they can be realized with very little infrastructure overhead. A set of end-nodes can decide to form an overlay, and cooperatively construct it, without any additional support from the network or the ISP's. However, this transparency comes at some cost. First, by being completely *oblivious* of the underlying network layer, there are certain inefficiencies that cannot be avoided — very often, an *overlay neighbor* could actually be very far away in terms of the IP level network. Secondly, it might be that a particular overlay provides some service that is mandated on a well behaved underlying network. In the present case, ISP's do not differentiate between packets that will be routed to an overlay (or packets being forwarded on an overlay network) and other packets. This could be to the detriment of the application. For example, in the instance of a multicast overlay used for conferencing, it is reasonable to expect that the overall experience would be benefited by some prioritization of packets that are being exchanged on this overlay. If the packets meant for the overlay are similar to all the other transiting packets, there is no way to provide this service differentiation. Now if we can imagine a situation where the ISP was in some sense "overlay-aware" and also that packets heading to the overlay could be identified, then it might be possible to ensure that a certain degree of service differentiation is provided, leading to a better experience on the overlay. For this to happen, in a realistic setting, the ISP would need some economic incentive to actually do this. Third, if we were to imagine a number of overlay networks in operation (over the same underlying network), each of the overlays would be replicating some common functions. For example, consider a situation where overlay A provides a streaming video service and overlay B is used for multicast video conferencing. Since both overlays are dealing with real-time traffic, they probably involve some active measurement component, running independent of each other. A far more efficient architecture would decouple the active measurement component from the overlay operation and allow the different overlays to share the the measurement infrastructure. A similar idea has been discussed in [1], where the authors advocate a *routing underlay* that takes over the common tasks.

The primary argument that we make through our architecture is that services can be deployed as overlays, but to address the performance limitations of the overlays and to ensure support for the requirements of newer applications, we also need an underlying infrastructure which addresses the shortcomings listed above.

In the rest of the paper, we focus on the details of the infrastructure and how it can be realized. To make the description complete, we also use examples to show how specific services can be realized and supported over the infrastructure.

2.1 Overview

In our architecture, we distinguish between the *data transport networks*, which roughly correspond to the existing autonomous systems (and the IP networks), and the *service overlay networks* (SON), each of which can be thought of as providing a well defined service. The role of the data transport networks is to provide bit-pipes as a service to the service overlay networks.

The service networks, on the other hand, are designed to provide specific value-added services to subscribers. These networks are operated by service providers and can be visualized as clouds which interface at multiple points with the data networks. Client requests are routed over the data network to the nearest (or most appropriate) point of entry into a particular service cloud. The client's request is then served from some host inside the cloud. This high level description is depicted in Figure 1, with the data networks shown towards the bottom of the figure and the service clouds near the top.

The *logical decoupling* between the data network domains and the service networks allows the independent evolution of each, allowing for flexible deployment of future Internet services while still supporting existing services. This logical independence is an artifact of completely separating the addressing, routing and forwarding mechanisms in the two realms. A service cloud could implement each of the mechanisms independently, as best suits its needs. There are three elements that are key to this separation, namely: a new *naming and addressing* scheme that is a significant departure from the existing IP addressing scheme, *service gateways (SG)*, and *service points-of-presence (S-PoP)*. Each of these will be described in this section.

2.2 Key Abstractions

The SOI architecture is built on top of the existing IP infrastructure, and provides *a common platform* for flexibly deploying new Internet services and effectively supporting their diverse requirements. The architecture is based on three key abstractions, as follows.

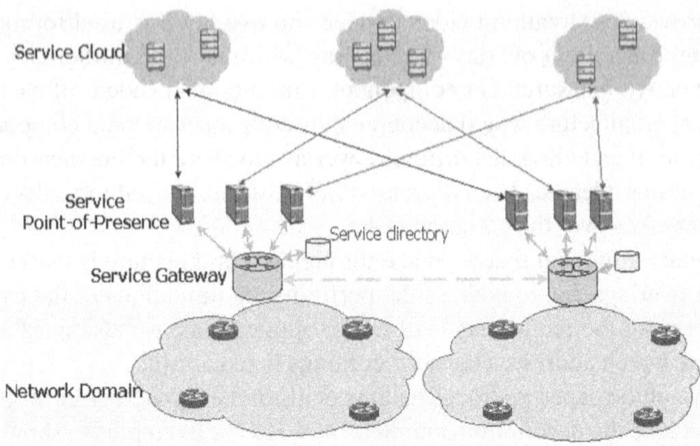

Fig. 1. Illustration of the SOI architecture.

Service Cloud abstraction: A service cloud is a collection of service entities (e.g., servers, proxies, caches and content switches) that are deployed over the Internet (typically at the network edges) to collectively and collaboratively provide a set of application/information services to users. It is a "virtual service overlay network" that is commonly owned and managed by a single provider or a consortium of application service providers, and it relies on the underlying IP data network domains for data delivery across the Internet[1]. Each service cloud has one or more points interfacing with the Internet, referred to as the *service points-of-presence* (S-PoPs). Objects enter or exit a service cloud *only* via its S-PoPs.

Service-oriented addressing scheme: The central idea of the SOI architecture is a new *two-level* addressing scheme that provides *location-independent* identification of service clouds and objects within these clouds. Each service cloud is uniquely identified by a fixed-length *service id* (**sid**); and an object within a service cloud is specified by a (generally variable-length) *object id* (**oid**). The syntax and semantics of **sid** is *globally defined* and *centrally administered*, just like today's IP addresses (or rather network prefixes); whereas the syntax and semantics of **oid** are defined by each individual service cloud, and thus are *service-specific*. Moreover, they are never interpreted outside the service cloud.

Service (routing/delivery) layer: Underlying the SOI architecture is a new *service layer* that resides above the IP network layer. Corresponding to the two-level $\langle$**sid**, **oid**$\rangle$ addressing scheme, the service layer comprises two new *network elements* with distinct functions: *service gateways* (SGs) and *service points-of-presence* (S-PoPs). SGs can be viewed as extensions of the underlying network domains who own and manage them, and are typically deployed at the edge of a network domain. They examine only the **sid** part of the two-level address and are responsible for routing and service delivery across

[1] Note that the separation between data transport domains and service clouds is purely logical. It may well be that the nodes in the service cloud use the IP networks to move data between them.

network domains. S-PoPs are the *interface* points of a service cloud with the network domains, and are thus logically a part of the service cloud (and hence are **oid**-aware). They are responsible for delivering objects within a service cloud. SGs and S-PoPs work together to support flexible end to end delivery.

All data destined for a service cloud passes through a particular service gateway, which is owned and managed by the network domain. This provides a way for the network domain to accurately identify and track traffic meant for the overlay networks. Also, since each service cloud has a distinct identifier, it is possible for a service gateway to perform service differentiation. This provides a framework in which economic incentives can be applied — and is one of the key features of our architecture. A concrete example of how this can be used is presented in Section 4.3.

3 SOI Architecture

In this section, we present the key components of the proposed SOI architecture, describe their basic operations and run through a typical transaction.

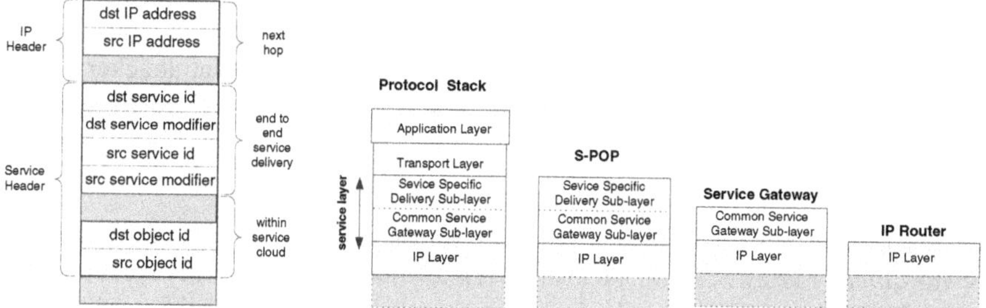

Fig. 2. Service object header format.

Fig. 3. Service layer and the SOI protocol stack.

3.1 Addressing and Name Resolution

The name resolution should return a two level address corresponding to the $\langle \mathbf{sid}, \mathbf{oid} \rangle$ addressing scheme. One of the key features of our architecture is that the resolution separates these two address components. At a very high level, we could say that the **sid** mapping is performed external to the service cloud, while the **oid** mapping is performed inside the cloud. The advantages of this should become clear shortly.

Under the proposed SOI architecture, each application/information service provider who wants to deploy services over the Internet is assigned a single fixed-length (32 bit) service id, which is administered by a central authority (just like IP addresses). This is a departure from the IP addressing scheme, where a "cloud" (network domain) is assigned a contiguous range of addresses (address block or network prefix). Each service cloud can be *roughly* thought of as corresponding to an organization currently having a second tier (e.g., yahoo.com, msn.com, real.com) or third tier (e.g., shop.msn.com, nu.ac.cn) domain name[2]. Such domain names will be retained in our SOI architecture as the names of service clouds, and are referred to as *service names*. To resolve the service name of a service cloud to its assigned **sid**, we can reuse the current DNS infrastructure (extending it so that names resolve to **sid**'s), or build a similar *service name resolution* system. The specific details of the service name resolution are out of the scope of this paper. It suffices to say that there are a number of existing approaches that can be readily adapted for our purpose. It is important to note that the mappings can be cached locally (with a reasonable sized cache), since the number of service names is significantly smaller than the number of domain names in the current DNS system, and service-name-to-**sid** mappings are essentially *static*. Hence, under the SOI architecture, service name resolution can be done with very little overhead (on the shared infrastructure).

In contrast to the **sid** space, the **oid** space is defined by each individual service cloud, with its own syntax and semantics. This gives each service cloud the maximum flexibility and efficiency for defining its own *object naming and addressing* system to meet its business needs. It also off-loads many service-specific functions (e.g., object resolution, internal routing, load balancing, etc.) to individual service clouds. This mechanism promotes a socially optimal solution. Providers that want more complicated mechanisms to perform the name resolution are forced to hide the complexity inside the service clouds. In addition, hiding the syntax and semantics of a service cloud's **oid** space from outsiders makes it more secure. This makes it very difficult for an attacker to lanch a DoS attack targeting a particular server, since the *corresponding* **oid** *can be dynamically re-mapped.*

Service Layer: For convenience, we refer to a service-layer protocol data unit as a *service object*. Figure 2 shows an abstract representation of a service object header. The header is partitioned into two logical sections, the **sid** part and **oid** part. Associated with both destination **sid** (**dst sid**) and source **sid** (**src sid**) is an additional 32-bit *service modifier*, which is defined by a service cloud to influence the forwarding of service objects. The service modifier contains two types of information: *S-PoP attribute* and *service attribute* (see Figure 8 for an example). The S-PoP attribute describes the properties of S-PoPs, and in general contains two sub-fields, an *S-PoP level* and an *S-PoP id*. For example, using S-PoP attributes, a service cloud can organize its S-PoPs in a certain hierarchy to best meet its service delivery needs[3]. The service attributes are used to indicate a preference for different service classes, next hops, etc. Multiple service attribute *sub-fields* can be defined as appropriate. One possible use of these attributes is explained in Section 4.

When a service object is generated, both the **sid** and **oid** parts of the header are filled *appropriately* by an application program (e.g., a browser). However, to ensure security we require that *the originating service cloud must verify the source* **sid** *of the object*

[2] This is not mandated by our architecture, and is just a suggestion that reflects the belief that most current service providers fall into these categories.

[3] It must be pointed out that this is but one possible interpretation. Since the SG does not need to understand the exact semantics of the modifiers, the service cloud can define them as appropriate.

before it passes outside the service cloud. In fact, we can even allow for in-flight **sid** resolution, i.e. the end-host sends a service object to the service gateway, the service gateway initiates the service name resolution, fills in the **sid** appropriately, and forwards the packet to the corresponding next-hop. These mechanisms enforce ingress filtering [2], and prevent address spoofing.

Figure 3 shows the relative position of the *service layer* in the protocol stack. Also shown in the figure are the layers of the stack that are interpreted by the different entities along the path. This should serve to clarify that the service layer lies above the IP layer and is completely independent of it.

The service layer consists of two sub-layers: the *common service gateway* layer where only **sid**'s are used to determine how to forward objects among service clouds; and the *service-specific delivery* layer where **oid**'s are used to decide how objects are delivered within a service cloud.

Service Gateway: The *data plane* function of an SG is to forward a service object to an appropriate *next-hop* on the path to the destined service cloud (this could either be an adjacent S-PoP, or another SG), using the **dst sid** (or both **dst sid** and **src sid**) and the associated service modifier(s). For this purpose, each SG maintains a *service routing* table (similar to an IP routing table), which is built by running the service gateway routing protocol (SGRP), the control plane function of an SG. The service routing table contains mappings from a **dst sid** (and, if specified, an associated service modifier) to a next-hop SG/S-PoP (specified by IP address). From an infrastructure point of view, we expect the SGs to be deployed by the Autonomous Systems.

Service Point-of-Presence: An S-PoP plays two major roles: 1) it cooperates with SGs to route and forward service objects to/from the service cloud it proxies for; and 2) it cooperates with other S-PoPs in the service cloud to route and forward a service object within the service cloud. The latter role is determined by the *service-specific* routing protocol and forwarding mechanisms employed by the service cloud. The internal operation of the service cloud will not be addressed here, but a brief discussion of some of the existing possibilities are listed in Section 5.

To begin receiving service objects from the data networks, an S-PoP participates in SGRP, advertising its presence and properties to neighboring SGs. It builds a (partial) service routing table which maps the service id space to appropriate neighboring SGs, and uses it to forward service objects out of its service cloud.

3.2 Service Gateway Routing Protocol

This protocol is mainly responsible for constructing the forwarding tables on all of the Service Gateways. At a very high level, SGRP involves two distinct functions, each of which is described in turn. The first component involves the individual *S-PoPs* registering themselves with the local *SG*. This has the effect of making them eligible to receive traffic for the cloud they represent. The second component, which is somewhat similar to the BGP protocol, distributes this reachability information to all the other *SGs*.

S-PoP registration and advertisement: When a new S-PoP of a service cloud is deployed in the Internet, it must announce its availability to the rest of world. This is done by the S-PoP advertising its presence to and registering itself with the SGs it is (logically) adjacent to[4]. In the registration process, the S-PoP sends the nearby SGs the **sid** of the service cloud it represents and *a set of service modifiers* it supports.

The set of service modifiers essentially describes the capabilities of the S-PoP and tells the SGs exactly what kind of traffic it can handle (as a subset of the traffic that is destined for its service cloud)[5]. Only service objects with a service modifier matching one of the service modifiers advertised should be forwarded to the S-PoP. A *null* set means that the S-PoP can handle all traffic destined to its service cloud.One operational possibility is that the set of service modifiers is represented as an ordered list of *bit-pattern matching rules* (e.g., using regular expressions).

Note that there is *no* need for an SG to understand the syntax or semantics of the advertised service modifiers in order to perform the bit-pattern matching. This is important, since the syntax and semantics of the advertised service modifiers are defined by each individual service cloud, and thus are *service-specific*.

Propagating Service Reachability: This component of *SGRP* uses a path vector protocol model similar to that used in BGP [3]. However, we use a novel mechanism to limit *path exploration* which is the fundamental cause of the slow convergence in path vector protocols. Due to a lack of space, we are forced to make this discussion brief, so we present a very high level overview of the *Service Reachability Propogation* mechanism of *SGRP*. A more detailed account of this idea is presented in [4].

SGs perform a function similar to that of BGP routers, albeit propagating *service reachability* (as opposed to *network reachability*). Each *SG* "learns" of a number of paths from neighboring *SGs*, from which it selects a single *best path*. This best path is announced to all its neighbors (with the exception of the neighbor that the best path was learnt from). The key departure from BGP is that in our architecture, distinct *S-PoPs* could be associated with the same **sid**, with the effect that multiple *SGs* announce reachability for the same **sid**. In the following, we describe some key concepts that are central to our scheme.

First, we introduce the notion of a *fesn* (or forward edge sequence number), which is an integer value associated with an *SG-SG* edge[6] (and a specific **sid**). Consider two *SGs*, A and B, which are adjacent. Suppose that A is announcing reachability for **sid** d to *SG* B for the first time. It initializes an *fesn* that is directly associated with the neighbor B and the service identifier d. The adjective *forward* signifies that these numbers are in the context of outgoing edges (i.e. the direction that messages are sent). The value of the *fesn* is modified only by the "owner" (which in the current case is *SG* A). In particular the value of the *fesn* is incremented when the edge between two *SGs* comes back up after a failure event, or when an *SG* re-advertises reachability for a **sid** (following a previous withdrawal) — *these are the only scenarios that could cause an* fesn *to change.* Note that an *fesn* is associated with a unique *SG-SG*, and essentially tracks the status of this edge over time. The monotonicity of the *fesn* allows an SG to determine if an advertisement is *new*.

[4] By this, we mean that the two *SGs* can talk to each other directly (at a layer above the network layer.)

[5] As an example, consider a content distribution cloud; here a particular S-PoP can declare via the service modifiers, that it can handle dynamic content.

[6] To simplify the description, we assume that there is at most one *SG* within an AS.

At any *SG* (say A), given an AS path P and a neighboring *SG* node, B, we associate with it a *fesnList*, which is the ordered list of *fesn*'s corresponding to *SG-SG* edges along the path from B to the destination. Note that for a given AS Path, the *fesnList* is unique. To make the distinction between a *path* and the *fesnList*, consider a simple example. Let SG A be adjacent to *SG*s B and C, to whom it is about to announce the same *selected best* path. The paths announced to B and C would be the same, but the associated *fesnList*s are distinct (since the *fesn*s that correspond to the edges $A - B$ and $A - C$ are distinct).

When an *SG* sends a service reachability announcement, it includes the **sid**, the AS Path, the associated *fesnList*, along with any service modifiers or additional attributes. If the *SG* is originating the reachability, as would happen if the **sid** was announced by a local *S-PoP*, the *fesnList* will only contain the single *fesn* (i.e. that of the outgoing edge.) On the other hand, if the announcement is being forwarded, i.e. the reachability was learnt from another *SG*, then the *fesn* (corresponding to the recipient of the announcement) is appended to the *fesnList* before being sent.

In the event that the edge between *SGs* A and B fails, or if A decides to stop accepting traffic from B for a **sid** d, then A generates a withdrawal message and sends it to B. The contents of this message include the **sid** being withdrawn, the path being withdrawn, and the *fesnList* associated with this path.

All service announcements and withdrawals carry the path being announced (or withdrawn) along with the associated *fesnList*. This is in contrast with the behavior in BGP, where withdrawal messages do not carry any path information.

The *fesnList* is used for two different purposes. First, it allows an *SG* to determine whether a message received corresponds to new information. By the monotonicity of the individual *fesn*s, only repair (or re-advertisement) events would cause the *fesnList* to change. Thus, an *SG* only needs to process the first message received with a different *fesnList* (from the one that it already knows about). Secondly, it allows an *SG* to correctly determine which paths to invalidate upon receiving a withdrawal. The *fesnList* for any two *SG* level paths are distinct even though the AS level paths might be the same. Thus, upon receiving a withdrawal, an *SG* can correctly invalidate *all paths* that it knows about which contain (as a prefix) the withdrawn path. This eliminates the problem of *path exploration* which causes the slow convergence in traditional path vector protocols.

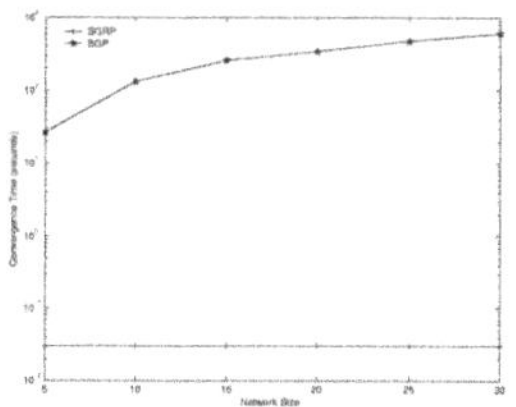

Fig. 4. Time complexity for Clique topologies

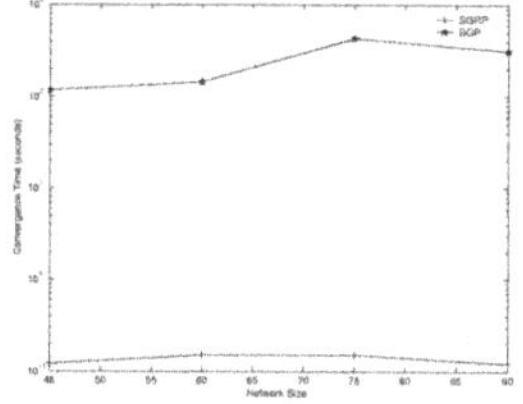

Fig. 5. Time Complexity for Power Law Random Graphs

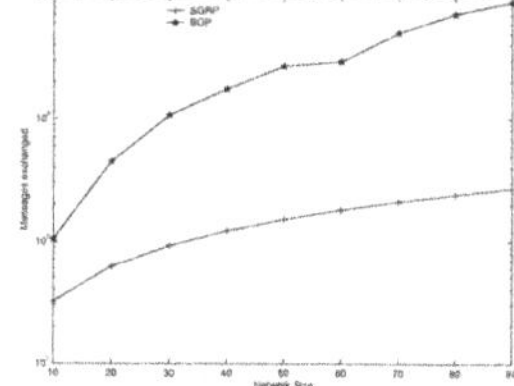

Fig. 6. Communication complexity for Random Network

When a withdrawal is received at *SG B* that causes *B*s *preferred* path to change, the (same) withdrawal is sent along with the announcement of the new path *in a single message*. Correspondingly, at the receiving node, the advertisement for a new path could have an attached withdrawal. In such a case, the withdrawal is processed first and subsequently the announced path is included in the path-set. On the other hand, if the received withdrawal causes all the available paths to be invalidated, indicating that there is no path to the destination, the withdrawal is propagated immediately. However, suppose only an announcement is received (without an accompanying withdrawal). Then the newly received path is included in the pathset and the best path recomputed. If the best path changes, then it is subsequently announced to the neighbors (along with the associated *fesnList*). Note that this announcement is subject to the hold timer constraint used to delay advertisements. Table 1 describes the step-by-step operations that are carried out when a withdrawal (or an announcement) is received at an *SG*.

In Figures. 4,5 and 6 we show the results of some simulations, carried out using the SSFNet simulation suite, comparing the performance of BGP and SGRP. In order to these protocols, we used only a single (unique) **sid** for each node. Each topology had nodes numbered from 0 through n. A special node, d (which originated some **sid**) was attached to node 0. At some time, d was disconnected from the network and two metrics were measured — convergence time and communication complexity. Figures 4,5 plot the size of the network (clique and power law topology, respectively) against the time taken (after d is disconnected from the network) for all the nodes to converge. In Figure 6, the x axis represents the size of the network (which is a random graph), while the y axis represents the number of messages that were exchanged in the network during the period of convergence. As can be seen in all the graphs, our scheme dramatically outperforms BGP for both of these metrics, and clearly demonstrates the advantage of limiting path exploration. We also carried out simulations with different topologies and failure scenarios, which we had to omit for lack of space. These results are presented in a related paper [4].

Table 1. Service Reachability Propogation

	Service Withdrawal	Service Announcement
1	validate the *fesnList*	validate the *fesnList*
2	update the pathset by marking dependent paths invalid	if withdrawal is defined, update the pathset by marking dependent paths invalid.
3		Include P into the pathset.
4	select best path	select best path
5	if best path is empty, then send withdrawal to all neighbors. Otherwise, (if best path changed) package best path and received withdrawal and send to all the neighbors	if best path changed, package best path and received withdrawal (if any), and send to all the neighbors.

4 Examples

In this section we present three generic situations in which our architecture provides a tangible benefit. In the first example, we detail how a multimedia content delivery service would be supported in our architecture. This example demonstrates how a service cloud could, by associating some consistent semantics with the service modifiers, dictate the forwarding behavior at the Service Gateways. The second application presented is that of an integrated communications service. This examples illustrates the powerful mechanisms that can be supported inside a service cloud, without any of the complexity being visible externally. The last example presented is that of a large scale VoIP service. This was chosen to illustrate the utility of the economic framework that is enabled by our architecture, and which can be used to provide QoS support to applications that require it.

4.1 Multimedia Content Delivery

Consider a service cloud that provides multimedia content delivery services. To support its services effectively, the service cloud deploys a collection of S-PoPs organized in a 3-level hierarchy as depicted in Figure 7. At the top of the hierarchy (level 1) are central S-PoPs, which are the front-ends to replicated *central* servers with a *complete* object repository. The intermediate level (level 2) are regional S-PoPs which are the front-ends to proxy servers that have a *partially replicated* object repository. At the bottom level (level 3) are local S-PoPs which are the front-ends for *local cache* servers. The local cache servers are only deployed inside network domains with large user bases. Hence not all level-2 S-PoPs have level-3 S-PoPs attached. The service cloud uses a one-byte field to specify the S-PoP attribute (see Figure 8), of which a 2-bit sub-field indicates the S-PoP level and a 6-bit sub-field indicates the S-PoP id within a level. S-PoP level 0 and S-PoP id 0 are *default* values, which are used to represent *wild-card* matching.

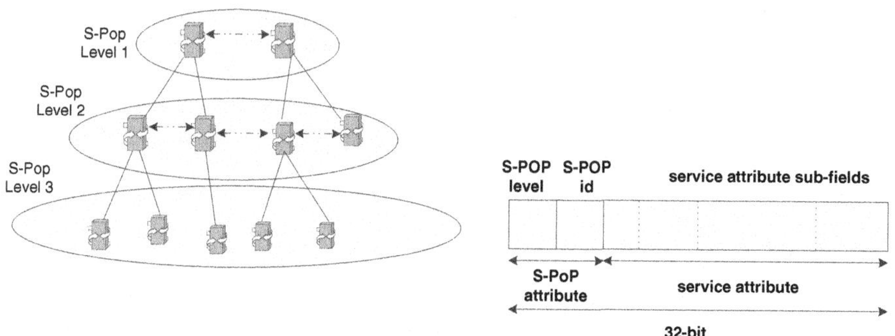

Fig. 7. A three-level S-PoP hierarchy.

Fig. 8. Service modifier.

To efficiently deliver its content using the S-PoP hierarchy, the service cloud defines a 2-bit *service attribute* sub-field to specify the *cacheability* of its content: popular (i.e., highly cacheable), normal (cacheable, the *default* value), rare (cacheable, but generally not cached), and dynamic (*not* cacheable). Popular content is preferably serviced from a local cache via a level-3 S-PoP if there is one close by, otherwise via a level-2 S-PoP. Normal content is generally serviced from a proxy server via level-2 S-PoP, while rare content from a central server via a level-1 S-PoP. Request for dynamic content is preferably processed by a proxy server via a level-2 S-PoP, which is responsible for forming the dynamic content, retrieving appropriate content from a central server if necessary. These guidelines for content delivery can be represented as a set of bit-pattern matching rules using the *S-PoP level* and the *cacheability* service attribute sub-field. *Regular expressions*, for instance, can be used for specifying such bit-pattern matching rules.

The S-PoPs register with the neighboring SGs of the underlying network domains, and advertise their presence and service capabilities (represented by a set of bit-pattern matching rules which specify the service modifiers it can handle). SGs formulate service reachability advertisements (SRAs) for the service cloud and propagate them after performing appropriate filtering and aggregation processing. From SRAs received, each SG can build corresponding entries in its service routing table. We want to emphasize that SGs do *not* need to understand the *syntax* and *semantics* of the service modifiers defined by the service clouds[7]. All that is required is *the ability to manipulate regular expressions and perform table look-ups*. This is a key feature of our SOI architecture, as it allows for simple and efficient SG implementation, while providing maximum flexibility in supporting diverse Internet services.

The cacheability service attribute of content can be embedded in an HTML (or XML) page publicized by the service cloud, and filled accordingly by a client program when a request is generated. Upon receiving a request for a popular object of the service cloud, an SG will forward it to a nearby level-3 S-PoP (a local cache), if one exists. On the other hand, requests for other content will always be forwarded to a level-2 S-PoP, or a level-1 S-PoP if there is one close by. If a request for a popular object cannot be satisfied by a local cache (i.e., a *cache miss*), the level-3 S-PoP will automatically re-direct the request to a nearby level-2 S-PoP by changing the value of the S-PoP level sub-field from 3 to 2. If a level-3 S-PoP fails, a nearby SG, upon learning of the failure, will cease forwarding requests to it, and instead will forward them to a nearby level-2 S-PoP. In case of a level-2 S-PoP failure, an SG can automatically forward requests to another level-2 or level-1 S-POP. In addition, an *overloaded* level-2 S-PoP can perform load-balancing by re-directing requests to a *light-loaded* level-2 S-PoP by specifying its S-PoP id (instead of the default value 0) in the S-PoP id sub-field.

4.2 Integrated Communications

We use this example to illustrate the advantages of the location-independent two-level addressing scheme in supporting user mobility and a variety of other value-added services such as personalized communications, anycasting and multicasting. The focus will be on the functions of S-PoPs.

Consider a service cloud offering integrated communication services to its users (subscribers of the services). It deploys a collection of S-PoPs organized in a flat, "peer-to-peer" architecture. It allows users to define a number of communication modes such

[7] In the present example, the SG is oblivious of the internal S-PoP hierarchy and content classification i.e. cacheability.

as *urgent*, *normal*, and *batch* modes. In the *urgent* mode a subscriber wants to be notified via *all possible* communication means such as cell phone, office/home phones at various locations, email and instant messaging, etc. In the normal mode, communication requests will be directed to *one of* its communication means, e.g., the one the user has turned on at a given moment, or if more than one have been turned on, the preferred one (say the cell phone.) If it is not picked up immediately, an "alert" message is generated afterwards and sent to all communication means within a pre-specified time (for example, 5 minutes). In the batch mode, communication requests are directed to the user's multimedia email-box, which the user may check at leisure.

Corresponding to these communication modes, separate user *object ids* (*oids*) will be created for each user. When logging on to the service cloud (e.g., by turning on one or more communication devices), a user registers with a nearby S-PoP that tracks and records the locations of his/her communication devices. The user can (pre-)specify the set of users he/she is willing to communicate in the different modes, making the corresponding user **oid**'s only visible to the specified users. For instance, the urgent mode is only for close family members and friends; normal mode for colleagues and acquaintances, etc. The personalized communication modes can be implemented by performing the appropriate mapping between the logical **oid** and the physical devices. For example, an S-PoP receiving an urgent call from a close family member will forward the call to the S-PoPs to which the user's communication devices are connected. The S-PoPs then direct the call to these devices, transforming the message formats if necessary, e.g., a voice call to the cell phone, an instant text message to the PDA, a voice email to the email account, etc. As the user moves around, the S-PoPs will update various mappings between the logical **oid**'s and physical devices.

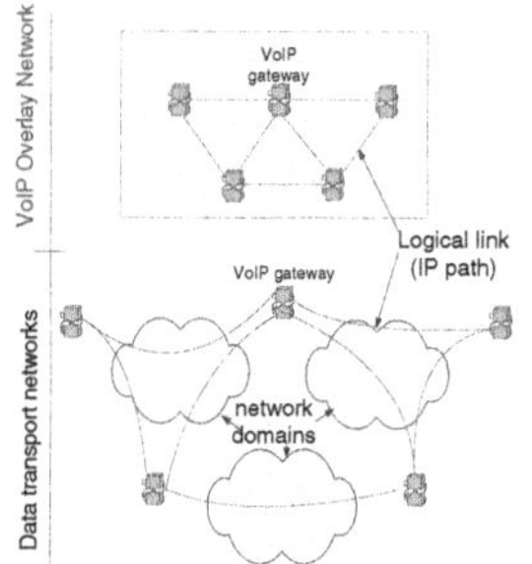

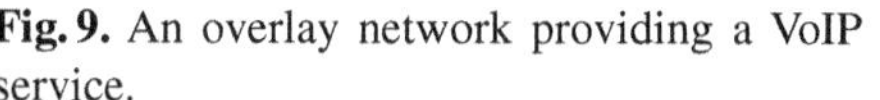
Fig. 9. An overlay network providing a VoIP service.

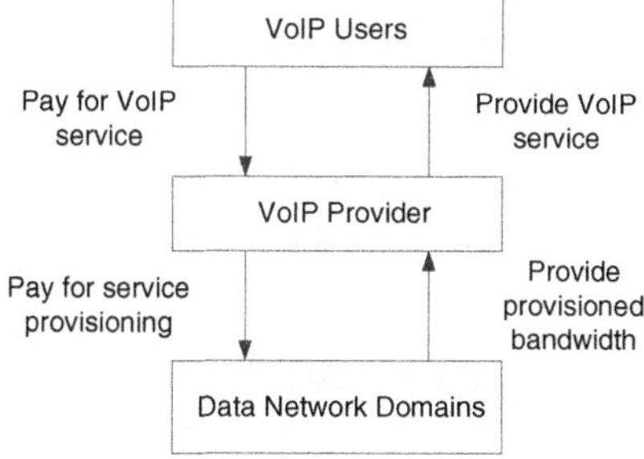

Fig. 10. Revenue flows and business relationships in the VoIP overlay network.

4.3 Voice over IP Service

This example particularly demonstrates how a service with QoS requirements can be deployed using our architecture. A provider wishing to deploy the VoIP service would first enter into agreements with the underlying data networks, and by means of SLA's or some such enforcing mechanism, obtain some network pipes between the regions where the service would be introduced. One possible service identifier space allocation could map users (or the particular device) to a unique **sid**. With the infrastructure in place, users of the service would place calls by identifying the person that will receive the call. This request is routed to the service provider, and the lookup service resolves this to a particular **sid**. Once the end points are mapped to the particular **sid**'s, the flow of packets corresponding to the call are routed to the closest S-PoP (in both directions). Once inside the service cloud, the packets are forwarded along the appropriate (pre-provisioned path) towards the S-PoP that is closest to the other end-point. A high level illustration of this is provided in Figure 9. In fact, the S-PoPs described in our architecture are very similar in functionality (in the context of a VoIP service) with the *gatekeeper* entities in the established **H.323** standard.

By means of purchasing pre-provisioned bandwidth pipes, the provider can get around the problem of transiting peering points, which have been anecdotally identified as the bottleneck areas. In the absence of the provider entering into agreements with both network domains (on two sides of a network boundary), there would have been no incentive for the network providers to provide a better service for packets being transited for the VoIP provider. [5] presents an architecture for providing Internet QoS using overlay networks, which can be used by the VoIP provider to construct the VoIP infrastructure. In fact, we argue that one of the benefits of our architecture is that it puts in place a framework over which bilateral agreements can be implemented. The economic relationships are illustrated in Figure 10.

The above examples help illustrate the *versatility* and *flexibility* afforded by our proposed SOI architecture. We also see that, with the help of the new location-independent two-level $\langle \mathbf{sid}, \mathbf{oid} \rangle$ addressing scheme as well as the SGRP protocol, this architecture provides better support for service availability, reliability and mobility. Furthermore, the SOI architecture facilitates the creation and deployment of new value-added services such as QoS-enhanced services, enabling rich business models and economic relations to be established among service clouds and network domains. Note in particular that, since service modifiers are defined by each individual service cloud, there is no need for a "global standard" such as IntServ [6] or DiffServ [7] – how the service is supported is decided by the *bilateral* service agreement between a service cloud and an underlying network domain. In addition, because of the location-independent addressing scheme, the "opaqueness" of service clouds, and the ease and efficacy of object verification and filtering based on **sid** and service modifier fields, our SOI architecture also greatly improves *security*, effectively vitiating such threats as DDoS attacks and IP spoofing.

5 Related Work

In this section, we contrast our own architecture with similar research in the area. We introduce the abstraction of a *service layer* that takes care of the service delivery from end to end. A somewhat similar abstraction has been mentioned in [8] where the authors advance the notion of a "content layer". The key idea in this work is that packets carry the resource name rather than IP address, and the corresponding forwarding is performed based on the carried name. However, given the unconstrained sizes of names, it is not realistic to think that packet forwarding will ever be based on names.

There has been much effort put into supporting more advanced service primitives. Overlay networks have been the most dominant mechanism to provide support for these services. Recent proposals advocate the use of overlays to provide an extremely diverse range of applications such as multicast [9,10], multimedia broadcast distribution [11], resilient routing [12] and content distribution. However, these proposals suffer from scalability and performance issues native to the current overlay paradigm. Our architecture provides a way to address these issues by means of a underlying substrate that would allow these applications to scale.

Within the domain of overlay networks, one of the interesting research issues has to do with locating objects in the network. Most peer to peer (*P2P*) applications use either a centralized directory, such as Napster or specify a flooding algorithm to propogate the search through the overlay (as in the Gnutella network). These approaches do not scale well with the size of the overlay, and there have been a number of recent proposals that address this. The most prominent are the algorithms based on *Distributed Hash Tables* [13,14]. Though originally intended as a way to address the scaling problems in existing *P2P* networks, they are complimentary to our architecture, since the algorithms can be used inside a service cloud to locate objects.

The idea of supporting QoS over the Internet by means of overlays is discussed in [15]. Such an idea fits very well into our framework, and suggest possible ways of deploying overlays that require QoS support such as multimedia delivery, VoIP etc.

Perhaps the idea that comes closest to ours is that of *i3* [16]. In this work, the overlay paradigm is taken further to provide a common "indirection infrastructure" that is interposed between the two parties in a transaction. This indirection decouples the sender and receiver — which enables essential service primitives such as multicast, anycast, host mobility etc. Our own work (in comparison) is broader in scope and addresses a slightly different set of problems.

6 Conclusions and Future Work

In this paper, we explored the inadequacies of the current Internet architecture — and its inability to satisfy the requirements of emerging applications, and also briefly described some capabilities that are currently lacking. It is our thesis that these capabilities are critical to the transformation of the Internet into a viable platform on which services can be delivered. The *SOI* architecture that we articulate in this paper has the capability to transform the Internet into a viable framework for the flexible deployment of new services. The architecture presented has the following properties.

1) Provides an infrastructure that can enable new Internet services that have requirements which cannot be currently satisfied —- such as reliability, security, service availability and QoS.

2) Leverages the existing IP infrastructure. It essentially introduces a service layer that is laid over the IP network layer, and which uses the IP network layer to transport the actual bits.

3) Extends the overlay network paradigm to be more efficient and scalable.

In our description, given the breadth of the architecture, we were forced to sacrifice detail when describing certain components of our architecture so as to present a coherent description in the limited space. At the same time, there are several details that were glossed over in the design of our architecture, such as the exact specifics of the packet forwarding, details of the service name resolution, and so on. In the future, we intend to flesh out the details of these components and construct a prototype of our architecture to evaluate its real world effectiveness.

References

1. Akihiro Nakao, Larry Peterson, A.B.: Routing underlay for overlay networks. In: Proc. ACM SIGCOMM, ACM Press (2003)
2. Ferguson, P., Senie, D.: RFC 2827: Network ingress filtering: Defeating denial of service attacks which employ ip source address spoofing. `http://www.ietf.org/rfc/rfc2827.txt` (2000) Best Current Practices.
3. Rekhter, Y., Li, T.: A Border Gateway Protocol 4 (BGP-4) (1995) RFC 1771.
4. Chandrashekar, J., Duan, Z., Zhang, Z.L., Krasky, J.: Limiting Path Exploration in Path Vector Protocols. Technical report, University of Minnesota (2003)
5. Subramanian, L., Stoica, I., Balakrishnan, H., Katz, R.H.: OverQoS: Offering internet QoS using overlays. In: First HotNets Workshop, Princeton, NJ (2002)
6. Braden, R., Clark, D., Shenker, S.: RFC 1633: integrated services in the internet architecture (1994)
7. Blake, S., Black, D., Carlson, M., Davies, E., Wang, Z., Weiss, W.: RFC 2475: an architecture for differentiated services (1998)
8. Gritter, M., Cheriton, D.R.: 'an Architecture for Content Routing support in the Internet. In: USITS. (2001)
9. Chu, Y.H., Rao, S.G., Zhang, H.: A case for End System Multicast. In: Proc. ACM SIGMETRICS, ACM (2000)
10. Banerjee, S., Bhattacharjee, B., Kommareddy, C.: Scalable application layer multicast. In: SIGCOMM, ACM Press (2002)
11. Chawathe, Y.: Scattercast: An Architecture for Internet Broadcast Distribution as an Infrastructure Service. PhD thesis, University of California, Berkeley (2000)
12. D. Andersen, H. Balakrishnan, M.K., Morris, R.: The case for resilient overlay networks. In: Proc. 8th Annual Workshop in Operating Systems. (2001)
13. Stoica, I., Morris, R., Karger, D., Kaashoek, M.F., Balakrishnan, H.: Chord: A scalable peer-to-peer lookup service for internet applications. In: Proc. ACM SIGCOMM, ACM Press (2001) 149–160
14. Ratnasamy, S., Francis, P., Handley, M., Karp, R., Shenker, S.: A scalable content addressable network. In: Proc. ACM SIGCOMM, ACM Press (2001)
15. Duan, Z., Zhang, Z.L., Hou, Y.T.: Service overlay networks: Slas, qos and bandwidth provisioning. In: Proc. International Conference on Network Protocols. (2002)
16. Stoica, I., Adkins, D., Zhuang, S., Shenker, S., Surana, S.: Internet indirection infrastructure. In: Proc. ACM SIGCOMM, ACM Press (2002) 73–86

Service-Oriented Device Ecology Workflows

Seng Wai Loke

School of Computer Science and Software Engineering
Monash University, Caulfield East, Victoria 3145, Australia
swloke@csse.monash.edu.au

Abstract. We address the need for a high level of abstraction to describe how devices should work together and to manage their interaction. Our perspective is from workflow, where business processes are managed by a workflow system that assigns tasks, passes them on, and tracks the progress. One can envision device ecologies for different purposes and situations but this paper focuses on a device ecology example within the home environment. We illustrate how a workflow model can be applied to describe and manage device ecologies – in particular, we treat devices as Web services and utilize the Business Process Execution Language for Web Services (BPEL4WS) for describing workflows in device ecologies. We also show how the DySCo workflow algebra can be employed to model device ecology workflows and discuss how to model the impact of these workflows on devices' observable states. The result of this work is a starting point for a workflow based programming model for device ecologies.

1 The Rise of Device Ecologies

We are surrounded by appliances, and increasingly so. The American Heritage Dictionary defines an appliance as "a device or instrument designed to perform a specific function, especially an electrical device, such as a toaster, for household use." Usability experts have advocated special-purpose devices (in contrast to general-purpose PCs) which, with their supporting computational and communication infrastructure, fit the person and tasks so well, are sufficiently unobtrusive and inter-connectivity seamless, that the technological details become virtually invisible compared to the task. These devices are often called *information appliances*, or *Internet appliances* if they have Internet-connectivity [5,16]. Part of "smart" behaviour is this interaction among devices and resources. The current Internet and networking technologies, and developments in wireless networking enable the "smart" devices to communicate with one another and with Internet or Web resources. The devices might need to interact effectively in order to accomplish the goals of its user(s), and such interaction ability, whether occurring over very short ranges or across continents, can open up tremendous possibilities for innovative applications.

The American Heritage Dictionary defines the word "ecology" as "the relationship between organisms and their environment." We perceive the above mentioned developments as yielding a computing platform of the 21st century that takes the form of *device ecologies* consisting of collections of devices (in the environment and on

M.E. Orlowska et al. (Eds.): ICSOC 2003, LNCS 2910, pp. 559–574, 2003.

users) interacting synergistically with one another, with users, and with Internet resources, undergirded by appropriate software and communication infrastructures that range from Internet-scale to very short range wireless networks. These devices will perform tasks and work together perhaps autonomously but will need to interact with the user from time to time.

There has been significant work in building the networking and integrative infrastructure for such devices, within the home, the office, and other environments and linking them to the global Internet. For example, AutoHan [19], UPnP [12], OSGI [13], Jini [21], and SIDRAH (with short range networking and failure detection) [8] define infrastructure and mechanisms at different levels (from networking to services) for devices to be inter-connected, find each other, and utilize each other's capabilities. Embedded Web Servers [3] are able to expose the functionality of devices as Web services. Embedding micro-servers into physical objects is considered in [15]. Approaches to modelling and programming such devices for the home have been investigated, where devices have been modelled as software components [9], as collections of objects [1], as Web services [14], and as agents [18,6]. However, there has been little work on specifying at a high level of abstraction (and representing this specification explicitly) how such devices would work together at the user-task or application level, and how such work can be managed.

In this paper, we address the need for a high level of abstraction to describe how devices should work together and to manage their interaction. Our perspective is from workflow, where business processes are managed by a workflow system that assigns tasks, passes them on, and tracks the progress. We can have device ecologies for different situations and purposes. Here, we focus on device ecologies within the home environment. We first provide some background in Section 2. Then, in Section 3, we illustrate how a workflow model can be applied to describe and manage device ecologies – in particular, we treat devices as Web services and utilize the Business Process Execution Language for Web Services (BPEL4WS) [2] for describing workflows in device ecologies. For short, we call such device ecology workflows *decoflows*. The idea of a DecoFlow Engine is outlined in Section 4. We also show, in Section 5, how the DySCo [17] workflow algebra can be employed to model decoflows and discuss how to model the impact of decoflows on devices' observable states. We conclude with future work in Section 6.

2 Preliminaries

2.1 Modelling Devices

We model the observable and controllable aspects of devices as Web services as done in [14]. Such device modeling is not inconsistent with emerging standard models for appliances such as the AHAM Appliance Models [1], where each appliance (such as clothes washer, refrigerator, over, room air conditioner, etc) is modelled as a collection of objects categorized according to subsystems. In this paper, we assume that aspects of devices can be directly observed and controlled by means of a collection of Web services, described using the Web Services Description Language (WSDL) [7]. We note that there will be aspects of the device which are not exposed as Web services.

2.2 BPEL4WS

BPEL4WS is an XML language for specifying business process behaviour based on Web services. Quoting from [22]:

"It (BPEL4WS) allows you to create complex processes by creating and wiring together different activities that can, for example, perform Web services invocations, manipulate data, throw faults, or terminate a process. These activities may be nested within structured activities that define how they may be run, such as in sequence, or in parallel, or depending on certain conditions."

BPEL4WS has language constructs for manipulating data, handling faults, compensating for irreversible actions, and various structured activities. BPEL4WS assumes that there is a central engine which is executing the workflow. A BPEL4WS process or workflow is viewed as the central entity invoking Web services associated with its (business) partners and having its own services invoked by partners (e.g., when the partner initiates the business process or receives results for a previously sent request). We describe the syntax and semantics of the BPEL4WS constructs together with our example below.

3 Modelling Device Ecology Workflows

3.1 An Example Decoflow

We consider a decoflow for someone we call Jane involving a television, a coffee-boiler, bedroom lights, bathroom lights, and a news Web service accessed over the Internet. Figure 1 describes this decoflow. The dashed arrows represent sequencing, the boxes are tasks, the solid arrow represents a control link for synchronization across concurrent activities, and free grouping of sequences (i.e., the boxes grouped into the large box) represents concurrent sequences.

This decoflow is initiated by a wake-up notice from Jane's alarm clock which we assume here is issued to the Device Ecology Workflow Engine (which we call the *Decoflow Engine*) when the alarm clock rings. This notice initiates the entire workflow. Subsequent to receiving this notice, five activities are concurrently started: retrieve news from the Internet and display is on the television, switch on the television, boil coffee, switch on the bedroom lights, and switch on the bathroom lights. Note the synchronization arrow from "Switch On TV" to "Display News on TV", which ensures that the television must be switched on before the news can be displayed on it. After all the concurrent activities have completed, the final task is to blink the bedroom lights, in order to indicate to Jane that the decoflow tasks have completed. This scenario was inspired by [4].

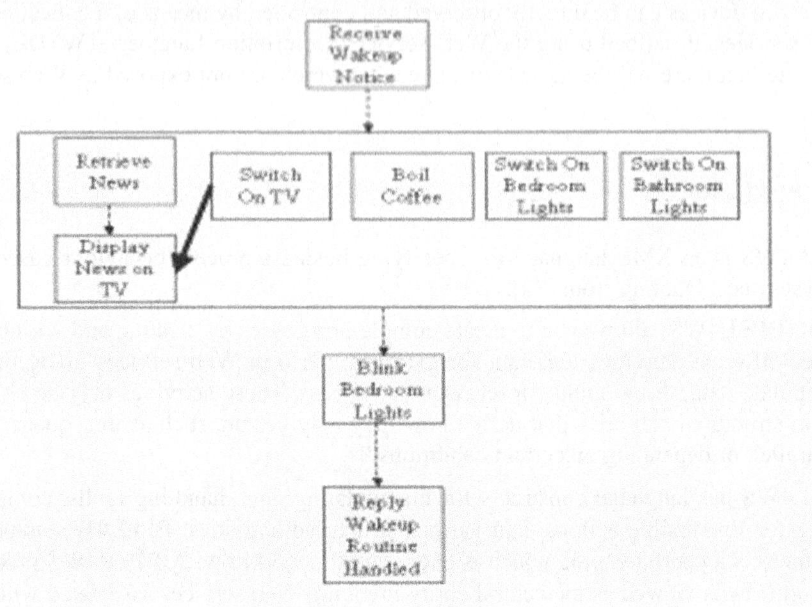

Fig. 1. A Device Ecology Workflow

3.2 The Decoflow in BPEL4WS

The above decoflow can be described using BPEL4WS. The process is given in outline as follows in Figure 2:

```
<sequence>
      <receive partnerLink="wakingUp"
                  portType="lns:wakeUpNoticePT"
                  operation="sendWakeUpNotice"
                  variable="WN">
      </receive>
      <flow>


            <links>
                  <link name="tv-to-news"/>
            </links>
            <sequence>

               <invoke partnerLink="newsRetrieval"
                   portType="lns:newsUpdatePT"
                   operation="requestNews"
                      inputVariable="newsRequest"
                            outputVariable="newsInfo">
               </invoke>

               <invoke partnerLink="tv"
                      portType="lns:tvControlPT"
                   operation="displayOnTV"
```

```
                inputVariable="newsInfo"
                <target linkName="tv-to-news"/>
            </invoke>
        </sequence>

        <invoke partnerLink="tv"
                portType="lns:tvControlPT"
                operation="sendTVCommand"
                inputVariable="switchOnTVRequest">
                <source linkName="tv-to-news"/>
                </invoke>

        <invoke partnerLink="coffeeBoiling"
                portType="lns:boilerControlPT"
                operation="sendCoffeeBoilerCommand"
                inputVariable="boilCoffeeRequest"">
        </invoke>

        <invoke partnerLink="bathroomLighting"
                portType="lns:bathroomLightControlPT"
                operation="sendLightCommand"
                inputVariable="switchOnLightRequest">
        </invoke>

        <invoke partnerLink="bedroomLighting"
                portType="lns:bedroomLightControlPT"
                operation="sendLightCommand"
                inputVariable="switchOnLightRequest">
        </invoke>
    </flow>

    <invoke partnerLink="bedroomLighting"
            portType="lns:bedroomLightControlPT"
            operation="sendLightCommand"
            inputVariable="blinkLightRequest">
    </invoke>
    <reply partnerLink="wakingUp"
           portType="lns:wakeUpNoticePT"
           operation="sendWakeUpNotice"
           variable="WNHandled"/>
    </reply>
</sequence>
```

Fig. 2. Outline of the process in BPEL4WS.

We first note the structure of the decoflow indicated by the following tags in Figure 2. The outermost `<sequence>…</sequence>` tags sequences the inner four activities encapsulated within the tags `<receive…>…</receive>`, `<flow>…</flow>`, `<invoke…>…</invoke>`, and `<reply…>…</reply>`:

1. The first `<receive…>…</receive>` activity and the final `<reply…>…</reply>` activity represents the DecoFlow Engine receiving the wake-up notice, and informing the alarm clock that the wake-up notice has been handled.
2. The `<flow>…</flow>` tags indicate that the five immediately nested activities, i.e., the `<sequence>…</sequence>` activity and the four `<invoke…>…</invoke>` activities are to be carried out concurrently.

3. The second last `<invoke...>...</invoke>` blinks the bedroom lights before replying the alarm clock.
4. The `<link>...</link>` from tv to news represents the dependency of the display news operation on the switch on television operation. Note that the switch on television operation is the source and the display news operation is the target, since the target depends on the source, and so, the source must complete before the target begins.

BPEL4WS has the notion of partner link, where a partner has a relationship with the business process, and represents both a consumer of a service provided by the business process and a provider of a service to the business process. In this context, a partner relationship between a decoflow and a device signifies that the device is used in the decoflow. A partner link can be defined by two roles, one to be played by the partner and the other by the business process. Sometimes only one role is given in a partner link definition implying that the partner expresses a willingness to link with the business process without placing any requirements on the business process, or conversely, i.e. the business process links with other partners without requirements on the partner. In this context, such roles provide semantics as to the role played by a device for that decoflow. For example, the following partner link is between the decoflow and the television, where the television is viewed as a service.

```
<plnk:partnerLinkType name="tvLT">
    <plnk:role name="tvService">
          <plnk:portType name="pos:tvControlPT"/>
    </plnk:role>
</plnk:partnerLinkType>
```

There is only one role in this definition, and it is to be taken up by the television. The port type given is a communication endpoint for accessing television controls. Note that only one role is given and is taken up by the device. The decoflow need not provide any services in this partnership with the television.

Associated with each port type is one or more operations, corresponding to Web service methods. For example, the tvControl port type has the displayOnTV operation.

```
<portType name="tvControlPT">
    <operation name="displayOnTV">
          <input message="pos:newsInfoMessage"/>
          <fault name="cannotCompleteWN"
    message="pos:WNFaultType"/>
    </operation>
</portType>
```

If there is fault with the invocation of this operation, the fault handler is invoked as explained later.

Using such partner link types, actual partner links can be defined. For example, the following partner link is an instance of the tv partner link type, where the partner or the device's role is specified as one offering the television service. Since there is only one role, no requirements are placed on the decoflow (or the DecoFlow Engine) in this partner relationship between the decoflow and the television.

```
<partnerLink name="tv"
       partnerLinkType="lns:tvLT"
       partnerRole="tvService"/>
```

But consider the following partner link type and its instance partner link.

```
<plnk:partnerLinkType name="wakingUpLT">
    <plnk:role name="wakingUpService">
          <plnk:portType name="pos:wakeUpNoticePT"/>
    </plnk:role>
</plnk:partnerLinkType>

    <partnerLink name="wakingUp"
          partnerLinkType="lns:wakingUpLT"
          myRole="wakeUpService"/>
```

The partner link type defines only one role but unlike the partner link type definition for the television, this role is taken up not by a device but by the decoflow instead. Also, since there is only one role, no requirements are placed on a partner device in this partner relationship between a device (which we have assumed is an alarm clock) and the decoflow. In other words, the decoflow offers this wakingUp-Service to any device, or any device can issue a wake up notice to initiate an instance of this decoflow, but only because we have defined the decoflow in this way.

Partner relationships with the other devices and their port types are similarly defined. We have not assumed an ontology for describing partner relationships and port types. In practice, device standards such as [1] can be used to specify the operations and port types for the respective devices. Through the use of such standards, such operations can be expected of different appliances (even of different manufacturers) as long as they adhere to the standards. We can view defining such partner relationships between a device and a decoflow as defining an abstraction (of some aspects) of the device which will be utilized in the decoflow, where this abstraction of the device is a subset of the device's capabilities (as accessed by their corresponding operations).

3.3 A Library of Decoflows

The above decoflow is only one example of how a wake-up routine can be captured. There could be other routines such as come-home-from-work routines or entertain-guests routines, etc, which can be captured in decoflows. A library of decoflows can be constructed, indexed on particular situations.

We also note that some of these decoflows might not be invoked by the user (or through the user's initiative) but by devices' own initiative. For example, a device might initiate a decoflow to further secure a home if it detects unwanted intruders when the owners are out for dinner, or initiate a decoflow to replenish (e.g. to order) certain household items based on a provided budget. A decoflow initiated by a device can be programmed to seek human approval for more critical tasks.

4 Decoflow Execution via the Device Ecology Workflow Engine

The above workflow can be executed by the DecoFlow Engine, as Figure 3 illustrates.

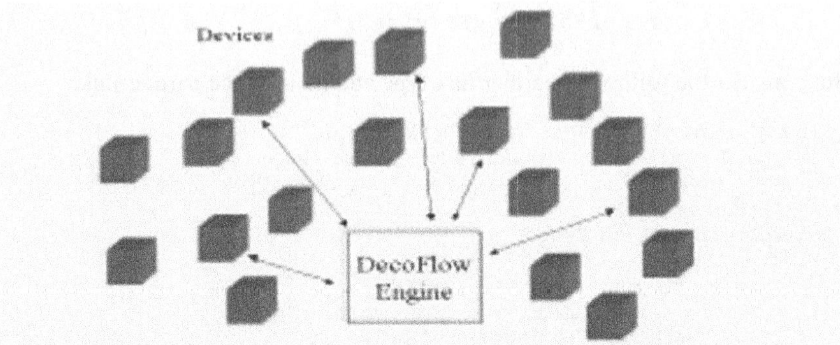

Fig. 3. DecoFlow Engine interacting with Device Ecology

The cubes represent devices and the bi-drectional arrows indicate messages exchanged with these devices while executing a decoflow specification. We assume the devices are described and connected to the DecoFlow Engine via some underlying networking and service infrastructure such as UPnP. The DecoFlow Engine is in charge of invoking the appropriate Web services on the devices, in order to request resources to perform tasks and maintaining the execution state of the process.

The execution state of the process are recorded in one or more declared variables such as the following, whose values can be used as inputs to operations or to store outputs of operations.

```
<variables>
        <variable name="WN" messageType="lns:WNMessage"/>
        <variable name="newsRequest"
              messageType="lns:newsRequestMessage"/>
        <variable name="newsInfo"
              messageType="lns:newsInfoMessage"/>
        <variable name="boilCoffeeRequest"
              messageType="lns:boilCoffeeRequestMessage"/>
        <variable name="switchOnLightRequest"

        messageType="lns:switchOnLightRequestMessage"/>
        <variable name="blinkLightRequest"
              messageType="lns:blinkLightRequestMessage"/>
        <variable name="switchOnTVRequest"
              messageType="lns:switchOnTVRequestMessage"/>
        <variable name="WNHandled"
              messageType="lns:WNHandledMessage"/>
        <variable name=
            "WNFault" messageType="lns:WNFaultType"/>
</variables>
```

It is too simplistic to assume that the decoflow will complete without any problems. BPEL4WS has constructs for defining fault handlers and for throwing exceptions. For example, the following description states that if a fault occurs in the invocation of an operation, i.e., the wake up routine (as defined by the decoflow) cannot be completed, a reply is sent to the alarm clock that there has been a fault.

```
<faultHandlers>
        <catch faultName="lns:cannotCompleteWN"
                faultVariable="WNFault">
                <reply partnerLink="wakingUp"
                        portType="lns:wakeUpNoticePT"
                        operation="sendWakeUpNotice"
                        variable="WNFault"
                        faultName="cannotCompleteWN"/>
        </catch>
</faultHandlers>
```

By including the following declaration in port type definitions

```
<fault name=
     "cannotCompleteWN" message="pos:WNFaultType"/>
```

operations can be associated with the fault handler by means of the common fault name.

5 Formal Modelling of Devices' Decoflow and Changes in Observable States

To the author's knowledge, BPEL4WS has not yet been given a formal semantics. But a basic formalization for workflow is given in a process algebraic manner for the DySCo framework [17], where the basic tasks in these workflows are Web service invocations. By modelling the controllable and observable aspects of devices as Web services, we can employ this formalisation in specifying decoflows.

From a given device's point of view, assuming that the device has an observable state, we would also like to model the changes to the device's observable state as the decoflow executes. Some of the activities of the decoflow can affect the device's observable state (for example, if the activity is one which invokes a Web service of the device) but there will be activities of the decoflow which does not affect the device's observable state (e.g., if the activity invokes a Web service of some other device). A device can also, with respect to external observers, spontaneously move from one observable state to another, that is, the device might change its observable state without sending or receiving any messages. Such *spontaneous moves* has been modelled in [20], where agents are modelled with observable states and the observable state of an agent can spontaneously change, spontaneous in the sense that it changed without the agent receiving any messages. The assumption there is that the spontaneous change is due to the agent's own internal processes, and represents the proactive nature of these agents. We can similarly model devices with such spontaneous changes, where spontaneity is with respect to a given decoflow and is in the sense that the change is not due to any of the activities of the decoflow being considered. In reality, such changes, thought spontaneous, might be due to some other decoflow that is concurrently executing, or due to actions of other users directly on the device – for example, before the decoflow instructs the bathroom lights to turn on, the user might have already turned it on.

Below, we present a basic formalization of decoflow including synchronization between concurrent activities based on the DySCo formalization in [17]. Other formalizations for service-oriented workflows might also be used. We need only consider global state in decoflows. We also provide transition rules that can be used to model changes in a device's observable state.

5.1 Decoflows with DySCo

The grammar for decoflows are given as follows.

W ::= ε	empty decoflow		
| T	task	where	
| W.W	sequence	T ::=	$t_d(\sigma).\lambda(n)$
| W $+_c$ W	choice		| $\lambda'(n).t_d(\sigma)$
| W || W	concurrency		| $t_d(\sigma)$
| !W	loop		

where W represents a decoflow, λ(n) and λ'(n) represents the source of a synchronization link named n and the target of the synchronization link, respectively, $t_d(\sigma)$ represents a task utilising device d with actual parameters given by σ: N –>V (where N is a set of variable names and V is a set of values), T is a task suffixed by a source of a synchronization link, a task prefixed by a target of a synchronization link, or a task without any synchronization links. The condition c for choice is a binary function with domain N. This formulation of workflows is the same as that in DySCo but with a definition of task that includes synchronization links, and resource is, in our case, a device. The task, in our case, assuming we use BPEL4WS operations, is an operation on a device, which is either an invoke, receive or reply.

The labelled transition system comprises the following rules of the form

$$(label)\frac{premises}{conclusion}$$

taken from [17]:

$$(step)\frac{\sigma' = \rho(t,d,\Omega \rhd \sigma)}{\Omega :: t_d(\sigma) \xrightarrow{\varphi} \Omega \lhd \sigma' :: \varepsilon}$$

where φ represents information to be made externally visible as a result of the action. In decoflows, we can interpret this to mean a signal given to the user that the task has been carried out. Ω represents the global state of the workflow. The functions (ω) and (ϖ) are used to extract information from the global state and to feed information into the global state respectively. ρ is a function representing the results of the execution of a task.

$$(loop)\frac{}{\Omega :: !W \xrightarrow{\tau} \Omega :: W(!W)}$$

where τ represents null visible information.

Sequence is represented as follows:

$$(seq1)\frac{\Omega::W1 \xrightarrow{\alpha} \Omega'::W1'}{\Omega::W1.W2 \xrightarrow{\alpha} \Omega'::W1'.W2}$$

$$(seq2)\frac{}{\Omega::\varepsilon.W2 \xrightarrow{\tau} \Omega::W2}$$

The symbol α represents visible information. Choice depends in the binary function c whose evaluation determines which alternative to execute. Two rule are given which represents the non-determinism.

$$(choice1)\frac{\text{eval(c)=1}}{\Omega::W1+_c W2 \xrightarrow{\tau} \Omega::W1}$$

$$(choice2)\frac{\text{eval(c)=2}}{\Omega::W1+_c W2 \xrightarrow{\tau} \Omega::W2}$$

Concurrency is given by the following four rules:

$$(conc1)\frac{}{\Omega::\lambda(n).W1 \| \lambda'(n).W2 \xrightarrow{\alpha} \Omega::W1 \| W2}$$

$$(conc2)\frac{\Omega::W1 \xrightarrow{\alpha} \Omega'::W1'}{\Omega::W1 \| W2 \xrightarrow{\alpha} \Omega'::W1' \| W2}$$

$$(conc3)\frac{\Omega::W2 \xrightarrow{\alpha} \Omega'::W2'}{\Omega::W1 \| W2 \xrightarrow{\alpha} \Omega'::W1 \| W2'}$$

$$(conc4)\frac{\Omega::W1 \xrightarrow{\alpha} \Omega'::W1' \quad \text{and} \quad \Omega::W2 \xrightarrow{\alpha} \Omega''::W2'}{\Omega::W1 \| W2 \xrightarrow{\alpha} \Omega' \nabla \Omega''::W1' \| W2'}$$

The four rules represent the different possibilities in concurrent execution, either we resolve a synchronization link, W1 executes first, W2 executes first, or both executes at the same time. The operator σcombines the two resulting states, perhaps serializing the updates. Note that concurrent access to Ω has not been represented explicitly. The first rule (conc1) is not in DySCo, but the rest are. (conc3) is not necessary since the concurrency operator is commutative (but is added for comparison with [17]). In addition, as observed from (conc1), execution cannot continue if the workflow is such that there is no matching source and target for each synchronization link.

The example decoflow given earlier can be expressed using the following expression:

$$rcv_a . ((inv_b.(\lambda'(tn).inv_c)) \| (inv_d.\lambda(tn)) \| inv_e \| inv_f \| inv_g) . inv_h . rep_a$$

where rcv_a is a receive via the sendWakeUpNotice operation,
inv_b is an invocation of the requestNews operation,
inv_c is an invocation of the displayOnTV operation prefixed by the link target,

inv_d is an invocation of the switchOnTVRequest operation suffixed by the link source,
inv_e is an invocation of the sendCoffeeBoilerCommand operation,
inv_f is an invocation of the sendLightCommand operation for the bathroom,
inv_g is an invocation of the sendLightCommand operation for the bedroom,
inv_h is an invocation of the sendLightCommand operation to blink the bedroom lights,

and rep_a is a reply to the sendWakeUpNotice operation. $\lambda(tn)$ and $\lambda'(tn)$ corresponds to the source and target of the "tv-to-news" link.

The execution proceeds as follows:

$$rcv_a . ((inv_b.(\lambda'(tn).inv_c)) \,||\, (inv_d.\lambda(tn)) \,||\, inv_e \,||\, inv_f \,||\, inv_g) . inv_h . rep_a$$

$\longrightarrow$ (using seq)

$$((inv_b.(\lambda'(tn).inv_c)) \,||\, (inv_d.\lambda(tn)) \,||\, inv_e \,||\, inv_f \,||\, inv_g) . inv_h . rep_a$$

$\longrightarrow$ (using conc repeatedly, and by commutativity of ||)

$$(\lambda(tn) \,||\, (\lambda'(tn).inv_c) \,||\, \varepsilon \,||\, \varepsilon \,||\, \varepsilon) . inv_h . rep_a$$

$\longrightarrow$ (using conc1)

$$(\varepsilon \,||\, inv_c \,||\, \varepsilon \,||\, \varepsilon \,||\, \varepsilon) . inv_h . rep_a$$

$\longrightarrow$ (using seq, and since $\varepsilon \,||\, W = W$)

$$inv_h . rep_a$$

$\longrightarrow$ (using seq)

$$rep_a$$

$\longrightarrow$ (using seq)

$$\varepsilon$$

5.2 Modelling Changes in Devices' Observable States

Now we turn to the modelling of a device's observable state. Given a device d, we can model d's possible changes in observable states as a decoflow is being executed. Suppose D represents d's initial observable state. Then, after executing a decoflow W, we would like to compute the series of observable states that d goes through when W is executing, i.e. $D^1, D^2, D^3, D^4, \ldots, D^n$, where $D \xrightarrow{W} D^n$. Note that not all the operations in W will affect d. Suppose that only two operations in W affects d, namely $t_d(\sigma)$ and $t'_{d'}(\sigma')$, and that these two operations are sequenced in W, i.e. $W = W' . t_d(\sigma) . W'' . t'_{d'}(\sigma') . W'''$, for some W', W'', and W'''. Also, suppose we have $D \xrightarrow{t_d(\sigma)} D'$ and $D' \xrightarrow{t'_{d'}(\sigma')} D''$. Then, $D \xrightarrow{W} D''$.

If we now consider a set of devices (d1, d2, d3, …, dk), we can work out the effect of a decoflow W on the collective observable state of the devices:

$$(D_1, D_2, \ldots, D_k) \xrightarrow{W} (D_1', D_2', \ldots, D_k')$$

If we perform analysis on $(D_1', D_2', ..., D_k')$, we can predict particular effects of the decoflow W. For example, we can define a function *num_lights_on* on the collective observable states of the devices, where $num\_lights\_on(D_1', D_2', ..., D_k')$ is the number of lights which have been switched on in the given state $(D_1', D_2', ..., D_k')$. By simulating the execution of W on the devices, we can determine if W will produce a collective observable state where $num\_lights\_on(D_1', D_2', ..., D_k') > 20$. A similar analysis technique can also be used to determine if a decoflow will ever switch a device on or off, and what circumstances will prevent a device from being switched off.

In reality, the problem is more complex. One complexity is due to two avenues by which a device can be controlled. One is via the system, and the other is direct control by a human user. For example, a light can be switched on manually by the user or automatically by the system in one or more decoflows. Thus, with respect to a decoflow, not all the changes in a device's observable state is due to actions of that decoflow. A user or another concurrently executing decoflow might have changed the device's observable state. To model changes in state not due to a given decoflow, we introduce the idea of *spontaneous state changes* analogous to the spontaneous moves mentioned earlier. With such spontaneous state changes, using the example of the effect of W on D above, we might not have $D \xrightarrow{W} D''$ anymore, but $D \xrightarrow{W} D'''$ for some $D''' \neq D''$, due to spontaneous state changes apart from the actions of W on d. Because it is practically impossible to predict when such spontaneous state changes might occur, when we analyse the effect of W, we do so with an assumption about the set of possible spontaneous moves that might occur during the execution of W, i.e. this set of spontaneous moves become a parameter to the analysis.

For example, suppose we have the following transition rule that defines only one possible spontaneous move of a device, which in this example, is a lamp with two observable states ("off", denoted by D, and "on", denoted by D'): $D' \xrightarrow{\text{user switch off}} D$. The user can only switch off the lamp but the system can switch it on or off automatically. The device can be switched on or off via a Web service invocation: $D \xrightarrow{\text{sendLightCommand(on)}} D'$ and $D' \xrightarrow{\text{sendLightCommand(off)}} D$. Given a decoflow W which includes these invocations, the transition rule for the user's possible action, and that the initial state of the lamp is "off", we can determine what possible states the lamp can be in at any point in the execution of W. Suppose, at a given point in time, W has partially executed, and so far, has not invoke any services on the lamp, then the lamp must be in the "off" state at this point, since the user cannot switch it on.

The above example is intentionally simple. More generally, analysis can be done to determine if a given decoflow will cause undesirable effects on the device ecology as a whole, i.e. to verify *safety properties* of the decoflow with respect to a device ecology, or whether the decoflow will result in intended effects, i.e. to ensure *liveness properties*. Liveness properties include the property of a decoflow completing, but also that it completes with intended effects. The user can pose "what-if" questions to the DecoFlow System situated between the user and the device ecology to examine properties of decoflows before executing them.

6 Conclusions and Further Issues

We have shown by example how BPEL4WS can be used to model device ecology workflows where devices are modelled as a collection of Web services. Note that these means that any other Internet based Web service can be integrated into the same workflow with these devices and existing Web service technology can be applied to interact with these devices. BPEL4WS is a practical language but has not been given a formal semantics. Hence, we have also adapted the DySCo algebraic workflow model for device ecology workflows or decoflows. Lastly, we have outlined how to analyse the effect of a decoflow on a collection of devices' observable states. We note that state space explosion can potentially occur and will require further experimentation to determine what size of device ecologies and device complexity can be tractably tackled. The result of this work is a basis for a workflow based programming model for device ecologies. Another contribution of this work is the proposal of a technique to analyze (e.g., by simulation) or to prove properties of decoflows, where a property of a decoflow is about an effect that a decoflow can have on a device or a collection of devices. We are currently investigating a prototype implementation over UPnP. A number of outstanding issues need to be addressed:

1. *When should a decoflow be triggered and stopped?* A decoflow may start a process involving a number of devices and have long lasting effects. Hence, there should not only be facilities to terminate a decoflow but perhaps also to compensate for a cancelled decoflow.
2. *How can the user perceive the progress of the workflow, and intervene freely?* This is as much a Human-Computer Interaction issue as it is a distributed computing one. Even non-technically minded users should be able to flexibly intervene, e.g., to terminate or alter, a decoflow.
3. *How can the decoflow deal with faults?* This is related to the problem of defining and executing compensations as stated above.
4. *How can we integrate event reporting with decoflows?* A spontaneous state change might result in the emission of an event message which should be handled by the DecoFlow Engine.
5. We have also not considered preconditions for tasks in a decoflow, in order to deal with situations where the task to perform is redundant.

Some devices might also exhibit more autonomous, proactive, and intelligent behaviour – we would like to see if such devices can be adequately modelled with spontaneous state changes. Also, we plan to identify further properties of decoflows and employ Petri net analysis techniques to analyze properties of decoflows as often used for analyzing workflows and multiagent interactions.

We have so far considered only a centralized engine for executing decoflows. Multiagent distributed workflows using a decentralized peer-to-peer model provides greater flexibility and facilitates on-the-fly just-in-time ad hoc workflows directly between devices without the mediation of a heavy-weight central engine. This would be another avenue of investigation. Lastly, recent work have considered Semantic Gadgets [11], using the Semantic Web framework to describe the semantics of devices, to discover new devices and to dynamically compose device coalitions. It would be interesting to consider semantics based extensions to dynamically compose decoflows, or less ambitious is, given an abstract description of a decoflow, dynamically bind the tasks mentioned in the decoflow to devices' Web services, thereby reducing the burden of composing a detailed decoflow prior to runtime, and providing flexibility by allowing alternative devices or resources to be selected and integrated into the decoflow at runtime.

References

[1] AHAM. Connected Home Appliances – Object Modelling, AHAM CHA-1-2002, 2002.

[2] T. Andrews, F. Curbera, H. Dholakia, Y. Goland, J. Klein, F. Leymann, K. Liu, D. Roller, D. Smith, S. Thatte, I. Trickovic, S. Weerawarana. Business Process Execution Language for Web Services (version 1.1), May 2003.

[3] J. Bentham. TCP/IP Lean: Web Servers for Embedded Systems (2nd Edition), 2002, CMP Books.

[4] S. Berger. Intelligent Appliances Give Automation A New Home, 2002. Available at http://www.aarp.org/computers-features/Articles/a2002-07-10-computers_features_appliances.html

[5] E. Bergman. Information Appliances and Beyond, 2000, Morgan Kaufmann Publishers.

[6] C. Carabelea and O.Boissier. Multi-agent Platforms for Smart Devices: Dream or Reality? In Proceedings of the Smart Objects Conference (SOC'03), Grenoble, May 2003. Available at http://turing.cs.pub.ro/~cosminc/papers/grenoble03.pdf.

[7] E. Christensen, F. Curbera, G. Meredith, S. Weerawarana. Web Services Description Language (WSDL) 1.1, March 2001. Available at http://www.w3.org/TR/wsdl.html.

[8] Y. Durand, S.P.J.-M. Vincent, C. Marchand, F.-G. Ottogalli, V. Olive, S. Martin, B. Dumant, and S. Chambon. SIDRAH: A Software Infrastructure for a Resilient Community of Wireless Devices. In Proceedings of the Smart Objects Conference (SOC'03), Grenoble, May 2003.

[9] J.H. Jahnke, M. D'Entremont, and J. Stier. Facilitating the Programming of the Smart Home, IEEE Wireless Communications, pp. 70–76, December 2002.

[10] O. Kasten and M. Langheinrich. First Experiences with Bluetooth in the Smart-Its Distributed Sensor Network. In Proceedings of the Workshop on Ubiquitous Computing and Communications at PACT 2001, October 2001.

[11] O. Lassila and M. Adler. Semantic Gadgets: Ubiquitous Computing Meets the Semantic Web, in D. Fensel et al. (eds.), Spinning the Semantic Web, pp. 363–376, 2003, MIT Press.

[12] Microsoft Corporation. Understanding UPnP™: A White Paper. Available at http://www.upnp.org/download/UPNP_UnderstandingUPNP.doc

[13] D. Marples, P. Kriens. The Open Services Gateway Initiative: An Introductory Overview, IEEE Communications Magazine, pp. 2–6, December 2001.

[14] K. Matsuura, T. Hara, A. Watanabe, and T. Nakajima. A New Architecture for Home Computing, In Proceedings of the IEEE Workshop on Software Technologies for Future Embedded Ssytems (WSTFES'03), pp. 71–74, Japan, May 2003.

[15] T. Nakajima. Pervasive Servers: A Framework for Creating a Society of Appliances. In Proceedings of the 1AD: First International Conference on Appliance Design, pp. 57-63, May 2003.

[16] D. Norman. The Invisible Computer, 1999, MIT Press.

[17] G. Piccinelli, A. Finkelstein, and S.L. Williams. Service-Oriented Workflows: the DySCo Framework. In Proceedings of the Euromicro Conference, Antalya, Turkey, 2003. *(to appear)* Available at http://www.cs.ucl.ac.uk/staff/A.Finkelstein/papers/euromicro2003.pdf
[18] F. Ramparany, O.Boissier, and H. Brouchoud. Cooperating Autonomous Smart Devices. In Proceedings of the Smart Objects Conference (SOC'03), Grenoble, May 2003.
[19] U. Saif, D. Gordon, and D.J. Greaves. Internet Access to a Home Area Network, IEEE Internet Computing, pp. 54–63, January-February, 2001.
[20] M. Viroli and A. Omicini. A Specification Language for Agents Observable Behaviour, in H.R. Arabnia and Y. Mun (eds.), International Conference on Artificial Intelligence (IC-AI'02), volume I, pp. 321–327, Las Vegas, NV, USA, 24–27 July 2002. CSREA Press.
[21] J. Waldo. The Jini Architecture for Network-Centric Computing, Communications of the ACM, pp. 76–82, July 1999.
[22] S. Weerawarana and F. Curbera. Business Process with BPEL4WS: Understanding BPEL4WS, Part 1, August 2002. Available at http://www-106.ibm.com/developerworks/webservices/library/ws-bpelcol1/.

Author Index

Lecture Notes in Computer Science

For information about Vols. 1–2828
please contact your bookseller or Springer-Verlag

Vol. 2629: A.E. Abdallah, P. Ryan, S. Schneider (Eds.), Formal Aspects of Security. Proceedings, 2002. X, 239 pages. 2003.

Vol. 2760: R. Dingledine (Ed.), Privacy Enhancing Technologies. Proceedings, 2003. VIII, 223 pages. 2003.

Vol. 2829: A. Cappelli, F. Turini (Eds.), AI*IA 2003: Advances in Artificial Intelligence. Proceedings, 2003. XIV, 552 pages. 2003. (Subseries LNAI).

Vol. 2830: F. Pfenning, Y. Smaragdakis (Eds.), Generative Programming and Component Engineering. Proceedings, 2003. IX, 397 pages. 2003.

Vol. 2831: M. Schillo, M. Klusch, J. Müller, H. Tianfield (Eds.), Multiagent System Technologies. Proceedings, 2003. X, 229 pages. 2003. (Subseries LNAI).

Vol. 2832: G. Di Battista, U. Zwick (Eds.), Algorithms – ESA 2003. Proceedings, 2003. XIV, 790 pages. 2003.

Vol. 2833: F. Rossi (Ed.), Principles and Practice of Constraint Programming – CP 2003. Proceedings, 2003. XIX, 1005 pages. 2003.

Vol. 2834: X. Zhou, S. Jähnichen, M. Xu, J. Cao (Eds.), Advanced Parallel Processing Technologies. Proceedings, 2003. XIV, 679 pages. 2003.

Vol. 2835: T. Horváth, A. Yamamoto (Eds.), Inductive Logic Programming. Proceedings, 2003. X, 401 pages. 2003. (Subseries LNAI).

Vol. 2836: S. Qing, D. Gollmann, J. Zhou (Eds.), Information and Communications Security. Proceedings, 2003. XI, 416 pages. 2003.

Vol. 2837: N. Lavrač, D. Gamberger, H. Blockeel, L. Todorovski (Eds.), Machine Learning: ECML 2003. Proceedings, 2003. XVI, 504 pages. 2003. (Subseries LNAI).

Vol. 2838: N. Lavrač, D. Gamberger, L. Todorovski, H. Blockeel (Eds.), Knowledge Discovery in Databases: PKDD 2003. Proceedings, 2003. XVI, 508 pages. 2003. (Subseries LNAI).

Vol. 2839: A. Marshall, N. Agoulmine (Eds.), Management of Multimedia Networks and Services. Proceedings, 2003. XIV, 532 pages. 2003.

Vol. 2840: J. Dongarra, D. Laforenza, S. Orlando (Eds.), Recent Advances in Parallel Virtual Machine and Message Passing Interface. Proceedings, 2003. XVIII, 693 pages. 2003.

Vol. 2841: C. Blundo, C. Laneve (Eds.), Theoretical Computer Science. Proceedings, 2003. XI, 397 pages. 2003.

Vol. 2842: R. Gavaldà, K.P. Jantke, E. Takimoto (Eds.), Algorithmic Learning Theory. Proceedings, 2003. XI, 313 pages. 2003. (Subseries LNAI).

Vol. 2843: G. Grieser, Y. Tanaka, A. Yamamoto (Eds.), Discovery Science. Proceedings, 2003. XII, 504 pages. 2003. (Subseries LNAI).

Vol. 2844: J.A. Jorge, N.J. Nunes, J.F. e Cunha (Eds.), Interactive Systems. Proceedings, 2003. XIII, 429 pages. 2003.

Vol. 2846: J. Zhou, M. Yung, Y. Han (Eds.), Applied Cryptography and Network Security. Proceedings, 2003. XI, 436 pages. 2003.

Vol. 2847: R. de Lemos, T.S. Weber, J.B. Camargo Jr. (Eds.), Dependable Computing. Proceedings, 2003. XIV, 371 pages. 2003.

Vol. 2848: F.E. Fich (Ed.), Distributed Computing. Proceedings, 2003. X, 367 pages. 2003.

Vol. 2849: N. García, J.M. Martínez, L. Salgado (Eds.), Visual Content Processing and Representation. Proceedings, 2003. XII, 352 pages. 2003.

Vol. 2850: M.Y. Vardi, A. Voronkov (Eds.), Logic for Programming, Artificial Intelligence, and Reasoning. Proceedings, 2003. XIII, 437 pages. 2003. (Subseries LNAI)

Vol. 2851: C. Boyd, W. Mao (Eds.), Information Security. Proceedings, 2003. XI, 443 pages. 2003.

Vol. 2852: F.S. de Boer, M.M. Bonsangue, S. Graf, W.-P. de Roever (Eds.), Formal Methods for Components and Objects. Proceedings, 2003. VIII, 509 pages. 2003.

Vol. 2853: M. Jeckle, L.-J. Zhang (Eds.), Web Services – ICWS-Europe 2003. Proceedings, 2003. VIII, 227 pages. 2003.

Vol. 2854: J. Hoffmann, Utilizing Problem Structure in Planning. XIII, 251 pages. 2003. (Subseries LNAI)

Vol. 2855: R. Alur, I. Lee (Eds.), Embedded Software. Proceedings, 2003. X, 373 pages. 2003.

Vol. 2856: M. Smirnov, E. Biersack, C. Blondia, O. Bonaventure, O. Casals, G. Karlsson, George Pavlou, B. Quoitin, J. Roberts, I. Stavrakakis, B. Stiller, P. Trimintzios, P. Van Mieghem (Eds.), Quality of Future Internet Services. IX, 293 pages. 2003.

Vol. 2857: M.A. Nascimento, E.S. de Moura, A.L. Oliveira (Eds.), String Processing and Information Retrieval. Proceedings, 2003. XI, 379 pages. 2003.

Vol. 2858: A. Veidenbaum, K. Joe, H. Amano, H. Aiso (Eds.), High Performance Computing. Proceedings, 2003. XV, 566 pages. 2003.

Vol. 2859: B. Apolloni, M. Marinaro, R. Tagliaferri (Eds.), Neural Nets. Proceedings, 2003. X, 376 pages. 2003.

Vol. 2860: D. Geist, E. Tronci (Eds.), Correct Hardware Design and Verification Methods. Proceedings, 2003. XII, 426 pages. 2003.

Vol. 2861: C. Bliek, C. Jermann, A. Neumaier (Eds.), Global Optimization and Constraint Satisfaction. Proceedings, 2002. XII, 239 pages. 2003.

Vol. 2862: D. Feitelson, L. Rudolph, U. Schwiegelshohn (Eds.), Job Scheduling Strategies for Parallel Processing. Proceedings, 2003. VII, 269 pages. 2003.

Vol. 2863: P. Stevens, J. Whittle, G. Booch (Eds.), «UML» 2003 – The Unified Modeling Language. Proceedings, 2003. XIV, 415 pages. 2003.

Vol. 2864: A.K. Dey, A. Schmidt, J.F. McCarthy (Eds.), UbiComp 2003: Ubiquitous Computing. Proceedings, 2003. XVII, 368 pages. 2003.

Vol. 2865: S. Pierre, M. Barbeau, E. Kranakis (Eds.), Ad-Hoc, Mobile, and Wireless Networks. Proceedings, 2003. X, 293 pages. 2003.

Vol. 2867: M. Brunner, A. Keller (Eds.), Self-Managing Distributed Systems. Proceedings, 2003. XIII, 274 pages. 2003.

Vol. 2868: P. Perner, R. Brause, H.-G. Holzhütter (Eds.), Medical Data Analysis. Proceedings, 2003. VIII, 127 pages. 2003.

Vol. 2869: A. Yazici, C. Şener (Eds.), Computer and Information Sciences – ISCIS 2003. Proceedings, 2003. XIX, 1110 pages. 2003.

Vol. 2870: D. Fensel, K. Sycara, J. Mylopoulos (Eds.), The Semantic Web - ISWC 2003. Proceedings, 2003. XV, 931 pages. 2003.

Vol. 2871: N. Zhong, Z.W. Raś, S. Tsumoto, E. Suzuki (Eds.), Foundations of Intelligent Systems. Proceedings, 2003. XV, 697 pages. 2003. (Subseries LNAI)

Vol. 2873: J. Lawry, J. Shanahan, A. Ralescu (Eds.), Modelling with Words. XIII, 229 pages. 2003. (Subseries LNAI)

Vol. 2874: C. Priami (Ed.), Global Computing. Proceedings, 2003. XIX, 255 pages. 2003.

Vol. 2875: E. Aarts, R. Collier, E. van Loenen, B. de Ruyter (Eds.), Ambient Intelligence. Proceedings, 2003. XI, 432 pages. 2003.

Vol. 2876: M. Schroeder, G. Wagner (Eds.), Rules and Rule Markup Languages for the Semantic Web. Proceedings, 2003. VII, 173 pages. 2003.

Vol. 2877: T. Böhme, G. Heyer, H. Unger (Eds.), Innovative Internet Community Systems. Proceedings, 2003. VIII, 263 pages. 2003.

Vol. 2878: R.E. Ellis, T.M. Peters (Eds.), Medical Image Computing and Computer-Assisted Intervention - MICCAI 2003. Part I. Proceedings, 2003. XXXIII, 819 pages. 2003.

Vol. 2879: R.E. Ellis, T.M. Peters (Eds.), Medical Image Computing and Computer-Assisted Intervention - MICCAI 2003. Part II. Proceedings, 2003. XXXIV, 1003 pages. 2003.

Vol. 2880: H.L. Bodlaender (Ed.), Graph-Theoretic Concepts in Computer Science. Proceedings, 2003. XI, 386 pages. 2003.

Vol. 2881: E. Horlait, T. Magedanz, R.H. Glitho (Eds.), Mobile Agents for Telecommunication Applications. Proceedings, 2003. IX, 297 pages. 2003.

Vol. 2882: D. Veit, Matchmaking in Electronic Markets. XV, 180 pages. 2003. (Subseries LNAI)

Vol. 2883: J. Schaeffer, M. Müller, Y. Björnsson (Eds.), Computers and Games. Proceedings, 2002. XI, 431 pages. 2003.

Vol. 2884: E. Najm, U. Nestmann, P. Stevens (Eds.), Formal Methods for Open Object-Based Distributed Systems. Proceedings, 2003. X, 293 pages. 2003.

Vol. 2885: J.S. Dong, J. Woodcock (Eds.), Formal Methods and Software Engineering. Proceedings, 2003. XI, 683 pages. 2003.

Vol. 2886: I. Nyström, G. Sanniti di Baja, S. Svensson (Eds.), Discrete Geometry for Computer Imagery. Proceedings, 2003. XII, 556 pages. 2003.

Vol. 2887: T. Johansson (Ed.), Fast Software Encryption. Proceedings, 2003. IX, 397 pages. 2003.

Vol. 2888: R. Meersman, Zahir Tari, D.C. Schmidt et al. (Eds.), On The Move to Meaningful Internet Systems 2003: CoopIS, DOA, and ODBASE. Proceedings, 2003. XXI, 1546 pages. 2003.

Vol. 2889: Robert Meersman, Zahir Tari et al. (Eds.), On The Move to Meaningful Internet Systems 2003: OTM 2003 Workshops. Proceedings, 2003. XXI, 1096 pages. 2003.

Vol. 2891: J. Lee, M. Barley (Eds.), Intelligent Agents and Multi-Agent Systems. Proceedings, 2003. X, 215 pages. 2003. (Subseries LNAI)

Vol. 2892: F. Dau, The Logic System of Concept Graphs with Negation. XI, 213 pages. 2003. (Subseries LNAI)

Vol. 2893: J.-B. Stefani, I. Demeure, D. Hagimont (Eds.), Distributed Applications and Interoperable Systems. Proceedings, 2003. XIII, 311 pages. 2003.

Vol. 2894: C.S. Laih (Ed.), Advances in Cryptology - ASIACRYPT 2003. Proceedings, 2003. XIII, 543 pages. 2003.

Vol. 2895: A. Ohori (Ed.), Programming Languages and Systems. Proceedings, 2003. XIII, 427 pages. 2003.

Vol. 2896: V.A. Saraswat (Ed.), Advances in Computing Science – ASIAN 2003. Proceedings, 2003. VIII, 305 pages. 2003.

Vol. 2897: O. Balet, G. Subsol, P. Torguet (Eds.), Virtual Storytelling. Proceedings, 2003. XI, 240 pages. 2003.

Vol. 2898: K.G. Paterson (Ed.), Cryptography and Coding. Proceedings, 2003. IX, 385 pages. 2003.

Vol. 2899: G. Ventre, R. Canonico (Eds.), Interactive Multimedia on Next Generation Networks. Proceedings, 2003. XIV, 420 pages. 2003.

Vol. 2901: F. Bry, N. Henze, J. Maluszyński (Eds.), Principles and Practice of Semantic Web Reasoning. Proceedings, 2003. X, 209 pages. 2003.

Vol. 2902: F. Moura Pires, S. Abreu (Eds.), Progress in Artificial Intelligence. Proceedings, 2003. XV, 504 pages. 2003. (Subseries LNAI).

Vol. 2903: T.D. Gedeon, L.C.C. Fung (Eds.), AI 2003: Advances in Artificial Intelligence. Proceedings, 2003. XVI, 1075 pages. 2003. (Subseries LNAI).

Vol. 2904: T. Johansson, S. Maitra (Eds.), Progress in Cryptology – INDOCRYPT 2003. Proceedings, 2003. XI, 431 pages. 2003.

Vol. 2905: A. Sanfeliu, J. Ruiz-Shulcloper (Eds.), Progress in Pattern Recognition, Speech and Image Analysis. Proceedings, 2003. XVII, 693 pages. 2003.

Vol. 2910: M.E. Orlowska, S. Weerawarana, M.P. Papazoglou, J. Yang (Eds.), Service-Oriented Computing – ICSOC 2003. Proceedings, 2003. XIV, 576 pages. 2003.

Vol. 2911: T.M.T. Sembok, H.B. Zaman, H. Chen, S.R. Urs, S.H.Myaeng (Eds.), Digital Libraries: Technology and Management of Indigenous Knowledge for Global Access. Proceedings, 2003. XX, 703 pages. 2003.

Vol. 2913: T.M. Pinkston, V.K. Prasanna (Eds.), High Performance Computing – HiPC 2003. Proceedings, 2003. XX, 512 pages. 2003.

Vol. 2914: P.K. Pandya, J. Radhakrishnan (Eds.), FST TCS 2003: Foundations of Software Technology and Theoretical Computer Science. Proceedings, 2003. XIII, 446 pages. 2003.

Vol. 2916: C. Palamidessi (Ed.), Logic Programming. Proceedings, 2003. XII, 520 pages. 2003.